D0227785

Cap

ee CHANGING
FOR THE FUTURE

PKTON   L

efore th   t date

Cape Verde

the Bradt Travel Guide

Aisling Irwin
Colum Wilson
Updated by Jacquie Cozens

edition
5

www.bradtguides.com

Bradt Travel Guides Ltd, UK
The Globe Pequot Press Inc, USA

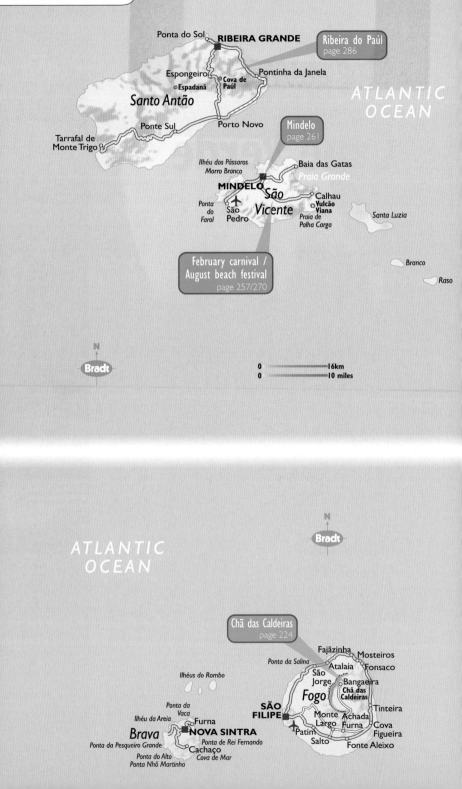

CAPE VERDE ISLANDS

Ponta do Sol · **RIBEIRA GRANDE**

Ribeira do Paúl
page 286

Espongeiro · Pontinha da Janela

Espadaná · Cova de Paúl

Santo Antão

ATLANTIC OCEAN

Ponte Sul · Porto Novo

Tarrafal de Monte Trigo

Mindelo
page 261

Ilhéu dos Pássaros
Morro Branco · Baia das Gatas

Praia Grande

MINDELO

São Vicente

Calhau
Vulcão Viana

Ponta do Farol · São Pedro

Praia de Palha Carga

Santa Luzia

February carnival / August beach festival
page 257/270

Branco

Raso

N

Bradt

| 0 | 16km |
| 0 | 10 miles |

ATLANTIC OCEAN

N

Bradt

Chã das Caldeiras
page 224

Fajãzinha · Mosteiros

Ponta da Salina · Atalaia · Fonsaco

São Jorge · Bangaeira
Chã das Caldeiras

Ilhéus do Rombo

Fogo

Ponta da Vaca
Ilhéu da Areia · Furna

SÃO FILIPE

Tinteira

Ponta da Pesqueiro Grande · **NOVA SINTRA**

Brava

Monte Largo · Achada · Cova
Furna · Figueira

Ponta de Rei Fernando

Cachaço · Patim

Ponta do Alto · Cova de Mar · Salto

Ponta Nhõ Martinho · Fonte Aleixo

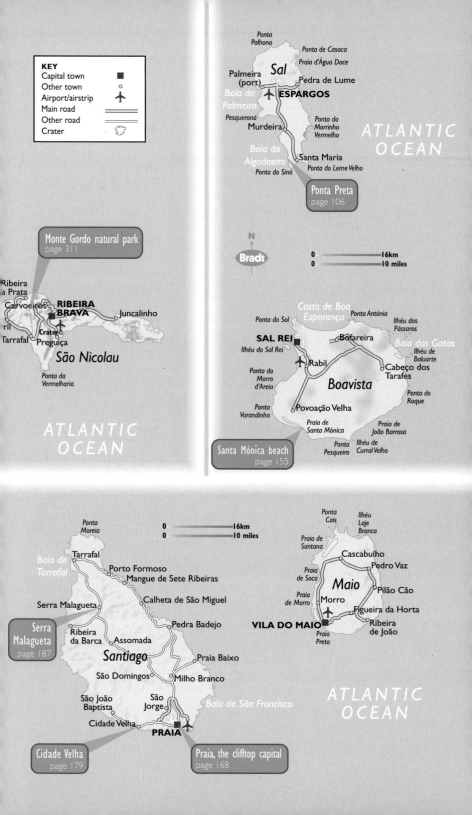

KEY
Capital town
Other town
Airport/airstrip
Main road
Other road
Crater

Sal

Ponta Palhona
Ponta de Casaca
Praia d'Água Doce
Palmeira (port)
Pedra de Lume
ESPARGOS
Baía da Palmeira
Pesquerona
Ponta do Morrinho Vermelho
Murdeira
Baía da Algodoeiro
Santa Maria
Ponta do Leme Velho
Ponta do Sinó

ATLANTIC OCEAN

Ponta Preta
page 106

Monte Gordo natural park
page 311

Ribeira a Prata
Carvoeiços
RIBEIRA BRAVA
Juncalinho
ril
Tarrafal
Crater
Preguiça
São Nicolau
Ponta da Vermelharia

ATLANTIC OCEAN

N
Bradt
0 ———— 16km
0 ———— 10 miles

Costa de Boa Esperança
Ponta do Sol
Ponta Antónia
Ilhéu dos Pássaros
SAL REI
Bofareira
Baía das Gatas
Ilhéu do Sal Rei
Rabil
Ilhéu de Baluarte
Cabeço dos Tarafes
Ponta do Morro d'Areia
Boavista
Ponta do Roque
Ponta Varandinha
Povoação Velha
Praia de Santa Mónica
Praia de João Barrosa
Ponta Pesqueiro
Ilhéu de Curral Velho

Santa Mónica beach
page 155

0 ———— 16km
0 ———— 10 miles

Ponta Moreia
Tarrafal
Baía de Tarrafal
Porto Formoso
Mangue de Sete Ribeiras
Calheta de São Miguel
Serra Malagueta
Pedra Badejo
Serra Malagueta
page 187
Ribeira da Barca
Assomada
Santiago
Praia Baixo
São Domingos
Milho Branco
São João Baptista
São Jorge
Baía de São Francisco
Cidade Velha
PRAIA

Cidade Velha
page 179

Praia, the clifftop capital
page 168

Ponta Cais
Ilhéu Laje Branca
Praia de Santana
Cascabulho
Pedro Vaz
Praia de Soca
Maio
Pilão Cão
Praia de Morro
Morro
Figueira da Horta
VILA DO MAIO
Ribeira de João
Praia Preta

ATLANTIC OCEAN

Cape Verde

Don't miss...

Pico de Fogo
One of the steepest and most spectacular volcanic cones in the world, with people carrying on an astonishing existence inside the crater (CN) page 228

Windsurfing
Catch the best breaks off the coasts of Sal or Boavista (JL/DT) page 48

Verdant *ribeiras*
The fertile Paúl Valley on Santo Antão is home to thousands of people and lush sugarcane, banana and breadfruit plantations, not to mention a prolific output of *grogue*
(PS/IB/FLPA) page 286

Rich music scene
Head to Mindelo on São Vicente for live music, including the haunting *morna* or upbeat *funaná*
(IB/A) page 261

Sweeping sand beaches
The stunning white sands of Santa Maria on Sal are popular with sunbathers and kitesurfers alike
(D/DT) page 113

top   Divers flock to Buracona on Sal, a 40m tunnel that emerges at a small pool dubbed the 'Blue Eye' (SS) page 127

above   It is thought that Sal was known by Moorish sailors for its saltpans before the island was first sighted by European sailors; today the Santa Maria saltpans are still in operation (SS) page 125

left   This isolated church serves the salt mines in Pedra de Lume, Sal (SS) page 127

above The endangered loggerhead turtle (*Caretta caretta*) populates the waters off Boavista and nests on the island's beaches (FB/MP/FLPA) page 136

right Fishing is a mainstay of several communities on Boavista; typical catches include big-game varieties such as tuna (SS) page 145

MORABEZA

the tradition of hospitality

Backed by more than forty years of success providing our guests with a relaxing vacation, we look forward to welcoming you.

90 Rooms & 30 Suites • Beach Club • 3 Bars • 3 Restaurants • 2 Swimming Pools • 2 Tennis Courts • 3 Pétanque courts • Fitness course • Archery range • Mini-Golf • Gymnasium • Games room • Excursions with Trimaran • Diving Centre • Wind /Kite/Surf Club • Fishing club • Car rental • Boutique

www.hotelmorabeza.com

Hotel Morabeza | Santa Maria, Ilha do Sal - Rep. de Cabo Verde
Tel: +238.242.10.20 | Fax: +238.242.10.21 | info@hotelmorabeza.com

Département Commercial | 207 Gasmeterlaan - 9000 Gand - Belgique
Tel: +32.9.226.19.47 | Fax: +32.9.226.94.72 | ciem.nv@skynet.be

AUTHORS

Colum and Aisling have been visiting Cape Verde for over a decade and their first guide to the country was published in 1988. Aisling is a journalist and writer, specialising in the environment, the developing world and science. A former *Daily Telegraph* correspondent, she has won several prizes for her feature-writing and has contributed to books on a variety of subjects, including Bradt's guide to solar eclipses over Africa. Colum is a relief worker. He worked for Médecins Sans Frontières and now works for the UK government's Department for International Development, specialising in humanitarian aid to west Africa. Colum  and Aisling have lived in, and written about, a range of countries including Zambia and Angola. Their other joint book is *In Quest of Livingstone: a Journey to the Four Fountains*, about their retracing of David Livingstone's last journey. See page IV for their authors' story.

UPDATER

Jacquie Cozens is a wildlife film-maker with credits on Discovery, BBC and Five, and she has also written many articles for travel and dive magazines. An ardent traveller and nature lover, Jacquie moved to Cape Verde some years ago when she became fascinated by the beauty and variety of the islands. Intrigued by the migratory routes between the UK and these islands not only of wildlife but also of people involved in piracy and slavery who visited the islands in the past, she intended to make a film exploring this theme. Walking on the beaches and finding only dead turtles, Jacquie quickly became involved in the battle to save Cape  Verde's loggerheads from imminent extinction, founding an NGO, SOS Tartarugas Cabo Verde (www.turtlesos.org). Jacquie lives in Sal but her work with the turtles frequently takes her to some of the most remote places in the country.

PUBLISHER'S FOREWORD   *Hilary Bradt*

When we commissioned the first edition of this guide in 1997 it seemed an impossibly obscure destination. But once the book was published, word got round that this was one of the best spots in the world for windsurfers and other watersports enthusiasts, and hikers were lured by the remote, volcanic interior. After that, the property market boomed as people sought a second home on an island with guaranteed sunshine. Since the fourth edition, the islands have shifted further still into the limelight. Marketing campaigns have promoted Cape Verde as the new 'cheap Caribbean', and some visitors have expected palm-fringed beaches and an azure ocean. But this isn't the Maldives. The islands are a raw mix of arid interiors, lush sugarcane plantations and clean windswept beaches. This forthright new edition shows you what to expect from each island, so you can pick and choose the best itinerary. Happy travelling!

Fifth edition published June 2011 First published 1998

Bradt Travel Guides Ltd, IDC House, The Vale, Chalfont St Peter, Bucks SL9 9RZ, England
www.bradtguides.com
Published in the USA by The Globe Pequot Press Inc, PO Box 480, Guilford, Connecticut 06437-0480

Text copyright © 2011 Aisling Irwin and Colum Wilson
Maps copyright © 2011 Bradt Travel Guides Ltd
Photographs copyright © 2011 Individual photographers (see below)
Project manager: Maisie Fitzpatrick

The authors and publishers have made every effort to ensure the accuracy of the information in this book at the time of going to press. However, the publishers cannot accept any responsibility for any loss, injury or inconvenience resulting from the use of information contained in this guide. All rights reserved. No part of this publication may be reproduced, stored in a retrieval system or transmitted in any form or by any means, electronic, mechanical, photocopying, recording or otherwise, without the prior consent of the publishers. Requests for permission should be addressed to Bradt Travel Guides Ltd, in the UK; or to The Globe Pequot Press Inc, in North and South America.

British Library Cataloguing in Publication Data
A catalogue record for this book is available from the British Library
ISBN 978 1 84162 350 4

Photographs Alamy: Imagebroker (IB/A), PKlandscape (PKL/A), Prisma Bildagentur AG (PB/A); Archipelago Cape Verde (ACV); Linda Aspden (LA); Dreamstime: Dareon (D/DT), J Lindsay (JL/DT); FLPA: Fred Bavendam/Minden Pictures (FB/MP/FLPA), Luciano Candisani/Minden Pictures (LC/MP/FLPA), Imagebroker (IB/FLPA), Imagebroker/Peter Schickert (PS/IB/FLPA), Fritz Polking (FP/FLPA), Martin B Withers (MBW/FLPA), Bernd Zoller/Imagebroker (BZ/IB/FLPA); Christian Nowak (CN); SuperStock (SS)

Front cover Coastline near Fontainhas, Santo Antão (CN)
Back cover Mindelo, São Vicente (CN); Girl in São Domingos, Santiago (SS)
Title page Windsurfing off Sal (LA); a grey-headed kingfisher (*Halcyon leucocephala*) (BZ/IB/FLPA); boats at Tarrafal, Santiago (SS)

Maps David McCutcheon

Typeset from the authors' disk by Wakewing
Production managed by Jellyfish Print Solutions and manufactured in India

Acknowledgements

This book is enriched by the fact that so many wise people were willing to set aside the time to discuss with me the changes going on in Cape Verde: for this I am deeply grateful. They include José Brito, then Minister for Economics, Jorge Sousa Brito, Rector of Jean Piaget University, Olugbenga Adesida, economics adviser to the government; Stahis Panagides, director of the Millennium Challenge Corporation in Cape Verde and his wife Joy, Raymond A Almeida, founder of the American committee for Cape Verde, Richard Lobban, chair of anthropology at Rhode Island College, former minister Xisto Almeida, Hank Weiss, director of Peace Corps, and his wife Beatriz, community liaison officer at the American embassy.

Paul Siegel and Ricardo Monteiro of the World Wildlife Fund, together with Abdelkader Bensada and José Levy of the UNDP, devoted much time to exploring the environmental situation in Cape Verde with me. Insights into the islands' wildlife came from Pedrin López, Jacquie Cozens and Cornelis Hazevoet. Thanks, too, for environmental insights from Tamas Szekeley, Luis Felipe López, Jorge Melo and Tommy Melo, Tali Jessamine, Iacopo Fortes and Peter Wirtz. Thanks to the head of water services in São Nicolau, Carlos Silva; to Agnelo Vieira de Andrade of Dj'ar Fogo; and to John Fernandez, ever-helpful resident of Brava. Bertholdt Siebert's insights into Fogo's crater were invaluable.

The archaeologists working in Cidade Velha – Christopher Evans, Konstantino Richter and Marie Louise Stig Sörensen – spared precious time to discuss their projects. Thanks to Alex Alper, Peace Corps worker, for her thorough research and perceptive contributions. Several other Peace Corps workers brought me up to date – Daron Christopher, Ross Guberman, Julia Kramer and Stephanie Locatelli. Araceli Ticó Rodriguez, researching in Maio, did the same.

There was a lot of much-needed practical help and local insight from Toi D'Armanda, Gerhard and Sibylle Schellmann, and from Paulo Lima, head of the Association of Cape Verdean Journalists, who came to my rescue in Achada Santo António. Also Monique, of Fogo Island.

It's hard to be expert in everything and one or two people have helped compensate for my deficiencies: James Ensor took the time to talk me through the realities of property-purchasing in Cape Verde and also shared his knowledge of sailing in the islands. Anna Etmanska set me right on some details of Jewish history.

Thanks are also due to Siân Pritchard-Jones and Bob Gibbons, who thoroughly updated the third edition of this guide, and to Ron Hughes of Cape Verde Travel: always on the end of the phone with the answer to a question and a kind word, too. And to his manageress, Lisa Newlove.

Writing a guidebook is certainly not done for financial reward. The following hotels softened the budgetary impact with complimentary nights – thank you: Hotel Bluebell and Santo Antão Art Resort in Santo Antão; Pensão Jardim, in São Nicolau; the Morabeza Hotel, Riu Funana and Odjo d'Agua in Sal; Parque das Dunas in

Boavista; Hotels Trópico and Pérola and Residencial Praia Maria in Santiago (and the Schellmanns, who put me up in the hotel they have now relinquished) and, in Fogo, Hotel Xaguate and Almada Inn View Point. TAP Portugal kindly provided the flights.

For assistance with the update we would also like to acknowledge the help of Jon Berg and Fu Mueller in Santiago, Jeanette and Stephen of Sunfish Scuba in Maio, Mic Dax in São Vicente, Harriette Taylor and Anderson Gammon, and the travel agency vista verde tours. The following hotels also helped with accommodation: Rosymar Inn (Praia, Santiago); Porto do Sol (Cidade Velha, Santiago); Quinta da Montanha (Rui Vaz, Santiago); ArcoIris (São Filipe, Fogo); Residencial Goa (Calhau, São Vicente); Aldeia Manga (Valé de Paúl, Santo Antão).

AUTHORS' STORY

When Colum and I first visited Cape Verde over a decade ago it was, for the British, an obscure destination. The annual number of tourists was a few tens of thousands, of which Brits were an infinitesimal fraction. Now tourism is in the hundreds of thousands and the development of hotels, apartments and condominiums surges ahead. The country is riding a rollercoaster with the added excitement that no-one knows how safe the structure is. I gaze through the estate agents' windows, at the developers' plans, at the construction sites and I try to extract meaning. Who will be living in these fairytale condominiums? What corners of the world will they come from? Will there be any Cape Verdeans in there? What will it mean if there aren't – and what will it mean if there are?

Now, when I visit, development has made things easier (though the air and ferry connections between the islands are worse than they were a decade ago). But now I am also finding disappointment among tourists. I have heard complaints about sullen service, about the endless wind, flies, the lack of anything to 'do', and the high cost of living. The main reason for their negativity is that they were oversold their holidays. Cape Verde is – hilariously – being touted as the 'new Caribbean' – when the islands for sale tend to have a barrenness approaching that of the moon.

So I find myself in a strange position now: instead of raving about Cape Verde I find myself sometimes advising people not to go. I've even inserted a small section in each island chapter entitled 'Lowlights' so you know what *not* to expect. Here is my reasoning: I want you to treasure Cape Verde, and if you're a person who won't find it treasurable, I want you to know beforehand.

So: go, if you love the sea and have a cracking watersports holiday on Sal or Boavista; go, if you love outstanding mountainous landscapes, particularly if you enjoy hiking in them: enjoy Santo Antão; go if something inside you responds to a barren land with a harsh black coastline pounded by a frothing white ocean; or to a convivial people with the time strike up a mournful tune over a glass of thick red wine.

I believe, though, that you will have your most fulfilling holiday if a little part of you goes as an anthropologist, interested in whatever the archipelago throws at you. Be like one of my contributors, who responds to notorious Cape Verdean punctuality with the words: 'It's great how these people refuse to be intimidated by time'. Cape Verde is, at heart, a place not to be consumed, but to be understood.

Contents

LIST OF MAPS

NOTE ABOUT MAPS

A couple of maps use grid lines to allow easy location of sites. Map grid references are listed in square brackets after listings in the text, with page number followed by grid number, eg: [116 B2].

FEEDBACK REQUEST

It means a lot to us when our readers take the time to tell us about their journeys: after all, we've written the book for you, and we're dying to know how you got on.

Cape Verde is changing so quickly now that updates, however tiny, are welcome. There are some remote corners we might have missed: let us know about those too. Even if it's just to laugh at an observation or groan at a bad joke: share it with us.

On Bradt's website we have a page where we keep the Cape Verde conversation going (*updates.bradtguides.com*). It's not a web forum but it contains updates and, with your permission and if appropriate, we'll feed your ideas in too. Maybe you'll meet the kind of visitor you resonate with: after all, you both bought the Bradt guide. Just email us on info@bradtguides.com, with 'Cape Verde' in the subject line, or call 01753 893444. The best and most useful contacts will be posted on our website.

LIST OF BOXES

Introduction

The flight to the island of Maio was full. As the tiny propeller plane bounced over Atlantic air currents, I was the only passenger to gaze out with a lick of fear at the mighty mid ocean below. Inside the plane everyone else seemed to have forgotten the sea. All was exuberance, chatter and a roaring laughter. The passengers were young men in polished shoes, expensive trousers and heavy gold jewellery. They spoke in a Creole that was too rapid for me to grasp and I wondered what interest Maio – flat, dry and quiet even by Cape Verdean standards – could hold for them.

A few days later I was driving through the north of Maio, mesmerised by its endless stony red plains where the goats eat rock and the people eat goats. I reached a village – a single street of dust, two rows of parched, single-storey houses. 'This is Alcatraz,' the driver said. The street was quiet apart from a few of the ragged, wide-eyed children who populate the poorer half of the world. Some of the houses were nothing more than bare concrete carcasses while others were painted in greens and pinks and blues and even had glass in their windows.

From the front door of one of the smarter houses a family appeared. I crossed the street and asked if I could take a photo.

'Not at all,' the man replied in perfect English. 'But don't you remember me? I was on your flight.'

My perception jolted and suddenly I saw the urbane passenger, representative of a richer world, gold still gleaming at his neck. And then my world altered again and I saw a poor village, forgotten even within Cape Verde. He must have noticed my perplexity: 'I live in Holland,' he explained. 'I work on the ships... I've come back to see my wife and children.' The woman at his side, uncomprehending, scooped a child on to her hip.

'How long have you been away?' I asked.

'Three years.'

'That's hard.'

'Yes,' he replied. 'But we Cape Verdeans – we have hard lives.'

That is one of the paradoxes of Cape Verde. There is a widespread cosmopolitanism that dates from centuries ago, but it lives side by side with poverty and isolation. For generations the young men have gone abroad – to the USA, to Europe, to the African mainland – because the land cannot sustain them, because their families need money. Back at home their relatives mourn not just the loss of their own sons and husbands but the painful emigrations of generations before. They mourn the peculiar lot of the Cape Verdean, stranded on outcrops in the Atlantic, abused over the centuries not just by the waves but by many nations. They mourn in a particularly beautiful way which I first discovered on Fogo, the volcano island.

I was clinging to the bench in the back of a small truck as it jolted up and down the steep cobbled roads of the old Portuguese town of São Filipe. Every so often the vehicle would halt in front of a house, the driver would shout and a man would appear in the doorway clutching a violin and scramble in beside me.

Soon we had gathered the band back together and we careered up into the foothills of Fogo's dark volcano till we reached the house of Agusto, a blind musician. Inside his white-painted, two-roomed home the men dragged chairs and benches together and I sat in a far corner as the violins made their awakening screeches and the guitars were tuned. Then the music began: sweet melodies and melancholy harmonies. The music was so sad, it was as if the sorrow of generations had erupted in the house.

The Cape Verdeans express through their *mornas* the sorrow of sons lost to the wider world, droughts, famines and relatives drowned at sea. Their music is exquisite, an Atlantic art form with influences from the four continents that surround it. But soon the sadness was done and there came the lively strains of a *funana*. Now we were celebrating... what, I wondered? I knew the answer, though. We were celebrating the same notion that had just made us cry – Caboverdeanidade, the essence of Cape Verde.

I absorbed it all in the dim room with its rough furniture and garish crocheted ornaments. Later I stepped outside where the sun was dissolving into the ocean. As I watched, the music still playing behind me, I thought: this is the reason to visit Cape Verde. There are fine mountains, wildernesses of desert dunes and warm waters. But what makes Cape Verde take hold of your heart is that rare moment, that flush of empathy, when you begin to understand what they mean by *sodade*.

If you would like information about advertising in Bradt Travel Guides please contact us on +44 (0)1753 893444 or email info@bradtguides.com

Part One

GENERAL INFORMATION

CAPE VERDE ISLANDS AT A GLANCE

Islands Santo Antão, São Vicente, Santa Luzia (uninhabited), São Nicolau, Sal, Boavista, Maio, Santiago, Fogo, Brava

Location Atlantic Ocean, approximately 1,000km southwest of the Canary Islands, and 460km from the Senegalese coast

Size Ten islands varying from 35km^2 (Santa Luzia) to 990km^2 (Santiago), spread over an east–west band of 370km of ocean

Status Independent republic

Government African Party for Independence of Cape Verde or PAICV

Population 505,606 (UN, 2009)

Life expectancy 71 years (UNDP, 2008)

Capital Praia, on Santiago (population around 128,000)

Economy Tourism an increasing earner; bananas most important export; heavy dependence on remittances

Language Officially Portuguese, commonly Creole

Religion Roman Catholic

Currency Cape Verdean escudo (CVE, written as $, after the numeral)

Exchange rate €1=111.85$ (March 2011)

International telephone code +238

Time GMT –1

Electricity supply 220V AC, 50Hz. Round, European two-pin sockets.

Flag Blue with white and red horizontal stripes and a circle of ten yellow stars

Public holidays 1 January, 20 January, 1 May, 5 July, 15 August, 12 September, 1 November, 25 December

Background Information

GEOGRAPHY AND CLIMATE

Just a few geographical oddities shape Cape Verde's natural history and economy to a profound degree: a combination of winds and currents that bring heat and cool, dust, dryness and the occasional monsoon. Drought is the key to everything and, as the Cape Verdeans say, 'the best governor is rain.'

LOCATION AND SIZE The Cape Verdes are an arrow-shaped archipelago of ten islands, five islets and various rocks and stacks that poke out of the eastern Atlantic on a band of latitude that runs between Senegal in the east and the Caribbean, 3,600km to the west. They stretch between 14°N and 18°N and 22°W and 26°W. The archipelago is the furthest south of the groups of islands known as Macaronesia. Others of that group include the Azores and the Canary Islands, but the distance between them is great. The Canaries, off Morocco, are over 1,000km away while the Azores, parallel with Portugal, are at a distance of about 2,500km. The islands are widely spaced. The most easterly is 460km from Senegal and the most westerly is 830km. The largest island is 990km^2, about twice the size of the Isle of Wight. The smallest is the 35km^2 pinprick of Santa Luzia. Brava is the smallest inhabited island at 64km^2. The total land area is 4,033km^2, scattered over 58,000km^2 of ocean.

The archipelago is popularly divided into two groups. The *Barlavento*, or windward, islands in the north are Santo Antão, São Vicente, Santa Luzia, São Nicolau, Sal and Boavista. The *Sotavento*, or leeward, islands to the south are Maio, Santiago, Fogo and Brava.

TERRAIN Another way of dividing the islands is longitudinally: the easterly islands of Sal, Boavista and Maio are extremely flat, while the rest are mountainous. There is extraordinary variation in height: Fogo's peak reaches 2,829m, and you can walk to the top of it, while Boavista musters only a small hill of 390m.

The variation in height reflects the huge age span of the islands and therefore the time available for erosion to take place. Their geological history is still controversial but the most popular theory estimates the flat ones to be up to 26 million years old, dating from the Miocene era. It has been shown that the central islands of São Nicolau and Maio appeared less than 12 million years ago, in the Pliocene. To the west Fogo and Brava, the youngest, have been around for a mere 100,000 years.

The theory is based on the drift of the African Plate, a section of the earth's crust that stretches well beyond the African landmass as far as the middle of the Atlantic. This tectonic plate began a slow drift to the east about 120 million years ago. Underneath it lies a 'hot spot'. As the plate above has drifted, this spot has periodically erupted, poking a series of holes like molehills through the crust. It is thought that the most eroded volcanoes can no longer be seen, submerged by the

3

Atlantic somewhere between Boavista and the mainland. It is even possible that the basalts of Cap Vert, the Senegal promontory, are remnants of the first eruption of the hot spot into the Atlantic.

But some of the islands are more complicated than that. Not all of the magma that erupted from below actually blasted through to the surface. Some of it became trapped within the crust and cooled there, forming large igneous intrusions. The intrusions swelled up and rose within the forming volcanoes, lifting with them the ancient marine sediments that had been deposited on the ocean floor long before any islands developed. The intrusions and the uplifted sediments remained hidden within the volcanoes for millions of years, but the distance between them and the surface has slowly been shrinking as wind and flash floods have eroded the volcanoes away. Now, like slicing the top from a boiled egg, the sediments are revealed, the yolk within. The result is that the flat land of some islands (Maio in particular) is, very roughly, young volcanic rock around the outside and much older sedimentary rock forming an uplifted ring around the intrusions that are exposed in the heart of the island.

The mountainous islands can be very rugged, sometimes with virtually no flat land. Dunes, both still and wandering, are present mainly in the flat islands, most visibly and beautifully in Boavista, where parts feel like true desert.

CLIMATE Caught in the Sahel zone, Cape Verde is really a marine extension of the Sahara. The northeast tradewind is responsible for much of its climate. It blows down particularly strongly from December to April, carrying so little moisture that only peaks of 600m or more can tease out any rain. The high peaks, particularly on Fogo, Santo Antão and Brava, can spend much of the year with their heads in the clouds.

Added to that wind are two other atmospheric factors. First is the **harmattan** – dry, hot winds from the Sahara that arrive in a series of blasts from October to June, laden with brown dust which fills the air like smog. The second factor is the **southwest monsoon**, which brings the longed-for rains between August and October. Often half the year's rainfall can tumble down in a single storm or series of storms. Unfortunately Cape Verde's position is a little too far north for the rains to be guaranteed each year: it lies just above the doldrums, the place where the northeast and southwest tradewinds meet and where there is guaranteed rainfall. The longest recorded time Cape Verde has gone without being watered by the southwest monsoon is 18 years. For 12 years from 1968 there was also a drought.

ANNUAL WEATHER STATISTICS

	Jan	Feb	Mar	Apr	May	Jun	Jul	Aug	Sep	Oct	Nov	Dec
Temperature °C day												
	24	25	25	25	26	27	27	28	30	29	28	27
Temperature °C night												
	8	17	18	18	19	20	22	23	24	23	22	20
Sea temperature °C												
	21	20	20	20	21	22	23	24	25	25	24	22
Hours of sunshine												
	8	9	10	10	10	8	7	6	8	8	9	8
Days of rain												
	0	0	0	0	0	2	3	3	7	4	1	0

In the ocean, the cool stream known as the **Canary Current** reaches the archipelago from the north and mitigates the heating effect of the northeast tradewind.

Temperature variation on the islands is small – it remains between 22°C and 27°C on Santiago throughout the year. But these figures mask big variations within and between islands. In the desert centre of some of the flat islands it can reach 40°C between July and September, while on the moist peaks of Santo Antão early in the year it can be as cool as 10°C.

Cape Verde's **rainfall** figures tell a similarly strange story. A recurring theme is the wide variation in rainfall even between different slopes of the same island – the northeastern slopes are the wettest. On Fogo for example, the average rainfall over 35 years for the northeastern slope of Monte Velha is 1,190mm, while the average on its leeward side is 167mm. Monte Velha's figures also reveal how precious rain can deluge an island over a very short period. In a single month, 20 years ago, 3,000mm of rain fell there. The lower islands, the flat ones, São Vicente and Santa Luzia, receive much less moisture, leaving them almost totally barren.

These chaotic figures can be processed to give mean average rainfalls in the range 10–900mm. Most regions of Cape Verde are classified as arid or semi-arid.

NATURAL HISTORY AND CONSERVATION

Many species on Cape Verde exist nowhere else in the world – the phenomenon known as endemicity. Unlike other islands such as the Caymans, which were once part of a bigger landmass and carry species left over from the greater continent, life here has arrived by chance. Which species completed the extraordinary journey was a lottery and the winners were a peculiar assortment. In addition, these species have had millions of years of isolation in which to branch out on their own, adapting to suit the oddities of the habitat. The grey-headed kingfisher (*Halcyon leucocephela*), for example, in the absence of much inland water in which to live up to its name, dines on insects instead.

The closest relatives of some of Cape Verde's plants are found in east Africa rather than the west. Scientists think that they were borne here from west Africa, which then itself became so dry that they disappeared from there.

FLORA Cape Verde has probably never been profusely covered in greenery. Lack of research and poor early records mean we know little about what it was like before humans arrived. The lower slopes were probably grassy and treeless (steppe) or with low vegetation dotted with trees (savanna). There are a few indigenous trees that still survive: the lovely blue-green, gnarled, flat-topped dragon tree (*Dracaena draco*), fast disappearing except on São Nicolau; the tamarisk palms, known locally as *tamareira* (*Phoenix atlantica*), that fill the lagoons and sunken deserts of Boavista (though some believe that it is just a feral version of another palm tree, *Phoenix dactyl*); the ironwood tree and perhaps a species of fig tree and one of acacia.

The indigenous plants are adapted to dryness (having small leaves, for example) and are small and sturdy to cope with strong winds.

Over the last 500 years, plants have been introduced from all over the world, and people have tried to cultivate wherever they can. Shrubs and trees have been cleared to make way for arable land. Poor farming techniques and the ubiquitous goat have combined with these forces to oust most of the original vegetation. The result is that, of the 600 species of plant growing in Cape Verde (aside from crops), only a quarter are natural to the islands and about half of those are endemic. Some of the endemic plants, such as *Língua da vaca* (*Echium vulcanorum*) are suited only to ranges of crazily small dimensions, as frustrated botanists will tell you.

Since independence in 1975, people have been making Herculean efforts to plant trees. The roots form a matrix that traps earth so that heavy rain cannot wash them away, and the branches prevent the wind scattering the precious soil. The trees are also supposed to create a moist microclimate. The reafforestation figures have been almost unbelievable: over some periods about three million new trees have been planted each year, or 7,000 a day. The result is pine trees, oaks and sweet chestnuts on the cool peaks of Santo Antão, eucalyptus on the heights of Fogo, and forests of acacia on Maio.

FAUNA

Birds Cape Verde has a dedicated following of ornithologists and amateur birdwatchers who can be found wedged into crevices high up mountainsides or, before new restrictions came into force, trying to secure passages with local fishermen across wild stretches of sea to some of the uninhabited islands. Their dedication stems from the fact that Cape Verde abounds in endemics and some of the seabirds living on cliffs around the islands are particularly important. The archipelago lies on the extreme southwestern corner of the western Palaearctic region and is thus the only place in that region where certain species, mainly African or tropical, can be found to breed regularly. There are about 130 migrants for whom Cape Verde is an important stopping point on their long journeys. Some 40 use the islands for nesting. The archipelago is host to four threatened marine bird species: the magnificent frigatebird, brown booby, Cape Verdean shearwater and red-billed tropicbird.

However, as with the plants, much of the natural birdlife has been wiped out, particularly by hungry locals tempted by succulent seabirds or by fishermen treading on their burrows as they search for shellfish along the beaches. A more modern threat comes from actual and proposed tourism developments close to important wetland areas, such as Rabil in Boavista and the Salinas de Porto Inglês in Maio.

The most prized birds to discover in the islands include the **raso lark** (*Alauda razae*) and the **magnificent frigatebird** (*Fregata magnificens*), both with extraordinarily restricted breeding areas. The entire eastern Atlantic population of the latter are to be found – all five of them – on the islet of Curral Velho off Boavista. The **Cape Verde petrel** (*Pterodroma feae*), or *ngon-ngon* bird, is disappearing fast and the elegant **red-billed tropicbird**, *rabo de junco* (*Phaethon aethereus*), with its red bill and streaming white tail, is also plunging in numbers. More common birds include the colourful **grey-headed kingfisher**, known locally as *passarinha*. It can be found on Santiago, Fogo and Brava, and has a red beak, and orange, black and blue plumage. You will also see plenty of **helmeted guineafowl** (*Numida meleagris*) on mountain slopes and even the distinctive white **Egyptian vultures** (*Neophron percnopterus*) at high altitudes. Waders frequent the few lagoons and saltpans, on Sal, Maio, Boavista and Santiago. If you miss the **brown booby** (*Sula leucogaster*) – known locally as the *alcatraz* and also an inhabitant of the islet of Curral Velho in Boavista – take a look at the 20-escudo piece. The **Cape Verde red kite** is probably extinct (see *Chapter 11, Santo Antão*, page 305) and the **Cape Verde purple heron**, *garça vermelha* (*Ardea (purpurea) bournei*) leads a particularly precarious existence in possibly just one mahogany tree in Ribeira Montagna in Santiago. There are 25 birds in that tree and that is thought to be it (see page 187). The **Cape Verde cane warbler** (*Acrocephalus brevipennis*) (endangered and brownish) lives mostly in Santiago, with about 500 breeding pairs left.

Some of the most compelling sites for rare birds in Cape Verde are the islets. On the Ilhéus do Rombo can be found **Bulwer's petrel** (*Bulweria bulwerii*), known locally as *João-petro*. These are known to breed only on Raso Island, which is near São Nicolau, and on Ilhéu de Cima. They are almost totally black with a strip of dark grey stretching along the middle of their wings.

The **Madeiran storm petrel** (*Oceanodroma castro*) is known locally as the *jaba-jaba* or the *pedreirinho*, and breeds only on these islands and on Branco, Raso and islets off Boavista. It is black apart from a white bit just before the tail. The **Cape Verde shearwater** (*Calonectris edwardsii*), imperilled by a mass annual culling of its chicks (see box, *A taste for baby shearwaters*, page 328), lives on Raso Island.

More information can be found on the website of the Sociedade Caboverdiana de Zoologia (*www.scvz.org/*).

Other fauna There are no large mammals and no snakes, but several species of bat can be found, and green monkeys inhabit Santiago. There are also many small, brown, endemic reptiles, geckos and skinks. The Cape Verde giant skink (*Macroscincus coctei*) – delicious, sadly – became extinct in the 1940s (see *Chapter 12, São Nicolau*, page 329). Many interesting endemic insects and beetles live on the islands and there are collections of them in the Natural History Museum in London (*www.nhm.ac.uk*).

MARINE LIFE According to the World Wildlife Fund, we are still ignorant of the riches that may lie in Cape Verde's waters. But the marine life here is probably globally significant. There is a high degree of endemism, which is unusual for oceanic islands, and the sea is full of corals – not true reefs but slabs, pinnacles and, importantly, coral mountains reaching up from the ocean floor and providing rare mid-ocean habitats at all depths. A recent study concluded that Cape Verde has one of the world's ten most important coral reefs – though that claim has since been disputed by other experts. The highest levels of marine biodiversity are around Boavista, Sal and Maio, which share a marine platform. Meanwhile, Boavista hosts one of the largest wetlands of the Macaronesia region (see page 136).

So far, scientists have catalogued 639 species of fish including mantas and whale sharks. More than 17 species of whale and dolphin have been reported, including the humpback whale, which breeds in Cape Verde. Five species of turtle frequent Cape Verdean waters, including the loggerhead (*Caretta caretta*) for whom Cape Verde is the third most important nesting ground in the world (see also page 8).

Marine life is more tropical than would be found at the same latitude of mainland Africa, on the coast of Senegal. This is because the archipelago is sufficiently far from the mainland to escape the cold 'winter upwellings', in which the turning of the globe causes water from deep in the ocean to surface at the coast. This would otherwise decrease the temperature of the 21°C waters to about 10°C.

There are several threats to the marine heritage of Cape Verde. One of them is fishing: overfishing by domestic and international commercial boats and the use of destructive fishing methods, such as spear guns, and fishing during spawning seasons, by local fishermen.

A second threat comes from coastal development. Many of the most important habitat areas along the coasts are just the places where people want to build hotels and marinas. The country plans tens of thousands of new tourist beds over the next 20 years. Problems from such developments include pollution, the disappearance of sand as it is siphoned off for construction (entire beaches have already disappeared), the effects of artificial light on turtle nesting and damage from quad bikes and the like roaring across fragile coastal land.

Turtles Marine turtles are some of the most important species on the islands. Cape Verde is an important feeding area for five species Recent research has shown that Cape Verde is a crucial participant in the life of the loggerhead turtle (*Caretta caretta*), the population being the third largest in the world after the Florida Keys in the United States and Oman's Massirah Island. In the Atlantic, it is the second largest. About 3,000 turtles are thought to breed in Cape Verde, overwhelmingly in Boavista, probably followed by Maio, then Sal and all the other islands.

Turtles face two threats. The first is hunting. This dates back possibly as far as 1479, when the French explorer Eustache de la Fosse reported that leprosy was treated locally with a diet of turtle meat and by rubbing the affected areas with turtle blood. King Louis XI, who believed he was suffering from leprosy, dispatched his representative to the Cape Verde Islands to investigate after learning of the cure.

Hunting continues today. Practices vary from island to island: sometimes the meat is cut out of the live turtles, sometimes the eggs are taken, sometimes both. Sometimes the blood is drained and added to wine as a fortifier, while on some islands males are prized for their penises which are added to *grogue* as an aphrodisiac. There are nesting beaches where the loss of turtles is 100%.

The threat to habitat is also increasing as land is used for tourism development and sand is removed illegally for building. A report on the effects of tourism on turtles can be downloaded from the Sociedade Caboverdiana de Zoologia website (*www.scvz.org*).

A recent report by the secretariat for the Convention on Migratory Species called for urgent attention to conserve west Africa's sea turtles. Klaus Toepfer, Executive Director of UNEP, said: 'In the western Atlantic and Pacific oceans, populations of sea turtles have been falling dramatically in recent years. This makes [recent] findings in western Africa doubly significant, given its now undoubted status as a globally important region for sea turtle species.'

The report recommended that conserving nesting sites for the loggerhead turtle on Cape Verde should be a priority. The loggerhead is categorised as endangered. The hawksbill (*Eretmochelys imbricata*), which is critically endangered, feeds at the islands. The green turtle (*Chelonia mydas*), which is endangered, calls at the islands, as do the critically endangered leatherback (*Dermochelys coriacea*) and the endangered Olive Ridley (*Lepidochelys olivacea*).

A national turtle plan was drawn up in 2008. Unfortunately, as of 2011 this plan has still not been ratified in parliament and therefore not funded or properly implemented. There are active turtle campaigns on several of the islands, notably Sal (see page 99) and Boavista (see page 136), as well as projects run by communities or city halls on all the other islands. In 2009, a coalition of organisations, called Taola, The Cape Verde Marine Turtle Network, was formed to synchronise activities and, hopefully, lobby parliament more successfully.

Whales North Atlantic humpback whales were driven almost to extinction during the whaling exploits of the 14th century. Now there are 10,000–12,000 worldwide and most breed in the West Indies. A few hundred, however, choose Cape Verde. This select group makes seasonal migrations between Iceland, Norway and Cape Verde. The archipelago is where they mate, after which the females travel north to feed, returning around a year later to give birth. March and April are the peak of the breeding season and also the time when the whales can be sighted – mostly off the west and southwestern coasts of Boavista, Sal and most other islands. Individuals can be identified from natural markings (ventral fluke patterns). Males sing songs, at least partly to attract females, and also to maintain distance from other males (see also *Chapter 5, Boavista*, page 137).

CONSERVATION EFFORTS Marine, coastal and inland areas do have friends in Cape Verde. The government has signed up to some key international conventions but implementation takes time and money. There are several programmes, including the National Research and Marine Biodiversity Conservation Programme and the Coastal Zone Management Project, which is establishing policies on how to use and manage coastal areas. The two marine-protected areas in Cape Verde – Murdeira Bay in Sal (see page 98) and the Santa Luzia complex (that island plus the surrounding islets, including Branco and Raso – see page 328) – have management plans. The two areas face threats from very different sources: in Murdeira, it's tourist development, whereas in the Santa Luzia complex it's artisanal fishing. Unfortunately, neither are patrolled nor properly protected.

Crucially – not just for marine and coastal areas but also for inland – in 2002 the government established the General Directorate for Environment – a framework from which environmental care can operate. They have built on a proposal by Cabo Verde Natura 2000 to create a network of 47 protected areas around Cape Verde. The areas were declared in law in 2003 but only one has had its precise boundaries enshrined in law.

Three of the protected areas are part of a UN Development Programme/Global Environment Facility project to develop parks with boundaries, services and income-generation activities for local people, including ecotourism (see *Chapter 8, Fogo*, page 217, *Chapter 12, São Nicolau*, page 214 and *Chapter 6, Santiago*, page 163). More are in the pipeline, including two on Santo Antão and one on São Vicente.

The government has taken other actions such as banning the removal of sand from the beaches for construction (with patchy enforcement). The Second Environmental Action plan (PANA II) published in 2007, included a proposal that new developments must submit an Environmental Impact Assessment. It's also against the law to build within 80m of the low tide mark.

The Sociedade Caboverdiana de Zoologia (*www.scvz.org*), which was founded with the aim of promoting zoological research in Cape Verde, publishes a scientific journal, and plans other activities such as organising scientific meetings. Descriptions of all Cape Verde's protected areas can be seen on the website (*www. areasprotegidas.cv/index.php*).

HISTORY

White lives in big house
Mulato lives in shop
Black lives in hut
Sancho lives in mountain:
But a day will come
When Sancho turn all upside down:
Horribly grimacing
Tail curled up
Sancho drag black from hut
Black drag mulato from shop
Mulato drag white from big house
White run to mountain and there he fall

A *batuque* of Santa Catarina, published in the magazine *Claridade* (1948)
Translated by Basil Davidson, *The Fortunate Isles* (Hutchinson, 1989)

When the first island of Cape Verde erupted from the ocean hundreds of kilometres from the African coast, the archipelago's fate was sealed. For, overwhelmingly, the islands' unique and often tragic history has been the result of their position. Their history is one of use and abuse by nations from the four corners of the Atlantic. The world has changed around them and has found fleeting uses for them: they have served until they are exhausted and then they have been forgotten until another convulsion in world affairs has produced a new use for them.

The archipelago's story has been a sad one but it has begun a hopeful chapter. For now the Cape Verdeans have their own identity, proclaim their own culture and, most importantly, govern themselves. Since the 1970s they have been able to act strategically. At the same time, the outside world has changed and has found new uses for Cape Verde: white beaches to serve the interests of mass tourism, and abundant fish when other seas are severely depleted. Whether the archipelago will be able to exploit these riches for itself, or whether the 21st century will be just another chapter in which it is sucked dry and thrown away, it is too early to tell.

ROCKS APPEAR AND LIFE ARRIVES According to local lore, when God was satisfied with Creation, and brushed his hands together, the crumbs that fell unnoticed from his fingers into the sea formed Cape Verde.

The geological explanation for their existence is just as beguiling. Under the plates of the Earth's crust lie 'hot spots' of bubbling magma, one of which is several hundred kilometres west of Senegal. Every so often, when the conditions of heat and pressure are right, this hot spot erupts as a volcano, leaving an island in the Atlantic to mark where it has been. In this way, some 15 million years ago, the island of Sal was created. It was a mountain which has since been the victim of the ocean winds and has eroded away until all that remains is flat, brown rock. The hot spot erupted every few millions of years to make another pimple on the Atlantic. Today it is still putting the final touches to youthful Fogo, which lies in the southwest. The island is 100,000 years old and one senses that brooding Fogo gazes east towards Sal preparing to spend the next ten million years weathering down to a similar fate.

Somehow, plant life found Cape Verde, carried there on winds from mainland Africa or by the ocean itself. Over such a distance there was only a tiny chance of such a voyage culminating in life reaching the islands – but millions of seeds over millions of years transformed that chance to a certainty. Once they had arrived they were cut off from their relatives and evolved into new species, as island life does.

Next came aquatic life. Washed into the Cape Verdean shallows by accident, many species remained to evolve their own identity in the same way as the plants. Other, more ocean-going species, such as turtles, have found the islands a useful transit point. The story of the birds is much the same.

Legend shrouds the tales of the first humans to arrive at the islands. They may have been Phoenician sea captains who landed there and left no trace except for some enigmatic inscriptions on a rock that survive until the present day. In 445BC, the Phoenician captain Hanno sailed from Cadiz and reported that he passed some small islands which scholars now believe may have been Cape Verde. He named them Hesperias. Once Hanno wrote that he had seen a large volcano off the west African coast: perhaps it was Fogo. West African sailors may have reached Cape Verde in their sea-going canoes, but they, too, left no trace.

And so the islands lay, effectively undiscovered, until the middle of the 15th century. The reason for their elusiveness is also the very reason why, when they were found, they were to prove so useful. For they lie below the latitude of the Canary

Islands, a region into which any ship that dared to venture would never return. Myths surrounded the fate of the ships from the north that vanished beyond the Canaries, but their disappearance has a simple explanation. The prevailing northeasterly wind drove them south but then, like a one-way valve, blocked their return.

RAISING CAPE VERDE'S HISTORY FROM THE OCEAN FLOOR

Divers investigating the shipwrecks around Cape Verde say it is the last great unexplored site in the world. They guess there may be up to 600 boats lost on the archipelago's reefs. Through them, it is possible to build up a vivid picture of the islands' trading history.

Already, after several years of exploration, researchers have a warehouse and museum in Chã d'Areia, Praia, which is stacked with treasures brought up from the sea. Coins and clay pipes help to date the wrecks; hoards of goods such as ivory tusks or silver coins testify to the ships' missions; while the odd treasure has been retrieved that is of great beauty or significance.

Perhaps the most spectacular find by the marine archaeologists – from Cape Verde, Oxford University and the Portuguese company Arqueonautas Worldwide – was an astrolabe. With the invention of the sextant the astrolabe, which had guided sailors for two millennia, abruptly lost its purpose and many were melted down. The few examples of this marvellous instrument that remain tend to have been found in shipwrecks.

The team found this beautiful example of a bronze and silver astrolabe in a 1650s' shipwreck. Despite their detective work, however, they still do not know the identity of the ship. The astrolabe was probably Portuguese, the cannons were Dutch, the coins Spanish.

Sadly Cape Verde no longer has the astrolabe, but only a copy – in 2001, it was sold at Sotheby's.

Piecing together a ship's history, and matching it with a known vessel, requires all sorts of lateral thinking. The cargo provides clues. Sometimes small collections of coins from a variety of countries – perhaps from the pocket of an individual sailor collecting a souvenir from every port – can help plot the ship's route.

'The quality of the cargoes is amazing,' says Piran Johnson of Arqueonautas Worldwide. A massive batch of ivory tusks – eaten away like long thin pieces of cheese – was brought up from the *Princess Louisa*, a 1743 ship that was on its way between London and Bombay. An intact bottle of wine 200 years old and, more irresistibly, several bottles of cognac, were retrieved from an unknown wreck in the harbour of Praia. One ship yielded huge copper plates that the Swedes once used as an unwieldy currency – the ship went down in 1781 on its way from Denmark to China.

Another ship – the *Hartwell* – contained a collection of watches: 'They were the Ratner's of the day,' says Johnson. 'Gold filigree on top but cheap tat underneath – they were being shipped out to the colonies to buy off the locals.'

Most of the treasures emerge looking most unpromising, in the form of ugly grey concretions formed by the build-up of iron, sand and other substances over the decades. It takes a professional eye to spot the underlying shape; then it takes weeks of painstaking work to remove the concretion without damaging the valuables inside.

To visit the collection, see *What to see and do*, page 178.

In the 15th century, this barrier to human ambition fell. The rig was invented, and allowed mariners to harness the wind so they could sail against as well as before it. It was one of the most significant of all inventions, enabling humans to emerge from their home continents and link every region of the globe. The west coast of Africa was now a prize for whichever nation could reach it first, and it was inevitable that the Portuguese, with the skills and vision of Prince Henry the Navigator behind them, would win.

Several famous mariners pushed ever further south in the 1460s and more than one claimed to have discovered Cape Verde. The debate will probably never be

JEWS IN CAPE VERDE *Anna Etmanska*

'See these? Old Jewish merchants' homes,' says Jorge Pires, pointing to the dilapidated edifices on the main street in the town of Ponta do Sol, Santo Antão. Buildings in different stages of decay line the quiet street leading towards the ocean. We get closer to examine a faded sign – Cohen. The once-magnificent house stands in ruin, windows and doors boarded up.

Jorge Pires, an official at the local *câmara municipal*, despairs at the sad state of Ponta do Sol's historical heritage. 'Jews built this town and now our past is left to crumble.'

Mr Pires dreams of turning the old Cohen house into a museum of Cape Verde's Jewish history, and Ponta do Sol into a heritage tourism destination. I understand his logic. This area of Santo Antão has more surviving Jewish sites than any other island in the country. The cemeteries in Ponta do Sol and Penha de França already attract curious visitors. The village of Sinagoga is just down the road. And in Ribeira Grande, the green mansion of Ruth Cohen de Marçal still occupies the central position in town.

'The old Jewish lady lived there,' explains a local storeowner. And then he proudly adds, 'My grandfather was Jewish, too.'

Though present-day Cape Verde does not have an organised Jewish community, or even any practising Jews, the islanders, like the storeowner in Ribeira Grande, are very much aware of their country's Sephardic heritage.

The two major waves of Jewish immigration left behind them not only names like Benros, Mendes and Levy, or gravestones with Hebrew inscriptions. Thanks to the centuries of intermarriage, the Sephardic culture became an important ingredient in shaping Cape Verde's modern Creole identity.

The first Jewish settlers came to the island of Santiago to escape religious persecution in 15th-century Portugal. Some came willingly, but an even greater number were deported by force, along with other undesirable elements that King Manuel I no longer tolerated in the country. Known as *degredados* (convicts), these Portuguese exiles worked as traders on the coast of Guinea. They lived initially in Praia but, because of their commercial activities, they spread throughout Cape Verde, married African women, and eventually became an integral part of the brand new, multi-cultural nation.

These Jewish traders acquired the name of *lançados* (outcasts), and quickly became the implementers of the slave trade. Working as intermediaries on the African coast, they traded with whom they pleased and ignored the commercial restrictions imposed on them by Portugal. Yet at the same time, in order to rid Portugal of Jews, the Crown not only allowed, but even encouraged the *lançados*'s activities. Of course not all *lançados* were of Jewish origin: the African trade, just

resolved. Perhaps it was the Venetian, Cadamosto, who said he sighted the islands first in 1456. More likely, it was the Genoese António de Noli who may have stumbled on them in 1455 or in 1461. Some reports say he was accompanied by the Portuguese Diogo Gomes.

Whatever the truth, all the islands were discovered between 1455 and 1461 and the credit generally goes to de Noli and to Gomes, for discovering Santiago and the other leeward isles. Diogo Afonso discovered the windward islands of Santo Antão, São Vicente and São Nicolau. The archipelago was named Cape Verde, not because it was verdant, but after the green butt of Senegal that lies across the sea.

like any other profitable occupation, attracted tough men from varied cultural backgrounds. Some of those traders, be it Jewish, Muslim, or Christian, became known as *ganagogas*, which in the African Biafada dialect means 'men who could speak many languages.'

By the end of the 17th century, Jewish presence on the islands was an important factor in the success of the colonial economy. However, with the establishment of a branch of the Portuguese Inquisition in Cape Verde in 1672, the Crown forcibly confiscated most of the Jewish trading enterprises. As a result, many of the affected merchants hid their true identities until the frenzy of religious persecution died out in the late 1770s.

In the early 1820s, a group of Jews involved in the Liberal Wars fled Portugal and settled in the mountains of Santo Antão. A few years later, they were joined by economic migrants from Morocco and Gibraltar. Following in the footsteps of their 15th-century predecessors, they also engaged in commerce, such as trading salt and hides, and used their skills to rejuvenate the local economy. And as those before them, they took local wives and successfully assimilated into Creole society. As a result, today the great majority of Cape Verdeans, including the country's former prime minister Carlos Alberto Wahnon de Carvalho Veiga, can claim Jewish ancestry.

Yet the Jewish past of Cape Verde is also a victim of this successful assimilation. While Jewish graves remain in Santo Antão, Santiago and Boavista, on Brava and Maio, they are long gone. All that is left in Brava are photos and framed pictures kept by the island's last surviving Jewish descendant – Eugénio Anahory Lobo.

'The people in the photos are either long dead or emigrated to America,' explains Mr Lobo.

Meanwhile, the cemetery on Boavista, where the Benoliel family is buried, is under threat from the rapid tourist development. The Jewish graves in Praia's main cemetery, and the burial sites in Ponta do Sol and Penha de França, all need attention.

There is hope that the initiative of Carol Castiel and her Cape Verde Jewish Heritage Project (*www.capeverdejewishheritage.org*) will improve this situation. However, due to the chronic lack of funds, the change is slow, and for now, the ambitious dreams of Mr Pires remain just that – dreams. (See *Appendix 2, Further Information*, page 339.)

Anna Etmanska is an independent filmmaker and a writer who became interested in the history of Cape Verde Jews after stumbling upon the cemetery in Penha de França on Santo Antão Island. She blogs at www.budgettrouble.com.

It is hard to understand now the value of such a discovery. Venturing over the seas with only the capricious wind for power, with no facility for measuring longitude and with limited water and food, the cry of 'land ahoy' could mean life rather than death.

The Portuguese realised that the islands could be of immense strategic power. And so colonisation began in 1462 when a small group of Portuguese, Spanish and Genoese settled on the most promising island, Santiago. The southern half was allotted to de Noli, who set up in Ribeira Grande on the south coast. The northern half fell to Afonso, who began less successfully in the northwest.

Lisbon wanted to entice talented men to live on the islands and develop them, so Cape Verde was awarded a valuable advantage over other Portuguese colonies. Settlers were given exclusive trading rights along the creeks and shores of the west African coast between Senegal and Sierra Leone. These rivers thus became known as the Rivers of Cape Verde, later to be known as the Rivers of Guinea.

At this time the Atlantic was dotted with Portuguese and Spanish ships making prolific discoveries in the Americas, Africa and beyond Africa's southern tip, as far as India and China. It was the beginning of the expansion of Europe, the spread of its civilisation around the globe and unprecedented mass migration. Over the next 300 years Europeans would emigrate to North and South America and Africa. Africans would fill the Americas, mainly as slaves. The Portuguese and Spanish had begun nothing less than a global redistribution of races, animals and plants and the beginnings of modern mass trade. Meanwhile, the few resources of Cape Verde were put to use, and trading began that would supply the Portuguese Crown with income for centuries.

FROM ROCK TO TRADING POST: THE 1500S The first desire of the colonisers of Santiago was to plant and reap, for which they sought the services of an unpaid labour force. They found what they wanted on the mainland coast of Africa: slaves. Over the next century these captives from the great tribes of west Africa arrived in their thousands, and were soon put to work growing food and cotton in the valleys. By 1582, there were 13,700 slaves labouring on Santiago and Fogo under a regime of 100 white men.

The settlers released goats on to the uninhabited islands where they devoured the scrub pasture and provided meat, hides, butter, milk and cheese, and some cattle were farmed. But barren Cape Verde would never provide enough food for prosperity. Wealth generation was to come from two other activities: resupply of ships, and the slave trade.

Cape Verde lies at the Atlantic crossroads, not just because of its position in relation to the landmasses of the Americas, Europe and Africa, but because of where it lies in relation to the north Atlantic wind patterns and to ocean currents. Both factors drew America-bound ships towards the archipelago. Increasingly, in the latter part of the 16th century, the Portuguese who stopped there were on their way to open up the treasure of Brazil. The Spanish were ferrying goods and people to and from the vast new empire they were creating in South America.

In 1580, Spain and Portugal united to create an Iberian empire with three powerful realms: the spice empire of the east, the sugar empire of the south Atlantic, and the silver empire of Spanish America. Iberian vessels often found it useful to stop at Cape Verde for food and water, for ship repair and for nautical supplies.

Thus, throughout the 1500s, **ship supply** was the islands' great function, and the most basic commodities – water and food – were its speciality. They charged a high price for fresh water and sold maize, beans and dried or salted goat meat. They also exported horses, donkeys, cattle and goat hides. Cape Verde's other commodity lay in sparkling white lakes on the three flat islands to the east: salt, and enough, it seemed, to supply mankind in perpetuity.

Once there were sufficient **slaves** working on the islands, the Portuguese looked west for new markets. They were in a unique position to sell slaves for labour in South American colonies and so the archipelago became a warehouse for human merchandise. For slave merchants who would otherwise have had to visit the African coast, Cape Verde was an expensive market but a sanitised one. Forays to the mainland could be dangerous and lengthy. Ships were often delayed, sometimes for months. Payment methods were elaborate: tribal leaders often demanded a multiplicity of items: iron bars, cloth, brandy, guns, knives, ribbons and beads. In addition, the land was rife with disease and the creeks and rivers of the coast were tricky to navigate. If a ship became stranded on the shore the local people would claim it for their own.

There were other advantages to be gained from shopping for slaves in Cape Verde. The negroes had been 'seasoned'. The sickly, unfit and obstinate had been weeded out or had died. Those who remained had given up hope of escape. They had also learned a few Portuguese words so they would understand orders, and they had been baptised. The Portuguese Church argued that a baptised slave was luckier than a free African because the former had achieved the chance of a place in heaven.

Thousands of slaves were Fula. They were victims of Gabu, a tributary kingdom to the Mandingo Empire of Mali. Gabu, founded in the mid 13th century, stretched through most of today's northeastern Guinea-Bissau. Its people were warriors and their battles generated many of the slaves who were then traded on the coast.

Alongside the business of slavery grew trade in other goods from the African coast: ivory, wax, hides, gum, amber, musk, honey and gold dust. Cape Verde took them and became a depot where these products were exchanged for goods coveted by wealthy Africans – Venetian beads and wine from Europe; silver from Spanish America; cloves and coral from the East. Cape Verde itself supplied the African coast with raw cotton, cloth, salted goat meat, horses and cattle.

The important islands in those first years were Santiago, where the settlers built a capital in the green valley of Ribeira Grande; Fogo, a live but fertile volcano; and the lonely salt island of Maio. Ribeira Grande was the first city built by Europeans in the tropics and became one of the highest-yielding cities of the Portuguese Kingdom. Visitors praised its comforts and in 1533, it was elevated from the rank of *vila* to *cidade*. In 1556, the Bishop of Cape Verde, whose jurisdiction extended to the mainland, began building his cathedral there, and in 1570, the king agreed to the founding of a seminary. All was optimism and prosperity.

Cape Verde mustered few home-produced goods with one major exception, mentioned above: **cotton**. It was grown by slaves who then wove it into cloth of the finest quality, which was marketed along the west African coast and in Brazil. Its skilful patterns became outstandingly popular amongst Africans and the cloth rose to be the chief currency for trading. This gave Cape Verde a continuing hold on the slave trade even when competition appeared from other nations. English and French ships were forced to stop at the archipelago to obtain cloth for barter on the mainland. Another trade was in the dye-yielding lichen orchil, which was collected in mountainous areas and transformed into a potion of vivid blue.

Thus, positioned between the Old World, Africa and South America, slicing taxes from every import and export, and with a monopoly on trade with the mainland, Cape Verde had become a viable community, with the slave trade its fundamental market and Portugal reaping as much as it could.

ORCHIL DYE

The mountains of Cape Verde yielded one important product – a lichen known as urzella, or orchil (*Litmus roccella*), which could be turned into a blue dye. Together with indigo it was used to colour cloth (see page 40). To make orchil dye, lichen was ground to a powder and mixed with stale urine to form a paste. Quicklime was added to make blues, violets and purples, and tin solution for scarlet.

Portugal made a healthy profit from the orchil business, which began as early as 1469. Rights to take the orchil were sold as a Crown Monopoly which was controlled first by a Brazilian group and then, beginning in the 18th century, by the English, because of that country's burgeoning textile trade. An English firm paid over £6,000 for six years' access to the orchil of Cape Verde, the Azores and Madeira and it was in demand into the 1830s but withered when huge quantities of the lichen were found in Angola and Mozambique, which sent prices plummeting.

During this period the botanical colonisation of the islands was completed as well. As a traffic junction, Cape Verde received plants from everywhere, particularly maize from Brazil, which became a staple, and cassava, which was later planted on the African mainland.

THE ATLANTIC GROWS BUSIER: THE 1600S

Driving the defenders before them they entered the City almost without resistance, where they sacked houses and destroyed them. The authorities fled to the hills and the English, carrying away their spoil, departed to Cartagena and San Domingo.
Contemporary account of the sacking of Ribeira Grande

As the 1600s began, rival nations appeared on the seas. The French, English and Dutch spilled into the Atlantic, and aggression on the ocean became more than the sporadic acts of piracy and smuggling that had characterised the second half of the previous century. Cape Verde became increasingly vulnerable to attack and Portugal foresaw this, responding in 1587 by appointing a governor-general for the islands who was directly responsible to the Crown for Cape Verde and the Guinea coast.

Now France, England and Holland were becoming serious forces in the Atlantic, making their discoveries mainly in North America. As they began to make settlements in their new lands they, too, started to look for slaves. Business across the Atlantic multiplied as the desire for sugar, slaves, salt and fish sent trading ships in a perpetual circle between the four continents.

As international affairs fluctuated so, too, did Cape Verdean fortunes. They fell for a while when the Dutch seized Portuguese slaving sources in west Africa, and when they were sacked and plundered by nations who were at odds with Spain or Portugal. Their fortunes rose after 1640 when Portugal achieved independence from Spain.

Overall, though, the archipelago still made money because the demand for slaves was rising. It was at its peak for Cape Verde during the 1600s and 1700s. Numbers are uncertain, partly because many slaves were not measured in whole 'units'. A 15–25 year old was a *peça*'s worth. A 30 year old in good health was two-thirds of a *peça*. Records are poor but it has been estimated that 3,000 slaves a year left Cape Verde in 1609 and 1610, although these were probably peak years. These slaves earned Cape Verde about £6,500 in import taxes and £1,300 in export taxes over the two years. Nearly three-quarters of the revenue the Portuguese Crown received from Cape Verde was from the slave trade.

RESENTMENT STIRS The question that exercised the people of the archipelago was why so much of its profit should go straight back to Lisbon. It was part of a wider question: what was the purpose of Cape Verde? If it was merely an overseas warehouse then the Portuguese were entitled to act as they wished. But Cape Verde was now a place that some called home and they were trying to make a living there in spite of increasingly tight controls from the Crown.

During the first 150 years of colonisation, blacks and whites came together to found the Cape Verdean ancestry, and the core of Cape Verdean society became remarkably stable. Other Portuguese were reluctant to follow as settlers because the islands were perceived as an arduous posting. In particular, few Portuguese women arrived. The black population was similarly stable, with the shiploads of slaves destined for distant lands mere transient visitors, isolated from the static population.

Black and white, isolated from the rest of the world by the ocean, developed complex layers of relationships. Intermarriage produced a race of *mestiços* who had nowhere else to call their motherland and who were not to assert a national identity until the 20th century.

Cape Verdean Creole heritage differed from other Creole cultures around the world for several reasons. The Cape Verdeans emerged in an empty place where there had been no indigenous population. They were the descendants of a smaller number of whites than is the case with other Creole cultures and so the European element was not sufficiently strong to exert cultural dominance.

It was these 'pre-Cape Verdeans' – whites and, increasingly, people of mixed race governing a large number of slaves – who complained bitterly and frequently about the way Lisbon organised the slave and other trades, and in particular about the rise of the Crown monopolies.

THE MONOPOLIES The right to extract slaves from the African coast was awarded by the Crown as a single, monopolistic contract which lasted for six years. The benefit for the Crown was that the contractor paid a lump sum and agreed to supply a few incidentals including slaves for the king, and some money donated to the Church.

Whoever bought this slaving right then subcontracted it to smaller enterprises. The Portuguese Crown received customs duties when contractors deposited slaves at Cape Verde, and also export duties from those who bought them. The people of Cape Verde were banned from engaging in other trade with non-Portuguese. This rule was resented and widely flouted.

The islanders began to feel seriously undermined in 1675, when the Crown handed out to various companies a series of crippling monopolistic rights over the west African and Cape Verdean trades. The terms seemed to bypass the role of the archipelago as middleman.

Under the rules of the first monopoly, the contractor possessed the sole right to take international products to the Guinea coast for trading: Cape Verdeans were permitted to trade only with homegrown products such as cloth and salt. Santiago's access to Africa, therefore, was deeply threatened. Further decrees were issued by Lisbon. Perhaps the most memorable was that of 1687 which banned anyone on Cape Verde from selling cloth to foreigners, under penalty of death.

The second monopoly was granted in 1690 to a newly formed organisation, the Company of the Islands of Cape Verde and Guiné (Compania Nacional de

Cabo Verde e Guiné). Even more restrictive conditions were included in the new contract, and two seemed almost guaranteed to ensure that Cape Verde was bypassed in the international slave trade. Firstly, the contractor bought the right to supply the Spanish Indies directly with slaves, so he had no need to find someone to buy them on the archipelago. Secondly, the Governor of Cape Verde was put in the pay of the new company. By 1700, Cape Verde felt that it had been ousted by the monopoly companies from its role as a slave-trading depot. It was increasingly left to concentrate on the more predictable business of victualling the hundred ships a year that called at Santiago for supplies in the second half of the 1600s.

CONFLICT: THE 1700S The 1700s began with a bang and the War of the Spanish Succession to prevent France gaining control of Spain. Fears that the fusion of the two countries would give them too much power over Atlantic possessions were typical of the concerns of other European powers at the time. The century was to be one of territorial expansion to the west of the Atlantic, consolidation, and the rise of the British as the supreme naval force.

Cape Verde would always be prey to the whims of the rest of the world, successful when exploiting the needs of a diversity of countries and unsuccessful when those needs suddenly changed. When Portugal was drawn into the War of Succession, the slave trade with the Spanish Indies came to a sudden end for Cape Verde but also for the monopoly companies.

That war did not finish until 1714 and was the cause of the sack of Santiago in 1712, a disastrous plunder by the French that robbed Ribeira Grande of all its riches. The people of Cape Verde urged Lisbon to liberalise its trade and finally, in 1721, Portugal relaxed the rules so that the people could trade with whom they wished. Business was reinvigorated, but the central problem remained – Portugal was not prepared to pour money into a string of rocks which could not guarantee much return. The people of the islands were left to live on their wits, thinking only from day to day.

This conflict was behind many of the background problems of the archipelago. Goats chomped inexorably at the fragile vegetation that had taken millions of years to win a hold in the face of Saharan winds. Without sophisticated, long-term land management it was inevitable that famine would increasingly afflict the islands. Every century there were one or two more famines than the century before and, in 1773–76, 44% of the population died.

Lack of investment in proper military protection also led to raids which were a perpetual drain on resources. Like a fleet of marooned ships the islands were unable to flee marauders of the high seas.

THE END OF SLAVERY: THE 1800S Towards the end of the 1700s the seeds were sown in America and Europe for convulsions that would end the 300-year-old Atlantic slave trade and transform life for most nations bordering that ocean. The changes were partly intellectual. The Enlightenment grew in Europe, with its faith in rationality and social progress; with it came concepts of the rights of man and the iniquity of slavery, both of which served to justify the French and American revolutions. After the French Revolution Napoleon's energies were unleashed on the oceans and one of the consequences was that Portugal and Spain were cut off from their colonies in South America. The effect of this was profound. A vacuum arose in 19th-century South America into which grew movements for liberation, followed by the abolition of slavery and, later, the rise of concepts such as African nationalism which would inspire countries such as Cape Verde to fight for independence.

Slavery was disappearing in North America as well, following independence in 1783. America became a land of promise that lured millions of emigrants fleeing starvation or unemployment in other parts of the world. The 1800s became an era of mass global migration.

Cape Verde was buffeted by these 19th-century Atlantic storms. One of the most bitter was the demise of its own slave-trading, abolished as a 'business' by the Portuguese in 1854, with private slavery ending in 1876.

During the 19th century the dominance of the sailing ship came to an end, and with it Cape Verde's prime function as a resupplier. But as Santiago suffered, two other islands began to emerge as arenas where profits could be made.

The first was São Vicente. It has a perfect and generous natural harbour, perhaps the safest place to pause in the entire eastern Atlantic. Other than that it is a sterile pile of stones and so it had been of little interest in previous centuries.

This deep harbour was just the place for the new steamships born of the Industrial Revolution to reload with coal on their journeys along the Atlantic shipping lanes. The British, riding the crest of the invention of the steam engine, flocked to São Vicente to set up coaling stations. Mindelo, its capital, grew at an astonishing rate.

The second island where epochal events were taking place was a tiny one: Brava. It was at this insignificant dot at the end of the archipelago that whaling ships from New England began to stop and pick up eager crews of young men. The ships offered the prospect of passage to America and in this way Cape Verdeans joined the mass migration to the New World.

They went on emigrating throughout the century and on into the next. In the first 20 years of the 1900s, 19,000 Cape Verdeans set up new homes there. Many of them still regarded the archipelago as their home, which would eventually bring great economic benefit to Cape Verde.

The structure of Cape Verdean society changed in the 19th century as homegrown slavery disappeared. In 1834, a rough count yielded 52,000 free or freed men and women, and 4,000 slaves. Yet for most people the 1870s declaration that, finally, slavery was to end, did not mean a better life, for slaves had to serve further years of forced labour which were to continue in various guises until well into the following century. Another social change occurred as Cape Verde became a place of exile for Portuguese convicts, from thieves to political dissidents. Between 1802 and 1882, according to the English historian Basil Davidson, nearly 2,500 such *degredados* arrived at the islands: 'They were at once absorbed into a population increasingly homogeneous in its culture and way of life, if notably various in the colours of its skin.'

Portugal ruled by skin colour. A census of 1856 listed 17 distinctions, ranging from various shades of 'very dark' to 'almost white'. Many lighter Cape Verdeans clung to their rank and despised the darker ones.

SUFFERING: THE BEGINNING OF THE 1900S The 20th century began with a very different Cape Verde. The cinder heap of São Vicente, not fertile Santiago, was its chief commercial centre. São Vicente attracted a hopeless migration of the desperate from other islands in search of work. But the island had virtually no natural resources and was incapable of sustaining a rural peasant population. So when the shipping business dipped, as it did from time to time, the consequences of drought became increasingly shocking. Some 17,000 died in 1921. In 1922, the Santiago journal *A Verdade* reported:

The schooner *Ernestina*, a beautiful, 112ft sailing vessel over a century old, is one of the most famous of the packet ships that connected Cape Verde with the USA in the early 20th century.

She was still working as a packet ship in the 1960s, making her last Atlantic voyage to Providence in 1965 in an era that had long been dominated by the steamship, which itself was fast losing trade to the aeroplane.

The *Ernestina* had many lives. After her launch in 1894 she became a Grand Banks fisher and then an Arctic expeditionary vessel. She sank after a galley fire in 1946, and that was when a Cape Verdean, Captain Henrique Mendes, stepped in. The schooner was raised, restored to seaworthiness, bought by Captain Mendes and then began her new life as a transatlantic packet ship. Her work was to carry passengers and goods between Cape Verde and the USA. Often she took seasonal workers to New England for the cranberry harvest. Hopeful immigrants would also come. Sometimes she would take successful immigrants on rare trips home; more often it was goods she ferried back to the motherland – bought with hard-won money earned on the bogs or in the textile mills of New Bedford.

For ten years this trade continued between Cape Verde and Providence, Rhode Island. After her last trip in 1965 she continued work between Cape Verde and the African mainland. She also worked the islands. One job was to ferry schoolchildren from Fogo and Brava to boarding school in Praia and Mindelo.

But even this work was being eclipsed by other, more modern ships, and eventually it was decided to return the *Ernestina* to the USA. But the trip home, in 1976, was a disaster – a storm dismasted her and she was forced to return to port. There, the government of the new republic had her rebuilt and, six years later, gave her to the USA as a symbol of friendship.

The *Ernestina* is now a sailing school, educational vessel and cultural icon. For more information on the schooner and a vivid history of the passage of Cape Verdeans to and from the USA as well as the campaign to restore her to the seas, see www.ernestina.org.

1921 was horrific... yet now follows this of 1922, equally horrific but with the addition that people have spent all they possess, whether in clothes or land, livestock or trinkets, and today are in the last stage of poverty, while emigration is carrying away all whom the steamers can embark.

The rains came in the end. In the 1930s, they were plentiful and the archipelago turned green. Emigrants, fleeing the Depression in the USA, returned to live with their families. But it did not last, and hunger returned in the early 1940s.

Outside the archipelago World War II began. On the islands, anti-Portuguese sentiment surged when Lisbon decided to garrison over 6,000 men amongst the islands' starving population. It is possible that Portugal feared that the British or the Germans were planning to seize the archipelago, and their fears were justified. Winston Churchill had well-developed plans to invade Cape Verde but called them off at the last minute. The matter of who controlled the islands was still of interest to the world.

Peace came in 1945 but for the Cape Verdeans the worst drought they were ever to face was looming. Some 30,000 people died. The hunger was exacerbated by the return of the emigrant Americans a few years before: they swelled the numbers and decreased the remittances.

This hideous cycle of drought and famine raises the question: could it have been avoided? After all, Cape Verdeans do not die of hunger today. The answer is still

TRACING THE ANCESTORS

Romantic stories abound of brave Cape Verdean men who risked their lives to sail across the Atlantic and find fortune for themselves and their families in the USA. But these days, many Cape Verdeans in the USA have lost track of their personal family histories. They may have a forgotten great-great-grandfather who toiled on whaling ships on the wild ocean, risking his life to harpoon whales, earn promotion and set up life on the east coast. They may be descended from a couple of lost generations who worked themselves to the bone in the cranberry bogs of New England, returning home with their earnings at the end of each season. You may be descended from a young man who left his sweetheart on Fogo; you may own a stone cottage or great *sobrado* house, now standing forgotten on Brava.

Of all the Africans who went to the USA in the era of mass migration, Cape Verdean Americans are the only ones who can trace their families back to their original villages, according to James Lopes, author of a genealogy website (*www.umassd.edu/specialprograms/caboverde/jlopes.html*). This is because there are excellent records of Cape Verdean arrivals in the USA. Those who have made the journey of rediscovery often find they have relatives, or ancestors, from all over the world, including Europe, Asia, and South America.

To decipher your family tree, begin by questioning your immediate family, advises Mr Lopes. Write down everything you unearth – in particular the dates of birth, marriage and death of each remembered person, and how they made a living.

Then, when a particularly dim but fascinating figure emerges from the past, there are several sources to help you investigate. For those whose families went to the USA before 1920 the arrival should have been recorded in the passenger and ships lists of the Port of New Bedford. Most Cape Verdeans passed through there, though Boston and Providence were other ports of entry. The voyages of all Cape Verdean whaling ships are also listed, and kept in New Bedford Free Public Library.

One mine of fascinating information is the Old Dartmouth Historical Society at the New Bedford Whaling Museum (*New Bedford, MA 02740, USA*). The original logbooks of many of the whaling expeditions that took Cape Verdeans to the USA are stored here. Details of the trip, including how much your ancestor was paid, might be found.

There are several other useful places to begin digging, including the Arquivo Histórico Nacional in Santiago (see *Appendix 2, Further Information*, page 342). Staff there will research birth records on request. For more information on where to search, see James Lopes's website, above.

Finally, Marilyn Halter's book *Race and Ethnicity* (see *Books*, page 339) gives spellbinding accounts of life in the cranberry bogs and other features of emigrant life.

Background Information HISTORY

obscure but it seems certain that an important ingredient of the famines was the way the land was owned and run. It was a system which discouraged peasants from planning more than a season ahead.

Agriculture was mired in a system of inheritance which split land with each generation until people farmed it in splinters in an inefficient way. Land that was not subject to this system was owned in great swathes by a small number of men who rented it out in patches a year at a time. The peasants who farmed this land had no incentive to improve it: they knew that the extra yield would be taken as rent.

SOCIAL STRUCTURE

Numerous categories defined the different elements of Cape Verdean society. *Fidalgos* were the noblemen, representing the king and making money for themselves and for the Crown through a system of royal charters, trade monopolies and land grants. They tended to be Portuguese, though there were some Genoese, Venetians and Spanish. *Capitãos* were military governors appointed by the Crown, with a high degree of local autonomy. *Feitors* were powerful private business agents who had won royal trade monopolies and also represented private mercantile concerns.

The pariahs of the slave trade were the *lançados*. They were, by definition, outcasts, but they were essential middlemen, embedding themselves in the tropical creeks of the west African coast where they channelled the trade in goods and humans. Portuguese, they were often political or religious criminals, and many of them were Jews who had fled the Inquisition. *Lançados* had an ambiguous relationship with the Crown: in theory they complied with royal trade monopolies, but in practice they had a pervasive power that the Crown could not control. They traded with whom they pleased and flouted Portuguese tax and other restrictions. *Ganagogas* were technically Jewish *lançados*, but in practice the term embraced anyone who could speak many local African languages.

Tangamãus were the public interface of the African involvement in the trade, and functioned mainly as translators; the name probably comes from *targuman*, the Arabic for translator. The mercenary bodyguards of the *lançados* and *tangamãus* were the *grumettas*.

Banished from Portugal for criminal or political reasons, *degredados* often became galley slaves in rowing boats. They lived either on Cape Verde or on the African coast, where some became *lançados*. Like the *lançados*, they became an important white ingredient in the founding of the Creole population. *Pretos* were free blacks, while *ladinos* were slaves who had been baptised and given a Latin name.

As slaves escaped or were freed, the peasant population grew. At its core was a group whom the Portuguese despised, as did the later *mestiço* class. These were the *Badius*, and they clung to their African culture. They were small-scale farmers generally living in the remote central regions of Santiago. *Parcerias* were colonial partnership share-cropping systems; share-croppers usually gave between a half and two-thirds of the crops they grew to their landowner. *Rendeiros* grew subsistence crops for themselves and worked on other people's land, generally for wages.

Later in history came *contratados*, contract labourers who worked in São Tomé and Príncipe and also in the United States.

So, at a time when the people could have been producing income for the islands by cultivating cash crops such as coffee for export, agriculture stagnated. This, combined with the dwindling of tree cover, imposed deep poverty. Cape Verde was becoming an increasingly unsustainable place. Population control was left to the crude device of starvation.

People escaped not just to America but also to work on other Portuguese islands. They left for São Tomé and Príncipe in their tens of thousands: 24,000 Cape Verdeans worked there between 1902 and 1922; 34,000 laboured there from 1950–70. In this way these *contratados* escaped starvation, though some said the labourers returned more emaciated than when they left.

Soon Cape Verde's only lingering use, as a coaling station, seemed to be vanishing as well; oil was replacing coal as the fuel for the high seas and, as a result, few ships needed to pause there. When they did stop, resupply with oil was an easier, smaller business than loading coal. There was no need to maintain great companies with armies of staff on the crescent of rock halfway to South America. The world had dumped Cape Verde.

REVOLT Ideas of independence began to grow in the minds of 20th-century Cape Verdeans as a result of several world events. The consequences of their uprising, when it eventually came, were momentous. It was probably the first time in Cape Verde's history that the rocks made a splash of their own, and the ripples spread far. For it was Cape Verdeans, unique in Portuguese Africa because of their education and cosmopolitanism, who led the ferment in other Portuguese African colonies. This in turn weakened Portugal and was the direct cause of the unseating of its fascist dictatorship.

One important force arose from the European 'scramble for Africa', which began in the late 1800s and had allocated most of the continent to colonial rule by the early 1900s. When World War I diverted the colonists' attention, resistance to colonial rule gathered pace, giving rise to the growing feeling that European reins could be thrown away. Cape Verde, unusual in having been subjugated for long centuries rather than mere decades, absorbed these ideas as they emerged in other European colonies. Allied to this was the rise of communism, which leaked into Africa and gave structure to undirected stirrings of antagonism amongst the people towards their rulers.

Another factor was necessary, however, for Cape Verdeans to begin to assimilate these ideas: they needed to hear about them and they needed to be educated enough to understand them. This impetus came, ironically, from the beneficence of Lisbon. Portugal had acknowledged the peculiarity of its Cape Verde colony and recognised its *mestiço* population as closer to its own than were the natives of mainland Africa. As a result, Cape Verdeans were granted a form of Portuguese citizenship, although it is unclear how this benefited most of them. The archipelago was also the intellectual centre of the Portuguese African colonies, with a secondary school which attracted pupils from the mainland, and a seminary.

There arose a small group of urbane, mixed-race Cape Verdeans whom the Portuguese employed as middlemen. They were halfway between black and white and so they could more easily administer the people of Portuguese Guinea, Angola, Mozambique and São Tomé, while being an acceptable interface with the true Portuguese. A select group of Cape Verdeans was thus educated, chosen as a literate class of administrators, and sent to work in diverse outposts of empire. From this group sprang poets and journalists who began to seek to express the nature of Cape Verdeanism. Their political objectives were limited: they prized the privilege of Portuguese citizenship and supported enlightened colonialism, defending the fledgling republic that was born in Portugal in 1910.

Perhaps if the liberalism that accompanied the new Portuguese republic had been allowed to continue, the movement for independence would have come earlier. Perhaps it would have fizzled out. We shall never know, for in 1926, the republic was overthrown by its own military, inaugurating 50 years of fascist dictatorship. Freedom of speech disappeared.

More visible twitchings of nationhood came with the publication of *Claridade*, a journal that called to the nation to realise the essence of 'Cape Verdeanness'. It published the work of some gifted writers in four issues between 1936 and 1941, and in another six after the end of World War II. For 500 years there had been no such race or culture as the Cape Verdean. There were Portuguese, there were slaves and there were *mestiços*. Yet the Cape Verdeans were there, incipient, infused with the knowledge of their African and European roots, endowed with a musical and poetic culture. *Claridade* helped them to see this – to define as Cape Verdean their laments and their poetry, the way they wore their clothes and their craftsmanship. *Claridade* reminded them that they had their own language: Creole.

It was those members of the educated class who were teenagers in the early 1940s who made the crucial step in the evolution of Cape Verdean thought. They were so angered by the mass of deaths in the droughts of that time that they began to believe that Cape Verde could be better off if it was independent from Portugal.

Amílcar Cabral was just 17, and in his second year at secondary school, when the 1941 famine ravaged the people of Mindelo. His later success in rousing the people of Cape Verde and Portuguese Guinea to rise against the Portuguese, and his effective fighting techniques, have been ascribed by historians to his profound knowledge of these countries and his ability to inspire Africans with a concept of their own nationality.

Born in 1924 of Cape Verdean parents, Cabral grew up in what is today Guinea-Bissau, then Portuguese Guinea, in great poverty, finding the money to attend school from the small profits of his needleworking mother, whom he greatly admired. He had at least 61 brothers and sisters, all sired by his father, Juvenal Cabral. After school he studied agrarian engineering at Lisbon where he graduated with honours. He had a sound colonial career at his feet.

But while he was a student he imbibed from various clandestine sources ideas of communism and liberalism as well as news from revolutionary intellectuals from other African colonies. After graduating, Cabral's career move must have seemed bizarre to outsiders. He buried himself in the backlands of Guinea, an employee of the farming and forestry service, making the first analysis of its agrarian and water resources. During this time he acquired an intimate knowledge of the country's landscape and social structure.

Cabral's battle was not just against the Portuguese. Cape Verdeans themselves accepted assimilation, and the cycles of drought and emigration, as an unavoidable consequence of the land. Cabral formed a tiny nationalist movement in 1954.

He made friends with another product of the Mindelo secondary school, Aristides Pereira, who worked in the posts-and-telegraph office in Guinea. They learned local languages, read literature on uprisings around the world and worked on until Cabral was deported from the country in 1955. The following year, the two formed a tiny party: the **PAIGC (Party for the Independence of Guinea and Cape Verde)**. Other members were educated people with administrative jobs in Portugal, Angola and Guinea. The party pursued peaceful means at first, appealing for better conditions. One of their group, Abilio Duarte, returned to Cape Verde to agitate there amongst the students and the dockers, while Cabral set up a base in Conakry, capital of ex-French Guinea.

The **insurrection** stumbled forward, manifesting itself publicly through graffiti at first and then through strikes, which inevitably led to sporadic massacres. A wages strike in Portuguese Guinea left 50 shot dead and the rest sentenced to 15 years' hard labour.

Throughout 1959 and 1960 the activists moved around the world, gaining confidence from news of uprisings outside Portuguese Africa while the islands suffered another drought. This time, however, the loss of life was not of disastrous proportions because of a more compassionate governor.

Fighting began in Portuguese Guinea in 1963 and Cape Verdeans made their way to the mainland to join the army. The war lasted for ten years, with the PAIGC, numerically tiny compared with the number of Portuguese troops, employing brilliant guerrilla tactics to lure the enemy into dispersing into numerous garrisons which it could then besiege. Arms from the USSR eventually arrived and by 1972 the PAIGC had control of half of the country, but not the air, where the commanding general, António de Spínola, retained supremacy.

Back in Cape Verde, nothing had happened superficially even by 1971. Abilio Duarte worked both at the Mindelo school, transforming the aspirations of the next generation, and amongst the dockers of Mindelo, more open to new ideas than their inland counterparts.

From 1966 a band of 30 of the most talented young men of Cape Verde had been living in Cuba, where they trained for a surprise landing on Santiago and Santo Antão which would begin the war on the archipelago. In fact the landings plan would never be executed, most critically because the group failed to find the transport they needed across the ocean.

It was just as well, because swooping arrests in 1967 eliminated any organised reception the rebels might have hoped for, while the drought of 1968 would have starved any guerrillas trying to survive in the highlands. So, back on the archipelago, there was no war, just the arrests of increasing numbers of suspected rebels. The peasants were waiting with messianic expectation for Amílcar Cabral to come from Portuguese Guinea and liberate them.

But they would never see him. Tragedy struck on 20 January 1973, when traitors from within the PAIGC's own ranks murdered the 52-year-old Cabral on the mainland, just a few months before the victory in Guinea. Anger at his death shook any stagnation out of the guerrilla ranks and this, together with the arrival of ground-to-air missiles from the USSR, triggered the final offensive which was to bring them victory. Guinea-Bissau became a member of the Organisation of African Unity on 19 November 1973.

Cabral had been right when he prophesied in 1961: 'We for our part are sure that the destruction of Portuguese colonialism is what will destroy Portuguese fascism.' Young officers in the Portuguese army in Guinea became convinced that they would never win their African wars. Portugal was becoming overburdened, economically and politically, by these African questions. The officers grouped to form the Armed Forces Movement, returning to Portugal to overthrow the dictator, António de Oliveira Salazar, just five months after Guinea's liberation. Independence followed quickly for some other Portuguese colonies, though for Cape Verde it was far from automatic. Spínola, head of the AMF and new leader of Portugal, wanted to hang on to the strategically positioned islands.

The USA was reluctant to help, fearing that an independent Cape Verde would become a Soviet base. Meanwhile all the leading militants on the islands were locked up and the remainder were still on the mainland. All Cape Verde had won was an agreement that it could have its own National Council.

Returning from the mainland war in August 1974, the Cape Verdean heroes were given a rapturous welcome. But they arrived in a country where Portuguese authority was not just intact but working overtime under the orders of Spínola.

There were those on the islands who wanted to remain with Portugal. Intellectuals from the old *Claridade* movement argued that Cape Verde could never be economically viable on its own and should remain associated with someone, Portugal or the United Nations. They supported the words of Eugénio Tavares, the poet:

> For Cape Verde? For these poor and abandoned rocks thrown up in the sea,
> independence? What sense is there in that? God have pity on thoughtless men!

But most could not bear to remain allied to the country that had caused them so much ill.

Rescue came in the form of the democrats in Portugal who overthrew Spínola and were more receptive to Cape Verdean demands. After a transitional joint government, a general election was held at the end of June 1975, and the PAIGC became the new government, a National Assembly proclaiming independence for the archipelago on 5 July 1975. The president was Aristides Pereira, Secretary-General of the PAIGC. Cape Verde and Guinea-Bissau were a joint country.

AFTER INDEPENDENCE Cape Verde was free but it was a wasteland: its resources plundered over centuries, its soil thin and disappearing with every gust of Saharan wind. Drought had come again in 1969 and afflicted the islands for six years. In 1977, the maize and bean harvest was nil. There was no work for wages and exports were almost non-existent. Over half of the islands' imports were of famine food, and emigration surged. The shock of the sudden assumption of responsibility for such a land must have been acute.

One of Cape Verde's few advantages was that it was not riven with tribal rivalries. In that sense it began rebuilding from a metaphorical, as well as a literal, bare ground. Another advantage lay in its good contacts with the outside world. The democrats of Portugal were on friendly terms with Cape Verde, a relationship that continues today.

Help came from many countries: once the USA was convinced that Cape Verde was indeed 'non-aligned' it sent a gift of US$7 million. The World Food Programme dispatched thousands of tonnes of maize, and a variety of countries, including Sweden, Holland and the USSR, also sent aid. Uniquely, the Cape Verdean government insisted that the WFP grain was not handed out as charity but was sold to people who did construction work on water-retention and anti-erosion dykes and on barrages in return for wages.

The government was a socialist one which attracted the interest of the USSR, China and Cuba. There are still strong ties with these countries: Cuba and Russia have been the destination of many Cape Verdean university students, while university links with China are underway. Indeed, the Chinese embassy is the most prestigious building in Praia, and sits opposite Cape Verde's parliament, and China's economic links with the country are growing. Guinea-Bissau, meanwhile, suffered more turbulence than Cape Verde, which led to a coup in 1980 that ruptured the link between the two countries. After that 'The Party', for there was only one, renamed itself the PAICV (Partido Africano da Independência de Cabo Verde).

The PAICV had a political monopoly enshrined in the country's constitution and which went unchallenged at first. One person within the party who objected to the lack of democracy, and also to the centralised control of the party and the limits placed on free enterprise, was one Carlos Veiga, who formed the MpD (Movimento para a Democracia) in 1990.

Things moved swiftly and by September 1990 Cape Verde had legally become a multi-party state. Elections the following January swept out the PAICV and handed power to Veiga, who was prime minister from 1991 to 2001. A month later the candidate the MpD supported for president, António Manuel Mascarenhas, was elected.

Flagship policies of the government in 1991 were a market economy with less public spending, opening up to foreign investment, and the development of fishing, tourism and service industries. A new national anthem and flag were adopted in September 1992.

A decade later, on 14 January 2001, the PAICV regained control in an overwhelming victory. The people then elected for president (with a margin of 12 votes) Pedro Pires, who had been prime minister of the first government in 1975. More importantly for the PAICV, it won in the Legislative Assembly. In the latest national elections the ruling party, PAICV won an historic victory when it was voted in for a third five-year term, the first party to achieve this.

So the islands survive to face a brighter future than ever before. The land now receives the love it needs. The people are trying to demonstrate that the islands' history has been due to incompetence, greed and neglect, not because of what they once were called: 'bitter bare rocks strung out in mid Atlantic like a crown of thorns floating on the sea.'

GOVERNMENT AND POLITICS

Cape Verde is a democratic republic with no political prisoners and a clean human rights record. The oldest party is the PAICV, which won independence for the country in 1975 and ruled it as a one-party state for many years. The MpD (Movimento para a Democracia), devoted to liberal economic and social reform, won democracy for Cape Verde in 1990 and was elected in 1991 and then again in December 1995. A sliver of the MpD broke away to form the Partido da Convergencia Democratica (PCD) in 1994. In late 2000, the PAICV came to power again and was re-elected in 2006 and 2011. The president is Pedro Pires, and the prime minister is José Maria Neves. The closest rival, Carlos Veiga, of the MpD, claimed that the results were fraudulent and filed a lawsuit, but international election monitors deemed them free and fair. MpD conceded the 2011 elections which PAICV once again won with a small margin. Municipal elections were held in 2008 with the majority of seats being taken by the MpD. Local elections will be held again in 2011. In many instances this has led to a lack of co-operation and a stalemate between central government (PAICV) and local government (MpD), and has sometimes hindered the economic and social development of the islands.

ECONOMY

DEVELOPMENT In the 2010 report for the United Nations' human development index, Cape Verde came in at 118 – beating almost every other country in mainland Africa. According to the World Bank, Gross Domestic Product was US$3,193 per head in 2008. Unemployment at the end of 2007 was 22%, although many of the unemployed are occupied for at least some of the time in fishing or farming.

According to the International Monetary Fund growth has slowed severely in recent years, reflecting the reduction in tourism and investment in property due to poor economic conditions in Europe. In 2009, GDP growth was reduced to 3%. During this period remittances from Cape Verdeans living overseas also slowed down (according to a US State Department report, these remittances account for 20% of GDP). In July 2010, the IMF was still rather pessimistic about a strong growth in the Cape Verdean economy during 2010, estimating GDP growth at a modest 4.1%. The government's finance minister, however, was more optimistic, forecasting 6–8%.

Inflation was 1% in 2009 according to the country's National Statistics Institute. Cape Verde is one of the few countries set to achieve its Millennium Development Goals.

Cape Verde forged a special partnership with the European Union in 2007, as well as membership of the World Trade Organization, and has been elevated by the UN to 'middle income' status.

In the long term, Cape Verde has extraordinary ambition. It hopes to transform itself into an international financial centre and an investment and transport gateway to continental Africa. The first stage in this plan is to get the money rolling in by the rapid development of tourism, on the back of which a service economy can be developed. For the moment, however, the major inputs into Cape Verde's economy are still aid and remittances.

AID Foreign aid and remittances together sustain about a quarter of Cape Verde's economy. The islands have been the recipients of one of the highest amounts of international aid, per capita, in the world (US$270 per person annually in 1997). Many sources of aid funding were withdrawn from 2007 when Cape Verde was upgraded by the United Nations to the status of 'middle income country' – one of only a handful that have ever achieved this elevation. However, there are still substantial – one might say, enormous – amounts of investment and aid coming from other nations.

One organisation that has stepped into the breach is the **Millennium Challenge Corporation**, a US government corporation that rewards good governance in poor countries with substantial investment in areas that will lead to economic growth. Through its Millennium Challenge Account, it is putting US$110 million into Cape Verde. The money is going towards developing agriculture on three islands by improving rainwater capture (and its storage and distribution) and soil conservation; improving the road and bridge infrastructure on some islands; and financial sector reform. In 2008, the World Bank announced US$6 million for the fight against poverty motivated partly, it said, by Cape Verde's inability to secure other sources of funding because of its new status. Portuguese co-operation with Cape Verde, meanwhile, will total €70 million from 2008–11.

But these helping hands are dwarfed by the agreements Cape Verde is reaching with China, whose relationship with the country goes back to the early days of independence. Agreements made in 2008 were so vast, embracing shipping, fishing, communications, electricity and construction, that they were dubbed the 'new Chinese wave'. The key project is with the China Ocean Shipping Companies Group (Cosco), one of the world's largest shipping companies, in partnership with Enapor, which looks after Cape Verde's port facilities. The investments will include several port redevelopments and the building of cargo facilities. Meanwhile there are plans for a major fishing supply centre in São Vicente followed by the conversion of São Vicente into a special economic area. China built Cape Verde its first dam (in Santiago) and will construct a national stadium with capacity for 20,000 people.

REMITTANCES Calculations vary, but it is believed by some that there may be more Cape Verdeans abroad than at home (see box, *The diaspora's influence on Cape Verde*, pages 30–1), and that between a third and two-thirds of families on the islands are receiving money from relatives overseas. Remittances contributed 20% of GDP in 2009.

FISHERIES Fishing contributes 1.1% of GDP. The archipelago is at the centre of one of the last great underused fishing grounds of the world. Tuna and lobster abound, but at present fishing is a trade of artisans, though there is some export of fish and crustaceans. Although the continental shelf area is relatively small, the Exclusive Economic Zone of Cape Verde covers an area of about 789,400km^2, much of which is not exploited by the national fisheries.

In spite of increased fishing efforts during the past decade, landings have reached a plateau at around 9,000–10,000 per year, and catches of some fish have decreased. However, new fishing agreements are on the horizon, particularly with China. New fish-processing facilities will be built in São Vicente.

TOURISM Tourism contributed 10% of GDP in 2005 (when the last available statistics were compiled) although it as yet generates little employment (0.4% for the same year). It is almost entirely responsible for Cape Verde's recent growth in GDP, and the construction boom is by far the major component of this. Plans for holiday resorts, condominiums and apartments, abound. The number of tourists coming to the islands has similarly risen. In 1991, there were 19,000 tourist arrivals. In 2009, reflecting the world economic crisis, the number of arrivals fell to 188,000 but the first quarter of 2010 saw a growth of 9.1%, with the majority of international arrivals landing in Sal. The island that saw the biggest increase was Boavista, growth that can be accounted for by the opening of a new all-inclusive resort. Inclusive packages operated by Thomson (UK) and TUI (Germany, Nordic) account for the majority of tourists arriving in Cape Verde, followed by TAP (Portugal). Tourists from the UK have now overtaken the number of visitors from Portugal.

AGRICULTURE 'It is heartbreaking,' says one expat scientist working in Cape Verde, 'to watch a peasant woman patiently prepare the ground and sow, then wait for months while it doesn't rain, then return to break the ground and sow again.'

Only a tenth of the land, 40,000ha, is suitable for cultivation. Of this, 34,000ha are cultivated and less than a tenth of that is irrigated, although this proportion has been rising (see box, *Energy and water in Cape Verde*, pages 34–5). Some 90% of the crop is maize and beans which are often grown together. The beans grow up the maize stalks which act as trellises and offer some shade. Other major crops are bananas, sugarcane, sweet potatoes, manioc and cassava. The only significant exported crop is the banana, although other cash crops are coffee, peanuts, castor beans and pineapples. More than half of the total irrigated land grows sugarcane, most of which is used in the production of *grogue*, the local rum.

Historical patterns of ownership have deterred investment in, and maintenance of, agricultural land (see *History*, page 9) but land reform has been very hard to implement. The PAICV's attempts in 1981 were so unpopular that the next government reversed them in 1993.

Farming on steep hillsides is another challenge to Cape Verdean agriculture. There are many devices in the Cape Verdean hills and valleys designed to keep precious water and topsoil from being flushed away. *Arretos* are lines of small stone walls around the hillsides, designed for erosion control. Although they are not supposed to be used for planting, crops grown behind them are producing double the yield of crops grown before the *arretos* were built. Terraces are much bigger walls, properly designed for the ubiquitous shelved farming seen all over Cape Verde.

Check dams of concrete or stone are built in the *ribeiras* to try and slow the rainwater's progress to the sea. At the moment, when it rains, about 85% of the water is lost. Concreted slopes on the hillside, and sometimes natural rock formations, catch water which then flows into a tank or reservoir at the bottom.

Another major problem for agriculture in Cape Verde is pests. The millipede in Santo Antão devours potatoes and carrots – as a result the island, which is agriculturally the most productive in the archipelago, has suffered an embargo on exports of its agricultural products for decades, although this was finally, and partially, lifted in 2008. Grasshoppers cause devastation on other islands.

There is one goat for every two people in Cape Verde. In the villages there are many pigs which forage for scraps, so they cost little and are an important source of meat.

THE DIASPORA'S INFLUENCE ON CAPE VERDE
Elizabeth Mistry

Since the archipelago was first populated, Cape Verdeans have taken to the seas in search of new opportunities abroad. More than 30,000 have emigrated to Portugal since the 1968 drought. Italy has up to 10,000 Cape Verdean immigrants, many of whom went to work there as domestics in the 1970s, a route opened up by the Church and which became self-perpetuating.

Senegal and Angola each have tens of thousands of Cape Verdeans. There are emigrants in Luxembourg, France (10,000–15,000) and Holland (8,000–10,000). There are substantial numbers in Argentina and Brazil and in Spain and Sweden.

But the largest group by far is in the United States, where there are approximately 300,000 Cape Verdean Americans. Numbers remain static although unemployment in the archipelago means that arrivals continue, many of whom do not register with the embassy. A new census was completed in 2010 which is expected to show an increase in numbers of emigrants as well as inter-island migration.

Today the community is spread right across the country but the strongholds remain the states of Massachusetts and Rhode Island. The US diaspora has two representatives in the Legislature in Praia. They represent the interests of the entire Americas, including the sizeable Brazilian population. Regardless of whether they are US-born or incomers, however, diaspora members in the US are fully integrated into the American way of life, with many prominent members of the community working in state and federal positions as well as at a grassroots level.

Yet they have also successfully fought to maintain as many traditions from home as possible – not least the use of Creole (which is taught in several universities, including Harvard) in various media, both print and broadcast, and the celebration of all the usual Cape Verdean festivals. Independence Day (on 5 July, just one day after the host nation) is one of the most important.

Families still get together to eat *cachupa* and drink imported *grogue* and to listen to *mornas* by B Leva and also, increasingly, the newer artists who regularly tour the US. The younger generation in particular has embraced cyberspace and there are a number of electronic fora and blogs that enable cousins on either side

PEOPLE

POPULATION Cape Verde has a population of 505,606 (UN, 2009) ranging in ethnicity from virtually white to black: about 70% are mixed race, 1% are white. Women outnumber men because of emigration, although there are localities where it is the women who are emigrating rather than the men. The lack of men, together with the intermittent returns and lengthy absences, are two of the reasons why marriage, and family units of father, mother and children, are unusual. Men typically have children by many women and are often married to none of them; the same applies to women. Responsibility for bringing up children invariably falls to the women, who may be dependent on remittances sent back from abroad by the various fathers.

Population growth is 2.1% and the government has campaigned hard to bring it down through birth control, including abortion. The Catholic Church has campaigned hard against the latter. Life expectancy is 68 for men and 74 for women. Some 81% of people are literate, and this rises to over 90% among the young. Some 38% of the population is under 14 years of age.

of the Atlantic to keep in closer contact than their parents' generation could ever have imagined.

'The importance of the diaspora's contribution to the islands cannot be underestimated,' says Raymond A Almeida, who has lived in the US for many years but who maintains close links with the islands. There is a symbiotic relationship, he suggests, with the remittances from the US a sizeable amount. In addition, the number of charitable associations and friendship groups that provide support, both financial and in kind, is impressive for so small a nation, he says. It is hard to find a school or organisation that does not receive some sort of help from a US-based community initiative.

The political clout, also, cannot be underestimated. It is popularly said that the cliffhanger presidential election in 2001, won by 12 votes, was decided by the diaspora.

The link works the other way, too. In 2008, Patrick Kennedy, nephew of John F Kennedy and the Congressional representative of Rhode Island, visited Cape Verde. There are 80,000 Cape Verdeans in Rhode Island – so it was a constituency visit. He joked that he had come from Cape Verde's tenth inhabited island.

Most American-born Cape Verdeans who return do so to maintain links with family and friends and, increasingly to invest in business, especially in the service industries and in small-scale property development.

'We are way behind the Europeans though,' says John Monteiro, who was born on Fogo and went to the US as a six year old. Almost 50 years later he is looking to build a small hotel but says land prices in the last few years have tripled. 'The only advantage we have over the Irish developers is that we speak the language and some of us have relatives who can help steer us through the red tape. But we're in it for the long term. Those coming from the Cape Verdean community in the US want to see the community on the islands benefit too – we want to see improved education and healthcare and are prepared to help make that happen. We're not just here to make money. I know a lot of people who have come back from visiting the islands and who say, "we've got to help".'

More than half the population lives on Santiago, and of these over 128,000 live in Praia, the capital of Cape Verde. The only other big population centre is Mindelo on São Vicente. The island of Santa Luzia is uninhabited.

SOCIAL ISSUES

AIDS A recent national study indicated that the prevalence of HIV in the population is 0.8% (1.1% for men and 0.4% for women). This means there are about 1,900 people across Cape Verde who are infected with HIV. This rate is

---

TURNING A COUNTRY ROUND   *Aisling Irwin*

'2007 was a golden year for Cape Verde,' says Jorge Sousa Brito, Rector of Cape Verde's Jean Piaget University. 'We forged a special agreement with the European Union; we achieved World Trade Organization membership and we were upgraded by the United Nations to a middle-income country.' He speaks from a comfortable office in his large and beautifully finished university, full of well-equipped lecture rooms, laboratories, auditorium and a library. 'Four years ago I was not optimistic about my country,' he confesses. 'But now? I am optimistic.'

The campus, on the outskirts of the capital Praia, is vibrant with the chirpy optimism of 1,500 students studying everything from pharmacy to architecture. They are on the crest of Cape Verde's transformation from unloved rocky outpost to thriving service economy. Jean Piaget, along with the newly created University of Cape Verde, is supplying the demand for educated people.

Praia itself is in frenzy. Buildings are shooting up willy-nilly, wherever there is spare land: whole new neighbourhoods seem to have emerged in just a few years.

I take a tour of Sambala Resort, to the northeast of the capital. It was the first of the many exclusive condominiums/holiday resorts to get started on the islands and I gaze at its three-storey townhouses towering incongruously over the rocky plain above Santiago's eastern coast. Justin Crowther, the resort director, is as optimistic as Jorge Sousa Brito, though in a more blustery, entrepreneurial kind of way. 'There will be a biofuel plantation here, a golf course there, vegetable plots, more villas, a hotel,' he waves exhaustingly at the relentlessly brown, hot plains. The prospect of lush vegetation here seems as unlikely as the idea of the glass-fronted skyscraper planned for the old, low-rise city of Praia. But Cape Verde seems to specialise in making the improbable happen. Even independence seemed a ridiculously foolish idea once, as the poet said.

Everyone wants a piece of Cape Verde now: China, the USA, Europe, Brazil, mainland Africa; investors, tourists, retirees, land speculators, emigrants, itinerant labourers, NGOs. They want its unused trading quotas with the USA, its fishing grounds, its proximity to Africa, its international relationships, its tax concessions. They want to retire there, to work there, they want a piece of its sun, its wind, its land, its stability. Some want the satisfaction of bringing aid to a country that is still poor but refreshingly helpable. It's a great place, it's on the up, its indicators are all buzzing, it's not corrupt. As Stahis Panagides, country director for the Millennium Challenge Corporation, which is investing millions in Cape Verde, says: 'It exports transparency.'

On the balcony of Panagides's beautiful house in the Prainha quarter of Praia, I sit with him and his wife to watch the nightly spectacle of hundreds of elegant white egrets congregating in a huge acacia tree in their garden. Why this tree? Because the others, which lined the main street of the old diplomatic quarter,

low for an African country. Rates may increase with the rise in the number of foreigners coming to the islands. Cape Verde has quite a frank attitude towards AIDS, however, so educational programmes have been able to operate openly.

Drugs When Caribbean and European nations got together a few years ago to crack down on drug trafficking they were so successful that the trade along direct routes dropped almost to nothing. Yet, like water, cocaine will always find a way. It continues to enter Europe in abundance because traffickers switched their

have all been cut down. No-one can tell me why: it must be something to do with progress that has lost these birds their homes.

Maybe the *favela*-dwellers of Santa Maria and Sal Rei towns would sympathise: the shanty towns seem to be growing as the sale of land restricts any legitimate expansion of the towns. Land prices are shooting up as foreigners buy what they can. There have been protests. Unemployment is still, stubbornly, at 22%. When is the bonanza coming for the locals – or will the profits just be siphoned out of the country? What's the plan?

I ask the Minister for Economy, Competitiveness and Growth, José Brito, what the plan is. It's this: to develop tourism as a matter of urgency. Then, to use it to create the demands on the rest of the economy that will stimulate wider growth. And then, when these other industries are sufficiently strong, to get them to diversify these markets so their reliance on tourism is not absolute.

Out of the dusty heat, in his office, we discuss the downsides. 'Doesn't the profit from this foreign investment just get siphoned straight out of the country?' It might, he agrees, but it can't help but change things here. It brings the opportunity to learn, to copy, to compete for business.

'What about the flight of land into foreign hands, and the choking of the landscape with endless apartments and hotels?' The government is tightening controls as demand increases, he says. It can't control the sale of private land, but no more public land will be released. And, in the future, freeholds will not be available: only 50-year concessions, he claims. And the government is slowly tightening regulations about the proportion of each development plot that can be built on.

Watching the birds flocking in their hundreds to that single tree I had asked Stahis Panagides whether he thought that the massive influx of foreigners into such a small nation could be an entirely positive thing. The key, he replied, is that they become part of the community: 'Then they will *care*,' he said.

Jorge Sousa Brito thinks 'Cape Verdeanness' will survive whatever is thrown at it. 'Cape Verdeans have a very strong identity,' he says. 'This is the oldest Creole culture in the world and the first Creole nation. Every culture that comes here will find something in common with us. Our strength is to absorb things, good and bad, and transform them into Cape Verdean culture.'

I'm not sure I agree. If Cape Verdeans prosper, the ocean will no longer be that enlarging, suffocating source of both sorrow and hope that is the essence of *sodade*. And without *sodade* some important part of the 'real' Cape Verde (as the specialist tour operators now call it) will be gone.

But who could object to that?

routes. They now use 'Highway 10', the 10th parallel transatlantic route from Latin America to west Africa and thence to Europe. Around ten west African countries are thought to be warehouses for cocaine en route to Europe, and Cape Verde is one of them. Until recently, its tiny navy and 965km of coastline have left it helpless. Now the international community is stepping in. There has been help from Brazil, and Cape Verde's new partnership with the European Union will give EU navies

ENERGY AND WATER IN CAPE VERDE *Alex Alper*

'Salt, basalt rock, limestone, kaolin, fish, clay, gypsum.' So reads the finite list of Cape Verde's natural resources, giving insight into the tremendous challenge that existence here has always posed. And yet, in a world where the price of fossil fuels climbs ever higher, Cape Verde has at least been blessed with the need to innovate. Critical deficiencies in water, agriculture and energy are compelling the country to become an innovator, and maybe a leader, in exciting new technologies, from growing plants without soil to capturing water from the fog.

But the difficulties are formidable, and the lack of water is perhaps the most. Rainfall averages 200mm per year, barely enough to replenish the natural springs that supply much of the rural population with water. As the springs slowly dry up, salt water is seeping into the aquifers, contaminating the sources that remain. Desalinisation technologies provide water to the majority of urban residents but are very expensive (see box, *A sip of the sea*, page 160).

Agriculture also presents challenges. Throughout Cape Verdean history, severe droughts have caused epic famines, killing thousands and driving many abroad. Erosion, caused by agriculture, grazing, and wood-gathering in a delicate ecosystem, has decreased the quality of the soil, while much of the country was originally sand and rocky mountain slope anyway. Indeed, only 10% of Cape Verde's 4,033km^2 of landmass is arable, and homegrown food provides only 10–20% of what is consumed. Nevertheless, a large number of Cape Verdeans are still involved in agricultural activities, planting corn, beans, peanuts, squash, sweet potatoes, sugarcane, bananas and other crops each year. Some farmers plant corn only for animal fodder, knowing it will not reach maturity.

The rest of Cape Verde's food is imported, and transportation requires energy – another scarce commodity for a country with no fuel reserves. The country also needs fuel for electricity, for cooking (butane gas) and for desalinisation. Cape Verde spent €54.4 million on petroleum derivatives in 2007 alone, and domestic fuel taxes are high compared with other African nations. When local prices for petrol and diesel climbed to €1.28 and €1.32 per litre respectively in early 2008, *hiace* drivers on Santiago called a strike, protesting at the government's high fuel tax. In the meantime, rural Cape Verdeans rely largely on dwindling forest resources for their cooking needs to supplement expensive butane gas. This constitutes a great pressure on Cape Verde's fragile ecosystem. With rising tourism, and annual population growth of about 2%, the demand for cheap, abundant energy will only continue to rise.

Precisely because of the gravity of these challenges, Cape Verde, with the help of foreign governments and NGOs, is trying to pioneer green technologies. The country promised to achieve 25% renewable energies by 2010, a figure that should rise to 50% by 2020. Cape Verde also hopes to have one island with 100% renewable electricity by 2020, and it is offering tax deductions for expenses related to renewable energies.

the ability to help police its waters. In addition the USA, as part of its controversial Africa Partnership Station initiative, is helping to patrol Cape Verdean waters and train and support the Cape Verde coastguards. In 2011, the US government will give Cape Verde US$397,000 to help combat drug trafficking and organised crime. Meanwhile, drug crime has entered Cape Verdean life, with at least two drug-related murders in Praia in 2007–08.

With 3,000 hours of sunlight per year, Cape Verde has promoted solar energy to pump and heat water, and to illuminate homes in remote areas. The Cape Verdean government and the European Union have begun a campaign to disseminate solar water pumps to 30 rural communities on Santiago. That will go far to help rural Cape Verdeans, most of whom make up the 40% of the population that still lacks electricity.

In one rural community in Serra Malagueta, a pilot project sponsored by the Protected Areas Programme is underway to disseminate more efficient wood stoves. It aims to reduce wood use among residents who can't afford butane gas for cooking, thereby protecting the endangered forests.

Wind energy is another promising technology (see box, *The answer is blowing…*, page 255). In consultation with the Danish company Wave Star, the government also began exploring the possibility of wave technology for electrical power generation. Still in the test phase, Wave Star's machine consists of 20 half-submerged hemisphere-shaped floats that float upward when a wave passes. Ocean waves offer a more potent and constant energy than wind. Still, wave technology must overcome the formidable challenge of keeping costs low while resisting storms and salt damage over the long term.

The government has also begun considering a floating nuclear island to supply 70MW of energy, which would meet Santiago and Maio's total energy needs. The nuclear material would be provided by the Russian Company Rosenergoatom, who would also be responsible for removing and treating the waste. Though it would provide cheap and abundant energy, the proposal is controversial and still in the early stages. Cape Verde is innovating in water too, through fog collectors (see box, *Have you ever drunk a cloud?*, page 198).

Agricultural innovations are perhaps even more promising, with the advent of hydroponics and the spread of drip irrigation. Drip irrigation, called *gota-gota* or 'drip-drip' locally, utilises a series of plastic tubes running the length of the plant bed. They feature tiny holes that allow water to pinpoint the plant roots alone, bringing water use down by 80% and diminishing weed growth. Materials are somewhat expensive and must be replaced after three to five years. However, the technology allows for year-round cultivation, and local governments and NGOs are helping to fund it, with the result that of the 17% of farming families who use some sort of irrigation, 45% use *gota-gota*.

Soil-less culture, or hydroponics, incurs astronomical start-up costs but cuts water use by 90–95%, land use by 90%, and produces much healthier crops (see box, *Cucumbers in the desert*, page 129). Cape Verde is still far from the paragon of green technologies it could be, and may need to become, to deal effectively with rising fuel prices and its own historic lack of resources. Hopefully by 2020 the efforts underway now will be paying off.

LANGUAGE

In the ethnic mosaic of Cape Verdean slave communities, the speaking of tribal languages was actively discouraged. To communicate with each other, slaves were forced to piece together words from Portuguese and a mélange of other sources. It was these fumblings that were the beginnings of the Cape Verdean mother tongue, Creole. It is at root Portuguese, primarily the 15th-century Portuguese of the Algarve, with a simplified grammar. Phonetics, and some words, have been added from some Mandingo and Senegambian languages, members of the large Niger–Congo family of African languages. Creole was the language in which Cape Verdean writers began to express themselves, sometimes in order to hide their ideas from Portuguese officials but principally as a way of defining themselves. Poems do not always translate easily. Eugénio Tavares of Brava, the legendary writer of *mornas*, was reported by the later luminary Baltasar Lopes to be 'a very mediocre poet in Portuguese but a very good poet in *Crioulo*'. Above all, Creole is the informal, spoken language that everyone understands. It is the language for sharing the Cape Verdean sentiment, the language of intimacy and feeling. The soul of Cape Verde speaks in Creole.

PORTUGUESE AND CREOLE: TWO OLD RIVALS   *Steve Maddocks*

Portuguese is the official language of Cape Verde. All business is conducted in Portuguese; it is used for correspondence, newspapers, road signs – in fact anything that needs to be written down. But only very rarely will Cape Verdeans speak Portuguese to each other. In the bank, the doctor's surgery, or the barber's, at work or after hours, everyone, be they president or peasant, uses Creole. It is their national language.

Creole (*Crioulo*) is not just a product of Cape Verdean history, it is an index of Cape Verdean identity. During Portuguese colonial rule it was forbidden to use Creole in public situations. Of course, this law was impossible to enforce, and the use of Creole became an act of defiance against the Portuguese.

Creole is now being used in more and more public situations. The DJs on the very popular Praia FM introduce Creole music in Creole. The tagline for one of the campaigns for the February 2001 presidential election was 'Nôs Presidente' – which is Creole for 'Our President'. And yet, despite the fact that many Cape Verdeans feel Portuguese to be an alien and difficult language for them, and despite the fact that the Portuguese of a lot of Cape Verdeans is not particularly good, Creole is perhaps even further now than it was 20 years ago from becoming the official language.

For a start, a lot of people, among them a number of Cape Verdeans, don't consider Creole to be worthy of the name 'language'. It is a dialect of Portuguese, or, as some would have it, badly spoken Portuguese (others counter that French is just a 'dialect' of Latin).

Secondly, Creole is a spoken language only. Written Creole exists, but it is very scarce. A handful of books have been written, among them collections of traditional stories and poems, a grammar, and a structural analysis. Attempts to settle upon a standard way of writing Creole, and more importantly to disseminate Creole texts and get people into the habit of writing Creole, have consistently failed.

The earliest attempt at an alphabet was an 1888 grammar written by António de Paula Brita. This was an etymological version, that is, it was based on Portuguese. The most recent was 1994's ALUPEC (Unified Alphabet for the Cape Verdean Language). In March 1979, a two-week colloquium was staged in Mindelo, and

See *Language*, page 78, for more information about Portuguese and English usage. For basic words and phrases and hints on pronunciation, see *Appendix 1, Language*, page 331.

RELIGION

The islands have been Catholic from the beginning and most other denominations have had little chance to win many converts. Some 95% of the nation is ostensibly Catholic, though the priests complain that they have lost their influence. The largest minority, less than 1%, is the Nazarene Church. This is a Protestant grouping introduced to Brava in the early 1900s by emigrants returning from the USA. The Nazarenes collaborated with another group, the Sabbatarians, to build two Protestant churches, and they translated the gospels into Creole, the local language. The islands are seen as fertile recruiting grounds by several groups, including the Church of Jesus Christ of Latter Day Saints (popularly known as the Mormons). The Church claims around 3,000 members in Cape Verde. Jehovah's Witnesses proselytise here as well. The Jews have a fascinating and formative history in Cape

the international team of linguists proposed an alphabet which is still the most widely used. But the situation remains that, although the vast majority of Cape Verdeans speak Creole with great passion, wit and intelligence, they are totally unaccustomed to, and even incapable of, reading or writing it.

There are powerful arguments both for and against making Creole the official language. By doing so, Cape Verdeans might finally break the colonial yoke, achieving cultural as well as political independence from Portugal. Thus the language of their folklore, of their poems, stories and songs, might also be the language of their business. The current situation is also damaging for young children. The first language they learn to read or write is not their mother tongue, but a foreign language, learnt in school. Illiteracy is widespread, and if Cape Verdeans want to express their imagination in writing, or conduct any kind of business, they are forced to resort to a foreign language, divorced from the home and the heart.

But, on the other hand, Portuguese is the sixth most commonly spoken language in the world. With it Cape Verdeans have immediate access to 170 million people, plus the possibility of a halting conversation with the world's 266 million Spanish speakers. What use is Creole in the global village?

Officialising Creole would be a mammoth task. It would mean a total overhaul of a whole host of current procedures from the highest levels down. A commission of international linguists would need to be assembled to settle upon an alphabet and a standard form, prepare an official grammar, and develop educational materials for teaching in schools. It would take years. And who would pay?

The most vexed question is that of a standard form. Creole differs greatly from island to island, and even within the islands. Tell someone from Mindelo that the standard form of Creole is *Badiu*? Or someone from Praia that he must start speaking and writing São Vicente Creole? You might as well tell a cat that it should bark.

Visitors to Cape Verde will communicate successfully in Portuguese. But if they want to participate in something that is unique to Cape Verde, if they really want to impress, flatter, and entertain Cape Verdeans, if they want to approach Cape Verdeans as friends, they will be richly rewarded by using just a few words of Creole.

Verde, fleeing there to escape persecution (see box, *Jews in Cape Verde*, pages 12–13). There is a small, new, Muslim population mostly comprising immigrants from the west African coast, with a mosque or two in Praia.

CULTURE

The faces of Cape Verde are numerous: blue eyes gazing out from above a brown cheek; green eyes below tight curls of black hair with a wisp of blonde; Chinese eyes set in a black face. Race in Cape Verde is not just Portugal mingled with the Rivers of Guinea, but also Italy and drops of Lebanon, China, Morocco and more. Pirates, sailors and merchants from Spain, France, England, Holland, Brazil and the USA deposited their genes here. Senegambians, Mandingos and Fulas gave variety to the African blood that arrived in the form of slaves.

This disorientation of racial types was regarded for centuries as a bastardisation. Then, in the very late 19th century, when the stirrings of nationalism began, the idea arose that Cape Verde had its own identity, not an unholy mixture but an exciting synthesis. This idea marked the emergence of Creole (*Crioulo*) nationhood. The Cape Verdean people have their own history, the result of a unique combination of social and natural forces.

LITERATURE '*Caboverdeanidade*' – 'Cape Verdeanness' – is expressed in poetry, the lyrics of *mornas*, folk stories and novels. The emotion that dominates is a sorrowful one, known as *sodade*. It is often translated as 'nostalgia', though that word has oversentimental connotations in English and does not convey the depth of feeling or the unsentimentality of expression. 'Longing' is a better word. *Sodade* is the longing of the emigrant looking across the sea to the motherland; the longing of mothers for their exiled children. Much Cape Verdean poetry focuses on the sea as the bringer of riches, but also of loneliness and sometimes death: 'Oh gold of the sea, you are dearly earned,' wrote Tavares.

The first Cape Verdean poetry arose in the 1890s and did not directly address the Cape Verdean condition. It followed Portuguese patterns with their rigidity of metre and verse. The movement began in São Nicolau, then the intellectual centre of the archipelago. Writers produced a literary annual and a book of poetry. This period, known as the Classical period, lasted until the 1930s. Amongst the writers were a very few who did not remain bound within Portuguese tradition. It was then, for example, that Tavares honed and popularised the art form of the *morna*, a combination of music, dance and poetry that expresses *sodade*. Another rebel, whose militant ideas would not be recognised for decades to come, was Pedro Cardoso, who signed himself 'Afro'. He named his journal *O Manduco* (*The Cudgel*), and he was the first Cape Verdean to try, albeit in a stumbling way, to articulate ideas such as pan-Africanism and Marxism.

With a clarion call in 1936, the Classical period was shattered and a new literary movement began. *Claridade*, a literary review, was published, addressing head-on the nature of Creole culture and the conditions people endured in the islands. Tales of the lives of Cape Verdeans appeared in the classic novel *Chiquinho* by Baltasar Lopes. It is a seminal work, one of the first novels from Portuguese Africa, and it was written in Creole.

Essays on Creole culture and language poured from the *Claridosos* in their irregularly published journal whose last edition appeared in 1960. Other leaders were Jorge Barbosa and Manuel Lopes. Barbosa introduced a new style of poetry which he thought reflected better the Cape Verdean character, a looser verse for a freer spirit. His book *Arquipélago*, published in 1935 when he was 33, was his pioneering work. It established the central axis of the Cape Verdean tragedy, the desire to leave while being forced to stay, and the desire to stay while being forced to leave.

More recently, literature has become more militant and artists and writers have turned to Africa for inspiration. Onésimo Silveira has written of the 'force which only the black man knows', and Kaoberdiano Dambara has produced some of the first Cape Verdean poems in the negritude tradition, though these concepts are far less commonly expressed than on mainland Africa.

Some critics believe that Creole is not a sufficiently complex language to be a literary vehicle and that the success of Tavares and Cardoso was an exception.

BADIU WITH CRACKED FEET, *SANPADJUDU* WITH POTATO BELLIES

Alex Alper

Ethnic conflict may be the story of many countries in Africa today, but the old saying in the title is perhaps the extent of ethnic rivalry in Cape Verde. It compares the *Badiu*, who inhabit the southern islands, with their northern counterparts, the *Sanpadjudu*. Both are descended from the mix of African tribes and Portuguese that settled the islands 500 years ago. They speak dialects of the same Creole, root for the same soccer teams, and the *Badiu* and *Sanpadjudu* vote for both political parties.

Yet there are notable differences. The quaint farmhouses, the lighter complexions, more lusophone Creole, and Portuguese-influenced *morna* of the north indicate the more 'European' aspect of northern culture. In contrast, the darker complexions, more African Creole, and the thriving traditions of continental origin – from the raw beats of the *batuk* dance to the intricate patterns of the *pano de terra* weaving – denote the vibrant African traditions still alive in the south.

It is said that *Sanpadjudus* look down on their southern counterparts as less 'sophisticated'. *Badius* would counter that their culture is more authentically Cape Verdean, pointing out that singers from both regions usually choose to sing in *Badiu* Creole. ALUPEC, the current Creole alphabet, is modelled on the *Badiu* dialect.

These time-old stereotypes are rooted in the very origins of the names. *Badiu* most likely comes from the Portuguese word '*vadiu*' or 'lazy'. It is said that the *Badiu* slaves ran away from their masters to farm their own plots along the steep ridges. When Portuguese masters would demand their labour, *Badius* would refuse. Their subsequent label '*Badiu*' persists as a proud symbol of defiance, while their alleged 'cracked feet' belie the myth of laziness: in reality there is a truly formidable *Badiu* work ethic (or lack of sophistication, as the *Sanpadjudu* might say).

The origins of the word '*Sanpadjudu*' are more obscure. Many think the term comes from the phrase '*são pa' ajuda*' ('they are for helping'). This may refer to those Santiago inhabitants who were convinced to emigrate northward, to populate and cultivate the *Barlavento* islands. Their 'potato bellies', according to *Badiu* lore, refer to the only crop that they managed to cultivate.

These stereotypes mostly serve as fuel for good-natured teasing. As Heavy H, a *Sanpadjudu* rapper sings, '*Sanpadjudu ku Badiu, nos tudo, nos e kul*' ('*Badiu* and *Sanpadjudu*, all of us, we are cool').

The slaves on Brava, Santiago and Fogo all wove fine cloth using skills learned on the African mainland. The cloth was in great demand in the 17th century among the upper classes along the Rivers of Guinea and it was also worn by the elite as far away as the Gold Coast and Brazil. The deep blues and beautiful patterns of Cape Verdean cloth were superior to what these people could produce themselves but they were familiar, with a west African aesthetic. It became one of the principal currencies underpinning the slave trade, more in demand than European, Indian or African alternatives.

The demand forced English and French slaving vessels that wished to avoid Cape Verde to call there first for rolls of cloth so that they could barter on the coast. In the late 17th century, a slave was worth 60 *barafulas*, cloths of standard length and width, which in turn were worth 30 iron bars. In the 18th century, Cape Verde exported 6,000 of the 2m-long cloths a year to the mainland.

The cloth was woven on a narrow loom made of cane, sticks and banana leaves, which produced strips never more than 7in wide. Dye was made from urzela, a lichen (see *Chapter 9, Brava*, page 235), and from the indigo plant. Female slaves pounded the leaves of the latter, pressed them into small loaves, dried them in the sun and then left them to ferment in a pot with water and ashes.

The standard design was a six-banded cloth (*pano*). Within that strict formula there were many variations. *Panos listrados*, for example, were alternating bands of white and indigo. *Panos simples* were simply white. Others interwove silk with the cotton. *Panos de bicho* interwove white, blue and black threads to make intricate geometric designs including the shapes of leopard and snakeskins and also of Portuguese crosses. The most expensive were cloths of a pure deep blue.

The desirability of such cloth continued for hundreds of years, from the 16th until the early 19th centuries. When the wealthy Diogo Ximenes Vargas died in Cape Verde in 1624, his estate consisted chiefly of hoards of the cloth: 1,800 *barafulas* in 45 large rolls and 840 plain white cloths in 21 rolls. Their value was recorded to be £630.

Today *panos* are worn by women either as shawls or as sashes tied just below the waist.

For more information see *Appendix 2, Further Information*, page 339; www.reisetraeume.de/kapverden/viadoso/c-a4/en00.html.

Serious Cape Verdean writers overwhelmingly use Portuguese, albeit the Creole-infused Portuguese of the islands.

MUSIC AND DANCE Music underpins Cape Verdean life, gives it continuity and draws meaning from collective, often brutal experience. A key element of the Cape Verdean experience is to hear the bittersweet *morna* wrought from a collection of guitars and violins in an evening café; or the more lively, escapist strains of the *funaná* embellished with the scratchings of some unique percussive instrument. Music-making happens everywhere – in the nightclubs of Mindelo where people dance into the small hours, in restaurants, in people's homes. There are several musical forms that have evolved over the last 500 years. Some are essentially European, some are African and many lie in between the two.

Traditional musical forms The *morna* and the *coladera* are the principal forms. Obscurity surrounds the origins of the *morna*, but it seems to have emerged in the mid 19th century on the island of Boavista, influenced by the *modinha* of Portugal and Brazil (see Chapter 5, Boavista, page 140). Of all the musical forms, it is the most European and literary; the lyrics are sophisticated expressions of tragedy, the instruments are similar to those played in Portuguese folk music. Technically, the *morna* is a poem set in four-line verses and put to music, but the name is also given to some music without words, and to some distinctive poems without music. The singer performs to the strains of stringed instruments, violins (*rabeças*), guitar-like violas and *cavaquinhos*, which resemble ukeleles. The singer tends to sing a line twice and then another line twice. This double pattern is then repeated.

The *coladera*, or *cola*, is a processional dance performed on festival days on São Vicente and Santo Antão. It has also over the last few decades come to mean a fast, danceable music with singing, influenced by Afro-American music.

More powerful rhythms, with less emphasis on melody, emanate from the *batuko*, *finaçon*, *funaná* and *tabanka*. These musical forms are more rooted in Africa and arose mainly on Santiago and on Fogo, where defiant, escaped slaves looked for inspiration eastwards in the land of their origins. The slaves were from a diversity of African ethnic backgrounds, so the resulting musical culture was a mixture with a Cape Verdean identity. In these musical forms the singer calls and the rest respond, the harmonies are simple and there is much repetition. The singing is open and coarser in tone and the words are often improvised.

Batuko dancing is the most reminiscent of Africa; the rhythm is often provided by surrogate drums: rolled-up cloth held between the legs and pounded with the hands. It is the music and dance of women in the inland villages of Santiago, who will sit round in a semi-circle and beat the *panos*, all taking different rhythms that layer together into a complex structure. The women sing and a woman dances, slowly at first, with gyrating hips and then faster and faster until there is a climax of the dancing, *panos*-pounding and chanting. Then another woman takes her place. The origins of the *batuko* are obscure. Some trace it back to a time when a slave owner would offer a guest the pick of his female slaves. Others believe it originates from within the women's culture itself – it is a way of coping with the grief of widowhood, or other loss, through a purging frenzy of dancing.

Tabanka is drummed out on conch-shell horns and drums. Again, it comes from Santiago, and it is repetitive, accompanied by women who play percussion on plastic sheets, bags, bottles and their thighs (see *Chapter 6, Santiago*, page 186).

If you hear an accordion, you are probably listening to a *funaná*. This is energetic, fast, joyful and sensuous – one of the most traditional expressions of resistance to Portuguese domination. Its home, again, is Santiago. The traditional instruments on which it is played are the *gaita*, a type of accordion, and the *ferro*, a stick of iron scraped with a table knife. The *gaita*-player alternates between just two chords and plays a melody on top. Modern musicians have replaced the *gaita* with keyboards or guitar, and the *ferro* with drums. The *funaná*'s popularity has led to the formation of a number of *funaná* dance bands.

There are many other musical forms, such as the *mazurka*, imported from Europe and given a new twist. Sadly, some of the most African of instruments that local people used to play have all but disappeared.

The international stage Cape Verdean music is flourishing. Cesária Evora, barefoot diva with the mellow, unschooled voice, is the figurehead of the *morna*

CESÁRIA EVORA

Cesária Evora, the 'barefoot diva', has a dedicated international following, particularly in Paris. Her appeal lies in the quality of her voice which, in addition to its mellow elements, is untrained, simple and unaffected – the perfect vehicle for expressing the poetry of the *morna*. It has earned her the names 'Aguadente' and 'Red Wine'. Evora is also loved because she sings as if she has just stepped into one of the Mindelo bars – lack of pretension, even bluntness, are her hallmarks. She sings the *morna* accompanied mainly by violin, acoustic guitar, accordion, piano, clarinet and the mandolin-like *cavaquinho*.

Evora was born in 1941. It was a friend of Evora's who remarked on her voice when she was a teenager. She joined a band at the age of 16 and sang in the bars of Mindelo. She made no money from it, apart from a little when she performed at Portuguese official functions – but even that source disappeared with independence in 1975. Her humble career seemed to have evaporated and for a decade she refused to sing.

In 1985, at the age of 45, Evora was invited to Portugal by the Organisation of Cape Verdean Women to contribute to a record. She went, but the record was not a hit. However, while she was there she met a businessman, José da Silva, who offered to work with her. Three years later she cut a record, *La Diva aux Pieds Nus* (*The Barefoot Diva*), in Paris. She has made several more albums, including *Destino di Belita*, *Cesária*, *Miss Perfumado*, *Mar Azul* (*Blue Sea*) and *Cabo Verde*. She lives in Paris and has houses in São Vicente.

(see box, *Cesária Evora*, above), who sells albums in the hundreds of thousands and is particularly popular in France.

Other musicians are increasingly better known on the international stage. In the 1960s, it was Bana, and the Voz di Cabo Verde, who popularised the *morna* in Europe. They were influenced by Latin American and Brazilian rhythms and styles, particularly *cumbia*.

Bands and singers with a long history in the archipelago include Luis Morais, Os Tubarões and its lead singer Ildo Lobo, Norberto Tavares, Bulimundo and Finaçon. The last three turned the accordion-based *funaná* into its high-energy offspring.

Other well-known Cape Verdean musicians are Paulino Vieira, Dany Silva and Tiro Paris. The Mendes brothers, emigrants from Fogo, set up in 1976 and have worked particularly with the *coladera*. They also work with Angolan music, introduced to them by natives of Fogo returning from doing their military service on the mainland.

Commercial Cape Verdean music has often incorporated new ideas from Latin America, and today it is filled with other styles to the extent that purists fear that true Cape Verdean musical culture could vanish. Optimists believe that the Cape Verdean nature, whose essence is to absorb and transform multi-national influences, will ensure that Cape Verdean music remains distinctive and fertile.

FOLKLORE Folklore is rich with tales of Sancho, the mischievous monkey who lives in the mountains and causes chaos wherever he goes. He remained in the hills throughout the Portuguese oppression, waiting until it was time to 'turn all upside down', as the poem on page 9 describes. Sancho's threat of confusion is generally a desirable one, a welcome anarchy upsetting those in power. But sometimes Sancho is purely an agent of trouble. He pops up in proverbs, such as the one reminding the lazy or naughty that they will go hungry if they don't till the soil: 'Beans don't grow where monkeys are.'

Another character is Nho Lobo, the lazy wolf, who appears in many cycles of tales in the oral tradition handed down through generations. A Nho Lobo story generally conveys a moral for children.

Bli Mundo is the ox who broke free from the yoke of the *trapiche*, and symbolises liberty. A charming recent children's book is *Do Tambor a blimundo*, available as an English translation (see *Appendix 2, Further Information*, page 339).

Speech is also rich in proverbs: 'A scratching chicken will meet its grandmother'; 'A man without a wife is a vase without flowers'; 'A lame goat does not take a siesta'; 'In cooking, eggs show up rotten' and 'They'll pay you to climb up the coconut palm but getting down again, that's your affair.'

FESTIVALS Traditional festivities are generally Catholic saints' days. They usually begin with church services and include processions, drumming and the eating of specially prepared foods. Many have their own traditions, some of which are described in the island chapters, and most occur in the summer. All the islands celebrate Christmas, Saint John (São João, 24 June) and Carnival (around 16 February).

STARTING YOUR CAPE VERDEAN MUSIC COLLECTION

If you want to buy some recordings of modern Cape Verdean music, here are some ideas to start you off. This list is designed to be small and of course there are many other bands and singers to look out for.

The *grande dame* is of course **Cesária Evora**, with at least ten albums, including *Miss Perfumado* and *São Vicente di Longe*. **Bau**, a musician who plays regularly in Mindelo, has produced *Djailza*, *Tope da Coroa*, *Inspiration* and *Bli Mundo*. Go for the last if you are buying only one.

Other, more recent, artists have one thing in common: mixing traditional Cape Verdean music with influences from around the world.

Lura, whom some critics have suggested is Evora's successor, has been well known since her first album release in 2004. Try *M'Bem di Fora* (I've come from far away). It has a rich mixture of her music, with influences from many of the islands.

Teófilo Chantre has composed several of Evora's songs, is a top guitarist and has a rich, baritone voice. Try his album *Viaja*, which includes some of his most famous pieces.

Mayra Andrade, born in 1985, is lauded for her lyrics as well as her music. Try her debut album *Navega*.

Tcheka, a guitarist and vocalist, is said to be able to reproduce the feel of all Cape Verdean instruments and rhythms on a single guitar. Try *Nu Monda*.

Cordas do Sol is a band from Santo Antão whose CD is widely on sale, especially in their home island. In Fogo, **Agostinho da Pina**, the blind violinist who inspired the introduction to the first edition of this book, now has his own CD *Augusto Cego*.

Simentera, a band founded in 1992 and greatly inspired by traditional Cape Verdean music, has three albums: *Raíz*, *Barro e Voz* and *Cabo Verde Serenade*. Perhaps the last is the best.

Finally, for some compilations try *Funaná*, an album dedicated to that musical form. Try also *The Soul of Cape Verde*, for a good mix of some of the bands above. *Travadinha* is a popular instrumental collection. Then there's also *The Rough Guide to the Music of Cape Verde*.

CAPE VERDE TRAVEL

Tour Operator & Retail Agent
Proprietor: Mr Ron Hughes P.Q.R.C
14 Market Place, Hornsea, East Yorkshire, HU18 1AW, England
Tel: 0044 1964 536191 Fax: 0044 1964 536192
www.capeverdetravel.com sales@capeverdetravel.com

Mindelo Office: Carlos Mondlane, Mindelo, Sao Vicente, Republic of
Cape Verde Tel: 00238 9982878 Capeverdetravel@cvtelecom.cv

Specialists in the Cape Verde Islands for 15 years we offer our clients tailor
made itineraries to each of the 9 islands as well as the traditional beach
holidays.

Discover the Real Cape Verde with its culture and beauty.

Our skills allow us to coordinate travel throughout the archipelago
providing many activities such as trekking, rambling, bird watching, diving,
deep sea fishing, mountain biking, sailing and other various sports., topped up
with wedding arrangements on some of the islands.

We offer the widest range of flights to our country including North and South
UK, Europe, USA, Brazil and West Africa including Fortaleza, Gabon,
Cameroon, Sao Tome & Principe, Angola and Senegal. We also provide
domestic air passes for the local airline.

Accommodation consists of character guest houses, established local hotels
and soon to appear are the more internationally recognised hotel chains. All
facilities are personally inspected.

Wherever you are in the world, plan your journey with us. Whether it be for
business or leisure, contact us.

**For more information on flights and holiday reservations please contact
our sales team on 0044 1964 536191**

**Also offering other
adventures to Sao Tome,
Cameroon, Senegal, Angola
and Brazil.**

2

Practical Information

WHEN TO VISIT

The islands are warm and sunny all year round so for many it doesn't really matter when they go. For **windsurfers** the best months are January and February while **divers** will find the calmest waters and peak visibility from June to December; **beach lovers** might wish to avoid the windy winter months. **Fishermen** after marlin should opt for May to October, while tuna fishing is at its best in August. For **hikers**, the mountainous islands are significantly more beautiful during and just after the rainy season of July to December, though flooding can impede some Santo Antão hikes. The heaviest rainfall is usually in August and September. For those concerned about the heat, the peak is in September (with an average daily temperature of 30°C), with the trough being in January (average 24°C). For those who wish to see **nesting turtles** the season is June to October, peaking in mid-July and August. Turtle hatchlings are born from mid-August until the end of November. **Photographers** should avoid December to March when the harmattan winds dull the light, and leave deposits of sand. **Partiers and music lovers** might choose February for the São Vicente Carnival, or for that in São Nicolau; August for the São Vicente Baía das Gatas music festival, or May for the Gamboa music festival in Santiago. Those on a **tight budget** will find hotels cheaper from April to June and in October, and should definitely avoid Christmas and Carnival time. **Peace seekers** might avoid July and August, when Cape Verde is full of both European holidaymakers and *emigrante* families taking their summer holidays back home. Christmas and Carnival times – in fact the whole period from November to March – are also high season.

HIGHLIGHTS

HIKING Cape Verde is a superb hiking destination – the vistas from the mountains of Santo Antão or from the depth of its gorges; the lonely slopes of Brava and the stunning interior of the brooding volcano crater of Fogo make for a unique experience. Much of the walking on Cape Verde is on the extraordinary cobbled paths that have been constructed in the most unlikely corners and up the steepest of slopes, making the walking much easier than might be construed from the map.

On Santo Antão the classic walks are up or down the *ribeiras*, taking transport at the beginning or end (see *Chapter 11, Santo Antão*, page 297). On Fogo the great challenge is to ascend the Pico, the 2,829m spectacular volcano cone and, for some, to spend the night with the villagers who make their home in its shadow. On Brava there are endless walks criss-crossing the steep 'flower' island where you are unlikely to meet any other travellers. São Nicolau is a gentle and quiet island with a hidden, green and mountainous heartland filled with beautiful walks, whilst Santiago has its own mountainous spine with some fine walks between it and the coast.

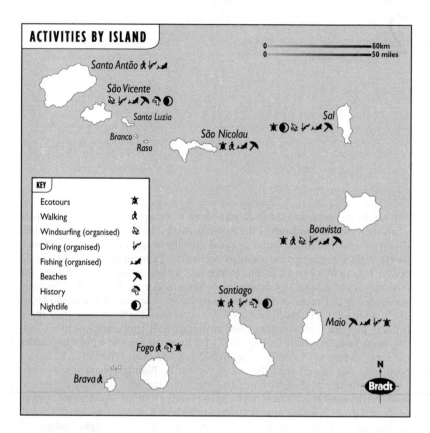

ACTIVITIES BY ISLAND

Santo Antão

São Vicente

Santa Luzia

Branco

Raso

São Nicolau

Sal

KEY

Ecotours	✹
Walking	⋔
Windsurfing (organised)	⮧
Diving (organised)	⅀
Fishing (organised)	⚓
Beaches	⛰
History	⚲
Nightlife	◑

Boavista

Santiago

Maio

Fogo

Brava

N

Bradt

0 — 60km
0 — 50 miles

Most of the walks require a certain amount of fitness because they are steep, and a certain elasticity of knee for the descents. In this book each is rated according to a rough scheme:

1 Easy path with little fitness required.
2 Medium fitness, with some bursts of steep ascent and/or the odd slippery stretch.
3 Prolonged steep walking and/or slippery, uncobbled paths.

While we attempt to make our assessments uniform, it is inevitable that our judgements of time lengths and difficulty are a little partial. Because of this, we have identified the writer of each hike description at the top: CW – fit male, mid-thirties; AI – unfit female, mid-thirties; AH – fit male, 20; HC – unfit female, mid-thirties. For those seeking very gentle hikes there are options in Santo Antão and Boavista, but few attractive flat walks on the other islands. You can penetrate quite far by vehicle, however – into Fogo's crater and far up one or two of Santo Antão's *ribeiras*.

SAILING, WINDSURFING AND SURFING With the trade winds providing a remarkably steady force 5 to 6 in winter falling to a gentler force 3 to 4 in summer, wind is never lacking, and Cape Verde has become an international windsurfing and kitesurfing destination.

Sailing Sailing around the islands is still quite unusual. At any one time there might be 20 boats moored in the main harbour of São Vicente, and a few more to be found in those of Sal and Santiago. Facilities are far inferior to the Azores or Canaries (see *Getting there and away*, page 54), but there are beautiful anchorages at Murdeira Bay on Sal, at the remote Fajã d'Água on Brava and at Tarrafal in north Santiago. In fact, each island has some sort of shelter but it may be a long trek to get provisions and an even longer one for spare parts.

There are many day excursions in large sailing boats and powerboats on Sal but less available on other islands. Yachts can also be rented, with or without skipper, in São Vicente. The *Itoma* (*www.itoma.at*) is a 23m (70ft) motor-catamaran with

---

CRUISING IN CAPE VERDE   *John Abbott*

Sailing to Cape Verde and spending some time sailing between islands is growing more popular. There is a wide variety of scenery and culture and incredibly friendly people. Many find it a convenient location to stop for a while before an Atlantic crossing.

All islands are suitable cruising destinations but the quality and suitability of the harbours and anchorages varies greatly. The Atlantic swell is all-pervasive and can make any of the anchorages uncomfortable, if not dangerous. A good pilot book, such as *Atlantic Islands* by Anne Hammick, is essential for visiting the less frequented islands and for guidance on working into some of the more tricky anchorages.

Given the prevailing northeast winds it is best to cruise from north to south and from east to west. The island of Sal makes a good and friendly arrival destination. The port of Palmeira is well sheltered from all but the southwest winds and there are excellent anchorages further south at Murdeira. Santa Maria Bay and Ponta Sino also offer shelter. There is a sail repair service on Sal (for contact details, see page 124).

Boavista is an easy day's sail from Sal and has an excellent, isolated anchorage in the shallows between the islet of Ilhéu do Sal Rei and the mainland. A short dinghy ride to the rustic town of Sal Rei allows you to sample the outstanding fish restaurants or, surf permitting, you can land the dinghy on the miles of sandy beach that line the west coast or visit the remains of the fort on Ilhéu do Sal Rei.

Tarrafal on São Nicolau is a pretty anchorage where the water is very clear. The island of Santa Luzia offers peace and isolation; in settled conditions anchor in Praia do Palmo a Tostão in the shelter of Ilhéu Zinho. The island of Maio in the southern group boasts plenty of fish, birds and deserted beaches; it is possible to anchor at Porto de Maio on the southwest side of the island. The swell often makes disembarking on the pier a bit tricky.

The country's capital, Praia, on Santiago, has good anchorage, and nearby Fogo is a spectacular island with a good settled weather anchorage on the west coast. Brava is another spectacular and pretty island where it is possible to anchor in the really tiny harbour of Furna; ashore you can visit the exceptionally charming village of Vila Nova Sintra.

São Vicente hosts the only marina in the island chain at Porto Grande, Mindelo. Shelter is excellent and a good range of facilities and a chandlery are available for those preparing to cross the Atlantic.

room for 16 passengers; its owners organise cruising, diving and windsurfing tours. (For further information, see *Mindelo*, page 259.)

Windsurfing Cape Verde is a popular destination for windsurfers from Europe to Hawaii, and regularly hosts championships. The two main islands for windsurfing are Boavista (see *Windsurfing and kitesurfing*, page 143) and Sal (see *Windsurfing and kitesurfing*, page 105), with São Vicente offering a lot of potential but little as yet in the way of facilities (see page 259).

November to the end of May is the windy season. During this time, the winds range from 18 knots to 22 knots and are good for both intermediate and advanced riders. Even during the windiest times there will be days that are good for beginners. If you want to avoid strong winds, the best time to learn is during the summer. Sal has a dedicated kitesurfing bay and also has Ponta Preta, whose huge breakers, kicked up by a strong offshore wind, led to the venue being added to the World Wave Circuit in 2007 and the Professional Windsurfers Association World Cup (*www.pwaworldtour.com*) in 2008, 2009 and 2010. In São Vicente, in the bay of Mindelo, the average wind speed between January and June is 16 knots, with gusts of up to 30 knots. Round the coast in São Pedro Bay, world windsurfing speed records have been set and the current record is over 40 knots.

Surfing Cape Verde has 965km of coastline, spotted with reefs and points and steady wind throughout the year, and its reputation as an international windsurfing, kitesurfing and surfing destination is growing. The water is warm and the swell from the open Atlantic, during the winter, can be big. It is similar to the Canaries and the Azores in the kind of swell it picks up – but it is warmer. The Barlavento – the islands in the north – are in the best position for winter surf, while the Sotavento – southern islands – pick up summer, tropical swells and swells from far away in the south Atlantic. The wind is strongest in the winter and calmest from May to September.

The winter swell season runs from January to March and at this time the average deep-swell height is about 1.8m. The swells tend to hit the western coasts of the islands and wrap around into spots heading south. The result is offshore conditions with northeast winds.

The best-known island for surfing is Sal, whose most famous wave is at Ponta Preta – a long, classic right-hand reef with 200m rides. There are also surfing spots on Santiago – Tarrafal, and the coast in the southeast, south of Ponte de Lobo. The surf is mostly reef breaks but there are some beach breaks. Boards are available for hire in Sal and São Vicente.

DIVING *with Jacquie Cozens*
Will Cape Verde soon rival the Red Sea for diving or is it all just hype? The marine life is certainly abundant and there is the novelty of being in the Atlantic yet encountering tropical fish such as parrotfish, angelfish or the occasional whale shark. In addition, flight times from Europe are relatively short, you are never likely to tie up on a crowded dive site and there are exciting seasonal events such as the migration of humpback whales and the breeding of turtles. That said, there are no classic coral reefs, there are occasional strong currents and wind, the water is colder and diving is in its infancy.

Although there are centres on five of the islands, most of the focus is on Sal which has a variety of sites in Santa Maria Bay within ten to 15 minutes' boat ride, a few along the west coast and some less frequently visited places on the east coast. The underground topography consists of rocky ridges, pinnacles and boulders and underwater arches and caves. On Sal there are five wrecks at between 5m and 30m, the latest having been sunk in April 2008 by Manta Diving Center. Sal also offers the opportunity to dive in caves that have been formed by lava in the north of the island. A classic dive is Buracona, a 40m tunnel that emerges at the 'Blue Eye', a pool where you can surface to see the surprised faces of land-based tourists looking down on you.

Dive sites in Cape Verde are usually ridges with big overhangs smothered in bright yellow polyps and populated with large aggregations of surgeonfish, goatfish, parrotfish, Atlantic bigeyes, enormous scribbled filefish and metre-long cornet fish. At certain times '*papaguia*' or Guinea grunts form huge balls of up to 1,000 fish. The macro life is also abundant, with numerous nudibranchs, tiny coral eels, sharpnose puffers and frogfish.

Large marine life you may encounter include dolphins and five species of turtles, including loggerheads which come ashore to nest between June and October. Species such as endangered tiger sharks and bull sharks were once common but are now more often seen being gutted on the pier. Sometimes there are nurse sharks, reef sharks and manta rays. Humpback whales visit in the spring.

In general the diving around all the islands is reliably good and, compellingly, it is very underexplored. The potential as a diving destination is huge, as the relative isolation in the middle of a vast ocean is likely to lead to exciting and unexpected encounters.

Water temperatures range from 21°C to 27°C. Diving and courses are available on Sal, Boavista, Santiago, São Vicente and Santo Antão. All the centres have rental gear. Be aware that there is no operational recompression chamber on any of the islands.

FISHING Cape Verde has superlative big-game fishing. Blue marlin, for example, is big both in numbers and in size (fish up to 750lb have been caught here). There are also tiger shark, sailfish, swordfish, kingfish and striped and white marlin. Closer in to shore there are wahoo, albacore, yellowfin tuna, grouper and dorado. Casual fishing is best done from Sal, where trips range from £30 to £50 for a half–full day (see page 106). Big-game fishing is best from São Nicolau (see page 314) and between São Vicente and Santo Antão (see page 260). Hiring a boat for the day for such a trip is around £500–900, depending on whether it is a local fishing boat or not, while booking an all-inclusive week's trip is around £1,600–2,400, depending on numbers. Around the archipelago

---

TIPS FOR PLANNING YOUR TRIP

- Don't use ferries (except to Santo Antão and Brava) unless you are on a long trip
- If you are on a tight schedule or already know exactly what you want to do, book your internal flights at home
- Visit no more than two islands (in a week) or three–four (two weeks)
- Minimise the number of flights
- Select your islands carefully: they differ wildly and it's hard to change your plans
- If you use a tour operator choose a specialist in Cape Verde

it is possible to join local fishermen on their trips. Often they go out a few hundred metres, drop anchor, and fish for goldfish, grouper and squirrelfish. Some go night-fishing for morays. The locals use harpoons to catch lobster, octopus and parrotfish. As sport fishing grows in popularity, so do less than ecologically sound practices. Many operators with limited knowledge of marine life take undersized fish and target marginal species such as sharks, marlin and other billfish. If you don't want to contribute to this indiscriminate practice look out for a skipper who practices catch and release.

BEACHES Cape Verde has miles and miles of virgin, white coastline, but without the palm trees. It is breathtakingly beautiful – and much of it is remote and desolate too. Luxury holiday resorts are now common on Sal and there are a few on Boavista and some likely to be in the pipeline for Maio. Beware, though, that some beach tourists complain about the wind and some seem to be plagued by flies, too; others have complained that swimming was not safe in front of their hotel: check before you book.

GETTING MARRIED IN CAPE VERDE As the islands develop, demand is growing amongst couples dreaming of a barefoot wedding on a beach. Although this kind of tourism is in its infancy, it has all the makings of a growth sector. The regulations are straightforward, the weather is virtually guaranteed, the setting beautiful and the cost, so far at least, is nowhere near the cost of other, more established destinations. Weddings or renewal of vows can be held in a church, on the beach, in hotels or other venues such as the volcano at Pedra de Lume on Sal. More information can be found on the Cape Verde Tips website.

SUGGESTED ITINERARIES

There's nothing more tragic to this guide writer than to meet grumpy tourists at the end of their holidays who, in essence, selected the wrong islands for their tastes. If all you want is mountains and greenery you will loathe Sal. If you are after a bit of luxury by the sea with watersports you will be frustrated in Fogo or São Nicolau. You can select islands to suit your interests from the map on page 46 and from the list below, which is followed by a few suggested itineraries. Bear in mind, however, the islands' internal flight system is centred on the hubs of Sal (to get to Boavista or São Nicolau), Santiago (to get to Fogo and thus Brava by boat, and to get to Maio), and São Vicente (to get to São Nicolau and Santo Antão – the latter by boat); so it might take two flights to get to your island.

CHOOSING YOUR ISLANDS

- **Santo Antão** Mountain walking; scenic driving; one luxury hotel; a small amount of adventure sports.
- **São Vicente** Barren; nightlife and restaurants in Mindelo, with some buildings of historical interest; one luxury hotel by a beautiful beach; game fishing; marina with yachts for hire.
- **São Nicolau** Very quiet; beautiful mountain walking; scenic driving; black-sand beaches; game fishing.
- **Sal** Barren, flat interior; superb watersports; beach resort hotels; nightlife; turtles.
- **Boavista** Flat with desert interior; superb watersports; miles of deserted beaches; a few beach hotels; turtles.

- **Maio** Flat, mostly barren interior; miles of deserted beaches; slow pace; gourmet restaurants; few hotels as yet.
- **Santiago** A balanced mix with no extremes; a city with some music and restaurants; one or two nice beaches; craggy mountainous interior with a few good walks; and the country's one major historical sight.
- **Fogo** The volcano; for sightseers and hikers; some history.
- **Brava** Very quiet; mountainous with some lovely walks.

SUGGESTED ITINERARIES
- **Hikers** Make straight for Santo Antão (three+ days) and Fogo (two–three days). If schedules permit, Brava and São Nicolau are also stunning and Santiago has one or two good hikes in its interior.
- **Watersports enthusiasts** Stick to Sal and Boavista. Boavista is quieter and arguably more beautiful but has fewer facilities.
- **All-round sightseers** Choose one of the flat islands (Maio, Boavista or Sal), one of the two extraordinary landscapes (Fogo or Santo Antão) and a day/evening in either Mindelo (if you're heading to Santo Antão) or Praia's Plateau (if you're heading to Fogo) to sample city life.

TOUR OPERATORS

There's a growing number of tour operators and travel agents who claim to understand Cape Verde but in reality have only a shallow knowledge. More than for other locations it is essential to choose an operator who understands the islands with all their peculiarities.

UK
Archipelago Cape Verde 1b Museum Sq, Keswick, Cumbria CA12 5DZ; 017687 75684; e info@archipelagocapeverde.com; www.archipelagocapeverde.com
Cape Verde Travel 14 Market Pl, Hornsea, East Yorkshire HU18 1AW; 01964 532679; e info@capeverdetravel.com; www.capeverdetravel.co.uk. Also, in São Vicente, Rua Carlos Mondlane; m +238 998 2878; e capeverdetravel@cvtelecom.cv. Run by Ron Hughes, who has been offering Cape Verde holidays for 20 years & knows every island & every hotel inside out.

He has done an enormous amount to promote Cape Verde as a destination & to encourage Cape Verdeans to set up their own tourist businesses. He offers a personal service, tailoring trips to your tastes & offering everything from ticket-only to a full package including activities. Welcomes orders from outside the UK.
Explore Worldwide 55 Victoria Rd, Farnborough, Hampshire GU14 7PA; 0845 013 1537; e hello@explore.co.uk; www.explore.co.uk. Offers an 11-day group tour of 2 islands, mostly hiking.

GERMANY
Olimar Reisen Unter Goldschmied 6, 50667 Cologne; +49 2212 05900; e service.center@olimar.de; www.olimar.de. A big operator doing mainly package seaside holidays in Sal. Its holidays can be booked from Britain with a credit card.
Reiseträume Bühlstrasse 22, 72458 Albstadt; +49 7431 763168; e kapverden@reisetraeume.de; www.reisetraeume.de/kapverden/reisebuero/angebote.html; 15.00–

17.00 Mon–Fri. Gerhard & Sibylle Schellmann live in Calheta in Santiago & have an office in Germany. They offer hiking tours around the archipelago, & specialist tours in Santiago. They also speak English.
Sun & Fun Sportreisen Franz-Josef-Strasse 43, D-80801 Munich; +49 8933 8833; e marion.henne@sportreisen.de; www.sportreisen.de. A good bet for watersports, including diving.

FRANCE

Nomade Aventure www.nomade-aventure.com. A specialist company.

Terres d'Aventure www.terdav.com. A large operator of adventure holidays.

CAPE VERDE

Alsatour CP 33, Paúl, Santo Antão; ☏ +238 223 1213; m +992 5875; e alfred@alsatour.de; www.alsatour.de. Based in Santo Antão for the last 20 years, Alsatour specialises in tailor-made trips including international flights (see box, Alfred Mandl, page 288). Particularly good with trekking tours in Santo Antão, including those to remote areas. English spoken.

CaboVerde No Limits Ponta do Sol, Santo Antão; ☏ +238 225 1031; m +238 997 9039; e info@caboverdenolimits.com; www.caboverdenolimits.com. Spanish- & French-run operator specialising in adventure activities in Santo Antão. English spoken.

vista verde tours ☏ +238 242 1261; e sal@vista-verde.com; www.vista-verde.com/. Well-established travel agency specialising in social & environmentally responsible tourism. Arranges small group tours or tailor-made holidays incorporating international & domestic flights, hotels & excursions. Offices in Fogo, Sal & Boavista. Part of the Oneworld travel agency (*www.kapverdischeinseln.de/*).

ONLINE BOOKINGS Flights and accommodation can be booked through websites such as www.greatlatedeals.co.uk, www.lastminute.com, www.thomson.co.uk, or www.tuifly.com. You might find good prices here for a week in the sun, but if you are planning anything more elaborate it is advisable to use a specialist operator.

RED TAPE

Every non-Cape Verdean visitor needs a visa unless they are married to, or are the offspring of, a Cape Verdean citizen – in which case they need their marriage or birth certificate. If there is a Cape Verdean embassy in your country you can obtain the visa from there. The cost varies from country to country.

In the UK, where there is no embassy, you have several options. Whoever books your air tickets in the UK will probably be able to arrange the visa for you, to be picked up at the airport on arrival. This is by far the most common scenario.

Alternatively, download an application form from the website of the Cape Verdean Honorary Consul (*www.capeverdebureau.com*), follow the instructions and dispatch. Be sure to allow plenty of time, as there are often delays. This website also has a lot of information about different types of visas.

The third option is to arrive without a visa and just buy one on arrival. This costs €25, so is cheaper than other options and is a straightforward operation. You will generally be given a visa for a week as this is the norm; make sure you ask for the length of time you need (usually a maximum of a month). You can renew your visa at a police station during your stay (you will need a passport photo), but it is much easier to go before your visa expires. Fines are often levied on departure if you have overstayed. Visas bought in advance are normally valid for 30 days unless a longer length is specified.

You are not usually required to show proof of a return ticket to purchase a visa on arrival or to arrange a visa in the UK, but some other consulates (such as the one in Italy) will insist on it.

In Italy, your travel agent or tour operator should arrange your visa for you. Check with them whether it is pre-paid or whether you will need to pay on receipt. If you are travelling independently, try the Cape Verdean embassy for a visa (for address, see opposite).

Anyone planning to visit Cape Verde from west Africa should if possible get a visa before leaving Europe, as it may add time and complications to get a visa in African capitals. In The Gambia, for example, there is no Cape Verdean representation, so organise a visa before leaving home or fly to Senegal.

CAPE VERDEAN EMBASSIES AND CONSULATES

Austria (consulate) Dornbacher Strasse 89, 1170 Vienna; +43 676 549 9114; e kv@meixner.at; www.kv.meixner.at

Belgium embassy) Av Jeanne 29, 1050 Brussels; +32 2 646 6270; e emb.caboverde@skynet.be

Brazil SHIS-QL 08 Conj 08, Casa 07 CEP: 71620-045; +55 61 3248 0543

Canada (consulate) 802 The Queensway, West Suite 103, Etobicoke, Ontario M8Z 1N5; +1 416 252 1082

France Rue Jouffroy D'Abbans, 80, 75017 Paris; +33 1 42 12 73 50

Germany Dorotheenstrasse 43, D 10117 Berlin; +49 30 2045 0955; e info@embassy-capeverde.de; www.embassy-capeverde.de

Italy Viale Giosué Carducci, 4-1° Interno 3, 00187 Rome; +39 06474 4678/4596; e elviofernandes@hotmail.com

Luxembourg 46, R Goethe, L-1637, Luxembourg; +352 2648 0948

Netherlands Baan 6, 3011 CB Rotterdam; +31 10 477 89 77; e cons.cverde-nl@wxs.nl; www.conscv.nl

Portugal Av do Restelo 33, 1400-025 Lisbon; + 351 213 041 440; e emb.caboverde@netcabo.pt

Russia Rubliovskoe Chaussé, 26 APT 180, Moscow; +7 095 415 4503

Senegal 3 Bd Djilly M'baye, Immeuble Fahd 13ème étage, Dakar; +221 821 1873; e acvc.sen@metissacana.sn

Spain (consulate) Calle Capitán Haya, 51 Planta 4, Of8, 28020 Madrid; +34 91 570 2568; e con.geral-cv@mad.servicom.es

Sweden (consulate) Tellusvägen 16, 135 47 Tyresö, Stockholm; +46 8 742 2927; e miguel.pinto@telia.com

Switzerland (consulate) Rümelinplatz 14, CH-4001 Basel; + 41 61 269 8095

UK (consulate) Cape Verde Bureau, 214 Smithdown Rd, Liverpool L15 3JT; +44 (0)7935 091509; www.capeverdebureau.com

USA 3415 Massachusetts Av NW, Washington, DC 20007; +1 202 965 6820; e ambacvus@sysnet.net; www.virtualcapeverde.net

USA (consulate) 607 Boston St. 4th Fl, Boston, Massachusetts 02116; +1 617 353 0014; e cgcvbost@aol.com (plus satellite office: University of Massachusetts Dartmouth, 800 Purchase St, Rm 109)

EMBASSIES AND CONSULATES IN CAPE VERDE

Belgium (consulate) Rua 5 de Julho, 86–88, Praia; 261 3892

Brazil (embassy) Chã D'Areia Nr 2, Praia; 261 5607/0809

Denmark (consulate) Mindelo; 232 1785

France (embassy) Prainha, Praia; 261 5591; www.ambafrance-cv.org

Germany (consulate) Av Da OUA, Praia; 262 3100/3102

Israel (consulate) Mindelo; 232 3353

Italy (consulate) Chã D'Areia, Praia; 261 9171

Netherlands (consulate) Rua Senador Vera Cruz, Mindelo; 232 1348; e consulmindelo@cvtelecom.cv

Norway (consulate) Tira-chapéu, Praia; 262 7555

Portugal (embassy) Achada Santo António, Praia; 262 6097

Senegal (embassy) Rua Abilio Macedo, Praia; 261 2024; e ambsenecvpraia@cvtelcom.cv

Spain (consulate) Prainha, Praia; 261 4342

Sweden (consulate) Av Andrade Corvo, Praia; 261 7969

Switzerland (consulate) Rue Césario Lacerda no 19; 261 9868; e jspencerlima@hotmail.com

UK (consulate) Shell Cabo Verde, Av Amílcar Cabral, Mindelo; 232 6625; e canutoantoniorc@yahoo.com

USA (embassy) CP 201, Rua Abilio Macedo 6, Praia; 261 5616; e emb.usa@cvtel:ecom.cv; http://praia.usembassy.gov/

The website www.embassiesabroad.com/embassies-in/CapeVerde also lists contact details for other embassies and consulates in Cape Verde.

GETTING THERE AND AWAY

BY AIR There are international airports on Sal, Santiago, Boavista and São Vicente. Most international flights land at Sal; however, this may change rapidly. As internal flights are a little unreliable, it can be an advantage to fly to the airport closest to the island of your holiday destination. For example, travellers making for Santo Antão will have a much shorter journey if they fly directly to São Vicente, while those heading for Fogo should choose Santiago.

Scheduled airlines flying to Cape Verde include TAP Portugal, the national carrier TACV, and Air Senegal. TACV has been subject to an enormous amount of disruption and although its safety record is exemplary it cannot be recommended as an international link, especially from the UK, because of its unreliability. You should, however, check whether the situation has improved. Charter flights come and go. ThomsonFly, TUIfly, TUI Nordic and Jetair are some of the names that operate many flights to Cape Verde from Europe. Monarch Airlines are also rumoured to be starting a service from the UK. Direct flights from Europe range from around six hours, from the north, to three hours from southern countries such as Portugal.

Despite TACV's unreliability, it may be cheaper to choose them because of the entitlement this gives you to a domestic airpass, allowing less expensive travel between the islands.

From the UK A stellar array of direct flights from the UK has been promised for years now – with a flight time of 5.5 hours – but has not materialised. However, as the number of tourists from the UK rises some of these promises may come true. Here is the current picture:

TACV www.flytacv.com. The airline operated direct flights from from Stansted to Santiago for a while, but currently they do not have direct flights. You can connect with TACV by flying to another European city, such as Lisbon. You cannot book directly through the airline in the UK or online, but instead through one of its agents, such as Cape Verde Travel (see page 51).
TAP Portugal www.flytap.com. Flights from London to either Sal or Praia via Lisbon.

Thomsonfly www.thomsonfly.com. Weekly & twice-weekly flights from Manchester to Sal & Boavista; Gatwick to Sal & Boavista; & Birmingham to Sal. Geared mostly towards those who book packages with the company, though it is sometimes possible to book a standalone flight. It can even be cheaper to book a package but use only the flight.

Alternatively, fly from London, Birmingham, Bristol, Liverpool and elsewhere to Lisbon, Germany or Belgium and pick up a charter flight to Sal or Boavista.

From Ireland There have been a few attempts to set up charter flights, with none functioning as this book went for publication. The best connections are via Manchester, Gatwick or Lisbon.

From Italy
Neos Air Via della Chiesa 68 20019, Somma Lombardo (Varese); e neos@neosair.it;

www.neosair.it. Flies from Bergamo, Milan Malpensa, Verona & Rome Fiumicino to Sal. The charter flights can also be booked through Cabo Verde Time (*Via Stretta 28, 25128, Brescia;* 030 370 0167; *www.caboverdetime.it*).

TACV Was operating flights from Bergamo to Sal that could be bought at the last minute for a low cost, but the route was temporarily taken over by an English charter company. Check with your travel agent.

From the rest of Europe

TACV The national carrier flies direct from France (Paris), the Netherlands (Amsterdam), Switzerland (Zurich), Germany (Munich, Düsseldorf, Frankfurt), Italy (Milan – Malpensa & Bergamo, Verona, Bologna, Rome – Fiumicino), Poland (Warsaw), Portugal (Porto & Lisbon), Finland (Helsinki), the Czech Republic (Prague) & Hungary (Budapest).

Jetair *www.jetairfly.com.* Flights from Brussels to Sal & Boavista.
TAP Portugal Connects most major European cities with Lisbon for the daily onward flight to Cape Verde (Sal or Santiago).
TUIfly *www.tuifly.com.* Flights from Frankfurt, Düsseldorf, Munich & Hanover to Sal & Boavista.

From North America
Some visitors from North America fly to a European capital and from there to Cape Verde.

Cape Verde Travel (see *Tour operators*, page 51) books flights from North America to Cape Verde.
Neves Travel 1545 Acushnet Av, New Bedford, MA; 508 996 1332; e info@nevestravel.com; www.nevestravel.com. Many years of experience arranging flights & holidays to Cape Verde.

Sun Travel 598 Warren Av, East Providence, RI; 401 434 7333. Experienced at getting people to & from Cape Verde on any available airlines, including occasional charters at competitive prices.
TACV Flies from Boston to Praia; some may be via Lisbon.
TAP Portugal Flights from New York & Boston–Lisbon–Sal.

From Africa

Air Senegal *www.air-senegal-international.com.* Flights to Praia from Dakar in Senegal with links to Bissau in Guinea-Bissau, & Banjul in The Gambia.

Angolan Airlines *www.taagangola.pages.web. com.* Stops in Cape Verde en route to Europe.
TACV Operates flights to/from Senegal (Dakar), Angola (Luanda), Banjul, Bissau, & São Tomé & Príncipe.

From the Canary Islands
TACV Operates 1 flight a week from Las Palmas to Praia.

From South America
TACV Flies to the Brazilian city of Fortaleza, on the northeast coast of Brazil, twice a week. It is also flying to Recife, capital of Pernambuco state.

BY SEA
By ships and cruise Arriving by sea and watching the Atlantic crags materialise from the ocean is an unusual and uplifting way of reaching the islands. Some ships stay for 48 hours, which is plenty of time in which to get across from Mindelo to see the highlights of Santo Antão. An increasing number of cruises are stopping in Cape Verde, mostly in Mindelo. These include Cunard (*0845 678 0013; www.cunard.co.uk*), P&O (*0845 678 0014; www.pocruises.com*), Celebrity Cruises

(↳ *0844 493 2043; www.celebritycruises.co.uk*), and Noble Caledonia (*www.noble-caledonia.co.uk*). Smaller cruise ships, such as the *Marco Polo*, sometimes go to Fogo.

For information about passage in a cargo ship to Cape Verde try the following:

Arca Verde CP 153, Rua Senador Vera-Cruz, Mindelo, São Vicente; ↳ 232 1349
Atlantic Shipping Cape Cod, MA; ↳ 508 672 1870. Sometimes offers sailings from the US to Cape Verde.

Strand Voyages 1 Adam St, London WC2N 6AB; ↳ 020 7766 8220; e voyages@strandtravel.co.uk; www.strandtravel.co.uk

By yacht Cape Verde is becoming better known to yachts on the Atlantic run: numbers are increasing, and it is not uncommon to see 20 boats at anchor in Mindelo harbour, a few at Palmeira on Sal and Sal Rei on Boavista, and one or two more dotting bays around the archipelago. One big draw is that pausing in Cape Verde, rather than the Canaries, can reduce the longest leg of the Atlantic crossing by a week.

There are three good harbours and these are on the best-resourced islands (Sal, São Vicente and Santiago). The other islands all have reasonable anchorages, some of them quite beautiful, but at some the safety or comfort depends on the weather.

Cape Verde is short on spares and repair skills compared with ports in the Azores or the Canaries. Boat repair facilities are limited: the best and only real maintenance and spares point is Mindelo. This has lifts for quite large craft and a tradition of woodworking and boatbuilding. There is a chandlery in the new marina in Mindelo with a lot of high-tech equipment for crossing the Atlantic. There is a sail repair service on Sal.

Food is expensive because it is imported, and it can sometimes be hard to find fresh meat and vegetables. Water and diesel are available by jerry can on jetties in the three good harbours but otherwise it can be a case of making journeys to the tap. Water is scarce on Cape Verde and much of it comes from desalinisation plants. Consumption is high in this warm climate so you need to plan your route with care unless you have a water-maker.

You do not need a visa unless you are planning to sleep onshore, or to stay for longer than three months. You must enter and clear at every island you visit.

In the island chapters, brief information is given as to anchorages and facilities. However, the approaches to many of the islands are tricky and it is best to consult the excellent *Atlantic Islands: Azores, Madeira, Canary and Cape Verde Islands* (see *Appendix 2, Further Information*, page 339). The most detailed charts are pre-1975 Portuguese; there are also British Admiralty charts but these have errors, sometimes dangerous ones. The British Admiralty Africa Pilot has lots of useful information about weather, sea conditions and currents. All these can be obtained from Imray, Laurie, Norie and Wilson's aforementioned guide.

➕ HEALTH   *with Dr Felicity Nicholson*

Cape Verde does not suffer from many of the diseases that are a menace in mainland Africa. There is a limited incidence of malaria and dengue fever – and polio, diphtheria and measles have successfully been combated. With increased immigration from west Africa there have been incidences of yellow fever and hepatitis A and B. Food-borne diseases, from diarrhoea to cholera, are common though, and for the tourist, accidents are a threat. The islands have a good number of doctors, trained overseas.

PREPARATION

Travel insurance Cape Verde's tourism is developing faster than its infrastructure. There are hospitals on São Vicente and Santiago, and there is a large private medical clinic on Sal, but bear in mind that if you are taken seriously ill elsewhere, treatment may be hard to find. That's why it's important to take out comprehensive travel insurance.

American travellers should remember that US medical insurance is not always valid outside their country. The Medicare/Medicaid programme does not provide payment for medical services outside the United States. You may need to take out supplementary medical insurance with specific overseas and medical evacuation coverage (see *Travel clinics and health information*, page 58).

Cape Verde does not have an operating hyperbaric chamber, so divers should take out proper diving insurance which will include being flown at low altitude to Europe for treatment for the bends.

Immunisations There are no compulsory vaccinations except that if you are going to Cape Verde from a country that has reported yellow fever infections over the last six years you must carry a certificate of vaccination unless there are specific contraindications. Several weeks – or, to be on the safe side, two months – before you go make sure you are up to date with the following: tetanus (ten-yearly), polio (ten-yearly), diphtheria (ten-yearly), and pertussis. Typhoid, hepatitis A and hepatitis B vaccinations are recommended for backpackers or those who will be in close contact with the local population. One dose of hepatitis A vaccine (eg: Havrix Mondose, Avaxim) gives protection for up to one year and can be given even close to the time of departure. A booster dose given at least six months after the first dose provides protection for up to 20 years, so is well worth having. Consult your doctor before you go, as it may be necessary to have an exemption certificate if the vaccine is deemed unsuitable.

Typhoid vaccine (Typhim Vi) is about 85% effective and needs boosting every three years. It is recommended unless you are travelling at short notice for a week or less, when the vaccine would have insufficient time to be effective.

Hepatitis B vaccination should be considered by anyone working within a medical setting or with children. It is also recommended for stays longer than four–six weeks. A course of three doses of the vaccine is ideal and can be taken over as little as 21 days (Engerix).

Rabies vaccine is also recommended for those working with animals or for longer trips (four weeks or more) when you are likely to be more than 24 hours from medical help. Again, three doses of the vaccine are ideal and like hepatitis B can be taken over 21 days (see below). Immunisation against cholera is not required unless specific outbreaks are reported. There is now an effective oral vaccine (Dukoral) available in the UK. Two doses of vaccine should be taken at least one week apart and at least one week before entry for those over six years of age. At the time of writing, however, there are no specific concerns in Cape Verde. Your family doctor or a commercial travel clinic (see page 58) can tell you if this list has changed recently.

If you need more than one of these immunisations then the cheapest approach should be through your family doctor, who may make an initial charge plus a small fee for each jab. Remember, however, that not all GPs offer these services, so you should contact your clinic to check. Travel clinics can also be faster and are used to dealing with the last-minute traveller. The rabies jab can also be about £20 cheaper from a commercial clinic.

Malaria All the islands except Santiago are free from malaria, and Santiago suffers only between September and December. The current advice is not to take any prophylaxis, but if a fever develops (in Cape Verde, or at home), it should be investigated promptly.

Dengue fever 2009 saw the first cases of dengue fever in Cape Verde following the heavy rains in August and September of that year. Some cases proved to be fatal. The main islands affected were those with the most rainwater, and thus most vegetation – Santiago, Fogo, and Brava. There were fewer cases in 2010. There is no immunisation for dengue, so prevention of mosquito bites is the only answer.

Medical kit Pharmacies are widespread and well stocked but, just in case, bring a small medical kit containing soluble aspirin or paracetamol (good for gargling when you have a sore throat and for reducing fever and pains), plasters, antiseptic, insect repellent and suncream. Many travellers are reassured by investing in a blood transfusion kit which contains sterile equipment such as needles for use during surgery. Some travel clinics will try to persuade you to take antibiotics but there is no need as doctors' prescriptions and the drugs themselves are readily available. Self-medication should only be a last resort.

TRAVEL CLINICS AND HEALTH INFORMATION A full list of current travel clinic websites worldwide is available from the International Society of Travel Medicine on www.istm.org. For other journey preparation information, consult www.tripprep.com. Information about various medications may be found on www.emedicine.com. For information on malaria prevention, see www.preventingmalaria.info.

UK

Berkeley Travel Clinic 32 Berkeley St, London W1J 8EL (near Green Park tube station); ☎ 020 7629 6233

Cambridge Travel Clinic 48a Mill Rd, Cambridge CB1 2AS; ☎ 01223 367362; e enquiries@travelcliniccambridge.co.uk; www.travelcliniccambridge.co.uk; ⊕ 12.00–19.00 Tue–Fri, 10.00–16.00 Sat

Edinburgh Travel Clinic Regional Infectious Diseases Unit, Ward 41 OPD, Western General Hospital, Crewe Rd South, Edinburgh EH4 2UX; ☎ 0131 537 2822; www.mvm.ed.ac.uk. Travel helpline (☎ 0906 589 0380) ⊕ 09.00–12.00 Mon–Fri. Provides inoculations & antimalarial prophylaxis, & advises on travel-related health risks.

Fleet Street Travel Clinic 29 Fleet St, London EC4Y 1AA; ☎ 020 7353 5678; www.fleetstreetclinic.com. Vaccinations, travel products & latest advice.

Hospital for Tropical Diseases Travel Clinic Mortimer Market Bldg, Capper St (off Tottenham Ct Rd), London WC1E 6AU; ☎ 020 7388 9600; www.thehtd.org. Offers consultations & advice, & is able to provide all necessary drugs &

vaccines for travellers. Runs a healthline (☎ 0906 133 7733) for country-specific information & health hazards. Also stocks nets, water-purification equipment & personal protection measures.

Interhealth Worldwide Partnership Hse, 157 Waterloo Rd, London SE1 8US; ☎ 020 7902 9000; www.interhealth.org.uk. Competitively priced, one-stop travel health service. All profits go to their affiliated company, InterHealth, which provides healthcare for overseas workers on Christian projects.

Liverpool School of Medicine Pembroke Pl, Liverpool L3 5QA; ☎ 0151 708 9393; www.liv.ac.uk/lstm

MASTA (Medical Advisory Service for Travellers Abroad) Moorfield Rd, Yeadon, Leeds, West Yorkshire LS19 7BN; ☎ 0113 238 7500; www.masta-travel-health.com. Provides travel health advice, antimalarials & vaccinations. There are over 25 MASTA pre-travel clinics in Britain; call or check online for the nearest. Clinics also sell mosquito nets, medical kits, insect protection & travel hygiene products.

NHS travel website
www.fitfortravel.scot.nhs.uk. Provides country-by-country advice on immunisation & malaria, plus details of recent developments, & a list of relevant health organisations.
Nomad Travel Store/Clinic 3–4 Wellington Terrace, Turnpike Lane, London N8 0PX; 020 8889 7014; travel-health line (office hours only) 0906 863 3414; e sales@nomadtravel.co.uk; www.nomadtravel.co.uk. Also at 40 Bernard St, London WC1N 1LJ; 020 7833 4114; 52 Grosvenor Gardens, London SW1W 0AG; 020 7823 5823; & 43 Queens Rd, Bristol BS8 1QH;

0117 922 6567. For health advice, equipment such as mosquito nets & other anti-bug devices, & an excellent range of adventure travel gear. Clinics also in Bristol & Southampton.
Trailfinders Travel Clinic 194 Kensington High St, London W8 7RG; 020 7938 3999; www. trailfinders.com/travelessentials/travelclinic.htm
Travelpharm The Travelpharm website www.travelpharm.com offers up-to-date guidance on travel-related health & has a range of medications available through their online mini pharmacy.

Irish Republic
Tropical Medical Bureau Grafton St Medical Centre, Grafton Bldgs, 34 Grafton St, Dublin 2; 1 671 9200; www.tmb.ie. A useful website

specific to tropical destinations. Also check website for other bureaux locations throughout Ireland.

USA
Centers for Disease Control 1600 Clifton Rd, Atlanta, GA 30333; 800 311 3435; www.cdc.gov/travel. The central source of travel information in the USA. The invaluable *Health Information for International Travel*, published annually, is available from the Division of Quarantine at this address.
Connaught Laboratories Pasteur Merieux Connaught, Route 611, PO Box 187, Swiftwater, PA 18370; 800 822 2463. They will send a free list of specialist tropical-medicine physicians in your state.

IAMAT (International Association for Medical Assistance to Travelers) 1623 Military Rd, 279, Niagara Falls, NY 14304-1745; 716 754 4883; e info@iamat.org; www.iamat.org. A non-profit organisation that provides lists of English-speaking doctors abroad.
International Medicine Center 915 Gessner Rd, Suite 525, Houston, TX 77024; 713 550 2000; www.traveldoc.com

Canada
IAMAT Suite 1, 1287 St Clair Av W, Toronto, Ontario M6E 1B8; 416 652 0137; www.iamat.org

TMVC Suite 314, 1030 W Georgia St, Vancouver, BC V6E 2Y3; 888 288 8682; www.tmvc.com. Private clinic with several outlets in Canada.

Australia, New Zealand, Singapore
IAMAT PO Box 5049, Christchurch 5, New Zealand; www.iamat.org
TMVC 1300 65 88 44; www.tmvc.com.au. Clinics in Australia, New Zealand & Singapore, including: Auckland Canterbury Arcade, 170 Queen St, Auckland; 9 373 3531 Brisbane 75a

Astor Terrace, Spring Hill, QLD 4000; 7 3815 6900 Melbourne 393 Little Bourke St, 2nd floor, Melbourne, VIC 3000; 3 9602 5788 Sydney Dymocks Bldg, 7th floor, 428 George St, Sydney, NSW 2000; 2 9221 7133

South Africa and Namibia
SAA-Netcare Travel Clinics Sanlam Bldg, 19 Fredman Drive, Sandton, P Bag X34, Benmore, JHB, Gauteng, 2010; www.travelclinic.co.za. Clinics throughout South Africa.

TMVC NHC Health Centre, Cnr Beyers Naude & Waugh Northcliff; PO Box 48499, Roosevelt Park, 2129 (postal address); 011 888 7488; www.tmvc.com.au. Consult website for details of other clinics in South Africa & Namibia.

Switzerland
IAMAT 57 Chemin des Voirets, 1212 Grand
Lancy, Geneva; www.iamat.org

COMMON MEDICAL PROBLEMS

Travellers' diarrhoea This afflicts half of all visitors to the developing world and can ruin a short holiday. The bacteria are borne on traces of faeces which get into food sometime between when it is growing in the soil and when it arrives at the table. If you are scrupulous you should be able to keep the bacteria from reaching your mouth. Only eat freshly cooked food or peeled raw fruit and vegetables. In particular avoid unpeelable raw food such as lettuce or cabbage and avoid raw seafood. Steer fruit juice, unless it is from a sealed bottle, and ice cream. Avoid the local water including ice cubes. Tea and coffee should be fine, simply because bringing water to the boil kills 99% of bacteria. Wash your hands after going to the toilet.

If you do fall ill then you should rest, stop eating your normal diet, avoid alcohol and take lots of clear fluids. If you are hungry then eat bland food such as biscuits and boiled rice or potatoes. The idea is to avoid stomach cramps caused by the belly trying to expel food. It is dehydration that makes you feel rotten during a bout of diarrhoea, and dehydration is also the principal danger, so it is of paramount importance to drink plenty of fluid. Sachets of oral rehydration salts such as Dioralyte, Electrolade or Rehidrat give the perfect biochemical mix – so put some in your medical kit. You can make your own such drink with eight teaspoons of sugar, one teaspoon of salt and one litre of safe water. A squeeze of lemon or orange juice improves the taste and adds another vital ingredient: potassium. You can create an approximation to this wonder-drink with flat Coca-Cola and a pinch of salt. Drink two large glasses after every bowel action and more if you are thirsty. If you are not eating you need to drink three litres every day plus enough fluid to compensate for what you are losing through diarrhoea.

Diarrhoea blockers such as Imodium, Lomotil and codeine phosphate are not a treatment and should be avoided: your body is trying to expel poisons, not lock them in. However, it may be necessary to use them if for example you are facing long bus rides. If the diarrhoea lasts more than 36 hours or you are passing blood or slime or have a fever you will probably need antibiotics. Seek medical advice as soon as you can, but if this is not possible then you may wish to take ciprofloxacin (one 500mg tablet should be taken and repeated ten–12 hours later).

Giardiasis is prevalent on Cape Verde. It can take about ten days to incubate. Stools are loose, greasy and sometimes watery; there can be pains in the upper abdomen, and sulphurous belches from both ends. If you suspect you have it, seek help.

Skin infections Any insect bite or cut gives bacteria the opportunity to foil the skin's usually strong defences. Skin infections start quickly in warm and humid climates so they are not such a problem in Cape Verde. Creams do not keep the wound dry so they are not as effective as a drying antiseptic such as dilute iodine, potassium permanganate (a few crystals in half a cup of water) or crystal violet applied three times a day. If the wound starts to throb, if it becomes red and the redness begins to spread, or if the wound oozes then you may need antibiotics and should seek a doctor. Fungal infections take hold easily in moist parts of the body so wear cotton socks and underwear and shower frequently, drying thoroughly. An itchy and often flaking rash in the groin or between the toes is likely to be a fungus and will require treatment with a cream such as Canesten (clotrimazole). If this is not available then try Whitfield's ointment (compound benzoic acid ointment) or crystal violet.

Dr Felicity Nicholson

There is growing evidence, albeit circumstantial, that long-haul air travel increases the risk of developing deep vein thrombosis. This condition is potentially life threatening, but it should be stressed that the danger to the average traveller is slight.

Certain risk factors specific to air travel have been identified. These include immobility, compression of the veins at the back of the knee by the edge of the seat, the decreased air pressure and slightly reduced oxygen in the cabin, and dehydration. Consuming alcohol may exacerbate the situation by increasing fluid loss and encouraging immobility.

In theory everyone is at risk, but those at highest risk are shown below:

- Passengers on journeys of longer than eight hours' duration
- People over 40
- People with heart disease
- People with cancer
- People with clotting disorders
- People who have had recent surgery, especially on the legs
- Women who are pregnant, or on the pill or other oestrogen therapy
- People who are very tall (over 6ft/1.8m) or short (under 5ft/1.5m)

A deep vein thrombosis (DVT) is a clot of blood that forms in the leg veins. Symptoms include swelling and pain in the calf or thigh. The skin may feel hot to touch and becomes discoloured (light blue-red). A DVT is not dangerous in itself, but if a clot breaks down then it may travel to the lungs (pulmonary embolus). Symptoms of a pulmonary embolus (PE) include chest pain, shortness of breath and coughing up small amounts of blood.

Symptoms of a DVT rarely occur during the flight, and typically occur within three days of arrival, although symptoms of a DVT or PE have been reported up to two weeks later.

Anyone who suspects that they have these symptoms should see a doctor immediately as anticoagulation (blood thinning) treatment can be given.

PREVENTION OF DVT General measures to reduce the risk of thrombosis are shown below. This advice also applies to long train or bus journeys.

- Whilst waiting to board the plane, try to walk around rather than sit
- During the flight drink plenty of water (at least two small glasses every hour)
- Avoid excessive tea, coffee and alcohol
- Perform leg-stretching exercises, such as pointing the toes up and down
- Move around the cabin when practicable

If you fit into the high-risk category (see above) ask your doctor if it is safe to travel. Additional protective measures such as graded compression stockings, aspirin or low molecular weight heparin can be given. No matter how tall you are, where possible request a seat with extra legroom.

Practical Information HEALTH

2

Insects and parasites

Insect bites There is a slight risk of malaria on Santiago Island, so it is worth protecting yourself against mosquito bites between dusk and dawn by covering up with trousers, a long-sleeved shirt and applying insect repellent containing the chemical DEET. Ideally you should sleep under a mosquito net. Cape Verde's waterless climate keeps insects down but they pop up all year round in odd places where there is stagnant water.

Tumbu flies or putsi The adult fly lays her eggs on soil or drying laundry. When those eggs come into contact with human flesh (when you put on your clothes or lie on a bed) they hatch and bury themselves under the skin. There they form a crop of boils, each of which hatches a grub after about eight days. Once they are hatched the inflammation will die down. Avoid putsi by drying clothes and sheets within a screened house or by drying them in direct sunshine until they are crisp or by ironing them.

Jiggers or sandfleas These bury into bare feet and set up home under the skin of the foot, usually at the side of a toenail where they cause a painful, boil-like swelling. A local expert must pick them out. If the distended flea bursts during eviction the wound should be doused in spirit, alcohol or kerosene to avoid more jiggers infesting you.

Ticks There are several nasty, tick-borne diseases, such as typhus. Avoid ticks by wearing long clothes and repellent, especially if walking takes you into scrubby countryside where you are brushing through vegetation.

Remove any tick as soon as you notice it – it will most likely be firmly attached to somewhere you would rather it was not – grasp the tick as close to your body as possible and pull steadily and firmly away at right angles to your skin. The tick will then come away complete as long as you do not jerk or twist. If possible douse the wound with alcohol (any spirit will do) or iodine. Spreading redness around the bite and/or fever and/or aching joints after a tick bite imply that you have an infection which requires antibiotic treatment, so seek advice.

Heat and sun

Dehydration It is easy to get dehydrated, especially in the first week. If you wake up in the morning feeling nauseous and tired that may be the reason. Water requirements depend on temperature, humidity, amount of exercise taken, and the length of time the person has been in the country. Those who get into trouble are people who do not allow themselves to acclimatise, a process that takes up to two weeks. Eager adolescents are particularly vulnerable. In the tropics you need to drink about three litres a day, more if you are exercising. Take it easy for the first week. In Cape Verde it is very likely you could end up on a long, hot and shadeless hike for a day. In those conditions you will need to have drunk five litres by the end of the day to avoid dehydration. If you are going on a day's hike drink plenty before you go, try to carry two litres per person, and fill up again in the evening.

Prickly heat A fine pimply rash on the trunk of the body is likely to be heat rash. Take cool showers and dab (do not rub) yourself dry, finishing off with a sprinkling of talc. If the rash doesn't improve it may be necessary to check into an air-conditioned room for a while, slow down, wear only loose, cotton clothes and sleep naked under a fan.

Sunburn Cape Verde is notoriously lacking in shade so you must bring your own in the form of a broad-brimmed hat, umbrella, or even a windbreak for a day on the beach. The best solution is to cover up: a light-coloured, loose cotton shirt and long skirt or trousers is also cooler than shorts and a T-shirt. Many visitors don't notice the sun burning them because of the cooling effect of the wind. Try and keep out of the sun between noon and 15.00 and, if you must expose yourself, build up gradually from 20 minutes per day. Be particularly careful of sun reflected from water and wear a T-shirt and plenty of waterproof suncream (SPF15) when snorkelling or swimming. Tanning ages your skin and can give you skin cancer.

Heat exhaustion and heat stroke Heat exhaustion develops gradually, caused by loss of salt and water through excessive sweating. It is most common in people new to the heat or new to exercise in the heat and in people who have recently had an illness in which they lost fluids (diarrhoea or vomiting). Sufferers have fast shallow breathing and a rapid weak pulse. They may feel dizzy and sick, be pale and sweating, have a headache and have cramps in the limbs and abdomen. Sit or lie the casualty down in a cool place, raise and support the legs to allow blood to flow to the brain. Give plenty of water.

Heat stroke is less common and is most likely to happen as a result of prolonged exposure to very hot surroundings. Symptoms include confusion, swiftly deteriorating to unconsciousness, a strong pulse and slow, deep breathing. The sufferer's skin will be hot, flushed and their temperature will be over 40°C. The essential thing is to cool the person quickly – do this by moving them to a cool place, removing their outer clothing, wrapping them in a cold, wet sheet and fanning them. Call for a doctor immediately.

SERIOUS ILLNESS
AIDS With a mobile population and no stable family structure Cape Verde is facing a big problem with AIDS. About 40% of HIV infections in British people are acquired abroad. Bring condoms or femidoms with you. If you notice any genital ulcers or discharge get them treated promptly. The presence of a sexually transmitted disease increases the chance of contracting AIDS.

Cholera This arises sporadically in Cape Verde and in 1995, killed 240 people and sickened 13,000. Avoid it through the precautions described under Travellers' diarrhoea, page 60. However, it is very unlikely to affect visitors. The severe form of cholera, which almost never hits travellers, is sudden and copious diarrhoea without any pain, very watery with white flecks in it. There is vomiting but usually no fever. Rehydration is vital – up to 20 litres a day in serious cases. Seek immediate help.

Typhoid Symptoms are fever, headache, loss of appetite, abdominal pain and sometimes pink spots on the skin. The heart rate may slow. Seek immediate help.

Elephantiasis Also known as filariasis, this is spread by mosquitoes and causes massive inflammation of the leg in long-standing sufferers: another reason to avoid insect bites between dusk and dawn.

Trachoma This is a disease of the very poor and not something that travellers get. However, in trachoma-affected countries the risk of travellers contracting ordinary conjunctivitis increases – so a course of antibiotic eye-drops might be useful in your medical kit.

ACCIDENTS Hospitals on the smaller islands can do little and have to evacuate to São Vicente or Santiago, even for the resetting of a broken leg. The hospital on São Vicente is the best. The inter-island planes always reserve space for medical emergencies.

Vehicles Vehicle accidents – not exotic diseases – are often the biggest killers of visitors to Africa. Cape Verde vehicles are in better condition than those on mainland Africa and many drivers are careful of their investments. But the roads are vertiginous and a few drivers compete with each other in heart-stopping races along the corkscrew routes – there is plenty of scope for 100m cliff plunges. Make sure your driver has not been drinking alcohol and try not to travel along precarious roads at night.

Swimming Swimming accidents are the other danger. The blue waters may be seductive but they are also the wild mid ocean, abounding with hidden reefs, strange currents and hungry wildlife. The golden rule is to ask local people whether it is safe to bathe (*Não é perigoso tomar banho?* – 'It's not dangerous to take a dip?'), and don't dive from boats that are far from the shore, or you could end up getting nibbled by a shark. In the shallows a pair of plimsolls will protect against coral, urchins and venomous fish spines. The trick after being stung by a venomous fish is to denature the poison by heating it – so stick your foot in a bucket of hot water until some time after the pain subsides – perhaps 20–30 minutes overall. If the pain returns, immerse the foot again. Then ask a doctor to check for fish spines in the wound.

Hiking Much of the classic walking on Cape Verde is through populated areas or at least on paths trodden regularly each day by local people, but some hikes are so deserted you will meet no-one. On Santo Antão in particular, once off the beaten track it is dangerous, with scree, gullies and landslides and no sign of water or food. It can be easy to leave the path in some of the Santo Antão *ribeiras*, particularly the many tributaries of Ribeira Grande, in which case you could get stuck on a path that has dwindled to a crevice, unable to descend without sliding along the rubble and unable to ascend because there are no footholds – and with the mist approaching. The really remote region is the west of Santo Antão where only experienced hikers should go.

Walking accidents are not uncommon. Cape Verdean terrain – hard, bone-dry soil sprinkled with tiny, rolling bits of grit – can be slippery even for those in good walking boots and even when it is flat. Sometimes you must watch each step, placing the foot on any available vegetation, stone or clear ground and avoiding the mini landslides waiting in the middle of the path. If you break a bone insist on having it set by a qualified doctor rather than a nurse, or you could end up needing it reset later.

If you go hiking don't forget the basic principles: it is essential to wear walking boots with ankle support; plan your route before you set off so that you know which villages to ask for along the way; tell someone who might care where you are going and when you are expecting to be back; drink plenty of water before you go and take two litres of water for a full day away (this assumes you can stock up beforehand and replenish in the evening); bring food – assume you will not find any on the way; take a whistle and protect yourself from the sun.

For walks in the Fogo crater and on Santo Antão's peaks take a jumper – it can get cold. Cuts and grazes can be avoided by wearing long trousers.

Animal bites The only mammals to watch out for on Cape Verde are village dogs, cats and monkeys. Some people keep monkeys as guards or pets on long stretches of rope. They are accustomed to being fed and may bite. Although the UK lists Cape Verde as a country free from rabies, it is best to assume these animals are rabid. Rabies can be carried by all mammals and is passed on to humans through a bite, or a lick of an open wound. If you are bitten, seek medical help as soon as is practicably possible. In the interim, scrub the wound thoroughly with soap and bottled/boiled water for five minutes, then pour on a strong iodine or alcohol solution. This can help to prevent the rabies virus from entering the body and will guard against wound infections, including tetanus. The decision whether or not to have the highly effective rabies vaccine will depend on the nature of your trip. It is definitely advised if you intend to handle animals, or if you are likely to be more than 24 hours away from medical help.

Ideally three pre-exposure doses should be taken over a three-week period although if time is short even one dose may be considered better than nothing. If you think you have been exposed to rabies by any of the routes described above then you should seek treatment as soon as possible. At least two post-bite rabies injections are needed, even by immunised people. Those who have not been immunised will need a full course of injections together with rabies immunoglobulin (RIG), but this product is expensive (around US$800) and may be hard to come by – another reason why pre-exposure vaccination should be encouraged in travellers who are planning to visit more remote areas. Treatment should be given as soon as possible, but it is never too late to seek help as the incubation period for rabies can be very long. Bites closer to the brain are always more serious. Remember if you contract rabies, mortality is 100% and death from rabies is probably one of the worst ways to go!

The other risk with animal bites is tetanus which is caught through deep, dirty wounds. Make sure your immunisation is up to date and clean wounds thoroughly.

SAFETY

CRIME Although Cape Verde remains a peaceful place with a very low incidence of crime, theft is increasing as a direct consequence of tourism. It is most common in Mindelo and Praia, as well as isolated spots on Sal. In São Vicente, tourists regularly fall victim to gangs of bag-snatchers. In Mindelo this kind of robbery seems common and blends with aggressive begging which occurs mostly on the waterfront (young men who may throw a stone at you if you fail to hand over money), and on the Amílcar Cabral Square (children who follow you until you retreat into a hotel, asking for money but also trying to take it from your pocket). In Praia the speciality theft venue is Sucupira Market, where pickpocketing is common, but people have had valuables such as laptops snatched from many different places in the city. In Sal it is Buracona, on the west coast, where the theme is to hide behind a rock and break into cars once their drivers have gone for a walk. In Boavista, in isolated spots, there is an increasing amount of violent crime against tourists. Other islands remain virtually crime-free.

Very recently Cape Verde has had to start to grapple with drug-related crime. Drugs are entering the country as drug-smuggling routes change (see page 34) and it is also said that tourism has increased the problem. A third cause is the US's deportation of criminals with Cape Verdean ancestry back to Cape Verde.

Follow the usual rules. Carry a purse in an inside pocket; when paying, don't open a purse stacked with cash. Keep valuables hidden in money belts, or leave them in the hotel safe where possible. If you are a victim, make a fuss so that people come to your aid. Also, it is irresponsible not to report it to the police, who are striving to fight crime (also, if you are to claim on your travel insurance you must have a police report).

HIKING SAFETY One of the joys in Cape Verde is the cobbled paths in the mountains, making some walks easier both underfoot and navigationally than they might appear. Nevertheless there are hazards. Dehydration and sunstroke are two: shade is sparse and, on some islands, non-existent, while water sources are scarce. Another is falls: where the paths are not cobbled they can be shingly, with small loose stones, and it is easy to tumble on the way down. The west of Santo Antão has its own special dangers born of remoteness (see *Chapter 11*, *Santo Antão*, page 280). Take the usual precautions: strong boots, several litres of water per person, sun protection, a map, and a message left at your hotel about where you've gone.

FOCUS ON SPECIFIC GROUPS

WOMEN TRAVELLERS Females can travel a lot on their own in Cape Verde and never feel threatened, although they might regularly feel mildly irritated. Cape Verdean men will flirt outrageously. If you're older there's less attention but always a few die-hard admirers hoping to become toy boys. The casual mention of a husband back in town makes most men lose interest pretty swiftly. However, if you reveal that you are childless – whether married, with a partner or single – you will attract huge sympathy, mystification and interest. You will have plenty of offers from potential fathers. If you go to a man's home, or invite him back to your place, he will expect to have sex even if you tell him it is not on the agenda.

Women who stay for a long time in one place – for example volunteers – can have more serious problems (see *Chapter 3*, page 81).

OLDER TRAVELLERS Increasing numbers of older people are holidaying in Cape Verde, and it poses no particular problems for them. There are a few caveats, though. The elderly may find the undulations of steep islands a little hard – there are one or two hotels that can be accessed only by foot up steep paths but these are indicated in the text. Make sure you understand about the distribution of medical facilities: if you keel over outside Sal, Santiago or São Vicente it will be a ferry journey or a plane ride to the nearest hospital. Most sights are accessible by car, but do bear in mind, if you are in need of a fairly sedentary holiday, that there are not many cultural 'sights' to go and see – just a tiny sprinkling of museums.

FAMILIES Cape Verde is increasingly attractive to families as beach tourism develops. Choose your hotel carefully though: some hotels are built in front of stretches of water in which it is not safe to bathe. Some of the resort hotels on Sal have dedicated children's facilities, such as playground, swimming pool and even activities. Many hotels are not near the water and the beaches have no shade. If a beach holiday was not what you had in mind, it's perhaps best only to take children if they are old enough to enjoy activities such as windsurfing or hiking.

DISABLED TRAVELLERS As far as we know there are no operators running specialised trips to Cape Verde for disabled people. It would be best to contact a specialist who really knows the islands you want to visit, knows the hoteliers personally and is interested in your quest: they can take the time to craft a journey for you. A good one, if you are visiting several islands, is Cape Verde Travel (see page 51).

The local minibuses are generally very crowded and hard to climb into. There are plenty of taxis in the capitals (Mindelo and Praia). In other towns the taxis may take the form of minibuses or 4x4s which may be harder to get into. For journeys by car discomfort is reduced by the fact that there are no great distances to cover anywhere in Cape Verde but most of the roads are cobbled, which can be bumpy. Some, non-cobbled, non-tarred roads can be pot-holed and uncomfortable (for example off the principal roads in Santiago, crossing the deserts in Boavista). It is best to take advice beforehand.

Because many trails, particularly in Santo Antão, are cobbled almost all the way, it is just conceivable that a disabled person in a tailored wheelchair could travel on them. One person who achieved this is Jean François Porret and his account of his experience is at www.bela-vista.net/Wheelchair.aspx.

Travel insurance can be purchased in the UK from Age UK (❀ 0845 601 2234; www.ageconcern.org.uk), who have no upper age limit, and Free Spirit (❀ 0845 230 5000; www.free-spirit.com), who cater for people with pre-existing medical conditions. Most insurance companies will insure disabled travellers, but it is essential that they are made aware of your disability.

Although the vast majority of people will only want to help you, it is worth remembering that, as a disabled person, you are more vulnerable. Stay aware of who is around you and where your bags are, especially in Mindelo and Praia where bag-snatching is on the increase.

WHAT TO TAKE

Clothing is overwhelmingly casual, though you might want to be smarter for the top restaurants. A sweater is necessary because evenings can be slightly chilly in the cooler seasons, and are always chilly higher up, for example in Rui Vaz in Santiago, or in Fogo's crater. Take walking boots if you are planning to hike.

Even the cheapest *pensão* is likely to provide towels, loo paper, soap and a basin plug. Those using a homestay might sometimes be thankful they brought a sheet sleeping bag and a pair of flip-flops for washing in. For overnight boat trips, which you may spend on deck, you must have a sleeping bag for warmth. The main towns – Santa Maria, Praia, Mindelo – should sell all other basics, including tampons (not necessarily with applicator), hair conditioner, razors, camera film, Imodium and painkillers.

Take suncream – expensive and not so easy to find – and a sunhat. Take insect repellent because there are biters about in the evenings. Although there are few mosquitoes there seems to be an average of one resident in every hotel bedroom, regardless of quality. A few hotels have mosquito nets but if it's very important to you not to be bitten, either take a net or buy some killer spray on arrival.

Cape Verde struggles with its electricity supply. Some hotels have generators but many hotels of a good standard do not. Take a torch and consider taking a lighter and candle.

The electricity supply is 220V 50Hz, which is standard in western Europe. The plug is a standard European two-pin type so a converter is necessary.

A Portuguese dictionary would be useful. Bring your own reading matter – there is little available in English in Cape Verde. Some hotels have a book swap scheme.

Sal is full of British expats desperate to see a copy of a recent newspaper or magazine from Blighty. Biros are useful presents for children (but see *Begging*, page 77). An ordinary driving licence suffices for car hire.

If you are happy to travel light with only hand luggage you will have the great advantage of whistling through airports much faster than everyone else.

2

MAPS Many of the maps that previously published by Goldstadt Verlag are out of print and will not be republished, but some, such as those for São Vicente, Santiago and São Nicolau, may still be found in speciality shops such as Stanfords (*www.stanfords.co.uk*) or The Map Shop in Upton-upon-Severn (*www.themapshop.co.uk*), or from www.reisetraeume.de/kapverden/reisefuehrer/en/bookshop.html. Newer maps can be ordered from Kartenverlag (*www.atlantic-islands.com*).

Cabo Verde 1:200,000 tourist map published by Kartenverlag. Cost: €14.80
Santo Antão Hiking map 1:50,000, AB Kartenverlag; €14.80
Fogo & Brava Hiking Map 1:50,000, AB Kartenverlag; €14.80

Boa Vista, Sal, Maio Hiking Map, AB Kartenverlag 1:50,000; €12.80
Sal Tourist Map 1:100,000 with city plans for Santa Maria & Espargos, AB Kartenverlag; €5.00

$ MONEY

The **currency** is the escudo, represented by the $ sign at the end of the number, or by the letters CVE. The escudo is officially set to a fixed exchange rate with the euro, currently €1=110.25$. In practice, banks and exchange bureaux/*cambios* vary the rates slightly. Rates are also varied – by as much as 110$ – by hotels charging in local currency. The euro is increasingly accepted in day-to-day transactions on Sal and Boavista; less so on other islands.

Credit cards are accepted only by some upmarket hotels – it is best to assume that hotels, restaurants and ATMs will not accept them. Visa cards can be used to withdraw funds at Banco Comercial do Atlântico for a minimum charge of 1,000$ with other charges of 0.5% of the amount withdrawn. Rates seem to vary throughout the different islands.

ATMs can be found at the major banks in most island capitals but not all. Those on less-frequented islands may not always be in operation.

Travellers' cheques are a safer way to carry money around and the three banks (Banco Comercial do Atlântico, Caixa Económica and Banco Interatlântico) all cash them. However, check the details of fees beforehand because some individual branches make perverse charges – up to €10 per transaction. (Note also that when you change travellers' cheques, if they are not consecutive numbers, you may have to pay a separate fee for each 'break' in the series.)

Money transfers can be done very quickly through Western Union to the Caixa Económica. High-street banks in the UK will transfer funds to Cape Verdean banks urgently (within two or three days) for a fee of about £20–25.

Given the above, it's best to take a mix of euros and travellers' cheques to the islands.

BUDGETING

Many goods and services approach European prices. The good hotels charge €60–100 per night with breakfast for a double room; hiring a vehicle and driver for a day will cost €70–80; a three-course meal in a good restaurant might cost about €16 without drinks; a guide for the day (without car) might cost about €30. At the other end of the scale, a basic hotel might cost about €30 for a double room with breakfast; a more basic restaurant charge around €9 for a two-course meal; and travelling around in the local *alugueres* will cost anything up to €2 depending on the distance.

Day trips and activities from Sal tend to cost €30–80, while going to another island for an organised day trip (by plane) can cost up to €200. Some tourists on package holidays who have run out of things to do complain that they did not budget for the cost of these entertainments and hadn't realised they would be so expensive. Here is a list of costs for common items:

water 1l	70–100$	chocolate bar	80$
coffee & a cake	200$	cheese triangles	115–125$
ice cream	100$	banana	15–20$ each
postcard	70$	Spam	135$
fruit juice	70–100$	cigarettes	400$
bread roll/baguette	10–30$		

GETTING AROUND

BY AIR The simplest and most convenient, as well as the most reliable way to travel between the islands, is to fly. Anyone with only two weeks in the archipelago should not consider taking a ferry, except to get to Santo Antão (for Brava, see page 237).

Flights with the national airline, TACV, cost about £60 (€85) per single journey, although there are substantial savings with a domestic airpass, available to those who book their international flight with TACV or, for the moment, TAP Portugal (see *Getting there and away*, page 54). Journeys take between 20 minutes and 50 minutes. Baggage allowance for internal flights is 20kg.

If you are on a very tight schedule or know exactly what you want to do, it is better to book internal flights before you go. If you leave it until you arrive you may not get the flight of your choice but there are usually other options if you are flexible. At certain times of the year (festivals or times when emigrants arrive for their holidays), flights get very busy – it may therefore be worth checking with a local travel agent. Flights are generally cheaper the further ahead you book and there are often promotional fares. You must book ahead to qualify for the domestic airpass.

TACV flies to all the islands except Santo Antão and Brava and its flights are orientated around three hubs. From Sal you can get directly to São Vicente, São Nicolau, Boavista and Santiago. From Santiago you can get directly to Fogo, Sal, Maio and São Vicente; from São Vicente you can get directly to Sal and Santiago. Flights can fill quickly, especially through the summer, so early booking is essential. There is nothing worse than being stuck on a remote island with an international flight looming in Sal and a TACV employee advising you to turn up on standby every day for the next week.

Halcyonair-CaboVerde Airways (*www.halcyonair.com*), a privately owned airline that began operations in mid 2008, flies between Sal and Boavista, Santiago, Maio and São Vicente and has prices a little lower than those of TACV if you are booking a single sector. If you are visiting several islands a ticket with TACV is likely to be cheaper. Halcyonair continues to expand its operations and sometimes operates routes such as Sal to Maio – check with a local travel agent for up-to-date information. Again, it is best to book before you leave your home country, using an operator that understands Cape Verde.

Cabo Verde Express (*www.caboverdeexpress.com*) operates charter day trips, in general from Sal and Boavista to Fogo. Unless you are planning to charter a whole plane, you will need to sign on to a group tour via one of the operators, who advertise everywhere in Sal. You can book a flight-only option if there is availability but this is only possible at the last minute.

Even being checked in is not a guarantee of getting on the flight because of overbooking; sometimes overbooked flights sneak away 15 minutes earlier than stated. Our advice is to be mildly paranoid. The golden rule is to reconfirm your flight 72 hours beforehand: this is absolutely essential to avoid your seat being given to someone else. It is also worth calling 24 hours or even 12 hours before the flight to check the time, as they can change quite suddenly. Make sure all your flights and times are booked as soon as possible; make sure TACV and/or your tour operator has your hotel details or phone number so it can alert you to changes in the schedule. Arrive early to beat the crowds; keep watch and be first in the queue to get on the plane; and avoid travelling in large groups.

If you run into problems and are told all flights are full it is worth persisting. Every flight has seats automatically reserved for government employees and, on the lesser islands, for medical emergencies. They regularly become available for standby passengers at the last minute.

BY FERRY These are not the Greek islands; we are in the middle of rough Atlantic waters with great distances between many centres.

Ferries do operate between some of the islands, although schedules are not always strictly adhered to, so it is worth double-checking the sailing times listed throughout the guide. The following website keeps reasonably abreast of the ferry situations: www.bela-vista.net/Ferry.aspx. In 2008, two ferries sank and before that, two newly introduced catamarans were withdrawn because they couldn't cope with the rough seas. When available, boats cost about £12 (€20) per journey. You are unlikely to find a ferry too full to take you, however boats can be delayed for days and journeys are long (typically 14 hours between all but the closest islands). The services between Mindelo on São Vicente and Porto Novo on Santo Antão, however, are reliable.

A new operator, Cabo Verde Fast Ferry (*www.cvfastferry.com*), started operations in January 2011 with an initial route linking the southerly islands of Santiago, Fogo and Brava. With the arrival of a second ferry later in the year more routes will be added. The brand new, custom built ferries are modern and comfortable and should improve the reliability of inter-island travel.

There is a national propensity towards seasickness, and it is advisable to keep your bags slightly off the floor and keep an eye on the passengers immediately beside you if you want to escape the consequences. Take food and drink and something warm to wear, particularly for night crossings.

BY CARGO BOAT There are sometimes a few cargo boats travelling between the islands, and the ferry ticket offices sell a few passenger tickets on these for reduced prices – typically about two-thirds of the full price.

BY YACHT AND CATAMARAN There are day trips from Sal to Boavista in various different craft (see *Excursions*, page 103). There are also yachts available for charter between the islands and even to Senegal and other west African countries (see *Chapter 7, Maio*, page 204).

BY BUS *Hiace* minibuses, and open trucks with seating in the back (*hiluxes*) constitute the public transport. They are recognisable by the sign '*aluguer*' and on most islands that is what they are called, though on Santiago the preferred term is *hiace* ('yasser'). They are typical African minibuses, often overloaded with people, chickens and packages and trundling along, perhaps rather fast, to the sound of happy-go-lucky tinkling music.

Generally, *alugueres* converge at a point in a town or village which anyone can point out to you; often they drive round town picking up passengers and few leave town before they are full. You shout when you want to get off and you pay after disembarking. *Alugueres* can be flagged down anywhere along the roads. In Cape Verde, unusually for west Africa, many of these vehicles are in good condition and consequently most of their drivers are careful and reasonably slow.

The great disadvantage for visitors is the timings of the *alugueres*. With some exceptions (noted in each chapter), they leave outlying villages at 05.00 or 06.00 to take people to town. They then leave town for the outlying villages between 11.00 and mid afternoon. Time and time again tourists pile into the 11.00 *aluguer* only to find they have no way of getting back to town in the evening without chartering a vehicle at great cost.

BY TAXI The term 'taxi' refers both to the cars with meters and taxi signs, found in towns, and to *hiaces* that have been chartered by an individual. Chartering costs about ten times the public fare and you may be forced to do it if you want to go somewhere at a different time of day from everyone else. Sometimes the fares can be bargained down and occasionally an opportunist will try to diddle you, but generally prices are fixed – they're just very high. Drivers in general love to be chartered by a tourist so watch out when they tell you there is no more public transport that day – hang around to check and say you want to travel *colectivo*. Tourists often get together to share a chartered minibus, which has the added advantage that they can control the speed of the driver.

BY HITCHHIKING Cars are likely to pick you up, except in Santiago. Offer the price of the *aluguer* fare if it seems appropriate, or ask if the journey is free (*buleia*). In remote areas there may be no traffic all day. Women travelling on their own should always exercise caution when attempting to hitchhike.

BY CAR RENTAL This is possible through local chain firms on São Vicente, Sal and Santiago and there are tiny firms on some of the other islands. International firms have opened on Sal and Santiago. For contact details see the relevant island chapters. Book several days ahead if you can and don't expect things to run smoothly – for example, the wrong car might arrive several hours late with no price reduction offered for the inconvenience.

BY CYCLING Keen cyclists do take their bicycles to the archipelago and return having had a good time. Bicycles can be transported between the islands on the larger TACV 46-seater planes. You pay by weight, just as with other baggage. Bicycles may be hired on Sal, Maio and Santo Antão.

However, there are several caveats about cycling in Cape Verde. Firstly, virtually all roads are cobbled, causing ceaseless, tiring vibrations to the hands as they clutch the handlebars, unless you have a very good bike. Secondly, the bulk of roads in Cape Verde are utterly devoid of shade and the constant sunshine can be exhausting. Thirdly, some of the most interesting islands have many stretches that are too steep for cycling – in particular, much of Santo Antão and many roads in Fogo. Fourthly, people trying to take their own bike to the islands have run into problems both with bike damage and with the aircraft unexpectedly refusing to take the bike.

⌂ ACCOMMODATION

The hotel star-rating system is an inflated one, internal to Cape Verde. The term 'hotel' implies a place of superior quality. The other terms, *pousada*, *pensão* and *residencial*, are interchangeable. Some establishments use the word *casa* to demonstrate the family atmosphere. At the bottom of the range there are some very cheap, grubby places that are not intended for tourists. No-one will mention them, they will not be marked, and even the proprietors may discourage you from staying for fear you'll complain about the conditions. Above this level accommodation is almost invariably clean, if basic, and en-suite bathrooms are the norm. Rooms can vary enormously in quality within the same hotel. In particular the windows of inner rooms in older buildings in Praia and Mindelo often open only on to a central shaft, which makes them dark and noisy.

Hotels are listed in descending order of price and are grouped into price categories (for the key, see the inside cover). There's an increasing number of good quality and luxury hotels in Cape Verde. At the time of writing this book there were many on Sal, several on Boavista, Santiago and São Vicente, one on Santo Antão and one on Fogo. Rooms in most three-star hotels will have hot water, telephone, fan or air conditioning, and often a fridge and television (often just local channels, though). Camping is permitted on the beaches, but finding a natural water supply may be difficult.

On Sal, Boavista and Maio, there are many apartments to rent and there will be villas. See island chapters for details.

HOMESTAYS On the two great hiking islands, Santo Antão and Fogo, local people are increasingly opening up their homes to walkers. In general you sleep in a spare (or hastily vacated) bedroom and are fed your evening meal as well as breakfast the next day. Sometimes local people have built concrete annexes on to their houses to accommodate tourists. A few homestays provide better facilities. The system has several advantages. It allows trekkers to do more ambitious journeys safe in the knowledge that they have places to stay along the way. It brings locals and visitors into closer contact – you experience a taste of the rural lifestyle while they derive entertainment and cash from you.

But rural homestays are not for every visitor. Conditions will be basic: perhaps there will be a room without windows, a very old mattress and some sort of shared washing facility without a huge amount of privacy. Although the price will be lower than that of hotels, it may be higher than you expected it to be. This can be because of the high cost of arranging special food for visitors (for example, some homestay hosts in Santo Antão have to spend a day travelling to town and back to purchase food for their guests). For some visitors, a homestay is the high spot of their trip and even a formative experience in their lives; for others it is a disaster from which they can't wait to escape. The key is to abandon your tourist-as-consumer mindset and become a tourist-as-anthropologist for the day, accepting what is given and taking an interest in everything you are privileged to witness. Contacts for homestays are given in the island chapters.

✗ EATING AND DRINKING

Fish lovers will be in heaven on Cape Verde. The grilled lobster is superb, as are the fresh tuna, octopus and a multitude of other delicacies. Vegetarians may find only omelette on the menu but can always ask for a plate of rice and beans. The very few places that welcome vegetarians are mentioned in the restaurant listings.

A speciality is *cachupa*, a delicious, hearty dish that comes in two varieties: poor-man's *cachupa* (boiled maize, beans, herbs, cassava, sweet potato) and rich-man's *cachupa* (the same but with chicken and other meat). *Cachupa* takes a long time to prepare: some restaurants put a sign in their windows to indicate when they will next be serving it. For the casual visitor it may be quite hard to sample this famous

GROGUE

Sugarcane, the sole ingredient of *grogue*, arrived in Cape Verde with the slaves from mainland Africa. The word '*grogue*' is derived from 'grog' – used by English seafarers. At first, the production of spirit from sugarcane was forbidden on the grounds that it presented a risk to public health. However, restrictive laws just drove the distillers underground and by 1866 the authorities relented and introduced a brandy tax instead. By 1900, there was even legislation dictating the safe design of sugarcane presses, or *trapiches*.

The *trapiche* is a large machine traditionally made of wood and driven by oxen or mules, plodding round in a never-ending circle. Men feed cut sugarcane through heavy metal rollers and sugar syrup runs out and is collected in large wooden barrels where it is allowed to ferment for five to ten days. No water is added, and neither is yeast – there is enough naturally occurring on the cane.

The still is partly buried in a loose stone oven, and the fermented syrup is brought to the boil, producing an aroma that wafts up the valley. After an hour, the steam is run through a curly pipe cooled by water, and the clear distilled spirit starts to flow. A skilled eye can tell from the froth in the distillate the point at which a palatable fraction is being produced. That's the theory, at least.

In practice, the *grogue* drunk in villages will not have been produced under controlled conditions. Distillation is likely to have been carried out in an old oil drum, and the spirit collected in a rusty tin. It will not kill you unless you binge on a particularly dodgy brew, but it may upset your stomach. After 20 years of sustained drinking, the accumulated methanol may make you blind.

For those who are not put off, *grogue* is an exciting and throaty drink. There are, of course, as many subtleties to *grogue* as there are distilleries in Cape Verde. To fully appreciate the eye-watering gaspiness of it, it is quite acceptable to sip it, although you may be left with the strange feeling that much of what you were going to swallow has already evaporated in your mouth.

If you find yourself recoiling at *grogue*'s rawness, ask for *ponche* (punch). In this amber-coloured liquid the spirit's kick is muffled by honey. For those who dislike the cough-mixture sweetness of this, *coupada* ('cut') is the halfway house – a mixture of *grogue* and punch.

Grogue is something close to the hearts of many Cape Verdeans – an invitation to share a glass in a remote village is not something to be turned down lightly. The drink is an important part of Cape Verdean culture to the extent that the pressing of the cane, with its steady repetitive rhythm, has proved to be a fertile source of inspiration for music. The most famous ballads sung while at work on the *trapiches* are the *abois* or *kola boi*. They dwell at some length on the socio-economic ills which beset the Cape Verdeans. It is said the melodies often reduce the oxen to tears.

dish. *Cachupa grelhada* is perhaps the most palatable – everything available all fried up together, often for breakfast.

A local speciality is jams (*doce*) and semi-dried fruits. These are often served as desserts along with fresh goat's cheese, making a delicious end to the meal.

Most towns will have local eateries where huge platefuls of rice, chips, beans and fish, or of *cachupa*, are served up for 300–500$; but they may not be open all day though. Restaurant prices are indexed in the rest of this book by the cost of their cheapest main meat or fish dish. In most places, these start at 500–900$. Lobster tends to be 1,200$ upwards. Tea is typically 50$ a cup and coffee 100$.

Food on the streets is fine, if unexciting. There are many women with trays of sweets, monkey nuts, sugared peanuts and popcorn. Sometimes they will have little *pastéis* (fish pastries). Trays of homemade sweets are ubiquitous. The confectionery is very sugary, and flavours are mainly coconut, peanut and papaya. Here and there ladies fry *moreia* – moray eel. Nice, but greasy – just spit the bones out, the dogs will get them.

Cheap picnic lunches can be bought from supermarkets, markets and from bakeries. These exist in every town but they can be hard to track down.

Outside the big towns try to call in at your chosen restaurant about two hours in advance to order your meal or you will be confined to the dish of the day.

Many villages have no eating places, but somewhere there will be a shop – often hard to distinguish from an ordinary house. There you can buy biscuits and drinks. For useful food terms see *Appendix 1, Language*, page 331.

Bottled water is widely available and in ordinary shops is cheap (80$ for a 1.5-litre bottle); prices are inflated at hotels (up to 180$). Some of the wine made on Fogo Island is distinctive and very quaffable and can be found for sale around the archipelago. There are three principal beers. Strela is a domestic brand, and has a sub-brand, Strela Ego, which is a high-strength lager (8%). The two brands imported from Portugal are the maltier Superbock and Sagres. Costs are typically 100$ for local beer and 250$ for imported brands. On Sal many familiar brands are available such as WKD, Heineken and Strongbow. These are usually quite expensive.

The drink that Cape Verdeans literally live and die for is **grogue**. It is locally produced (see box, *Grogue*, page 73) and abundantly available – in any dwelling carrying a sign above its door prohibiting children under 18 from entering.

On quieter islands such as Maio and São Nicolau, food shops and restaurants may open erratically and only for short periods. To avoid hours of hunger, always have provisions with you.

PUBLIC HOLIDAYS AND FESTIVALS

Each island has a calendar of festivals, many of which originated as saints' days and all of which offer a great excuse for music and dancing. The most renowned is the São Vicente Carnival in mid-February. Others of particular interest are described in the island chapters.

The following dates are public holidays, including Mardi Gras and Good Friday.

1 January	New Year
20 January	National Heroes Day
1 May	Labour Day
5 July	Independence Day
15 August	Nossa Senhora da Graça (Our Lady of Grace)

12 September	Nationality Day
1 November	All Saints' Day
25 December	Christmas Day

🏛 SHOPPING

Shopping outside the towns is almost non-existent. The most colourful market is in Assomada, on Santiago, a flavour of mainland Africa. Most island capitals have some sort of fruit and vegetable market though the only one of touristic interest is on the Plateau in Praia, Santiago.

Local crafts can be bought in Mindelo, in São Vicente, where there have been revivals of skills such as the weaving of cloth and baskets. Baskets and clay figures can also be bought in São Domingos on Santiago. Santo Antão and São Nicolau are also good places to find a lot of local crafts and home produce. Locally made souvenirs are becoming increasingly common in the main tourism centres, particularly at Genuine Cabo Verde on Sal (see page 125). For excellent souvenirs of the islands, buy bottles of *grogue* (available in any small shop in a town), or its more exotic variants (try more touristy shops for these), Fogo wine and coffee beans, little bags of the abundant local sweets, and CDs of Cape Verdean music (in Mindelo, Praia and the airport duty-free shop).

Everything is closed on public holidays and on Sundays, and many shops also close early on Fridays. Opening hours tend to be Mediterranean – that is, 08.00/08.30–12.00/12.30 and 14.00/14.30–18.00/18.30 Monday–Friday, 08.30–12.00 Saturday. Banks tend to be open until 15.00, without a lunch break. Restaurants operate from about 19.00 to 23.00.

🎭 ARTS AND ENTERTAINMENT

MUSEUMS AND HISTORICAL SITES Despite the archipelago's fascinating history there is little to see in the form of buildings or museums. The one exception to this is on Santiago. In the capital, Praia, there is a fascinating museum documenting what is known of the many shipwrecks around the islands; another, general museum and a museum in the Santiago hills is devoted to the *Tabanka* musical and dance form.

Cape Verde has one historical site of international stature: the old city of Ribeira Grande (Cidade Velha) on Santo Antão, the first European city in the tropics and a pivotal arena in the transatlantic slave trade. The capital of Fogo, São Filipe, is a fine town full of *sobrado* architecture.

Most island capitals have southern European architecture and ambience, and some have a faded Portuguese feel to them with narrow cobbled streets, ochre-tiled roofs and abundant flowers in well-tended public gardens.

MUSIC AND DANCING Music and dancing are the Cape Verdeans' principal means of cultural expression. The Cape Verdean music scene is thriving, with an increasing number of bands making the international break and joining the renowned Cesária Evora (see box, *Cesária Evora*, page 42) on the world scene. The music is a blend of African, European and more recently, Latin. Music is everywhere in the archipelago: in Fogo crater, in every little village, down the *ribeiras* and of course in the cities of Praia and Mindelo. There are an astonishing number of outstandingly talented musicians for such a small group of islands.

To hear the music in a planned way, spend time in Mindelo (see page 261) and Praia (see page 168). Musicians play every night in Fogo crater and many restaurants in Sal have live music in the evenings. The islands have six or seven key dances and you may be lucky enough to see them all demonstrated by a troupe in Boavista (see page 133). Other than that, you might pick up different dances on different islands, at local nightclubs, for example. *Possada* is a favourite of Mindelo clubs, danced to zouk music; *funaná*, a fast dance done mainly to the strains of the accordion, is a more southern dance form, not really accepted in Mindelo; *cola* (which means 'glue') is a slow and amorous pelvic grind. Nightclubs tend to open at midnight.

MEDIA AND COMMUNICATIONS

TELEPHONE It is straightforward to make calls from numerous phone call centres with booths where you phone first and pay afterwards. Most of the island capitals have them. Cheaper is to call from the post office. You can also buy cards from the post office to use in the public phones. Telephone cards cost 750$ or 1,000$.

If you are likely to make quite a few calls in Cape Verde, it's worth buying a SIM card from CV Telecom, or its rival TMais (t+). The latter is still rolling out across the archipelago and may not have reached remoter islands by the time of your trip. To avail yourself of this service you should get your mobile unlocked back home before your trip, although there are organisations in Praia that claim to be able to unblock phones. SIM cards, including some initial free credit, are cheap, at €5. Mobile phones themselves are expensive.

Local calls are cheap but it's expensive to make and receive international calls on Cape Verdean mobiles. For cheap international calls also consider using Skype.

INTERNET Internet access is readily available in almost all towns and is usually high speed and reliable. There are many internet cafés all over the place offering pretty cheap services – which can be triple the price in hotels. If you have your laptop with you, there is wireless internet (Wi-Fi) on Sal for which you need to buy vouchers. Many of the *praças* (town squares) have free internet access, including the two on the Plateau in Praia, São Filipe on Fogo, Ribeira Brava on São Nicolau, and Mindelo on São Vicente. All of the international airports have free Wi-Fi (Sal, Boavista, São Vicente and Santiago).

POST OFFICE Cape Verdean post offices are well equipped and it is possible to transfer money, send and receive faxes, make phone calls and often make photocopies there – as well as buying stamps. Opening times vary considerably but tend to be 08.00–12.00 and 14.00–18.00 Monday–Friday.

RADIO AND TELEVISION Local television is provided by **RTC** (12.00–00.00), which broadcasts English-language films and series all afternoon on Saturdays and Sundays and late at night. A wide range of satellite channels is available. These include, as well as all the film channels, BBC, CNN, RAI, French and German stations, Portuguese and even Brazilian soap operas. Voice of America, RDP and BBC (Portuguese and English versions) are rebroadcast on FM radio. The Portuguese channel SportTV shows a wide variety of sports and can be seen in a lot of bars throughout the country. Radio Cape Verde has an office in the cultural centre in Mindelo.

CULTURAL ETIQUETTE

In many practical ways travelling around the islands is a joy, and in general the people are keen to encourage tourism. As one visitor put it: the people have the carefree approach to life of South America combined with the family orientation of Africa. Culturally there is little corruption and bribery.

Cape Verde has a history of cosmopolitanism; people know about the outside world because their sons and brothers live there. Nevertheless, tourism always brings with it crime, envy, loss of dignity, hassle and some despoiling of nature. It also remains to be seen what impact widespread foreign ownership of land and apartments will have on local people. An influx of richer people can often send prices soaring in the shops.

SCAMS It may be worth giving suspected 'rip-off merchants' the benefit of the doubt in Cape Verde. Often when you think you are being mistreated it is really a problem with the language barrier, or the local custom (as, for example, with a two-hour wait in a restaurant), or the fact that prices are genuinely high for everyone (for example with taxi fares).

BEGGING In a small but growing number of places in Cape Verde – the waterfront in Santa Maria, the streets of Cidade Velha, the Fogo crater – the children have become beggars, pursuing passers-by with persistent demands for money, sweets, pens or photos. Responding to these demands gives the donor a brief feeling of beneficence but does nothing to alleviate poverty. Instead it

---

SOCIAL INTERACTION
Steven Maddocks and Gabi Woolf

GREETINGS In social situations, men shake hands with men. Sometimes the handshake lasts for as long as the conversation, so a man may hold onto your hand while he's speaking to you. It takes some getting used to, especially for frigid, contact-shy Brits, but go with it. A man and a woman, or two women, generally shake hands plus a kiss on each cheek, even on first meeting.

SMALL TALK This is the name of the game. Conversations tend to run round in circles. Each person will enquire about the other's wellbeing, the wellbeing of each member of the other's family, then their colleagues. Then the questions turn to life in general, work, health. Neither will actually answer any questions – they just keep asking each other. So the response to 'How are you?' is 'How are you?'

'TUDU BON?' There are about 50 variations on '*Tudu bon?*' (which means 'everything OK?') The *tudu* can be followed by *bon, ben, dretu, fixe, em forma, sabi,* or OK, tranquil, cool, fine, nice, and a million others.

NO The gesture for 'no' is a waggle of the index finger with a 'no' look on your face. It seems rude, but isn't.

HISSING If someone wants to get your attention, they will hiss at you. Sometimes this comes out as 'sss', sometimes more like 'pssssssyeoh'! This can strike the newcomer as incredibly rude, but it's not meant to be, and it's a lot more effective than 'Ahem, excuse me… ahem… excuse me! Hello, excuse me?'

'OI' This means 'Hi' and is very friendly.

causes rivalry amongst children, upsets the family balance (in the case of cash gifts) and, worse, instils a vigorous sense among the children that tourists owe them gifts.

Think of the next batch of tourists that will pass through: successful hassle breeds more hassle, which can ruin an otherwise peaceful outing. We suggest you do not hand out money unless it is to people who have earned it – for example through employment as guides. If you would like to help the children, then seek out the local school and give a box of biros or paper to the ill-supplied teachers. Alternatively, consult *Travelling positively*, opposite, for bodies looking for donations for Cape Verdean good works.

There are some effective ways of replying to demands for money – smiles and good humour being the best accompaniments to whatever you say: '*Desculpe (deshculp)*' – 'sorry'; '*Não tenho (Now tenyu) livro/stilo/caneta/dinheiro*' – 'I don't have a book/pen/money'; '*Sem trabalho, não dinheiro*' – 'no pay without work'.

One form of apparent begging is children who are merely asking to change the euros they've received from other tourists into useable escudos.

STREET SELLERS There have been a lot of complaints from tourists about west African street sellers, mostly in Sal. They've arrived because of the tourists and they operate very differently from the more laid-back Cape Verdeans. (See box, *Aggressive vendors*, page 114, for more information.)

TAKING PHOTOGRAPHS It is best to ask people before you take their photo; smile and say hello, pause, ask to take a photo, offer to take their address and send them a copy. Then, when they are relaxed, you can take the real atmospheric ones. Do not try to photograph the *rebelados* in Santiago, who have scruples about photography; or the hot-tempered market women in Praia. Some old people may have objections as well. Photographing TACV aircraft sometimes provokes an angry response on the runway.

HIRING GUIDES We indicate in the text whether a guide is necessary or not. Where a guide is not absolutely essential, you may still prefer to hire one in order to get to know a local person, embellish the walk with more information and help the local economy.

LOCAL RESOURCES Water is scarce and has invariably taken toil and money to reach your basin. It is very important not to waste it.

There are many endangered plant species on the archipelago (see *Chapter 1, Background Information*, page 5). Ultimately, the goats may get them all. Nonetheless, picking flowers is absolutely out of the question.

Don't buy products made of turtle shells, coral or other endangered resources.

LANGUAGE Everyone speaks *Crioulo*, an Africanised Creole Portuguese. Portuguese (the official language) is spoken fluently by most townspeople but is not well understood in outlying villages – some people do not speak it at all. Everything official and everything written is in Portuguese. The most common second European language is French, spoken widely by officials, with English third. If you are struggling then keep asking people if they speak English or French (*fala inglês?, fala francês?* – fowle eenglaysh?, fowle frensaysh?). It's astonishing how often such a speaker can be found even in the remotest village. For words and phrases and a discussion of Creole see *Appendix 1, Language*, page 331.

You can give something back simply by venturing out and about, using local tour operators, staying in the many family-run *pensões* and eating in local restaurants.

If you would like to contribute to charitable work in Cape Verde you could contact one of the following:

Anjos (Angels) m 995 3734. Run by local people who live in Santa Maria & Espargos, Anjos began as a group of friends & has now become an official charity. Its goal is to help the poor in whatever obvious ways arise: for example, a Christmas party in the shanty town, or the distribution of TVs from an Italian developer to a local school. Visitors can help by taking with them clothes, pens, books & so forth.

Boernenfonden www.bornefonden.dk. This Danish organisation helps children with their education in Santiago. Founded in 1989, it supports children with goods rather than money – materials, health products & so forth, on the condition that the mother attends educational events, such as health meetings. It is possible to sponsor a child. BF is part of Child Fund International (www.childfundinternational.org) & money can be given directly to them or via their German supporters, Kinderhilfswerk (*www.ccf-kinderhilfswerk.de*).

Cabo Verde Children www.cvchildren.com. Run jointly by the website CaboVerdeOnline. com & the Cape Verde embassy in Washington, DC, this organisation seeks to help children in poverty, principally through sponsorship. The main goals are to ensure children are nourished & get to attend school.

Peace Corps www.peacecorps.gov/ index.cfm?shell=donate. Peace Corps lists on its website those of its projects for which it is soliciting donations. You may find some based in Cape Verde. Peace Corps says that 100% of the donation goes to the project &, if you are in the US, the donation is tax-deductible.

SOS Children's Villages www.sos-childrensvillages.org/Where-we-help/ Africa/Cape-Verde/Pages/default.aspx. This international social development organisation has 2 SOS children's villages, 1 SOS youth facility & 2 SOS kindergartens on Santiago, & focuses on family-based, long-term care of children who can no longer grow up with their biological families.

SOS Tartarugas www.turtlesos.org. The plight of turtles internationally is dependent largely on how they are treated at their key breeding grounds, which include Cape Verde. SOS Tartarugas needs money to train wildlife rangers & support grass-roots projects throughout the country. It also needs donations of equipment such as radios & phones (there's a list on the website). You can also volunteer long term or short term & participate as part of your holiday.

The Cape Verdean Society 53 Ty Mawr Av, Cardiff CF3 8AG; +44 029 2021 2787. This charity (registration number 1018138) seeks

2

STUFF YOUR RUCKSACK – AND MAKE A DIFFERENCE

www.stuffyourrucksack.com is a website set up by television's Kate Humble which enables travellers to give direct help to small charities, schools or other organisations in the country they are visiting. Maybe a local school needs books, a map or pencils, or an orphanage needs children's clothes or toys – all things that can easily be 'stuffed in a rucksack' before departure. The charities get exactly what they need and travellers have the chance to meet local people and see how and where their gifts will be used.

The website describes organisations that need your help and lists the items they most need. Check what's needed in Cape Verde, contact the organisation to say you're coming and bring not only the much-needed goods but an extra dimension to your travels and the knowledge that in a small way you have made a difference.

to help with education, relieve need & provide facilities for Cape Verdeans, including expatriates in Cardiff. In the past it has contributed to the upkeep of schools, orphanages, a children's hospital & a malnutrition centre.

ANIMAL WELFARE There is increasing concern over the treatment of animals in Cape Verde, particularly cats and dogs. A lack of veterinarians on all the islands has led to a large population of feral and free-roaming animals, many of which are in dire need of treatment for a variety of diseases and injuries. The government's only answer is indiscriminate poisoning by laying strychnine during the night and collecting the bodies the following morning. This has led to several concerned individuals setting up shelters and organising neutering clinics with vets from overseas. All are desperately short of funds and will welcome donations of money, medicine, tick and flea treatment and even simple things such as collars and leads. If you are a visiting vet, you could do untold good by helping out for a few days. Even if you have no experience most will welcome your assistance for long or short periods. Contact the organisation in question to find out exactly what they need.

Amigos Animais Bubista Sal Rei, Boavista; m 992 2864
Bons Amigos Praia, Santiago; 264 1578; m 984 1339; e info@abacv.org; www.abacv.org
Cape Verde Cats and Dogs Santa Maria, Sal; m 957 2162; e info@cvcatsanddogs.org; www.cvcatsanddogs.org

Si Ma Bo Mindelo, São Vicente; 231 2465; m 993 7347; e info@simabo.org; www.simabo.org. Provides accommodation for volunteers.

3

Living and Working in Cape Verde

This chapter covers business visits to Cape Verde, investing in Cape Verdean property, setting up a business, gaining residency and working as a volunteer. Regulations are liable to change so you need to contact the relevant agencies to get the latest information.

BUSINESS VISITS

People who are used to the tribulations of mainland west Africa generally find Cape Verde to be 'Africa lite'. Transparency is a key 'export', and of the three perceived vices among governments – corruption, nepotism and cronyism – there's a near unanimous verdict that the first is very hard to find. Deals tend to be reasonably straightforward. The administration can be slow and bureaucratic but it's a small administration dealing with enormous changes and generally they are just trying to get it right.

PREPARATIONS Much of the information contained in *Chapter 2, Practical Information*, page 45, applies here, particularly the sections on *Getting there and away*, *Red tape*, *Money*, and *Getting around*.

You obtain a visa with the same form and for the same price as a tourist visa. You must submit, however, a letter of guarantee from your company or a copy of an invitation from a Cape Verdean organisation.

Flights European travel agents recommend that business travellers use **TAP Portugal**. While it can be good to support a national airline **TACV**'s deficiencies are even more frustrating for those on business than for tourists. However, TACV offers various discount schemes to regular travellers to Cape Verde.

Money Business hotels generally accept Visa. Acceptance of MasterCard is rare, though the company says it will be introducing the service soon. It is advisable to carry euros, which are widely accepted in hotels, restaurants and by taxi drivers (often at rather approximate exchange rates). The TACV airline office in Praia will accept payment directly with major credit cards and travellers' cheques.

Where to stay The details of all hotels mentioned below are in the relevant island chapters. In Praia the business hotels are all off the Plateau to the south, a taxi ride from the business centres on the Plateau and Achada Santo António. Hotels that cater for business travellers (eg: telephones in rooms capable of making international calls, business centre, Wi-Fi hub, generator, conference facilities) are the Hotel Pestana Trópico and Hotel Praia Mar, although you can get most of these facilities from the cheaper Hotel Perola as well.

In São Vicente, in Mindelo, the business hotels are the Hotel Porto Grande and the Mindel Hotel. The Foya Branca, near the airport, offers business, conference and secretarial facilities for up to 30 people and corporate rates but it's also a resort hotel.

In Sal the business hotel, the rather faded Atlântico, is in Espargos. In the resort of Santa Maria there is Wi-Fi across the town. The big beach hotels have good facilities, but are very much geared towards sun holidays. In Fogo the Hotel Xaguate can provide good accommodation for business travellers. In Boavista, try the Hotel Luca Calema. Near the airport is the tranquil Parque das Dunas, but it's a taxi ride from town.

Communications If you are planning to make a good number of mobile calls from Cape Verde it's worth buying a SIM card there (see *Chapter 2, Practical Information*, page 76). If your phone is blocked, and the new SIM card doesn't work, the mobile-phone company can advise you where to get it unblocked, but this is not always straightforward. Many people have email and a lot of businesses have websites. Wi-Fi is available in top hotels, in the two praças on the Plateau in Praia and across Santa Maria, Murdeira and Espargos in Sal.

INVESTING IN CAPE VERDE

There are many reasons to invest in Cape Verde but the most powerful one lies in its governance: the government is passionate about making its country succeed and there is little corruption around to sap these intentions. In 2007, Cape Verde achieved three economic successes: elevation to the status of 'middle income country' by the United Nations; membership of the World Trade Organization and the establishment of special status in relation to the European Union. In 2010, Cape Verde was praised by the Millennium Challenge Corporation for completing the first African Compact and setting a good example in the region through good governance and policy reforms. There is, therefore, a lot of optimism.

On the downside, Cape Verde is still a developing country. It still makes requests to the international community for emergency food aid. Its Achilles heel is its oil dependency which, in a sense, is a triple whammy. Not only does Cape Verde have to import all its own fuel for the usual purposes but also in order to desalinate much of its water, a fuel-intensive process. Thirdly, the oil price affects the food price. Since Cape Verde relies heavily on food imports, being too barren for self-sufficiency, it is deeply affected by soaring food prices as well. Measures are being implemented to try to reduce these dependencies (see page 28).

Infrastructure is still poor, though there are many projects underway to expand ports, construct international airports, build roads, energy plants and so forth. To fund these, Cape Verde is dependent on foreign aid and foreign investors. And as tourism keeps growing, the demands on the infrastructure keep growing, too. So long as everyone remains confident, the wheel can keep turning.

Foreign investment in property is taking its toll on the locals. Some are benefiting from lucrative land sales and employment opportunities. Others can no longer afford to buy land because of soaring prices – or are angry that important public areas needed in order to accommodate expanding towns have apparently been sold off. There have been land disputes on Boavista, Sal and São Vicente and possibly on other islands. The government is taking steps to deal with this, partly by releasing less government-owned land for sale, and partly by controversial plans to switch the terms of sale to lease only.

INVESTMENT OPPORTUNITIES

Buying property The number and size of proposed developments is stunning. Despite the slowdown after 2008 which left many investors high and dry and many construction sites devoid of activity, there are still huge areas that are earmarked for massive complexes. On Sal, Paradise Beach and the huge complex of Cotton Bay are making progress, Tortuga Beach is open, and its sister complex, Dunas Beach, is being constructed, all on the west coast. Meanwhile, several others have ground to a halt (eg: Esmerelda Beach on Ponta Preta, Murdeira Beach). But that's not all in Sal. To the east there are supposed to be two developments on Ponta Sirena (to the distress of the local community, many of whom say the land should be for Santa Maria), and there is another enormous development at Pedra de Lume which has ground to a halt after being partially built.

In Santiago, the gigantic development of Sambala is in a state of limbo and there are developments around Cidade Velha, as well as the Santiago Golf Resort (which has seen little movement for years) and Ponta Bicuda just up the coast from Praia as well as Tarrafal Sands up in the north. In Boavista, proposed developments are even more ambitious: the vision is for hotels and apartments down Chaves Beach, Estoril Beach, north of town and down in Santa Monica (see *Chapter 5, Boavista*, page 155). Then there is Sabi Sands, just outside Sal Rei, and Palm Beach, advertised as Cape Verde's first 'true' six-star resort (now vanished without trace). But the king of them all must be the massive complex planned for Lacação Beach in Boavista, starting with a new RIU hotel and ending with miles and miles of apartments, hotels, shops and golf courses. In São Vicente, investors from Dubai are proposing a resort of over 8,000 apartments and villas, with five hotels as well (see *Chapter 10, São Vicente*, page 253), and there are resorts planned for Baia das Gatas and Calhau. Few of these have taken shape. There are apartments and resorts planned for Santo Antão and Maio. It's hard to avoid media articles and websites frenziedly trying to persuade people to buy apartments and villas in Cape Verde. The advantages of the islands are obvious but increasingly the web forums are full of investors who have had their fingers burned and those who simply have had little or no information about the properties to which they have made partial payments.

During the last couple of years the high-profile sales talk about Cape Verde being the next Caribbean has died down and the second wave of purchasers who have more realistic expectations have arrived. Investors still recognise that Cape Verde has the potential to be a good, profitable destination (climate, stability, accessibility, incentives to investors), but now there is an element of caution due to financial market changes in credit, mortgages and exchange rates.

Many of the agents and property sales companies have moved on, leaving the more experienced developers and agents providing stability and better advice to clients. The government is also stimulating the market by introducing incentives through reductions in property registration fees.

Overall the market in the most popular investment island, Sal, has become more professional and organised but there is still a large amount of property unoccupied and a question mark hangs over whether there will ever be enough tourists to fill them.

Buying in Cape Verde remains speculative, in a market that is flooded with apartments. It might end up being a lucrative investment but it is not recommended for ordinary people who cannot afford to take a risk with their capital.

Other investments For more than a decade, the country has had legislation designed to encourage foreign investment, particularly in fishing, light industry

Up to 90% of people investing in Cape Verdean property place deposits on properties that they have never seen. This is inherently risky. Here are some of the things to consider.

GO TO CAPE VERDE Overseas property is not regulated like pension selling. Quite fanciful, artistic impressions of future development can be seen on the internet. Some carry photos from other islands in Cape Verde, or even the Caribbean. The best possible investment before deciding anything is to take an independent trip to check things out, pace the site, check the views, listen to the noise, feel the wind and smell the scent, see the building progress (if any) and make up your mind about the island.

CHECK THE DEVELOPMENT FINANCE Developers can be undercapitalised. For many their project is their first ever development abroad. They rely on a steady stream of deposits from investors to fund the purchase of land and the building of apartments. If this dries up, work may cease. They may even start selling property before land ownership is secured or planning approved.

FIND OUT ABOUT THE LAND OWNERSHIP Some claims to land ownership have turned out to be false, thus undermining its sale to developers. The government has in the past had to cancel land deals and reassign parcels of land already allocated. You can make some checks on ownership yourself: white stone markers are placed on plots of land to delineate them – and plans are lodged at the town hall for public scrutiny. Developments may claim to be beachfront or that there is protected land between the plot and the beach. This should be checked with care. Some developers do not provide access roads and owners may have to pay for this later.

LOOK FOR THE ROUND STAMP Outline planning permission for development is given by the government. Detailed plans for design must be approved by the town hall on each island, which adds a round stamp to the blueprint. This is not always done.

GET THE CORRECT PAPERS Cape Verde, unlike English-speaking countries, uses a notary system. A buyer receives a sales contract in Portuguese which stipulates when a property will be finished and when stage payments are to be made. On completion, the buyer and vendor meet at the notary`s office, pay the 3% sales tax and sign the deeds. The notary acts as an independent arbitrator and tax collector. Without the correct papers you are not the legal owner.

CHOOSE YOUR SALES AGENCY WELL Many developments are sold during subsidised weekend inspection trips. These agents have been known to mark up prices by

and tourism. It has promoted Cape Verde's advantages as the following: a strategic position close to Europe, west Africa and the Americas; a large, young and motivated unskilled workforce which is largely literate; a professional workforce whose members generally have degrees from foreign universities (and local universities as the education sector improves); a stable political system with an unblemished human rights record and low crime rate; and a moderate tropical climate.

The fishing industry needs substantial investment but is said to have huge potential. Cape Verde has an Exclusive Economic Zone of 180 times its land area

10–20% to more than cover extra selling costs and also to use subtle tricks to hustle sales. If the agent who takes initial payments and commissions is not well financed your deposit money or stage payments may be at risk.

CHECK THE MANAGEMENT CONTRACT Find out how a property is to be managed. Owners have the legal right to an annual meeting to discuss issues. But this is not so easy when owners are absent and speak different languages or want different things. Ideally annual charges and an inflation clause should be agreed in advance in writing. In some developments water or electricity have not been connected for months after building completion. In some cases developers will inflate utility bills – a problem that has to be resolved legally.

BE SCEPTICAL ABOUT GUARANTEED RENTALS Some developers quote a guaranteed return and a prospective rate of capital gain. Unless this is in writing it is worthless. Some of the figures quoted are very optimistic. Long-term rents on most islands are low. Letting to holidaymakers is hard work and most developers are not equipped to do this. Property prices rise and fall with supply and demand and whilst Sal prices have certainly increased you need to buy at the right price to show a gain after sales tax and exchange rate shifts.

USE A CAPE VERDEAN LAWYER This is the best possible insurance policy. Charges are usually less than €1,000 and they can check land ownership, planning, road access and other key issues that are recorded locally. Unfortunately few answer email or telephone calls, as their English can be poor, so you should call in person. Lawyers from outside Cape Verde charge more and delegate the work to a local lawyer. It is important to choose your own and not take one selected by the developer.

INVESTIGATE MORTGAGE FINANCE This is rarely available on off-plan property until it has been completed. Interest rates from Cape Verde banks can be almost 20%. Cheaper sources of new capital are to borrow on an asset such as your main home.

WHAT IS YOUR LEGAL REDRESS? If the contract is signed in Cape Verde then any arguments are settled in a Cape Verdean Court, which is very slow. The law allows for a 7% interest payment by the developer once a building is more than six months delayed, as they often are. Alternatively it provides for a full refund if required, but many developers are loath to comply.

James and Claire Ensor were the first Britons to buy villas in Sal.

and is therefore one of the last significantly underused fishing zones in the world. The estimated annual sustainable catch is 45,000 tonnes, of which 6,000 tonnes is caught at present, mainly by artisanal fishermen. There is potential for large catches of tuna, lobster, shark and molluscs.

Over the last few years there has been substantial investment in ports, including wharves, warehousing, cold storage and repair facilities. A business park has been built at Praia.

TOURISM Various regions have been earmarked for beach tourism development (zones on Sal, Boavista, Maio, Santiago and São Vicente). Other regions have been targeted for adventure tourism (in particular Santo Antão, Fogo and São Nicolau) and there is also believed to be scope for cultural tourism in Santiago, São Vicente and São Nicolau.

Investors must provide their own, desalinated water and meet various architectural standards, amongst other requirements. In return there are tax exemptions mentioned below.

LIGHT INDUSTRY Cape Verde has unfulfilled quotas for products sent to the USA through the Most Favoured Nation status and the Generalised System of Preferences. It has preferential access to European markets through the Lomé Convention; and to west African markets through the Economic Community of West African States (ECOWAS).

INFRASTRUCTURE The lack of adequate infrastructure, in particular inter-island transport, sanitation and water, has put a significant brake on tourism development. However, many ports have been modernised, including Porto Grande on São Vicente and Porto Vale de Cavaleiros on Fogo, and the harbours on Sal, Boavista and Maio.

The Amílcar Cabral International Airport on Sal has a main runway 3,270m long and another, 1,500m long. There are also international airports on Santiago, Boavista and São Vicente. Marine connections between the islands are under a lot of pressure. Ferries taking passengers have received a number of blows, including the sinking of two in 2008 and the withdrawal of certain boats and catamarans because of an inability to cope with the rough seas. Cargo transport to the mainland is seen as a problem. A limited number of vessels operate between Mindelo or Praia and the African mainland. Water is a perpetual problem and more desalinisation plants are being built.

INDUCEMENTS A foreigner with a regular monthly income of at least US$1,300 and private health insurance can apply for residency in Cape Verde. Citizenship is available to any foreigners on payment of at least US$35,000, or if they are resident for two years, or if they set up an 'external investment company' and employ a minimum number of Cape Verdeans.

The important step is to achieve status as an 'external investor'. Once registered in this way, a business qualifies for various privileges. It is allowed duty-free import and export of materials, which is essential because tariffs are otherwise extremely high – in the case of a car they can equal its cost, for example. Registered businesses are also supposed to receive streamlined customs procedures.

Foreign businesses also qualify for total tax exemption for the first five years and, after that, pay 10% tax. Exports qualify for tax incentives and there are special tax deals on industrial, tourism and fishery projects. If you train Cape Verdean staff the costs are exempt from tax. There is Free-Zone Enterprise status for companies producing goods and services exclusively for export.

HOW TO GO ABOUT IT An application for foreign or external investment must be made to Cape Verde Investments (*www.virtualcapeverde.net*), from whom forms and instructions can be obtained. Once you have obtained a certificate of external investment (in the case of a tourism facility, *autorização turístico*) you have access to the tax incentives. This can be quite a laborious process. It is useful to cultivate a good relationship with the president of the town hall of the relevant island. It is also essential to speak Portuguese or it will be very difficult to oversee the project.

LABOUR SYSTEM Local people can be employed either on 'limited time' or 'unlimited time' contracts. If your staff are on the latter type, and you wish to fire them, you have to compensate them with three months' salary for every year you employed them. This can make an extraordinary total in the case of long-serving employees. There is no minimum wage.

HELP In Praia contact Cabo Verde Investimentos (262 2621/2689; e *isabel.duarte@ cvinvest.cv*). It is out on the headland near the upmarket hotels in Praia. In smaller islands contact the town hall (*câmara*), which is generally the biggest, smartest building in town. Ask to speak to a councillor (*vereador*). The following is a list of telephone numbers to contact:

Boavista Fundo Figueiras; 252 1255
Brava Nova Sintra; 285 1314
Fogo São Filipe; 281 1295; Mosteiros; 283 1038
Maio Vila do Maio; 255 1334
Sal Santa Maria; 242 1136; Espargos; 241 9000

Santiago Praia – see Promex; 622736
Santo Antão Porto Novo; 225 1169; Ribeira Grande; 222 1223; Ponta do Sol; 225 1179
São Nicolau Ribeira Brava; 235 1242
São Vicente Mindelo; 232 5218

Other suggested contact links:

Banco de Cabo Verde www.bcv.cv
Cabo Verde Investimentos www.virtualcapeverde.net

Cabo Verde Telecom ww.cvtelecom.cv
Governo de Cabo Verde www.governo.cv

OBSTACLES Cape Verdean culture is complex – at once west African, European, American, cosmopolitan and parochial. Politically it is still coming to terms with the liberalisation of its economy. For this and many other reasons it will take a while to understand the people around you.

The following are tips from people who have recently set up businesses in Cape Verde:

- Try to learn the language as soon as possible
- Cultivate a good relationship with the president of the town hall (*câmara*) on your chosen island
- Even small investors should employ a lawyer for dealing with Cabo Verde Investimentos and other bodies
- Although imports made by 'external investors' are exempt from tax, they are not free from a variety of fees. For example, one must pay for each day the goods spend at the harbour, and for the compulsory hiring of a lawyer to deal with freight. One small-scale investor has calculated that these charges have cost him 5–10% of the value of each batch of imported goods.
- Customs bureaucracy can delay the release of imported items, sometimes by up to six months
- Cultivate the virtue of patience

RETURNING *EMIGRANTES* Many Cape Verdeans overseas long to return home one day, either to work or in retirement. On the one hand the flourishing economy is

3

Steven Maddocks and Gabi Woolf

Life in Cape Verde has some of the characteristics traditionally associated with life in Africa, so things that are quick and easy in Europe or the US might be expected to take a long time here and be fraught with difficulties. But anyone who has travelled beyond Europe, especially to regions like Africa, South America, India, or China, will find life in Cape Verde a comparatively smooth ride.

People who consider themselves officials – behind counters, in uniforms, with name badges – refuse to be hurried. The more impatient you look, the more they will seem to enjoy taking their time. Lots of apparently simple procedures are unnecessarily complicated, involving baffling bureaucracy and pointless paper. Be prepared to wait around a lot, maybe even to have to come back tomorrow. People have a lot of time on their hands. If they have to sit in a waiting room for three hours to pay their electricity bill, so be it. What's the rush?

Queuing is a fluid art form. People will go to the bank, stand in the queue for five minutes, go away, do some shopping, have lunch, come back, and expect to reclaim their place. You may have been standing there in the queue for an hour and a half, finally reach the front, only to find two or three women suddenly appear from nowhere and 'reclaim' their places in front of you. Very frustrating. Women (yes, unfortunately it's always women who do this) go into the supermarket and grab three empty baskets. They put those baskets on the floor in the queue. They then walk round the shop, grabbing this and that, bring it back to their baskets, and go back for some more things, ingeniously moving forward in the queue and doing their shopping at the same time.

Cape Verdeans accept situations without feeling the need to enquire into the whys and wherefores. So if you find yourself in a crazy predicament, and want to know why the post office hasn't got any stamps, or why the baker doesn't sell bread, or why you can't buy the cheese even though it's there in the fridge with a price on it, don't expect an explanation. That's just the way it is.

creating opportunities, on the other rising land prices and the state of the dollar may make a return financially difficult, if not impossible. For *emigrantes* from Europe, whose savings are in euros, the situation is better. The Instituto das Comunidades (*www.ic.cv*) is publishing a guide for *emigrantes*. In this guide you can find out how to buy land or property; how to invest elsewhere; how to open an *emigrante* bank account and the benefits this brings (eg: interest rates; automatic payment of utility bills while you are away). The booklet also lists those banks outside Cape Verde that have links with banks in the motherland, to facilitate money transfers. For further information follow the blogs on www.caboverdeonline.com.

BECOMING A CAPE VERDE RESIDENT

If you are thinking of settling permanently in Cape Verde, particularly if you are retired, the government claims it can process your application within 30 days. Once you have a residence permit, you qualify for certain privileges, including the import of personal effects such as a car and electrical equipment free from taxes and fees; exemption from property tax when buying your house; and no tax on any financial resource brought in from outside the country. Also, if you decide to invest any of your savings in a Cape Verdean business, you will qualify for foreign investor status (see page 82).

To qualify, you must have a monthly income of no less than US$1,300 (this figure is sometimes reviewed) and provide your own medical insurance. Contact the Ministério dos Negócios Estrangeiros e das Comunidades, Gabinete de Estudos, Documentação e Assessoria (261 5733). Also you may contact the *câmara* (*Rua Cesário Lacerda No 6, Tenis, CP 105 Praia;* 261 7234/5352; e *cciss@cvtelecom.cv*).

VOLUNTEER AND DEVELOPMENT WORK

Many volunteers and other development workers in Cape Verde have a superb, and sometimes life-changing, time. They have the opportunity to absorb the people and landscape in a way that tourists can only dream of. They have the chance to understand this singular people, impoverished in some ways yet deeply resilient and formidably artistic. Some who have spent time in Cape Verde say they feel it has qualities that Europe and the USA have lost in the stampede for material success. Returning *emigrantes* from the USA, as well as foreigners, enjoy the peace, the relaxed pace of life, and the high value given to (and consequently time invested in) friendships, free time, parties and making music.

Trying to work in such a culture can pose problems, however, which are all the more frustrating if your work is designed to help local communities rather than produce a successful business for yourself. Your success is uniquely dependent on the enthusiasm and co-operation of the people with whom you work, and if they are not co-operative, you may end up with nothing to show for your efforts. The ability to motivate and inspire is essential.

'The culture here is a double-edged sword,' says one volunteer. 'They are an island nation, which makes them somewhat isolated and entrenched in their own

BRINGING YOUR POSSESSIONS WITH YOU

Victoria Abbott, Cape Verde Imports

Cape Verde allows the tax-free importation of used personal items for people moving here on a long-term basis. With the limited shopping available in Cape Verde, many prefer to transport their belongings from their own country rather than purchase new goods. Shipping items to Cape Verde is relatively straightforward as long as you contact an appropriate agent to organise the shipping and customs clearance on your behalf. Goods can be sent via both air and sea; air freight is the better option for small quantities that are required quickly but the most cost-effective method, and much more appropriate for large consignments, is sea freight.

Shipping from the UK to Cape Verde takes roughly three–six weeks by sea whilst air-freight consignments leave weekly. Some companies offer a full door-to-door service.

It should be noted that Cape Verdean law only permits tax-free importation of personal used household effects and this depends on provision of the appropriate paperwork. New items are classified as commercial cargo and must be cleared by an authorised import agent and will be subject to import taxes. The taxes vary according to category and it is worth finding out the relevant duties prior to shipment.

For more information, contact Cape Verde Imports (+44 (0)208 123 6487 (UK); m +238 993 3843 (Cape Verde); e *info@capeverdeimports.com; www. capeverdeimports.com*).

ways. Yet by African standards they are sophisticated, better educated, and more European.' Some volunteers arrive with an idealistic notion that the people will greet them with 'outstretched arms, waiting for them to teach, train, and show them a better way of life,' he says. It can be a shock to discover indifference – or pride in the current way of life – combined with a reluctance to change.

English teachers may find that schoolchildren do not have the docile enthusiasm to learn that is found in mainland Africa. Pupils – adult or children – are also unlikely to have come across educational methods we take for granted in the West. 'A lot of the people trying to learn English have had very little formal education and find learning itself extremely difficult,' says one teacher. Community workers may find their job descriptions have changed by the time they arrive, or the job disappears totally after a few months. Unless you have the type of character that can deal with this type of disruption you may come unstuck.

An invaluable attitude derives from realising that you are in Cape Verde to learn as well as to give. Every new situation, however discomfiting, can provide insights into this foreign culture. Ask why it has happened, search for the answers in the history and culture, find it interesting. In this way you will derive a deeper understanding of another culture – one that only comes when you spend time in a place and which will be invaluable through life.

Another approach to irritation is to do some mental gymnastics and find something to admire in, for example, the failure to turn up to a meeting. 'My ploy is to think not "where the hell are they?" but "Ah yes, these people are great the way they refuse to be intimidated by time"', says another English-teacher.

Above all you must be able to switch off. This does not rule out caring deeply about your work, and putting in more than 100%. But it does mean that when things get beyond your control you can shrug, laugh and say: 'I did my best, and the rest is out of my hands.'

ESSENTIAL CHARACTERISTICS Consider whether you have the following before you go:

- Linguistic ability, especially the ability to pick up a spoken-only language like Creole, but also the wherewithal to learn a formal written language like Portuguese, used for all official purposes
- Patience
- Sensitivity to other cultures
- People skills

VOLUNTEER PROGRAMMES The British honorary consul arranges for volunteers to come on short postings to teach English on the islands. Contact him (see *Chapter 2, Practical Information*, page 53) or the British embassy in Senegal.

Many volunteers in Cape Verde have been sent there by the US Peace Corps on two-year postings. The Peace Corps (\ +1 800 424 8580; *www.peacecorps.gov*) is active in the national programme to combat the HIV/AIDS epidemic, and all volunteers are trained in HIV/AIDS prevention education. Volunteers also work with youth through the programme's other cross-cutting themes – women/gender, rural and business development, education and information technology. Other volunteer activities include environmental education, organisation of youth/sports groups and summer camps, income generation initiatives, vocational education, English clubs and language as well as computer classes. A recent example of volunteer work is the design and construction, with their students and faculty, of prototype water desalinisation units using solar energy to reduce the use of petroleum (see page 160). The United Nations (*www.unv.org*) also sends volunteers to Cape Verde.

ENVIRONMENTAL PROJECTS SOS Tartarugas (Turtle SOS) (m *974 5019;* e *info@ turtlesos.org; www.turtlesos.org*) accepts volunteers for its conservation programme from June to December.

FINDING OTHER WORK Many Europeans disillusioned with life and the weather back home make their way to islands such as Sal and Boavista hoping to be able to pick up work, open a bar or buy a boat. For many who have not done much research, disappointment is rapid. There are very limited opportunities for jobs at a salary Europeans would call a living wage and bureaucracy and language barriers make it even harder to start and run a small business. Just like in other countries, to succeed you need to understand the system, follow the regulations and work hard.

TEACHING ENGLISH AS A FOREIGN LANGUAGE (TEFL)

The English Language Institute (*Rua 5 de Julho;* ℡ *261 2672*) has schools in Praia, Mindelo and Sal. Lessons are generally business or general English, taught to adults, although there are some classes for children. The pay can sustain a good lifestyle in Cape Verde and the institute helps people get started – for example by organising a flat to be ready on your arrival. They are looking for Celta-qualified TEFL teachers. Some would-be teachers have just walked in off the street with their certificates and secured jobs, but it is probably best to arrange it beforehand.

Language link (℡ *262 5101;* e *languagelinkcv@gmail.com; www.languagelinkcv. com*) is based in Praia and may have vacancies for people with TEFL or ESP qualifications.

High schools are desperate for English teachers, so it might be quite easy to find such work. The pay would be about 50,000$ a month and you are likely to be left to sort out issues such as accommodation and medical insurance yourself. The work can be tiring, with classes of 40, and those who do not already speak Portuguese may have problems with class control.

It may be possible to give **private classes**, charging 1,000–2,000$ per hour. There are plenty of people who want to learn English for work or to visit the USA, but they might be hard to find until you have links with the local community.

WOMEN WORKING IN CAPE VERDE

Unattached women who stay for a long time in one place in Cape Verde report a very different experience from that of female tourists. The concept of an unattached woman is incomprehensible in Cape Verdean society and it seems that some communities just cannot tolerate it, so sexual predation can build up until it is, in some cases, quite frightening. Several unattached expatriate women working long term in Cape Verde have been sexually attacked in recent years. Meanwhile, local women can become angry with visitors who take a boyfriend from their already limited supply of men.

archipelago°
cape verde

Adventure, activity and tailor made holidays to Cape Verde

Away from the beach resorts and the better known islands, Cape Verde is an archipelago of dramatic beauty and cultural vibrancy.

With its warm all year round climate, direct flights from the UK and beautiful beaches, it is quickly becoming a popular holiday destination.

We specialise in off the beaten track holidays to Cape Verde by offering a wide range if interesting experiences. You can go walking and mountain biking on Santo Antao, try kite surfing and windsurfing on Sal, quad bike across the sand dunes on Boavista, experience a guided ascent of Mount Fogo, have Capoeira dance class on Sao Vicente and scuba dive from Santiago.

For our brochure or more information on holidays to Cape Verde call us on **017687 75684**

or e-mail info@archipelagocapeverde.com

www.archipelagocapeverde.com

All of our holidays are financially protected – ATOL 6059

Part Two

THE GUIDE

SURF ZONE
KITE SURF
WIND SURF
SURF

For more information or to pre book please email us at info@surfcabovderde.com or visit our website www.surfcaboverde.com

SURF ZONE CABO VERDE:

- Cabo Verde's largest professional kite, wind and surf school
- High quality instruction provided at all levels: beginners to advanced
- Languages: English, Portuguese, French, Italian, German and Spanish
- Rental and lesson equipment graded every year
- Location: Beach Club Morabeza Hotel and Watersports Centre Riu Hotel

---

Property Rentals & Management

We have the largest portfolio of properties to rent in the Cape Verde Islands. Whether you are here on vacation or planning to stay for several months – be it a studio or a large multi-bedroom apartment with a pool – we will be able to find something to suit your needs.

We also offer a full and comprehensive property management service, covering all aspects of the letting process, from general maintenance and upkeep to all the local legal procedures, to ensure total peace of mind for your investment.

Tel: 00238 242 1658
email: info@sal4rent.com
www.sal4rent.com

SAL4RENT

4

Sal

You live – sleeping mother
Naked and forgotten
Arid, Whipped by the winds
Cradled in the music without music
Of the waters that chain us in…
Amílcar Cabral, quoted in Basil Davidson, *The Fortunate Isles* (Hutchinson, 1989)

There can be nowhere on earth as elemental as Sal. It lies like an oil slick on the Atlantic – any mountains, streams or vegetation that may have adorned it in the past have been obliterated by the wind over millions of years. Now Sal is just rock, sand and salt, still blasted by the same winds. On Sal the transience of life – animal or vegetable – becomes dismally clear.

The arrival at Sal on an international flight is a deliciously depressing descent. For hours the traveller has scanned the Atlantic from the aeroplane window, searching for the lost islands of Cape Verde with a growing sense of their isolation. Then Sal appears: relentlessly brown and featureless, etched with dry cracks through which rain might occasionally flow. Disembarking from the aircraft to cross the heat of the runway you will gaze at the rocky plains in puzzlement, trying to remember why you decided to come. Three types of travellers come to Sal: those seeking year-round sunshine, beautiful beaches and blue sea who head for the all-inclusive resorts or their own holiday apartments; watersports enthusiasts craving world-class wind- and kitesurfing and diving; or those who use it as a relaxing and comfortable base from which to explore other islands.

HIGHLIGHTS

Sal is a top windsurfing, kitesurfing and surfing destination and also offers good diving and fishing and the largest number of organised tourist activities. You can sunbathe and swim, and enjoy the international hotels with their pools and other facilities. Those based on Sal can glimpse other Cape Verdean islands through day trips by boat or plane. You can fill a day by visiting the imposing volcano crater and salt lake of Pedra de Lume (a candidate UNESCO World Heritage Site), the foaming lagoon and Blue Eye at Buracona, see the mirages at Terra Boa or take a boat ride to view whales and dolphins. Other possibilities include taking lonely walks to watch the turquoise sea from its treeless, rugged coastline or crossing the rocky interior with a 4x4 or quad bike. Sal abounds in interesting birds and shells and there are opportunities to watch turtles. The island also has many restaurants, bars, live-music bars and nightclubs.

SUGGESTED ITINERARY AND NUMBER OF DAYS If you are dedicated to a watersport or two, are a real sun lizard, or enjoy the prospect of the resort hotels you should aim to spend at least a week here. If you are a sightseer, or crave mountains or greenery go for one to two days, maximum.

If you are passing through Sal between flights, we suggest one of the following, all of which are described below: a walk up and around Monte Curral in Espargos (one hour); a trip to Pedra de Lume (two–four hours); a day pass at the Morabeza Hotel in Santa Maria; or an organised excursion around the island (three–six hours).

LOWLIGHTS

Sal is still developing as a tourist destination and some tour operators and travel agents oversell it as some verdant, undiscovered paradise. It's not: though its beaches are beautiful, and it has the occasional small mountain, its interior is a brown desert with very little vegetation. Visitors who book under false impressions sometimes return disappointed with what they see as substandard service, the small number of sights on Sal, relatively high prices and the abundant wind. Many others, of course, have had a happy, sunny holiday.

Those who love Sal tend to be sea lovers rather than land lovers. It is not the place for hikers, those in search of verdant scenery or who seek to immerse themselves in the rustic Cape Verdean way of life. If your goal is to see several islands you may regret having allocated precious days to Sal. Instead, get on with your journey – you can fit Sal into transit times at the beginning and end of the holiday.

BACKGROUND INFORMATION

HISTORY On Sal the living was always marginal, based on whatever demand could be found for its four specialities: sun, sand, wind and salt. Today, for the first time in its history, it is flourishing as the result of three of those commodities. Sand and sun are in demand from beach-loving tourists. And the wind now catches the sails of delighted windsurfers who have discovered one of the best places in the world for their sport.

For the last five centuries Sal's economy has risen (always modestly) and fallen with international demands for its fourth element: salt. It is thought that even before the island was sighted by Gomes and de Noli in 1460 it was known by Moorish sailors for its rich saltpans.

The colonisation of the rest of Cape Verde had little consequence for Sal for hundreds of years – salt was procured more easily from the island of Maio, closer to the capital island, Santiago. Nothing much disturbed Sal except perhaps the offloading of some perplexed goats in the 16th century as part of the archipelago's drive to increase meat production. For much of the time there were probably also a few slaves on Sal, digging for salt. Early reports from passing sailors reveal that people sometimes hunted marine turtles on Sal.

Even by 1683 the passing English sailor William Dampier reported just six men, a governor… and an abundance of flamingoes. There are no longer any of the last – it is believed they disappeared with the rise of the salt industry. The men survived by trading with the odd passing ship – salt and goat skins in exchange for food and old clothes.

It wasn't until 150 years ago, when Cape Verdean businessman Manuel António Martins set up a salt export business, that Sal's population began to grow. A thousand souls came to join the 100 occupants between 1827 and 1882 – 'souls' was the word used by the British businessman from São Vicente, John Rendall, to describe both free men, of whom there were 300, and slaves.

The salt business was based at two sites: Pedra de Lume in the east and Santa Maria in the south. Its fortunes fluctuated with the rise and fall of trade barriers in Brazil, the African mainland and even Portugal itself. Eventually the business ceased in the first half of the 20th century and the island returned to desolation. Archibald Lyall, an English journalist who visited in 1936, reported:

> Not even the most rudimentary garden is possible among the shifting dunes, and all the landward windows of the houses have to be kept perpetually shuttered against the penetrating yellow grit.

Sal's 20th-century prosperity began when the Italian dictator Benito Mussolini was looking for a site where aircraft could stop to refuel between Europe and South America. Portugal sold him the right to build an airport on Sal, then bought back the resulting

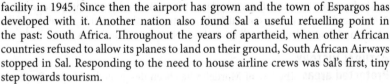

facility in 1945. Since then the airport has grown and the town of Espargos has developed with it. Another nation also found Sal a useful refuelling point in the past: South Africa. Throughout the years of apartheid, when other African countries refused to allow its planes to land on their ground, South African Airways stopped in Sal. Responding to the need to house airline crews was Sal's first, tiny step towards tourism.

SAL TODAY Sal draws income from its airport, its petrol-storage facilities, and the fish-processing factory in its harbour, Palmeira. But it is tourism and real estate where the economic potential is thought to lie.

Over the last few years, thanks to generous tax concessions and an unquenchable European thirst for virgin destinations, tourism on Sal has surged. Tourist arrivals in Cape Verde in the first half of 2010, for example, were up 5.6% on the same period in the previous year, with the majority, 190,000, arriving at Sal. If national development plans are followed some 17% of Sal's land will be taken up with tourism developments and services over the next few years.

Echoing this is a boom in apartment building. The thought of owning a few square metres of real estate in Sal have caught the imaginations of mostly British and Irish nationals who want both a place in the sun and a financial stake in the 'Next Big Thing'. Following the worldwide economic crisis in 2009, many inexperienced speculators had their fingers burned and many developments lie unfinished.

4

Sal today has a purpose, a place in the world. Its population has soared from just 5,500 in 1970 to around 20,000 in 2009. Wander around Sal today and you will find not just the indigenous inhabitants but their compatriots from most other islands; you will find construction workers, trinket salesmen and musicians from west Africa; estate agents, developers, gardeners, plumbers, restaurateurs and furniture importers from Britain and Ireland; and Italians, Spanish, Portuguese and French.

But though Sal may be the crucible of Cape Verde's economic transformation, it is in some ways its sacrificial victim. It is providing, in the national government's eyes, the quick economic boost thought to be needed in order both to diversify the economy and fund more sensitive touristic development on other islands.

The danger is that Sal will lose its allure in the longer term unless efforts are made to preserve what makes it unique: thick margins of undeveloped beach, dunes, unique birds, turtles and coral mounts in the sea. Even Sal's celebrated windsurfing spots need a custodian, now that they are jeopardised by new buildings blocking the wind.

The government has taken some decisive national protective measures: for example, it has banned the use of sand from beaches for construction; it now insists that potential developers make environmental impact assessments; it is tightening up on what they can build and is proposing to replace freehold purchases with leasehold. Sadly, the enforcement of these environmental laws rarely happens.

Unfortunately, mass tourism and unsympathetic development on Sal have set the tone for the rest of the archipelago's sandy islands, with Boavista and Maio heading along the same road. With some imagination tourism could have been redirected so that it treasures, rather than exploits.

GEOGRAPHY Sal is the most barren of the inhabited islands. Its highest peak, Monte Grande, in the northeast, reaches just 406m. The island is 30km long and nowhere more than 12km wide. Its landscape is of brown, stony plains and desert sands deposited by winds from mainland Africa. Around 20,000 people occupy its 216km^2 and they live almost exclusively in Espargos, the capital in the centre of the island, and Santa Maria, the village and tourist resort on the south coast.

NATURAL HISTORY
Protected areas The bay of Murdeira has been designated a Marine Protected Area but no monitoring or patrolling has taken place, making it an MPA in name only. Known to some as the 'bay of corals' it is home to diverse life, including around 45 types of small fish, many of them endemic (but no big fish). Although Murdeira is rocky it has very small beaches where loggerhead turtles (*Caretta caretta*) come to nest, but numbers are dwindling due to development and hunting. For both fish and turtles it is a place to hide and feed, and offers perfect conditions as a nursery for fish stocks. Humpback whales can sometimes be seen in the bay, as can melon-headed whales (*Peponocephala electra*). Widespread throughout the world's tropical and sub-tropical waters, they often go unseen by humans because of their preference for deep water. In 2005, however, a group became stranded in Murdeira Bay. People managed to guide them back to sea.

The salina of Pedra de Lume is a protected landscape. It is also a candidate for designation as a World Heritage Site. Other protected landscapes are the salina of Santa Maria, Monte Grande (the island's tallest mountain) and the lagoon of Buracona. The natural reserves on Sal are Monte Leão (a small hill at the northern end of Murdeira Bay also known as Rabo de Junco); the southeastern stretch of

SAVING TURTLES ON SAL

There's a common refrain that turtles are doomed on Sal. If the locals don't get them for supper, the quad bikes will crush their nests; and if the bikes don't get them, hotel and apartment lights will lure them into a deathly inland wander.

SOS Tartarugas (*www.turtlesos.org*), a local NGO, is resisting this mentality. It points out that there are fine laws already in existence for the protection of turtles: it's just the implementation that's missing. And implementation needs three things: a willingness on behalf of the authorities, resources, plus manic drive. The willingness is there; shoestring resources have been cobbled together, and the three-strong team running SOS Tartarugas certainly verges on the manic. Since its inception in 2008, it has brought together groups including Cape Verdean soldiers and volunteers to do night beach patrols during the nesting season to prevent turtle hunting. Quad-bike trails were developed so that bikers can enjoy themselves without unwittingly going on illegal beach jaunts. Hotels and tour operators are being persuaded to sign up to turtle philosophy – issuing codes of conduct and putting turtle stickers on their bikes. Turtles are also entering the tourist itinerary with the launch of night trips to witness egg laying and afternoon hatchery visits to see the release onto the beach of babes born from rescued eggs. Groups of concerned locals and expats have been out cleaning up crucial beaches.

Jacquie Cozens, co-founder of SOS Tartarugas, says that one of their more solvable problems is, simply, ignorance. 'I don't think tourists *want* to destroy turtle nests. And so if we publicise this information I think most visitors will comply. Similarly, I think developers want to be turtle-friendly. And the government wants to do it: they know they've got a really good resource here, there's little else to do on Sal. That's why I'm so ridiculously optimistic that we can do something here.'

SOS Tartarugas has also begun nagging developers who look set to infringe the law (for example because they have erected fences less than 80m from the coastline) or infringe the philosophy (for example by over-illuminating the beaches they overlook). Problems raised by proposed new developments are probably the most intractable and are generally thought to be what will get the turtles in the end.

'Almost every bit of land on the west coast is earmarked for development,' says Cozens. 'But we do have a big opportunity on the east coast, which is a nature reserve.'

coast known as Costa da Fragata; the beaches of Serra Negra and Ponta Sino. Morrinho do Açúcar and Morrinho do Filho are natural monuments.

Birds Birdwatchers will find interesting waders in the saltpans including, if they are lucky in Pedra de Lume, the black-winged stilt (*Himantopus himantopus*), known locally as *pernalonga*. This extraordinary, elegant creature has long red legs that extend behind it as it flies, as well as a long, thin beak. It breeds only on Sal. Following the rains in August and September many more birds can be seen in the temporary pools that are left dotted around the island. Species you may see include turnstones, sanderlings, Kentish plovers, greenshanks, egrets, kestrels, ospreys and herons.

Turtles About 300 endangered loggerhead turtles (*Caretta caretta*) nest on Sal (compared with around 3,000 on Boavista Island), mostly along the southwestern and southeastern coasts. Turtles face two major threats on Sal: from tourism and from hunting.

Tourism development has been occurring on exactly the beaches that are important for turtles. Illumination from beachfront hotels and apartments disorientates adults and hatchlings. Although the law stipulates that there should be no construction within 80m of the high-tide mark, some developments have flouted this. And the rising number of tourists is leading to more noise, rubbish and adverse types of beach use, particularly as they have not, until recently, been given any advice on how to minimise their impact. In 2007, for example, quad bikes crushed around 70% of turtle nests laid on Sal's beaches, according to research by Cape Verdean biologist Euclides Gonçalves, an environmental adviser working for Sal's local government and a director of SOS Tartarugas (see box, *Saving turtles on Sal*, page 98).

Meanwhile the hunting of female turtles has been prolific on quieter, eastern and northern beaches, with some beaches losing 100% of their turtles.

While some experts believe that tourism will drive every last turtle from Sal, others believe that tourists offer the only hope of salvation – their interest in the matter may convince all parties to change their behaviour. (For more on turtles see *Chapter 1, Turtles*, page 8.)

HAZARDS Take care when swimming: Currents are milder than in the UK, but when the wave height is great there can be a powerful undertow. Swimming on the east coast needs care. For unfrequented beaches take local advice.

Theft is common in parts of Sal, mostly of possessions left in unattended vehicles and on beaches. Violent muggings involving theft are unusual, but use common sense if you go to remote places, and don't walk on unlit streets late at night.

FESTIVALS Festivals, when everything may be closed, are as follows:

19 March	São Jose (Palmeira)
3 May	Santa Cruz (Espargos)
9 June	Santo António (Espargos)
24 June	São João (Espargos)
29 June	São Pedro (Hortela, Espargos)
Last week of July	Santa Ana (Fontona)
15 August	Nossa Senhora de Piedade (Pedra de Lume)
15 September	Nossa Senhora das Dores (Santa Maria)

GETTING THERE AND AWAY

BY AIR Most international flights land in Sal, although there are also international airports on Santiago, Boavista and São Vicente. The arrivals hall at **Amílcar Cabral International Airport** can feel chaotic, with a long queue at passport control, but in reality there is almost none of the hassle commonly found in airports in mainland Africa.

If you already have a visa or have prearranged a visa you should join the main queue for passport control. If you have no arrangements for a visa go to the office to the left of the passport barriers to get one for €25. Customs officers are used to giving visas for one week but if you state how long you will stay they will usually extend the time. If that office is closed join the main queue and they'll deal with you when everyone else has been sorted (for more information on visas see *Chapter 2, Practical Information, page 52*).

There are several banks, one of which has an ATM (use these and avoid the queues in Santa Maria); ticket sales offices for TACV, TAP (only open during the night when the flights arrive from Lisbon), TAAG and Halcyonair; a few tour operators; two car-hire firms, some cafés, a photography shop and a left-luggage office (100$ per item).

You can pay for your taxi from the airport in euros (€10 (day)/€12 (night)) to Santa Maria).

Airlines

✈ **Airport** ☎ 241 1468/1305
✈ **TAAG** Airport & Rua 3 Agosto, Espargos; ☎ 241 1355

✈ **TACV (Cabo Verde Airlines)** Airport; ☎ 241 1305
✈ **TAP Portugal** Airport; ☎ 241 3129; e tapreservas.cv@tap.pt

International departures from Sal Get your hotel to obtain updates from the airline about the time of your international departure – better to sit out a delay on the beach than in the airport.

In transit through Sal If you are in transit to Praia Airport on Santiago with TACV then your baggage may well have been checked all the way through. You will, however, have to go through immigration and customs yourself, after which you should check in immediately for your onward flight. If you are in transit to any island other than Santiago you may have to collect and re-check in your baggage. Currently only Sal, São Vicente, Praia and Boavista airports have money-changing facilities so if you are in transit to another island consider obtaining local currency in Sal Airport. If you have a long wait you can leave your luggage at the airport and take a five-minute ride into Espargos or a 15-minute taxi ride to Santa Maria.

Domestic flights TACV flies from Sal to Santiago (about three flights a day); São Vicente (two flights a day); Boavista (daily) and São Nicolau (three times a week). Fly to Santiago for connections to Maio and Fogo. If you need to book TACV flights in Sal, it is best to go to the airport office (⊕ *08.00–11.30 & 14.00–17.00 Mon–Fri*) or to Barracuda Tours or vista verde tours in Santa Maria (see page 104). Flights can be paid for with Visa or MasterCard. Be warned, however, that flights book up quickly and if you are on a tight schedule it is best to pre-book internal connections before leaving home, through your tour operator or travel agent.

Cabo Verde Express is a charter airline that mostly flies tour groups on day trips to other islands. Enquire at the airport or through tour operators in Santa Maria. Flights only go ahead if the plane is full. Halcyonair (*www.halcyonair.com*) offers flights from Sal to Santiago, Maio, Boavista, São Nicolau and São Vicente.

From the airport Most of the big tourist hotels meet international flights with buses. Santa Maria is a 15-minute journey from the airport, Murdeira less than ten minutes and Espargos only two minutes. From the airport there are always plenty of **taxis** to Espargos (250$, or 300$ at night) or Santa Maria (1,000$, or 1,200$ at night). You probably won't find **public transport** (an *aluguer*) waiting at the airport, but if you walk out of the airport and stand on the main road you can catch an *aluguer* (100$ to Santa Maria); be aware that you may wait some time as most *alugueres* leave Espargos full. Alternatively take a taxi only as far as Espargos and pick up an *aluguer* there. Relying on finding an *aluguer* is not recommended if your flight lands late at night.

BY BOAT There are no regular ferries between Sal and the other islands, but the new Cabo Verde Fast Ferry may mean that this changes (to check the latest situation see websites listed under *Getting around*, page 69). There are day trips by boat to Boavista (see *Excursions to other islands*, page 103) but you may have to pay for a return fare even if you are only going one way. If any ferries are running they will be operating through the island's main harbour, Palmeira.

BY YACHT Sal is the most upwind of the islands. There is a very good anchorage in the western harbour of Palmeira. It is a useful place for making crew changes because of the international airport. Yachts generally need to fill up with jerry cans. There is no pump at the pontoon. There is a small shipyard where they can do welding. If this is the first island you visit you will be dispatched in a taxi to the airport for an immigration stamp – an easy process. Other anchorages lie in the broad Baía da Murdeira in the west (where a marina may be built); just south of the promontory of Monte Leão and in the southern bay of Santa Maria, which is a good anchorage except in southerlies.

GETTING AROUND

A tarmac road links the airport to the capital, Espargos, and runs down the spine of the island between Espargos and Santa Maria. The journey takes 20 minutes by car. The other paved roads run from Espargos to Pedra de Lume, and Espargos to Palmeira. There are many tracks, some of them pretty rocky, criss-crossing the island, and one can drive straight across much of its inland terrain in a 4x4.

BY PUBLIC TRANSPORT *Alugueres* run regularly between Espargos and Santa Maria (100$) and between Espargos and the airport; less regularly from Espargos to Palmeira (50$) and infrequently to Pedra de Lume. In Espargos they depart from the square beside the town hall and Hotel Atlântico (although they tend to bump around town shouting for custom, so it's hard to miss them); in Santa Maria they depart from near the BCA Bank at the entrance to the town.

BY TAXI Taxis (or public *alugueres* chartered as taxis) from Espargos, or the airport, to Santa Maria cost 800–1,000$; and from Espargos to the airport 200–300$. There is a 30% surcharge after dark. Taxis may also be chartered for a half- or full-day's sightseeing (see *Sightseeing by car or quad bike*, page 109).

BY CAR Hiring at the airport is costly and not to be relied upon because cars get booked up quickly. There are several car-hire firms of varying standards: try to get a personal recommendation and check the car's tyres, brakes and lights before setting off.

Prices start at about €50 per day. Many firms require a deposit of at least €100 in cash. Make sure you hire a 4x4 or much of Sal will be inaccessible to you. Take care not to leave valuables unattended in the vehicle as smash-and-grab is a speciality in quieter parts of Sal (some rental cars have the locks disabled in order to discourage you from leaving things in the car and getting the windows smashed). The police sometimes stop vehicles in Sal, checking front-seat passengers are wearing seat belts, documentation is correct (proof of ownership or hire; driving licence), and lights are working. Cars do break down more frequently than in Europe so take basic precautions: take water, a hat, a spade to dig yourself out when you get stuck in sand, relevant telephone numbers and a mobile phone.

Car-hire companies

🚗 **Alucar** Inside the Morabeza Hotel, Santa Maria; ☏ 242 1187; m 991 5586; ⊕ 08.00–13.00 & 15.00–18.00 Mon–Sat, closed Sat pm & Sun. A local firm with a good reputation & usually the cheapest prices. A Suzuki Jimny is €50/day but you could probably negotiate a lower rate for more days.
🚗 **Avis** Hotel Belorizonte, Santa Maria; ☏ 242 1551
🚗 **Joel Evora** Espargos; ☏ 241 3636; e stand@joelevora.com

🚗 **Melicar** Espargos; ☏ 241 1666
🚗 **Mendes and Mendes** Hotel Pontão; ☏ 241 2860; m 991 8756; e mendesemendes@cvtelecom.cv; Santa Maria: ☏ 242 1415; e ctpontao@cvtelecom.cv
🚗 **Sulcar** On the road behind the Supermercado Central; ☏ 242 1941; m 992 7755; e sulcar@cvtelecom.cv; ⊕ 08.00–13.00 & 15.00–18.00 Mon–Sat, closed Sat pm & Sun. Smallest car is €53/day.

🏠 WHERE TO STAY

There are two main places to stay: Espargos and Santa Maria. Espargos is cheaper, near the airport and almost entirely unaffected by the tourism in the south. Staying in Espargos and commuting to Santa Maria, however, carries the added cost of the transport.

The third option is to take a villa in Murdeira village, halfway between the airport and Santa Maria (see *Baía da Murdeira*, page 126). It's an attractive hideaway with facilities, but it's a vehicle trip to the action in Santa Maria or to anywhere with local ambience.

With the explosion in apartment-building, there are many self-catering options in Santa Maria. Renting an apartment can be a much cheaper option than staying in a hotel, especially if you are in a group. Self-catering in Santa Maria is not always straightforward however, as it is sometimes hard to find all the ingredients you need for a meal. Renting an apartment for a week starts at around €200.

There are enormous development plans for Sal, with multitudes of apartments, villas, townhouses and resorts being built in and around Santa Maria, up the west coast and in Pedra de Lume.

ACTIVITIES

EXCURSIONS TO OTHER ISLANDS If you have just a week in Sal, and did not take the preferable step of booking any inter-island trips beforehand, time constraints mean that day excursions are your only sensible option. They will whet your appetite for a return trip to Cape Verde.

There are day trips by plane to Boavista (like Sal but with a slightly prettier interior), Santiago (a microcosm of the rest of Cape Verde), Fogo (dramatic volcano), São Nicolau (gentle, mountainous beauty hard to discern on a day trip), and Maio (tranquil town and deserted beaches). These are group tours and they don't give you too much time to look around by yourself. Costs are around €160–220 depending on the island. They can be booked through the tour operators listed below and the flight is with the charter airline Cabo Verde Express. If you want a tailor-made, private tour with your own local guide, vista verde tours (see below) can set this up for you. Sometimes there are day trips by boat and trimaran to Boavista for around €150; check with local tour operators or your hotels.

LOCAL TOUR OPERATORS AND TRAVEL AGENTS

Barracuda Tours 242 2033 (Santa Maria)/241 2452 (airport); m 921 4708; e geral@barracudatours.com; www.barracudatours.com. Long-established Cape Verdean operator situated just east of the pier that can organise most activities, including trips to other islands & excursions on Sal including island tours (approximately €36), boat trips (€40–70), fishing trips, diving, & car rentals. They also arrange cookery lessons where you can learn to cook the traditional dish of *cachupa*.

Hotel Morabeza (for contact information, see page 115) The hotel has an office between the main reception & swimming pool which can organise most activities, with discounts for guests.

Morabitur At Sal Airport & in Santa Maria, on the road down to Hotel Morabeza; 241 2070; e morabitur@morabitur.com; www.morabitur.com. Offers round-island trips, day trips to other islands, fishing, quad bikes, etc.

SalMine Tourist Office Outside Bombay Brasserie, Santa Maria; m 983 0712; e jeanette.mathers@mail.com; 09:00–17.30 Mon–Sat. Friendly advice & information & a booking point for land & sea excursions. Booking agent for SOS Tartarugas turtle walks & turtle adoptions.

Morgana Arcadia/The Arcade; 242 1480; e morgana@cvtelecom.cv. Italian-run travel agency that books cheap last-minute flights to Italy.

TUI/Thomson Djadsal Moridias; 09.00–12.30 & 14.00–18.00 Mon–Sat, closed Sat pm. Flight changes or information about booking flights.

Turtle Shack Tourist Office m 959 2030; 09.00–17.00 daily. On the walkway running along the main beach in Santa Maria near the Morabeza Hotel, they organise excursions on land & sea, including an island tour by minibus (€15), sailing/snorkelling trips (€35), & whale watching (€40). Friendly, helpful service in English & other languages.

Unotur Rua 15 de Agosto, CP 97, Santa Maria; 242 1771; e unotur@cvtelecom.cv. A non-profit agency that seeks to promote Cape Verde, it is sponsored by a number of hotels, agencies, car-hire companies, island promoters & real-estate agents. It therefore doubles as a tourist office & tourism promotion organisation but it is rarely open.

vista verde tours m 993 0788; e office@vista-verde.com; www.vista-verde.com; 10.00–13.00 & 16.00–19.30 Mon–Fri, 10.00–13.00 & 16.00-18.30 Sat. Next to Les Alizes Hotel, just off the main square in Santa Maria, is this well-established travel agency specialising in social & environmentally responsible tourism. Arranges small-group tours or tailor-made holidays incorporating accommodation, flights, hiking & excursions. Offices in Fogo, Sal & Boavista.

SAILING AND BOAT TRIPS There are usually many ways to get out on the sea in Sal. Boats including catamarans, traditional wooden sailing ships and powerboats offer whale watching, cruising, snorkelling and fishing. They leave from either the pier in Santa Maria or the dock in Palmeira. If it is the latter, transport to Palmeira is usually included. Boats come and go so check with a local booking office or your hotel when you arrive.

⚠ **Fidel** Book via the main hotels or tour operator. Charters available. A 25m Turkish Caicco. Offers daily trips around the west coast of Sal, departing from Palmeira & stopping in Murdeira Bay for snorkelling & swimming. Day trips from €60.

⚠ **King Boa** m 994 9248; powerboat trips.

⚠ **Madrugada** 242 1505; m 984 0302; e nauticamadrugada@yahoo.es. Day trips to Boavista & trips around Sal; €115 for a trip to Boavista including an island tour. Book at your hotel or a tour operator.

⚠ **Neptunus** m 999 4200; or contact via a tour operator. Day & night trips in a boat with a glass undercarriage that allows you to see the reefs, fish & wrecks in Santa Maria without getting wet. The latest attraction is a statue of Christ in 6m of water off Porto Antigo.

⚠ **SalMine Tourist Office** Outside Bombay Brasserie; ▢ 983 0712. See page 120 for details.

WINDSURFING AND KITESURFING For a discussion of Cape Verde's wind- and kitesurfing potential, see *Chapter 2, Practical Information*, page 48.

Sal is a great destination for these sports and Cape Verde is now included in the Professional Windsurfing Association's competition circuit. Winds can be strong from November to May, however, and beginners need to be careful. For surfers, the best surf comes between November and the end of March. All kite, wind and surf locations are deep-water locations; there are no shallow areas for kitesurfing here. All schools have rescue boats and a rescue will cost you €30–50.

Sal is favoured by many because it has five major locations all within a 15-minute drive from Santa Maria. A wide range of conditions can be found between these five locations including waves, flat water, offshore winds and onshore winds. There are a number of places along the west coast for more advanced surfers and windsurfers. (For further information, see www.surfcaboverde.com/bottommenu/kitesurfing_sal_cape_verde.html.)

Spares and items such as leashes, helmets and fins are not usually available, so bring your own.

The main spots are:

Santa Maria Bay A 3km of white sandy beach and no rocks. The most convenient spot because it's likely to be walking distance from your accommodation and it's where the kite- and windsurfing schools are. The water is generally flat with gentle swells but the wind can gust a bit close to shore. Near the pier is suitable for beginner windsurfers, the middle of the bay for all levels of windsurfers, and the far end (Ponta Sino) is popular with kitesurfers. Ponta Sino also has a lovely wave when the swell is right. Schools teach kite- and windsurfing in this area, where the wind is more side offshore at the start of the bay and side onshore at the end. Further out, the wind becomes stronger and more steady; nowadays, the wind closer in to shore is more gusty due to the increase in construction. For this reason, more advanced windsurfers prefer Lem Bedje Beach or round the corner in front of the RIU Hotel.

In front of the RIU Hotel A three-minute taxi ride from Santa Maria, this area is growing in popularity with kitesurfers and windsurfers. The area in front of the hotel offers some of the strongest side offshore winds on the island and the sea becomes more wavy the further out you go. More advanced kite- and windsurfers enjoy this location as the wind is more consistent, however, from January to March there can be a strong shorebreak. Surfzone have a base there and can take you there or rent you equipment once you are there.

Punta Lembje Many windsurfers start out in the bay and make their way to this point at the eastern end of Santa Maria. Lembje is great for more advanced windsurfers; the water is flatter on the inside of the bay and wavier outside. There are some rocks (more in the winter time) when entering the water, so shoes are advisable. When there are waves at this beach, they are great clean waves. It is also a good spot for more advanced kitesurfers, as it is difficult to enter the water from this beach, because of the rocks and the gusty wind (once you are out in the water the wind is more constant).

Kite Beach Formerly known as Shark Bay, this 2km stretch of nature reserve on the southeastern coast has stronger and more constant side onshore winds but gentler waves. It's shallow for hundreds of metres out to sea. There is a small reef providing a stretch that is useful for beginners and intermediate wave riders, and a deeper area further south for the more advanced (but watch for the occasional rock). It is growing in popularity with windsurfers, but at present mostly kitesurfers are seen here.

It's a bit too far to walk but you can get there in 15 minutes by taxi from Santa Maria (€10 round trip). There are no schools at Kite Beach but the schools in Santa Maria will often allow you to rent equipment to take there. There is a small shack that sometimes sells drinks.

Ponta Preta Now on the world wave-jumping circuit, Ponta Preta is suitable only for the experienced with huge, hollow, perfectly formed waves, that can reach 6m in height. Ponta Preta presents a number of challenges including an offshore (or side offshore) wind, waves breaking mostly onto sharp rocks (though finishing on sand), and strong undercurrents. There are no schools here or rescue boats and it is rare that a school will rent you equipment to take there, since the risk of damage is so high. Ponta Preta has a restaurant (see page 126).

There are several schools offering equipment hire and/or tuition. Sample prices are: kitesurfing introductory lessons €60, full course €345 (11 hours), one day's rental €70; windsurfing lessons: one hour €53, one day's rental €15, one week's rental €345; one hour's surfboard rental €10.

Angulo Watersports Praia António de Sousa; 242 1899; www.angulocaboverde.com. Close to the Hotel Sab Sab, it offers windsurfing, kite rentals, private tuition & island trips.
Bravo Club At the Vila do Farol Hotel; e bcfarol.recep@renthotel.org. Offers windsurfing.
Club Mistral On the beach near Hotel Belorizonte, this centre offers tuition & equipment hire for kite- & windsurfing.

Surf Zone 242 1700; m 982 7910/997 8804; e info@surfcaboverde.com; www.surfcaboverde.com; ⊕ 09.00–17.00 daily. Located outside the Morabeza Hotel & on the beach at the RIU Hotel, it offers kitesurfing, windsurfing & surfing; instruction & kit hire. Its website has excellent information for independent kite- & windsurfers on the most popular spots on the island.

SURFING Surfing in Cape Verde is discussed in *Chapter 2, Practical Information*, page 48. The surf is mostly reef breaks but there are some beach breaks too, and there are breaks suitable for all abilities, but it is particularly good for advanced surfers. The big waves tend to be between January and March. In Santa Maria Bay the area beside the pier is one of the major wave spots for surfers. This wave, like all the waves on the island, are dependent on an ocean swell and when the waves do come in they average in size from 1m to 2m and offer a great ride. The other wave spot is at Ponta Sino at the far end of the bay. For equipment hire see the listings in *Windsurfing and kitesurfing*, page 105.

FISHING For a description of Cape Verdean fish, see *Chapter 2, Practical Information*, page 49. Fishing is best done between July and October, but wahoo is available almost nine months of the year. There is a good wahoo fishery about 20 minutes away, by sea, from Santa Maria. Big-game fishing (for tuna, shark and blue marlin; €250–400 per boat), trawl fishing (for wahoo, tuna, barracuda and bonito; about €250 for a boat) bottom fishing (bonita, sargo and more), pier fishing, and surf casting (about €30 per person for two hours) are available from some of the companies below.

⚓ Big Game Fishing/Fishing Dream
📞242 2080; m 991 5505; e info@ fishingdream.it; www.fishingdream.it. At the end of the pier, it offers quad fishing (drive down to behind the dunes & walk to the beach from there). Half a day's big-game fishing €250; other types from €75.

⚓ Club Odissea
m 999 1062; e caboverdeaquasport@hotmail.com;

www.salsportfishing.com. Offers big-game fishing & bottom fishing. You can also book your trip on *Neptunus* (glass-bottomed boat) here & trips to Boavista on the *Madrugada*.

⚓ Fishing Centre
📞242 2050; m 993 1332; e caboverdefishingcenter@yahoo.it. On the walkway running along the main beach. Trolling, jigging & big-game fishing with a long-established Italian-owned centre.

In addition, local fishermen at the pier might be recruited more cheaply for interesting fishing trips.

DIVING Diving in Cape Verde is discussed in *Chapter 2, Practical Information*, page 48. There are some exciting dives on Sal, including five wrecks. There is the 1966 freighter *Santo Antão* sitting at a depth of only 11m but full of large, colourful fish, and the Russian fishing trawler *Kwarcit*, which was confiscated after being caught transporting illegal immigrants from Africa, and which now sits at 28m. Manta Diving Center, in conjunction with the Oceanário de Lisboa, has developed a project called 'Rebuilding Nature', which aims to create artificial reefs as a means of increasing fish life and developing sustainable tourism. The latest wreck sunk as part of this project is the *Sargo*, a decommissioned Cape Verdean naval vessel. The artificial reefs are being evaluated to determine their role in improving biodiversity and raising awareness of threats to the marine environment. (For more information, see www.rebuildingnature.org/uk/index.php.)

Within the bay of Santa Maria and along the west coast there is a range of reef dives suitable for all levels. A highlight is Cavala (40m), a dramatic wall dive ending in a large cave.

There are several cave dives in the north, including one at Buracona where, 20m down, you swim into lava tubes and journey through caves for about 80m until the tunnel turns upwards, revealing a chink of light. Following it further you reach a huge, open-topped cave, 10m in diameter where you can surface to the surprise of land-based tourists looking in from the top. There are also good dives at the many other small caves and inlets north of Palmeira (10–15m drops). Salão Azul, 200m off Pedra de Lume, is a reef with a wall that stretches to a depth of 45m, peppered with recesses full of marine life, but the northwesterly winds mean it is rarely dived.

Dive centres based at hotels are also open to non-guests and all the dive centres offer PADI (Professional Association of Diving Instructors) courses including try dives. Manta Diving Center is a BSAC (British Sub Aqua Club) centre as well. All have equipment to rent. Prices are around €90 for a two-tank dive including equipment, €90 for a try dive, and €360 for an Open Water course.

🐟 Cabo Verde Diving
m 997 8824; e info@ caboverdediving.net; www.caboverdediving.net. PADI resort behind the Djadsal & Crioula Hotels; Italian-run, offering PADI courses & guiding in English & other languages.

🐟 Manta Diving Center
Between Hotels Novorizonte & Belorizonte; 📞242 1540; e info@ mantadivingcenter.cv; www.mantadivingcenter. com. Visits Buracona & Palmeira on a big boat. Also runs fishing & snorkelling trips from Palmeira (€40 including refreshments).

Scuba Caribe At Hotel Riu Funana & Riu Garopa; 242 1002 (town office); 242 9060, ext 8235 (dive centre on beach); www.scubacaribe.com

Scuba Team Cabo Verde On Santa Maria Beach near the pier; m 991 1811; e scubateamcaboverde@yahoo.fr; www.scubateamcaboverde.com/en/centre.html. Offers guided dive trips in small groups & PADI courses, as well as equipment rental.

SWIMMING There are plenty of lovely swimming areas on Sal, but it's not by any means uniformly safe. The swell and the shore breaks vary depending on the time of year, so ask at your hotel for advice. The *câmara municipal* has employed members of the civil guard to work as lifeguards on some beaches. The beaches east of the pier including Praia António de Sousa are often calm when the west coast is rough. Igrejinha, at the far eastern end of Santa Maria, is a 20-minute walk or a few minutes in a taxi and has a small lagoon, a lovely beach which is perfect for children, and a bar. Ponta Preta has a wide beach and stunning dunes as well as a restaurant. Calheta Funda, north of Santa Maria, is favoured by locals and is good for swimming when it is calm (see *Cycling*, below, for directions). The small coves north and south of the residential complex at Murdeira usually offer calm conditions and clear water.

SNORKELLING There are a couple of good spots for snorkelling but the sea floor off the main beaches is mostly sandy. Look for areas that have rocky outcrops but take care if there is surf. The area directly east of the pier and around Porto Antigo and Papaia's Restaurant in Santa Maria are good spots (there is a statue of Jesus 50m straight out from Papaia's). Further out of town Calheta Funda and Cadjatinha are local favourites. Some of the boat excursions will also include snorkelling, most notably with Manta Diving Center who organise snorkelling and fishing excursions to Palmeira (see *Diving*, page 107, for contact information). Other boat excursions may take you to Murdeira Bay (a Marine Protected Area) where the fish life is good, but they often anchor in a deep part and you will have to swim to the reef – ask where to go before you jump in or you might be disappointed. You can also snorkel in Murdeira Bay from the shore; there are good beaches north and south of the residential complex ten minutes' drive from Santa Maria.

SHARK WATCHING South of Pedra de Lume is an area where it is possible to see nurse sharks (*Ginglymostoma cirratum*) in 2–3m of water. You can get in the water with these relatively docile, toothless species which have more in common with stingrays than great white sharks. Some tour companies organise excursions but you could drive yourself there if you get good directions.

CYCLING Some people say that Sal is an excellent place to train for cycling or for triathlons. You could do a fairly relaxed trip from Santa Maria past the RIU and up to the restaurant at Ponta Preta, all on good roads. If you wanted to carry on you could cycle on the main road until you reach Murdeira and then turn off and follow a small road and then a track around the bay to Monte Leão (a half-day trip).

A trip following the road through Santa Maria to the east, past the Sab Sab will take you on a good track that follows the coastline to Igrejinha (little church), a favourite barbecue spot for locals. You will find a small lagoon protected from big waves by a line of rocks. There is also a bar and plenty of shade (one hour).

Carrying on from Igrejinha you could find the track behind the dunes and pass by the old salina on the way to Kite Beach (less than one hour). After Kite Beach there is a dry, dusty, rocky, red sand track that will take you all the way to the beach at Serra Negra (two hours approximately). Follow the coastline so you don't end up on the track heading to the town dump.

A trip to Calheta Funda, where you could swim and snorkel in the protected cove, could make a pleasant half-day excursion. Alternatively you could visit Calheta Funda and then head a little further south to the residential complex of Murdeira where there is a restaurant, bar and pool. To get there, head north from Santa Maria towards the airport until you reach the roundabout with Calheta Funda signposted to the left. Head west along the dirt track (you will appear to be going through private property; it is in fact a cement factory and the road is a public road). Keep heading straight on until the road turns to the left to run alongside the coast. Calheta Funda is a small bay that is signposted.

Bikes can be rented from **Ponta Preta Apartments** (see page 119) for €5/day and **Baileys** for €10/day. There may be others; ask a tour operator or your hotel.

HIKING You can go for lonely long walks virtually anywhere on the island. See page 130 for details of suggested hikes.

TURTLE WATCHING The only authorised turtle walks on Sal are run by the charity **SOS Tartarugas** (m *974 5019;* e *info@turtlesos.org; www.turtlesos.org;* ⏱ *mid-Jun–late Sep, or book through your hotel, vista verde tours or the Turtle Shack Information Centre*). The walks are guided by a biologist or biology student, for groups no larger than ten people, and begin around 20.30 with a short talk about turtles followed by a two-hour period on the beach (or longer, depending on laying time). The walking is not strenuous but you should be able to walk 3km on soft sand. It is not suitable for young children who can find it hard to be still and quiet on demand. The cost is approximately €20, which goes straight into turtle conservation and booking in advance is advised. Many unauthorised and untrained guides will also want to take you to the beach at night but as this has the potential to disturb turtles and may be dangerous, it is not recommended.

There are also hatchery visits on the beach outside the Riu Hotel and on Praia António de Sousa (⏱ *1 Jun–30 Nov 16.00–18.00 daily; no charge*). There may be the opportunity to see hatchlings being released mid-August–mid-November. Please report any sightings of turtles or tracks on the number above.

SIGHTSEEING BY CAR OR QUAD BIKE There are organised island tours by vehicle for a half day (approximately €20) or full day including lunch (approximately €40). These take in the two key sights of Buracona and Pedra de Lume, and other points of interest. Contact local tour operators (see *Local tour operators and travel agents*, page 104). To see the island you have a number of options: rent a car and see the island in a day without a guide, taking in Pedra de Lume, Buracona, Espargos and perhaps Palmeira and one or two remoter locations described below (for information on car hire, see page 102); charter a taxi for €25 for half a day; or take a round-island tour in a pick-up – the local guides are popular and usually receive good reviews. The pick-ups are normally marked *Volta ilha* or can be found outside your hotel (from €20 per person for a half day). If you don't fancy bouncing around in the back of a pick-up, Turtle Shack Tourist Office does a minibus tour.

Some tour operators offer a tour of Santa Maria, but the village is so small and safe it hardly seems worth it. A few combine this with a visit to a school in order for you to donate small items such as pens and books.

You can rent a quad bike (€70/day, €40/half day) or take an organised tour (€45–65). It is possible to take a quad-bike tour around the southern part of the island through some interesting terrain that would not be possible by car (€60–70). It is illegal to drive on any beach or dune, so stick to the road or tracks. Quad bikes are available from Cabo Quad.

Cabo Quad Near Enacol; 242 1590; m 996 8271; e caboquad@cvtelecom.cv; 08.30–12.30 & 14.00–18.00 Mon–Sat, closed Sun

ESPARGOS

Poor Espargos has an undeserved reputation for dreariness. In fact, it is just an ordinary town of middling size, with no great attractions but no major hassles for the visitor either. There is no reason to visit it but then it didn't invite you: you are meant to be in Santa Maria. Still, Espargos has an increasingly bustling feel thanks to Sal's economic growth. It has some good restaurants and at night it is pleasantly lively in the main square and around Bom Dia.

Espargos draws its unlikely name from the wild, yellow-flowered, red-berried asparagus bushes that are said to grow on sandy parts of the island. There is nothing touristic to do in town except perhaps walk up Monte Curral, the mound covered in communications equipment, where you can circle the outside wall for a 360° panorama that will eloquently impart some understanding of the island. To get there, go east from Hotel Atlântico, straight across the roundabout and then take the left turn immediately after the church. Head uphill, passing a sign for the *miradouro* (viewpoint).

WHERE TO STAY

Hotel Atlântico (80 rooms) CP 74, Rua Amílcar Cabral; 241 1210; e hotelatlantico@cvtelecom.cv. On the airport side of town, this is Espargos's only hotel & caters mainly for flight crews & heavily delayed passengers. Terraced bungalows around the grounds are attractive & well kept; rooms are large & each has its own veranda. Sadly the grounds themselves are in a state of neglect, the endless concrete, ruptured only by a hopeful weed, giving the hotel an air of abandonment. There is a restaurant & 1st-floor bar with a view. English spoken. **$$**

Pousada Paz e Bem (16 rooms) CP 161, Rua Jorge Barbosa; 241 1782; e pensaopazbem@cvtelecom.cv. West of the main square in a fairly modern building, all rooms are en suite with hot water; some have AC, some balconies. **$$**

Residencial Central (12 rooms) CP 27, Rua 5 de Julho; 241 1113. On Espargos's main street, facing the square; the entrance is down a side road. Adequate rooms arranged around a courtyard, some with balconies, some with only internal windows. English spoken. **$$**

Residencial Monte Sentinha (13 rooms) Zona Travessa; 241 1446; m 994 3459/991 8671. Towards the northern end of town, this has large, good-quality, AC rooms; the more expensive are en suite with hot water & fridge. Restaurant Amelia on the ground floor. The owner speaks English. **$$**

Residencial Santos (15 rooms) Morro de Curral; 241 1900; m 992 3850; e residencialsantos@hotmail.com. Modern & in good condition with large rooms & upper terrace. Restaurant Panorama is closed but may well reopen. B/fast inc. **$$**

Casa da Angela (19 rooms) Rua Abel Djassy 20; 241 1327; m 997 7440; e casangela20@hotmail.com. Friendly simple place in a quiet location towards the north of town. En-suite rooms with fans; hot water & TV. Some rooms have fridge & spare bed. Restaurant 07.30–10.00 & 12.30–21.00. **$**

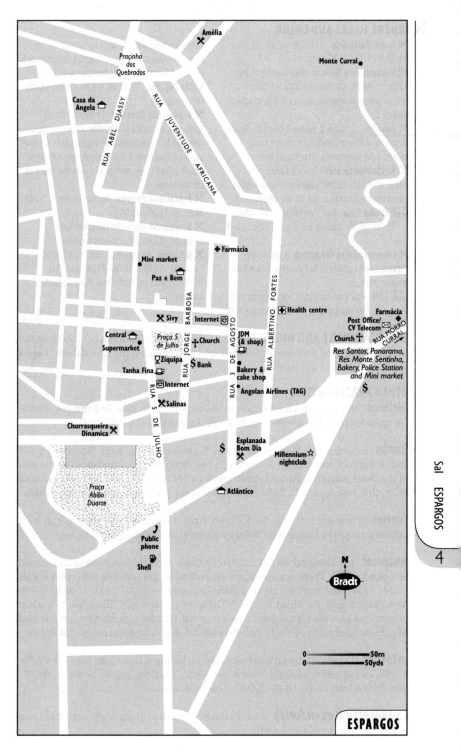

Sal ESPARGOS

4

ESPARGOS

111

✖ WHERE TO EAT AND DRINK

✖ **Hotel Atlântico** ⏲ 07.30–10.00, 12.30–14.30 & 19.30–21.30 daily. $$$$

✖ **Restaurante Salinas** Rua 5 Julho; ☎ 241 1799; ⏲ 08.00–00.00 daily. Airy 1st-floor restaurant serving good-quality fish & spaghetti dishes. $$$

✖ **Amélia** ⏲ lunch & dinner Mon–Sat. Beside Residencial Monte Sentinha with the same owner, who sometimes plays music here. $$

✖ **Restaurante Sivy** Praça 5 Julho; ☎ 241 1427; ⏲ 11.00–02.00. Traditional local menu; eat in the cool inside or out on the square. $$

🍺 **Tanha Fina** Rua 5 de Julho; ☎ 241 2822; ⏲ 08.00–00.00. A snack bar & good b/fast place. $$

✖ **Churrasqueira Dinamica** A local café serving hearty plates of fish or stew. Behind the *aluguer* park. $

🍺 **JDM** Rua 3 de Agosto; ⏲ afternoons only Mon–Sat. One road east of the main square, this café is on a shaded 1st-floor terrace above the souvenir shop of the same name. It serves local & fast food from *cachupa* to hamburgers. $

🍷 **Bar Ziquipa** ⏲ 10.00–02.00. On the square, serving drinks.

✖ **Esplanada Bom Dia** ⏲ 07.00–00.00 Mon–Sat. Just east of the Hotel Atlântico, this café-bar has a large outside seating area & serves snacks & ice cream & is extremely popular with round-island tours, which take over the place at certain times. $$

✖ **Esplanada Pedera** Hortela de Cima; ☎ 241 2620; ⏲ 16.00–02.00. $

✖ **Scalabrod** Opposite the town hall; ⏲ 08.00–03.00 daily. Snacks & drinks. $

✖ **O Sonho** Av Marcelo Leito; ☎ 241 3030; ⏲ 10.00–15.00 & 17.00–21.00 Mon–Sat, 10.00–17.00 Sun. Traditional dishes & buffet lunches. $

ENTERTAINMENT AND NIGHTLIFE The **Millennium Nightclub** (⏲ *23.00–06.00*) is several minutes' walk east from the Hotel Atlântico, on the roundabout. **Lagoa** (⏲ *23.00–06.00*) is in Hortela.

OTHER PRACTICALITIES

Airlines Major airlines have offices at the airport rather than in Espargos. TAAG (Angola Airlines) has an office on Rua 3 de Agosto (☎ *241 1355*).

Banks Espargos has four banks: Caixa Económica, Rua Jorge Barbosa (☎ *241 2608*); Banco Comercial do Atlântico (☎ *241 1491*), on the roundabout to the east of the Hotel Atlântico; Banco Interatlantico (☎ *241 8085*), behind the town hall; and BCN, Rua 3 de Agosto (☎ *241 3299*). All are open ⏲ 08.00–15.00 Monday–Friday.

Ferries If any are running, they depart from Palmeira. Each ferry is run by a different company that sells its tickets separately, from Espargos.

Hospital The **Hospital do Sal** (☎ *241 1130*) was recently inaugurated and should be open in 2011. There is a small government-run clinic on Rua Albertino Fortes (☎ *241 1130*), and a private clinic, Sahida Consultorio (☎ *241 2551*; ⏲ *08.00–17.00 Mon–Sat*), across the street from CV Telecom in Espargos. There are two more private clinics with reasonable facilities on Sal (see listings for Santa Maria and Murdeira), and many of the large hotels will be able to find you an on-call doctor.

Internet There are several internet cafés, including Cyber Café Suzy (⏲ *09.30–00.00*), in the centre of town; Snack Bar Cyber Pretoria, Barrio Novo (⏲ *08.00–00.00*); and Inforsal (⏲ *08.00–22.00*), near BCA Bank.

Laundrette (*Lavandaria*) With Residencial Santos on the right, turn right and follow the road round to the left.

Optician
Optico Nho São Filipe Rua 3 de Agosto; ✆ 241 8142; ⊕ 09.00–12.00 & 15.00–18.00 Mon–Fri.

Pharmacy
Farmácia Ivete Santos Rua 3 de Agosto; ✆ 241 1417; ⊕ 08.00–20.00 Mon–Sat   **Alianca** Zona Centro; ✆ 241 1109; ⊕ 08.00–18.00 Mon–Sat

Police With your back to the Hotel Atlântico, follow the main road to the right for ten minutes (going straight on at the roundabout). The police station (✆ *241 1132*) is on the right almost at the bottom of the road.

Shopping JDM in Espargos and Genuine Cabo Verde in Santa Maria are two of the few souvenir shops in Sal that sell strictly Cape Verdean products, including wine from Fogo, *grogue* and *ponche* in their endless variations, salt from Sal, and assorted handicrafts. There are two music shops: Tropical Dance, Rua 5 de Julho, the main road through town, on the right, and west off the main road heading towards Casa da Angela. *Minimercados* are to be found opposite the church, just off the main square, and under Residencial Santos, in the southeast of town. There is a supermarket under Residencial Central. There are two bakeries. Sabores do Sal (m *594 5008;* ⊕ *07.00–13.00 & 15.00–20.00*) in Barrio Novo has Portuguese-style breads and pastries.

Travel agencies There are two small agencies in Espargos: ISI, Rua 1 de Maio (✆ *241 1954;* ⊕ *09.00–12.00 & 14.00–18.00 Mon–Fri*); and Trans-Toda Hora, Barrio Novo (✆ *241 3424;* ⊕ *09.00–12.00 & 15.00–18.00 Mon–Fri*).

SANTA MARIA DAS DORES

For all the international hype about Cape Verde, Santa Maria, its key tourist town on the main tourist island, remains small and unassuming. Its coastal road, and those just behind it, are lined with low pastel-coloured buildings housing restaurants, bars, hotels and souvenir shops and the occasional home – lively, but nevertheless often struggling in the shadow of the giant, all-inclusive resorts that lure most of Sal's market.

In 1938 Archibald Lyall, the English journalist, reported:

Never was a place better named than these two or three dozen little houses by the sad seashore. There is no vegetation and nothing to do but steel oneself against the unceasing wind which blows the sand into food and throat and clothes. At night, when the red-eyed people retire to their shuttered, oil-lit houses, the great white crabs come out of the sea and march through the streets like a regiment of soldiers.

But Santa Maria is more cheerful now. The big thing has happened: tourism. And instead of crabs it is tourists that walk the streets at night.

HISTORY While the bay at the south of the island was probably frequented over the centuries by salt diggers and sailors, Santa Maria only officially came into existence at the beginning of the 19th century, when Manuel António Martins of Boavista arrived to exploit the saltpans that lie behind the village.

Martins's workforce scraped away the sand to the rock beneath. They guided seawater inland along little trenches and then pumped it by means of wooden

AGGRESSIVE VENDORS

Tourism has attracted many types to Santa Maria including souvenir vendors from west Africa whose tactics some Europeans find disconcerting. Their methods differ greatly from the laid-back approach of local Cape Verdeans though probably, at heart, they differ little from the time-honoured techniques used by European estate agents flogging Sal apartments to visitors on inspection trips.

Unlike the agents, however, the Senegalese curio seller is out on the main street hassling YOU, and will often start to follow you the minute you set foot outside your hotel. If you are not interested in their wares you need to give a firm 'no', avoid being drawn into conversation and resist invitations to follow them to their stall at the local market or into their shop. Some people recommend ignoring them completely but, if you feel awkward doing this, wave your arm dismissively, laugh loud and long to avoid giving offence and keep walking, without answering questions. Do not allow a vendor of African souvenirs to adorn you with a sample piece of jewellery. Some of those priceless pieces don't unfasten. You can shop for products from Cape Verde at your own pace in Genuine Cabo Verde (for more information, see page 125).

windmills into the rows of broad shallow pans. The water would gradually evaporate leaving white sheets of salt which were dug into pyramids. These were loaded into carts which were pulled by mule, along the first railway tracks to be built in Portuguese Africa, to a newly built harbour. Around 30,000 tonnes of salt were exported each year from the port of Santa Maria and much of it went to Brazil until the late 1880s when that country imposed a high customs tax to protect its own new industry.

In the early 1900s, several new ventures with European companies collapsed, forcing the people of Sal to leave in search of work on other islands. Just a few peasants were left, making a living from salting fish and exporting it to other islands.

Santa Maria's fortunes surged again in the 1920s, when a new market for salt opened up in the Belgian Congo and some Portuguese companies revived the business. By the mid 1900s, Sal was exporting 13,000 tonnes a year and there was enough money to build the Santa Maria of today but, as always, international events were to snatch away whatever prosperity they had bestowed. Independence for the Belgian Congo, changes in Portugal and then independence in Cape Verde brought an end to the business. By 1984, even the routine maintenance of the saltpans ceased.

Santa Maria had a small but significant role to play in Cape Verde's liberation. In September 1974, hearing that Spínola, the new Portuguese ruler, was secretly to visit Sal, Cape Verdeans immediately hired whatever planes and boats they could find. They arrived in Sal and picketed him, daubing slogans on the road from the airport and braving threats that they would be shot. In return an embarrassed Spínola sacked the Cape Verdean governor on the spot and ordered a stronger one to the colony.

ORIENTATION The bay of Santa Maria takes up most of the southern coast of Sal. The town of Santa Maria begins roughly at a point in the middle of this coastline, and extends to the east. To the west of this midpoint is a line of bigger hotels.

Santa Maria Town has three 'layers': hotels make the topping, lining the beach; affluent locals live along parallel streets behind, where there are some tourist restaurants, bars and shops; beyond that the poor part of Santa Maria stretches inland. Here people live in half-finished and unpainted houses made of breeze blocks. To the east there is a new district (Zona António Sousa) of smart apartment buildings being bought by Europeans, tourists and investors.

The heart of the town consists of three main roads running east to west and centred on the main *praça* and the pier; the hotel zone is to the west of the village, and to the north and east are the residential districts where most of the self-catering accommodation can be found.

WHERE TO STAY Most of the big, upmarket resort hotels lie on a road running parallel with the beach, west from Santa Maria, and currently all but two are beachfront. There's also a large, once-upmarket hotel at the eastern end of town whose advantage is its superb, quiet beach location. Most of the other hotels, ranging from budget to boutique, are in town, at varying distances from the beach, though Santa Maria is still so small that nowhere is more than five minutes' walk from the sea. Many new hotels and apartment blocks are still planned but the boom is over for the time being. Santa Maria has a glut of accommodation, so you are likely to find a room in your price range. For an explanation of the $ rating, see the inside cover.

Increasing numbers of tourists, particularly watersports enthusiasts, are choosing self-catering apartments, which can be cheaper. Bear in mind, however, that food shopping in Santa Maria is not that straightforward: food is expensive and the range is limited.

The following hotels are to the west of Santa Maria:

Hotel Dunas de Sal [117 F2] (48 rooms) 242 9050; e geral@hoteldunasdesal.com; www.hoteldunasdesal.com. Located on the landward side of the road that runs west of Santa Maria, this is a designer hotel & the design is minimalist. A stylish hotel with a good restaurant. In addition to the usual facilities, including massage & beauty centre, it also has a business centre. **$$$$$**

Hotel Morabeza [117 H1] (140 rooms) CP 33; 242 1020; e info@ hotelmorabeza.com; www.hotelmorabeza.com. Reservations in Belgium: 15–17 Kaarderijstraat, 9000 Ghent; +32 9 226 1947; e ciem.nv@ skynet.be; www.hotelmorabeza.com. Built in the 1960s as a private house for a pioneering Belgian couple long before tourism hit Sal, the Morabeza has expanded over the years & is now a centrally positioned, 4-star hotel run by their granddaughter. The hotel was recently given a facelift & a new elegant reception was built which gives it the air of a gentlemen's club. Attractively laid out, each room has a veranda giving sea or garden views. There is a large open-air swimming pool. The usual activities & excursions are offered, plus massage, archery, minigolf, watersports, tennis & even traditional dancing & the Creole language. There are 3 restaurants & a bar, including a rooftop venue serving local-style food. This is the most sought-after hotel with a great reputation & is a good choice for those who want resort facilities & safe beach swimming without feeling cut off from local life. **$$$$$**

Crioula Hotel [117 F2] (242 rooms) 242 1615/1647/1654; e crioulahotel@ cvtelecom.cv. Reservations in Italy: +39 030 370 0630; e vilacrio@tin.it; www.caboverde.com/ pages/421615.htm. Santa Maria's first 5-star hotel lies to the west of town, constructed of pleasant, muted terracotta & stone architecture with quiet rooms arranged around gardens. It has a large freshwater pool, plus the usual array of excursions & entertainments, & is an all-inclusive establishment. **$$$$**

Hotel Oasis Atlântico Belorizonte [117 G1] (230 rooms) 242 1045; e hborizonte@ cvtelecom.cv; www.oasisatlantico.com. Just beyond the Morabeza, this is a newly refurbished package hotel with a mixture of rooms – bungalows or conventional rooms arranged around a pool, with mature planting. It also

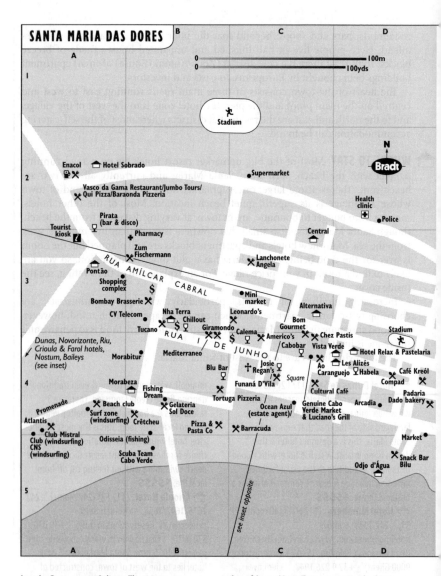

SANTA MARIA DAS DORES

Stadium

Enacol — Hotel Sobrado

Vasco da Gama Restaurant/Jumbo Tours/
Qui Pizza/Baraonda Pizzeria

Supermarket

Health
clinic

Police

Pirata
(bar & disco)

Tourist
kiosk

Pharmacy

Zum
Fischermann

Central

RUA AMÍLCAR CABRAL

Lanchonete
Angela

Pontão

Shopping
complex

Mini
market

Alternativa

Bombay Brasserie

CV Telecom

Nha Terra

Chillout

Leonardo's

Bom
Gourmet

Tucano

Giramondo

Calema

Americo's

Chez Pastis

Dunas, Novorizonte, Riu,
Crioula & Farol hotels,
Nostum, Baileys
(see inset)

RUA 1 DE JUNHO

Cabobar

Vista Verde

Hotel Relax & Pastelaria

Stadium

Morabitur

Mediterraneo

Blu Bar

Josie
Regan's

Square

Ao
Caranguejo

Habela

Les Alizés

Café Kreól

Compad

Morabeza

Fishing
Dream

Funaná D'Vila

Cultural Café

Arcadia

Padaria
Dado bakery

Promenade

Beach club

Gelateria
Sol Doce

Tortuga Pizzeria

Ocean Azul
(estate agent)/

Genuine Cabo
Verde Market
& Luciano's Grill

Atlantis

Club Mistral
Club (windsurfing)
CNS
(windsurfing)

Surf zone
(windsurfing)

Crêtcheu

Odisseia (fishing)

Pizza &
Pasta Co

Barracuda

Market

Snack Bar
Bilu

Scuba Team
Cabo Verde

Odjo d'Água

see inset opposite

---

has the Restaurante Salinas. There is an array
of entertainments & watersports, as well as
children's activities & a children's pool. You can
book B&B, HB or FB (its sister hotel, Novorizonte,
which is next door, is similar but package only).
$$$$

⌂ Farol Hotel [117 F2] (236 rooms)
📞 242 1725; e farol.recep@alpitourworld.it.
Large Italian all-inclusive resort, big gardens,
swimming pool & watersports facilities. **$$$**

⌂ Hotel Pontão [116 A3] (36 rooms) 📞 242
8060; e ctpontao@cvtelecom.cv. At the western

edge of Santa Maria Town, opposite the Pirata
Nightclub & thus near the main street & a few
mins' walk of the beginning of the western
beach, the balconied rooms are en suite with AC
& TV. There's an unexpected garden with a pool of
reasonable size. Good value. **$$$**

⌂ Riu Funaná/Riu Garopa [117 E1] (500 +
500 rooms) 📞 242 9060/9040;
e clubhotelfunana@riu.com, clubhotelgaropa@
riu.com; www.riu.com. Twin resort hotels
enclosed behind vast walls beside the beach
about 1.5km west of Santa Maria with assorted

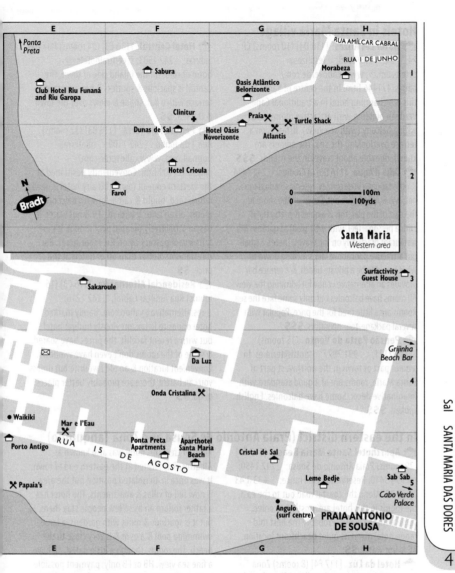

restaurants, pools, spa & watersports centre.
Accommodation is in a series of buildings around
the grounds. They provide entertainment & a
wide variety of activities & excursions. Heated
children's swimming pool. Caters mostly for a
variety of Europeans (including British) on all-
inclusive package holidays. The buffet restaurant
has an enormous variety of food as the Riu tries
to cater for its many nationalities of visitor.
You either love it or hate it. Book directly on
the website or as part of a package with, for
example, Thomson Holidays. From Sal, just go

to the sales office. All-inclusive rate only. Day-
passes are available for approximately €60. **$$$**

🏠 **Hotel Sabura** [117 F1] (40 rooms, 8 suites)
📞 242 1515; e direccion@hotelsabura.com;
www.hotelsabura.com. Opened in 2009, rooms
in this bright modern hotel are centred on a lush
garden & swimming pool. The rooms don't have
numbers but instead are named after musicians.
Suites are only slightly larger than standard
rooms. All rooms have AC, minibar, safe, veranda,
TV & internet access. Restaurant open all day
(vegetarian meals available). **$$$**

Hotels in Santa Maria village

🏠 **Hotel Les Alizés** [116 D4] (10 rooms) CP 74; 242 1446/1008; e lesalizes@cvtelecom.cv; www.caboverde.com/pages/421446.htm. In the centre of Santa Maria, this is a charming hotel in a traditional Cape Verdean building with attractive rooms, each with a balcony (with sea view). B/fast is on a terrace overlooking the sea. The owners are knowledgeable about travel in the islands. **$$$**

🏠 **Odjo d'Água** [116 D5] (47 rooms) 242 1414; e odjodagua@cvtelecom.cv, reservas@odjodagua.net; www.odjodagua.net. Down on the shore to the east of the pier, this is a quiet & pretty hotel with a personal feel, with well-planted gardens & a restaurant practically on the waves. There's a small but attractive pool above steps leading down to what is said to be a private beach, & a terrace bar provides an alternative venue for admiring the view. All rooms have balconies but only some face the sea. Rooms are a little tired for the price. Popular with several package-tour operators. **$$$**

🏠 **Pensão Porta do Vento** (15 rooms) 242 2121; m 991 7877; e ciotti@terra.es. In a quiet part of town in the northwest part of Santa Maria, rooms are of a good standard with imaginative décor. Some have balconies. English spoken. **$$$**

🏠 **Hotel Central** [116 C3] (24 rooms) Rua das Salinas; 242 1503; e centralhotelcv@hotmail.com. On the inland side of town, the Central is spacious & spotless & has a rooftop terrace with a bar, shade & views over the town & the sea. **$$**

🏠 **Pensão Nha Terra** [116 B3] (12 rooms) Rua 1 de Junho; 242 1109; e nhaterra@hotmail.com; www.caboverde.com/pages/421109.htm. Conveniently positioned at the western edge of town, this airy hotel is newly refurbished, bright & cared-for with balconied rooms, all en suite & with AC, TV & hot water. It has an attractively planted pool though it's in full view of passers-by on the main street. Bar & restaurant. Better than other hotels at this price. **$$**

🏠 **Residencial Alternativa** [116 C3] (16 rooms) Rua Amílcar Cabral; 242 1216; e res.alternativa@yahoo.com. Barely marked hotel opposite Relax, previously budget hotel but with a recent facelift, the prices have soared & some of the rooms don't even have windows. Convenient location & an old favourite but unless you can barter, there are probably better places to go. **$$**

In the eastern district (Praia António de Sousa and Zona Tanquinho)

🏠 **Aparthotel Santa Maria Beach** [117 F5] (29 rooms) Praia Antonio de Sousa; 242 1450; m 994 3410. Reservations in France: +33 1 43 00 87 32. Along the coastal road out to the east, the rooms in this hotel are mostly balconied, some with sea views. Probably the best mid-range hotel given its quiet beachfront location. AC & hot water. **$$**

🏠 **Hotel da Luz** [117 F4] (8 rooms) Zona Tanquinho, north Santa Maria; 242 1138; e pousadadaluz@mail.cvtelecom.cv. Basic hotel but a popular choice amongst those on a budget. Quiet location & small swimming pool. **$$**

🏠 **Residencial Cristal de Sal** [117 G5] (8 rooms) 242 1851; m 991 5960; e gabs@cvtelecom.cv. Popular with surfers, this is good value. Hot water is via solar panels so can be limited in the morning. **$$**

🏠 **Sab Sab Hotel** [117 H5] (50 rooms) 242 13010/242 8046; e reservations@hotelsabsab.com; www.hotelsabsab.com. Built to house Aeroflot crew this hotel was also known as Albatros, & is located at the eastern end of town. It was once in an isolated position but the area is now full of villas & apartments. The hotel has a rather forlorn air as so few people stay there, but it is spacious & quiet with gardens, a large swimming pool & a gym & is very close to the beach. The rooms, though a little dated, all have a fine sea view. HB or FB only; payment possible by Visa, MasterCard or American Express. **$$**

🏠 **Surfactivity Guest House** [117 H3] (8 rooms) Zona Tanquinho, north Santa Maria; m 992 6282; e info@surfactivity.it; www.surfactivity.it. Imaginatively conceived & highly recommended rooms & apartments rented by the week or night & aimed mostly at the watersports crowd. Beautiful communal living areas with kitchens, games room & outside space with hammocks. The owner is a windsurfer & can store your equipment & help you with arrangements. **$$**

🏠 **Sakaroule** [117 E3] (7 rooms) m 979 8838/954 1630; e sakaroule1999@yahoo.it; www.sakaroule.com. Tucked away at the back of Santa Maria, this colourful Italian-owned *residencial* is a traditional Cape Verdean building with an interior courtyard that has been expanded & improved. Some of the rooms have kitchens & balconies. Has internet service & a place to store wind- & kite-surfing equipment. Friendly, helpful service from live-in managers. An excellent price because of its location; some love it because it's not in the tourist areas, but it can be a little noisy at w/ends. **$**

Self-catering apartments
Agencies

🏠 **Aquisal/Sal4Rent** Edifício Fogo, Santa Maria; ✆ 242 1658; e info@sal4rent.com; www.sal4rent.com. Rents holiday apartments from €5 per night & long-term rentals from €200 per month. Also offers property management, keyholding service & commercial units.

🏠 **Cabo Direct** Next to Blu Bar; m 995 9308; e pamela@cabo-direct.com; www.cabo-direct.com. Long- & short-term rents, many suitable for watersports enthusiasts.

🏠 **Infocasa** Rua Amílcar Cabral; ✆ 242 2131; m 997 1216; e residencecv@ yahoo.it; ⏰ 09.30–12.30 & 16.00–19.00. Italian-owned propertycompany offering rentals & management.

Apartments

🏠 **Residencial Porto Antigo** [117 E5] ✆ 242 1815; m 997 1701; e portoantigoreservas@hotmail.com; www.portoantigo.com. This pretty, beautifully planted apartment & villa complex on the edge of the sea has now expanded to include Porto Antigo II just down the road towards the pier, & soon there will be a Porto Antigo III. 1- & 2-bedroomed apartments with living room, kitchenette & balcony. You can rent from the management company but agents in town may be cheaper. Attractive pool. Weekly rentals. **$$$**

🏠 **Cabo Verde Palace** ✆ 242 1238; m 991 2040; e palace@cvtelecom.cv; www.caboverdepalace.com. At the far eastern end of town (past the Sab Sab & the new residential district). This fanciful, fairytale building offers an unfettered view of the ocean & the feeling that you are no longer in a busy tourist centre. Rooms are filled with heavy, Baroque furniture giving an air of grandeur, & the largest has a jacuzzi. 1 tiny room is tucked into the turret where you can glimpse the ocean through circular windows. There's a spacious veranda. A unique place. **$$**

🏠 **Ponta Preta Apartments** [117 F5] (25 apts) Praia Antonio de Sousa; ✆ 242 9020; e info@pontapreta.info; www.pontapreta.info. In the east of town some 20m from the beach, all apartments are spacious & have balconies with a view of either the sea or the garden. All have TV, phone & internet, safe, AC, bed linen, towels & cleaning service. Good value & good location. Bikes & mopeds to rent. **$$**

🏠 **Leme Bedje** [117 H5] e info@ lemebedje.com. A long way behind schedule, this refurbishment is still under construction. When it finally opens it may have bars & restaurants as well as apartments.

4

✖ **WHERE TO EAT AND DRINK** There are many restaurants in Santa Maria, but most visitors stick to a favourite few along Rua 1 de Junho. It is, however, worth hunting out some more of Santa Maria's 50 eating establishments. Some tourists complain that there is nowhere really special to eat in Santa Maria; some are quite happy, particularly those who like seafood and experimenting with local fare.

Most of the upmarket hotels – the **Crioula, Belorizonte, Dunas** and **Morabeza** – have restaurants that welcome non-residents and generally have live music. If you wander along the beach in front of them you will find several restaurants on the shore. Most of the bars have happy hours at differing times, therefore potentially you could drink cheaply for most of the evening. The Morabeza's bar has a happy hour between 18.30 and 19.30 when *caiprinhas* and beers are very cheap and Blu Bar has a happy hour that lasts almost all day on a Sunday. The most popular tourist restaurants and the upmarket hotels that line the beach have live music most nights.

Best for watching sports
Cape Verdeans love sport, especially football, so there is always somewhere to watch a game. Apart from the national station, sports can be watched on three Portuguese channels as well as African, French and Brazilian services.

- **Cabobar** [116 C4] Big screen upstairs.
- **Enacol petrol station** [116 A2] Believe it or not, there is a terrace where you can eat and drink cheaply and watch TV as well as getting your car filled.
- **Luciano's Grill** [116 C4] Cheap beer and eats in the open air.
- **Tim Tam** Several small screens showing all the big games; lively atmosphere.
- **Turtle Shack** [117 G1] Big-screen and internet streaming.

Best for vegetarians
Choices are fairly limited in Cape Verde but you can always get an omelette or plate of rice and beans. In Santa Maria you can always get pizza or pasta, but a few places do something different.

- **Ao Caranguejo** [116 C4] Try the *ortalano*, packed with fresh vegetables.
- **Bombay Brasserie** [116 B2] Several vegetable and chickpea dishes. The owner is vegetarian and will often have something special available. Ask in advance if you want something different.
- **Papaia's** [117 E5] Quesadillas and falafel with hummus are just two options.
- **Pizza & Pasta Co** [116 B4] Several different vegetarian pasta dishes.

Restaurants and cafés

✕ **Beach Club** [116 A4] 242 1020; ⏱ lunch till 15.00. One of Hotel Morabeza's 3 restaurants, it's on the beach with both conventional seating & sun loungers. Excellent service, fairly cheap drinks but pricier food & a great brunch on Sun. $$$$$

✕ **Leonardo's** [116 C3] Off Rua Amílcar Cabral; m 981 0057; ⏱ 12.30–15.00 & 19.00–22.30. This upmarket Italian restaurant has had mixed reviews. $$$$$

✕ **Odjo d'Água** [116 D5] Beside the hotel of the same name. Mixed reviews but even the more negative enjoy their evening because of the restaurant's invigorating location almost overhanging the sea. Specialises in grilled fish. $$$$$

✕ **Praia** [117 G1] On the beach in front of the Hotel Belorizonte; ⏱ 12.00–15.00 daily. Serving sandwiches & grills; bar open all day. $$$$$

✕ **Americo's** [116 C4] Rua 1 de Junho; 242 1011; e soaresamerico@gmail.com; ⏱ 12.00–15.00 & 18.00–22.00 daily. On the main street beyond Calema Bar, this is a Santa Maria landmark & tourist favourite. It serves seafood & grilled fish, lobster, kebabs & charcoal-grilled meat from South Africa. *Cachupa* on Thu; live music most days. $$$$

✕ **Ao Caranguejo** [116 C4] Rua 1 de Junho; 242 1231; m 997 1216; e caranguejocv@yahoo.it; ⏱ 19.00–late Tue–Sun. Don't be put off by the entrance which looks like a corridor – it opens up into a courtyard bedecked with fairylights. Enjoy delicious pasta & great pizza under the stars. Take-aways available. $$$$

✕ **Atlantis** [117 G2] On the beach outside Hotel Belorizonte; 242 1879; e wcv.pat@gmx.net; ⏱ 10.00–22.00. Open-air fish restaurant with good sea views. A blend of Italian, French & Creole cooking. $$$$

✕ **Bombay Brasserie** [116 B2] Next to BCA Bank on the road running south to Hotel Morabeza; m 994 4878/991 8666; ⏱ 12.00–15.00 & 18.00–23.30. Indian dishes. Good for vegetarians. $$$$

✘ Chez Pastis [116 C4] Rua Amílcar Cabral; ✆984 3696; ⊕ 18.30–23.00 daily. Good reviews for this tiny, Italian-run concern offering food with a French influence, mostly meat & seafood dishes. Book ahead. $$$$

✘ Crêtcheu Pizzeria [116 B4] ✆242 1062; ⊕ 10.00–22.00 daily. At the bottom of the pier. Pasta, pizza & grilled fish from a pleasant terrace with a view of the sea, the pier & all the boats moored nearby. $$$$

✘ Dunas de Sal [117 F2] On the western hotel road; ✆242 9050; e geral@hoteldunasdesal.com; www.hoteldunasdesal.com. Worth the taxi ride out to dine in elegant poolside surroundings. A varied menu & daily specials. $$$$

✘ Mediterraneo [116 C4] Rua 1 de Junho; m 979 8219. Italian restaurant with tables on the street. $$$$

✘ Nostum Djadsal Moridias Block B; m 985 9291; e itasaloman@hotmail.com; ⊕ 11.00–15.00 & 18.30–22.00, closed Sun lunchtime. Cosy Sardinian restaurant with the usual pasta dishes & fish. Will prepare vegetarian dishes if ordered in advance. Also has a small deli. $$$$

✘ Papaia's [117 E5] Porto Antigo Hotel; m 973 3482; ⊕ 08.00–23.00 daily. Newly refurbished & rebranded as a café/deli, this is still a wonderful setting at the edge of the water. Homemade bread & cakes & a diverse menu including meals for kids & vegetarians. $$$$

✘ Baileys Djadsal Moradias; m 951 4761; e bailey-s@hotmail.co.uk; ⊕ 08.00–22.00 Mon–Fri, 10.00–22.00 Sat/Sun. Cheap pints & British food as well as curry nights and other themed evenings for the growing expat community in the western part of town. There is also a Chinese restaurant on the premises. $$$

✘ Barracuda Restaurant [116 C4] Beachfront location just east of the pier; ⊕ Tue–Sun. It has a good choice & a good reputation. $$$

✘ Café Kréol [116 D4] Travessa Patrice Lumumba; ✆242 1774; m 995 3690; ⊕ 12.00–15.00 & evenings Mon–Sat. Small, busy, established venue with a veranda & a varied menu; proud of its homemade yoghurt. $$$

✘ Cultural Café [116 C4] Main praça; ✆242 2154; ⊕ 08.00–00.00, closed Tue in low season. Hip venue, of mixed Cape Verdean/European design, tumbling out on to the square in the centre of Santa Maria. Promotes a lot of local

foods & drinks such as punches, grogues, cakes & a classy cachupa (they will also teach you how to cook it). A must-try. $$$

✘ Funaná d'Vila [116 C4] Main praça; ✆242 1238; e funana@cvtelecom.cv; ⊕ 08.00–00.00 Mon–Sat. This bar/restaurant is a scaled-down version of the well-known Funaná that is now Turtle Shack. The same format works well in the centre of town & the Cape Verdean nights with music & dancing (Fri & Sat) draws a large crowd of locals & tourists. Offers Cape Verdean & international evening meals as well as a more limited menu through the afternoon & later at night. $$$

✘ Lanchonete Angela [116 C3] Behind the main street; ⊕ 07.30–22.30 Mon–Sat. This little diner is always popular with residents. $$$

✘ Onda Cristalina [117 F4] Zona Tanquinho; m 983 7630; ⊕ 07.30–23.00 daily. From the moment this restaurant opened it has been packed. Large restaurant & terrace serving the usual fare of meat & fish & cheap pints. The only restaurant in this residential zone. $$$

✘ Pizza & Pasta Co [116 B4] On the beach to the east of the pier; m 983 0286; ⊕ 14.00–22.00. Sit under the stars surrounded by palm trees with your feet in the sand & enjoy perfect homemade pasta & delicious sauces. $$$

✘ Snack Bar Bilu [116 D5] Down the side road as you leave the Hotel Odjo d'Água, this unmarked restaurant serves local food & continues to be popular. $$$

✘ Tortuga Pizzeria [116 B4] Next to Blu Bar; m 986 6220; ⊕ 08.30–20.30 Tue–Sun. Terrace & indoor seating. Take-away available. $$$

✘ Turtle Shack [117 G1] On the beach walkway heading west from the pier; ✆242 1637; from the UK +44 (0)161 408 0176; e steve@turtle-shack.com; www.turtle-shack.com; ⊕ 09.00–late daily. Large bar/restaurant popular with British holidaymakers venturing out of all-inclusive hotels. Familiar food served all day, big-screen sports & evening entertainment. Sun loungers available & the only place on Sal with free Wi-Fi. Market every Sun. $$$

✘ Zum Fischermann [116 B3] m 991 7500; ⊕ 18.00–23.00. Large building with a huge sign just to the east of Pirata, this restaurant is German owned & specialises in fish & seafood. $$$

✘ Baraonda [116 A2] In the parade of shops on the left after Enacol; m 985 9350; ⊕ 18.30–23.00 daily. Colourful pizzeria. $$

✕ **Compad** [116 D4] Av Amílcar Cabral. Perennial favourite with locals. Good simple food, served quickly. $$

✕ **Mar e l'Eau** [117 D4] Rua 15 de Agosto; ☎ 242 1134. Known locally as Tud Fixe, this unassuming courtyard café could easily be missed. Friendly & cheap, but some meals may need to be ordered in advance. $$

✕ **Padaria Dâdo** [116 D4] Rua 1 de Junho; ☎ 242 1516; e padariadado@yahoo.com.br; ⏲ 07.00–01.00. Mainly a local haunt, this is an excellent venue for inexpensive b/fast, *cachupa* & cakes. $$

✕ **Tucano** [116 B3] Downstairs at Pensão Nha Terra on Rua 1 de Junho; ☎ 242 1019; ⏲ 08.00–23.00 daily. Sit poolside & watch the world go by as you enjoy pasta & fish dishes. Also does delicious pancakes & muffins for b/fast & sandwiches for lunch. Good-value 2-course menu for €9. $–$$$

✕ **Enacol petrol station** [116 A2] As you enter Santa Maria; ⏲ 08.00–22.00. Perhaps not the most scenic place to eat & drink, but you can't do better than a *prato de dia* of chicken, rice & salad for 350$. The café & little terrace beside the shop is a popular choice for a quick, tasty meal. $

🍨 **Gelataria Sol Doce** [116 B4] Beside the pier; ⏲ 07.00–19.00 daily. Café serving Portuguese pastries, crêpes, sandwiches & coffee. $

✕ **Kiosque Beach Bar** To the west of the pier; ⏲ 09.30–20.00. Simple, cheap food & drinks sitting on the beach watching the world go by. $

✕ **Luciano's Grill** [116 C4] At the Genuine Cabo Verde Market off the main *praça*; ⏲ 07.00–23.00 daily. Simple, quick food with a great reputation. The burgers are particularly recommended & the cheapest in town. $

✕ **Giramondo** [116 B4] Rua 1 de Junho. The best ice cream in town. Also serves coffee, smoothies, slices of pizza & pastries. $

Fresh bread can be bought from **Padaria Dâdo**, **Bom Gourmet**, **Minimercado Andrade** and **Minimercado RG**.

ENTERTAINMENT AND NIGHTLIFE

🍸 **Bar Habela** [116 D4] Rua 1 de Junho. Rooftop bar with music, films, live music or a DJ.

🍸 **Blu Bar** [116 B4] Rua 15 de Agosto; e info@blubarcapeverde.com; www.blubarcapeverde.com. Smart cocktail bar with live music & great atmosphere. Ladies' Night on Fri (buy 1 get 1 free) & the longest happy hour on the island (16.30–21.30 on Sun). Available for private parties.

🍸 **Cabobar** [116 C4] Opposite the main *praça*; ⏲ 18.00–04.00 Tue–Sun. Breezy bar on 2 floors with music every night, chillout lounge & happy hour 19.00–21.00. Big screen showing sports & music videos.

🍸 **Calema** [116 C4] Rua 1 de Junho. Famous late nightspot with live music.

🍸 **Chillout** [116 B3] At the end of Rua 1 de Junho. Outside seating area.

🍸 **Cultural Centre** Behind the Cultural Café, this often has free (but poorly advertised) events such as concerts, plays or capoeira displays. You can check the notices on its door.

🍸 **Funaná d'Vila** [116 C4] Main *praça*; ☎ 242 1238; e funana@cvtelecom.cv; ⏲ 12.00–15.00 & 19.00–22.00 Fri–Wed. Live Cape Verdean nights at the w/end.

🍸 **Grijinha Beach Bar** m 985 9318; e grijinha@msn.com; ⏲ 11.00–18.00 Thu–Sun. A lovely open-air bar/restaurant at the eastern end of Santa Maria with a natural lagoon for swimming & a cooling breeze. Snacks served daily & a barbecue available all day Sat & Sun. Also organises private parties. Follow the surfboard signs (10min walk) or take a taxi.

🍸 **Josie Regan's Irish Bar** [116 C4] Above Funaná d'Vila on the main *praça*; ⏲ 19.00–03.00 Mon–Sat, closed Tue & Sun. The first games bar in Sal offers poker, blackjack & live music & barbecues on the rooftop terrace.

🍸 **Pirata** [116 A2] Near Enacol petrol station; nightclub ⏲ late night–early morning at w/ends. Entrance fee.

🍸 **Tam Tam's** Rua Amílcar Cabral; ⏲ 08.00–01.00 Mon–Sat. A bar frequented by European expats.

🍸 **Turtle Shack** [117 G1] Cabaret & other entertainment each night (see *Where to eat* for details).

OTHER PRACTICALITIES

Airlines Book internal flights directly with the airline at the airport. At its office you take a queuing ticket, but you should still keep an eye out for queue-jumpers. In Santa Maria try vista verde tours, Barracuda or Morabitur.

Banks

$ **Banco Comercial do Atlântico** Opposite Nha Terra; ⊕ 09.00–15.00 Mon–Fri.

$ **Banco Interâtlantico** Rua 1 de Junho; ⊕ 09.00–15.00 Mon–Fri). Less busy than the Banco Comercial do Atlântico.

$ **Caixa Económica** Rua 1 de Junho; ✆ 242 1616; ⊕ 08.00–15.00 Mon–Fri.

Beauty therapy/hairdressers

Waikiki Spa [117 E4] Rua 1 de Agosto near Porto Antigo; m 977 6178; e waikikispa@ gmail.com; ⊕ 09.00–13.00 & 15.00–17.00 Mon–Sat. Manicure, pedicure, waxing, massage with Brazilian therapists.

Unica Rua 15 de Agosto; ✆ 242 1596; ⊕ 09.00–20.00 Mon–Sat. Beauty therapy & hairdressing.

Dentist

La Sourire Zona Tanquinho, near Leme Bedje, Santa Maria; ✆ 242 1919

Food shopping There is a wide range of good-quality food available in *minimercados* on Sal but availability varies. Many of the *lojas chineses* have also started selling food cheaply. Here are a few shops that usually have a good supply.

Bom Gourmet Rua Amílcar Cabral; ⊕ 09.30–13.00 & 16.30–20.00 Mon–Sat. Italian-owned deli selling meat, parmesan & other Italian cheeses & fresh fruit & vegetables including such rarities as rocket & cauliflower. They make their own delicious baguettes & sesame loaves (usually stocked around 12.00 & sold quickly).

Delta Eastern end of Rua Amílcar Cabral; ⊕ 08.00–20.00 Mon–Sat. Owned by the large food importer that supplies many of the big hotels, this shop occasionally stocks British foods & has a range of cheeses & wines, but isn't cheap.

Enacol [116 A2] Garage at the entrance to Santa Maria. Has a shop that often has things you won't find elsewhere.

Garrafeira do Sal Behind the main road. An off-licence with a wide variety of wines, spirits & imported beers & cider.

Kazu Just to the east of Enacol petrol station on the big tarmac road. Brand new, large supermarket with the usual tinned foods, plus bread, fresh fruit & vegetables & occasionally some European imports.

Merceria RG/Mateus Opposite Porto Antigo; ⊕ early until late Mon–Sat. A wide range of tinned, dry & fresh foods as well as bread & ice cream.

Minimercado Andrade [116 C3] Rua Amílcar Cabral; ⊕ early until late daily. Good for staples such as rice, milk, eggs & tinned foods, they sell bread & fresh food, but sometimes the fruit & vegetables are past their best.

Wind Shop Rua Amílcar Cabral; ⊕ 08.00–20.00 daily. Usually has a good range of fruit & vegetables at reasonable prices as well as butter & cheese.

Shirley's La Piazza, Zona António de Sousa; m 972 1485; ⊕ 09.00–19.00 Mon–Sat. At the far end of Santa Maria's eastern residential area this British-owned *minimercado* stocks familiar British foods including Bird's custard, stir-fry sauces & Bisto. The owner also makes & freezes ready meals such as lasagne, sweet-&-sour chicken & pies, as well as vegetarian sausages & quiche. Will cook to order if contacted in advance. Walk past the Sab Sab Hotel & ask for directions or take a taxi.

Furniture and household items There are several options for furnishing your newly completed apartment.

Aiga Beach side of the main *praça*; m 918 3330; ☉ 09.00–20.00 Mon–Fri. Wicker furniture, lights & soft furnishings.

Archangelo [116 D4] The Arcade/Arcadia; ☏ 242 1686; e arcangelo@cvtelecom.cv; ☉ 09.30–13.00 & 16.00–19.00 Mon–Fri. Furniture & soft furnishings.

Boa Vista Property Services Zona Tanquinho; ☏ 242 2036; m 985 7031; e info@boavsitapropertyservices.com. Furniture & household goods imported from the UK.

Sal Holiday Near the post office; ☏ 242 1190; e sales@salholiday.com; ☉ 08.30–12.30 & 14.30–18.30 Mon–Sat. Large items of furniture & fitted kitchens.

Smythe Interiors [116 D4] The Arcade/Arcadia opposite Porto Antigo II; m 987 0369; www.smytheineriors.com. Furniture packs, blinds, curtains, mosquito screens & bedding.

Veranda On the main road out of town towards Espargos; e veranda@verandafurniture.com. Expensive Italian furniture from Cotton Bay's partner.

Zanadoo Djadsal Moridias ☉ 10.00–13.00 & 15.30–19.30 Mon–Sat. Soft furnishings, crockery & kitchen items.

Hospital Clinitur [117 F1], a large private clinic, is on the road from Santa Maria to the resort hotels (☏ *242 9090;* m *988 7075;* ☉ *08.00–15.00 Mon–Sat (on call for emergencies)).* Murdeira has a medical centre (☏*241 2451;* m *592 3464;* ☉ *09.00–13.00 & 15.00–20.00 Mon–Fri, 09.00–12.00 Sat)* with services ranging from gynaecology and physiotherapy to dentistry. Alternatively, try the Posto Sanitário de Santa Maria (☏ *242 1130);* or the new hospital just outside Espargos (see page 112).

Internet There are several cafés (price per hour in brackets): on Rua 1 de Junho, Protect Cabo Verde (200$); on Rua Amílcar Cabral, IPNet (*www.ipnetsal.com*) (200$); Cybershop, near the post office (200$); and Access Net, behind the sports stadium (150$). Santa Maria has Wi-Fi in most places provided by Cabocom (*www.cabocom.cv*). Vouchers to access this service from your own laptop or mobile device are available from their office and various outlets. A voucher for one hour is €5 and for a monthly subscription prices start at €40. Turtle Shack offers free Wi-Fi (you need your own laptop). There is free internet in the town square which can be picked up in the bars and restaurants nearby.

Laundry Serilimpo, next to Bar Onda [116 A2] on the left-hand side just as you come into Santa Maria (m *995 3494;* ☉ *08.00–17.00 Mon–Sat).*

Pharmacy [116 B3] The green building opposite Djadsal apartments at the entrance to town.

Police [116 D3] (☏ *242 1132).* The big new building on the new tarmac road in the northern part of Santa Maria.

Post office [117 E4] (☉ *08.00–12.00 & 14.00–17.00 Mon–Fri).* The large, pink building to the east of town.

Sail repair Sal Sail Repairs (m *988 7386;* e *sal.sail.repairs@gmail.com)* offers windsurf, sail and kite repairs or any other heavy-duty items.

Shopping Souvenirs can be bought at shops dotted all over town. The vast majority of these souvenirs are imported from Senegal and other parts of west Africa, but if

GENUINE CABO VERDE

Fed up with the lack of Cape Verdean products available and growing tired of tourists complaining of being hassled by street vendors claiming that their imported knick-knacks were from Cape Verde, the owner of the Cultural Café found his own solution. Genuine Cabo Verde is an open-air market just off the main *praça*. Open 09.00–23.00 daily, this charming market only sells Cape Verdean handicrafts, *grogue*, the best *piri-piri* (hot sauce) in town, and other produce from the islands. Even better, no-one will induce you to buy as this kind of sales technique is anathema to Cape Verdeans. You can also have a drink and eat a highly recommended burger here (for details, see *Where to eat*, page 122).

you look around you can find a few products made in Cape Verde. One of the best places to go is Genuine Cabo Verde [116 C4] (see above for more information), an open-air market with a laid-back approach. Sol e Sal and Artesanto Cerâmica on Rua 1 de Junho are also recommended. Music can be bought at a number of places (and at the airport shop). Fruit and vegetables can be bought from street vendors opposite the bakery or on Rua Amílcar Cabral. Surf clothes, accessories and a few boards are for sale at Angulo's [117 G5] and Pura Vida (near the taxi rank). Suncream and other toiletries can be found in, often unmarked, Chinese stores (*lojas chineses*), where you can also find cheap clothes, shoes and household items.

Telephone The cheapest rates are from the post office. Calls are also possible from several internet cafés, including Protect Cabo Verde, Turtle Shack and opposite Relax Café on Rua Amílcar Cabral. You can make calls for 30$/minute to most European countries from Access Net behind the sports stadium. If you are staying for a while or you need to make a lot of calls you could consider buying a local SIM card. These are available from the CV Telecom (near BCA bank, English spoken) for €3–5 and include credit. You will need an unlocked phone and your passport. You can also make calls and purchase credit from the wooden booth in the middle of the main square.

Tourist information [116 A3] There is a booth operated by the Câmara Municipal do Sal at the entrance to Santa Maria, near the roundabout with information about hotels and excursions (⊕ *09.00–12.00 & 15.30–21.00 daily*).

WHAT TO SEE AND DO Santa Maria is a base for the surfing, windsurfing and fishing that are the chief activities of the island. (See *Activities*, page 103.) Beach basking on its stunning white sands is popular. You can also visit the Santa Maria saltpans – walk inland through the northern part of Santa Maria, and they are on the other side.

OTHER PLACES TO VISIT

These are arranged in clockwise order beginning at Santa Maria, to be of use to those doing a tour of the island.

SANTA MARIA SALINA Located behind Costa Fragata, the salina can be found by walking directly north from the Sab Sab Hotel. The salina is still worked by hand by a small community; unfortunately they cannot sell the fruits of their labour since it does not meet required regulations for quality and sanitary control. You can walk between the saltpans and early in the morning it is possible to see a variety of birds.

PONTA PRETA A stunning beach with a restaurant from which to appreciate it, Ponta Preta is a favourite of windsurfers and surfers (see *Surfing*, page 106). It is possible to reach the beach by walking for about an hour around the coast from Santa Maria. Alternatively, drive along the road that goes west from Santa Maria towards the resort hotels, turn right opposite Hotel Crioula and go straight ahead for approximately 2km. You will see, after a few minutes, the timber-built restaurant, and a minute after that you should find a rough track leading towards the water.

✕ Where to eat

✕ **Ponta Preta** 242 1774; m 991 8613; ⊕ 10.00–17.00 Tue–Sun. Large wooden building with a big deck & sunbeds serving salads, snacks, fish, seafood, meat & spaghetti overlooking the beach. Owned by the same people as Café Kréol in Santa Maria. $$

BAIA DA MURDEIRA This bay lies about 8km north of Santa Maria. The coast here is quite rocky, with some smaller sandy areas and a fine, quiet beach just to the south. There is a resort here – Murdeira Village. It is gated but you can enter and use the beach, pool and so forth if you are a customer of the bar or restaurant.

⌂ Where to stay

⌂ **Murdeira Village** (40 rooms + apts & villas) Espargos (office); 241 1604/2308; e reservas@murdeiravillage.com; www.murdeiravillage.com. Some tourists have experienced problems trying to book directly with Murdeira management or with certain online agencies. Hotel rooms are high quality with AC, TV & verandas, but apartments are small. But the beachfront villas are pleasant with wonderful views out to Monte Leão. They have all the kit, such as dishwasher, CD player & washing machine. Facilities at the resort include a swimming pool & children's pool, snack bars, a restaurant with a sunset view, gym & car rental but check these are operational before booking. $$$$

CALHETA FUNDA A favourite with locals at the weekend, this lovely little beach is usually deserted and is a fine place for a swim, snorkel and picnic. See *Cycling*, page 108, for a description of how to get there.

MURDEIRA TO PALMEIRA A few places of interest or beauty (and sometimes both) lie hidden within the land that stretches, like a vast natural car park, between Murdeira and Palmeira.

Monte Leão At the far northern end of Murdeira Bay there is a dead-end track to the west, which leads to the coastal foot of Monte Leão, the unmistakable 'lion' gazing out to sea. It is known on the maps as Rabo de Junco.

Ponta da Parede There is a small, secluded beach here, about 0.5km before the end of the track to Monte Leão. There's a small blowhole and some pretty rockpools.

Viewpoint After visiting Monte Leão, about 2.5km back along the track, there is another track branching to the north, which later joins a bigger track to the left that leads to this viewpoint which stands some 45m above sea level. There's a good view over Monte Leão and down to Santa Maria.

Fontona This is a pretty, tree-filled oasis that lies about 3km south of Palmeira. It can be reached by following the track from the viewpoint (above) for a further 2.5km, in a northwesterly and then northerly direction. Alternatively, it can be reached from Palmeira (take the signposted turning to the left off the road into Palmeira).

PALMEIRA Palmeira is a friendly little place which is on the route of many round-island tours. Other than at these times, it is a peaceful village with a couple of excellent restaurants. At the harbour you can lounge at the bar overlooking the water with the locals and watch them frolic in the water (and join in) on public holidays, or chat to visiting yachties taking a break on their passage across the Atlantic. Get there by *aluguer* from Espargos (50$) or by walking or hitching.

There is an **internet café**, Cyber Internet Patrica, next to Snack Bar Gomes (℡ *241 3184;* ⊕ *08.00–22.00 daily*).

✗ Where to eat and drink

✗ **Siempre Insieme Italian Restaurant**
Near the town hall building; ℡ 241 2300;
⊕ 12.00–15.00 & 19.00–23.00. $$$

✗ **Da Romano's** A little Italian spaghetteria on the left as you drive in on the main road but often closed. $

✗ **La Cantinha** Just past the church; ⊕ 12.00–15.00 & 19.00–23.00. Italian-run restaurant with good food. $$$

✗ **Taverna Restaurant** Near the beach; ⊕ 12.00–22.00. $$

✗ **Minimercado Continental** ℡ 241 3366; ⊕ 08.00–19.00. $

✗ **Minimercado Musmarra** ℡ 241 1534; ⊕ 08.00–19.00. $

✗ **Snack Bar Gomes** m 986 5214; ⊕ 08.00–00.00. On the main street on the left as you enter Palmeira. $

BURACONA This is an exhilarating natural swimming pool encased in black lava rock over which white foam cascades every few minutes. Nearby is the Blue Eye, an underground pool reached through a large hole in the ground. Divers can swim along an underground tunnel out into the sea.

If you are not in a car you'll have to walk the 6km from Palmeira. Follow the main road into Palmeira until just before the port gates. On the right is the yellow customs building. Turn right before you pass it. Immediately, take the left fork which goes round the front of a desalinisation plant, and take a turn left towards the sea. The road continues, past a boat yard, and then into a land which is about 25 shades of brown (including chocolate, wine-stain and rusted) covered with a few bent-over trees. Superimposed on this is a disused wind farm, a few scavenging goats and the odd anti-litter sign with plastic bags caught round it. The coastline itself is wildly beautiful, a jumble of black lava rock and waves. You pass a lesser pool but walk the full 6km to reach Buracona, which is just before **Monte Leste** (263m). It's a great place for a swim and a picnic (but don't leave belongings unattended).

There are the ubiquitous African craft sellers and a small snack bar selling cold drinks. Unfortunately this has led to an increase in litter and the beauty of the Blue Eye is increasingly spoiled by plastic bags and bottles floating on the surface. Go early if you want to avoid large tour groups.

PEDRA DE LUME This is a spectacular place, and best appreciated in silence, so the poetic should rise early to reach it before anyone else. Inside a ring of low mountains lies a sweeping geometry of saltpans in blue, pink and green depending on their stage of salt formation, all separated by stone walls. The old rusted cables and a dirty mountain of salt testify to more prosperous days. You can sit on the crater slope in the shade listening to the water lapping in the lakes below and the cry of an occasional bird circling the crater rim.

There is nowhere to stay in this area, and the planned Stefanina development is now an ugly concrete half-finished monstrosity marring the previously beautiful vista from the small town.

History Manuel Martins, who developed Santa Maria, had a business here as well. Bags of salt were strapped to pack animals, which had to climb up the slopes of the volcano and down the other side to reach the port. In 1804, a tunnel was cut through the volcano wall, and in 1919 transport was made easier when a businessman from Santa Maria and a French firm bought the salt company and built the tramway, the remnants of which can be seen today. They could then transfer 25 tonnes an hour to the port, from where it was shipped to Africa. But markets shifted and the saltpans fell into disuse by 1985: today they do not even produce enough salt for Sal. Pedra de Lume is still inhabited but it feels like a ghost town except on public holidays.

There is disagreement about how salt water rises into the bottom of this crater – some believe it comes from deep in the earth, but the most orthodox explanation is that it infiltrates through the natural holes in volcanic rock along the kilometre distance from the sea.

Getting there The village is off the main Santa Maria to Espargos road and you can reach it by taxi from Espargos (300$; if you are being driven into the crater and then back to town, from 600$) or, sometimes, by *aluguer* from Espargos. A taxi from Santa Maria costs 1,500$. You can try hitching but you might end up walking all the way.

✗ Where to eat and drink

✗ **Cadamosto Restaurant** 〵241 2210;
⊕ 09.00–18.00 daily. This large seaside
restaurant down by the shore has an inviting
terrace, good seafood, pizzas & ice cream. $$$$

✗ **Café** In the crater, serving drinks & snacks.

What to see and do When you have looked around the village with its important-looking housing blocks and its little white church you can examine the relics of the pulley system for taking salt from the crater and loading ships. Then turn inland, along a track that lies just after the church, and follow the old overhead cables uphill. After a few minutes the track arrives at a car park. Ahead is the tunnel into the crater.

Inside the crater a centre has been built where it is possible to receive treatments such as thalassotherapy (€13 for eight minutes); antioxidant treatment to face and feet (€11 for 13 minutes); or an application of water, salina salt and aromatic oil, said to be draining and nourishing (€11 for ten minutes). There are also toilets, and a shower for those who have bathed in the salt lakes, and a café serving drinks and snacks.

It is possible to walk at least halfway round the crater rim by leaving the crater through the tunnel, taking a track to the right and just choosing a shallow part of the slope to ascend.

Since the salina is in private hands you are also obliged to pay to go in. The cost is €5 per person and includes a drink.

The old wreck Head south from Pedra de Lume following the rough tracks along the coast and you will see the remains of a wreck sticking out of the sea. It

CUCUMBERS IN THE DESERT   *Alex Alper*

Deep in the heart of Sal's waterless moonscape, cucumbers, tomatoes, lettuce, peppers and other crops are being harvested year round thanks to hydroponics.

Hydroponics is soil-less culture. Developed by Germans in the 1860s, it uses nutrient solution in place of soil, which increases yields and greatly reduces water use. While hydroponics is practised widely in Europe, the Americas and the Middle East, it is nascent in Cape Verde. There are farms in São Francisco (Tom Drescher's 'VenteSol Cultura Hidroponica e Turistica') and São Domingos on Santiago in addition to Sal. A popular method is the Nutrient Film Technique (NFT). A shallow stream of nutrient-rich water flows constantly along a slightly tilted trough, which holds the plants. A non-soil medium like gravel may be used to anchor the plants. Usually a mesh encloses the crop, retaining moisture and protecting against insects.

The advantages are tremendous. Water input is reportedly between 5% and 10% of that necessary for normal agriculture, even less than what is used by drip irrigation. That's because no water is wasted through soil absorption or excess evaporation, and because water can be recycled through the trough. Hydroponics also uses only 10% of the land required for normal agriculture and there is no need for weeding or ground preparation. Crops are usually healthy and mature quickly, because the microbes that cause weak plant growth reside only in soil.

Start-up costs are high. One farmer estimates having spent €6,000–7,000 to set up his 500m farm. And the method requires constant energy as the water must keep flowing to prevent rapid plant death. Nevertheless, monthly yields were so good that he claims to have recouped his investment after only seven months.

is possible to snorkel here although it is a bit of a walk across slippery rocks. Take care as the sea can be very rough on this side. A little further on you will see a small sandbank. At certain times it is possible to spot the fins of schools of nurse sharks (*Ginglymostoma cirratum*) that swim into this area which is less than 1m deep. Further south are some pleasant bays and coves but, ultimately, a dead end.

SERRA NEGRA This is a stunning stretch of coast. Beaches alternate with black rocks lashed by white waves and the cliffs of Serra Negra rise behind them providing a touch of topographical grandeur unusual for Sal. This is a good place for a peaceful day away from the crowds. You can swim here, but note that the northern end of the beach gets cut off by high tide so, in common with the whole of the eastern coast, you should take care. It's a lonely spot, except on public holidays, so take the usual precautions against opportunistic theft. There are no facilities.

Getting there requires a 4x4 or quad bike and is hard (but not impossible) to navigate, over slightly tricky terrain, if you've never been there before. The driver must negotiate the sparse network of rough tracks and rocky ground that lies between the main road and the east coast. Coming from Santa Maria, turn right at the roundabout just before the chapel on the hill on to a dirt track. Follow the track as it forks to the right and head for Restaurant Demiflor (signposted but now closed); there will be another fork to the right, marked with painted rocks, which you should follow (going straight on will bring you to the town dump). When

Sal OTHER PLACES TO VISIT

4

you are past the restaurant, turn left and follow the coast. You will cross some dry *ribeiras* which look steeper than they actually are. You will see a sign when you have reached Serra Negra. (See also *Hikes*, below.)

COSTA DA FRAGATA This wild coast is hardly visited, most people preferring the calmer western and southern beaches. Its designation as a nature reserve should ensure some degree of protection for the important dune ecosystem. It is home to many native plants and an important turtle-nesting area. (See below for a description of where to start and finish.)

HIKES

Hikers can go more or less anywhere on Sal – the important thing is to take plenty of water and a hat. Even on the very quiet beaches it is rare for muggings or theft to take place, but take minimal possessions and ask for advice. A good, 1:50,000 map is published by Goldstadt (see *Chapter 2, Practical Information*, page 68).

1 SAB SAB HOTEL–IGREJINHA
Distance: 2km (circuit); time: 1 hour; difficulty: 1 (JC)
Follow the instructions for the bike trail (20 minutes) (see *Cycling*, page 108). You can make this a circuit by continuing north to the start of the beach on Costa Fragata, turning left and walking through the dunes back to Santa Maria (20 minutes).

2 COSTA FRAGATA
Distance: 6km (circuit); time: 1 hour; difficulty: 1 (JC)
Costa Fragata is a natural reserve and in theory is protected from development. Along the wildest coast, subject to strong northwesterlies and with attractive dunes and some birdlife, walking one way will take around one hour. In the summer you will see many turtle tracks, and in the winter dozens of sails of kitesurfers flying in the sky. Start at Grijinha beach bar or take a taxi to Kite Beach (500$) and walk southwards along the coast to Santa Maria. Don't rely on getting a taxi back from Kite Beach unless it is during the windsurfing season.

3 SERRA NEGRA
Distance: 1km (one way); time: 30 minutes; difficulty: 1 (JC)
To many, this is the most beautiful beach on Sal. It consists of three secluded bays surrounded by tall cliffs. Other than at weekends in the summer it is deserted. The area is home to many types of birds including the red-billed tropicbird (*Phaethon aethereus*), known locally as Rabo de Junco, and is an important turtle-nesting beach. It is possible to walk to Serra Negra from Santa Maria but it is a dry, dusty and rocky walk. Much better to drive to the start of the beach and then take a walk to the end (30 minutes) – to reach the last bay you need to walk over a rocky area. You can also drive along a track around the back of the cliffs, park and walk to the top for a magnificent view of the coastline. There is a bit of scrambling to get to the top, so you need to be in reasonable shape to do this. At the top you will see cairns and tributes built from stones and shells to friends, family and lost loves.

4 SANTA MARIA PIER–PONTA PRETA
Distance: 4km (one way); time: 1.5 hours; difficulty: 1 (JC)
A big favourite with locals and resident expats alike, this is a delight first thing in the morning. Heading west out of Santa Maria, this takes you past all the big hotels and

on to Ponta Sino, a long, unspoilt nature reserve with Sal's only lighthouse. Turning north you will pass the RIU Hotel; continue up past the dune until you reach the Ponta Preta Restaurant. You can either return the same way or walk beside the road directly inland from the restaurant, where you can easily stop a taxi.

5 MONTE LEÃO
Distance: 2km (circuit); time: 1.5 hours; difficulty: 2 (JC)
Follow the trail to the top of Monte Leão at the northwestern end of Murdeira Bay for an amazing view of the surrounding area (one hour). Eagles and their nests are frequently seen here. You will need a rental car or hire a taxi driver to reach Monte Leão.

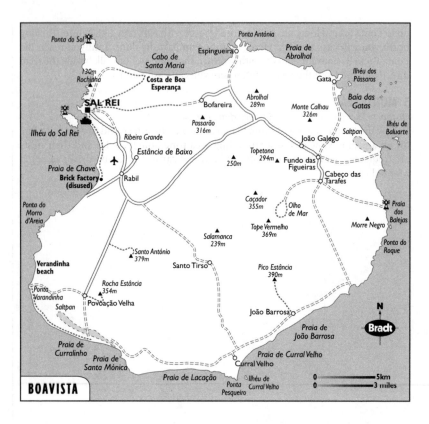

Ponta do Sol

Ponta Antónia

Espingueira

Praia de Abrolhal

Cabo de Santa Maria

Ilhéu dos Pássaros

130m
Rochinha

Gata

Costa de Boa Esperança

Baía das Gatas

SAL REI

Abrolhal
289m

Monte Calhau
326m

Bofareira

Ilhéu de Baluarte

Ilhéu do Sal Rei

Ribeira Grande

Passarão
316m

Estância de Baixo

João Galego

Saltpan

Praia de Chave

Topetona
294m

Fundo das Figueiras

Brick Factory
(disused)

Rabil

250m

Cabeço das Tarafes

Ponta do Morro d'Areia

Caçador
355m

Olho de Mar

Praia dos Balejas

Tope Vermelho
369m

Morre Negro

Salamanca
239m

Ponta do Roque

Verandinha beach

Santo António
379m

Santo Tirso

Pico Estância
390m

Ponta Varandinha

Rocha Estância
354m

Saltpan

Povoação Velha

João Barrosa

N

Bradt

Praia de João Barrosa

Praia de Curralinho

Praia de Santa Mónica

Praia de Curral Velho

Praia de Lacação

Curral Velho

Ponta Pesqueiro

Ilhéu de Curral Velho

0 ——— 5km
0 ——— 3 miles

BOAVISTA

AGENCIA DE VIAGENS
ISLAND TOUR · FLIGHT TICKET · HORSE RIDING · RENT A CAR

Morena LDA

tel - fax 2511445   e-mail: boavistapoint@cvtelecom.cv

5

Boavista

Mornas Dancing
In the sensuous bodies of the sensuous girls
In the dyspnoea of the brave waves
Dying in the sand
In the rolling of the
Languid and gentle waves,
Boa Vista,
The unforeseen
Scenery
Of sands marching on the village

Jorge Barbosa

Boavista is the siren island. For many seafarers down the years, it was the first sight of land for months. The white dunes, like cusps of icing, must have been an alluring sight but Boavista's beaches have drawn many to a watery grave. It is ringed by reefs and its iron-rich rock formations send ships' compasses spinning. Over 40 ships have foundered here, within sight of land.

Beyond the idyllic beaches another story unfolds. The bleached land has a terrible beauty but it will leave you feeling parched and a little crazed by the sun. The only forests are petrified remnants on the shores: aeons ago, Boavista was a moister place.

In many parts the struggle for existence has become too much. Villages are abandoned, and sand drifts across the floors of their empty houses.

HIGHLIGHTS

Go for walks along deserted, searingly beautiful beaches, drifting dunes and desert oases; go for wind- and kitesurfing and go for game fishing. There is diving, though currents and wind can make it hard to explore many shipwrecks and can impair the clarity of the water. Go for fledgling ecotourism centred on birds, turtles, corals and whales.

SUGGESTED ITINERARY AND NUMBER OF DAYS You can see Boavista in a day by 4x4, although you will be hot and exhausted by the end of it. Three full days would be an ideal period in which to do a more relaxed vehicle tour that encompasses some of the remoter beaches; do a hike, perhaps to the north and/or a quad-bike expedition, perhaps to the Viana Desert, with maybe a watersports session or an eco trip thrown in as well.

Don't expect any mountain walking. If the landscape or the watersports do not appeal then the only other reason to come here is sunbathing: there is little in the way of conventional tourist 'attractions' to visit.

BACKGROUND INFORMATION

HISTORY With little to offer but salt, Boavista, like Sal, did not receive much attention after its discovery on 14 May 1460. It was named Saint Cristovão until, it is said, a storm-tossed sailor's triumphant cry: *'Boa vista!'*, the equivalent of 'Land ahoy!', led to its present name.

Island life has been punctuated by shipwrecks – tragedies that were often fortuitous for the starving islanders who would clamber over the rocks after a stormy night to retrieve food and goods from the debris. It is said that in times of starvation the people would tie a lamp to a donkey's tail and send it in the darkness along the coastal reefs in the hope of luring ships to their doom.

Most ships were wrecked by a strange conflation of circumstances. A strong and gusty tradewind combined with a powerful current pulled sailing ships towards the island. Flat, and often shrouded in a dusty haze, Boavista could be invisible until those boats rammed into the hidden rocks of its northern and eastern coasts. Meanwhile, maps and charts consistently placed Boavista several miles to the west of where it actually is.

Against this background, modern life began very slowly. It was visited early in its history, in 1498, by Christopher Columbus on his third voyage. By then the island already had a few inhabitants and was also used as a leper colony for well-to-do Europeans. After three days Columbus left, made a brief stop at Santiago and went on, reporting that the islands had: 'a false name... since they are so barren that I saw no green thing in them and all the people were infirm, so that I did not dare to remain in them.'

Apart from that, little happened on the island for the first 150 years after its discovery except desecration by goats. In 1580, there were only 50 people living there and in 1619, there was just a group of hunters (after the goats).

Then English sailors discovered Boavista's high-quality salt and an economy began in about 1620, based at Povoação Velha – its first village. By 1677, Boavista even had a priest, but periodic sackings shook its economy. English sailors attacked the island in 1684, taking chalices from the churches to trade on the African coast. There was another attack in 1697, and by 1702, the population of Povoação Velha was routinely armed.

Nearing the 1800s, Porto Inglês (now Sal Rei) became the most important town on the island and salt production was increasing, reaching its zenith in the first half of the 19th century. But the pillages continued in 1815 and 1817. The final desecration came in 1818 when the town was razed. As a result a fort was built on the Ilhéu do Sal Rei, and with this protection Boavista began an era of relative prosperity, becoming an important cultural centre. In 1834, it was even argued that the town should become the capital of Cape Verde. The Luso-British anti-slavery commission made Boavista its base in 1843.

The fortunes of even the prosperous dwindled, however, when the building of the port at Mindelo transformed the island of São Vicente into the new trading centre. When Charles Thomas, chaplain to the American Africa Squadron (an anti-slavery police) visited in 1855 he found the inhabitants to be starving and the cattle 'with sad faces and tears in their eyes, walking solemnly in cudless rumination over grassless fields'. The chief amusements of the people, he reported, were 'fishing, salt-making and going to funerals'. Fortunes changed again towards the end of the 19th century with increasing business in lime, clay tiles and castor oil. Over the last hundred years or so the island has been the victim of drought, famine and grasshopper infestation which has led to emigration.

Perhaps the island's most famous son is Aristides Pereira, the 12th son of the priest of Boavista, who became the first president of Cape Verde in 1975.

BOAVISTA TODAY Boavista is an island marked by tragedy and struggle. There is little in its history, though, to guide it through the pressures it faces today. On the one hand it is poised to participate, for the first time, in international prosperity, through mass tourism. On the other it seems ready to fall headlong into destruction – plundered by the same industry and with little to show financially as a result.

Boavista's beaches have an almost traumatic beauty. In these days when so many bewitching landscapes have been consumed by tourism, and the European palate is jaded, Boavista has allure. Exploiting this, most people seem to believe, means to build, build, build massive hotels and streetfuls of apartment blocks and condominiums, hence the prediction that this island of just over 6,000 people could be welcoming a million visitors a year by 2020. This is the rationale behind the projected construction of 15,000 beds at Santa Mónica Beach; 18,000 beds in total for Chaves Beach; nearly 3,000 beds for Morro de Areia: in total a possible 50,000 beds. The coast from Sal Rei to Curral Velho could be filled with hotels and apartments. What Boavistan, laden with an ancestry of famine and isolation, could fail to be dazzled?

But over the last few years some voices have questioned Boavista's direction. There is the economic question: how much does an all-inclusive resort hotel under foreign ownership, built under generous tax concessions, actually make for Boavista? Then there is the more subtle question: might Boavista's progress destroy its very capital and thus, ultimately, extinguish itself?

One group that has spoken out about this is the World Wildlife Fund (WWF), concerned mainly about Boavista's role in the international fight against species collapse. 'The planning process lacks transparency,' said Ricardo Monteiro in 2006. 'Nothing has been done to assess the potential effect of land speculation, inflation, and increased immigration to the island. And, it does not address the likely negative impact on the natural beauty and biodiversity of the island.' 'The plans for Boavista,' added Arona Soumare, WWF's Marine Protected Areas Programme Officer, based in Dakar, Senegal, are 'massive, destructive, operations'.

To develop a vision for Boavista and regain some control, the government formed the Society for the Development of Boavista and Maio (*www.sdtibm.cv*), a state-owned company with the power to decide who gets to invest in what, within the tourism development zones. 'We don't want to make the same mistakes as were made in Sal,' said a society representative in Boavista. 'We want quality tourism and benefit to the local people.' The society, launched in 2005 and rejigged in 2007, has strict criteria to apply to developments.

Since then, however, development has begun on yet another beach, Lacação, where a massive complex of hotels, apartments and golf courses, taking up an area of 3,432ha, is planned. Construction of the massive new all-inclusive RIU Hotel has already had a significant impact on this important turtle-nesting beach, while further building phases mean there is no untouched land on this section of the southern coast. It seems that the island's government is merely ushering Boavista towards her own destruction.

5

GEOGRAPHY Boavista is the closest island to the African mainland, and 50km from Sal. It is the third largest, at 620km², and sparsely populated, with only 6,000 inhabitants. The island is very flat with the highest point, Pico Estância, at only 390m. The barren, stony landscape is covered in many areas with white sand and drifting dunes, which pile up on its western coast. The dunes have swallowed various buildings and covered the once-busy saltpans just outside Sal Rei.

There are 55km of white beaches and, in the centre, Sahara-like oases filled with date palms. Since independence, environmental measures have been taken such as the building of catchment dams and planting of trees.

NATURAL HISTORY Boavista's biodiversity is of global importance as it includes endemic species of plants, birds and insects, as well as marine species. Its shores provide important nesting sites and feeding grounds for endangered marine turtles. Humpback whales come here to breed. A broad swathe of eastern Boavista is a hugely important coastal ecosystem, encompassing wetlands and nesting sites for thousands of turtles. It is scattered with temporary wetlands all the way from Curral Velho at its southern tip to Ponta Antónia in the north. There are breeding colonies for a variety of seabirds along this shore and its offshore islets (Pássaros, Baluarte and Curral Velho). Corals grow in small bays and coves of the north and northeast coasts, protected from high swell and strong currents. These quiet and warm inshore waters are often frequented by nurse sharks (*Ginglymostoma cirratum*), juvenile hawksbill turtles (*Eretmochelys imbricata*) and green turtles (*Chelonia mydas*).

Protected areas In 2003, a law was passed approving 47 protected areas across the archipelago, including 14 on Boavista. The technical work carried out to delineate these areas has not, however, been approved, which has left them vulnerable.

After 2003, the government published its zones for integrated tourist development (ZDTIs). Land that was part of the protected areas was reallocated to ZDTI areas

WORKING WITH TURTLES ON BOAVISTA

Each season, European and Cape Verdean researchers led by Professor Luis Felipe Lopez Jurado of Las Palmas University gather under the umbrella of Cabo Verde Natura 2000, a conservation group, to study the loggerhead turtles (*Caretta caretta*) that nest at Ervatão Beach. They want to understand the status, distribution and numbers of the turtles. It's a night job, and as soon as volunteers spot a turtle coming ashore they lie on the ground and crawl towards her. After she has laid her eggs and is on her way back to the sea, they put a chip in the turtle and ID attached with tags on the flippers. Turtles equipped with satellite transmitters send information about their migratory routes and feeding areas back to scientists. Meanwhile, hatchlings are counted, weighed and measured before being released into the sea.

Since 2008 another group, Turtle Foundation, has also become active, concentrating on preventing the slaughter of the turtles as they nest. Patrols by international volunteers and Cape Verdean soldiers are made through the night on Canto, Boa Esperança, Norte and Lacação.

The growth of tourism is bringing increasing problems for this endangered species through loss of habitat, light pollution and increasing numbers of cars, quad bikes and dune buggies driving on nesting beaches.

WHALES

Interest is growing in the whales that frequent the waters around Boavista and other islands. Over the last decade Beatrice Jann, a biologist from the University of Basel in Switzerland, has been documenting sightings of humpbacks and other species. Sometimes Pedro López, a naturalist who has been living in Boavista for a decade, gathers what information he can for her during the whale-watching trips he organises for tourists. Other groups such as the Irish Whale and Dolphin Group have organised research trips to try to uncover a link between the Cape Verdean whales and the whales sighted around Ireland.

Whales are identified by the undersides of their tail flukes. Each underside is unique to that whale. Their shifting patches of black and white look like an ink-blot pattern. Researchers photograph these patterns and send them to a store at Bar Harbour in Maine, USA, where there are now 'fingerprints' of 5,000 whales. 'It's sort of an Interpol of the humpbacks,' says Beatrice. By matching observations, scientists can piece together the whales' migrations. They have found whales photographed in Norway turning up in the Dominican Republic, and whales from western Canada appearing in Japan.

– most notably the coastal part of the Morro de Areia area in the southwest of the island and much of Praia da Lacação, the beach to the east of Santa Mónica.

The protected areas are Curral Velho, Monte Caçador and Pico Forçado. There are nature reserves at Boa Esperança in the north and Ponta do Sol at the northwest tip, Tartaruga, and Morro de Areia on the southwestern coast. An expanse of the northwest has been made into a natural park. Many of these areas will be affected by roads designed to link the island's villages. National monuments are: Monte Santo António, Monte Estância, Rocha Estância and Ilhéu do Sal Rei (the islet opposite Sal Rei). The islets of Baluarte, Pássaros and Curral Velho are Integral Nature Reserves (RNIs)

Ramsar sites It may seem counterintuitive, but Boavista has one of the largest wetlands in the Macaronesia region. It stretches from Curral Velho, at its southern tip, up to Ervatão, and this region has been designated a Ramsar site – that is, a wetland of international interest.

It's not wet all the year round – just over the rainy season and during extreme spring tides. But this is enough for it to be an important host to many migratory birds coming from Europe and west Africa.

A second Ramsar site is Rabil Lagoon, which acquired this status in 2005 and is also categorised by BirdLife International as one of 12 important bird areas in Cape Verde. This site seems doomed, however, by the noise of aircraft arriving at the new international airport, quad bikes tripping through the area, quarrying and general developments on the coast.

Marine Boavista shares with Maio and Sal a single large marine platform that harbours the country's highest levels of marine biodiversity. The nearby João Valente seamount, an underwater mountain between Boavista and Maio, hosts a particularly rich biodiversity. Seamounts are known to fishermen for high concentrations of fish, and to researchers as rare and unique habitats.

Turtles Thousands of loggerhead turtles (*Caretta caretta*) nest on Boavista's east coast and especially its southeastern beaches annually, making it the second most important nesting site in the Atlantic Ocean and the third most important in the world, after the Florida Keys and Oman's Massirah Island. The key stretch for turtles is from Curral Velho in the south to As Gatas in the northeast.

The mother turtles crawl up the beaches between mid-June and late October. Once they have laid their eggs they disappear, leaving the hatchlings to fend for themselves. When the baby turtles emerge from their eggs in late August to late December, they make a frenzied dash for the sea. It is thought that the glimmering surface of the ocean is what attracts them – hence the problem that lights from houses and hotels could lure them in the wrong direction.

But development is not the only threat to turtles. There remains a strong local culture of turtle consumption, and dead turtles, the relics of this, sometimes litter the beaches. This is not done out of hunger, says Professor Luis Felipe Lopez Jurado, who has been studying turtles in Boavista since 1998, currently for the NGO Cabo Verde Natura 2000. 'The people killing turtles have big cars and jobs,' he says. 'They come down on a Friday night. Nobody needs the meat of the turtle to survive.'

Whales Sal Rei is the bay of choice for many humpback whales as a place to give birth and nurse their young. They arrive between December and April, nurse their

MASS WHALE STRANDINGS

The bodies of hundreds of melon-headed whales (*Peponocephala electra*) lay in an unending line, flippers pointing helplessly at the sky, along the sands of Chaves and Estoril beaches. How they came to die, *en masse*, within a 36-hour period in November 2007, is still unexplained.

It was late in the evening when some 265 whales washed up on Chaves Beach. Locals tried to refloat them but every time they did so the whales just swam back to the shore. There they died.

Just 36 hours later, another 70 whales beached themselves further north at Boca da Salina in front of the Riu Karamboa Hotel. Locals and tourists alike scrambled to help them, refloating them and swimming and boating with them into deeper water. This time, some 65 of them were saved.

By the time international experts arrived to help assess the situation, the bodies had been buried and advanced decay had destroyed much in the way of potential clues to what had happened. Scientists have managed to exclude many possible causes of the strandings, such as entanglement with fishing gear, disease, hunger or predation by sharks.

The whales were stranded just as the US nuclear submarine USS *Annapolis*, on a visit to Cape Verde, is thought to have been leaving the island of São Vicente. Might the use of active sonar have disrupted the whales' navigation or caused them to panic and seek to escape the noise? No-one knows.

Another mass whale stranding occurred in June 2010 when 50 pilot whales beached themselves on the northeastern coast of Sal, while at the same time another 40 became stranded on Santiago Island. This was followed by 50 dolphins stranding themselves on Chaves Beach in October 2010. Despite efforts by residents and tourists to refloat them, the group stranded themselves a further two times, and all perished. No-one understands the reason for these tragic events.

calves in a shallow haven free from waves, and then depart for the deep ocean (for more on whales, see *Natural history and conservation*, page 8).

Sharks The quiet bays and coves of the north are often frequented by nurse sharks (*Ginglymostoma cirratum*).

Birds The emblematic species of Boavista are the white-faced storm petrel (*Pelagodroma marina*) and the magnificent frigatebird (*Fregata magnificens*). Other sought-after birds are the cream-coloured courser (*Cursorius cursor*), and the Egyptian vulture (*Neophron percnopterus*). There are also breeding colonies of red-billed tropicbirds (*Phaethon aethereus*). The Cape Verde sparrow (*Passer iagoensis*), one of four endemic Cape Verdean birds, is found in Rabil Lagoon.

For the non-specialist the most eye-catching birds to watch for are perhaps the magnificent frigatebird, black with a 2m wing span and a long beak, hooked at the end. Males have a scarlet throat pouch which inflates in the breeding season. Secondly, look for the red-billed tropicbird, white with its eponymous red bill and a long, streaming white tail following behind.

Overall there are more than 20 species of bird breeding on Boavista. The areas of most interest are perhaps Ilhéu de Curral Velho, Ilhéu dos Pássaros, and the wetland areas, both fresh water and salty.

Flora The tamareira (*Phoenix atlantica*) and the date palm (*Phoenix dactilifera*) fill the lagoons and *ribeiras* of the island (see *Flora*, page 5, for more information on palm trees in Cape Verde).

ECONOMY Apart from the growing business of tourism, there is some business exporting dates and fishing (limited because of lack of investment in the large boats needed to withstand the stormy seas). An unusually poor soil thwarts agriculture. Villages across Boavista are supplied with water by tanker from a desalinisation plant in Sal Rei. Some water is drawn from the ground by windmills (many of which are broken) but this is brackish and not suitable for drinking. It is used for washing, and also for agriculture, although the salt content constrains the type of vegetable that can be grown. Salt production ceased in 1979.

HAZARDS
Crime Unfortunately robberies, some of them violent, are becoming increasingly frequent on Boavista. Many of these incidents take place on remote beaches with tourists being violently robbed in the dunes along Chaves Beach or in the vicinity of the wreck of the *Santa Maria*. There have also been instances of mass robberies of quad tours. The City Hall of Boavista has responded by calling in the army to work with the police and are working on the development of a programme of safe tourism. Take basic precautions – don't go walking alone in these areas and don't carry valuables with you. Also, try asking around about the security situation, because it would be a shame to restrict yourself unnecessarily.

Hiking Boavista is a parched landscape, bereft of shade, and could cause serious dehydration or sunburn for the unwary, particularly hikers. Kit must include several litres of water (as many as five for a full day's walking); boots for dealing with the stony ground and frequent, short hilly scrambles; and sun protection. The interior is empty: most folks gave up on the possibility of living there many years ago. Learn from them and take at least a map and preferably a compass. Swathes of Boavista have no mobile-phone coverage.

Driving If you rent a 4x4 remember that it is illegal to drive on beaches and dunes; stick to the tracks. If you become stranded help may be hard to find. Carry food, water and a spade – and leave details of your journey at your hotel.

Swimming Offshore winds and swells in the north make swimming periodically hazardous. In places (for example stretches of Chaves Beach or north of Espingueira) the beach slopes steeply and there can be a strong undertow. Check before you dip.

FESTIVALS

1 January	New Year (whole island)
6 January	Twelfth Night (João Galego and other northern villages)
3 May	Santa Cruz (Rabil slave liberation)
	Parades, drumming and whistling
4 May	Pidrona (Rabil)
8 May	São Roque (Povoação Velha)
Last weekend of May	Cruz Nhô Lolo (Estância de Baixo)
	Horse racing, *coladeras*, goat fighting
13 June	Santo António
	Procession to a church near the deserted Rock of Santo António
24 June	São João Baptista (northern area)
	Procession and offerings
4 July	Santa Isobel (Sal Rei)
	Boavista's most important feast day, attracting visitors from around the archipelago
15 August	Nossa Sra da Piedade (João Galego)
16 August	Saint Roque (Rabil) Praia da Cruz festival
	A week after the Baía das Gatas festival in São Vicente, this beach festival attracts national and international musicians.
8 December	Imaculada Conceição (Povoação Velha)

THE ORIGINS OF THE *MORNA*

The origins of the *morna* are obscure but it is said to have emerged on Boavista, named after the English word 'mourn' or perhaps the French word *'morne'*, meaning 'sad'. There are a multitude of theories as to how its characteristic melodies arose. According to the Cape Verdean historian António Germano Lima, one theory is that it came from the sound of fishermen's oars hitting the water on their long journeys, and their marking of the rhythm of the rowing with the call *'vo-ga... vo-ga'*. Others say it came from a mixture of musical types, such as the medieval Portuguese ballad, the *cancioneiro*, the Portuguese–Brazilian *modinhas* and the priests' liturgical chants. Lima himself favours the idea that the melancholy music must have been born from the hearts of slaves longing for home.

The modern *morna* was developed by Eugénio Tavares (see *Chapter 8, Brava*, page 240). Boavistan *mornas* are much livelier than Tavares's tearful versions. They can be full of satire, caricature, ridicule and dreams of revenge.

BY AIR There are direct international flights from Italy, the UK and Portugal, with more in the pipeline. There is a daily flight to and from Sal, with TACV and also a few times a week with Halcyonair. As with all internal flights it is best to book from home in order to be sufficiently early get a seat. It's cheaper, however, to book in-country.

Boavista International Airport The airport (↖ *251 1313*) is 6km south of the capital, Sal Rei, near to the town of Rabil. It's a pretty place with laid-back architecture and an endearing welcome notice in the arrivals hall. Not very airport-like at all, really. Facilities include a bar, ice-cream kiosk, bank, souvenir shops and two tour-operator offices (Morena and Barracuda). There is free Wi-Fi access if you have your own laptop.

Some hotels meet their clients with a minibus. *Hiaces* and *hiluxes* wait outside and can be hired as taxis. The charge to town is €10; the fare to the Marine Club (see *Where to stay*, page 148) is higher.

Transport back to the airport from Sal Rei can be found by loitering in the main square, but if your flight is at an odd time (eg: on a Sunday) it's better to ask your hotelier to arrange a vehicle.

BY FERRY Ferries come and ferries go. At the time of writing there is no regular ferry service to Boavista, and certainly none from Sal, whence many tourists want to come. The only ocean option, therefore, is a day trip from Sal – either by catamaran (faster, which maximises time on the island) or by boat (slower but cheaper).

BY YACHT The waters off Sal Rei offer a very good anchorage. Most people anchor between the southern end of the islet and the shore. Harbour officials are generally on the pier. There are few facilities for yachts; try the shop beside the Oasis Bar.

GETTING AROUND

BY PUBLIC TRANSPORT *Alugueres* run frequently between Sal Rei and Rabil (100$); and between Sal Rei and the airport at relevant times. To other destinations they leave Sal Rei in the afternoon, and do not return until the following morning, generally arriving in Sal Rei at about 07.00. Don't get stranded. Buses for the northeast leave from the west side of the main square in Sal Rei at about 13.00. Those heading south depart from the south of the square.

BY TAXI In the form of chartered *alugueres*, these can be hired for about ten times the public fare (eg: to Rabil 500$; to Santa Mónica 5,000$; to Morre Negro 6,000$; one day around the island 9,000$). To do a thorough tour of Boavista it is essential to have a 4x4.

BY CAR Most of the hotels can put you in touch with a car-hire firm and driver.

🚗 **Alucar** ↖ 251 1445; m 991 9204; e boavistapoint@cvtelecom.cv. Charges around €50/day.
🚗 **Mendes and Mendes** ↖ 251 1145. Prices start at €50/day.

🚗 **Olicar** Largo Santa Isabel; ↖ 251 1743. Charges around €60/day, or more with a driver.

Most accommodation, including all of the cheaper places, is in the capital Sal Rei. There are a few hotels some kilometres to the south, along Chaves Beach. There is one hotel 2km north of Sal Rei, along the coast. And there is one, remote hotel in Espingueira. There are plans for many more hotels along Chaves Beach and along Santa Mónica Beach in the south. There are an increasing number of apartments available for long- and short-term rental. Try asking tour operators or rental agencies such as Blue Banana (for contact information, see page 150).

To be within walking distance of any external facilities, such as local restaurants or the watersports establishments, it's best to stay in Sal Rei. A hotel along Chaves Beach such as the Parque das Dunas (see page 156) is a beautiful and isolated option but it is too far (and, at certain times of day, dangerous) to walk to Sal Rei, so you will be reliant on the hotel shuttle or a taxi (€10).

ACTIVITIES

EXCURSIONS TO OTHER ISLANDS There are day trips to Santiago, Fogo and Sal on offer. These won't allow you much time on the island but will give you a flavour. The companies listed in the following sections can assist with tours and activities on the island.

Local tour operators

Barracuda Tours Av 4 de Julho, Zona de João Cristovão, Sal Rei; 251 1907; e geral@ barracudatours.com; ☺ 09.00–13.00 & 15.00–18.00 Mon–Fri, 09.00–13.00 Sat. Southwest of town on a road running towards the beach from opposite one of the fuel stations. Offers half- & full-day trips around the island (from €26), quad tours (from €45) & buggy tours (from €65), & a day trip to Fogo.

Clamtour Av 4 de Julho; 251 2121/1982; m 918 7351/7352. Offers walks (€25), 4x4 tours

(from €25), boat tours (from €30), & day trips to Santiago (€189) & Fogo (€225).

vista verde tours Riba D'Olte, Sal Rei near the rock gardens; m 983 2550; e boavista@ vista-verde.com; www.vista-verde.com; ☺ 10.00–13.00 Mon–Fri. Specialising in social & environmentally responsible tourism, this agency can arrange small group tours or tailor-made holidays incorporating accommodation, flights, hiking & excursions. Offices in Fogo, Sal & Boavista.

Excursions

ATC Scooter Largo Santa Isabel; 251 1872; m 992 7306/994 6139; e l_ripa@yahoo.it, fuji_em@tiscali.it; www.quadland-boavista.com. On the southeast corner of the main square. Offers quad & scooter rental, & also guided quad excursions (4hrs; €85).

Morena Tourist Agency Largo Santa Isabel; 251 1445; e boavistapoint@cvtelecom.cv; ☺ 09.00–12.30 & 16.00–19.00 Mon–Fri. In the north of the main square. It offers day trips to the dunes & further afield to Santa Mónica Beach, horseriding & other activities. Also has internet.

Naturalia 251 1558; m 994 1070/998 6650; e naturalia.cv@hotmail.com. Offers whale-watching, snorkelling among corals & nurse sharks, turtle-watching & birding trips. The company, set up in 2008, is one outcome of the EU's Naturalia Project to restore ecosystems & test whether they can be used sustainably & profitably in ecotourist activities. See individual entries below.

Olitour Largo Santa Isabel; 251 1743. It offers half- & full-day tours into the dunes, etc from €25pp.

DIVING See *Chapter 2, Practical Information*, page 48, for a discussion of diving in Cape Verde.

A few years ago, divers plunged into Cape Verde's waters on a hunt for shipwrecks, and surfaced clutching a gold coin bearing the date 1760. They believe they discovered the remains of the *Dromadaire*, a French trading ship that sank in 1762, carrying more than £3 million of gold and silver. It is said the crew of the *Dromadaire* only realised their plight when they saw the reef surf under the prow. Some 17 miles south of Boavista lies the notorious reef, Baixo de João Leitão: it has wrecked many a vessel. One man who spent tormented hours battling (successfully) to avoid it was Captain James Cook on his third and last voyage to the South Seas, in 1776.

Old people on Boavista still tell of a legendary cargo of gold brought to their ancestors by shipwreck. This may have been the wreck of the English vessel *Hartwell* on 24 May 1787. The ship suffered a mutiny while on the seas and in the confusion the crew let the boat stray to Boavista's shallows. The reef that sank it is now called the Hartwell Reef and lies at the northeast side of the island – it is partly above water, and extends for about 6km.

Cape Verde's version of the *Titanic* disaster occurred in the 19th century – the tragedy of the *Cicília*. It was the night of 5 November 1863, and the Italian ship was carrying emigrants destined for South America. Their spirits were high and there was a dance going on in the ballroom when the ship foundered near Boavista. When the captain realised what had happened he commanded the door of the ballroom to be locked. He made a great error. According to the poet José Lopes: 'There inside was true horror… a dance of life was transformed into a macabre dance of death…'. Passengers were later found dead in the act of struggling to get out of the portholes; in all 72 died.

The *Santa Maria* was wrecked in August 1968 on the northwest coast. It was *en route* from Spain to Brazil with a cargo of cars, drink, melons, cork and cheese. The year 1968 had until then been a bad one for Boavistans: they spent the next 12 months salvaging booty.

✈ **Dive School Submarine Center** Located along the beach south of the Hotel Estoril near Tortuga Beach; m 992 4865/7866; e atilros@hotmail.com; www.caboverde.com/pages/924865.htm. Atila & Rose have lived on Boavista since 1997 & offer PADI & NAUI courses at all levels, including try dives for adults (€100) & PADI Bubblemaker for kids (€70). They also organise snorkelling trips (€35) & rent windsurfing (€25/hr), surfing (€20/half day) & bodyboard equipment & lessons from €50/hr.

Between them they speak English, Portuguese, Italian, Spanish & French.

✈ **Watersports Center Scubacaribe** Located at RIU Karamboa, Bahía de Chaves; ☎ 251 9100, ext 9070 (dive centre); 251 1999 (office); e info@scubacaribe.com; www.scubacaribe.com. PADI Gold Palm Resort offering scuba diving, snorkelling, quad tours, fishing trips, kitesurfing & windsurfing in many different languages. Prices & reservations available on the website.

WINDSURFING AND KITESURFING The excellent windsurfing potential of Cape Verde is discussed in *Chapter 2, Practical Information*, page 48. Boavista has many great spots but not everywhere is suitable: rescue facilities are non-existent in most places so beaches like Santa Mónica, with a strong offshore wind, are not recommended. The northern shore has a heavy wind swell, and though wind- and kitesurfing are possible there are better places elsewhere. The island is good for independent and advanced kitesurfers, windsurfers and surfers looking for a variety of conditions, but beginners should stick to Sal Rei Bay. For many of the spots you will need a hire car or arrange a pick-up or taxi. Key spots are:

1 Sal Rei Bay A long white sandy beach stretching south of town, with the wind increasingly stable as you move south, and the ground increasingly sandy once you have left town behind. The wind is offshore, so make sure you know how you will be rescued. There's a reef with small break waves. Apart from that the water is flat.

2 Chaves You can windsurf or kitesurf on the beach outside the RIU Karamboa but in the winter this often has a large shorebreak and to find a good place to enter the water you will have to go much further down the beach.

3 Baía Varandinha Reached by 4x4 overland this remains a lonely place with stable, side-shore winds, beach break waves and sand below. Not suitable for beginners.

4 East coast Out of the turtle season it should be possible to windsurf and kitesurf on many of the beaches here. Again the wind is stable and side-shore to side-on. There is some wind swell out of the protected bay areas. Not suitable for beginners.

Kit hire and lessons are available from the following:

Boavista Wind Club e Boavista012@yahoo. com; www.boavistawindclub.com. Located at Tortuga Beach on the south side, this long-established club is run by François Guy, a Frenchman with a stellar windsurfing history. Offers windsurfing & rents windsurfing, kayaking & surfing kit. Also offers surf safaris to 'secret' surfing spots on the island. 3hrs of windsurf hire come to just over €40, with lessons at €30 for 90mins. Kayak hire at €12/hr, surfboards at €5/hr; catamaran Dart at €30/hr (insurance included, where relevant).
Dive School Submarine Center (see *Diving*, page 143). Also rents watersports kit.

Fruits of Cabo Verde Estoril Beach m 980 2741; www.fruitsofcaboverde.com; ☺ 10.00–18.00. Surf lessons from €30 for 90mins. Also sells boards, surf gear & original T-shirts as well as an interesting line of herbal suncreams.
Vista Surf On the beach in front of the RIU. Offers rentals & lessons. However, in winter even though the waves are fantastic, the shorebreak can be very large, making it difficult to enter the water. At other times it can be a great spot for advanced windsurfing & kitesurfing. Kite lessons are often given in a shallow lagoon near the school.

SURFING Cabral Beach, where the swell is greatest, is the most popular venue for surfers. Surfing is best from November to March in terms of waves and swell, but calmest in May to September. Boards can be hired from the Boavista Wind Club or Dive School Submarine Center (for further details, see page 143).

BEACHES AND SWIMMING The vast strands of Chaves, Curralinho, Santa Mónica, Curral Velho and many others make Boavista into one huge, ravenously beautiful beach. There are endless opportunities for sunbathing, dipping and swimming. Opposite Ilhéu do Sal Rei is a lovely option – the water is never more than 3m deep and it is only 1,000m to the island. Another possibility close to Sal Rei is Praia da Cruz Beach which is just before the beach used by the Marine Club, and is divided from it by a little spit of land (although as complexes spring up behind it, it may get busy).

There are also many protected coves around the island – for example Praia de Ponta Antónia in the north (see also *Hazards*, page 139).

FISHING Both line fishing and deep-sea fishing are available.

Boapesca m 994 1060/991 8778; e info@ boavista2000.com, luca@boavista2000.com. Deep-sea fishing. Catch your fish with Boapesca & get it cooked at the Blue Marlin Restaurant (see *Where to eat and drink*, page 151).

Charterpesca m 982 7761; e info@ sampeifish.com. Based at the Quadland office (see *Quad biking*, page 146), it offers deep-sea fishing.
Morena Tourist Agency (see page 142)
Olitour (see page 142)

WHALE WATCHING Humpback whales come to Boavista to have their young and to nurse their calves until they are strong enough for the open ocean. Journeying out on a catamaran in search of them, watching their great masses surging and looping effortlessly through the water, and catching glimpses of their signature tail flukes, is a magical experience, as is taking a dip on the way back to shore. You may be accompanied by scientists photographing, recording and collecting skin samples, which adds even more interest to the trip.

Naturalia For contact details, see page 142; available Sep–Apr 08.30–11.00 & 14.00–16.30 approximately, several days a week, depending on the wind & swell; adult/under 12 €50/30 including transfers, although this may differ depending on the number of people.

BIRDWATCHING Local fishermen can be recruited to take tourists to the various islets.

Naturalia For contact details, see page 142; half & full-day tours €35–80.

TURTLE WATCHING Watching nesting loggerhead turtles is a night-time experience, with August the peak of the nesting season. There is an 80-minute journey to the southeastern coast. A guide gives a briefing on turtle biology and conservation work in Cape Verde as well as the basic rules to follow to minimise disturbance to the animals. Seeing turtles is guaranteed; witnessing their egg laying is more hit-and-miss as it depends on their finding a suitable nesting site.

Naturalia For contact details, see page 142; available Jul–Oct 20.00–01.00 approximately; adult/under 12 €50/20. Book directly or via travel agent.

Turtle Foundation www.turtle-foundation. org. The foundation may be offering tours in conjunction with local travel agents.

CORAL SNORKELLING Snorkelling takes place at Gatas Bay, on the northeast shore of Boavista, where, in the summer, you may find yourself nose-to-nose with nurse sharks as well as exploring the corals.

Naturalia For contact details, see page 142; available at high tide; adult/under 12 €40/18 (min 4 people); price includes equipment & transfers.

HORSERIDING Perhaps this is the perfect way of seeing Boavista. Treks go mostly along the beach or inland to oases.

Morena Tourist Agency For contact details, see page 142; €8–30 for 30mins–2hrs.

QUAD BIKING Motoquad is increasingly popular and a compelling way to see the sights. It is, however, frowned on by some who wish to preserve the peace of Boavista's beaches. It is illegal to take vehicles, including quad bikes, onto the beaches or the dunes.

Caboquad Excursions to Boa Esperança & Santa Mónica on buggies & quad bikes from €60.

Quadland m 994 1922. Organises tours & rentals from €60/day.

HIKING Although Boavista lacks the verdant mountainous scenery of the more traditional hiking islands, its white deserts, pretty coastline and serendipitous oases, combined with its emptiness, make it a rewarding place to explore on foot (provided the hiker is properly shod, hatted and watered – see *Hazards*, page 139).

There are several short hikes around the north of Sal Rei, and three of these can be joined together to make a full-day excursion. There are a couple of short hikes up small peaks in the southwest, near Povoação Velha, and a charming hike down Chaves Beach and around Rabil Lagoon.

For hike descriptions, and further hiking ideas, see *Hiking*, page 146.

CULTURE A small dance group does a rip-roaring trip through the main dance forms of Cape Verde, performing weekly at some of the resort hotels. Some of these performances are open to non-residents (try asking at Marine Club or Venta Club; see page 148).

SIGHTSEEING BY VEHICLE Contact Olicar Rental (*Largo Santa Isabel, beside Olitour* (see page 142). *4x4 rental from €60/day*). Alternatively, 4x4 taxis can be picked up at the east end of Largo Santa Isabel.

A popular activity is to join a half- or full-day tour of the island, using one of the tour operators listed on page 142, or to hire your own car, or taxi with driver, for the day. The latter option, of course, has the advantage that you can dawdle where you please. Another option is to hire a quad bike and set out on your own, but if you are new to quad bikes take advice on how to extract yourself from the sand. A possible route is: go south from Sal Rei, northeast along the main road after Rabil, branch off north to see Espingueira and Bofareira and then return to the main road; follow it to Fundo das Figueiras and Cabeço das Tarafes; take the track south to Curral Velho, northwest back up to the main road, then southwest on the main road to Povoação Velha, where a new road is being built. Most of the sights along this route are described below. Exercise extreme caution if travelling alone as there have been incidents of violent mugging on deserted beaches. Listen to advice about the current situation before venturing

---

THE BOAVISTA ULTRAMARATHON

Running for three days through the dunes, beaches and oases of Boavista, testing themselves in the bone-dry heat and under the desert night skies, is the experience of a lifetime for many of the contestants in the annual ultramarathon. Launched in 2000, the 150km race lasts for up to 60 hours. Sleep as you go. For more information contact Boavista Ultramarathon Club, Crioula Bar, just south of the main square in Sal Rei (e *info@boavistaultramarathon.com*; *www.boavistaultramarathon.com/english/homepage.asp*).

I left Cabeço das Tarafes and the scant vegetation of a *ribeira*, and the road deteriorated to a dusty track. Now I was in open upland dominated by Pico Estância on the right. It is not a large mountain but in this emptiness I had lost all sense of scale and as it shimmered in the heat it seemed massive.

All around was dry rock. Once, I stopped and there was no movement except for the drifting trail of dust thrown out by the jeep. There was silence except for the droning of the hot wind. The land was an endless brown and the skull of a donkey gleamed like a white flower amongst the rocks. At last, after an eternity on the plateau of dry bones, the track swung towards the coast and soon I was driving just above the white sand.

Curral Velho is a crumbling village next to a salt lagoon just behind the shore. It is built in warm honey-coloured stone: a place of stone, built on stone, amongst stone. The wind murmured through the gaping windows. Two of the largest, blackest crows I had ever seen watched me from a broken gable as I picked my way round the ruins. I found a path over the dunes amongst the twisted roots and stumps of a fossilised forest. At the beach I sat for a little and watched the patterns of fine sand stream over the ground. Beyond, the sea crashed on to the steep shore.

From Curral Velho I drove inland. Walls criss-crossed the dry landscape – impressive monuments to generations of Boavistans who have put to good use the two resources that are not in short supply here: rock and time. From time to time I passed the ruins of farmhouses and here and there an abandoned well – there is water, but it is bitter now.

In places the track threatened to disappear altogether beneath thick drifts of dust. Elsewhere, the route was no more than a cleared path across boulder fields.

The sun sank and Santo António became an outlandish silhouette. I passed a tree blasted into a tortured sculpture by the prevailing wind – it was the first living thing since the crows, hours before. There were low scrubby bushes and then, at last, an attempt at cultivation. The field was more like a fortress than a garden: first there were walls to keep the goats out and then there was an embankment around each plant to keep the water in.

to remote places. Remember that it is illegal to drive on the beach anywhere in Cape Verde.

Take local advice about the state of the track directly linking Curral Velho to Povoação Velha and, if you are taking a driver, check with him beforehand that he is happy to follow your route. Don't embark on the venture on your own without a good map.

SAL REI

There is a charm about this town that seeps in slowly, as you sit in the main square watching life go by or drink coffee in thankful shade overlooking the beach. The water is a glorious turquoise and the mounds of sand are a true, desert-island yellow. Men maintain their painted boats and children shout and play around the decrepit ones or hurl themselves into the water from the old pier. From the town, the hillocks of Boavista appear like craggy mountains.

At night, you may become aware of a canine sub-culture, characterised by ferocious barking matches and brawling in the empty streets. Next morning traces of fur in the square are all that remain.

Sal Rei is quietly busy. Town planners made the cobbled roads wide and planted acacias, their trunks painted a tidy white. The main square is vast, with bandstands, children's play areas, benches and even urinals.

So far the influx of visitors to the all-inclusive hotels has made little impact on Sal Rei, which has not experienced a sudden boom in restaurants and bars in the same way as the neighbouring island, Sal. There are, however, far more souvenir sellers from west Africa than ever before. In common with every other island, the town has seen an influx of Chinese shops.

⌂ WHERE TO STAY

⌂ **Estoril Beach Resort Hotel** [149 A7] (21 rooms) ☎251 1078; m 991 8663; e info@ estorilbeachresort.com; www.estorilbeachresort. com. Near the beach but no longer with a sea view, down the road opposite the Shell petrol station, the hotel is attractively laid out around a central courtyard & faced in a pleasant stone, but has deteriorated in service over the years. Next door are apartments in a similar style – perhaps a good option for proximity to the windsurfing & diving clubs. Has an outdoor restaurant open for lunch & dinner. **$$$$**

⌂ **Marine Club** (76 rooms) ☎251 1285; e marineclub@cvtelecom.cv. A 20min walk along a straight cobbled road that leads from the north of Sal Rei, this is the oldest resort in Boavista & occupies a prime position overlooking the water. It was once out of town, but the town is now creeping towards it. Marine Club's mature planting & chalet-style layout give it a village feel. It is used mostly by Italian holidaymakers on all-inclusive packages. As well as the chalets there are 2- & 3-room villas. There's a beautiful pool & small playground, & the hotel makes use of the adjacent small beach. There is a buffet restaurant open to non-guests for a set price of €20. Non-guests can also pay to spend a half day enjoying the facilities (€30). Entertainment includes a weekly performance by Cape Verdean musicians & dancers, also open to non-guests. **$$$$**

⌂ **Hotel Boa Vista** [149 C5] (34 rooms) Rua dos Emigrantes, CP 40 Sal Rei; ☎251 1145. Positioned on the right as you enter Sal Rei from the airport. Large, bright, mostly balconied rooms & with a communal terrace offering views over Sal Rei to the sea. Back rooms have no sea view but are more modern. **$$$**

⌂ **Hotel Luca Calema** [149 A4] (20 rooms) Av Amílcar Cabral, CP 30 Sal Rei; ☎251 1225/1088; e dunas@bwscv.com. Previously called Hotel Dunas, this is a bright, spacious hotel on the seafront with a courtyard restaurant. **$$$**

⌂ **Guest House Orquidea** [149 A6] (10 rooms) ☎251 1041; e domorguidea@hotmail. com. A charming guesthouse only a few metres from the sea featuring delightfully decorated rooms, each with bathroom, balcony, fridge, television & safe. There is also a gym & internet & laundry service. Upstairs rooms have a wonderful sea view. B/fast is served in a shady courtyard & the welcoming owners, long-term residents of Sal Rei, will arrange all the excursions you could want. A safe & comfy place to base yourself while exploring Boavista. **$$$**

⌂ **Migrante Guesthouse** [149 A2] (5 rooms) Av Amílcar Cabral, CP 80 Sal Rei; ☎251 1143; m 995 3655; e info@migrante-guesthouse. com; www.migrante-guesthouse.com. On a road to the west of the main square, this is the most atmospheric guesthouse in town, a traditional house set around a courtyard, all lovingly restored & tastefully decorated. Many people are captivated by its charm, but some complain that the rooms are too hot. Rooms are en suite with hot water & fan. English spoken. There's a bar (⊕ early–22.00 daily), & dinner is available if requested in advance; there is also Wi-Fi. **$$$**

⌂ **A Paz** [149 C5] (7 rooms) Av 5 de Julho; ☎251 1643; m 958 5704; e info@a-paz.it; www.apazboavista.com. Near the main square, this small, Italian-run house has been decorated with some charm & much bamboo. Comfortable enough, all rooms are en suite with hot water & a fan, & some have a sea view. B/fast is on a roof terrace, currently with a view of the ocean. **$$**

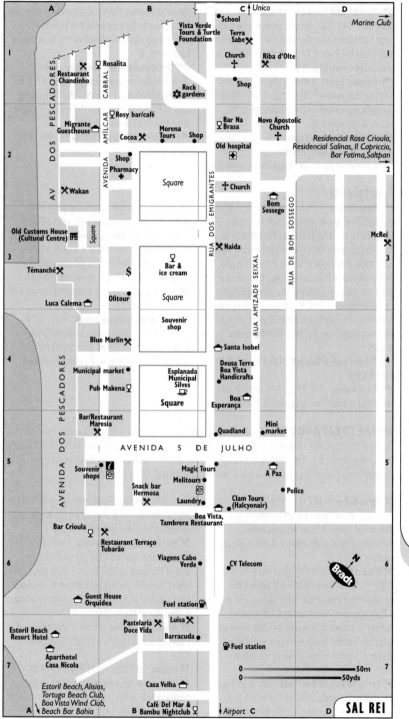

SAL REI

0 —————— 50m
0 —————— 50yds

Marine Club

Unico

School
Vista Verde Tours & Turtle Foundation
Terra Sabe
Church
Riba d'Olte
Shop
Rock gardens

Rosalita
Restaurant Chandinho
Migrante Guesthouse
Rosy bar/café
Cocoa
Morena Tours
Shop
Bar Na Brasa
Old hospital
Novo Apostolic Church

Shop
Pharmacy
Square
Church
Wakan

Old Customs House (Cultural Centre)
Square
Bar & ice cream
Square
Naida
Bom Sossego

Residencial Rosa Crioula, Residencial Salinas, Il Capriccio, Bar Fatima, Saltpan

McRei

Témanché
Olitour
Luca Calema
Souvenir shop
Blue Marlin
Santa Isobel
Deusa Terra Boa Vista Handicrafts
Boa Esperança

Municipal market
Pub Makena
Esplanada Municipal Silves
Square
Boa Esperança
Quadland
Mini market

Bar/Restaurant Maresia

AVENIDA 5 DE JULHO

Souvenir shops
Snack bar Hermosa
Magic Tours
Melitours
Laundry
Clam Tours (Halcyonair)
A Paz
Police

Boa Vista, Tambrera Restaurant

Bar Crioula
Restaurant Terraço Tubarão
Viagens Cabo Verde
CV Telecom

Guest House Orquidea
Fuel station

Estoril Beach Resort Hotel
Aparthotel Casa Nicola
Pastelaria Doce Vida
Luisa
Barracuda
Fuel station

Estoril Beach, Alisios, Tortuga Beach Club, Boa Vista Wind Club, Beach Bar Bahia

Casa Velha
Café Del Mar & Bambu Nightclub
Airport

RUA DOS EMIGRANTES
RUA AMIZADE SEIXAL
RUA DE BOM SOSSEGO
AVENIDA AMILCAR CABRAL
AV DOS PESCADORES
AVENIDA DOS PESCADORES

N

🏠 **Residencial Salinas** (14 rooms) Rua Bom Sossego; ☎ 241 1563. Simple, clean rooms with large bathrooms near the salinas in the northern part of Sal Rei. Fans & TVs in all rooms & a bar & restaurant downstairs. **$$**

🏠 **Pensão Santa Isobel** [149 C4] (6 rooms) Rua dos Emigrantes; ☎ 251 1252; m 992 7990. Centrally positioned on the inland side of the square & renovated. **$**

🏠 **Residencial Boa Esperança** [149 C4] (8 rooms) Rua Tavares Almeida; ☎ 251 1252. In the road east of the main square. Proud to be the cheapest in town, this establishment is definitely just a place to lay your head & is becoming increasingly rundown. Some rooms have shared bathrooms. **$**

🏠 **Residencial Bom Sossego** [149 C2] (7 rooms) Rua de Bom Sossego; ☎ 251 1155. In the block behind the church – the lively owner lives at Bar Sossego around the corner. A couple of bedrooms have verandas. **$**

🏠 **Residencial Rosa Crioula** m 994 0090. Basic facilities. **$**

Apartments

🏠 **Casa Nicola** [149 A7] ☎ 251 1793; e info@ canicola.com; www.canicola.com. Attractive, stone-faced block built around 2 courtyards & just 50m from the water, with a panoramic view from its rooftop terrace. Serves b/fast & snacks, with a reception that can organise tours, & in a good situation very close to the windsurfing & diving outfits on Estoril Beach but also very close to Sal Rei. Pleasantly decorated & with verandas, all apartments have kitchens & living rooms. **$$$$**

🏠 **Estoril Beach Resort** [149 A7] (see page 148) **$$$$**

🏠 **Casa Velha** [149 B7] m 995 8197; e info@ casavelha.it; http://en.casavelha.it. A newly developed, managed apartment block built in the Portuguese colonial style with a central courtyard overlooked by wooden balconies. Casa Velha's publicity states that it 'blends a classic hotel with the freedom of a private residence'. The building has a large communal terrace & there is a penthouse with a secluded terrace with sea views. **$$$**

🏠 **The Blue Banana Group** ☎ 251 1978; m 974 2349; e bluebanana.cv@gmail.com; skype sabine2429. Offers apartments for short- or long-term rental as well as maintenance & management.

✗ **WHERE TO EAT AND DRINK** Island specialities include *chicharro assado* (saurel fish coated in olive oil and roasted); *canja de capado* (boar broth) and *botchada* (sheep or goat stomach). The restaurants of several hotels are open to non-residents – for example the buffet at the Marine Club or the Hotel Luca Calema.

✗ **Terra Sabe** [149 C1] m 993 9078; ⏱ 10.00–00.00 Mon–Fri, 19.00–00.00 Sun. Mixture of Italian & Cape Verdean dishes, including grilled goat's cheese. Rooftop terrace seating. **$$$$$**

✗ **Riba d'Olte** [149 C1] ☎ 251 1015; m 992 4292; ⏱ Wed–Mon. Up the hill behind the northeastern end of the main square, this is a Portuguese-run restaurant & offers some variety in a town dominated by Cape Verdean & Italian cuisine. There are some vegetarian dishes & a good-value 3-course set menu. **$$$$**

✗ **Tortuga Beach Bar/Café** This is an open-air, Italian-run restaurant on the beach just south of town & serving mainly Italian dishes, meat & fish cooked on an open-air grill. You can rent a sun lounger & parasol on the beach just in front of the restaurant for €8/day. **$$$$**

✗ **Bar/Restaurant Maresia** [149 A5] ☎ 251 1430. 1 road seaward from the southwestern end of the main square, this is a good place from which to watch the fishing boats in the harbour over a dish of their fresh catch – perhaps lobster, a speciality of the restaurant. **$$$**

✗ **Beach Bar Bahia** At the southern end of Estoril Beach & thus in a beautiful location. **$$$**

✗ **Cocoa** [149 B2] m 981 7191; ⏱ 08.00– 00.00. A colourful, breezy Italian café on the northern side of the town square. Serves slightly pricey pizza, salads, omelettes & pasta. **$$$**

above The elegant red-billed tropicbird (*Phaethon aethereus*) is identified by its long central tail feather (IB/FLPA) page 6

above right Helmeted guineafowl (*Numida meleagris*) are commonly sighted on mountain slopes (MBW/FLPA) page 6

right The male magnificent frigatebird (*Fregata magnificens*) inflates its scarlet throat pouch in the breeding season (FP/FLPA) page 6

far right The grey-headed kingfisher (*Halcyon leucocephala*) is relatively common on the islands, but is highly territorial; it will dive-bomb intruders who get too close to its nest (BZ/IB/FLPA) page 6

below The brown booby (*Sula leucogaster*) is known locally as the *alcatraz* and appears on the 20-escudo piece (LC/MP/FLPA) page 6

above left The main draw of São Filipe, Fogo's capital, is its *sobrado* architecture, decorated with fine wood and tiles imported from Portugal and west Africa (SS) page 224

above right The youngest island in the archipelago, Fogo presents a dramatic landscape formed by successive lava flows (SS) page 211

THE COLONIAL GUESTHOUSE

Restaurant Bar Rooms Pool Spa Massage

**Big game fishing
Volcano excursions
Island Tours
Transfers**

www.thecolonialguesthouse.com

Caixa Postal 123 S. Filipe Ilha do Fogo, Cabo Verde
Tel.: +238 991 4566 Fax: +238 281 3102
info@zebratravel.net

zebra
travel
turismo&viagens

www.zebratravel.net

✗ **Estoril Beach** [149 A7] ⊕ all day. Serving a high standard of mainly local & Italian cuisine, including pasta that is handmade on site, the restaurant can be found in the hotel of the same name. It's open air, but there's not much of a view & it can overheat during the day. $$$

✗ **McRei** [149 D3] ✆ 251 1631. Burgers & meat with a delightful fruit salad to compensate. $$$

✗ **Restaurant Luisa** [149 B7] m 981 7191. Located on the road that runs towards Estoril Beach after the fuel station, this is a happy Italian concern serving pizza. Another good place for vegetarians. $$$

✗ **Alisios** Estoril Beach; m 987 7881; ⊕ 09.00–18.00 Thu–Tue. Spacious, colourful café on the beach with a large deck, run by an Italian/English couple. Features delicious meals from ingredients sourced locally & freshly squeezed juices. There is a plan to open a fitness & beauty centre soon. $$

✗ **Bar Naida** [149 C3] ✆ 251 1173; m 993 4804. This is a simple, local establishment on the north side of the main square which has been running for over a decade & may be the oldest restaurant in Sal Rei. Varied food served in a whitewashed yard with a banana-leaf roof. Book in advance. $$

✗ **Blue Marlin** [149 B4] ✆ 251 1099. This small restaurant & bar is on the main square & popular with locals & expats, serving traditional Cape Verdean dishes, especially freshly caught fish & seafood. Also has a good selection of wines. Book in advance. $$

✗ **Café Del Mar** [149 B7] m 981 0145; e carlo.stefani@libero.it. Beyond the petrol station on the way to the airport, this delightful rooftop bar has been furnished using recycled materials. A great place to chill out & watch the sun going down. The restaurant serves delicious food with specialities such as *filet mignon* &

risotto, & downstairs is Bambu, a disco open every night; ✆ 972 7231. $$

⊑ **Esplanada Municipal Silves** [149 B4] Largo Santa Isabel; ⊕ day & night. A refuge from the sun if it's impeding your journey across the parched main square, this café serves snacks & drinks during the day & hosts music & dancing at night, with local traditional music on Sun. $$

⌷ **Rosy Bar/Café** [149 B2] Close to the Migrante Guesthouse. This is popular, & used by some day-tripping groups from Boavista. Advance booking compulsory. $$

✗ **Témanché** [149 A3] A pier kiosk run from a container serving straightforward, basic dishes. Lounge here in the shade & watch the children playing in the water & the odd fishing trip come in, or conduct your local business. Service is pretty slow. $$

✗ **Tortuga Beach Club** Estoril Beach; m 993 0811; ⊕ 10.00–18.00 daily. Restaurant & watersports centre. $$

✗ **Unico Café Cabral** m 993 4213; ⊕ 17.00–until late. Breezy bar & café with sofas & great views over the bay towards the Marine Club. Simple food such as Spanish omelette, fish & pasta served between 19.00 & 23.00. Themed nights such as Ladies' Night, Latin Night & Cocktail Night. $$

✗ **Wakan** [149 A2] Kiosk close to the pier where you can sit in the shade & watch the fishermen's daily activities. Simple food including freshly caught fish. $$

✗ **Il Capriccio** m 999 6894; ⊕ 08.00–18.30 daily. At the north end of town, this Italian-run concern serves fresh pasta & a variety of salads. Comfortable place popular with local Italians, & good for vegetarians. $

✗ **Pastelaria Doce Vida** [149 B7] ✆ 251 1533. Good-value pizzas & sandwiches as well as Italian specialities such as crêpes, cakes & focaccia. Near Estoril Beach. $

You can buy fresh bread from the *padaria* east of the Bom Sossego Bar in the mornings, and generally cheese and vegetables from the women at one corner of the square.

ENTERTAINMENT AND NIGHTLIFE

☆ **Crystal Disco Rabil** ⊕ 22.00–02.00 Sun. Transport to this Rabil disco generally materialises in the main square of Sal Rei at about 23.00–00.00. The *aluguer* drivers will sell

you an all-in-one ticket to take you there, get entry, & transport you home afterwards. Cape Verdean music & disco.

☆ **Disco Mazurka** ⏲ 00.00–05.30 Wed & Sat; 400$ entry which includes free transport to & from Sal Rei. A green, warehouse-like building with red writing on it on the road between Sal Rei & Rabil. Mixture of music including Cape Verdean, hip hop & disco.

OTHER PRACTICALITIES

Airlines TACV (*At the airport;* ⏲ *08.00–12.00 & 14.30–17.00 Mon–Fri, 09.00–11.00 Sat*).

Banks BCA and BCN (⏲ *08.00–15.00 Mon–Fri*). Both on the main square.

Hospital [149 C2] Beside the church, on the square (☏ *251 1167*). This is more of a clinic than a hospital and is due to be replaced by a new hospital in the east of town.

Internet Several points, including Morena Tourist Agency [149 B2] and Hotel Boa Vista [149 C5].

Pharmacy Drogeria Rodrigues [149 B2] on the square.

Police Av 5 de Julho [149 C5] (☏ *251 1132*). Round the corner from Residencial A Paz [149 C5].

Post office (⏲ *08.00–15.30 Mon–Fri*). Up the hill to the north of town.

Shopping Traditional Boavista crafts include hats made from palm leaves (a speciality of Povoação Velha) and ceramics (from Rabil). There are a few small craft and souvenir shops in the back streets of Sal Rei, for example one street north of Rua dos Emigrantes, near the old hospital. There's also a complex of shops selling the ubiquitous West African souvenirs down near Restaurant Maresia [149 A5] and a Cape Verdean souvenir shop in the middle of the main square (⏲ *08.00–19.00*). There is a *minimercado* on the southeast corner of the square. Maps, including the Goldstadt 'Wanderkarte' 1:50,000 map of Boavista (see *Maps*, page 68) can be bought at the Shell garage in Sal Rei and Morena Tourist Agency [149 B2] in the main square.

WHAT TO SEE For activities, see page 142. In Sal Rei itself there is little to do of a non-sporting nature except soak up the quiet atmosphere, or bask on the beach south of town. However, there are quite a few places to visit within walking distance of Sal Rei (or walking plus a short spell on public transport). These are listed below and can be visited individually or put together into hikes.

The Ben'Oliel graves These lie near the Marine Club (though there is some pressure to move them), which you reach by following the signs out of Sal Rei and along a road across what was a brown wasteland – the sand-covered saltpans – and is now a building site.

Before you reach the hotel, on the right, are the graves of the Jewish Ben'Oliel family, who fled here from the Moroccan persecution of the Jews in 1872. There is also the tomb of a young English woman, Julia Maria Pettingall, daughter of Charles Pettingall, who was one of the administrators of the Luso-British Commission. Julia was the 19-year-old victim of a plague of yellow fever that struck Boavista in the 1840s. She left with her family to the safety of another island, but her father later decided the threat had receded and returned to

Boavista. He was wrong. Julia died in November 1845. While on board the boat returning to São Nicolau after her death, Pettingall himself died, and later his daughter's fiancé died too.

Igreja Nossa Senhora de Fátima This is a little hike – 15 minutes from the Marine Club, or 45 minutes from the centre of Sal Rei. (See *Hiking*, page 146, for a description.)

Islet of Sal Rei This islet is nearly 2km at its longest, and up to 700m wide. It was the site of the fort of the Duque de Bragança, though all that remains of the 19th-century construction is some circular stonework and some cannons. In the north of the island there are also some ruins and a lighthouse. It is uninhabited apart from crabs, lizards and litter left by previous visitors. Along the western side are little sandy coves, while to the east there are views over the anchored boats. Looking back, there are beautiful views of Sal Rei and down Chaves Beach.

You should be able to persuade a fisherman to take you out there for a fee (about 1,500$). Alternatively you could swim the 1,000m: locals say the water is never deeper than 1.5m.

Cultural Centre Near the pier is the charmingly refurbished old Customs House [149 A3]. It now houses a cultural display of interesting Cape Verdean artefacts and objects, and features art shows and temporary exhibitions.

OTHER PLACES TO VISIT

The rest of the island is described in a clockwise order, beginning at Sal Rei.

COSTA DE BOA ESPERANÇA This long and beautiful, windswept and deserted beach stretches from the lighthouse in the northwest (Ponta do Sol) to Ponta Antónia in the northeast. Along it is the unmistakeable wreck of the *Santa Maria* (see box, *Shipwrecks on Boavista*, page 143). At its western tip is Ponta do Sol, where there is a lighthouse reachable on foot (see *Hikes*, page 157). This area is usually deserted and has been the scene of many muggings. Be wary and do not take valuables with you.

BOFAREIRA AND ESPINGUEIRA These villages can be reached by hiking northeast from Sal Rei along a track marked on the map, or by 4x4 along a road from Rabil. After leaving Sal Rei, bear left at the fork south of Rabil and take the road to João Galego. After about 11km turn left at the small, incongruous shrine to the Virgin Mary at the side of the road. Stay on the cobbled track and after 20 minutes you will emerge at the tiny village of Bofareira. This place is serviced by a daily *aluguer* but there is not much else happening – there's a shop and a telephone box. The focal point of the village is the standpipe, when there's any water (it all has to be tankered in from Sal Rei).

From the Bofareira road it is possible to get to the shore: about 4km from the village take the rough track, signposted to Spinguera, which resembles the bed of a river. This leads to the coast and the ruined village of Espingueira, now partly transformed into a hotel. There is a small fishing camp out on the Ponta Antónia and, just east of the point in a semi-circular cove, lovely snorkelling – if you're lucky, among nurse sharks (*Ginglymostoma cirratum*). Looking west along the beach there is a good view of the hulk of the *Santa Maria*.

Where to stay

Spinguera (13 rooms) 251 1941; m 997 8943; e info@spinguera.com; www.spinguera.com. The ruined cottages of an abandoned village inspirationally transformed into the designer chalets of a small hotel. This is a deeply quiet, lonely & evocative stretch of coast & the hotel has been created by an artist in a sparsely beautiful style that echoes its environment. No phone, internet or mobile connection; electricity is available from 07.00 until 02.00 using solar panels & a generator. Accommodation includes 2 apartments & a villa – the latter can be a self-catering option & ingredients for cooking can be ordered from the owner. There is also a bar, open to non-guests, & a restaurant, which must be booked in the morning. The owners can organise activities. The hotel is about 1km from the coast but swimming is not recommended in the winter. **$$$$$**

JOÃO GALEGO, FUNDO DAS FIGUEIRAS, CABEÇO DAS TARAFES Accessed along the road that leads south and then east from Rabil, these three villages are strung out at the fertile end of a *ribeira*. After the flat, dry plain you have crossed from Rabil, it is refreshing to be near vegetation again. The villages are centred on the most agriculturally productive part of Boavista and enjoy modest renown as the source of delicious goat's cheese. João Galego has a smattering of shops, a bar (Moirasa Bar) and a nightclub. In Fundo das Figueiras, a few kilometres further on, there are shops and a snack bar (Bons-Irmãos). You must phone ahead to Gracinda at the Tiéta Restaurant (252 1111) to have a hope of tasting her grilled fish and meat; the same goes for the other restaurant, Nha Terra (252 1105).

What to see

Baía das Gatas The bay is a 15-minute drive by 4x4 along a reasonable track 7km from Fundo das Figueiras. It is named after the tiger sharks that have been seen from the point. There is a small, semi-permanent fishing camp here, with racks of salted fish hung out to dry. The fishermen will let you have a piece very cheaply – it is probably best to strap it outside the vehicle on the way home. You can see dolphins here.

The largest of the islets in the bay is Ilhéu dos Pássaros, home to the white-faced storm petrel or *pedreiro-azul* (*Pelagodroma marina*). Travel to the islets is prohibited.

Olho de Mar A small natural pool overlooked by a cliff with a remarkably human face. It lies to the southwest of Cabeço das Tarafes, along a track and then a path.

Morro Negro Lighthouse The most easterly point of Cape Verde, this lighthouse sits on a 150m-high promontory accessed along a track southwest from Cabeço das Tarafes. It offers a great panorama of the east coast.

Oasis of Santo Tirso This is the greenest part of the island, where you will find coconut palms, acacia and baobab trees. Owing to good rains in the last couple of years, it is a nice shady spot for a break.

Ponta do Roque and Praia dos Balejas From the lighthouse, the path continues to the south to this point and to the dolphin graveyard. Here lie the bones of nature's equivalent of the Boavista shipwrecks. They litter the sand near Morre Negro, which is alleged to have magnetic properties that draw the creatures to their deaths.

PRAIA DE CURRAL VELHO This beach is glorious but exposed and remote. Come prepared for a day in the desert. At 15km from the nearest civilisation, it is probably too far to attempt by foot. Curral Velho is, however, accessible by 4x4 from Povoação Velha, from Cabeço das Tarafes, or directly across the heart of the island from Sal Rei. This last route is 43km from town and takes just over an hour by jeep. On the road south from Rabil, bear left at the fork towards Fundo das Figueiras, and after about 1.5km, strike right on a track. For the next hour or so, you will feel as if you are driving across the surface of the moon, and then at last you will reach a T-junction near the coast. Turn right and, after about 300m, take the rough track down to the left through the deserted village of Curral Velho (see box, *Driving in Boavista*, page 147). Then head round to the right of the salt lagoon until the track runs out at the back of the dunes. Beyond is a blindingly white beach, with extensive, Sahara-like dunes to your right, providing the unwary motorist with ample opportunity to get stuck.

There is only one islet in the whole of the eastern Atlantic where the magnificent frigatebird or rabil (*Fregata magnificens*) deigns to breed. You can see that islet ahead: Ilhéu de Curral Velho. Watch out for the bird with its long, slim, black wings that have a span of around 2m. The female has a white breast and the male's is red. There are thought to be only about ten.

PRAIA DE LACAÇÃO This can be reached by following the track from Santa Mónica. This impossibly beautiful beach is the site of the new RIU Hotel, currently under construction (the first phase is due to open in May 2011). This massive development will change this remote area into a destination for all-inclusive mass tourism – and that is only the first stage.

PRAIA DE SANTA MÓNICA This beach is well worth a visit, but do come prepared, particularly if you are walking. You will need food, suncream and loads of water (see *Health*, page 62). In a 4x4, follow the road through Povoação Velha. After 6km a very rough track deposits you on the beach, named after the famous Californian strand. The Boavistan version is undeniably magnificent but a good deal bleaker. Swimming is possible here because of its southern aspect.

PRAIA DE CURRALINHO This is a beautiful beach and, like Santa Mónica, is reasonably accessible – a two-hour walk from Povoação Velha. Don't expect ice-cream kiosks – the most Curralinho Beach offers is the possibility of shelter from the wind in the lee of rocky outcrops. Bring your own shade.

As you enter Povoação Velha on the main road, turn right by the bright-green school and head towards the hill that looks like a large slag heap. The track is uncobbled, but the surface stays good for 4–5km until you reach the sand. This is not the beginning of the beach – you are still about 3km away. Beyond the dunes there is a dusty flat land, pock-marked with a reafforestation programme. Then, at last, is the sea. The shore is steep, so take care when swimming.

POVOAÇÃO VELHA In the words of a Povoação Velha landlord: 'It's a slow place, this.' It doesn't look much, but a settlement has endured here for almost 500 years and today it has a sleepy appeal: old folk ruminate on doorsteps, dogs scratch in the sun and donkeys twitch their ears on street corners.

There are two main, parallel streets with a handful of shops. Both the Bar António and the Club di Africa will prepare food on request; they need about two hours' notice so you could place your order before you ascend Rocha Estância, and return to the village as the meal arrives on the table.

You can reach Povoação Velha from Sal Rei by *aluguer* – there's one at 13.00 and one at 16.00 – and hope to hitch back later in the day. *Alugueres* from Povoação Velha to Sal Rei go only very early in the morning.

To ascend Rocha Estância or Pico Santo António see *Hikes*, opposite.

VERANDINHA BEACH An exposed beach with fantastic conditions for wind- and kitesurfing (though not for beginners). Another attraction is the caves behind the beach. Reach it along a track heading west from Povoação Velha. Much to the locals' dismay the area has become a racing track for quad tours, ripping through the village of Povoação Velha and destroying crops on the way to the beach. If you drive yourself there, take care as the dunes constantly change and require a 4x4.

RABIL This was the capital of Boavista until the early 19th century. It is a bit short on attractions, but has a pottery open to visitors. Look inside the imposing church of São Roque, built in 1801, the oldest church on Boavista. You can visit Rabil by *aluguer* (see *Getting around*, page 141) or as part of the hike on page 158. The canyon east of town is very Saharan in scenery, with palm trees and the dunes to the northeast enhancing the atmosphere.

✗ Where to eat and drink

✗ **Restaurante Sodade di Nha Terra** 251 1048. A large building with a flight of steps in front, this is a happening place serving local food including the renowned Boavista goat's cheese & much-praised lobster & goat. Some consider this the best restaurant in Boavista. $$

✗ **Rosi** 251 1242. A homely place serving either a dish of the day or what you have ordered in advance. Try the octopus. $

Entertainment and nightlife

☆ **Crystal Disco** (see page 151)

What to see

Viana Desert A much-praised desert to the northeast of Rabil, loved for its fine white sands and its oasis filled with coconut and date palms. This is a vast place covering about a quarter of the island and extending for about 15km north–south and 10km east–west.

CHAVES BEACH One of the most exhilarating beaches of Cape Verde, Chaves lies to the south of Sal Rei and stretches forever down the coast. The walk from Sal Rei is wonderful although the return journey can be a bit sand-blown.

⌂ Where to stay

⌂ **ClubHotel Riu Karamboa** (750 rooms) www.riu.com/index.php. Vast, all-inclusive resort hotel stretching like a desert palace along Chaves Beach, 7km from Sal Rei. It offers the usual resort facilities including 4 restaurants, children's & adults' pools, spa, a daytime activity programme for children & sports from tennis to scuba diving, & so forth. Inclusive packages only. $$$$
⌂ **Royal Decameron** (300 rooms) Previously the Venta Club, this is an all-inclusive resort hotel on Chaves Beach. The stunning panorama & the stepped construction of its rooms means that each one has a private terrace with sea view. The food is pretty good & varied. There are tennis courts, activities for children & various sports & entertainments, several pools, spa & a beauty centre. $$$$
⌂ **Parque das Dunas Village** (28 rooms) 251 1283/1288/1290; e info@ parquedasdunas.com; www.parquedasdunas.com.

Located at the southern end of Chaves Beach, south of the brick factory chimney, this is a quiet retreat with shady trees & an airy bar/restaurant area with a large pool. Although the rooms are not really luxurious (& have no TV, AC or phone) the hotel's position on the beach, & the setting of the terraced chalets, many patios of which open directly onto the shore, create a peaceful & evocative atmosphere. Sea bathing is often dangerous (see *Hazards*, page 139). Free shuttles to Sal Rei depart at 10.00 & 19.30; return at 12.00 & 22.30. Internet access is also available. $$$

✗ Where to eat
✗ **Parque das Dunas Village** ☻ lunchtime & 19.45– late. Bar serving light snacks 07.00– 23.00. $$$$

What to see
Brick factory This eerie building is slowly being submerged by the dunes. It takes just over an hour to walk to it from Sal Rei down Estoril Beach to the south, crossing Rabil Lagoon after about 35 minutes and continuing towards the chimney, which you will see poking out of the sand. There is a track leading inland from the factory to Rabil from where you can travel back to Sal Rei.

Rabil Lagoon Ribeira do Rabil is the main watercourse on the island and its water content varies through the year – sometimes dry, sometimes brackish pools, sometimes a good stream.

The lagoon itself has water all year round. It's a pretty, lonely, place surrounded by shifting sand dunes and popular with birdwatchers for its wintering migrant waders and for the Iago sparrow (*Passer iagoensis*). In fact, BirdLife International has designated it one of 12 Important Bird Areas in Cape Verde and it is a Ramsar site – a wetland of international importance.

The area stretches from the airport road to the sea. The quickest way to reach it is to take an *aluguer* destined for the airport and ask to be deposited at the bridge (*ponte*), after about 3km. From the road, however, the lagoon looks rather uninviting, so it is better explored from the beautiful beach end. You can do this by walking down from Sal Rei (see *Hikes*, below).

HIKES *Aisling Irwin (AI); Colum Wilson (CW*

In the northwest of the island is a triangle of hikes: Sal Rei–Ponta do Sol Lighthouse (7km); Ponta do Sol Lighthouse–wreck of the *Santa Maria* (5km); and Sal Rei–wreck of the *Santa Maria* (7km). Combining them yields a satisfying hike of 21km, which should take at least six hours and requires several litres of water per person as well as hiking boots and sun protection.

1 SAL REI–PONTA DO SOL LIGHTHOUSE (FAROL)
Distance: 7km; time: 2 hours; difficulty: 1 (AI)
The first part of this walk is not particularly scenic. Walk along the road to the Marine Club until you are 200m from it, at which point fork right along a road that runs for just over 2km to the cemetery. Just after the cemetery the road becomes an ascending track and bends to the left. Continue for 500m until you reach a fork: straight on leads to the church of Nossa Senhora de Fátima; branch to the right instead, and continue uphill. The view of old rubbish dumps is not edifying – but look on the bright side: they enhance the magnificence of the end of the walk. Stick to this track even, after 2.5km, when you pass another that forks to the left and

appears to be a more direct route. Less than 1km after that fork you will come to Chã de Agua Doce where the path turns left for the lighthouse (or right for the wreck of the *Santa Maria*). Continue for another 2km, through Curral Preto and its further litter dumps. Finally, you ascend to the etiolated structure that passes for a lighthouse. It's a lonely, atmospheric place.

2 PONTA DO SOL LIGHTHOUSE–WRECK OF THE SANTA MARIA

Distance: 5km; time: 1.5 hours; difficulty: 2 (AI)
The first 2km of this walk are a reversal of the final 2km of the previous walk. Follow the track from the lighthouse, through Curral Preto, and on to a fork. The right track leads back to Sal Rei. The left track takes you down, past lime kilns and onto the beach. You have a choice of following this track to its bitter end – it bends inland and then out again in a 'U' shape – or descending to the beach as soon as you have reached white sand. The two routes take about the same amount of time. After this the hulk of the wreck can be your guide.

3 SAL REI–WRECK OF THE SANTA MARIA

Distance: 7km; time: 2 hours; difficulty: 1 (CW)
The old hulk of the *Santa Maria* dominates the beach to the north of the island and is within walking distance of Sal Rei. Looking northeast out of town from a high point you will see a ridge – it lies over that.

Head south out of town towards Rabil and just past the small houses at the edge of town you will see the old road to Rabil (signposted Via Pitoresca) branching off on your left. Follow the old road for about 2km until a left turning. Take this rough track for about 7km. You will pass through Floresta Clotilde, an oasis filled with various species of palm including the endemic *tamareira* (*Phoenix atlantica*), and then through Boa Esperança. At times now the road is almost entirely obscured by sand but the route is straight. About 1.5km after leaving the oasis the paving gives way to sandy track. Just keep going until you hit the beach where you cannot miss the wreck.

(Following this route in the other direction (ie: starting at the wreck), the track is signposted; in the oasis avoid a track branching off to the left: keep right.)

4 SAL REI–MARINE CLUB–IGREJA NOSSA SENHORA DE FÁTIMA

Distance: 2.5km; time: 45 minutes; difficulty: 1 (AI)
Walk northeast out of Sal Rei on the straight road that leads to the Marine Club. At the front of this hotel there is a vehicle barrier. Don't go through this but instead take the little path that has been built down the left-hand side. This takes you around the coast, at first on a nicely crafted passageway. At the end of this walkway it becomes a rough little path and then a track along a pretty coastline including a sandy beach that would fit perhaps one person. By this time you will be able to see the ruins of the chapel and the path towards it. Beside it there was once a house with steps leading down to the beach.

5 SAL REI–ESTORIL BEACH–RABIL LAGOON–ESTÂNCIA DE BAIXO–RABIL

Distance: 10km (18km if done as circular walk); time: 3 hours (circular walk: 5 hours); difficulty: 1 (AI)
This walk begins down the beach and over high dunes with views over the sea, inland up a bird-filled lagoon and up a silent *ribeira* filled with *tamareira* trees and surrounded by sand hills. There's a hill to ascend up to Rabil but in general it is a flat and easy walk. At Rabil it should be possible to organise transport back

to Sal Rei – the alternative is to walk. (Guard against sun and theft, however – see *Hazards*, page 139.)

Go to the beach at Sal Rei and turn left (south), following the coast. After ten minutes you'll pass Tortuga Beach Resort, where you can pick up a drink and watch people skidding across the bay.

Set off again south, walking up the dunes until you reach a disorientating world composed of nothing but expanses of hard-packed white sand. From those high dunes there is a vertical drop to the beach below and superb views of the cobalt sea and the islet of Sal Rei. There are often whales in the bay, in season, and you may spot turtles on the beach. Further on you will see the black masts of a shipwreck poking out of the water.

Half an hour from the windsurfers is the lagoon. All you can hear is the waves, the wind on the dunes and, increasingly, the tweets of a multiplicity of birds who thrive on the salty water. The mud is covered in millions of their footprints.

Walk inland up the side of the lagoon. If you choose the left side then ascend a great beer-belly of a dune and after that follow your instinct – there is no path and sometimes you must leave the lagoon edge out of sight in order to find a way between the thick trees. After 20 minutes there is a rough track to the main Sal Rei–Rabil road. Follow the road south as far as the bridge and then clamber down into the *ribeira* on the landward side and follow it inland.

It is a broad, dry riverbed full of *tamareira* trees (*Phoenix atlantica*), a speciality of Boavista. After the rain it is lush, full of grass and small plants. The *ribeira* is hauntingly quiet except for the sounds of goats and the occasional child on a donkey collecting water.

The *ribeira* broadens and turns to the right; at times it must be 200m wide. Soon you are between two ridges – inland the hills look as if they are covered in snow with just the tips of plants poking through. Always stay where the trees are thickest. To the left appears a cliff with the village of **Estância de Baixo** on top. Keep well away from that side of the *ribeira* and stick to the right until, eventually, you see Rabil Church, on the ridge; tracks lead up to it.

From Rabil you may find transport back to Sal Rei or you can walk down to the airport (look for the windsock), before beginning the 8km trek back to town, hopefully picking up a lift on the way. If you want to walk back to Sal Rei, it's more scenic to take the old road (now called the scenic route), which begins after the main road crosses the *ribeira*, and goes straight on where the main road bends to the left.

6 SANTO ANTÓNIO (379M)
Distance: approximately 8km round trip; time: approximately 2.5 hours; difficulty: 2 (CW)
From the waterfront at Sal Rei, Santo António can be seen on the left. Take an *aluguer* towards **Povoação Velha** and disembark at the point which seems closest to the mountain. The castellation near the summit means that it cannot be ascended from this side, so cross the rough ground to the mountain (past the men breaking rocks) and skirt round its north side, past some small ruins, before beginning the ascent from the east, which is straightforward.

7 ROCHA ESTÂNCIA (354M)
Distance: 3km round trip; time: 1 hour; difficulty: 2 (CW)
From the waterfront at Sal Rei, Rocha Estância is on the right, with the antennae on top. There are two routes to the summit. The first involves a scramble. Go straight out of the back of the village of **Povoação Velha** near the Bar di Africa and strike

A SIP OF THE SEA   *Alex Alper*

Salt water is fast becoming a widespread source of drinking water for Cape Verdeans. Plants on Sal, Boavista, Santiago, Maio and São Vicente – managed by Electra, the state-owned energy company, and Aguas da Ponta Preta, a private enterprise – produce roughly four million m³ of water annually. That supplies almost 30,000 Cape Verdeans.

The most common technology used in Cape Verde is reverse osmosis (RO). Osmosis is a natural phenomenon in which the substance dissolved in the water (in this case, salt) naturally moves from an area of high concentration to an area of lower concentration through a semi-permeable membrane, equalising its distribution between the two. During reverse osmosis, the salt water is pressurised so that the salt moves towards an area of high concentration. What's left behind is clean water. RO is cheaper, but more high-tech, than vapour-compression distillation and multi-effect distillation, two other technologies used in Cape Verde. Still, it is far more expensive than other water-collection methods, such as drilling or rainwater harvesting. The most energy-efficient RO plants still require between 2kWh and 3kWh per m³ of water. For a 1,000m³-capacity plant, that's about US$600–900 a day.

Moreover, it is possible that the highly saline leftover 'brine' dumped back into the ocean is harmful to marine life.

Other forms of desalinisation are being tested to address these problems. Two volunteers are working with students at Assomada's technical school to develop solar stills that use sunlight alone to convert seawater into fresh water through evaporation. Construction costs are low and materials readily available – but the so far the prototype produces only about two litres a day.

Nevertheless, Cape Verde is counting on desalinisation for the future. Two new RO plants are under construction in Santiago's interior, while private golf courses and hotels will continue to run their own plants. If all goes according to plan, underground water sources will be left exclusively to agriculture and Cape Verdeans will drink seawater every day.

slightly up to the right towards the saddle. Once on the saddle, head left towards the summit. Alternatively, go towards the church on the low ridge to your right as you are looking north at the mountain, and then follow the shoulder up to the left. It is longer this way but more gentle.

For a less arduous walk around the base of the mountain, continue past the church and go round the *rocha*'s north side. It is not possible to reach the summit from this side.

8 MORE HIKING IDEAS

Armed with a good map (see *Maps*, page 68) it is possible to walk to remote Bofareira in the northeast. There is a round-trip hike from Povoação Velha west to Varandinha and then southeast along the coast to Praia de Santa Mónica, followed by a northern leg back to Povoação Velha. Finally, you can create another trip by hiking from Cabeço das Tarafes west and then southwest, first along a track and then a path, to the pool at Olho de Mar. Some of these hikes are described on www.bela-vista.net/Boa-Vista-Reviere-e.htm.

6

Santiago

The sea
You enlarge our dreams
and suffocate our desires

Jorge Barbosa, born on Santiago Island, 1902

Among the extremes of the Cape Verdean archipelago – the desert islands and the islands so mountainous there is barely a scrap of level ground – Santiago stands out as the normal relation. It is more balanced, more varied – it has a bit of everything. At its heart are craggy mountains cut into exotic outlines and afforested on their lower slopes. Sliced in between are green valleys alive with agriculture. To the south lie irrigated plantations; to the southwest a sterile and gravelly landscape where nothing grows; and in the north and southeast there are some pretty beaches.

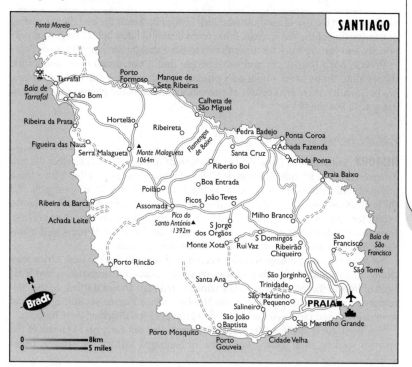

In Santiago the black and the white ingredients of the archipelago's past are at their most vivid. On the southern shore is the old capital of Cape Verde – Ribeira Grande – the first European city in the tropics whose pivotal importance in the Atlantic slave trade is still being uncovered. Up in the mountains, in contrast, the people are as African as Cape Verdeans can be – their ancestors were escaped slaves from the city below.

HIGHLIGHTS

Cidade Velha, the 500-year-old city, is the most important historic site in the archipelago and is of such international significance that in 2009 it became a World Heritage Site. The landscape in central and northern Santiago, and down much of its east coast is stunning and worthy of exploration at least by vehicle and preferably with a couple of hikes as well. Santiago also gives a good overall sample of what Cape Verde has to offer if you are very limited in time.

SUGGESTED ITINERARY AND NUMBER OF DAYS You could 'do' Santiago in a day and a half – half a day for Cidade Velha and a full day for an organised, round-island excursion. For a richer experience, take two days for the round-island tour, spending the night in either Assomada or Tarrafal. Those with more time and inclination could easily find two or three good hikes to do, spend a day on the beach in Tarrafal or at one of the few hotels with some coastal ambience (eg: Pôr do Sol or Mariberto) and visit some of the other attractions listed below.

LOWLIGHTS

Santiago is not the island for those who seek idyllic beaches or the best diving, surfing or windsurfing of the archipelago. It has some beautiful hikes but if that is your only priority, and you are stuck for time, it's best to head straight for Santo Antão or Fogo.

Praia is not a tourist city and some people find it hot, unattractive and a little threatening. Yet its heart – built on a plateau with sheer sides overlooking the sea, has personality; there are a couple of interesting museums and plenty of restaurants, many with live music.

BACKGROUND INFORMATION

HISTORY Santiago *was* Cape Verde for hundreds of years. It was here that the two discoverers of the islands, António de Noli and Diogo Gomes, together with a small group of settlers from the Algarve in Portugal, set up in 1462. Their town grew and the business of resupplying ships and trading in slaves flourished. The other islands, except for Fogo, remained unexplored or were exploited merely for salt or grazing. Even today, inhabitants of Santiago refer to the island as Cabo Verde – as if it was the mainland – and to the other islands as just that: '*as ilhas*'.

Yet from early on Santiago was also a centre of dissent. Its links to west Africa were strong. The *rebelados* and other African renegades escaped miscegenation and lived isolated lives in the interior where they remembered their ancestral tribes. In the 20th century, rebellion stirred primarily in São Nicolau and São Vicente, yet Santiago too had its uprisings – and produced the islands' first great poet and dissenter, Jorge Barbosa.

The Portuguese spelling São Tiago (St James) died out early on in favour of the Spanish spelling used today. (For more on Santiago's history see *History*, pages 9–27.)

SANTIAGO TODAY Today Praia, the political centre of Cape Verde, is undergoing enormous expansion while its infrastructure struggles to keep up. The south of the island is changing quickly, with a new ring road, a few enormous condominium developments and the general spread of the city and its attendant services, from universities to sewage plants. New roads have also been completed in the north recently but the island still feels very much like rural Africa. Here there is a slower pace of life, permeated with donkeys and carts, pigs, hens, dogs and goats. Much of the economic development of the country is concentrated in Santiago, with many foreign NGOs working on diverse projects designed to stimulate the economy and improve the standard of living.

GEOGRAPHY The largest island in the archipelago, at 990km², Santiago has two mountain ranges: the Serra do Pico do António, which rises to a peak of 1,392m, and the more northern Serra Malagueta, rising to a height of 1,064m. There are lush valleys in the centre and several permanent sources of water. Some 290,000 people live here – about 128,000 in Praia, the capital.

The volcanic rocks on Santiago are four–five million years old while the rocks from the sea floor are older, at 8.5–9.5 million years. An important feature of Praia's landscape is the *achadas* (elevated plains) on which the different districts of the city are built. Santiago is the principal agricultural producer of Cape Verde.

NATURAL HISTORY
Protected areas There are two protected areas in Santiago: Serra Malagueta and Serra do Pico do António, both of which are natural parks.

Serra Malagueta is one of three protected areas in the archipelago where there is a team (the Cape Verdean government working with United Nations Development Programme (UNDP) and the Global Environment Facility (GEF)) actively working to breathe some life into the protection through a combination of conservation measures and development of local economic opportunities.

It boasts a large number of endemic plant and bird species, including erva-cidreira (*Melissa officinalis*), used to treat a wide range of illnesses, aipo (*Lavandula rodindifolia*) and losna (*Artemisia gorgonum*).

Birds There are five Important Bird Areas, as designated by BirdLife International:
Three trees – a huge kapok tree in Boa Entrada and two mahogany trees near Banana – constitute two of them. The first tree, a single, huge, 25m-high kapok tree (*Ceiba pentandra*), lies at the heart of a valley near Boa Entrada village. The two mahogany (*Khaya senegalensis*) trees are of moderate height, and also stand at the valley bottom in Santa Catarina. Here are the only two breeding colonies of the endemic Cape Verde purple heron (*Ardea (purpurea) bournei*), although it is said that the occupants of the mahogany trees have moved north to Serra Malagueta.

Some 8km of rugged cliffs along the southwestern coast of the island of Santiago, from the fishermen's village of Porto Mosquito to Baía do Inferno (Baía de Santa Clara), make the third area, which is known for its brown booby (*Sula leucogaster*) and red-billed tropicbird (*Phaethon aethereus*) populations, among others.

The fourth site is made up of two lagoons and their environs south of Pedra Badejo on Santiago, where about 20 species of wader have been recorded.

The final site is the central mountain range including Pico do Santo António, a breeding haven for many endemic birds including Cape Verde little shearwater

(*Puffinus* (*assimilis*) *boydi*), Cape Verde buzzard (*Buteo* ('*buteo*') *bannermani*), Alexander's kestrel (*Falco* (*tinnunculus*) *alexandri*), Cape Verde peregrine (*Falco* (*peregrinus*) *madens*), Cape Verde swift (*Apus alexandri*), Cape Verde cane warbler (*Acrocephalus brevipennis*) and the Iago sparrow (*Passer iagoensis*).

HAZARDS Bag-snatching and pickpocketing are becoming more audacious in Praia, with anecdotal evidence that females are more at risk than males. Take the usual precautions (no visible or accessible laptops, cameras, purses, etc). Sucupira Market is the most notorious for theft and Achada Santo António has a bad reputation, particularly at the northern end. Taxis are everywhere: it's worth hailing one if you're not sure about where you're going.

FESTIVALS

15 January	Municipality Day (Tarrafal)
2 February	Nho Fenrero Festival (São Domingos)
Wednesday after Carnival	Ashes Day
13 March	Municipality Day (São Domingos)
15 days after Easter	São Salvador do Mundo (Picos)
23 April	São Jorge
1 May	São Jose
May	Music festival (Gamboa Beach)
	A three-day-long jamboree
8 May	São Miguel Arcanjo Feast
	(Ribeira Calheta de São Miguel)
13 May	Nossa Sra de Fátima (Assomada)
31 May	Imaculada Conceição
June and July	*Tabanka* processions (see page 186)
15 August	Nossa Sra do Socorro
25 November	Municipality Day (Santa Catarina area)

GETTING THERE AND AWAY

BY AIR
International flights You can fly direct from Lisbon to Santiago. For information on international flights see *Chapter 2, Practical Information*, page 54.

Domestic flights There are TACV flights to and from Sal, São Vicente, Maio and Fogo (for ticket purchase, see *Other practicalities*, page 186). There is a regular day trip from Sal to Santiago with Cabo Verde Express which can be booked through the major tour operators on Sal and involves an island tour. There are also flights between Sal and Santiago with Halcyonair.

Praia International Airport The airport and terminal building are new. Facilities include: money-changing (⏰ *15.00–19.30 Mon–Sat & a variety of morning hours, depending on the day*); international car-hire firms; a somewhat underwhelming tourist information kiosk; tour operators (Orbitur, Morabitur); internet access (supposedly open 24/7); a bank and a 24-hour café.

If you arrive on an international flight and do not have a visa you will need to buy one on arrival (see *Chapter 2, Practical Information*, page 52).

Taxis from the airport wait in a mostly orderly queue. A taxi from the airport to town will cost around 700$.

BY FERRY A new service operated by Cabo Verde Fast Ferry (*www.cvfastferry. com*) started operations in January 2011 with a service between Praia, Fogo & Brava. Other routes are to follow. The brand new boat has comfortable seats, a refreshment kiosk and entertainment on plasma screens. This new company looks set to revolutionise inter-island travel, offering some much-needed competition to the two domestic airlines. Check the latest with the ferry agencies, listed below, with a tour operator in Praia, or on www.bela-vista.net/ferry.aspx, which updates ferry news regularly.

The port is at the northern end of the harbour. Taxis there or back cost 200–500$ depending on the destination.

Agentur STM ✆ 261 2564
ANAV Shipping CP 58, Rua Serpa Pinto; ✆ 261 7858/260 3100; e anavpraia@cvtelecom.cv
Cabo Verde Fast Ferry Chã de Areia, Praia; ✆ 261 7552; e cvff.info@cvfastferry.com; www.cvfastferry.com

Cabo Verde Shipping Agency ✆ 261 1179; e csa.rai@cvtelecom.cv
Polar Shipping CP 120, Rua Candido dos Reis, Praia Plateau; also try Rua Serpa Pinto 141; ✆ 261 5223/5225/7177/7224; e polarp@cvtelecom.cv
Viagens Cabo Verde Also on Rua Candido dos Reis, for shipping.

BY YACHT Praia provides a well-sheltered harbour where yachts are asked to anchor in the west between the two jetties. It is essential to follow all the entry procedures with the port captain and immigration office, whether or not this is your first stop in Cape Verde; on departure get clearance again from the port captain. Yacht facilities are poor. There is no boatyard or chandlery. Fuel and water have to be collected by can. Ask the port captain for a watchman, at around €4 per day.

The next-best anchorage is Tarrafal, at the north of the island. Visit the harbour office on arrival. Another anchorage is at Ribeira da Barca (but there is swell and northeast winds funnelling off the island).

GETTING AROUND

BY PUBLIC TRANSPORT *Alugueres* (on this island, more commonly referred to as *hiaces*) travel up and down the spine of the island – the road between Praia and Tarrafal – all day and evening. Villages down the west coast are reached on roads extending from this central spine, so catch one of these *alugueres* and change at the relevant junction. *Alugueres* are also frequent along the slower, eastern coastal road between Praia and Tarrafal. They all leave from the Sucupira Market west of the Plateau. For Cidade Velha there are regular *alugueres* leaving from Terra Branca in Praia, southwest of the Plateau. Sucupira Market is a noisy melée of drivers and their assistants trying to get you to choose their *alugueres*. Pick the one with the most people inside, as they don't leave until they are full.

Many of the roads have been improved with money from the Millennium Challenge, making travel in Santiago more comfortable and faster as well as improving the lives of the residents by providing small communities with better links to main towns. A grey-haired driver is the safest bet.

BY TAXI The taxis in Praia are marked and are cream-coloured; a journey within town costs 150–200$, sometimes 300$ (especially after 23.00). A taxi for the day costs about 7,000$.

🚗 **Eurotaxi** ✆ 262 6000. A 24hr taxi service.   🚗 **Taxi Lopez** ✆ 262 1043

BY CAR There is quite a choice in Praia. Remember that only a 4x4 can take you on the dirt tracks down to the west coast. One day's hire should cost around €50–60. It is cheaper to hire a car in town (many companies are in the Prainha area), but not as convenient as picking one up at the airport. There are two rental kiosks (Inter-Cidades and Avis) at the airport but they are not always open.

🚗 **Abreu** Fazenda district; ☎ 261 2757

🚗 **Alucar Chã d'Areia** ☎ 261 5801

🚗 **Atlântico** Prainha ☎ 261 6424; m 993 9630; e rentcaratlantic@cvtelecom.cv

🚗 **Autobraza** Fazenda

🚗 **Avis** At the Hotel Oasis Praia-Mar in Prainha; ☎ 261 8748

🚗 **Classic Auto Rental** Achada Santo António, Praia; ☎ 262 1808; e rentcarclassic@cvtelecom.cv

🚗 **CV Rent a Car** Prainha; m 989 9545; e cvrent@cvtelecom.cv

🚗 **Hertz** At the Hotel Pestana Trópico in Prainha; ☎ 261 4200

🚗 **Inter Cidades Rent-a-Car** Achada Santo António, Praia; ☎ 261 2525; m 994 353; e comercial@intercidadesrentacar.cv

🏠 **WHERE TO STAY**

Most people stay in the capital Praia because anywhere on the rest of the island can be reached in a day trip. Here there are two smart international hotels each with a pool and most of the trimmings, and many others encompassing a great range of quality, though none of the latter are places in which to laze for a day.

There are two other hotel centres. The growing city of Assomada has six or seven hotels, some of which are pretty smart, but none of them have any potential for lazy touristic enjoyment. Assomada is a growing staging post though – a departure point for hikes, with a museum and a vibrant market. The other centre is Tarrafal where, in addition to budget hotels, there are a few choices for those who want to enjoy this quiet town in more comfort.

There are a few enjoyable hotels in odd, interesting places: most notably the inland Quinta da Montanha and Pousada Mariberto on the east coast. If you have a car you could comfortably base yourself at these locations and make day trips to other parts of the island.

ACTIVITIES

EXCURSIONS Try the following operators for guided tours to highlights of the island.

Girassol Tours Rua Serpa Pinto, Plateau, Praia; ☎ 261 2899; e girassoltours@cvtelecom.cv. Offers transfers around the island, excursions to Cidade Velha (2 people; €20 each) or Achada Leite (2 people; €45 each), & a round-island tour (2 people; €40 each), as well as the usual hotel reservations, car rental & national & international air tickets.

G and S Schellmann Esplanada Silibell, Ponta Calhetona, Calheta de São Miguel; ☎ 273 2078; m 996 7930; www.reisetraeume.de, www.reisetraeume.de/kapverden/viadoso/enindex.html. Gerhard & Sibylle have lived in the islands for years now & specialise in small-group

hiking holidays in Santiago. They also operate on an international level, organising the entire holiday in the archipelago including international flights. At their base in Calheta de São Miguel (see page 126), they offer an open-air, sea-view restaurant, bar & tourist information & can direct you, for example, to finding out more about the weaving of *pano de terra*.

Hotel Prestige Assomada (for contact details, see Assomada, page 186). Offers a 2-day round-island tour beginning in Praia, with the intervening night spent at its hotel in Assomada, & other excursions in & around Assomada.

Orbitur Rua Cândido dos Reis No 9; ☎261 5736/7; m 991 8331; e orbitur@cvtelcom.cv; www.orbitur.cv. Arranges tours in Santiago as well as travel to other islands.

Praiatur Av Amílcar Cabral ☎261 5746/7; e praiatur.lda@cvtelecom.cv; ⏰ 08.00–12.00 & 14.00–16.30 Mon–Fri. This established agency has been running for over 20 years in Praia. It offers a round-island tour of Praia, does a 1-day tour of Santiago (3,170$); half-day or full-day tour of Cidade Velha; a trip to Praia Baixo for swimming & lunch. Price per person drops considerably for groups of 5 or more. Guides speak a variety of languages.

Soul Tours Ponta d'Atum, Serra Malagueta, close to King Fisher Resort; ☎266 2435; m 917 8529/8520; e soultours@soultours.ch. Arranges hotels, transport, excursions & tours in Santiago & elsewhere.

HIKING The interior of Santiago is filled with spectacular craggy mountains, *ribeiras* and plantations. Though it does not have the breathtaking drama of Santo Antão, or the sheer strangeness of Fogo, it has walks that are both beautiful and rewarding, for which it is definitely worth putting aside some time. Many walks consist of finding a point along the spine of the island and walking down a *ribeira* to the coast (or vice versa). The two, perhaps classic, hikes are to descend from Serra Malagueta down towards Tarrafal (about six hours – you could get yourself dropped off and your luggage taken on to a hotel in Tarrafal) and the hike down Ribeira Principal, towards the east coast.

The biggest hike is to the top of Pico do Santo António – a twin peak that protrudes from the landscape like a canine tooth. Unfortunately the path to the Pico is not clear, the final ascent borders on the hazardous and knowledgeable guides are hard to find. See *Health*, page 64, for advice on hiking. New hikes are opening up in Serra Malagueta, with the development of the natural park. See *Serra Malagueta*, page 187.

FISHING You can link up with local fishermen in almost any village (try Tarrafal or Pedra Badejo) - pay them about 1,000$ if they take you out on one of their trips. See *Chapter 2, Practical Information*, page 49, for a discussion of fishing. Sambala (see *São Francisco*, page 192) plans to offer big-game fishing.

DIVING Most diving is done in Tarrafal where there are several interesting diving spots all reachable within 15 minutes of Tarrafal by boat. There is also diving off Cidade Velha (interesting for the relics of centuries of ships that anchored there) and at Baixa de Janeia. A dive centre is opening in Praia, based at Hotel Praia Mar.

Divecenter-Santiago Based at King Fisher Resort, Tarrafal; m 993 6407; e divecenter-santiago@email.de; www.divecenter-santiago.de/start/?language=en. The website gives a good description of diving spots off Santiago.

King Bay Tarrafal; ☎266 1100; m 992 3050; e hrolfs1@gmx.net. Run by Monaya, a marine biologist & expert in Cape Verde's marine history. 4 languages spoken. €35 per dive.

Underwater Cape Verde Hotel Praia Mar, Prainha; m 977 9769; e nuno@underwater.cv; www.underwatercapeverde.com. PADI centre offering courses & diving around Praia & Cidade Velha.

SURFING There are some reasonable surfing spots in Santiago, though it is not worth coming to Cape Verde especially for them. The swell is best between January and March.

In Tarrafal, a short walk southwest from the main bay, there are some reef breaks, in particular at Ponta do Atum and at Chão Bom. The other well-known spots are in the southeast of the island: the coast south of Ponta do Lobo Lighthouse which marks the easternmost point of Santiago (accessible only by 4x4) and the local bodyboarding beach at Praia itself, just in front of the Plateau. See *Chapter 2, Practical Information*, page 46, for general surfing information.

BEACHES Santiago's beaches fade into insignificance compared with the exhilarating expanses of Boavista and Sal, and the beaches on Maio. Nevertheless there are some to enjoy: Tarrafal has perhaps the best, a pretty cove and white-sand beach, busy at the weekends with local day trippers. Also try Ribeira da Prata, a short journey south of Tarrafal, a long black-sand turtle-nesting beach set in front of lush green palms. The Câmara Municipal operates a turtle hatchery on this beach during the summer. São Francisco is another, currently hard to get to except, again, at weekends when locals head down there from Praia. There is a beach at Praia Baixo and there are several in Praia. You may well find other undiscovered gems if you explore the island in depth.

CULTURE The whole city of Cidade Velha is a museum; Praia has a small general museum on the Plateau and an interesting archaeological museum, which includes many trophies from the diving of wrecks. Heading north, Assomada has its *Tabanka* Museum documenting this fascinating traditional dance and music form, and Tarrafal has its more sombre Museum of the Resistance, in the former concentration camp there. You can also seek out the cloth-weaving tradition (see *Shopping*, page 178, and *Excursions, G and S Schellmann*, page 166), and enjoy traditional and modern Cape Verdean music at Quintal da Música, which has done so much to shepherd the country's musicians.

SIGHTSEEING BY VEHICLE A one- or, less often, two-day tour of the island by vehicle is a popular thing to do and well worth it, though it leaves a tantalising amount unseen off the main roads. If you hire your own vehicle or taxi for exploration try to get a 4x4 so you can go down some of the quieter roads, though an ordinary car will easily take you on the circuit and to and from Cidade Velha.

PRAIA

Built on a tableland of rock, with the city overflowing on to the land below its steep cliffs, the centre of Praia – its Plateau – is attractive. It has a disorientating feel: it is indisputably African and yet Mediterranean as well.

Praia is undergoing rapid growth and the population is around 128,000. Infrastructure – from sewage treatment to electricity generation – is finding it impossible to keep pace with this chaotic expansion. Journey to the outskirts of Palmarejo, where there is frenetic building, and you will see an entire hill being gradually, and illegally, hand-mined away. Some of the miners live in little caves in the hillside.

During the day, people of every shade of skin go about their business on the Plateau. At night, though, the Plateau is empty – life continues in the scattered regions beyond. To its south rises another level plain, the Achada Santo António, where the more affluent live in apartment blocks and where the huge parliament building is. Between the two lies Chã de Areia, and, in front of Achada, Prainha, where there are embassies, expensive hotels and nightclubs. Other districts include Terra Branca to the west and Fazenda district to the north. Palmarejo is a new, middle-class residential area to the west of central Praia. To the northwest is a huge sprawl of half-built houses and burning litter – Cape Verde's version of the urban drift from the countryside.

HISTORY From the early 1600s, Portugal tried both to entice and to force its citizens to make Praia da Santa Maria their capital instead of Ribeira Grande (now Cidade Velha). But the colonisers ignored instructions and stuck to their preferred settlement, 13km away. By ignoring Praia, they left themselves open to attack from behind: Praia, with its poorly fortified beaches, was a place where pirates could land. From there it was an easy overland march to attack the capital.

This happened on two disastrous occasions. Francis Drake used the tactic in 1585 and the Frenchman Jacques Cassard did exactly the same more than a century later in 1712. After the first assault the population built the fort, which survives to this day just outside Cidade Velha. The second sacking signalled the demise of Ribeira Grande as investment was made in the fortification of Praia. Praia's shacks were replaced by permanent buildings and it grew. By 1770, it was the official capital achieving, in 1858, the rank of *cidade*. Today Praia remains the administrative centre while culture seems to gravitate towards Mindelo.

One of Praia's most distinguished visitors was Charles Darwin, who anchored there at the start of his famous voyage on the *Beagle* on 16 January 1832, and spent some time examining the flora and fauna, as well as making forays to Cidade Velha and São Domingos. He reported that he 'feasted' upon oranges and 'likewise tasted a Banana: but did not like it, being maukish and sweet with little flavour'. He wandered through a valley near Praia:

> Here I saw the glory of tropical vegetation: Tamarinds, Bananas and Palms were flourishing at my feet. I expected a good deal, for I had read Humboldt's descriptions, and I was afraid of disappointments: how utterly vain such fear is, none can tell but those who have experienced what I today have. It is not only the gracefulness of their forms or the novel richness of their colours. It is the numberless and confused associations that rush together on the mind, and produce the effect. I returned to the shore, treading on Volcanic rocks, hearing the notes of unknown birds, and seeing new insects fluttering about still newer flowers… It has been for me a glorious day, like giving to a blind man eyes, he is overwhelmed with what he sees and cannot justly comprehend it.

He also wrote about the more barren slopes of Cape Verde:

> A single green leaf can scarcely be discovered over wide tracts of the lava plains; yet flocks of goats, together with a few cows, contrive to exist. It rains very seldom, but during a short portion of the year heavy torrents fall, and immediately afterwards

THE LINDBERGHS

Charles and Anne Morrow Lindbergh, the famous aviators, arrived in Praia while trying to circumnavigate the north Atlantic. Their plane was named the *Tingmissartoq* ('big flying bird' in a Greenland Inuit language). They took six hours to come from Morocco, arriving on 27 November 1933. They were not impressed with the island, which Anne said was 'boring'. In Santiago they recalculated their course and returned to the African mainland, deciding instead to attempt the transatlantic leg to Brazil from The Gambia.

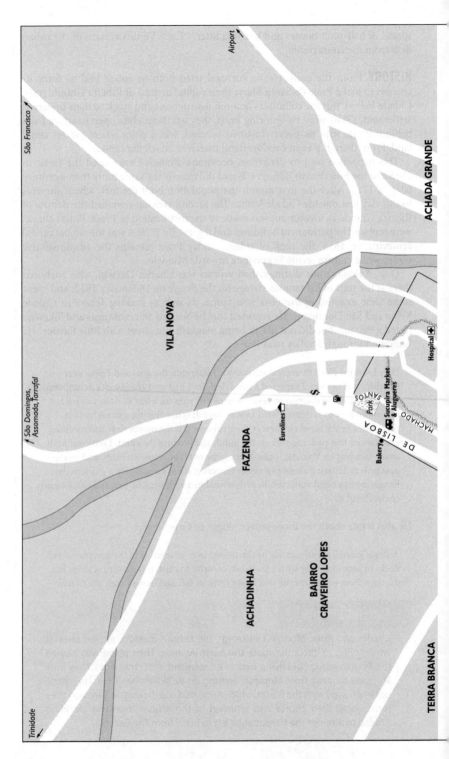

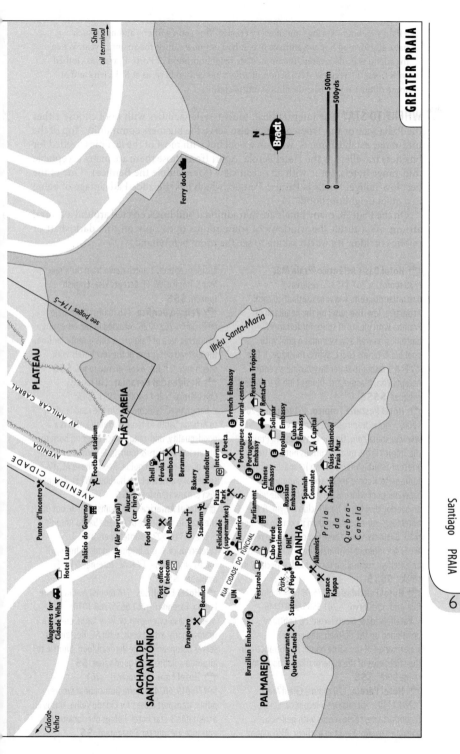

GREATER PRAIA

Shell oil terminal

Ferry dock

Ilhéu Santa-Maria

see pages 174–5

PLATÉAU

CHÃ D'AREIA

AVENIDA CIDADE
AVENIDA AMÍLCAR CABRAL

Punto d'Incontro

Hotel Luar

Alugueres for Cidade Velha

Palácio do Governo

Football stadium

TAP (Air Portugal)

Alucar (car hire)

Food shop

Shell
Pérola
Gamboa
Beramar
Bakery
Mundioltur
Internet
O Poeta
French Embassy
Portuguese cultural-centre
Pestana Trópico
CV RentaCar
Solimar
Portuguese Embassy
Angolan Embassy
Cuban Embassy
A Capital
Oásis Atlántico/ Praia Mar

A Bolha

Church

Stadium

Plaza Park

Felicidade (supermarket)
América
Parliament
Chinese Embassy
Russian Embassy
Spanish Consulate

A Falésia

Praia da Quebra-Canela

ACHADA DE SANTO ANTÓNIO

Dragoeiro

Benfica

Post office & CV telecom

RUA CIDADE DO FUNCHAL

UN

Festarola

Cabo Verde Investimentos

DHL

Park

Statue of Pope

Alikemist

Espace Kappa

PRAINHA

PALMAREJO

Brazilian Embassy

Restaurante Quebra-Canela

Cidade Velha

Bradt

N

0 ___ 500m
0 ___ 500yds

a light vegetation springs out of every crevice. This soon withers; and upon such naturally formed hay the animals live. It had not now rained for an entire year. When the island was discovered, the immediate neighbourhood of Porto Praya was clothed with trees, the reckless destruction of which has caused here, as at St Helena and at some of the Canary islands, almost entire sterility.

WHERE TO STAY For international, tourist-style facilities with pool choose either the Praia Mar or the Trópico, which also serve the business community. Top of the mid-range establishments, without a pool but with most of the facilities needed for business travellers, is the Hotel Pérola. Apart from those there are many acceptable mid-range hotels, some with an ocean view (for example the Benfica). One of the best low-budget hotels is Paraiso Pensão, which has the added advantage of being in a quiet neighbourhood.

On the Plateau, many hotels are in traditional buildings, erected around a central atrium. As a result the windows of some rooms open only on to a dark shaft or public corridor: it's worth asking to see the room beforehand.

Hotel Oásis Atlântico/Praia Mar
(130 rooms) 261 4153; e reservas@ oasisatlantico.com; www.oasisatlantico.com. Attractive, low-rise hotel on the headland of Prainha with plenty of space for terraces & balconies, as well as a swimming pool with pool bar & tennis court, gym & massage. It has Wi-Fi & a rather rudimentary business centre. Accepts Visa, MasterCard, Diners Club & travellers' cheques. **$$$$**

Hotel Pestana Trópico (51 rooms) 261 4200; e hotel.tropico@cvtelecom.cv; www.pestana.com. On the coast road in Prainha, the Trópico is the most luxurious hotel in town, a recent refurbishment giving its spacious rooms some style. Rooms are arranged around the seawater pool which is very comfortable with an overlooking bar, a health club & gym, & the hotel feels more peaceful than its cousin up the road. Business-wise, there is a conference room, Wi-Fi & 1 internet terminal. The restaurant has an excellent reputation for its food, especially its steaks. **$$$$**

Hotel Felicidade [175 D5] (24 rooms) Rua Andrade Corvo; 261 5585/260 0246; e hotelfelicidade@cvtelecom.cv. Centrally positioned on the Plateau, above the supermarket of the same name, its entrance is in the street east of the supermarket. A good, mid-range hotel. **$$$**

Hotel Pérola (20 rooms) Chã d'Areia; 260 1440; e perola@cvtelecom.cv. Smart & comfortable, some rooms with generous balconies overlooking the harbour. Also a good

business option, 1 notch down from the Praia Mar & Trópico. Wi-Fi. Accepts Visa. English spoken. **$$$**

Pensão Benfica (16 rooms) Palmarejo de Baixo; 262 7226. Situated in the emerging, bourgeois area of Palmarejo, this is quite far from the Plateau but is one of the few hotels with ocean views. It has a conference room. **$$$**

Residencial Beramar (10 rooms) Chã d'Areia; 261 6400; m 991 7343; e beramar@cvtelecom.cv. On the road leading to Achada Santo António & Prainha, this is a good-quality, mid-range place catering both to business travellers & tourists, & owned by an ex-taxi driver & tourist guide. Rooms have AC, TV & some have a view of the harbour. Wi-Fi. Accepts Visa & bank transfers. **$$$**

Hotel América (19 rooms) A little out of the way, in the peace of Achada Santo António; 262 1431/1527; e hotelamerica@ cvtelecom.cv. It is a bright & modern hotel, all rooms with fridge, TV & AC. Internet & Wi-Fi available. **$$**

Hotel Eurolines (14 rooms) Av Cidade de Lisboa, Fazenda; 261 6655/260 3010; e eurolines@cvtelecom.cv. Very large, en-suite rooms, many with 2 beds, with AC. Restaurant serves European & Cape Verdean food. Shuttle to airport available. Very good value. **$$**

Hotel Luar (28 rooms) 261 5947/6019/6024. In Terra Branca near where public transport leaves for Cidade Velha, this is an acceptable 3-star hotel. Rooms overlooking the entrance are quieter. Restaurant. **$$**

⌂ **Residencial Praia Maria** [174 D4] (16 rooms) Rua 5 de Julho; ☎ 261 4178; ▯ 993 3323; e res.praiamaria@sapo.cv; www.praiamaria.com. A bright & fresh 3-star hotel on the Plateau with large rooms, with TV, hot water, AC, fridge. Some rooms have no external windows. A good mid-range choice. Wi-Fi. Accepts Visa. Some staff speak English. **$$**

⌂ **Rosymar Inn** [175 E5] (10 rooms) 15 Rua Correio, Plateau; ☎ 261 6345; ▯ 916 3112; e info@rosymarinn.com; www.rosymarinn.com. Owned by a returned US citizen, this is one of the longest-established hotels & is currently being remodelled with plans for a café. Convenient location directly behind Pão Quente. Rooms are en suite with hot water. **$$**

⌂ **Residencial Santa Maria** [174 D3] (12 rooms) Rua Serpa Pinto, Plateau; ☎ 261

4337; e res.praiamaria@cvtelecom.cv. Sister of the Residencial Praia Maria, this offers a similar standard though without the airy central atrium that uplifts the other. Rooms are en suite with TV, hot water, AC, fridge. Accepts Visa. **$$**

⌂ **Pensão Paraiso** [174 D2] (14 rooms) Rua Serpa Pinto; ☎ 261 3539. In a quiet setting at the northern end of the Plateau, this is not bad for those on a budget. All rooms are en suite with hot water. **$**

⌂ **Residencial Sol Atlântico** [175 C7] (16 rooms) Av Amílcar Cabral; ☎ 261 2872. Overlooking the main square on the Plateau, ths is above the Sol Atlântico agency, but has no sign. It's probably the cheapest place in town, & the quality is definitely reflected in the price. Some rooms are en suite, all have fans, hot water. **$**

✕ WHERE TO EAT AND DRINK
On the Plateau

⊑ **French Cultural Centre** [175 E6] ⊕ 08.00–19.00. Now situated in Prainha opposite the Angolan embassy there is a café inside the centre, which also sells postcards & books. **$$$**

⊑ **Pão Quente de Cabo Verde** [175 E5] ⊕ 06.00–22.00 daily. A wide variety of delicious cakes, snacks & sandwiches in a busy, spacious European-style café. **$$$**

✕ **Quintal da Música** [174 C2] Av Amílcar Cabral; ☎ 261 7282; ⊕ from 08.30 Mon–Thu, from 21.00 Fri/Sat. Live music Tue–Sat. One of the classic places to spend an evening in Praia, this restaurant was founded by musician Mario Lucio along with the Cape Verdean band Simentera to promote traditional music & stimulate local musicians. Its courtyard & little stage make an evocative place to while away a Praia evening. Can get chilly later on – take a jumper. **$$$**

⊑ **Sofia Cyber Café** [174 D4] ⊕ 07.00–23.00. This restaurant is one of the few places on the Plateau where you can sit outside under a parasol & enjoy watching life go by, with the added advantage that you can check your emails & make national & international calls inside while your meal is cooked. A good varied menu & an assortment of desserts. Be warned: service is notoriously slow. **$$$**

✕ **Splab Grill** [174 E4] Rua Candido dos Reis; ⊕ 08.00–00.00 Mon–Fri, 08.00–03.00 Sat.

Popular place with spectacular beach view. Snacks, lunches, dinner. **$$$**

✕ **Restaurante Panorama** [175 D5] ⊕ 11.00–15.00 & 19.00–22.00 daily. Above the Hotel Felicidade on the Plateau but with an entrance in Rua Serpa Pinto, not Av Corvo. This rooftop restaurant is an escape from the noise & heat below, with plenty of seating including an open-air terrace at the back looking east. Popular with white-collar workers for its speed, conviviality & price rather than its cuisine. **$$**

✕ **Restaurant Plateau** [174 D4] (known as the Chinese Pink Palace) Av Eduardo Mondlane; ⊕ 08.00–21.00 Mon–Sat. Basic Chinese food & one of the few places in Cape Verde where you can find tofu. **$$**

✕ **Café Chocolate** [175 D5] Rua Serpa Pinto. Colourful café serving the usual sandwiches. **$**

⊑ **Café Sodade** [175 D5] Rua Andrade Corvo. Simple snacks & drinks & a plate of the day. **$**

✕ **Casa Bela** [174 D2] Rua Miguel Bombarda. Pleasant café with 3 plates of the day & vegetarian options. **$**

✕ **Casa Pasta António** [174 D3] Rua Miguel Bombarda. Bustling café serving *cachupa*, pizzas & soup. **$**

✕ **Restaurant Lim** [174 D2] Rua Serpa Pinto. Otherwise known as the 'Chinese Hole in the Wall'

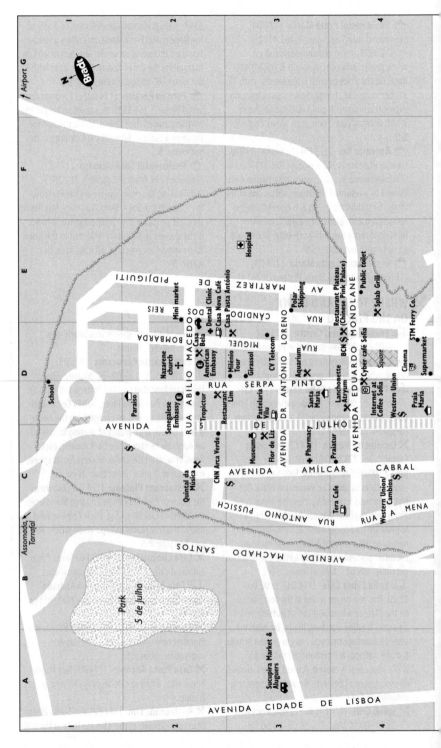

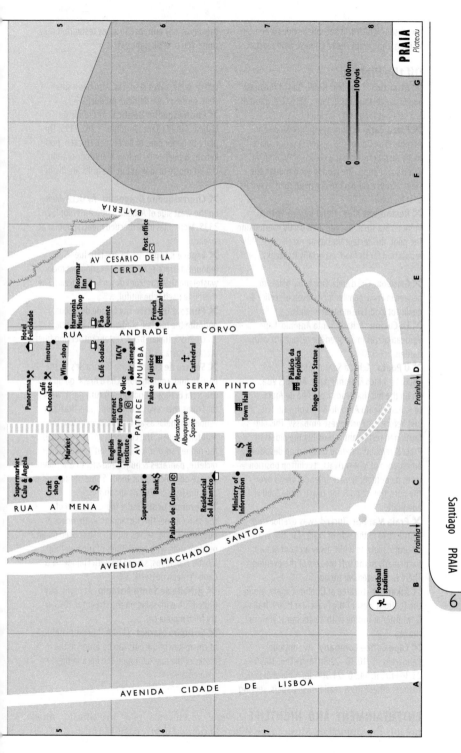

PRAIA
Plateau

Santiago PRAIA

6

175

for reasons which will become obvious when visiting, this serves cheap Chinese food most of the day. A tiny entrance to a tiny restaurant may cause you to walk right past it. $

Off the Plateau

✗ **Atlântico** Praia Mar Hotel. One of the most expensive restaurants in Praia, this AC restaurant is a safe bet for quality & variety. $$$$$

✗ **Plaza Park** ☼ lunch & dinner Mon–Sat. Accepts Visa. One of the newer, smarter, place-to-be restaurants it has a choice of AC, non-AC & terrace seating. The food is good though the view, across a car park to the main road, is not its best feature. $$$$$

✗ **Restaurant Alex** Hotel Trópico. With AC indoors, & a small outside area partly overlooking the pool, this restaurant has an excellent reputation for its food, especially its steaks. $$$$$

✗ **Gamboa** Chã d'Areia. One of *the* places to be seen in Praia, popular for its levels of service & quality of food. Live music at w/ends. $$$$

✗ **La Cucina** Achada Santo António. Cape Verdean pizzas in an open-air restaurant with garden. $$$$

✗ **O Poeta** Achada Santo António; ☎ 261 3800; ☼ lunch & dinner daily. Accepts Visa. Go up the hill that leads from Chã de Areia to Achada Santo António & it is on your left, just before the Portuguese embassy. This old-fashioned restaurant is possibly the oldest in Praia & remains a fixture on the map despite the emergence of newer rivals. Its clifftop position gives its outdoor terrace splendid views over the port, the island & the coast; & the food is adequate. $$$$

✗ **Praia Mar Bar** Tucked away overlooking a little cove to the side of Praia Mar, this is a beautiful place to while away an hour or two, particularly in the soft breezes of the evening. There is a limited bar menu. $$$$

✗ **Alkemist** Located at Quebra-Canela, along the seafront west of the Praia Mar Hotel; Italian & traditional cuisine with a panoramic view of the sea. $$$

✗ **Cape Coffee Company** Av Santiago, Palmarejo; ☼ 10.30–22.30 Mon–Thu, 10.30–23.30 Fri/Sat, 14.30–21.30 Sun. A place in which to meet other Brits & read British papers, serving coffee, wine, cakes & snacks. Also has a small shop serving Cape Verdean products. $$$

✗ **Churrasqueiro Benfica** Av Cidade de Lisboa, Achada Santo António; ☎ 262 2195. The place to go for piles of barbecued chicken, pork kebabs & beefsteak. Indoor & outdoor seating. It is a bit grotty to look at but the grills are divine. $$$

✗ **Churrasqueiro Dragoeiro** Av UCLA-Meio, on the west side of Achada Santo António; ☎ 262 3335. More piles of barbecued meats, popular at w/ends. $$$

✗ **Espace Kappa** ☼ 18.30–late Tue–Sun. Indoor & terrace seating that overlooks a rocky wasteland that stretches down to the ocean. The shoreline itself is beautiful. $$$

✗ **Punto d'Incontro** Av Cidade de Lisboa, opposite the football stadium in Chã d'Areia; ☎ 261 7090. Italian bar & restaurant serving fine pizzas & pasta. $$$

✗ **Sovaco de Cobra** Terra Branca. It's a little hard to find: coming from Chã d'Areia, go up to the Terra Branca roundabout & turn right, walk for 5mins then ask for directions. This Brazilian venue is popular as an interim stop before the nightclubs open. The cuisine is as interesting as the name ('*sovaco*' means 'armpit'), with crêpes, raclette, pancakes & huge sandwiches & a small terrace on which to eat them. Some of the food is a bit greasy. *Caipirinhas* abound. $$$

✗ **Beramar Grill** Under the *residencial* of the same name, this restaurant, with indoor & outdoor seating, serves superb fish cooked on an outdoor grill, with specialities of tuna, garoupa, lobster & octopus, served up with Fogo wine & Cape Verdean desserts. $$

✗ **Achada de Santo António** At night, buy grilled fish with salad on the street for 100$ or try fried moreia eel. $

✗ **Sucupira Market** [174 A3] Great platefuls of cheap lunchtime eats can be found in the kiosks of the market, round the back in the covered area. $

ENTERTAINMENT AND NIGHTLIFE Several restaurants play live music, most notably the Quintal da Música (see *Where to eat and drink*, page 173).

♀ **A Capital** Prainha; part of the Hotel Praia Mar complex. There is a small dance floor but plenty of tables & chairs. It appeals to a slightly older, more affluent crowd & is popular with both tourists & those seeking tourists; busy Fri/Sat nights.

♀ **Bomba–H** Off the road to Cidade Velha: turn left at the Terra Branca–Hotel Luar roundabout. Playing zouk, hip-hop & rap, this open-air place appeals to the teenage crowd.

♀ **Cockpit** Achada Grande, near the airport & Ponta Bicuda. A smart place frequented by anyone who is anyone.

♀ **Discoteca Zero Horas** Achada Grande. On the road to the airport take the right turn past some warehouses & it is about 400m down on the right, a large purple building. For young clubbers: sweaty, crowded & loud. It plays a mixture of Cape Verdean, South American, American & European music (entry 500$).

♀ **Flampa** Bomba's more mature twin, this is for people in their thirties upwards, with music more salsa than hip-hop.

♀ **Tabanka Mar** Live music at the Hotel Praia Mar Fri/Sat evenings.

OTHER PRACTICALITIES

Airlines TACV [175 D5], Rua Serra Pinto (☎ 260 8241/8200/261 7529; ☉ 08.00–17.00 Mon–Fri, 09.00–12.00 Sat). TAP, Chã d'Areia (☎ 261 5826), overlooking the roundabout beside the vast Palácio do Governo. Air Senegal [175 D6], Av Amílcar Cabral, at the northern end of the Plateau (☎ 261 7529/4795/7539; e praia@airsenegalinternational.sn; www.airsenegalinternational.com). Many travel agents and tour operators will book flights.

Banks On the Plateau: Banco Comercial do Atlântico, Praça Alexander Albuquerque (☉ 08.00–14.30 Mon–Fri); Caixa Económica, Av Amílcar Cabral, at the northern end (☉ 08.00–13.00 & 14.00–15.00 Mon–Fri). In Fazenda: Caixa Económica, Av Cidade de Lisboa (☉ 08.00–13.00 & 14.00–15.00 Mon–Fri); Banco Comercial do Atlântico, Av Cidade de Lisboa (☉ 08.00–14.30 Mon–Fri); Banco Cabo-Verdiano de Negro, Av Eduardo Montlane; various cambios along Av Amílcar Cabral.

Dentist Rua Miguel Bombarda (☎ 261 8364).

DHL Av OUA, Achada Santo António, CP 303A (☎ 262 3124; e dhl_praia@vtelecom.cv).

Embassies See Chapter 2, Practical Information, page 53.

Ferries

Polar Shipping [174 E3] Rua Candido dos Reis, Rua Serpa Pinto, Plateau; ☎261 5223; e polarp@cvtelecom.cv. Operates the Barlavento.
STM [174 D4] Rua Andrade Corvo, Plateau; ☎261 4180. Operates the Tarrafal and the Sal Rei.
Agencia Nacional de Viagens (ANAV) Rua Serpa Pinto, Plateau; ☎260 3107; e anavpraia@cvtelecom.cv. Operates the Djon Dade.

CNN Arca Verde [174 C2] Av 5 de Julho; ☎261 5497. At the northern end of the Plateau.
Moura Company Via Solatlântico, Praça Albuquerque, Plateau; ☎261 6692; e agencia_solatlantico@hotmail.com
Cabo Verde Fast Ferry Chã de Areia, Praia; ☎261 7552; e cvff.info@cvfastferry.com; www.cvfastferry.com

Food shopping There are many minimercardos on the Plateau. The largest supermarket on the Plateau, Leader Price, where you can sometimes find a surprising number of familiar brands and a variety of cheese, is by the main square on Av Amílcar Cabral. On the same road heading north, a small branch of Kalu e Angela also has a wide range of goods. The main branch of Kalu e Angela in the suburb of Achadinha is a megastore by Cape Verdean standards; any taxi driver will take you there.

Hospital [174 E3] Av Martirez de Pidjiguiti (◌ 261 2462). Situated at the northeastern edge of the Plateau, overlooking the airport road, this has a mixed reputation though it is well equipped. One recommendation is to use its facilities via a private doctor.

Internet Praia Ouro, Praça Alexander Albuquerque, northeast side; Cyber Café Sofia. Wi-Fi available on the two Plateau squares.

Pharmacy Various places throughout the city, including: Av Amílcar Cabral [174 C3] (◌ *08.15–12.30 & 14.30–17.00 Mon–Sat*); Africana (◌ *261 2776*); Central (◌ *261 1167*); Farmácia 2000 (◌ *261 5655*); Moderna (◌ *261 2719*); and Santa Isabel (◌ *261 3747*).

Police [175 D6] (◌ *261 1332*). Rua Serpa Pinto, close to the Palace of Justice.

Post office On the Plateau, behind the Palace of Justice, and in Fazenda near the big roundabout (◌ *08.00–12.00 & 14.00–18.00 Mon–Fri*).

Shopping Cape Verdean literature in Portuguese and French, music, jewellery, postcards and artefacts are on sale in Palácio de Cultura [175 C6] on the main square on the Plateau (Praça Alexander Albuquerque). There's a craft shop [175 C5] on Av Amílcar Cabral, nearly opposite the municipal market. Music shops include Harmonia Music Shop [175 E5] and Quintal da Música [174 C2] (see *Entertainment and nightlife*, page 176) on the Plateau, but the best is Tropical Dance in Sucupira.

If you are interested in the traditional weaving of *pano de terra*, visit Fatima Almeida (*Pano de Terra, Rua Cidade da Figueira da Foz, No 1, Achada de Santo António;* ◌ *262 3660*), a successful designer who incorporates *panos* into her clothes designs. She achieved fame after a fashion show in 2002 and now makes linen and cotton clothing adorned with *panos*, as well as ties, bags, lampshades and curtains. Prices are high: weaving *panos* is expensive and so is the Italian linen.

Telephone There are many booths on the Plateau from which to make national and international calls.

Tourist information None on the Plateau. Along Av OAU in Achada Santo António, near the Brazilian embassy, is the Agencia de Promoção de Investimentos de Cabo Verde, which incorporates Promex (◌ *262 2621/260 4110/260 4111;* e *promex@cvtelecom.cv*). Taxi drivers and officials know it as Promex. It may sell you some booklets but is not set up to hand out information to passers-by. The French Cultural Centre at Rua Andrade Corvo, on the Plateau, east of the main square, sells some guidebooks.

WHAT TO SEE AND DO
Museum [174 C3] (*Av 5 de Julho, Plateau;* ◌ *08.30–12.00 & 14.30–18.00 Mon–Fri; admission 100$*) Small but well laid-out display in a restored 18th-century building on the Plateau, with some interpretations translated into English. One of the few places you will see the beautifully woven *pano* cloth that was so important in Cape Verde's history (for this, see also *Shopping*, page 53). There are also relics from shipwrecks and artefacts from rural life.

Centro de Restauração e Museologia (*Rua da Alfândega, 3 Chã de Areia;* \ *261 1528;* e *crm@arq.de; www.arq.de;* ⊙ *09.00–12.00 & 15.00–17.00 Mon–Fri*) The museum of archaeology. Stunning display of treasure retrieved by the company Arqueonautas from various shipwrecks around Cape Verde, with exhibits demonstrating the detective work done in piecing together the histories of the various wrecks and their painstaking restorative efforts (see box, *Raising Cape Verde's history from the ocean floor*, page 11).

Main square On the Plateau, this houses the old Catholic cathedral, the old Palace of the Council, the Presidential Palace and the newest building, the Palace of Justice. Behind the square is the statue of Diogo Gomes, one of the two discoverers of the southern islands. Wander a little further and enjoy the views off the Plateau down to the sea.

Art Gallery (*Achada de Santo António;* \ *262 3882;* e *artgallery.cv@gmail.com;* ⊙ *08.00–20.00 Mon–Fri, 09.00–21.00 Sat/Sun*) Displays the work of Domingos Luísa, who created some of the sculptures around the archipelago such as *Homem de Pedra*, in the roundabout of Av Cidade de Lisboa, and the statue of Pope John Paul II in Achada de Santo António.

Beaches
Prainha A pleasant little yellow-sand cove, popular with locals, between the Hotel Praia Mar and the Hotel Trópico in an upmarket part of town, but with no facilities.

Quebra-Canela To the west of the Hotel Praia Mar, larger and less busy.

Other places of interest The wild and windswept lighthouse has a good view of the town; the caretaker should let you climb to the top.

CIDADE VELHA

This once-proud town has had nearly 300 years to decay since the French robbed it of its wealth in 1712. Now there is just an ordinary village population living amongst the ruins of numerous churches, the great and useless fort watching over them from a hill behind. Its inhabitants are still poor but there have been efforts to develop some tourist potential in town and it is becoming a delightful place, with a café on the shore, bright fishing boats in the harbour and a tourist information office. It is magical to wander through the vegetation in the *ribeira* and in the surrounding hills to discover the ruins of what was once a pivot of the Portuguese Empire.

HISTORY Ribeira Grande is where the history of Cape Verde began – where the first Cape Verdeans were born. It was chosen by António de Noli as the centre of his portion of Santiago and it flourished. It had a reasonable and defensible harbour that was the second safest in all of Cape Verde, Madeira and the Azores. It had ample fresh water and a stony landing beach. One of its early illustrious visitors was Vasco da Gama, in July 1497, who discovered India later on the same journey. Just 70 years after the *ribeira* was settled it was granted the status of *cidade*, and by 1572, some 1,500 people walked its streets (many of them slaves whose job was to till the plantations up the valley). They were watched over by a bishop, dean, archdeacon and 12 canons. Portuguese ships called there on their way to India and Brazil.

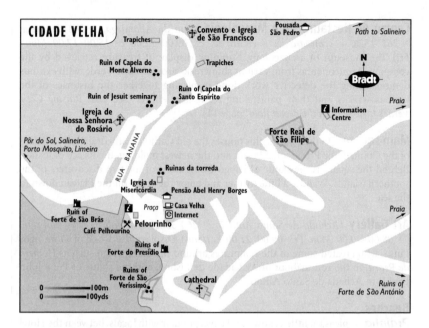

CIDADE VELHA

Trapiches

Convento e Igreja de São Francisco

Pousada São Pedro

Path to Salineiro

Ruin of Capela do Monte Álverne

Trapiches

N

Bradt

Ruin of Jesuit seminary

Ruin of Capela do Santo Espírito

Praia

Igreja de Nossa Senhora do Rosário

Information Centre

Pôr do Sol, Salineiro, Porto Mosquito, Limeira

RUA BANANA

Forte Real de São Filipe

Ruinas da torreda

Igreja da Misericórdia

Pensão Abel Henry Borges

Casa Velha

Praça

Internet

Praia

Ruin of Forte de São Brás

Pelourinho

Café Pelhourino

Ruins of Forte do Presídio

Ruins of Forte de São Veríssimo

Cathedral

Ruins of Forte de São António

0 ——100m
0 ——100yds

The upper valleys were planted with 'vast groves... of oranges, cedars, lemons, pomegranates, figs of every kind, and... palms which produce coconuts', according to one 16th-century account. Although there are still plantations in the valley it is hard to imagine such foliage there today.

But this was an isolated outpost, helpless under attack and victim of any country that happened to have a grudge against its colonial masters. In 1585, forces supporting the Prior of Crato, fighting for the succession to the throne of Portugal, attacked the town.

When Francis Drake's force landed in mid-November 1585, his 1,000 men found the city deserted. Everyone had fled into the mountains, where they remained for two weeks while the Englishmen were below. Drake marched 600 men inland to São Domingos but they found it too deserted. They torched the settlement, went on to Praia and did the same and then left, having acquired food and water but none of the gold they were after. Two weeks later a fever contracted on the island killed hundreds of Drake's crew.

Nevertheless Ribeira Grande continued to grow. By the end of the 1600s, it had a population of about 2,000. The grand cathedral was completed in 1693, but little did the people know that the demise of their city was imminent. The French raid of 1712, led by Jacques Cassard, began the drain to Praia and the city's fate was sealed by the decision of a new bishop in 1754 not to live at Ribeira Grande. Soon it was to be known only as Cidade Velha.

CIDADE VELHA TODAY Today archaeologists are trying to piece together what the city was like. They are finding there is a rich buried history that could shed light on the origins of Cape Verdean culture, the history of slavery, and on Jesuit history as well. This, the first European city in the tropics, is more than just a national treasure. And, in recognition of this, in June 2009, Cidade Velha became Cape Verde's first UNESCO World Heritage Site. It seems that very little has changed since this status was bestowed, but the Ministry for Culture, together with Promitur, are promoting the benefits of preserving this historic site and have so far trained ten young people to work as guides.

Increased demand for new housing in the town could threaten future excavations. 'The whole area is potentially at risk – including the nearby town of São Pedro,' warns Konstantino Richter of Cape Verde's Jean Piaget University. Where new buildings are going up, potentially valuable data is being lost as basements are excavated before sufficient exploratory work is carried out.

GETTING THERE AND AWAY Take the approximately hourly *aluguer* (30 minutes; 80$) from Sucupira Market or from Terra Branca in Praia. A taxi costs 1,000$ one-way. *Alugueres* depart from Cidade Velha from the tree in the centre of the square. Don't worry about finding one: it will find you.

WHERE TO STAY

Hotel Limeira (30 rooms) 267 1104. A brand-new hotel with a variety of rooms, suites & apartments, & a restaurant. Spread out along the side of the hill with great views & a few mins' walk to Cidade Velha. Bar & swimming pool. **$$$**

Pôr do Sol (8 rooms, 2 villas) Santa Marta, Cidade Velha; 267 1622; m 991 2136; e pordosol@cvtelecom.cv, dama@ cvtelecom.cv; www.pordosol.com.cv. Some 2km west of Cidade Velha. A taxi from the airport costs 1,500$ (or 1,000$ if arranged with the proprietor beforehand). Pôr do Sol is a haven of white tiles, bougainvillea & terracing, currently in an isolated spot on the rocky coast north of the town. There's a small pool, a good restaurant & a super view. Rooms are en suite with AC, TV, fridge. Internet available. The owner is developing the land &

it will soon become a gated community with several privately owned villas – the ones that are built already are available to rent & are spacious & well equipped. The restaurant serves delicious local dishes including *cachupa* & its speciality, a seafood & bean dish (*feijoada de mariscos*). There is sometimes live music. The owner will organise excursions. **$$**

Pousada São Pedro (6 rooms) 267 1681; e proimtur@gmail.com. A charming *pensão* in the heart of Cidade Velha's *ribeira*, constructed sympathetically in stone with red-tile roofing inset in the traditional way. Rooms are attractive & simple, with fridge, fan & hot water. **$$**

Pensão Abel Henry Borges (3 rooms) 267 1374. Simple rooms with a shared bathroom run by an elderly Cape Verdean couple. **$**

WHERE TO EAT There are several cafés, including Kuska, on the right as the road enters Cidade Velha from Praia, and Casa Velha, on the land-side of the square. There is also Café Pelourinho on the Esplanade, a great place to watch beach life. Or retreat to Pôr do Sol (see *Where to stay*, above).

OTHER PRACTICALITIES
Hospital 267 1111
Internet Next to Casa Velha
Police 267 1132

WHAT TO SEE AND DO
The key ruins in Cidade Velha
Fort Real do São Filipe (267 1681; e proimtur@cvtelecom.cv; guided tours 10.00 & 16.00 daily) Most easily reached from the main road from Praia, from where it is an 800m walk; the tourist information centre offers a pamphlet, video and café.

The fort was built after the 1585 sacking and was intended to guard primarily against attack from overland. Its extraordinarily thick walls were built with brick from Lisbon; its turrets with their little windows give a wide view over the Atlantic and the village. Behind are long views over flat-topped hills and lonely, rocky moors, and also deep into the canyon of Ribeira Grande with its sprinkling of plantations spreading up the valley floor. Inside the fort are some of the old cannons.

Cathedral (Enter through a gap in the fencing) Inside are the remains of its 1m-thick walls, begun by the third bishop of Cape Verde, Francisco da Cruz, in 1556. After his initial impetus, the work was half-hearted and construction funds were diverted elsewhere. In 1676, the ambitious original plans were scaled down and it was proposed to build only a sanctuary about 24m long. But the energetic Bishop Vitoriano Portuense, who arrived in 1688, returned to the original design and it was completed in 1693. Its life was short, however: in 1712, it was attacked and virtually destroyed by French pirate Jacques Cassard.

Archaeologists have done occasional digs here and revealed the gravestones in the floor; the balustrade between the central nave and the transept; the baptistry, with red-tiled floors and the foundations of the font; and the tomb of António José Xavier, first bishop of Cape Verde. Once the cathedral had a gabled façade, a tower on either side and a flight of steps which led down to the square.

Pelourinho This 16th-century pillory was used for the punishment of slaves. It is not much more than a century since slavery was abolished in Brazil and the pillory is an arresting symbol of inhumanity – as long as it is there the memory will never slip away.

Igreja de Nossa Senhora do Rosário This is the earliest documented church in the tropics. This church served as the settlement's principal place of worship until the cathedral was built, and is still full on Sundays. Laid in the floor are 17th-century tombstones of noblemen from the time of the reign of Philip of Spain. For more information, see box, *A church gives up its secrets*, opposite.

Igreja e Convento de São Francisco Built in about 1640, this was a monastery and later a cultural and training centre. Another victim of Jacques Cassard, it was destroyed in 1712.

A walk through Cidade Velha Start at the fort, then walk down into town either along the main road or via the zig-zag path down the mountainside. The **cathedral** is on the right of the main road, surrounded by high wire netting. Returning to the road and descending into town you will find the **pelourinho** at the far left of the square.

Leave the square at the pillory end, by the coastal road, and turn right into the wide and dry *ribeira*. This was once a great stream, which, before it reached the sea, formed a wide pool which was dammed at the mouth by a maze of pebbles through which the water trickled out slowly to the ocean. Fresh water was loaded from it into small boats and brought out to the ships, for which a huge charge was made.

You can walk up the *ribeira*, turning left on to a track that joins it after about 100m, after the ruins. The track bends round to the right and peters out into the valley above after five minutes.

Up on the right is **Igreja e Convento de São Francisco**. The ruins of this church hide among the trees up to the right and include a bell tower. Returning to the track, walk up amongst the trees of the valley to reach, after 15 minutes, a small water tank in which the local people bathe and which used to supply water to Praia. You can return to town along the concrete water channel that leads from the water tank just below you. It follows a contour round the hill and affords good views of the town and the hills behind. When the channel turns to the right at a road, jump off it and follow the track back to the main road.

As you return to town, after 50m, you will see a narrow path between stone walls off to the left. This leads up and then to the right to the church of Santa Luzia. There's little left of it, but there's a good view up to the fort and the cathedral.

Before crossing the *ribeira* to return to town, take the road on the left which leads to Nossa Senhora do Rosário. Wander through the few little roads here: Rua Banana is a pretty one, as is its neighbour, Rua Carrera. If you have time you can also wander further up Ribeira Grande among the plantations. The road continues up the coast for about 20km as far as the small village of Porto Mosquito.

Hiking Hike No 8, page 197, finishes at Cidade Velha.

SÃO DOMINGOS

The main reason to stop here is for drives or walks up to the west into the hills. Look out for the *Artesanatos* of São Domingos and their pottery, *pano de terra* (literally 'bread of the earth'), and other local arts and crafts.

GETTING THERE AND AWAY *Alugueres* leave Sucupira Market all day for São Domingos (60$). Any Tarrafal or Assomada *aluguer* will stop there. They run back to Praia well into the evening. By hire car from Praia, take the road north, signposted São Domingos, Assomada and Tarrafal, passing through the urban

Santiago SÃO DOMINGOS

6

A CHURCH GIVES UP ITS SECRETS

When archaeologists first started work on the Igreja de Nossa Senhora do Rosário, all that was visible were some foundations protruding into the neighbouring track and some walls that had been incorporated into drystone terracing. Since then the team, led by Konstantino Richter of Cape Verde's Jean Piaget University, and Christopher Evans, director of Cambridge University's Archaeological Unit, has exposed the church's massive foundations and reconstructed its outline. It was 26m long and 11m wide with, on its north side, a Gothic-style side chapel (discovered to great excitement in 2007). They have found some very early 'relief-style' tiles dating from about 1500, nearby, which they believe were the first tiles used in the church. They have also uncovered an early 16th-century inscribed grave-slab set into the church's floor, and an enormous tombstone, dating to the mid 16th century, laid into the floor of the side chapel. They have found late 16th–17th-century tiles in the nave – which must have been the result of a later recladding job.

'All this indicates that we certainly have found a very early church here, one dating from at least the early 16th century,' say the researchers. It is even possible that there is an even earlier phase of the church still buried underneath: the archaeologists estimate that they have found the remains of over 1,000 people sealed below the church floor. This number is very high, given the population at the time, and demonstrates 'just how high the mortality was during the first half century of the settlement's history'. Isotope analysis of the teeth, which is only at an early stage, suggests that the remains are of two or three distinct populations, at least one of which seems to be of west African origin.

The researchers have found all sorts of objects on the site, too, including Chinese porcelain, Portuguese earthenware and what looks like west African pottery.

sprawl and into the countryside. About 12km later there is a sharp bend to the right at which you take the main road to São Domingos.

🏠 **WHERE TO STAY AND EAT** There is little accommodation actually in São Domingos, but nearby Rui Vaz offers a pleasant hotel; otherwise it is probably best to stay in Praia.

🏠 **Quinta da Montanha** (18 rooms) Rui Vaz; 📞 268 5002/3; m 992 4013; e quintamontanha@ cvtelecom.cv; www.reisetraeume.de/kapverden/ viadoso/c-u2/00.html. In an unrivalled position high in the mountains with a dramatic view of the lush plantations below, this hotel is a great place to stay & a good base for visits to the botanical gardens, hiking & birdwatching. If you don't want to stay in Praia, this is a good alternative since it is only a 20min taxi ride from the airport (€18), & the hotel will arrange pickup. The owner, a returned Cape Verdean *emigrante*, is an agriculturalist, so the hotel grows its own

produce including an array of vegetables &, in season, strawberries. There is a telescope for star-gazers. Rooms are en suite with TV, hot water &, unusually for Cape Verde, baths. Internet is offered & there is a 100-seater conference room. FB possible; hiking excursions arranged. Its **restaurant** ($$$$; *€14 for a whole meal*) is often packed with day trippers from Sal so booking is advisable. It operates a buffet at the w/ends. Take a jumper for the evenings. **$$**
🏠 **El Dourado** 📞 265 1865. **$$**
✗ **Restaurante Morena** In Cutelo Branco; 📞 268 1159. $$

WHAT TO SEE AND DO The **Artisan Centre** (🕓 *08.30–12.00 & 14.00–18.00 Mon–Sat*) At this centre Cape Verdeans are trying to rejuvenate old crafts, in particular the weaving of *pano* cloth and the production of ceramics. You can watch them practising their skills around the back. In the front is the craft shop selling locally made dolls, as well as trinkets made from coconut and cow horn. Crafts imported from Senegal are also for sale. The centre waxes and wanes – sometimes there is not much there.

Rui Vaz and Monte Xota The road up into the mountains to this village and up to the peak is magnificent. Take a left turn towards the end of São Domingos, then take the first right. *Alugueres* go as far as Rui Vaz fairly regularly – the rest of the journey can be completed on foot. Alternatively, charter an *aluguer* in São Domingos (630$ one-way). At the top it is sometimes possible to enter the antennae complex and go up to the viewpoint for a panorama of the interior of Santiago. (See also *Hikes*, page 192.)

Barragem Poilão Just before João Teves, in São Lourenço dos Orgãos at the roundabout where there is a large, new school, turn right and follow the road down. This dam, funded by the Chinese, was inaugurated in 2006, and is already altering the ecology in the area – there are anecdotal reports that birds are congregating to enjoy the environment there. It cost 38 million Cape Verdean escudos to build and has a potential capacity of 1.7 million m³. The dam wall is 26m high.

Botanical gardens and São Jorge dos Orgãos Cool, verdant and pretty, this village is reached by going up the main road as far as the village of João Teves (*aluguer* from Praia 150$; one hour) and turning left. Above you tower the mountains of the Serra do Pico do António.

Here, houses rise up the crevices between the mountains, all relying on a single little mountain spring for the watering of their many crops. The agricultural research station here, Inida, just near the blue church, has a national botanical garden (Jardim Botânico Nacional), which lies up a turning to the left just beyond its main buildings. Here they are trying to study endemic species and conserve those threatened with extinction. Inida, meanwhile, selectively breeds plants in the quest for ever hardier species and develops more efficient irrigation techniques. If the researchers are not busy they sometimes show visitors around the garden. Look out for *língua de vaca* (*Echium vulcanorum*), if they've managed to get this inhabitant of Fogo volcano to grow, and the purple flowers of *contra-bruxas-azul* (*Campanula jacobea*).

ASSOMADA

Recently granted the rank of *cidade* (city), Assomada nevertheless still feels like a country town and does not possess the infrastructure of the two other Cape Verdean cities, Praia and Mindelo. It is the capital of the region of Santa Catarina, the grain basket of Santiago. It is an ancient town, as old as Cape Verde's human history, and was often more highly populated than Cidade Velha.

GETTING THERE AND AWAY By public transport, the journey from Praia takes 1.5 hours (50$). *Alugueres* leave all day from Sucupira Market, returning to Praia until late at night. Private taxis cost 3,000–5,000$ for half a day.

The drive to Assomada is spectacular, particularly after João Teves, when jagged clifftops rear into view and there are vistas into valleys on both sides of the road. A rock formation that looks like the profile of a recumbent face has been christened the Marquês de Pombal rock, after a statue of that nobleman in Lisbon. Climbing out of the Pico you can see the island of Maio to the east, before the descent into Assomada.

Car hire
🚗 **Garagem Monteiro** ☎ 265 1351   🚗 **Veiga Car** ☎ 265 4590
🚗 **Hotel Prestige** (see *Where to stay and eat*, below)

BADIUS AND REBELADOS

The *badius* were at the heart of the Santiago peasant population. Whenever there was a pirate attack, or drought caused some social chaos on the island, some of the slaves would seize the opportunity and flee into the mountainous interior. There, though in exile in a restricted and infertile area, they had freedom. The *badius* form the African core of Cape Verdean society, reflected in their music, which harks back to the African coast for inspiration, and in other aspects of culture. Because of this they have been despised by many. It was from the *badius* that the *rebelados* movement arose as a reaction against the arrival in the 1940s of the Portuguese Catholic priests of the Holy Spirit Congregation. They wished to purify Catholicism, eliminating the many native practices which were based on a clashing personal spiritualism. It is said that those who stuck to the old methods in regard to baptisms, marriages and other rituals were imprisoned or persecuted.

Ultimately the movement coalesced around practices such as the communal farming of land, the refusal to deal with money and a prohibition on killing living creatures. As their rebellion centred on treasuring traditions and rejecting change, they also renounced many of today's luxuries such as television and radio. When they thwarted an antimalarial campaign by refusing the fumigation of their homes, their leaders were arrested and dispersed to other islands. Some still live in the Santiago highlands in distinctive dwellings; their houses can be seen from the main road. They object to being photographed.

WHERE TO STAY AND EAT There are many places to stay in Assomada, ranging from budget to smart mid range. Not all are listed here.

⌂ **Hotel Cosmos** (17 rooms) ☎ 265 3915; e ccomercialcosmos@cvtelecom.cv. Spacious hotel in the middle of town with a tad of atmosphere created by the use of carved wood & an attention to detail. FB available. Also has a top-floor restaurant, Restaurante Panorâmico Cosmos, with live music on Sat nights & panoramic views. **$$**

⌂ **Hotel Prestige** (16 rooms) Smart rooms, including 6 enormous suites with kitchenettes & sofa beds. AC, TV, fridge. Internet available. Offers some interesting round-island & Assomada tours (see *Excursions*, page 166). **$$**

⌂ **Pensão Avenida** (16 rooms) Av Amílcar Cabral; ☎ 265 3462; www.reisetraeume.de/ kapverden/reisebuero/hotels/santiago/ avenida.html. Clean, sanitary & bright with large rooms & good-quality bathrooms. Some rooms are let down by the lack of a view – ask for a top-floor room with a mountain view. The Avenida also has a rooftop restaurant. FB available. **$$**

OTHER PRACTICALITIES

Airlines TACV tickets are available from Orbitur, left of the *aluguer* stop.

Bank BCA, BCN and Caixa Económica.

Hospital There is a large, new hospital (☎ *265 1130*).

Pharmacy Farmacia Santa Catarina (☎ *265 2121*).

Police (☎ *265 1132*). Near the Palace of Justice.

WHAT TO SEE AND DO

Excursions The Hotel Prestige offers various activities and trips as well as car hire (see *Where to stay*, above).

Museu de Tabanka This museum is in a former treasury and mail government building in the centre of town near the big market, yellow-walled with a large, overhanging red-tiled roof. It covers the history of Assomada and Santa Catarina and gives extensive coverage to the musical form of *tabanka*. There are also interesting displays of pictures, instruments and other objects.

African market This has all the colours, smells and noise of a west African market, and is held on Wednesdays and Saturdays. On the same days, near the schools in the southernmost part of town, there is a livestock market. Pigs, cows, goats and the smell of freshly cooking *chouriço* makes this worth the trip.

Porto Rincão This little fishing village is reached by turning west at Assomada (or catching an *aluguer* from beside the market or from the road junction) and following a fantastic road to the coast. There are deep red canyons and a stunning view of Fogo sitting on its cloud cushion across the water. Halfway along, the cobbled road turns to dirt. It's a 24km round trip, but if you have time for just one foray down to the west coast, we recommend the more northerly one, to Ribeira da Barca.

Boa Entrada North along the main road from Assomada, just slightly out of town lies a turning to this village, which lies in the green valley that meanders down to the east. You can walk down to Boa Entrada from Assomada. Dominating the valley is a magnificent, centuries-old kapok tree, in which nests one of the only two known colonies of Cape Verde heron, known locally as *garça vermelha* (*Ardea (purpurea) bournei*). (For more on this bird, see *Birds*, earlier in this chapter, page 163, and *Birds*, page 6.) The other colony is at Banana de Ribeira Montanha, near Pedra Badejo. This tree might be the biggest you will ever see and is said to have been there when the island was discovered.

The valley can be reached by several obvious paths. One leads down to a white church with pinnacles and a green door and from there to the tree. There is also a cobbled road that leads down from the main road about 100m further on.

House of Amílcar Cabral National hero Amílcar Cabral lived as a child in a yellow-walled, red-roofed house set back from the main road that leads north from Boa Entrada, on the left-hand side. However, he spent most of his short life in São Vicente, Portugal and the African mainland. The house is not open to the public.

Ribeira da Barca and Achada Leite It should be possible to reach this village by *aluguer* but there may be some long waits at the road junction. It's a 6km walk so it could make a pleasant day trip.

As you leave the vicinity of Boa Entrada start counting churches that possess separate bell towers. After the second one on the left there is a fork in the road – turn left and follow the cobbled track as it swings past a dramatic canyon on the left and continues past deeply carved *ribeiras* all the way to this beautiful beachside village. There are two restaurants.

SERRA MALAGUETA

Situated in northern-central Santiago, Serra Malagueta is an important area ecologically and one of the last remaining forest resources on Santiago. It is the starting point for some classic Santiago hikes.

The heart of the area is now a natural park (e *ecotourism.pnsm@gmail.com; www.ecoserramalagueta.cv*), which spans 774ha and reaches a height of 1,064m at the peak of Monte Malagueta. The park houses important threatened and endemic species (see *Natural history*, page 163). The ecotourist facilities offered are not as well advanced as those in Fogo or São Nicolau but the management has created campsites, is developing homestay possibilities, has trained guides and marked out (on a map at least) suggested hikes covering in total 55km and with a wide range of difficulty and times.

While hiking in the area, watch out for vervet monkeys and for the rare endemic Cape Verde purple heron or *garça vermelha* (*Ardea (purpurea) bournei*), which used to live further south in the island but is said to have moved here. Santiago is its only home.

The development of the park has included an excellent website (see above), where you can read more about the ecology and find information on trails, visitor centres and places to stay.

WHERE TO STAY AND EAT

✗ **Côte France** Achada Lem; 265 7431; e barbosacorreia3@yahoo.fr. On the right-hand side of the road in the direction of Tarrafal, this is a restaurant with some rooms. $$

WHAT TO SEE AND DO

Casa do Ambiente (265 4473; e *ecoserramalagueta@gmail.com; www.areasprotegidas.cv*) A renovated Portuguese house at the entrance to the park, reached by following a dirt track for 400m from the left side of the road to Tarrafal near the Serra Malagueta School. The park information centre is the place to obtain a guide, buy handicrafts and organise accommodation.

TARRAFAL

A cobalt sea, a string of little coves and a flat land under the forbidding mountains are what make Tarrafal. The beach is of lovely soft sand and there's a jumble of life going on there: fishermen, local sports fanatics, sunbathers, and lots of dogs. This place becomes packed at weekends but is very quiet midweek. It can be a bit windy and depressing during the harmattan period from December to March.

It is a good base for doing some of the walks the island offers and it is easy to laze away a few days here – the beach is cosier and more lived-in than Santa Maria in Sal, though it has none of the awesome splendour of beaches on the flat islands. There can be quite a few mosquitoes at night.

Tarrafal's mention in the history books comes from its notorious prison, 3km before town on the main Praia road, on the west side (see page 190).

GETTING THERE AND AWAY The 80km trip from Praia along the central road takes two hours and *alugueres* leave all day from Sucupira Market (200–250$); you may have to change in Assomada. To return to Praia on the same, inland road catch an *aluguer* from where the Praia road joins the main square of Tarrafal. They run until early evening. To return along the coastal road find an *aluguer* behind the church in the main square along with women returning from their early forays to Tarrafal beach to buy fish. *Alugueres* on this road rarely go all the way to Praia so you will have to change where necessary (150$ to Calheta; 200$ Calheta to Praia).

🏠 WHERE TO STAY

🏠 **King Fisher Resort** (9 lodges & apts) ✆ 266 1100; e hrolfs1@gmx.net; www.king-fisher.de/english/e-start.html. In western Tarrafal, this is a beautiful, imaginatively conceived set of lodges built into the rocky promontory of Ponta d'Atum, each with a terrace & its own surprises (one, for example, is built over a wave-washed grotto). King Fisher consists of apartments with kitchens rather than a hotel, & at some times of year there is a minimum booking period of 4 days. B/fast & dinner are available, however, & the owner, a German who has been in Cape Verde for 30 years, has plenty of information for guests, as well as a dive centre on site. There's a ladder directly into the sea. **$$$**

🏠 **Vila Botânico** (2 rooms) A 15min walk from the town, this luxurious villa (pink, with a cascade of white steps up the front), owned by a German family, has 2 elegant rooms set in a garden with pool & a roof terrace with panoramic views. Serves a substantial b/fast. **$$$**

🏠 **Hotel Baía Verde** (46 rooms) ✆ 266 1128. The chalets scattered in the shade of coconut palms on Tarrafal beach are an appealing prospect but for some the dream is spoilt by the tattiness & the management's lack of interest in either the buildings or the guests. The chalets' isolation is an attraction but may also create a feeling of insecurity. Each chalet has a TV, fridge & minibar. Some have hot water. **$$**

🏠 **Pensão Nôs Dôs** Modern accommodation in the centre of Tarrafal near the old market. Most rooms have balcony & AC, some budget rooms without AC. There is also a 2-bed apartment available for 6 people (4,700$). **$$**

🏠 **Hotel Sol Marina** (9 rooms) ✆ 266 1219; e gilbertofvieira19666@hotmail.com. Located on the beach with a nice sea view. Most of the rooms have a private terrace. B/fast is served on the roof terrace. **$**

🏠 **Pensão Mille Nuits** (12 rooms) ✆ 266 1463. At the heart of town with respectable, budget-type rooms arranged around a bright atrium. The cheapest have shared bathrooms. All have fans, hot water. Has a restaurant serving lunch & dinner. **$**

🏠 **Pensão Tata** ☎ 266 1125. Simple guesthouse in the centre of town. Has a restaurant serving lunch & dinner. **$**

✖ WHERE TO EAT AND DRINK

✖ **Altomira** ☎ 266 2251; m 996 3865. Through an unprepossessing doorway is a little courtyard with a bamboo roof in which is a very good restaurant run by a Frenchman, François. He serves mainly pizza & fresh fish. To get there from the now-closed Hotel Tarrafal turn left & go towards the main square. Turn left on the next street, in the direction of the Baía Verde. Then turn immediately right & it is the second house on the right. **$$**

✖ **Baía do Tarrafal** Spanish restaurant, between the Caixa Económica & the BCA. **$$**

✖ **Boka Boka** Behind the church. Although it doesn't look much, it offers a variety of meals at good prices. **$$**

✖ **Dragoeiro** ☎ 266 2616. On the right-hand side of the old market, across the street from the Girrasol office. Fast service, a couple of *pratos do dias* & a chicken grill at the front. **$$**

✖ **Hotel Baía Verde** Open-air restaurant overlooking the beach, with main dishes starting at 700$ & sandwiches & snacks for less. The place of choice because of its location. Advance ordering is advised if there are more than a couple of people. **$$**

✖ **Sol e Luna** ☎ 266 2339; m 997 9535. Breezy Italian restaurant overlooking a small beach serving great fresh fish & pasta. Reasonably priced & good food. **$$**

✖ **Bar Mama** Known for the best cakes in Tarrafal. **$**

✖ **Bar Rosa** Head south from Hotel Tarrafal to the south; only 2 tables but serves *cachupa* & good coffee. **$**

✖ **Churrasqueira Mangui Baxo** m 994 1404. Also south of the Hotel Tarrafal. Pre-order your barbecue or be prepared to wait a couple of hours. **$**

✖ **Sopa de Pedra** Before the petrol station. Simple & cheap with 1 or 2 *pratos do dia*. **$**

✖ **Sucupira Market** In & around the new market hall there are several small restaurants & snack bars that offer simple Creole dishes & cakes at very low prices. Probably the best spot to have lunch when you are on a low budget. **$**

✖ **Zenit** Main *praça*. Grilled chicken, hamburgers & chips, & a good place to watch local residents meeting in the square. **$**

ENTERTAINMENT AND NIGHTLIFE There are two late-night places: Discoteca Sagres, near the new market, and Discoteca Baía Verde, in the restaurant of the same name.

OTHER PRACTICALITIES

Bank Banco Comercial do Atlântico (☎ 266 1170; ⏱ 08.00–15.00 Mon–Fri).

Hospital (☎ 266 1130)

Police (☎ 266 1132)

Post office (⏱ 08.00–15.30 Mon–Fri). On the Assomada road, on the right as you leave town.

WHAT TO SEE AND DO

Diving There are two diving outfits in Tarrafal, both operating from King Fisher Resort. For further details, see *Diving*, page 167.

Boating Local fishermen can take you down the coast, for example to Ribeira da Barca and on to Achada Leite (see *Ribeira da Barca and Achada Leite*, page 187). One hour can cost 2,000$.

Surfing Before midday the break to the west of the bay is good and extends all the way down to Ribeira da Prata.

Hiking Tarrafal is a good starting point for several hikes, including the short walk to the lighthouse and the walk down Ribeira Principal (see *Hikes*, page 192).

Museum Close to Tarrafal is the **Museum of Resistance of Tarrafal**. It has now been restored and opened for visitors, taking them through the history of Cape Verde's fight for independence.

OTHER PLACES TO VISIT

CALHETA DE SÃO MIGUEL There's no particular reason for stopping the night here, although it is a pretty enough coastal town. It is a useful starting and end point for some hikes to and from the interior. To get there from Praia take an *aluguer* from Sucupira Market that is travelling up the coastal road; from Tarrafal catch an *aluguer* from behind the church in the main square. From Assomada you can catch an *aluguer* that takes an interesting route down a cross-country road to Calheta.

Where to stay

Mira Maio At the southern end of town, off a road leading down to the shore. Varied rooms, some large, some with balconies, some with TV & fridge. Rooftop terrace with coastal views. **$$**

Pensão Morgana Budget place behind the Mira Maio. **$$**

Where to eat

Esplanada Silibell Ponta Calhetona; 273 2078; m 996 7930; www.reisetraeume.de, www. reisetraeume.de/kapverden/viadoso/enindex. html; ⏰ 12.00–22.00 Mon–Sat. Situated at the

---

THE CONCENTRATION CAMP AT TARRAFAL

It was known as the *Campo da morte lenta* (slow death camp) to some; *Aldeia da morte* (death village) to others. The concentration camp just outside Tarrafal had at its centre a cemented building whose temperature would soar during the day. Each cell was a completely enclosed cement box about 3m long by 2.5m wide. At one end was the iron door. The only ventilation was a few holes of less than 1cm in diameter in the door, and a small, grilled hole up near the ceiling.

Into this camp, after it was built in 1936, were put 150 Portuguese anti-fascists. The prison continued to house such political prisoners until 1954, when it closed after international protest. But it opened again in the 1960s, this time to be host to independence fighters from Angola, Cape Verde and Guinea-Bissau.

The camp's history as an active prison came to an end on 1 May 1974, a few days after the Carnation Revolution in Lisbon which was to usher in democracy. The gates were thrown open and out tottered a bewildered group, many of them crying. Waiting for them was a crowd of thousands who had rushed from Praia in cars, trucks and on bicycles as soon as they heard of the telegram ordering their release.

southern end of Calheta, on a road leading off the main road, this is an open-air restaurant & bar with a sea view. It's the place to recover from the heat of the day & mull over what you have seen with Gerhard & Sibylle Schellmann, the German owners. The Schellmanns have been in Calheta for years & offer tourist information as well as tour operator services, specialising in hiking in

the hinterland (see also *Excursions*, page 166). $$$

✗ **Loja Casa Tute and Bar Esperança**
⏰ 08.00–late daily. Friendly, thatched open-air bar with good-quality local dishes made from fresh ingredients (order a meal a day beforehand). $$

PEDRA BADEJO This growing settlement is located a little north of Praia Baixo along the northeast coast. Some people love this coastal settlement but it can be hard to see beyond the sprawl, rocks, litter and cement-block buildings, many unfinished. A collaboration between local community groups and the Austrian town of Leibnitz has resulted in a nature-guide service based at Casa Ecotec (m *989 5914*; e *geovision.boedendorfer@aon.at; http://ecotec.geo-vision.info/hikes_en.php*) (see *Where to stay and eat*, below) in order to encourage sustainable ecotourism in this area. Multilingual guides will take you on bird-spotting beach walks and more strenuous hikes all over the island as well as cultural tours.

Where to stay and eat

🏠 **Palm Beach** (16 rooms) ☎ 269 2888; m 995 6942; e palmbeachs.cruz@hotmail.com; http://pedrabadejo.com/2_engelsk/index_e.htm. A large yellow building on the coastal side of the main road, this is smart, vast & new, if a bit soulless. Rooms are huge & finished to a high standard. There's a restaurant on the ground floor with terraces overlooking the beach, & 2 conference rooms. The hotel can arrange local excursions, for example in fishing boats. There are plans to build 80 apartments, a swimming pool & minigolf. $$$

🏠 **Pousada Mariberto 'A La Française'** (5 rooms) Punta Coroa; ☎ 269 1900; m 991 2298; e bernardlorac@yahoo.fr; www.hotelmariberto.com. On the road from Praia, 5km before Pedra Badejo, is Achada Fazenda, where a turning to the east, near the Restaurant Belavista, leads to lonely Punta Coroa. This quiet, single-storey guesthouse is the opposite of brash, its sensitive architecture blending almost imperceptibly into the rocky landscape. Inside is a huge living

room with a terrace overlooking the water & rockpools. Bedrooms are finished to a high standard. There's a conference/function room & a swimming pool under construction. The owner will facilitate organisation of treks, guides & birdwatching. Electricity evenings only, until the day the public connection arrives. English spoken. No children under 13. There is also a restaurant with an extensive range of wines & champagnes; reservations are required. $$$

🏠 **Casa Ecotec** (5 rooms) ☎ 269 1064; m 989 5914; e geovision.boedendorfer@aon.at; http://ecotec.geo-vision.info/house_en.php. Simple accommodation in pleasant rooms overlooking a courtyard facing the sea 2km south of Pedra Badejo in the village of Achada Igreja. The drive through the village is a little offputting as there are no signs, so make sure you ask for directions. Part of an Austrian project to develop sustainable tourism in the area; guided walks, hiking & cultural tours can be arranged in many languages. Meals can be arranged. $

PRAIA BAIXO Located on the northeast coast of Santiago about 20km from Praia, this spot is noted for its safe beach. Sir Francis Drake is thought to have made a landfall here.

Where to stay

🏠 **ApartHotel Praia Baixo** (8 rooms, 2 apts) ☎ 268 7105. On the beach. There are small rooms & also apartments. There is a

rooftop restaurant that is a popular destination at w/ends. $$

SÃO FRANCISCO With superb beaches and deserted coves, this is the best place near Praia for a day in the sun.

Getting there *Alugueres* leave approximately every 30 minutes from Paul, behind Fazenda in Praia and cost about 60$. They drop you in the village of São Francisco from where it is a walk of several kilometres downhill to the beach. A taxi costs about 1,400$ each way.

🏠 Where to stay

🏠 **Sambala** 📞264 8000; 01608 813160 (UK Office); e info@sambaladevelopments. Overlooking the beach is the development of Sambala, an entire holiday town in the making. The envisioned shops, cafés & golf courses have

not proceeded according to plan & at the time of writing, work appears to have ceased altogether. This may change, however, & there may be an option to stay at Sambala during the lifetime of this guide.

✖ Where to eat

✖ **Catumbela** m 991 5459. A restaurant on the beach.

DRIVES

ROUND-ISLAND DRIVE This is highly recommended as the interior of Santiago is a drama worth making the effort to see. It could be accomplished in one day but this would be pretty exhausting – it is better, if possible, to travel from Praia to Tarrafal, Assomada or another location with accommodation on the first day and return down the coast road on the second. If you have time take the left turn after Assomada (just before Fundura) and visit Ribeira da Barca for a vivid glimpse of the terrain leading to the west coast. There is a cursory description of the landscape below – for more information see the entries above.

The drive begins through the urban sprawl of Praia – ever expanding as people move from the villages to the city. As you reach the countryside you should see the long yellow flowers of aloe vera lining the roadside, along with, at the right time of year, maize and haricot beans. About 12km from the centre of Praia, where you take the left turn, you begin to gaze down into a green valley. The road passes through São Domingos and Assomada – springboards for visiting all the places described above. After marvelling at the Pico do Santo António and its surrounding craggy peaks you will later come to the Serra Malagueta – the other high point of Santiago.

From Tarrafal, the journey to Praia along the coast is 2.5 hours. There is less to stop for than on the inland road but the drive is spectacular, tracing hairpin bends that take you into verdant creeks and out again into the dry mountainsides. The houses have hay piled high on their flat roofs and sometimes goats live there too. Wires stick out of the top of every house in anticipation of the building of the next storey. Pigs forage round the houses and the dry landscape.

After Calheta the land becomes almost lush with great banana plantations, coconut trees and always the yellow of aloe vera poking up from cacti-like leaves.

HIKES *Alexander Hirtle (AH); Aisling Irwin (AI); Colum Wilson (CW)*

1 SERRA MALAGUETA–HORTELÃO–RIBEIRA PRINCIPAL (LONGER ROUTE)
Distance: 13km; time: 4.5 hours; difficulty: 3 (AH)
This is a beautiful walk, and the peak time for it is between mid-August and early

December (late October is probably the greenest and most picturesque). Beware, though, that during the rainy season that usually starts mid/late July and ends mid-October, trails can be slippery and, in a good year for rain, wiped out with streams rushing through them. Visibility can also be limited due to cloud cover and the rain itself. The walks are mainly downhill, but continual downhill jaunts can be very stressful on knees and ankles. You need to get transport up to the area of Serra Malagueta. From Assomada, an *aluguer* costs 100$. Tell the driver to drop you off at the secondary road with the gate (*portão*), before the primary school (*escola*).

Follow the secondary road, which is clear and wide with generally good footing, up several hundred feet; it makes winding turns, some so sharp and steep you'll wonder how vehicles get up there. There are some excellent views of the *ribeira* off to the left. As you continue upwards, the flora changes. You'll see groups of pine trees, part of a continual reafforestation project in which the locals participate. It is a necessary programme, because local residents are always collecting firewood from the area (you may pass several people coming down the road carrying loads of wood on their heads). Continue up the road and it begins to level off. You are near one of the highest points on the island, **Serra Malagueta**. There are spectacular views to the right; you may even be above the cloud cover, depending on the day. Watch the sides of the cliffs though: a misplaced step will send you hundreds of feet down. Continue on the road, and past a small clearing where at times vehicles are parked.

Stay to the right, along the drop-off, but not too close to it. The paths to the left lead to somewhat dangerous wooded areas. You will begin to descend, as the path takes a left turn and leads you into very green and beautiful woods: thus begins the decline to Ribeira Principal.

The path switchbacks several times; it is important to stay on the main path that generally goes to the left of the ridge and eventually to the bottom of the *ribeira*. If you find yourself going down to the right of the ridge, you will need to retrace your steps and find the correct path again. You will descend to an area with some enclosed animal pens and houses. Most residents here are very friendly, but it's wise to respect their privacy and property as on occasion you may meet a local who is not always happy with foreigners passing by. After entering the first area of houses, continue through another area with sets of houses and, as the path veers to the right, walk along an area that is a small ridge where the drop-off is steep to the left, shallow on the right. You will reach an area where the path quickly drops down, makes a slight turn to the right, and then a sharp turn to the left. This place can be dangerous when it is wet, so take it slow and steady. The path then takes you along a lower terrace that brings you to the left side of the *ribeira*. You will descend further to more houses, again staying along the lower ridge that overlooks the *ribeira*. There are very good views here: you can see the terracing of the agricultural areas, and the isolated *vilas* below. In several places there are diverging paths, so you need constantly to ask the locals the way to Hortelão, the *vila* just past Ribeira Principal. You will come to a converging area that will bring you across to the right side of the *ribeira*. You may not notice it at first, but once you leave the more dense areas with houses, you will be following the lower ridge on the right side of **Ribeira Principal**.

Continue to descend, past some fantastic rock structures on the right including a keyhole in one part of the ridge. Your final climb down is full of tricky switchbacks. The path eventually takes you to the bottom of the *ribeira*, to **Hortelão**. Waiting vehicles can take you to Tarrafal, or Calheta, where you can change vehicles to return to Assomada, or Praia. Alternatively, you can walk the extra 30–40 minutes along the road to the main road, but it is not the most scenic part of the trip, and may take longer if you are tired and hungry.

2 SERRA MALAGUETA–RIBEIRA PRINCIPAL (SHORTER ROUTE)

Distance: 8km; time: 3.5 hours; difficulty: 2 (AH)

The second, and shorter, way down the pretty Ribeira Principal starts from the *vila* of Serra, at the small market, or *mercearia*. The owner, Marcilino, can point out the path that starts your descent.

The first part is tricky: steep switchbacks where it is easy to slip. Take it slowly, and when you come to the first major fork (about 0.5km from the road) take a left. This second path is much simpler than the first: the higher part of the walk stays to the left of the *ribeira* the entire time. The path levels off quickly as it leads you on to a lower ridge, again staying on the left side of the *ribeira*. You can see the beautiful terracing of the lower gorge, the isolated houses, and the forested view of the opposite side of the *ribeira* – the route for the longer hike to Ribeira Principal (see previous hike). The path follows the ridge and then cuts inward (to the right), descending towards the centre of the *ribeira*. It cuts back and forth but leads mainly to the right, ending up at the bottom centre of the *ribeira* in a lush oasis of mango trees and sugarcane.

This is a good area to stop and have lunch. You will probably see locals coming and going, carrying water from the tank, or maybe sugarcane: give them passing space with their heavy loads. As you follow the path, you will pass several *grogue* distilleries. Many owners enjoy demonstrating how their distillery operates; feel free to enquire, but you may find they are at a tricky moment and can't take a break just now. Follow the path that climbs just a bit to the higher area of the oasis and goes through several small *vilas*. The path continues a little longer, again descending slightly to the lowest part of the *ribeira* where it ends at a large *grogue* distillery. By showing interest in the facility, and some friendly rapport in Portuguese, Creole, or maybe limited English, you may be invited to sample some of their *grogue*. Nearby vehicles can take you on to the main Tarrafal–Calheta road.

3 CHÃO BOM–RIBEIRA DA PRATA–FIGUEIRA DAS NAUS

Distance: 9km; time: 3.5 hours; difficulty: 2 (AI)

This is an attractive, if lonely, walk that begins on the level, following the coast as far as Ribeira da Prata. It then toils uphill along a remorselessly shadeless track, relieved by the drama of the canyons and the vista back towards the sea. The walk is on road and track and there are no problems with slipperiness or steep slopes, but the 1.5-hour upward slog from Ribeira da Prata requires a certain amount of fitness if it is to be enjoyable. To get to the beginning of the walk at Chão Bom (pronounced 'shambome'), travel for about five minutes by *aluguer* from Tarrafal along the Assomada road. The turning to Ribeira da Prata is signposted, on the right, at the beginning of Chão Bom.

From the Tarrafal side of Chão Bom, take the road signposted **Ribeira da Prata**, passing initially through slums. Leaving habitation behind, the lonely road passes in and out of the coastal fractals for about an hour, revealing eventually the black-sand beach of the *ribeira* with acacia and coconut palms offering a bit of shade. The bottom of the valley is where people pause in the shade to rest. Follow the road out, up, into the village and out of the other side after which it will do a great loop backwards and upwards to ascend into the hills.

This is an extremely quiet road and, as it ascends, there are views back to Tarrafal, to the harshly bright sea and over the rocky ground that characterises the western side of Santiago. There is a huge amount of reafforestation here. Some 1.5 hours after leaving Ribeira da Prata the track begins to pass through a series of villages, including Figueira Muite and Marmulano, most of which have bars tucked away –

all you have to do is ask for them. Some 2.5 hours from Ribeira da Prata you reach **Figueira das Naus** with its pretty church. Here the road divides and you can wait for an *aluguer* (there are three or four a day) to take you along the right fork and back to the main Tarrafal–Assomada road.

Alternatively, if you have a taste for more of this rocky, inland drama, you can walk the 8km to the main road. Just take the right fork and remain on the same track, ignoring a single right turn.

4 MONTE XOTA–PICO DO SANTO ANTÓNIO–MONTE XOTA
Time: 6 hours; difficulty: 3 (AI)
This walk is quite dangerous and only for the fit and sure-footed. Even then, the final ascent is up a dangerously steep and crumbling slope. All the rules of hiking apply (see *Health*, page 64), in particular that you should go in a group of at least three and wear boots with good grip. Take two litres of water for each person. Set off before 11.00. For the middle third of the journey the path is obscure or non-existent and one needs to trust to an understanding of the topography to find the way up the ridge to the top. Sadly, it is hard to find a competent guide. There are many local men who will agree to take you but few know the way or understand that most Westerners are less fleet of foot than they – so they may give you a false sense of security. The soldiers at the telecommunications station at the start of the walk work on rotation and may never have been up the Pico.

The walk begins at the telecommunications installation, on a path opposite its entrance. The path disappears into the vegetation and winds back behind the station. Almost immediately there's a view of the curved pincers of the Pico. Climb down the low wall ahead of you and follow the path that goes round the installation and then branches away to the northwest. You emerge on a little ridge and already the views are spectacular, with Fogo visible to the west and within five minutes, views of São Domingos and Serra Malagueta.

For the next half hour the path is clear, descending through pleasant forest, past a couple of smallholdings and in and out of the valleys until you are in the position from which to begin the ascent up the spur that leads to the top.

The ascent will take two–three hours, depending on fitness and agility. After the first 1.5–two hours, you reach the lesser peak.

5 MONTE XOTA ANTENNAE–SÃO DOMINGOS
Distance: 5km; time: 2 hours; difficulty: 1 (AI)
Spectacular views accompany this downhill walk from the antennae station at the peak of Monte Xota to the town of São Domingos on the main road. The road is cobbled throughout and navigation is simple: just head downwards. If you become tired at any point, you can just sit and wait for the next *aluguer* – these are fairly frequent from Rui Vaz downwards. To reach Monte Xota for the beginning of the walk either take a public *aluguer* as far as the Rui Vaz turning and walk, or charter an *aluguer* in São Domingos, which should cost around 700$.

Try to kick off the walk by gaining entry to the grounds of the Monte Xota telecommunications station and climbing the knoll to the right. The soldiers there may let you in if you ask nicely and they are not too busy. From the knoll you can see spread before you the heart of Santiago. Retracing your steps, join the road and enjoy the greenery and the sharply scented, cool air before it fades as you descend. The magnificent cobbled road takes you through sheer cliffs and craggy rock formations with occasional glimpses of Pico do Santo António, the canine tooth poking up behind them. Watch out for Pico de João Teves, one of many raw, majestic shapes, which looks like the top of a submarine. You will also pass the president's holiday home, on the left.

Further down the road descends towards the valley and travels parallel with it before a left and a right turn deposit you on the main road just in the north of São Domingos.

6 ASSOMADA–POILÃO–RIBERÃO BOI–SANTA CRUZ

Distance: 16km; time: 5 hours; difficulty: 1 (CW)

This is a long, gentle walk down a shallow *ribeira*. If you want to see rural corners of Santiago without tackling tougher peaks, this is a good walk to do, though it is not as interesting as many of the others. There are several active *grogue* distilleries along the route, where people will be only too happy to let you try some of the raw spirit, often still warm from the still. Your path is an easy, valley-floor track throughout. But if you want to avoid a one-off scramble down a rock face, you have to take a brief detour up the valley side.

The track out of Assomada is a little tricky to find – the best thing to do is to ask for **Poilão** (not to be confused with the location near the dam further south, of the same name), where there is a tourist-friendly distillery (or *trapiche*) (see box, *Grogue*, page 73). The track to Poilão threads along the right-hand side of the head of the *ribeira*, and finally brings you down to the valley floor about 1.5km out of Assomada.

You will know you have arrived because you will pass two large concrete tanks on your right. Turn right along the *ribeira* floor – the beginning of the path does not look promising, but does improve.

After about 500m, you will pass the Poilão *trapiche* on your right. There is usually pressing or distillation in progress (except Saturday, when the week's produce is taken to market).

From the *trapiche*, follow the track along the valley floor. Before the track bears round to the east, you will pass the outskirts of **Boa Entrada** on your left. After about 3km of easy walking from the *trapiche* you will see a line of houses on a high crag which projects into the valley from your left. Just before the track cuts up to the left, stay on the valley floor by taking a small path down to the right at the point where the track crosses a riverbed. There is a small concrete-lined spring directly beside the track.

Approximately 1km from the turning you will pass another *trapiche* on your left. If you continue on at this point, the path enters a tight gorge, and you will have to scramble down a 2m drop that interrupts the path.

You can avoid this by turning right, out of the valley floor, opposite the *trapiche*. After about 15m, take a steep path leading up a ridge on your left. After about ten minutes, this path passes over the shoulder, and you can take a small steep path on the left which will bring you back down to the valley floor, on the other side of the 2m drop.

Continue along the track in the valley floor for another 6.5km (about one hour 40 minutes), and you will reach **Riberão Boi**. Just before you arrive, you will pass beneath a high cliff face on your left, where the rock has formed into dramatic faceted columns.

From Riberão Boi to the Calheta–Pedra Badejo road it is about 3.5km. On the road, you can pick up an *aluguer*.

7 CALHETA–FLAMENGOS DE BAIXO–RIBEIRETA–CALHETA

Distance: 11km; time: 3.25 hours; difficulty: 1 (AI)

This is a pleasant little walk with no great ascents or descents, although it is quite rocky underfoot. It is not a walk of great drama but it shows off plenty of Santiago rural life on the way: from *trapiches* to terracing, and water extraction to traditional stone housing. The middle of the walk, up in the verdant hills, is very pretty.

Walk south out of Calheta along the main road as far as the big bridge across Ribeira dos Flamengos. Descend the rocky track into the *ribeira* and turn inland, among the palm trees. Wander up the *ribeira* for 1.5 hours, past three windmills in total, until you confront an earth road that crosses the *ribeira* and heads up to the right, becoming cobbled very quickly. Now you are walking uphill in pretty countryside. Some 15 minutes after joining the road, you reach a 'crossroads'. Go straight across, and then turn right, down the riverbed, disturbing clusters of butterflies as you go.

The descent down this second *ribeira* involves negotiating your way round several barrages. See the tiny, drystone terraces and hear the dogs, cockerels, goats and people, whose echoes help to make *ribeira* life a noisy experience.

Some 15 minutes after passing a pumping station on your right you will reach the main road. Turn right and walk for another 15 minutes through Calheta to reach the bridge again.

8 TARRAFAL–LIGHTHOUSE–TARRAFAL
Distance: 6km; time: 2.5 hours; difficulty: 2 (AI)
☞ **Note:** there have been muggings on this route; ask locally about safety and/or take a guide.

This walk will take you from the Tarrafal cove to the lighthouse at the foot of the big headland to the north of Tarrafal, which you can see from the beach. It involves a steep scramble at the end and there is no shade – take at least 1.5 litres of water and a hat.

Go to the north end of the most northerly cove of the beach and follow a little sand path up through the rocks and past the last of the holiday bungalows. You can see the path cut into the cliff side ahead. Keep an eye on it as it often disappears underfoot. After 30 minutes clinging to the headland, the path turns inland to face an inhospitable ravine strewn with huge boulders from a landslide. There is a path, though it turns to a scramble at times. When you have reached the end of it follow a path out along the big bulge of land, past deserted drystone walls built to keep cattle.

Instead of turning to the lighthouse you can continue up the coast and walk for hours, even as far as a distant cove (about three hours). It really is empty and there are exhilarating views down green stone canyons and up the coastline.

9 SALINEIRO–CIDADE VELHA
Distance: 4km; time: 1.5 hours; difficulty: 2 (AI)
This walk plunges you from a dry, impoverished village up on the escarpment down into the verdant *ribeira* of Cidade Velha and past a few of the old city's important ruins before depositing you in the main square. This *ribeira* is quite lush with a wide variety of trees and the canyons on either side are magnificently striated. It's not hard but the initial descent is steep and shingly underfoot.

Take an *aluguer* from the old town up to the village of Salineiro for 100$, or charter a taxi for around 500–600$. At the village, ask to be set down as close as possible to the *caminho* to Cidade Velha, a path that lies a little beyond the village's water source. The path is inauspicious, rocky, steep and rubbish strewn, but persist as it winds into the canyon, and watch the greenery of the acacias and palm trees below.

HAVE YOU EVER DRUNK A CLOUD?   *Alex Alper*

High along the jagged cliffs of Serra Malagueta Natural Park, green nets billow in the wind, like a half-erected modern art installation. They are, in reality, fog collectors, harvesting water from the clouds that shroud the park in almost year-round mist. The technology is simple: water vapour condenses along the mesh surface, forming droplets that fall into a gutter below and on to a holding tank. How much water could that possibly provide? More than you might think. Fog contains 0.05–3ml of water per m^3. Serra Malagueta, which receives only about 900mm of rainfall per year, has a semi-permanent layer of 'stratocumulus' – low-lying clouds – pushed upwards from the coast by the mountains themselves. Thanks to these clouds, Serra Malagueta's 120 metres of netting (suspended on eight separate frames) produce approximately 1,440 litres per day, with production reaching 75 litres per metre of net per day in the rainy season. That's a big help for the park's 488 families, who rely principally on local springs, wells, and private cisterns for their water. Rainfall is decreasing and underground sources are drying up, but 80% of Serra Malaguetans still earn their livelihood in agriculture.

Fog water is free from the microbes that contaminate ground water, requiring no treatment. Construction materials – mesh, plastic tubing, and wood or metal poles – are cheap and readily accessible worldwide. The most challenging aspect is positioning the nets accurately, and scientists say that fog harvesting will not damage the microclimate.

Despite these benefits, fog harvesting does not constitute a major source of water in Cape Verde. While 1,133ha of Cape Verde's territory are considered suitable, fog is currently harvested only on Santiago (though efforts are currently underway to install them on São Nicolau). Yet potential national output is estimated at roughly 14 million m^3 of water per year.

After about ten minutes of descent you reach a T-junction of paths, more or less at the treeline. Turn right towards the sea. Some 5m later you will pass piping and a barrage across the *ribeira*: there are several ways down to the *ribeira* floor.

As with many *ribeira* walks, the path emerges and fades and walkers have to negotiate themselves around the great barriers erected against the rain. Here there are mango trees, a stream, and an unusual sensation of humidity. Keep heading seaward, passing a mighty baobab, and finally the route becomes a track, about an hour after the start of the walk. Some ten minutes later you will round a bend and the fort will be in sight, and a few minutes later you will pass a *grogue* distillery on your left, the Pousada São Pedro on the right. After another 5m you will find yourself in the main square of Cidade Velha.

7

Maio

Huge heaps of salt like drifts of snow, and most fine and perfect in nature, the abundance whereof is such, and the daily increase so exceeding great, that they serve all countryes and lands about them, and is impossible to be consumed.

Sir Francis Drake, British sailor, pirate and slave trader, 1578

Maio was until recently the forgotten island. Its quiet dunes and secret beaches have been overshadowed by the more boisterous Sal and beguiling Boavista. It has been waiting to be lifted by the tide, and now its time has come. Maio is being eyed by developers, keen to snap up land for condominiums, apartments and hotels.

HIGHLIGHTS AND LOWLIGHTS

Much of Maio is flat, desolate brown desert, broken by unexpected patches of acacia forest and, in the east, relief for the eye from the odd fertile valley planted with crops and palm trees. The main town of Vila do Maio is charming and quaint with narrow cobbled streets and brightly painted houses.

It lacks the development of Sal or as generous a supply of beautiful dunes and oases as Boavista. It has little gripping walking. But it is this quiet that attracts some people – there are some lovely white and lonely beaches. There is the biggest acacia plantation of the archipelago – and the trees are mature and green although they make surprisingly little impact on the eye, perhaps because the soil itself remains dry and bare. For naturalists there are turtles in the summer and some interesting birds, particularly seabirds on Ilhéu Laje Branca off the north of the island. There are several very good restaurants in the capital.

SUGGESTED ITINERARY AND NUMBER OF DAYS There is little point in visiting Maio if your goal is to tick off the sights of Cape Verde: there's so little here, but combining it with a trip to Santiago could be the perfect combination of islands: Santiago for hiking and mountains, a strong African flavour and a bustling capital city, and Maio for the old Cape Verde, peace and tranquillity, beautiful empty beaches and a selection of great restaurants. Maio is really a place for wandering and musing among the dunes and beaches. This could take half a day to a lifetime.

BACKGROUND INFORMATION

HISTORY Maio's one resource is its prolific salt and for this reason it was a bustling island from the late 16th century until the 19th. In a good year it exported 11,000 tonnes. Before this treasure was discovered, Maio was a grazing ground for cattle

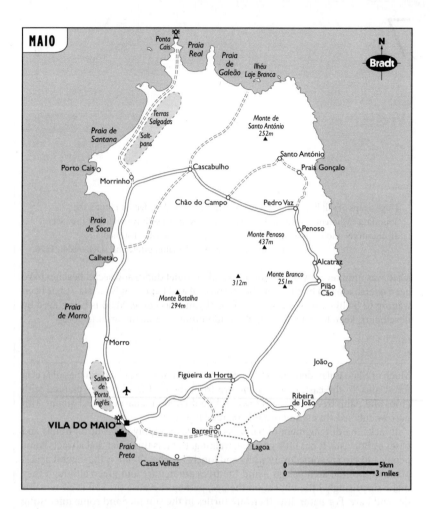

and goats, producing 4,000 head a year at its peak. But soon the fragile vegetation was eaten and there was little left to sell but salt and lime.

It was the English who commandeered the salt production because the Portuguese never had much interest in Maio. One Englishman even made a profit by loading salt at Maio and bartering it at Santiago. The salt was shovelled into sacks at the salt lake, fastened to donkeys and carried to the beach where it was loaded into boats specially designed to cope with the heavy swells in the bay. They would travel out to the boats belonging to the big ships which would themselves be anchored well away from the shore.

The English ships, each laden with about 200 tonnes of salt, would leave for Newfoundland to pick up cod, salt it, and take it to Europe. Other ships took salt on journeys between Europe and the West Indies and between America and Africa. Maio's fort was built by English sailors left behind by Sir Francis Drake in 1588.

All through the 17th century, about 80 English ships a year called at Maio for salt; there was usually a battleship standing by to guard English interests. The Maio people were paid with some money but also with old clothes and food. It is said their houses were full of English ornaments.

By the 19th century, the principal market for salt switched to Brazil, where thousands of tonnes were sent annually. That business was killed when Brazil introduced protective tariffs at the end of the 19th century.

Maio did not escape plunder. In 1818, a pirate ship from Baltimore sacked the port, and a South American ship sacked it in 1827. In the 20th century, there were repeated droughts and emigrations.

MAIO TODAY Farming occupies about 15% of the population and fishing about 7%. The people use their now plentiful wood to turn to charcoal in underground ovens for export to other islands. There are large lime reserves and there is some gypsum. A co-operative, launched in 2003, gathers a little salt from the salina at Porto Inglés. Several holiday complexes have opened in the last couple of years. With the construction of the huge complex of Salinas Beach Resort well underway, and the promise of a new Fast Ferry service connecting all the islands, it looks as if Maio's sleepy status may finally be changing. Salinas Beach will dominate the western part of Vila do Maio and will include a hotel, apartments, restaurants and shops. The publicity even promises a golf course. When it is complete it may also mean that transport to Maio will become more frequent and reliable. Or, like many other all-inclusive resorts, it may have a negative impact on the local economy. The website www.maiocv.com has up-to-date news, maps and photos.

GEOGRAPHY Maio, like the other islands, is an old volcano that has slowly been eroded by the wind. But Maio is unusual because beneath the volcano that welled up out of the ocean floor was ocean sediment that ballooned up behind it. Subsequent erosion of the volcanic rock has exposed vast amounts of marine sediments that are 190 million years old, which is why some texts refer to it as the oldest island.

Maio is small, at 268km², with a population of about 4,000. It lies 25km to the east of Santiago. Its terrain is similar to Sal and Boavista with one big difference: it has been heavily reafforested in parts, almost exclusively with acacias. The highest peak is Monte Penoso at 437m. There are saltpans in the southwest and northwest and there is more fertile, agricultural land in the east.

NATURAL HISTORY Terras Salgadas, Casas Velhas, Lagoa Cimidor and Praia de Morro are natural reserves. Barreiro e Figueira is a natural park and the Salina de Porto Inglês, Monte Penoso, Monte Branco and Monte de Santo António are protected landscapes. For the natural history of Maio's great salina, see *Salina de Porto Inglês*, page 208.

Turtles Maio has the second-largest nesting population of loggerhead turtles (Caretta caretta) in the archipelago. Its long sandy beaches and the limited amount of development have, in the past, made it an ideal habitat. Their survival, as elsewhere in Cape Verde, is threatened by the hunting of females for food, nest poaching and, increasingly, new beachfront development. There are programmes for their protection and it is possible to take a guided walk to see them nesting. Ask around for more information when you are there.

HAZARDS Maio boasts that it is crime-free. Northern beaches are not safe for swimming.

FESTIVALS The festival of Santa Cruz on 3 May, and those in June, are the biggest celebrations.

A BIRD'S-EYE VIEW OF LOVE

Some birds stay faithful for life, some have a roving eye – and it was always thought that this varied according to their species. Now researchers have discovered that even within the same species you get different types of behaviour. Just as with humans, some look after their kids and some are too busy elsewhere. What intrigues scientists is what makes one bird's attitude to its eggs or chicks so different from the next.

'The classic situation is who (mother or father) should go to the disco and who should provide care for the young,' says Tamas Szekely, Professor of biodiversity at the University of Bath, UK. 'If they both go to the disco then the babies die.'

Maio may be the place to answer this question because it is home to the Kentish plover (*Charadrius alexandrius*), the object of this research. Unlike elsewhere in the world, the Kentish plover stays in Maio all year round.

Wander down to the salinas outside the *vila* and you might find Szekely, or one of his students or volunteers manning their mobile hide, documenting behaviour, ringing birds, counting nests and taking genetic samples.

So far, it appears that the birds are remarkably good at varying their behaviour depending on what's going on around them. In Saudi Arabia, where they lay their eggs in the heat of the desert, it takes two parents to run the show: one to sit on the eggs to keep them cool and the other to fetch food. In less demanding environments like Maio two parents may not be so vital – might this liberate one, and if so is it mum or dad who gets to play around? Even more intriguingly, it looks as if even one individual bird may behave differently from one relationship to another.

'If you are a good mother in one family it doesn't mean you will be a good mother in a different family,' says Szekely.

Kentish plovers nest on the ground and start to breed after the annual rains (usually from September onwards). This is when Szekely and his team start their work. In addition to the plovers, the salina harbours breeding populations of cream-coloured courser (*Cursorius cursor exsul*) and the greater hoopoe lark (*Alaemon alaudipes*). It also hosts migratory waders and waterbirds. Protection of the salina is urgently needed because both the research and the habitat may be threatened by a massive new construction site right on the edge of the salina.

2 February	Nossa Sra do Rosário
19 March	São José (Calheta)
3 May	Santa Cruz (Maio)
13 June	Santo António (Santo António)
24 June	São João (Ribeira de João)
29 June	São Pedro (Pedro Vaz)
26 July	Santa Ana (Morrinho)

GETTING THERE AND AWAY

BY AIR There's a ten-minute TACV flight four times a week to and from Praia. Halcyonair also runs a service that connects to Sal, São Vicente, Fogo and Boavista (these services often change, so check before you go). *Hiaces* wait at the airport

(✆ 255 1108) and can be chartered as taxis. It is easy to walk the few kilometres into town: facing the sea, the capital, Vila do Maio, can be seen to the left. Take the only road, towards the sea, and turn left at the T-junction. Pass the saltpans and in about 40 minutes you are in town. On departure, ask around the hotels for transport back to the airport or allow time to walk.

BY FERRY Ferries come and ferries go and Maio has suffered from their vagaries more than most. There is generally some sort of service from Praia. Check with the ferry companies on the Plateau in Praia. At the time of writing the Fast Ferry service was about to start operating (for more information, see *Praia*, page 177). When you are ready to leave Maio ask around or keep an eye on the port – there is no booking office.

BY YACHT There is good anchorage in the rocky, sandy bay in front of Vila de Maio, but it can be difficult to disembark on the pier on account of the big swell. Clear in with the police in advance.

GETTING AROUND

BY PUBLIC TRANSPORT It is just about possible to do a circuit of the entire island in a day by picking up *alugueres* and hitching. But there is always the small chance of being left stranded and the desire not to end up in this situation will prevent you from exploring off the main road. Hitchhiking is an option and if there is passing traffic it will normally stop for you.

Several of the good beaches lie within walking distance either of the *vila* or of Figueira da Horta, which is easy to reach by *aluguer*. For other sights take a chance, hire transport, or ask your hotel owner to come and look for you in his car late in the day if you haven't returned.

Alugueres depart from villages such as Morrinho and Alcatraz very early in the morning to come to the *vila*. They return to Alcatraz at around 11.00 and to Morrinho between 08.00 and 10.00, departing from near the hospital.

BY CAR Find a 4x4: a minibus or car will substantially restrict where you can go. A car can be rented for about 4,800–5,800$ a day. A car plus driver will cost more – about 6,500$.

🚐 **Bemvindo** A *hiace* driver who can often be found at the airport when a flight is due, Bemvindo has a good reputation for safe driving. As well as his *hiace* he has a 4x4 to rent, with or without driver, & he offers a good round-island excursion (6,000$ with driver for the whole day).

🚐 **Ellcar** Vila do Maio; ✆ 255 1900; m 992 4273; e ellcar@cvtelecom.cv. On the way out of town towards the airport.
🚐 **MaioCar** Vila do Maio; ✆ 255 1700. On the street continuing northeast of the post/telecom building.

BY BICYCLE A great way to see Maio is by bicycle, but one would need a mountain bike for cushioning against the cobbled roads. You can rent bikes from IMO-Hire (m *995 5701*) for €10/day. Take several litres of water and remember that every village has a shop somewhere, often indistinguishable from a private home – so ask.

⌂ WHERE TO STAY

There is a growing assortment of apartments and condominiums in the *vila* and the Hotel Belavista up the coast (closed at the time of writing, but due to reopen in 2011). If you don't fancy one of the small hotels or *pensões* in the *vila* there are plenty of apartments or villas to rent, and some are very pleasant.

ACTIVITIES

EXCURSIONS Maio is a place for resting and taking early-morning walks along the beaches and around the saltpans. **Bemvindo** and others offer a round-island excursion (see page 203).

HIKING Maio is not really the island for hiking but it is possible to go for a couple of pleasant walks. In particular, you can head out from Morro towards Monte Batalha or try the more challenging walk to the top of Monte Penoso for which you almost certainly need a guide. Ask around in Vila do Maio for more information when you arrive.

BEACHES Maio has many accessible and inaccessible beaches, some of them breathtakingly deserted and remote. Near the *vila* are Ponta Preta and Bitcharocha. Up the west coast it is sandy way past Morro until just before Calheta. The beautiful half-moon-shaped Santana Beach, northwest of Morrinho, is usually deserted. You will make your own enchanting and personal discoveries.

CAMPING If you are self-sufficient you will find many quiet places to pitch a tent. You can arrange with an *aluguer* driver to be dropped off and collected.

DIVING English couple Stephen and Janette Frankland are in the process of opening Sunfish Scuba Diving Academy (m *954 9562;* e *sunfish.scuba@yahoo.com; www.capeverdediving.com*). When the paperwork is complete they will offer guided dives and try dives. Maio Fishing Club (see *Fishing*, below) had a diving school – currently closed, but which may reopen.

WHALE WATCHING Winter and spring are the times when humpback whales pass by with their newly born calves. Ask around if there are any boats (try *Fleumel* – see below for contact details), that will take you to see them – you may even be lucky enough to see them from the shore.

SAILING Day charters for fishing, snorkelling, sailing or whale watching can be arranged on the *Fleumel* with experienced skipper, Milan (€200/day), as well as longer charters to other islands or even as far afield as west Africa. Going to Senegal takes four–five days and costs €800 – Milan (m *977 0852;* e *sy-fleumel@web.de*) will take care of all the formalities.

FISHING Maio Fishing Club (m *988 9160/971 0006;* e *michela*@maiofishingclub. *com; www.maiofishingclub.com*) offers various types of sport fishing, from the shore and on boats.

VILA DO MAIO

There is a well-kept and gracious town centre with a large square endowed with extra drama because it rises up a small but steep hill to a huge, white Baroque church built in 1872. At the southeast edge of town is an 18th-century fort, now restored and including some cannons.

WHERE TO STAY

Casita Verde (2 rooms) 10mins' walk along the road to Morro; m 996 0633; e info@casita-verde.de; www.casita-verde.de/index_en.htm. Overlooking the beach, this is a private house owned by a German artist who offers 2 very comfortable & beautifully conceived rooms that are en suite with hot water, fan, mosquito net & fridge. You are welcome to join in her creative activities or sit on the shaded terrace admiring the garden & the sea view. Excursions offered. You can download a colourful brochure about Maio from the website. **$$**

Hotel Marilú [207 G5] (12 rooms) Rua 24 de Septembre; 255 1198. Facing the church, the hotel is to the right. Reasonable quality here with upstairs terrace, games room & fine views. Rooms are en suite with fan, & 2 are suites with fridge. **$$**

Residencial Bom Sossego [207 E6] (14 rooms) CP 34; 255 1365. A recently refurbished *pensão* with a restaurant underneath. **$$**

Residencial Porto Inglês [206 D7] (4 rooms) 255 1698; e rpingles@cvtelecom.cv. A blue building close to the new health centre, this is a newly built guesthouse with good rooms, some of them with AC & all en suite with hot water. **$$**

Apartments

Maio Fishing Club m 988 9160/971 0006; e michela@maiofishingclub.com; www.maiofishingclub.com. Catch-&-release fishing trips for wahoo, dorado & sailfish. Offers apartments & B&B which can be part of a fishing package (see Fishing, opposite). It will arrange collection from the airport. **$$$**

Salinas Village www.capeverdeholiday.com/rentsalinas_village.htm. 2-, 3- or 4-bedroom villas finished to a high standard, some with private swimming pools. **$$$**

Stella Maris [207 H5] (c20 apts) 255 1558; m 983 4671; e maiocasa@ymail.com; www.maiocapoverde.com. Overlooking Ponta Preta Beach in the south of town, Stella Maris offers a relaxing place to stay with beautiful views in well-appointed villas & apartments. A swimming pool juts out over the ocean, there is a mini market close by, & it is close to Vila de Maio's restaurants. Many apartments have uninterrupted ocean views. Studios, 2-bed villas with kitchen & living room, 1-bed apartments with kitchen, bathroom & bedroom are all available for short & long-term rental. **$$**

Residencial Solemar [206 A6] (11 apts) 255 1312; e gianniselva.bonino@libero.it. A few hundred metres from the beach, the Solemar is on the way to the meteorological station, below Montinho do Lume. **$$**

Ilha do Maio Imobilária [206 A6] m 993 7022; e info@ilhadomaio.it; www.ilhadomaio.it. Agency with helpful staff. They manage property & are able to find you an apartment or villa to rent. Their list of properties includes Stella Maris, the very popular Residencial Inês, Residencial Solemar & various other villas. Will arrange collection from the airport for 250$. **$–$$$**

WHERE TO EAT AND DRINK

For a small, unfrequented island, Maio has some restaurant treasures. Some of its expats claim they are the best fed in the archipelago.

Bar Tropical [206 D7] On the main beach, Bitcherocha; 12.00–18.00 Wed, 10.00–18.00 Thu–Sun. This snack bar is popular for its homemade pizza, ice cream & snow cones. It also serves sandwiches, hamburgers & French fries. Picturesque because of its clear walls which afford a super view of the sea. **$$$**

Chez Pastis [206 C7] Av Amílcar Cabral. A branch of the restaurant that has long been regarded as one of the best in Sal is now building a good reputation in Maio. **$$$**

Kulor [207 H4] Rua 3 de Maio; m 981 1303; e kulorcafe.maio@voila.fr; 10.00–15.00 & 18.00 until late Mon–Sat. Towards Ponta Preta Beach, this French-owned restaurant is popular, with a rooftop dining area. The food is varied & good quality, & may include chilli, *buzio*, pork caramel & various pastas. There are also some mouth-watering desserts. Sebastian will prepare vegetarian dishes on request. **$$$**

Lanterna [207 E6] Rua 1 de Maio; 255 1358; m 923 4949;

e lanterna7@yahoo,com. Another little gem. Recently opened by a Swiss couple, you will find some unexpected treats on the menu, including specialities such as fondue. $$$

✖ **Restaurant Tutti Frutti** [206 B7] 🕿 255 1575; m 997 9195. Along the main road towards the airport. Alberto & his wife serve excellent pizza & other fine food using imported ingredients, mainly from Portugal. $$$

✖ **Ana Rita's** [207 H6] Rua 1 de Maio; m 994 8561. New location for a popular restaurant serving the usual fare of chicken & pork. $$

✖ **Bom Sossego** [207 E6] This *pensão* has a reasonable restaurant downstairs. $$

✖ **Culinaria** [206 D3] Close to the football pitch near the post office; m 985 1518. A typical menu with varying *pratos do dia*. $$

☕ **Esplanada Miramar Café** [207 F7] A small kiosk opposite the hospital near the phone booth, with a beach view. $$

✖ **Kabana Beach Bar** [206 D7] Also on the main beach; m 993 7270. *Cachupa*, snacks & sandwiches as you watch the world go by. $$

ENTERTAINMENT AND NIGHTLIFE
🍷 **Bar Esperança Disco** [206 C7] Av Amílcar Cabral.
🍷 **Disco Tarrachinha** [207 E3] Near the sports ground.

OTHER PRACTICALITIES
Airlines TACV (🕿 255 1256). Along the road from the post/telecom building further out towards the town of Figueira da Horta.

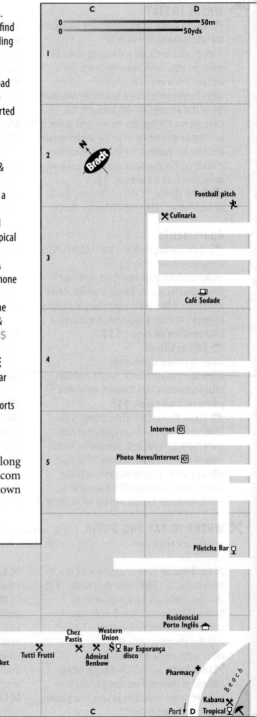

Bank (⏰ *08.00–15.00 Mon–Fri*). One on the square and the other close to the church. A branch of Western Union is on Av Amílcar Cabral (Rua Principal).

Hospital None, but there is a health centre (📞 *255 1130*).

Internet Photo Neves [206 D5], on Rua da Liberadade; Henry's, on the next street north (at the back of the hardware store); and a further one on the way to the post office. At Henry's you can plug in your laptop and at the one close to the post office you can connect wirelessly if you pay for a keycode voucher. Prices are around €1 for an hour. You can also make cheap international calls at Henry's.

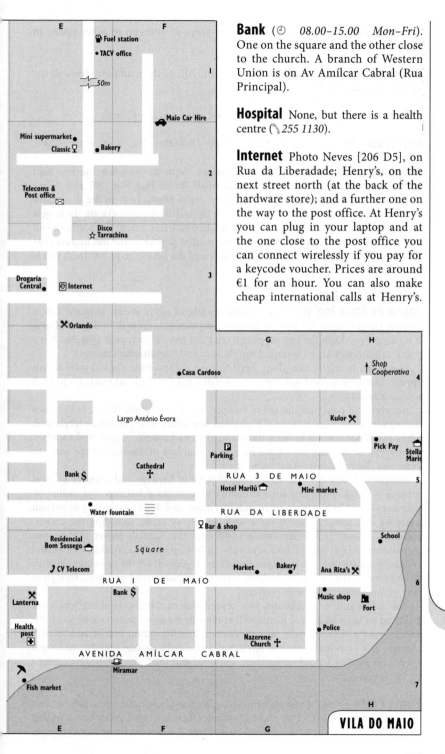

VILA DO MAIO

You cannot connect for free in the main *praça* as you can in other towns in Cape Verde.

Pharmacy Farmacia Forte [206 D7] (✆ *255 1370*), on the road down towards the salinas and main beach.

Police [207 H7] (✆ *255 1132*). At the far end of Av Amílcar Cabral.

Post office [207 E2] (☉ *08.00–12.00 & 14.00–18.00 Mon–Fri*). North of the square.

Shopping Whether the market has produce depends on when the last boat arrived from Praia, but there are several small shops: Pick Pay [207 H5] (close to Stella Maris); the Co-operative (north of Stella Maris, next to the distinctive beehive buildings); and Ramos [206 B7] (on the way to the airport), are the largest and probably have the best choice. There are two bakeries: one at the northern end of town [207 E2], and the other close to the market [207 G6]. The fish market [207 E7] is situated at the start of the main beach and the best time to buy fresh fish is around midday.

WHAT TO SEE AND DO
Salina de Porto Inglês This extraordinary lake of salt is, at 5km long and 1.5km wide, the largest salina in Cape Verde, stretching almost as far as the village of Morro. It no longer produces the vast supplies it once did (see *History*, page 199), but it is a poetic reminder of Maio's historical significance and thus an island treasure.

The salina is still in use: from April to June endless little conical piles of salt appear around it as local women work to make salt for the local market – just 1.5 tonnes a year.

Between the pans and the sea is a raised beach over which the seawater rises during spring tides and at times of high swell. Seawater also infiltrates underground, while rainwater trickles in from mainland streams between August and October. For the rest of the time the intense heat, wind and lack of shade allow the water to evaporate, leaving crusts of salt behind.

But the salina is not just Maio's biggest piece of heritage and a source of local income – it has important natural history as well. As a wetland it is visited by migrant waders. Its situation, surrounded by dunes and desert, make it an important breeding and feeding habitat for a wide variety of birds, including the cream-coloured courser (*Cursorius cursor exsul*) and the Kentish plover (*Charadrius alexandrinus*) (see box, *A bird's-eye view of love*, page 202). Alexander's kestrel (*Falco alexandrii*) and the Iago sparrow (*Passer iagoensis*) are the two endemic birds to be found in the salina. Loggerhead turtles (*Caretta caretta*) nest here, though in tiny numbers compared with Boavista.

The salina and its inhabitants face several threats. Firstly, sand extraction for building on both Maio and Santiago threatens to remove the barrier between the salina and the sea. Secondly, it is threatened by burgeoning tourist ambitions – though, as it is in itself a tourist attraction, one would assume that the salina will eventually be ring-fenced rather than destroyed and the town hall is developing a conservation plan.

Ponta Preta From the *vila* walk east along the coast, across the refuse tips and past the cemetery on the left – after about 15 minutes there is a small, pretty bay. A further 30 minutes will take you to the beach at Ponta Preta. Ask in town for further directions.

Turtle walks Biosfera 1 (e *tommymelo@hotmail.com; www.biosferaum*) is working with the Câmara Municipal do Maio to protect and monitor turtles on Maio. It may be possible to arrange to see nesting turtles by contacting Biosfera in advance. It is not a good idea to go to the beach alone at night as you may disturb the turtles.

OTHER PLACES TO VISIT

MORRO Morro is a small settlement with very little going on, but its beach is worth a look. In common with many beaches in Cape Verde, it fluctuates in size with the season's changing currents; in winter about 3m depth of sand vanishes, and the sea as a result comes many metres further in. The beach is safe for swimming apart from the odd day when the waves come from the south. From the town of Morro it is quite a long walk to the beach, so make sure that you ask to be dropped off at the beach rather than in the village.

From Morro there is a two-hour walk up the nearby hill with good views at the top and a walk along the stunning beach to Calheta.

Where to stay There are several resorts and hotels under construction.

Hotel Belavista (22 villas) 256 1388; m 972 6584; e info@belavistamaio.com. On the beach just before Morro, the Belavista, a Spanish-owned 3-star hotel, is a series of square stone villas surrounded by abundant planting. Villas have 2 bedrooms, a living room & a terrace. Facilities include tennis, swimming pool, car rental, excursions & a fine restaurant. This hotel was closed at the time of writing but may reopen in 2011.

Where to eat and drink There is a surprisingly large supermarket in Morro, underneath the planned hotel, Casa Blanca. You can buy drinks and snacks there but there is no restaurant.

CALHETA About 3km north of Morro is this pretty fishing village, reached by turning left off the main road. At the end of its street, lined with red-tiled pitched roofs and white-painted stones, is the bay. You can swim here, though it is probably cleaner away from the settlement. Bashona Beach is one of the calmest on the island. This is also the place to buy locally woven bags, for about 1,000$.

Where to eat and drink There are no restaurants in Calheta but several small bars. You may find someone willing to cook for you if you ask around.

MORRINHO About 4km north of Calheta is Morrinho. There is a rough track that leads from here northwest to Praia de Santana, a wild and desolate beach that remains invisible from the long road, hidden by a ridge of dunes. These endless, evocative dunes are well worth exploring. In the middle of them is a patch of palm trees which the locals think of as an oasis. It is possible to drive along the track by the beach for a few kilometres, after which it peters out: if you want to go further you must walk. Eventually, you reach Praia Real: bear in mind that northern beaches are not safe for swimming.

CASCABULHO AND PEDRO VAZ This area in the north is filled with more green and mature forest followed by a landscape that feels like an abandoned opencast mine. Pedro Vaz feels like it could be the end of the earth but it's not – there's

MAIO'S MYSTERIOUS BEACH BOULDERS

On the beach are a series of boulders that have intrigued visitors for years because they do not originate from anywhere in the archipelago. One academic thought they harboured clues to the whereabouts of Atlantis – it was once argued that the islands of Cape Verde might be the tips of a submerged continent. The mystery was solved by a vulcanologist who demonstrated that the boulders were from Brazil and were used as ballast – thrown onto the beach when the boat was loaded with salt.

another two rough kilometres to the beach, possible by car. This is perhaps the loneliest and wildest beach, enlivened occasionally by women who come to meet the returning fishermen. There is a restaurant that serves pizza in Pedro Vaz.

PENOSO This is an old village where all that remains is a little white church. They hold a service here on the last Sunday of each month. Just after the church you can walk up the slopes of Monte Penoso. Even a short stroll will be rewarded with good views.

ALCATRAZ The land between Pedro Vaz and Alcatraz feels increasingly isolated – abandoned stony plains and lifeless land. Alcatraz lies 4km from Pedro Vaz – a single wide and dusty street.

FIGUEIRA DA HORTA AND RIBEIRA DE JOÃO Ribeira de João is reached by a turning to the south, east of Figueira da Horta. It's a road past pretty oases. On arrival, turn right off the main street, down a footpath, and it is a ten-minute walk past the football pitch and along an enormously wide *ribeira* to find a magnificent beach with unbearably turquoise water. Look behind you – the village nestles like some Arabian desert town on the top of the bare brown hills.

BARREIRO AND LAGOA Barreiro is a neat settlement built on two sides of a valley. It is possible to drive from here to Lagoa and onto the beach. Locals say they walk to the beach from the *vila* (about 9km along the coast).

8

Fogo

It is all of it one large mountain of a good height, out of the top whereof issues Flames of Fire, yet only discerned in the Night: and then it may be seen a great way at Sea.

William Dampier, 1683

Fogo rises steeply from the ocean, pokes through the clouds and towers above them. From the coast of Santiago or the peaks of São Nicolau it looks as forbidding as a fortress. Fogo is a volcano, still active, and inside the crater the latest eruption still smokes gently.

Fogo is a menacing place: dark lava rivers from centuries of eruptions reach down its eastern side to the ocean. But it has a soft heart. Amongst the clods of cold lava that have covered much of the floor of the crater are fertile fields. Spilling over its northeast side are woods of eucalyptus and cool valleys in which grow coffee and vines. Inside the crater lives a race of people who have defied government orders to evacuate and instead live and farm below the smouldering peak that last erupted in 1995.

HIGHLIGHTS

The crater is a highlight of the archipelago, its drama matched only by the mountains of Santo Antão. Fogo is thus one of the principal hiking islands, but it is also fascinating for its anthropology and its natural history. Much of the island's splendour can be reached by vehicle. There are caves to explore.

SUGGESTED ITINERARY AND NUMBER OF DAYS Many visitors spend two nights in Fogo, wandering round São Filipe on their first afternoon, spending their one full day travelling to the crater for an ascent of the Pico, and departing the next day. The crater is rewarding enough to merit a little longer than this. We suggest four nights: on the first day look at São Filipe and perhaps visit one of Fogo's lesser sights such as its lagoon, at Salina. On day two head to the crater and climb the Pico. Day three, another of the crater walks. Day four, a descent to the northeast, to Mosteiros. After a night in Mosteiros an *aluguer* should be able to take you to your flight. You can arrange a day trip from Sal (and sometimes from Santiago or Boavista) with several travel agents and, although this won't allow you much time to get to know the island, it does, at least, give you a flavour. The tours usually include a quick trip to view the crater and walk around São Filipe.

LOWLIGHTS

There are only modest opportunities for swimming and no white-sand beaches. Apart from fishing, there are no organised watersports. The capital is quiet and it's not big on top-quality restaurants.

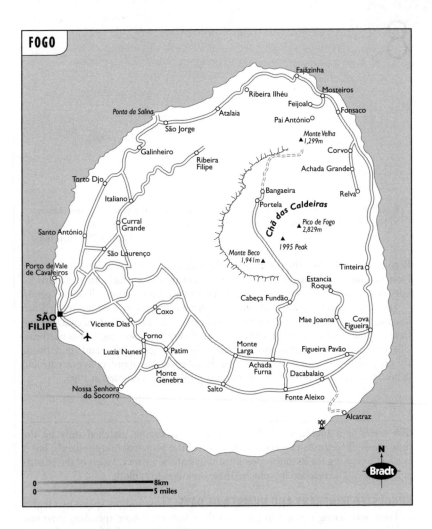

FOGO

Fajãzinha
Ribeira Ilhéu
Mosteiros
Feijoal
Fonsaco
Ponta da Salina
Atalaia
Pai António
São Jorge
Monte Velha
▲ 1,299m
Corvo
Galinheiro
Achada Grande
Ribeira
Filipe
Torto Djo
Bangaeira
Relva
Italiano
Portela *Chã das Caldeiras*
Santo António
Curral
Grande
Pico de Fogo
2,829m
▲
São Lourenço
1995 Peak
Porto de Vale
de Cavaleiros
Monte Beco
1,941m ▲
Tinteira
Estancia
Roque
Cabeça Fundão
SÃO
FILIPE
Coxo
Mae Joanna
Cova
Figueira
Vicente Dias
Forno
Monte
Larga
Figueira Pavão
Luzia Nunes
Patim
Achada
Furna
Dacabalaio
Monte
Genebra
Nossa Senhora
do Socorro
Salto
Fonte Aleixo
Alcatraz

N

Bradt

0 ——————— 8km
0 ——————— 5 miles

BACKGROUND INFORMATION

HISTORY Geologists have done intricate work to piece together the volcano's history by extrapolating from the directions of lava flows of different ages and combining that information with literary descriptions of the appearance of the volcano at different times.

Fogo erupted from the sea a few hundred thousand years ago, a single volcano reaching a mighty 3.5km high. Its walls were steep and unstable and so, sometime within the last 10,000 years, a great section in the east collapsed towards the sea – reducing the height of its walls by about 300m in one giant avalanche. After the first eruption there were numerous smaller ones, all making craters in the floor of the original large crater, which is now about 10km long and 7km wide.

Volcanoes are fertile places and Fogo's agricultural potential was harnessed from early on – it had acquired a population of 2,000 within the first 120 years of its discovery. It was the second island of the archipelago to be settled and was populated with slaves who grew cotton and developed the skill of weaving

– the island was famed for its ***pano preta***, or deep indigo cloth (see *Chapter 1, Background Information*, page 40). The cloth was shipped to Santiago, and because of this the island remained remote from the trans-oceanic ship trade. But it did not escape attack: the Dutch had a four-day spree there in 1655. Lisbon's response to the ensuing plea for more Portuguese settlers was to dispatch convicts. Fogo was regarded as a hardship posting and, though it is only 50km from Santiago, it was the threatened place of exile for the people of the greater island.

For much of this time the volcano in the background was growing: it appears to have put on several hundred metres between 1450 and 1750, and in the early 1600s, black clouds swathed its heights. An eruption in 1680 was savage and gave the island its name, which means 'fire' – before that it had been called, as usual, after the saint's day on which it was discovered. Much fertile land was ruined in that 1680 eruption and many people emigrated permanently to neighbouring Brava. From the end of the 1600s into the 1700s, the fire of Fogo could be seen from afar and was used by ships to aid their navigation.

It was into the open space left by the giant ancient collapse that, in 1785, Pico de Fogo erupted. Lava spewed down the northeastern slopes creating the bulge on which the town of Mosteiros is situated today, and the Pico became the highest point of the archipelago.

Against this tempestuous background the people of Fogo welcomed the crews of American whaling ships who came ashore in search of supplies and personnel, as they were doing on Brava. Thus began the **emigration to the United States** and the creation of the great Cape Verdean diaspora.

Since 1785, all eruptions have been inside the old crater. There was one in 1799 and three in the following century, in 1847, 1852 and 1857, after which there was a century's gap. Each eruption leaves cones in the crater floor, which is how it earned its name, Chã das Caldeiras or Plain of Craters. In 1847 there were fatalities caused not by lava flows but by the associated earthquakes. The eruption of 1852 created the cone known as Monte Preto de Baixo.

In the 20th century there were two eruptions. Lava spewed from one of the two chimneys on the southern side of the volcano in 1951, and also created cones to the north and south of the Pico – such as Monte Orlando, Monte Rendall and Monte Preto de Cima. These eruptions all began along a line of volcanic fissures extending from the flank of the Pico de Fogo summit cone across the floor of Chã das Caldeiras. The lava flows that issued from these vents spread over the northern and southern parts of Chã das Caldeiras and down the eastern flank of the island.

It was just a few years ago that the last eruption occurred, on the night of 2 April 1995. For a week before, the villages had been shaken with small but increasingly powerful earthquakes. Just after midnight the flank of the Pico split apart as a line of fissures opened. It was as if the Pico had been 'cut by a knife', said one villager. The eruption began and a curtain of fire issued from the volcano and poured down into the crater. Thousands of inhabitants fled. By daylight the whole island was covered by a thick cloud of dark ash extending 5km into the sky; lava bombs up to 4m wide landed half a kilometre from the eruption and a day later lava fountains were spurting 400m high: it is estimated that at its height the volcano ejected between four and 8.5 million m³ of lava per day.

One month later the lava had thickened but was still flowing at 15cm per hour. It was another month before the flow stopped. Miraculously nobody died; perhaps the luckiest escape was made by two guitarists who are said to have climbed the Pico the day before the eruption, to make music and enjoy the view.

The 1995 eruption was different from the others. Unusually, it occurred southwest of the Pico, through a system of fissures that lay in a broadly south-to-west orientation. As a result the lava flows spread west and then north, covering an area of fertile volcanic soils and ultimately much of the small village of Boca Fonte. Today, shells of its houses remain, invaded by monstrous clumps of lava as high as their roofs.

Alternative housing was quickly built on the southern slopes – it can be seen from the road as you ascend to the crater. It was assumed that the people would move there permanently but most of them have returned to their crater homes to cultivate whatever land escaped the lava flow. The road across Chã has been rebuilt.

For most of the duration of the eruption (from 10 April to the end of May) the only active vent was at the northeastern end of the fissure system and it is here that the largest volcanic cone of the eruption grew – the yellow-streaked, smoking black slope that lies at the foot of the Pico de Fogo. You pass it on the right soon after entering the crater by road.

FOGO TODAY Today Fogo has been boosted by development work, much of it funded by Germany. It has a fine new harbour, and acres of terracing, catchment dams and reafforestation.

Agriculture is the main activity, though fishing occupies a small number of people. There's plenty of water underground but hoisting it to the surface is expensive, and directing it higher – to the slopes that carry much of the agriculture – is even more costly. Some rainwater catchment tanks have been built to address this. The islanders grow coffee and produce wine. The coffee is grown on the outer northern slopes near Mosteiros. Grapes are grown in the crater by digging pits amongst the little black pieces of basaltic rock known as *lapilli* and planting a vine in each: at night the moisture condenses on the rock and dribbles into the holes. A collaboration between the people of the crater and an Italian NGO, COSPE, has led to the production of some really very quaffable wines, and they have now branched out into juices and various liquors.

Fogo is thought to have potential for geothermal energy for electricity production. Rainwater filters through the permeable volcanic rock and reaches underground reservoirs. The water samples taken during investigations have reached as high as 200–300°C.

GEOGRAPHY The fourth-largest island, with an area of 480km², Fogo's highest point is the Pico de Fogo which reaches 2,829m. Fogo has a population of about 39,000. São Filipe is the third-largest town in Cape Verde.

NATURAL HISTORY
Flora There are eight plant species endemic to Fogo. Two to watch out for are *língua de vaca* (*Echium vulcanorum*), a white flower with a broad leaf, which is confined not just to Fogo volcano but only to the volcano's rim; and *cravo-brabo babo* (*Erysimum caboverdeanum*), a delicate pink flower with long pointed leaves, which is found only inside the crater.

Birds The crater is designated an Important Bird Area by BirdLife International. Fogo is one of four islands in Cape Verde where the endemic Fea's petrel (*Pterodroma feae*) is known to breed, and it likes the inner walls of the crater best. The Cape Verde little shearwater (*Puffinus (assimilis) boydi*) breeds on the outer slopes of the crater and it has the largest population of Alexander's swift (*Apus alexandri*). Other breeding species include the grey-headed kingfisher (*Halcyon leucocephala*), the spectacled warbler (*Sylvia conspicillata*) and probably the Cape Verde peregrine (*Falco madens*). (For more on birds, see Natural history and conservation, page 6.)

Turtles As with all the Cape Verdean islands, Fogo is home to nesting loggerhead turtles (*Caretta caretta*) from June to October. The island has a fledgling turtle conservation project, Projeto Vitó; you may be able to arrange a visit to the beach to see them nest, or to a hatchery. Contact SOS Tartarugas (e *info@turtlesos.org*) for advice.

HAZARDS You should take care if **swimming**: the land drops steeply away and removal of sand for construction has not helped this. Take local advice.

Hikers should be aware that the Pico is pretty challenging and some walks, like the crater rim, are dangerous without a guide.

CONSERVING THE CRATER

The crater was deemed a natural park in 2003. The park extends over a large part of the landmass of the island: its 8,469ha include a margin around the south and north of the crater and a western section that extends quite close to the coast at some points. Some areas are under greater restrictions than others: for example any land use is banned on the Pico and on the inner wall of the crater, but some uses are permissible elsewhere. A project to conserve and develop the crater has been in progress, in one form or another, for some years. Berthold Seibert, a consultant for the project, says that the true value of the crater is geological, rather than to do with its flora and fauna, and so the priorities lie with conserving its rocks. 'Geological tourism' is a principal focus, he says.

Since the crater houses two expanding villages, and there are increasing numbers of visitors, some activities threaten the crater while others do not. 'The areas where people are growing vines are just ash, and there is no problem with this,' says Seibert. Conversely, large quantities of ash and sand in the crater are being shovelled away and used in the construction boom. It's valued because, compared with sand from the shore, it has a low salt content. And lava stone is used for roof tiles. On a small scale this would be no problem, he says. But the expansion now is 'aggressive'. It is thought that the crater population has grown from 500 to 1,000 people since 2000.

Conservation plans extend to the crater slopes. On the outer northern slopes of the volcano, there are eucalyptus, pines and acacias, planted during job-creation activities in the 1940s after the famine. In an area of the southwest, the project has planted fruit trees watered by drip irrigation and by reservoirs which fill over two–three months and then are used over the rest of the year.

To deal with the goat problem, the project did a deal with local people: they were given 'beautiful, big' goats from the Canaries that produce a lot of milk, if they agreed to build stables for them and prevent them roaming the countryside.

'Now we have about 70 stables built and huge demand,' Seibert says. The hills feel greener, though there's no scientific evidence yet to show that they are.

FESTIVALS The end of April is the time for Fogo's big party, Bandeira (Flag) de São Filipe. There is horse racing, held on the black sandy terrace outside Le Bistro Restaurant, dancing and processions. Special dishes are made. The island has a distinctive music known as *pilão*, a bit like *batuko*, a chanting and beating of drums that forms the background to the grinding of corn in the run-up to the festival.

20 January	São Sebastião
end April	Bandeira de São Filipe
24 June	São João
29 June	São Pedro
Second Sunday in July	Santa Rainha de Cabo Verde (Chã das Caldeiras)
5 August	Nossa Sra do Socorro
10 August	São Lourenço
15 August	Municipality Day (Mosteiros)
24 November	Santa Catarina (Cova Figueira)

GETTING THERE AND AWAY

BY AIR Flying over the flanks of the volcano and landing on a sliver of flat land between the grey slopes and the blue sea is one of the most spectacular experiences you will have on the archipelago. Coming from Praia, sit on the right-hand side. There is a daily flight with TACV from Santiago.

There are also well-established day trips from Sal (advertised all over the island of Sal) in planes owned by Cabo Verde Express.

It's 2km into the capital, a 20-minute walk downhill into town. A shared *aluguer* from the airport to São Filipe should not cost more than 100$ (taxi 500$). Some hotels collect their guests if they have booked in advance. There is an *aluguer* for Mosteiros which meets every São Filipe flight.

BY FERRY Ferries come and ferries go. Check the situation with the ferry agencies or tour operators. At the time of publication there was a daily connection with Brava and somewhat less frequent connections with Praia. The port (Barca Balêro) lies to the north of São Filipe and a taxi to town costs 200$ (but from town to the port costs 500$). Tickets can be bought in advance from the ferry ticket office in the docks.

BY YACHT Fogo is bathed in a swell that can only be avoided by anchoring at the harbour to the north of the capital. Unfortunately it is so small that the presence of two ferries or cargo ships may lead to an order for yachts to leave. Mosteiros is not suitable for yachts. Register with the port captain's office in São Filipe.

GETTING AROUND

BY PUBLIC TRANSPORT *Alugueres* leave Mosteiros, the villages in the crater and other outlying villages between 04.00 and 05.30. They generally head north, travelling anticlockwise around the coast, and arrive in São Filipe about an hour later. They depart from São Filipe mid morning and also at midday and at 14.00 for the crater (250$): don't get stranded. There are no *alugueres* to and from the crater on a Sunday. An *aluguer* leaves São Filipe for São Jorge sometime between 09.30 and 11.00 and one returns to São Filipe at 13.00.

Alugueres for the crater and for Mosteiros leave from beside the block that houses the town hall (*câmara municipal*) and the market. Those for São Jorge, Salina, the airport and the port leave from outside Pousada Belavista. To go to Monte Genebra, take an *aluguer* from outside the post office.

BY TAXI Taxis or chartered *alugueres* will go most places (the taxi rank in São Filipe is at the top of town, opposite the post office). Fares are relatively fixed – for example, to the crater 8,000$; around the island 8,000$; to Mosteiros 6,000$; to São Lourenço 1,000$; to Curral Grande 1,300$.

🚗 **Alino** 📞 281 1931; 📱 995 8057   🚗 **Vergilio** 📞 283 1711; 📱 996 7018

BY CAR
🚗 **BBAS** São Filipe 📞 281 1089
🚗 **Discount Auto Rent and Parts** [221 E6] São Filipe, next to Qualitur, which will handle the payment; 📞 281 1480; 📱 991 4597;

e discountautorent@hotmail.com. Charges €60/ day; you may be asked to pay a deposit.
🚗 **RL** São Filipe; 📞 281 1050; 📱 983 0947; e info.rl@cvtelecom.cv

🏠 WHERE TO STAY

Almost all the accommodation is in São Filipe where you have a choice between the relatively upmarket Hotel Xaguate and an array of *pensões* of varing quality, some of them situated in traditional *sobrado* houses and some with views of the ocean. The other major place to stay is in the crater, where the choice is between homestays, a humble *pensão* and the legendary Pensão Pedra Brabo. There are now a few options elsewhere, all classed as 'out of town'. They vary enormously in character but are mostly in beautiful, extremely quiet locations.

ACTIVITIES

EXCURSIONS AND TOUR OPERATORS

Dja'r Fogo [221 F6] Rua Dr Costa, São Filipe; 📞 281 2879; 📱 991 9713; e agnelo@djarfogo. net; www.djarfogo.net. Descended from an old Fogo family, Agnelo, the proprietor, is deeply interested in the traditional Fogo way of life & this is reflected in his tours. Specialising in small groups & individuals, he can arrange any itineraries to suit, including a visit to his country house (see *Quinta das Saudades*, page 222). Dja'r Fogo also sells crafts, maps & Fogo coffee which Agnelo roasts & grinds himself, & he is active in promoting cultural events.

Qualitur [221 E6] Praça Câmara Municipal, São Filipe; 📞 281 1089; 📱 997 1142; e qualitur@ cvtelecom.cv, qualitur@gmail.com; www.qualitur.cv. An efficient little outfit organising mainly group trips to Chã das Caldeiras, the salina, Monte Genebra, & a variety of walks in & out of the crater, with guides. Sample prices: day trip to the crater, climb the

Pico, return, €80–100pp (minimum 2 people – 4 people is cheaper); half-day tours, for example to Nossa Senhora or the salina, €25 (4 people or more). English spoken.

vista verde tours Close to the blue church, São Filipe; 📞 281 2380; e office@ vista-verde.com; www.vista-verde.com; ⏰ 10.00–12.00 & 15.00–19.00 Mon–Fri. Well-established travel agency specialising in socially & environmentally responsible tourism. Arranges small-group tours or tailor-made holidays incorporating accommodation, flights, hiking & excursions. Offices in Fogo, Sal & Boavista.

Zebra Travel [221 D5] On the main square; 📱 991 4566; e info@zebratravel.net; www.zebratravel.net. An agent for Halcyonair, can arrange flights, tours & excursions. It also rents cars. Connected to Colonial B&B & Fogo Lounge (see below). Internet service.

Round-island tours can be arranged with *aluguer* drivers. Try Vergilio (m *996 7018*) or Irlando (m *986 4574*).

HIKING This is the great activity of Fogo. As well as the big hike up to the Pico in the crater, there are several delightful, and arguably more rewarding, walks from various points in and around the crater (see *Hikes*, page 228).

FISHING The game fishing around Fogo's waters is high quality, with plenty of blue marlin, sharks and tuna. Zebra Travel can organise fishing trips.

CYCLING Fogo is steep and cobbled, and cycling anywhere but along contours or downhill can be unbearable without a good, comfy, mountain bike.

BEACHES AND SWIMMING It is often dangerous to swim off Fogo, but when the sea looks really calm it is safe at the beach at the port, and at Praia Nossa Senhora. The best place to swim, however, is Ponta do Salina – a stunning cove with black rock formations smothered by white seaspray and riddled with grottos and reefs. It can be reached on the São Jorge *aluguer* – ask to be dropped off there and check what time the *aluguer* is returning.

CAVES There are at least three volcanic tubes to explore on Fogo and the Parque Natural do Fogo is opening more to visitors. The tubes are lava flows that solidify on the outside, after which the inner liquid flows away leaving them hollow inside. Inside they are beautiful, with frozen lava in streams down the inner walls like melted chocolate.

Two of the caves lie on an imaginary line drawn roughly between Pico de Fogo and São Lourenço, on the slopes of Fogo a bit higher than the roads. To reach them ask one of the tour operators or check with the Park office. You should be taken to Ribeira de Aguadinha, to a large concrete water tank and then on to the caves. Access to one involves a 5m crawl before it opens out into a larger area. Bring a good head torch and don't go alone or if you are not an experienced caver. The floors of the caves are uneven.

CULTURE The *sobrado* architecture is the main draw, plus a visit to Casa da Memória.

SIGHTSEEING BY VEHICLE The volcano crater's grandeur is eminently appreciable from a vehicle if you don't mind a slightly hair-raising ascent to the crater. Once that has been done it is pleasant to trace other roads, enjoying the gentle western slopes and visiting a few further sights, all accessible by vehicle (see *Other places to visit*, page 227).

SÃO FILIPE

São Filipe is a large and pretty town full of Portuguese squares, esplanades and *sobrado* houses (see *Architecture*, below) – some of them collapsing, a few lovingly restored. The streets are cobbled, the buildings are pastel with terracotta tiles, and vegetation springs from pots on every fragile wooden balcony. Bougainvillea abounds and trees are a healthy size. The town could do with some more outdoor cafés from which its architecture and the views of Brava could be enjoyed. Until then, there is a promenade, adorned with busts of Portuguese heroes, which lines the clifftops and from which you can gaze down the harsh drop to the black sands and the violent sea below. There's also a large terrace on which to sit, halfway up the hill at the top of a flight of steps (marked on the map). Cafés with views are mentioned in the following listings.

🏠 **WHERE TO STAY** Some hotels raise their prices threefold in April to capitalise on the island's annual festival.

🏠 **Hotel Xaguate** [220 A2] (18 rooms)
📞 281 1222; e hotelxaguate@
hotelxaguate.com; www.hotelxaguate.com.
The hotel is set in a spectacular position on the headland, which can be enjoyed from the balconies of some of the rooms, or from the swimming pool terrace. This is the smartest hotel in town, with AC & most mod cons. Internet access via a terminal. Not all rooms have a sea view: it is worth paying the 5% extra for this. Offers massage. Non-residents may swim there for a reasonable fee. Visa accepted. **$$$$**

🏠 **Arco Iris** [221 E6] (8 rooms) Walk past the town hall & turn right; 📞 281 2526;
e arkoiris.fogo@gmail.com. Don't expect stunning views here; just a good-value, modest hotel. Vibrant & colourful with modern fixtures & cosy atmosphere. Rooms have AC, TV & good storage. Rooms are above the café of the same name. Portuguese owned; English spoken. **$$**

🏠 **Colonial B&B** [221 D5] (9 rooms) Part of Zebra Travel (for contact information, see page 217), this tastefully restored colonial building has a swimming pool & great views. A pleasant & peaceful place to stay. **$$**

🏠 **Hotel Savana** [221 D5] (16 rooms) 📞 281 1490; e reservasavana@yahoo.com; http://hotelsavana.homestead.com/index03.html. Head north from the town hall. A beautifully restored traditional sobrado house with great sea views in a quiet location. AC & TV. Good value. **$$**

🏠 **Pensão Inacio** [220 E3] (15 rooms)
📞 281 2746; m 991 7917. A new pensão in the orange building just off the airport road. An airy place, with lots of windows & shared veranda offering views either of the sea or of the volcano; fitted with most of the mod cons. There are better places for the same price but this one is convenient for the airport. **$$**

🏠 **Pensão Las Vegas** [221 C6] (12 rooms)
📞 281 2223; m 995 6873; www.caboverde.com. The Las Vegas has friendly management & a variety of rooms, some with balconies giving sea views. **$$**

🏠 **Pensão Open Skies** [220 E3] (8 rooms)
📞 281 2726/2012; m 991 4595; e majortelo@yahoo.com. At the top of town east of the main square. Some rooms are down at heel with internal windows, others are bright, offering views of the volcano or the sea. Pleasant rooftop terrace. **$$**

🏠 **Pousada Belavista** [221 C5] (11 rooms)
📞 281 1734/1220; e p_belavista@yahoo.com; www.pbelavista.com. It is around the corner of the same block that houses the TACV office. This friendly, excellent-value hotel is a popular choice in an immaculately kept sobrado house. Rooms are en suite & vary in their equipment: some have AC, some have fans; some have fridge & TV; some have hot water. Front rooms have balconies but can get a little noisy because alugueres stop in front. **$$**

🏠 **Pensão Cristina** [220 F4] (4 rooms) 📞 281 2623. On the east side of town, the rooms are basic but en suite & there's a small restaurant. It is linked with the hotel in Mosteiros. **$**

🏠 **Residencial Luanda** [221 D6] (6 rooms) Near the town hall; 📞 281 1181;
e reservasavana@yahoo.com. Connected with Savana Hotel, this small residencial has comfortable clean rooms with AC & TV. **$**

🏠 **Casa Renate** [221 F7] (3 apts, 1 room)
📞 281 2518; m 994 5939; e RenateFogo@hotmail.com; www.cabo-verde.ch. Opposite the cathedral, this is a beautiful, restored sobrado with views of the ocean. Rooms are simple but en suite & have access to a shaded courtyard in the centre. Currently closed, but may reopen.

Apartments

🏠 **Le Bistro** [221 D5] (1 apt) 📞 281 2518. Located above the Bistro Café (see Where to eat, below), this is a spacious apartment whose main selling point is an enormous, shaded terrace with

uninterrupted views across the ocean towards Brava. Another great advantage is that you have all the facilities of Le Bistro to support you. The apartment has private bathroom & kitchenette. **$$**

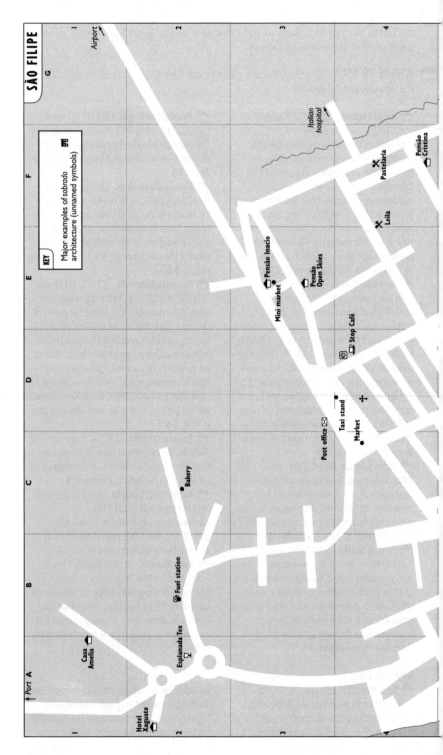

SÃO FILIPE

KEY

Major examples of *sobrado* architecture (unnamed symbols)

Airport

Port

Hotel Xaguate

Casa Amelia

Esplanada Tex

Fuel station

Bakery

Post office

Taxi stand

Market

Mini market

Pensão Inacio

Pensão Open Skies

Stop Café

Italian hospital

Leila

Pastelaria

Pensão Cristina

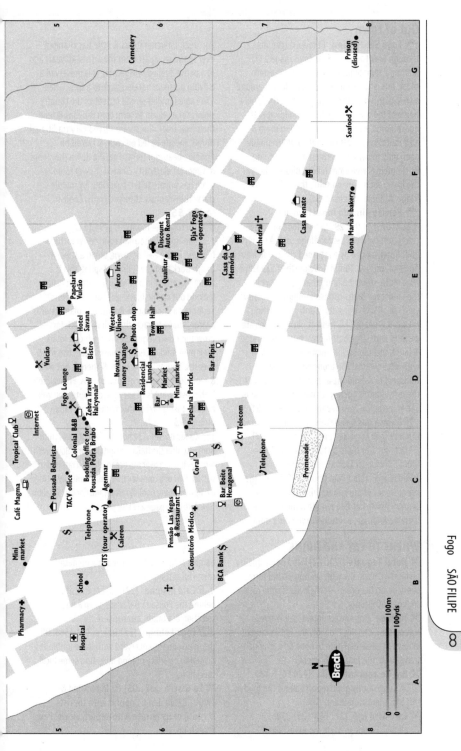

Cemetery

Prison
(disused)

Seafood

Dja' Fogo
(Tour operator)

Discount
Auto Rental

Qualitur
(Tour operator)

Arco Iris

Casa da
Memória

Cathedral

Casa Renate

Dona Maria's bakery

Papelaria
Vulcão

Western
Union

Photo shop

Town Hall

Hotel
Savana

Le
Bistro

Vulcão

Fogo Lounge

Colonial B&B

Zebra Travel/
Halcyonair

Booking office for
Pousada Pedra Brabo

Novatur,
money change

Residencial
Luanda

Bar

Market

Mini market

Bar Pipis

Papelaria Patrick

CV Telecom

Telephone

Promenade

Tropical Club

Internet

Pousada Belavista

Café Magma

TACV office

Agenmar

Coral

Bar Boite
Hexagonal

Telephone

Caleron

CITS (tour operator)

Pensão Las Vegas
& Restaurant

Consultório Médico

BCA Bank

Mini
market

School

Pharmacy

Hospital

N

Bradt

0   100m
0   100yds

8

Out of town

⌂ **Fogo Sea Fishing** (4 rooms) (contact through Dja'r Fogo, see *Excursions*, page 217). Built on a remote part of Fogo's northeastern coast, this is an attractive set of buildings around a well-planted garden, incorporating the family home of the owners, a separate building with guest rooms, a communal bar/dining room & a TV room. There's also a small pool. Originally open only to game fishermen it is expanding its clientele & welcomes hikers, birdwatchers & the like. 2 rooms are en suite, there's hot water, fridge, & dinner is served. **$$**

⌂ **Pensão Almada Inn** (16 rooms) ☏ 281 4075; m 992 2981; e seafoodalmada@ cvtelecom.cv; www.seafoodfogo.com. A newly built hotel, owned by a returned *emigrante* from America, this is a 10min drive north of São Filipe. It's a multi-storey building that stands out in the landscape & has correspondingly panoramic views in all directions. Its countryside setting means it is peaceful & fresh at night. Rooms are en suite with large bathrooms, hot water, fridge & fan, & include 8 triple rooms & 2 apartments with kitchenettes. The proprietor offers free transport to & from the airport. Check whether the restaurant is open: you might need to eat in São Filipe before you depart for the hotel. **$$**

⌂ **Quinta das Saudades** (2 rooms) (contact through Dja'r Fogo, see *Excursions*, page 217) ☉ Oct–Jul. Get there by taxi from São Filipe (800$) or *aluguer* (130$). A quiet retreat in Tchada Lapa, about 8km from São Filipe on the lower slopes of the crater. This 18th-century country house has been in the family of Agnelo Viera de Andrade, a returned *emigrante* from Portugal, for generations & little has changed over the years, apart from the arrival 40 years ago of a petrol-fuelled refrigerator. It is preserved as a living museum harking back to a time when São Filipe families would retreat to the country slopes for a season to farm corn & beans & tend their fruit trees. Guests are served very traditional dishes, mostly based on corn, & can sit on Agnelo's beautiful terrace gazing down the slopes of Fogo. No electricity. Shared shower room. 1 room has private toilet. Luxurious by middle-class, 18th-century standards only. English spoken. **$$**

⌂ **Tortuga** (4 rooms) m 994 1512; e casamarelacv@hotmail.com; www.tortuga-fogo.eu. To the east of town, down a steep & rough track past the Italian hospital, this is a stunning retreat in a quiet & beautiful location looking out on the black-sand beach of Nossa Senhora da Encarnaçao. Beautifully planted with a large, shady terrace, the Italian proprietors grow their own vegetables & produce a lot of their own food, including marmalade, fish roe & cheeses. Rooms are en suite, & there is hot water & electricity courtesy of solar panels. FB available & the restaurant is of very good repute. You will need to take a taxi or the owner can arrange pickup. **$$**

⌂ **Casas do Sol** (24 houses) East of town (turn right just after the Italian hospital). Bungalows with terraces looking over the ocean, though rather dark within. Part of a complex that will eventually include a bar, swimming pool, & restaurant. Contact Qualitur (see *Activities*, page 217) for prices.

✕ WHERE TO EAT AND DRINK

✕ **Hotel Xaguate** [220 A2] Has a good-quality restaurant, normally with seating on the terrace overlooking the ocean – otherwise it's the rather soulless, AC interior. **$$$$**

✕ **Tortuga** (for contact details, see *Where to stay*, above) ☉ daily. Probably the top restaurant in town, it's essential both to book & to arrange transport to this inaccessible spot. **$$$**

✕ **Bar Restaurante Leila** [220 F4] ☏ 281 1214. Consistently good reports about the food in this basement restaurant. **$$**

✕ **Café Arco Iris** [221 E6] ☏ 281 2526; ☉ all day. European-style menu including burgers & sandwiches served in a modern & colourful setting. **$$**

⊐ᑒ **Café Magma** [221 C5] Located above/ behind the Pousada Belavista, with a good selection & a bright atmosphere. **$$**

⊐ᑒ **Fogo Lounge** [221 D5] m 991 4566. Off the main square, courtyard with large umbrellas & serving a variety of food including some local specialities. **$$**

✕ **Le Bistro** [221 D5] ☉ lunchtime & 17.00–22.00 daily. Popular with tourists because of its terrace with superb views. Pasta & seafood. **$$**

✘ **Open Skies** [220 E3] ⏲ 17.00–late daily. Rooftop restaurant at the top of town, in the *pensão* of the same name. Can be crowded. $$
✘ **Pensão Las Vegas** [221 C6] ⏲ all day. Has a restaurant & bar on an esplanade. $$
✘ **Restaurante Caleron** [221 B6] An excellent open-air place for barbecued chicken & other tasty delights. $$
✘ **Restaurante Seafood** [221 G8] ✆ 283 1045; e seafoodalmada@cvtelecom.cv; www.seafoodfogo.com; ⏲ for b/fast, lunch & dinner. Down near the prison with a good view of the sea, & receiving good reports. $$
♀ **Tropical Club** [221 D5] Snacks at a bar with an outside terrace. With occasional live music, it's south of the Pousada Belavista between 2 streets. $$
✘ **Pastelaria** [220 F4] A little off the beaten track but well worth the effort. Sweet & savoury, Brazilian-style pastries, chocolates & snacks. Filling, delicious & good value. $
✘ **Restaurante Vulcão** [221 D5] Copious local fare. $

Find freshly made bread, cakes & warm ginger biscuits at Dona Maria's bakery on the edge of the cliff, just up from the old prison. It's around the back in an alley next to the sea wall. There is also a bakery in the north of town.

Fresh goat's cheese, fruit & tomatoes can be found in the municipal market in the middle of town, in the same block as the town hall.

ENTERTAINMENT AND NIGHTLIFE
♀ **Bar Boite Hexagonal** [221 C7] ✆ 281 2175. Next to the Cape Cod Restaurant.
♀ **Coral Bar** [221 C6] A watering hole in the centre of town.
♀ **Esplanada Tex** [220 A2] Traditional music most Fri nights. On the roundabout at the northwest of town.
♀ **Tropical** [221 D5] Traditional music every Fri night. Discos the rest of the time (see *Where to eat and drink*, above).
☆ **Discoteca Rabelado** Lem de Baixo, São Filipe; ✆ 281 1468; ⏲ w/ends

OTHER PRACTICALITIES
Airlines TACV [221 C5] (✆ *281 1340/1701; ⏲ 08.00–13.00 & 15.00–18.00 Mon–Fri*). Novatur sells national and international air tickets.

Banks Banco Comercial do Atlântico, Rua do Hospital (⏲ *08.00–15.00 Mon–Fri*). On the road that runs up the cliff edge of town, away from the esplanades.

Ferries Agenmar [221 C6] (✆ *281 1012; ⏲ 08.00–12.00 & 15.00–18.00 Mon–Fri*). Across the square from Pousada Belavista.

Hospital [221 A5] (✆ *281 1130*). On the same road as the bank, further up on the left. There is also a private Italian hospital which has an operating theatre and a good reputation – to the east of town.

Internet Free Wi-Fi is available in the main *praça* if you have your laptop. Also available at Zebra Travel, Microcenter and Terra Nova near the market.

Pharmacy [221 B5] Head up the hill from the main *praça*.

Police (✆ *281 1132*).

Post office [220 D3] (⏲ *08.00–12.00 & 14.00–16.00 Mon–Fri*). Large pink building at the top of town on the big square with a candle sculpture.

Fogo SÃO FILIPE

8

Shopping Souvenirs, including Fogo wine and coffee, and crafts, are on sale at Qualitur [221 E6] *and* Dja'r Fogo [221 F6] (see *Excursions*, page 217). Food supplies can be found at various small mini supermarkets.

Tourist information None, but the tour operators (see *Excursions*, page 217) are very helpful. There is a useful information kiosk in Chã das Caldeiras.

Miscellaneous Water is a very scarce resource on Fogo, so be sparing.

WHAT TO SEE AND DO

Architecture Wander the streets admiring the *sobrado* architecture. About 100 of these houses remain – built by the rich and decorated with fine woods and tiles imported from Portugal and west Africa. If you can peek into one of them take the opportunity: a central courtyard planted with trees and vines gave coolness and shade and around it, on the ground floor, were the working rooms. The next floor was more beautiful, lined with an inside balcony that overlooked the courtyard on three sides – this was the floor for the master and his family. On the street side there was a balcony of carved wood. It is said that slaves did not ascend to the first floor except once a year, on the festival of Santa Cruz. During the summer the town house was closed and the family went inland to oversee the farming. See map (page 221) for the location of some more prominent examples.

Casa da Memória [221 E7] (✆ 281 2765; e *moniquewidmer@yahoo.com.br; www. chez.com/ casadamemoria;* ◷ *10.00–12.00 Wed–Fri or by appointment)* A private museum in a restored family house, run by Monique, who has lived in Cape Verde for over 20 years. It depicts the history of Fogo from the early to mid 1800s. Full of photos, domestic objects and a patio in which there was Fogo's first cinema, now restored. Cultural events are held there, as well as some conferences. The Casa also has a library packed with interesting literature about the islands, including a handful of books in English.

The beach and swimming A walk down the grotty ribeira road to the black beach is interesting, if not a conventional tourist attraction. This is a poor part of town, with goats foraging and pigs tethered in makeshift shelters. Below lies a strip of black sand under the ominous Fogo cliffs, lashed by Atlantic breakers. As you begin your descent you will see the prison. Perched on the cliff, with a view of both the ocean and the cemetery, it must have afforded many a prisoner an inspirational setting in which to reflect on his misdemeanours. A hotel may be built here.

Take a swim at the Hotel Xaguate [220 A2], which has an enjoyable poolside terrace.

CHÃ DAS CALDEIRAS

The road to the volcano passes first through pleasant countryside dotted with abandoned Portuguese farms, and old volcano cones, and filled with cashew, banana and papaya trees. Just after a left fork, where the sign says '14km to Parc Natural de Fogo' is the 1951 lava spill down the right-hand slope.

Later the road becomes a series of terrifyingly steep hairpin bends with views down the massive ancient lava spills to the coast. Then it enters the echoing silence of the crater. Its sinister dark walls, and the vast clods of lava scattered over it, make one feel very small.

The people are as of a different race – light skinned, straight haired, some of them even blond and blue eyed. These are the descendants of the fecund Duc de Montrond (see box, *The Duke of Montrond*, page 226), a French nobleman who came here in the 19th century and brought the vines that began Fogo's wine production.

There are attempts to improve the crater's fragile ecology and geology, and develop an economy (see box, *Conserving the crater*, page 215). One step has been to define the crater as a natural park; another has been to set up small-scale tourism. The park office is at the entrance to the crater.

The town is traditionally split into two districts: Portela (upper), and Bangaeira (lower), though there is actually very little to distinguish them from each other.

In many places in Chã das Caldeiras the power is turned off at 21.00.

A non-profit organisation, Châtour, has been set up to support and develop the communities on Fogo and to help to promote tourism and development. Châtour is part of an Italian NGO, COSPE, and has an excellent website (*www.chatourfogo.com*) where you can find out more about the area and book accommodation and guides.

GETTING THERE AND AWAY There is a midday *aluguer* from São Filipe (300–500$). The return journey starts very early: listen for the horn which sounds loudly in the village at about 05.00. For a small supplement, you can ask to be dropped at the airport first. Pedra Brabo has its own vehicle for daily transfers.

If you prefer to walk some of the way to the volcano, then catch an *aluguer* from town to Achada Furna; it takes three hours to cover the steep road from there.

A day trip to the volcano is tricky by public transport, though there are cars in the crater which can be chartered as taxis for the trip back to São Filipe for several thousand escudos. Many people organise their visit through Qualitur or Dja'r Fogo.

WHERE TO STAY

Sirio Bed & Breakfast (6 rooms) 282 1586; e chatour@chatourfogo.com; www.chatourfogo.com. A newly constructed B&B at the foot of the volcano. **$$**

Casa Fernando (6 rooms) 282 1531. Mountain guide Fernando offers rooms adjacent to his family's house. Separate bathroom & no hot water. **$**

Chez Mariza (4 rooms) (book through Chã Tours at the homestay co-operative or through Pedra Brabo). Basic but newly built en-suite rooms in a lava-brick style similar to Pedra Brabo, plus a bar. **$**

Pousada Pedra Brabo (12 rooms) 282 1521; e pedrabrabo@cvtelecom.cv. A single-storey lava-brick guesthouse, its rooms arranged around a pretty courtyard – it manages to be both basic & tasteful at the same time.

The food is excellent, the view stunning. There is electricity from a generator. Rooms share a communal bathroom & water is often cold & not always abundant. Patrick, the congenial French proprietor, has a wealth of stories about crater life. Bookings can be made via his office in São Filipe. **$**

Homestays Book via an agent in São Filipe or through Chã Tours, the homestay co-operative, at the tourism kiosk. Accommodation is either in the houses of local people or in rooms they have built alongside especially for tourists. Accommodation is pretty basic; within people's houses it is sometimes just a windowless room made of lava blocks. But the best are clean & careful preparations are made for visitors, who are received with great delight & good spirits. Range of prices.

WHERE TO EAT AND DRINK

Chez Mariza (see *Where to stay*, above) **$$$**

Pousada Pedra Brabo (see *Where to stay*, above) ⏰ for lunch & dinner, though it can be chaotic with day trippers at lunchtime. **$$$**

Bar Restaurante Antares 282 1528; m 994 9128. Serves traditional food, Italian food & pizza & boasts an internet point. Hosts cultural events such as live music, poems, theatre & traditional dancing. **$$**

ENTERTAINMENT AND NIGHTLIFE Head for the *Cooperativa* (see *Information centre*, opposite), where there is often wine, music and dancing into the small hours.

WHAT TO SEE AND DO

Hiking The highlights are the walk up the Pico (which can take anything between three and six hours depending on your fitness and your proficiency at running back down through the lava powder – see box, *Climbing the Pico*, page 228), and the walk down to Mosteiros. Many visitors walk up the smaller, 1995 peak for a less demanding hike or in order to limber up for the big one. New trails are being developed by the park offices, and it should be possible to traverse the crater rim, which will be a major attraction, and also to enter the crater over the rim from Ponte Alto do Sul, in the southwest. Some of these walks are described in *Hikes*, page 228.

For some walks it is essential to have a guide. An example is climbing the Pico de Fogo, because the path shifts with the movements of the ash. The crater rim, to be negotiated at times by clipping oneself to a cable handrail, should also involve a guide.

There are several guides conversant with the natural history of the volcano, having worked with botanists and geologists. The park offices have been training guides in climbing and mountain safety. Guides cost around 3,000$ per group to ascend the big Pico, 1,500$ to ascend the 1995 peak. For walks where a guide is not essential, you might consider employing one to embellish the experience.

Winery As you walk towards Bangeiro from Pedra Brabo, the winery is on your left.

THE DUKE OF MONTROND

Most of the inhabitants of the volcano crater can trace their ancestry back to an eccentric French duke who made Fogo his home in the 1870s.

The scattering of blue eyes, light skin and yellowy hair among the people of the crater can be traced back to the prolific duke. He had at least 11 children – and now has 300 descendants in the USA alone.

François Louis Armand Montrond was on his way to Brazil when he arrived in Cape Verde in 1872 – and stayed. After testing most of the islands he found Fogo was the one he preferred and he spent the rest of his life there, returning to France several times for visits.

The duke has left more behind him than the intriguing people of the crater: he put to use his background in engineering and medicine. He oversaw the construction of a road from São Filipe to Mosteiros, and he sank wells, some of which are still in use today.

A wealthy man, he supported at least three wives and adopted two children as well. He also imported medicinal herbs and, it is said, the vines that kicked off wine production on the volcano slopes.

At age 60, he fell off his horse, broke his leg, and died of an infection.

At first he was not credited for his achievements because the Portuguese felt he showed them up, claims Alberto Montrond, a great-great-grandson who lives in the USA and regularly visits Fogo. 'He did great things for the people on the island,' he says. Alberto's work tracing the Montrond ancestry and investigating the duke's story has been the subject of a French documentary film.

Information centre (⊕ *08.00–12.00 & 15.00–17.00 daily*) Almost in the centre of the settlement this rondavel is the place for booking rooms, hiring guides and finding out about crater life through some exhibits. There is for example an exhibit on the genealogy of the Montrond family, including profiles of some of its more colourful characters; there are also displays about endemic species, and old and new photographs of the landscape, through which you can trace its changing topography.

Shop On the Bangaeira side of Portela the shop sells an array of Fogo wines as well as Manecom wine (homemade by Tito Montrond), various spirits, fruit juices and crafts made from junk.

MOSTEIROS

The town, also known as Igreja, is a useful stopping-off point during trips around the island but otherwise is not worth a visit. It has a pretty centre, squashed between the mountain and the sea, and a depressing suburbia of black, lava-block houses built on black lava rock.

GETTING THERE AND AWAY The southern *aluguer* run to and from São Filipe is a fantastic journey along the precipitous eastern slope of the island but since the opening of the road around the north, that is the direction that most of the public transport goes. The proprietor of Pensão Christine will arrange for one of the drivers to call at the hotel for you at about 04.45. *Alugueres* leave São Filipe for Mosteiros at about midday.

WHERE TO STAY

🏠 **Pensão Restaurante Christine e Irmãos** (7 rooms) ☎ 283 1045. In a green building on the main road through town; it has lovely, airy rooms & a big restaurant. **$**

🏠 **Pensão Tchon de Café** (12 rooms) ☎ 283 1610. Rooms are pleasant, en suite with hot water in this *pensão* nestled at the foot of a hill. There's a small restaurant with courtyard. **$**

OTHER PRACTICALITIES

Airlines TACV (☎ 283 1033; ⊕ *08.00–12.00 & 14.00–16.00 Mon–Fri*). In one of Mosteiros's two squares.

Bank (⊕ *08.00–14.00 Mon–Fri*).

Hospital (☎ 283 1034). In the same square as the TACV office.

Post office (⊕ *08.00–12.00 & 14.00–16.00 Mon–Fri*). In the other square.

OTHER PLACES TO VISIT

Nothing else on Fogo matches a crater visit, but all of the visits below are pleasant ways of filling spare days on the island.

SÃO LOURENÇO A large church and a peaceful graveyard – clusters of white crosses all with stunning views of Brava. Visiting it is a pleasant way of enjoying the green Fogo lowlands. It is a 12km round trip but you will probably find lifts for parts of the way. Leave São Filipe from the roundabout opposite the Hotel Xaguate, and, with your back to the hotel, take the second turning on the left (the first leads down to the port).

MONTE GENEBRA AND NOSSA SENHORA DO SOCORRO Find an *aluguer* to Forno and from there walk to the village of Luzia Nunes, then take the left fork to Monte Genebra. German development workers helped to build these gardens in 1976. Pumping stations take hundreds of cubic metres of water from a natural spring near the sea, to water tomatoes, potatoes, cabbages and fruits. You can go to the top of Monte Genebra, while down towards the sea is the little chapel of Nossa Senhora do Socorro.

PONTO DO SALINA This is one of the few possible swimming creeks on Fogo where the lava here has formed a natural pool. It is located close to São Jorge north of São Filipe. Take an *aluguer* to São Jorge and walk down to the sea. The walk there and back takes about two hours.

HIKES *Colum Wilson (CW); Aisling Irwin (AI); Hannah Cruttenden (HC)*

1 THE PICO This hike is described in the box below. Note that it requires energy and fitness particularly because there is no going back: to return halfway along requires a guide, but so does continuing to the top and there is generally only one guide per group.

CLIMBING THE PICO   *Simon Day*

The Pico de Fogo is one of the steepest and most spectacular volcanic cones in the world. I climbed it one January with a group of geophysicists from Lisbon. The 1,200m ascent and descent took seven hours. Although it was the coolest time of the year, we planned the climb to start at dawn. This meant leaving our hotel in Mosteiros at 05.00, driving up the steep mountain road in the pre-dawn twilight and reaching Portela before 07.00.

In Portela we met up with António and Jose António, two local men who work as guides and have also been field assistants for my Portuguese colleagues. They are good friends but António, who has lived all his life in Chã das Caldeiras, has a hard time adjusting to the idea that not everyone can run (literally) up mountains.

The usual route up the Pico starts from a track on its northern side, and begins with a long march up a gullied slope that is hampered by thick deposits of volcanic *lapilli*. These are fine fragments of lava, a bit like sand or gravel, which were ejected explosively from the vent during the volcanic eruption. It is like walking through deep sandbanks. By the time that we reached a group of small volcanic spatter cones marking the foot of the main ascent – a continuous slope inclined at 30–40° and over 1,000m high – we were already tired. One of the advantages of being with geologists, though, is that whenever you need to rest you stop walking and start discussing the rocks.

Higher up the slope the *lapilli* beds thinned out, leaving a treacherous veneer of loose ash and gravel underfoot: it was like walking on marbles. However, as the going became harder the views grew better: the northern half of the great crater was spread like a map below us: a vast field of lava flows dotted with small volcanic craters now clogged with bits of lava and known as *scoria*. It is truly a 'plain of craters'.

2 PORTELA–1995 PEAK–PORTELA

Distance: 7km; time: 2 hours 10 minutes; difficulty: 2 (CW)

You will never have done a walk like this. Walking through this lava field is like walking through a nightmarish black sea that has frozen in mid storm. Slabs of dark rock rest at jagged angles like buckled plates of ice; elsewhere, rivulets of molten rock have hardened in place. Beyond the lava field, you crunch across a glittering black landscape of *lapilli* that seems to muffle sound and life. The tricky bit is to find the rough path that takes you across the lava field up towards the peak.

From Portela, take the cobbled road that leads to São Filipe. After about 40 minutes you will pass just beyond the 9km² lava field that flows down in an ever-widening river from the 1995 peak and reach a point that is directly between Pico Beco on your right, and the 1995 peak on your left. Looking up at the cone you will see it is made of black, chilled fragments of lava, known as *scoria*. These have been turned a rusty red by exposure to the hot sulphur dioxide that poured out in the first few years after the eruption. The yellow patches are sulphur, precipitated from the gas as it cooled.

A few hundred metres before the road does an obvious turn to the left followed directly by an obvious turn to the right, strike out from the road to the left across the black sand (there is no path) towards the 1995 peak. About 600m from the road, you should join the edge of the lava field, and immediately start ascending on a rough path. This path takes you in a northerly direction across the side of the Pico for a few hundred metres before starting to bear northeast.

Beyond that, in the haze that had already begun to form, were the immense cliffs of the original volcano crater. Known as the Bordeira, it once rose another few hundred metres before it was destroyed in a great rockslide towards the ocean floor to the east.

The collapse left a scar which has been as much as half filled by the lavas which today form Chã das Caldeiras. The Pico rises out of the centre of the scar. But the old walls still ascend around the Pico as sheer rock faces, 1km high in places. Of all the volcanoes in the world, I know of no other where the evidence of a giant lateral collapse, involving hundreds of cubic kilometres of rock, is so spectacularly preserved. Even for professional vulcanologists, this is an awesome place.

We reached the summit after five hours of climbing (and a couple more hours of geological arguments *en route*). The lavas of the crater walls were coloured every shade from red through oranges and yellows to bleached whites – the result of corrosive attack by the acid gases that still fume from vents on its floor and walls although there has been no eruption in the Pico since 1785.

We did not have long to study them though: the day was hot and humid, and the Pico is not a place to be in a thunderstorm. Fortunately, the thick beds of *lapilli* that had hampered our ascent made the descent quick if not easy: we ran down the scree slopes, braking by ploughing into the *lapilli* up to our knees whenever the pace became too alarming. This is the only way to descend: if you try to go down the bare rock slopes you are liable to have an accident.

António was rather disgusted when we stopped to talk about another outcrop that caught my eye; but even so we reached the track where we had parked the jeep within 40 minutes of leaving the summit. We were just in time: a few minutes later the heavens opened and claps of thunder rattled around the cliffs of the Bordeira.

The crater of the 1995 peak is a gash a few hundred metres long running in a northeast direction. You are approaching the crater at the point where the lava spilled out and down the side from the southwest end. Twenty minutes after leaving the road, you will be at a low rim within the open southwest end of the crater. If you are prepared to scramble over loose rock and lava for another 50m, you will be able to look into the very eye of the crater, a jumble of massive yellow streaked boulders and lumps of lava.

You must return the same way you arrived, which should take about 40 minutes.

As an alternative, you can approach the northern rim of the 1995 crater from the northeast, where there is no path.

3 BANGAEIRA–CRATER RIM–BANGAEIRA

Distance: approximately 14km; time: 5 hours; difficulty: 2 (AI)
This trip takes you up to the rim of the volcano for a stunning bird's-eye view of the crater. Parts of the path are steep and slippery.

From the *Cooperativa* walk the 5km north along the road to the barrier that marks the protected forest. Continue down the road for 15 minutes to a fork. The road to the right leads to Mosteiros. Follow the left-hand road which becomes a dirt track, quite precarious in places. It winds its way up the side of the volcano. Soon you find yourself above the low cloud, gazing at a superb view of Santiago. The road eventually climbs steeply upwards to a large white building used to store rice and grain: this is where cars must stop. Walk past the front of the storehouse and on to a path running along the left-hand side of the building and up towards the volcano rim. It's a steep climb and the path is slippery in places but it shouldn't take longer than half an hour to get to the top.

This part of the crater is very green and you will see women from the villages gathering firewood. Recent eruptions are 'mapped out' in the vast area below, covered by lava, which pushes right up to the edge of the villages of **Bangaeira** and **Portela** to the right. The darkest lava is from the most recent 1995 eruption. Closer to you, the slightly lighter coloured lava is from 1951; the lightest-coloured lava, directly in front of you, is oldest of all. It is possible to continue walking round the rim – take a guide.

4 COOPERATIVA–PORTELA–1995 LAVA FLOW–BOCA FONTE–COOPERATIVA

Distance: 6km; time: 2 hours; difficulty: 1 (HC)
This two-hour walk starts at the *Cooperativa*. Head back towards the village of **Portela**, but as you leave the village, turn off to the right following the car tracks in the grey soil. The track leads you towards the west walls of the crater and continues round the edge of the 1995 lava to the former village of Boca Fonte – now destroyed except for the colonnaded façade of a *Cooperativa* which still stands at the edge of the flow. About 100m further on, climb up on to the lava and clamber across it to get a view of a house marooned in the flow. A short walk later you arrive at the vineyards – the vines look almost pitiful, straggling along the ground like weeds. Next, after curving round to the left and on to the southern side, you'll see several small agricultural and fruit farms. Their produce goes to the market in São Filipe. Shortly afterwards there's a chance to turn back towards the Pico and the main road back to Portela.

5 CRATER–MONTEBARRO–PAI ANTÓNIO–MOSTEIROS

Distance: approximately 10km; time: 4.5 hours; difficulty: 2 (AI)
This delightful walk takes you out of the crater and down the volcano's steep northeastern side, with views across the sea to Santiago, and a host of pretty

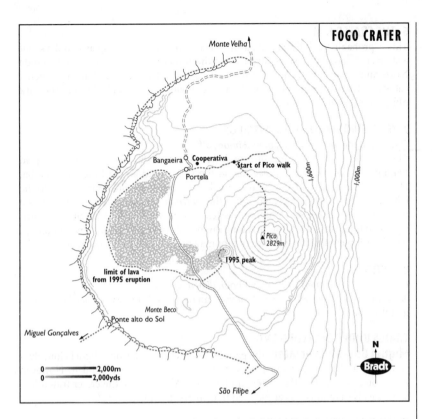

Monte Velha

Bangaeira Cooperativa
Start of Pico walk
Portela

1,600m
1,000m

Pico
2829m

1995 peak

limit of lava
from 1995 eruption

Monte Beco
Ponte alto do Sol

Miguel Gonçalves

0   2,000m
0   2,000yds

N

Bradt

São Filipe

plantations, in particular oranges and coffee. The hike involves some steep descents likely to produce aching and shaking knees, and those who find such descents difficult could find the walk takes five hours. Navigationally it is pretty easy.

Begin with a 5km walk north along the road through the crater which takes you out, past a road barrier that marks the protected forest and on past a road to the left that goes to **Montinho**. Two minutes after this turning there is a steep little path down to the right. You can stick with the road or follow this short cut, in which case you will rejoin the road after ten minutes, turning right. Some 15 minutes past this point you arrive in Monte Velho. The road bends to the right over the bridge where there are a few small houses. After crossing the bridge leave the road and turn right, down the right-hand side of the first house. The path takes you down the side of a ravine, across which can be seen the president's house. Giant *carapate* plants stack the sides of the path. Descend through **Pede Pranta**, after which the ban on farming expires. You enter little valleys planted with coffee, mango and orange plants.

Mist drifts upwards and the view of the ocean through the vegetation is beautiful. After a while, descending past little dwellings built on terraces of lava rock you reach the first region of Mosteiros – **Montebarro** – and the air is filled with the scents of oranges and fires and the noise of children and cockerels. Three hours into the walk you reach **Pai António**, with a steeply cobbled street, from where it is a 40-minute walk down the cobbled road (ignoring the left turning to Feijoal) to the centre of Mosteiros. Alternatively, it should be possible to pick up a lift in Pai António to save your knees that last steep descent.

Fogo HIKES 8

231

6 THE CRATER RIM

This is probably the longest walk available as it could take as long as two days, but a shorter version is possible. Stretches of the rim are so precarious (Ponte Alto de Norte and Ponte Alto do Sol are the worst sections) that the park staff have erected cable handrails to which you can clip yourself with a hoop available from the park offices. It is essential to have a guide.

7 MOSTEIROS–FEIJOAL–MOSTEIROS

Distance: approximately 5km; time: 2 hours; difficulty: 2 (Al)

There are various strolls up into the lower slopes of the volcano. To walk up to **Feijoal** for a drink, leave Mosteiros on the south road and, a little after the big Delegação de Fogo, take the cobbled road on the right (ignore a turning up to the left just before Feijoal). After a drink at the *mercado*, find a little footpath (*caminho para Igreja*) back into the centre of Mosteiros: with your back to the *mercado* turn right and the path is a few metres along on the left, running between two buildings. It's a bit slippery and the less sure of foot may prefer to return by the road.

8 CAVES

Distance: approximately 1km; time: 1 hour; difficulty: 1 (JC)

A simple walk to see some caves that you can look inside but would need a guide to go into. The caves are quite deep.

TRAILS UNDER DEVELOPMENT

Miguel Gonçalves–crater The path up to the crater rim from Miguel Gonçalves is shingly and unpleasant in places, and there are plans to rebuild it. However, once you have reached the crater rim (at Ponte Alto do Sol), the crater trail to the southeast is easy and ends at the road that enters the crater.

WALKING ROUND THE NORTH From the Mosteiros end, the first 2km north along the coast are dismal – save your legs and hitch if you can. Just before the disused airport, there is a left turning uphill. This is the beginning of a spectacular road, which goes up to Ribeira Ilhéu and then continues as a 9km track to São Jorge. From there you have to try and hitch back to São Filipe – there is supposed to be an *aluguer* at 13.00. The better alternative is to take a mid-morning *aluguer* to São Jorge from São Filipe and walk in the other direction, staying in Mosteiros at the end of the walk.

9

Brava

Swallows of the wide seas
What wind of loyalty
Brings you on this bitter journey
To our land of *Sodade*

Eugénio Tavares, quoted in Archibald Lyall,
Black and White Make Brown (Heinemann, 1938)

Brava is the most secret of the islands – a volcano crater hides its town, rough seas encircle it and the winds that buffet it are so strong that its airport has been closed. Brava lies only 20km from Fogo, but many visitors will merely glimpse it from the greater island's western slopes.

Brava – or 'wild' island – appears at first to live up to the meaning of its name. Approaching by boat, the dark mass resolves itself into sheer cliffs with painted houses dotting the heights above. A few fishing hamlets huddle at sea level.

But its unpromising slopes hide a fertile and moist hinterland filled with hibiscus flowers and cultivation. At least that is how it was: today, after years of drought, its flowers are less visible and its food more likely to be imported than grown.

This tiny, westerly island, dropping off the end of the archipelago into the Atlantic, seems to hide from its companions and look instead towards where the sun sets – it is dreaming of the wealth of the USA. For Brava is the island where the great 19th-century American whaling ships called to pick up crews and spirit hopeful young men away to new lives in another continent (see box, *Whalers and the packet trade*, page 250). The legacy is an island full of empty houses waiting for the return of the *Americanos* who have built them for their retirement. Meanwhile, a big container ship from Boston visits twice a year and American goods appear in the streets. Brava Creole is peppered with American expressions.

HIGHLIGHTS AND LOWLIGHTS

Go for the walking, for the peace and for the sheer intrigue of a place that is so out of the way.

Don't go for beaches or watersports, don't expect any conventional tourist attractions, and don't go if you are pushed for time.

SUGGESTED ITINERARY AND NUMBER OF DAYS Brava is small. Someone who wants to just grab the sights and go could see the island in less than a day by vehicle. A hiker will find several days' worth of walks to do.

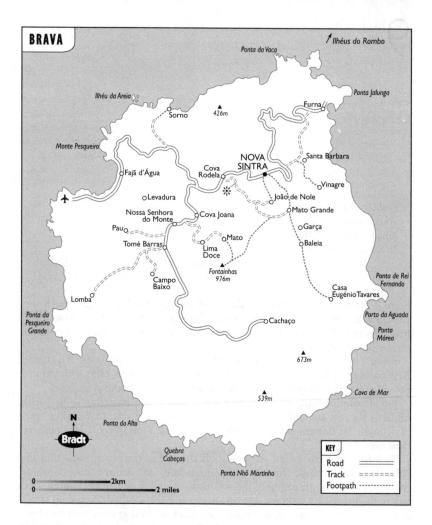

BRAVA

Ilhéus do Rombo

Ponta da Vaca

Ponta Jalunga

Ilhéu da Areia

Sorno

426m

Furna

Monte Pesqueiro

Santa Barbara

NOVA
SINTRA

Fajã d'Água

Cova
Rodela

Vinagre

Levadura

João de Nole

Mato Grande

Nossa Senhora
do Monte

Cova Joana

Pau

Garça

Tomé Barras

Mato

Baleia

Lima
Doce

Campo
Baixo

Fontainhas
976m

Ponta de Rei
Fernando

Lomba

Casa
Eugénio Tavares

Ponta da
Pesqueiro
Grande

Cachaço

Porto da Aguada

Ponta
Mórea

673m

539m

Cova de Mar

N

Bradt

Ponta do Alto

Quebra
Cabeças

Ponta Nhõ Martinho

KEY

Road

Track

Footpath

0 ——— 2km
0 ——— 2 miles

BACKGROUND INFORMATION

HISTORY Brava is, geologically speaking, part of Fogo. The channel between them is just a few hundred metres deep – shallow compared with the ocean floor that surrounds the rest of Brava, whose cliffs plunge 4km down beyond sea level. The oldest rocks of Fogo lie on the side that faces Brava and are very similar to Bravan rock, which is how their relationship has been deduced.

There are no volcanic eruptions now, but the land is not completely calm – clusters of earthquakes shake it, although most are too gentle to be noticed. Yet its active history was recent and its volcano cones are all less than 10,000 years old.

There is a legend about the first settlers of Brava. A young Portuguese aristocrat fell in love with a girl well below him in social class. To prevent their marriage, his parents banished the girl and her family to Fogo, but he pursued her on another ship and escaped with her to the haven of Brava. There they settled in the valley of Fajã d'Água, living with some of the loyal sailors who accompanied them.

Brava was discovered on 24 June 1462, on the saint's day of St John the Baptist (São João Baptista), after whom it was originally named. Settlers arrived in 1573 and included many fishermen from Madeira and the Azores. This, and the fact that Brava never really took part in the slave trade, are held to be responsible for there being a greater proportion of white skins on Brava than anywhere else.

When Sir Francis Drake's mariners passed by in 1578 they found only one of its 100 inhabitants – a hermit who looked after a small chapel. They probably never discovered the villages hidden in the volcano's crater. By the 1620s, there was a proper community there, which swelled 60 years later with desperate boatloads of refugees from Fogo fleeing volcanic eruptions on their own island. Many of them never returned.

By this time the island was owned by Luis de Castro Pereira, who also owned Santa Luzia near São Vicente. In 1686, the population was sufficiently large to merit a pirate attack in which its governor was killed.

Yet Brava remained a relative secret and took almost no part in Cape Verde's thriving 17th-century businesses. Its first major dabble with trade was in 1730 when the Englishman Captain George Roberts bought the rights to the *urzela* lichen that covered its slopes. The population was to double in the following 50 years to 3,200.

It was not until the end of the 18th century that Brava became of much interest to the outside world. It was the springboard for the great emigration of Cape Verdeans to the USA: an exile that was to be an important shaper of the whole economy of the archipelago.

That was when the whalers of New Bedford and Rhode Island, venturing further south and east, discovered in Brava a place where they could replenish their ships and recruit eager new crews. English whaling boats recruited there as well – it was easy for the ships to land in Brava's small but secluded harbours. Many of the young men disembarked at New England and set up new lives there (see box, *Whalers and the packet trade*, page 250).

Withstanding an attack in 1798 by the French, who were trying to oust the Portuguese from the islands, Brava continued to prosper into the first decades of the 19th century. Intellectually, Brava became the place to be. The parish of Our Lady of the Mountain was created; an American consul arrived in 1843 and a secondary school opened in the 1850s to which students came from throughout the archipelago and from Guinea-Bissau. It was into this environment that the poet Eugénio Tavares was born in 1867 (see box, *Eugénio Tavares*, page 240).

By the late 19th century, Brava was considered one of the most pleasant islands in which to live and its population peaked at 9,200. Income surged into the 20th century, as American *emigrantes* sent their money home. But the prosperity was not to last. The depression came; remittances from abroad dwindled and, confident that the rainy years of the 1930s would continue, many *Americanos* returned home.

It was a mistake. A drought was looming that was to prove the worst catastrophe in Brava's history. It squeezed the island just as World War II caused foreign remittances to dry up completely. Hundreds died in the ensuing famine.

Brava's ageing population rose to 10,000 in the 1960s and then fell back to 7,000. A recent disaster was Hurricane Beryl, which destroyed much of the infrastructure in 1982.

BRAVA TODAY On the surface little has changed in Brava and the march of developers and property speculators has, as yet, made few ripples. Nevertheless land prices have surged. This may partly be in anticipation of what has happened on other islands, or because Cape Verde's prosperity is attracting more *emigrantes* from Brava to return. Also, there is anecdotal evidence that the building of schools in Brava has combined with general optimism about the future to reduce the flow of emigration. The population is just over 6,000. Nevertheless, many people depend on government aid and the island relies heavily on fruit and vegetables imported from Fogo, Praia and Portugal. Maize is planted every year but often turns brown and dies. In better times the islanders grow coffee, bananas, sugarcane, cassava, maize and potatoes. Fishing is the base of the economy.

GEOGRAPHY The archipelago's smallest inhabited island, Brava is 64km² and just 10km across at its widest point. Much of the coastline is steep cliffs, which rise to a dry central tableland with some mountains rising out of it. In the west there is a lush valley – Fajã d'Água – with a small, semi-permanent stream. Offshore there are several rocks and stacks. The highest point is Monte Fontainhas at 976m, and often swathed in mist. Even a little lower down, within the crater, there is generally moisture and coolness.

NATURAL HISTORY Brava hosts none of Cape Verde's 47 protected areas but the adjacent Ilhéus do Rombo are a protected reserve. There are 24 endemic species on the island. The Cape Verde warbler (*Acrocephalus brevipennis*) once made Brava its home but is thought to have gone now, with dwindling agriculture. However, it was also thought to have disappeared from São Nicolau but was later rediscovered, so keep a lookout. The endangered Cape Verde shearwater, most famous for its occupancy of Ilhéu Raso, also dwells within the Ilhéus do Rombo.

Flowering garden plants found on Brava include plumeira, bougainvillea and jasmine. Vila Nova Sintra abounds with planted dragon trees (*Dracaena draco*).

It is cold between December and April in the *vila* and in higher zones.

HAZARDS Swimmers should ask locals about any hazards before taking a dip.

FESTIVALS The festival of São João is held on 24 June and many emigrants return for it. Several days before the festival the women begin a ritual pounding of the corn, joined by others who sing with a high-pitched chanting and clap to a complex beat until the preparation is finished. Another preparation for the festival is the dressing of the mast of *Cutelo Grande* – decorating it with intricately woven breads and also cakes, fruit and drinks and guarding it against pilfering by children. On the day, the mast – all greenery and red flowers and edible ornaments – is raised with a pulley. At the right moment the pulleys are cut, the mast comes plummeting to the ground and the children run to grab what plunder they can. Other festivals are as follows:

5 January	Twelfth Night
20 January	São Sebastião
24 June	São João (main festival: see above)
First Sunday in July	São Paulo
Second Sunday in July	São Paulinho
Last Sunday in July	Santaninha
Last Sunday in July	Santa Ana
First fortnight in August	Nossa Senhora do Monte (Fuma)
15 August	Nossa Senhora da Graça

GETTING THERE AND AWAY

Historically, Brava has been very hard to reach. There is no air service to Brava because of dangerously strong crosswinds. Every so often there is an innovation, such as a new ferry service, but after a while something goes wrong and Brava subsides into isolation again. Even when regular ferry services exist they can be severely delayed by bad weather. In 2008, the government put into service a strong, 27m fishing boat to reside in Brava's port and journey to Fogo at least once a day (500$). This transformed Brava's accessibility as well as being useful for emergency evacuations. Promises of new boats come and go and Cabo Verde Fast Ferry is the latest hope for an improved service. The current service between Fogo and Brava runs daily except Sundays (15.00 from Fogo and 08.00 from Brava) and has been fairly reliable. Be sure of your exit strategy because trying to leave Brava with an international flight looming in Sal or Santiago is not only stressful but also fairly certain to end in trouble. There are sometimes ferries from Santiago; check with an agency in Praia.

BY FERRY Ferry tickets to Brava can be bought either from Agenmar in Fogo, next to TACV (℡ *281 1012*), or Polar in Santiago, but can also be bought at the dock in Fogo. In Vila Nova Sintra in Brava, go to Agencia Brava in the main street (℡ *285 1270*). You can also enquire at the ferry offices in Praia (see page 165) or São Filipe (see page 223) or check www.bela-vista.net/Ferry.aspx, which keeps reasonably abreast of ferries. The price should be around 500$ one-way and it may only be possible to buy single tickets.

On arrival at Furna get to Vila Nova Sintra either by chartered *aluguer* or shared *aluguer* (100–150$). Alternatively you could walk the steep 3km up the old road, the reverse of the hike described on page 251.

BY YACHT Some of the best anchorages in the archipelago are here. Fajã d'Água is secure and beautiful and Furna is secure, except during southeasterly winds.

GETTING AROUND

Alugueres, in the form of trucks or *carrinhos*, travel between Furna and Vila Nova Sintra for 150$ (600–800$ when chartered as taxis); from Vila Nova Sintra to Nossa Senhora do Monte a charter is around 500$ and from Vila Nova Sintra to Fajã d'Água a charter is about 1,000$.

WHERE TO STAY

There are a couple of options outside Vila Nova Sintra, but the capital has the biggest range (see page 238).

ACTIVITIES

EXCURSIONS These are best organised on Fogo with **Dja'r Fogo** or **Qualitur** (see page 217). Pepe (m *999 9764*) is known for island tours and is recommended.

HIKING Brava is a superb hiking destination, with numerous circular walks, most of which can start and finish at the *vila* (see page 244).

SWIMMING Brava is not really a place for swimming, but there are a few safe lagoons, including one in between Fajã d'Água and the airport.

SIGHTSEEING BY VEHICLE You could probably see Brava in half a day by vehicle.

FURNA

Furna is the main port and lies in an extinct volcano crater, encircled with rocks on three sides. The bay is just a few hundred metres in diameter – sailing ships used to find it easy to get in but trickier to escape. It is more bustling than the *vila* but not as attractive.

From Furna the road winds up the slopes of the mountain. The sea and the harbour sink far below until, about 0.5km above and after endless hairpins, it drops suddenly over the rim of a small depression and into Vila Nova Sintra.

There is a restaurant near the waterside in Furna and one past the bank on the left-hand side.

VILA NOVA SINTRA

…an enchanted garden hanging by invisible cords from the clouds

Archibald Lyall

Named after the Portuguese town of Sintra, the *vila* is 520m above sea level. For weeks it can labour under a *Brigadoon*-like fog, inspiring melancholy in the visitor. On a clear day, though, there is a view across the ocean to Fogo: it is said that if you have good eyes you can see the women in São Filipe cleaning rice.

Nova Sintra is a quaint town nestled among the volcanic rocks. Hibiscus trees line many of the streets, scarlet against the ancient cobblestones. In wet years its gardens are jumbles of blue plumbago and bougainvillea, almond trees and jacaranda. The houses of the town – all Portuguese whitewash with red tiles – are covered in flowering vegetation, and fruit trees intersperse with fields of corn and cabbage.

The *vila* is very quiet and sometimes you can be the only person in the square. But before meal times the fish vendors are there, crying 'Nhos cumpra peixe' – 'you all buy fish'. Each of the three fishing communities has its own signature cry so that potential customers will know where their dinner is from before they buy it.

⌂ WHERE TO STAY

⌂ **Pousada Vivi** (formerly Municipal) (8 rooms) ⑆ 285 2562; e pousadavivisplace@hotmail.com. Recently renovated, off the road with the town hall on it, a friendly place with a communal veranda & bar. B/fast included & evening meals available. Internet also available. **$$**

⌂ **Residencial Nazareth** (5 rooms) ⑆ 285 1375; m 993 1162. Some of the Nazareth's rooms have TV & minibar. There is a family apartment with 2 bedrooms, kitchenette & separate bathroom/shower. **$$**

⌂ **Casa Silva** (ask for Johnny Silva's place). To the south of town, these are a good standard of room though not en suite. **$**

⌂ **Pensão Bragança** ⑆ 285 1305. Modern rooms with hot water & private bathroom. **$**

⌂ **Residencial Castello** Close to the main square; m 982 5786. A comfortable B&B with a bar & restaurant, but currently closed for renovation.

✘ WHERE TO EAT AND DRINK

✘ **Restaurante Bar Pôr do Sol** The blue building on the main square. Also known as Casa Mensa, this is a pleasant old building serving adequate food including cheap platefuls of beans, beef & potatoes for 300$. It also has internet, international phone & a gift shop. **$**

✘ **Sossego** Off the main road. May be better to order in advance. **$**

✘ **O Poeta** Outdoor seating & sometimes music. **$**

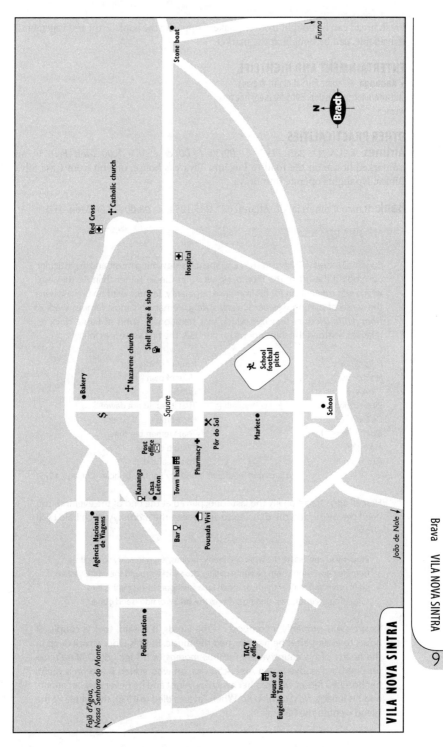

VILA NOVA SINTRA

*Fajã d'Água,
Nossa Senhora do Monte*

Police station ●

Agência Nacional
de Viagens ●

TACV
office ●

House of
Eugénio Tavares

João de Nole

Bar

Pousada Vivi

Kananga
Casa
Leiton ●

Post
office

$

Town hall

Pharmacy

Pôr do Sol

Market ●

School ✗
football
pitch

School

Square

Bakery ●

✝ Nazarene church

Shell garage & shop

Hospital

Red Cross

✝ Catholic church

Stone boat ●

→ *Furna*

N ←

Bradt

239

Fresh bread can be bought from the bakery opposite the bank. Fruit and vegetables, if available, can be bought at the market.

ENTERTAINMENT AND NIGHTLIFE
♀**Kananga** ☉ some Fri/Sat nights & every Sun afternoon; admission: 300$ for men; free for women

OTHER PRACTICALITIES
Airlines TACV (✆ 285 1192; ☉ 09.30–14.00 & 15.00–18.00 Mon–Fri). In an unmarked house on the road to Eugénio Tavares's house, one up from Casa Silva Bibica. No flights operate into Brava.

Bank Banco Comercial do Atlântico (✆ 285 1254; ☉ 08.00–14.30 Mon–Fri).

EUGÉNIO TAVARES

Eugénio Tavares was born in 1867 and spent his life writing music and in particular developing the art of the *morna*. He wrote in Creole rather than Portuguese, which was one reason for his immense popularity. Tavares lived on Brava where the sense of parting was particularly strong. Perhaps his most famous work is *Hora di Bai* (*Hour of Leaving*), which was traditionally sung at Furna dock as relatives boarded the ships bound for the USA. The first verse is as follows:

Hora di bai	Hour of going
Hora de dor	Hour of pain
Dja'n q'ré	I wish
Pa el ca mantché	That it would not dawn!
De cada bêz	Each time
Que'n ta lembrâ	That I remember thee,
Ma'n q'ré	I would choose
Fica 'n morrê	To stay and die!

Translated in *Atlantic Islands* by Bentley Duncan (Chicago, 1972)

Hora di Bai is traditionally the last song, played at the end of the evening. You need the music and the dancing to appreciate the *morna*. As Archibald Lyall wrote:

Properly to appreciate the work of Eugénio Tavares, it is necessary to see the humble people for whom he wrote gliding close-locked round the whitewashed, oil-lit room and to hear them, drugged for a few hours by his genius into forgetting their sorrows, singing softly to the strains of fiddle and guitar.

Tavares was primarily a composer – the words, it is said, took a couple of hours to invent after he had finished the music. But his lyrics struck deep in the hearts of his countrymen. Famous *mornas* of his include *O Mar Eterno* (inspired by his love for an American woman who visited Brava on a yacht; her horrified father whisked her away one night and he never saw her again), and his lullaby, *Ná ó menino ná*. When Tavares died in 1930, the whole of the island went to the funeral.

Hospital (✆ 285 1130). Brava's health post is on the Furna road out of the square, on the right. There is no capacity for complex interventions like transfusions or surgery.

Internet The post office provides an internet service, as does Casa Mensa (Bar Pôr do Sol). Also try the Shell shop, which provides a faxing and photocopying service.

Pharmacy Look for the well-stocked Farmácia Irene (✆ 285 1223).

Police (✆ 285 1132).

Post office (⏲ 08.00–16.00 Mon–Fri). On the square.

Shopping *Minimercados* are often better stocked than those in Fogo because of the American connection. Postcards are on sale in the post office. For Fogo wine, *grogue* and certain food and drink products unavailable elsewhere try the Shell shop (⏲ 07.00–21.00 daily), on the road leading from the square to the Furna road, which may also have maps in stock. Casa Mensa has a gift shop. The *papelaria* on the main square sells books on Cape Verde (in Portuguese).

Tourist information None, but road maps of Brava may be available from the Shell shop. Staff at the town hall (*câmara*) (✆ 285 1314) are very helpful to visitors looking for guidance.

WHAT TO SEE AND DO The house of Eugénio Tavares is at the top of the town just off the main road. There are plans to turn it into a museum. In the square is a kiosk with a plaque commemorating Tavares. In English it reads:

There above in planetary spheres
Shine brilliant and amazing stars:
But here on earth, one shines
For ever: Eugénio Tavares

FAJÃ D'ÁGUA

This is probably the most beautiful bay in Cape Verde – a little village at the foot of the mountains, sheltered from the northeast winds and always green. There is not much to do in the village but all the surrounding area is great for hiking.

Fajã is where the whaling boats used to anchor and here lies a monument to the passengers of the *Mathilde*. In 1943, a group of men – some American emigrants on a visit home, others young men who had never been out of Brava – bought the 55ft sloop. They all wanted to flee famine and go to New England. The *Mathilde* was in bad shape but this did not deter them; they made a few repairs and set sail on 21 August 1943.

Their voyage was a clandestine one because there were wartime restrictions on maritime travel. To make matters worse, they had chosen the beginning of the hurricane season.

Just after the boat left the harbour, a 12-year-old boy on board noticed that it was leaking. He took fright, jumped overboard and swam for the shore, half an hour away. 'There,' says Ray Almeida, an American Cape Verdean, 'he wept as he watched the sloop disappear over the horizon, carrying his compatriots to what he knew was certain death.' It is believed that the *Mathilde* went down in rough weather near Bermuda.

GETTING THERE AND AWAY Look out for the one *aluguer*, which leaves Fajã for the *vila* at 07.00, returning at 12.00 (200$). It is supposed to do an afternoon journey as well, leaving Fajã in the early afternoon and arriving back at 18.00. To charter an *aluguer* there or back costs around 2,000$. Fajã to Furna costs 2,000$.

WHERE TO STAY

🏠 **Pensão Sol na Baia** (4 rooms) 🤳 285 2070; e pensao_sol_na_baia@hotmail. com. A beautifully refurbished traditional house overlooking the sea, run by artist José Andrade, who speaks French, Italian, Spanish & Portuguese. Rooms are en suite with hot water but apart from that they are resolutely, & attractively, simple. FB available. **$$**

🏠 **Pensão Burgos/Motel Fajã d'Água** (6 rooms) 🤳 285 1321. About midway along Fajã's only road, the hotel consists of 3 rooms, basic but clean with a communal balcony gazing directly over the ocean. Sleep to the sound of the waves. Manuel will collect you from the port & entertain you with his stories of Brava. **$**

WHERE TO EAT AND DRINK

✖ **Pensão Sol na Baia** Fresh Cape Verdean produce with French style. **$$$$**

✖ **Pensão Burgos/Motel Fajã d'Água** May serve snacks (cake, bananas & coffee) plus meals of fish or meat. **$$**

OTHER PLACES TO VISIT

COVA JOANA Cova Joana is a small settlement west of Vila Nova Sintra, just south of the road to Fajã.

Where to stay

🏠 **Casa da Isabel** (5 rooms) 🤳 285 1081. Run by Jose & Isabel Teixeira, who lived in the USA for 5 years. It has shared bathrooms with hot water,

a bar & a pleasant aspect over the countryside. FB available. Good b/fast. **$**

VINAGRE This village derives its name from the mineral water which still bubbles up here from deep below the mountains. There is not much going on here now – a few broken-down donkeys and some ancient farmers, and an air of faded glory. The elaborate stone irrigation system and the extensive terracing are crumbling and largely overgrown. At the heart of the village is a bridge and a huge bougainvillea – a welcome splash of vermilion against the greys and browns.

On the left before the bridge is a majestic old water tank, fully equipped with gargoyle water spouts and large oval windows. Take a look inside to see how the water used to course through a carefully made tunnel under the road. To sample the water yourself, turn left just before the bridge, and follow the cobbled path down to where the piped spring water issues from a wall.

Further round on the left is the shell of a magnificent old house, inhabited within living memory. There are as many as four lime kilns around the settlement, once used to make whitewash for the houses – look out for their tall brick chimneys.

You can reach Vinagre by following a hike, or part of a hike (see page 244).

NOSSA SENHORA DO MONTE This village was founded as a place of pilgrimage in 1826 and, within a decade, had become a bishop's palace. Earlier in the last century travellers said that the road from Nova Sintra to Nossa Senhora do Monte was as thickly populated as the Thames Valley. Now emigration has left just a couple of tiny villages.

DRIVES

Brava is very small, so small that in just half a day you can cover all the driveable roads by car. This is well worth doing if you are pressed for time, but also to get a feel for the island – from its plunging mountains scored with deep *ribeiras* above Fajã d'Água, to the lively fishing village at Lomba, and the dusty poverty at the end of the road in Cachaço.

Take the road west out of the *vila*. A sharp hairpin in the first kilometre takes you out of the *caldeira* and through the pretty village of **Cova Rodela**. Just past the telephone box in the heart of Cova, the road forks – the left-hand fork takes you round the rim of the crater, past **João de Nole**, to where the road ends at **Mato Grande**. It is worth a brief detour along this road: after about 700m, there is a viewing point (*miradouro*) looking out over Vila Nova Sintra towards Fogo.

Continuing from Cova, bear left at a second fork (the right fork will take you to Fajã d'Água) and descend beneath a hill where there is a large water tank – this is one of a series that serves all of Brava. If you look down the *ribeira* to your right at this point, you will see Fajã d'Água nestling in a bay far, far below. Below the water tank, you pass through the attractive village of **Cova Joana**, where one aspect of Brava's economy becomes apparent: while emigré money has allowed many of the houses to be restored, the others are just left to crumble away.

A hairpin bend brings you up out of the valley into **Nossa Senhora do Monte**. A turning to the left on the hairpin below the school will take you into the labyrinthine tracks and pathways that make up the villages of **Lima Doce** and **Mato**, further south. Standing over Mato is **Fontainhas** peak, which you will see if the mist is not down. At 976m, this is the highest peak on Brava. Nossa Senhora do Monte is a winding cobbled street between whitewashed houses, where the red flowers of the cardeal bushes spill down the walls. The village commands spectacular views down the *ribeiras* to the north, with the sea beyond. The village is more or less continuous with Tomé Barras, where the road divides. Take the left fork to continue on to Cachaço. At this point, the countryside seems to change, and it starts to feel wilder, emptier and drier. As the road weaves in and out amongst the ridges, note the rows of acacia trees – planted to maintain a semblance of green during the dry season.

Cachaço is where the road stops – less than 10km from Vila Nova Sintra. It is a poor place, and epitomises the economic problems besetting rural communities in many parts of Cape Verde. Dependent exclusively on farming, it has been reduced almost to a ghost village. Although the volcanic soil is very fertile, increases in the price of seed and labour, and the unpredictability of the rains over a number of years are factors that have been felt keenly in Cachaço. Look about you and you will see traces of old field markings and terracing high up the slopes – all abandoned now – and shattered farmhouses left to the elements.

Returning from Cachaço, take the left turning at Tomé Barras. After about 900m, a small turning on the left goes to the small settlement of **Campo Baixo**. Carrying straight on, you will arrive at the fishing settlement of **Lomba**, after about 3km. Although the cobbled road surface stops after about 1km, this journey is worth making just to marvel at the road engineering – in places the track has been cut through ridges of solid rock.

The village of Lomba is strung out along a thin, exposed ridge. Bravans have remarkably limited access to the sea because of the steepness of their volcano. If you have a good head for heights, and are prepared to crane your neck, you will see the fishing boats drawn up hundreds of metres below. The women carry the fish in basins on their heads up an interminable zig-zagging path back up to the village. Depending on the season, they may be carrying bright orange groupers, or swordfish and tuna which, from far off, look like slabs of silver. There is a single shop in the village, selling cold beers. Lomba is a great place to watch the mist rolling down the *ribeiras*, or just to sit on the crumbling white rock of the ridge and try to see where the sea meets the horizon.

Returning along the road, pass the turning to Cachação on your right, go through Tomé Barras, into Nossa Senhora do Monte and on towards the *vila*. Winding up out of Cova Joana, you will come to the turning to Fajã d'Água on your left. This is another spectacular road – completed only in 1989 – cut through living rock. You will reach Fajã after about 4km. It is a wild and beautiful place, a well-protected harbour where yachts frequently drop anchor beneath mountains which seem to stretch upwards for ever.

A few houses line the waterfront, where, on windy days, you will be wet by the spray. At 1km beyond the village there is the ill-fated Bravan airport, wedged in between the mountains and the sea. Fickle crosswinds and a runway that is not quite long enough conspire to make the airstrip unsafe – one of the last planes to land here almost ended up in the sea.

On the road back out of Fajã look out for a turning on your left after about 3km. This road is not for the faint-hearted. After just over 2km, you will have to abandon your car, and continue to **Sorno** by foot, but it is well worth it (see *Hikes*, page 249, for a description of Sorno).

HIKES *Colum Wilson (CW); Aisling Irwin (AI)*

Several of the hikes below pass through Mato Grande, and hikers can therefore mix and match parts of routes.

1 VILA NOVA SINTRA–MATO GRANDE–MIRADOURO–COVA RODELA– VILA NOVA SINTRA

Distance: 5km; time: 1.5 hours; difficulty: 1 (CW)

This walk takes you up a steep path and then around the ring of hills to the south and west of Vila Nova Sintra on a well-surfaced road. You are always in sight of the *vila*, but you pass through the picturesque village of Mato Grande, clinging to the hillside, and you get some excellent views of Fogo. The *miradouro* (viewing point) is the highlight of this walk, giving an amazing view of the *vila*, spread out beneath you like a map.

From the southeast corner of the main square, take the road out past the building labelled **Casa Teixeira**. After about 100m you will come to a crossroads, where you go straight on. Bear right at a fork after a further 20m. After another 20m, the cobbled road turns sharp left. Go right on an unmade path that heads down to the bottom of the valley. After about 100m you will reach the valley floor.

Almost directly, go past a turning on your right leading up to a white house. After another 30m, turn right up a steep cobbled path between stone walls. This is a steep climb between houses that seem to be built on platforms carved out of the hillside. After about five minutes, the path bears left and you go round a rocky outcrop with a ruin below you on your left. From this point, and if the mist is not swirling around you, you get your first uninterrupted view of Fogo.

The path winds on around the hillside, passing houses in various states of repair. After another five minutes, it crosses a small valley and, directly, you reach a T-junction in front of a two-storey house. Turn right, following the path uphill. As you get higher, you will get glimpses down into the neat courtyards of some of the houses, where bougainvillea spills across ancient walls.

Five minutes later you cross a second small valley, and then bear left at a fork. Several minutes after that there is a white cross standing on a wall on your right beside a white house. Pass in front of the house on your right, and immediately turn right up beside the house, following the path uphill. Within a couple of minutes you will reach a telephone box, and a larger cobbled path through **Mato Grande**, which is spread out below you on your right as a maze of little paths between crumbling houses. Turn left at the phone box, and after five minutes of ascending, you will reach the Centro Social de Mato Grande (the social centre) on your left. Opposite, there is a table-football table, and a small bar selling fizzy drinks and *grogue*. Inside the shop, the youth of Mato Grande gather to while away the time with a pack of cards.

Looking south (with your back to the social centre), you will see the village of **Garça** down in the valley (look for the bright-green house) and, close by, the white outline of one of a series of stone ships dotted around the mountainside. On the far ridge is the village of **Baleia**, and at the east end of the ridge you will see a further ship.

A few hundred metres down the slope to the left of where you are standing, there is a third ship. If you would like a close look at one, ask at the bar for directions to the *barco*. On 24 June, it is these boats that are decorated with leaves and fruit to celebrate the festival of São João (see *Festivals*, page 236).

From the Mato Grande social centre, take the road that leads up to the left of the tapstand, with the *vila* visible on your right. Follow the road around the ridge, past old houses and small areas of cultivation squeezed in amongst the folds of land. After 1km (about 20 minutes), you will reach a T-junction in the road, where the right turning leads down to **João de Nole**. Turn left to continue to the *miradouro*.

Just 100m beyond the T-junction is a small, rough and steep path down on the right. (If you trust your knees, this is a quick way to descend to the *vila*.) The *miradouro* is another 200m beyond this, and gives a breathtaking view over the *vila*.

Continuing beyond the viewpoint, another 600m will bring you to a second T-junction, in the pretty village of **Cova Rodela**. Turn right here and follow the winding road back down to the *vila*. You will reach the western end of the main street after about ten minutes.

2 VILA NOVA SINTRA–MATO GRANDE–BALEIA–CASA EUGÉNIO TAVARES–BALEIA–MATO GRANDE–VILA NOVA SINTRA

Distance: 10km; time: 4 hours; difficulty: 3 (CW)

This walk south of the *vila* is a demanding sequence of ascents and descents, with spectacular views of Fogo out to the east. For much of this walk, the path is unmade and rough, and, particularly on the final steep zig-zag descent to the *casa*, care needs to be taken. Baleia is an attractive, if remote, spot to pause and gaze down vertiginous *ribeiras*. If you want to experience the unspeakable desolation of Brava's dryness, look no further than the *ribeira* where Tavares built his house.

Walk from the *vila* to Mato Grande (35 minutes) using the directions in the first five paragraphs of the previous walk.

In Mato Grande, looking south (with your back to the social centre), take the small path directly in front of you, which leads down in the direction of **Garça**.

At Garça, you can take a detour along the ridge to visit the stone boat (*barco*), which looks like it has been stranded at the end of the ridge in some cataclysmic flood. The path continues up to **Baleia** on the next ridge, about 1km from Mato Grande. Immediately on entering the village, you will see a house on your left that sells biscuits and *grogue*.

Baleia has the feel of a bird's nest perched high on a windswept ridge. The village comprises a single cobbled street and a few houses huddled together against the mist and the ceaseless purring of the wind.

It takes two hours to get from here to Casa Eugénio Tavares and return. People in Baleia will readily point you towards the path to the *casa*. Follow the cobbled path along the ridge through Baleia. Just before you reach the last two houses, turn right and immediately start to descend on an unmade path.

After about five minutes, the path branches. Going left will bring you in a few minutes to Baleia's stone boat. Bear right for the *casa*, down the side of the ridge. After about 20 minutes, you will reach a few scattered houses, mostly ruined. At a fork in the path bear left. You will see some rudimentary crosses on a cairn some tens of metres up the right turning. This is a homemade chapel, and means that the locals do not have to hike over to Mato Grande every Sunday.

You are heading towards what looks like a ruin (but is actually inhabited). Watch out for the dog, which may make you feel less than welcome. Cut close past the right side of this building (where the locals will point you in the right direction for Tavares's house), and descend a few hundred metres along the next ridge. If it is the dry season, you will enter a lunar landscape at this point, where there is nothing but rock and sand. The ruined huts look as if they have grown out of the landscape, rather than been built by human hand.

After less than ten minutes from the inhabited building, the path passes to the right through a small notch in a rocky ridge a few metres high. From here you will see the *casa* a long way below you on the other side of the valley. After a further five minutes, you will pass a ruin on your left. About 50m beyond this, there is a small (and easy-to-miss) turning on your right down the side of the *ribeira*. It is a very rough zig-zagging path, so watch your step. It will take you about ten or 15 minutes.

The ruin of Eugénio Tavares's house is reached by a five-minute scramble up from the floor of the *ribeira*. His house is surprisingly big – there are two storeys and outhouses. There is also a patio, and what looks like a small swimming pool, but was probably a water tank. In the dry season, you look out across a mind-numbing grey and brown panorama of splintered rock. But it clearly inspired Tavares and, apparently, a host of latter-day scribblers, who have left their poetic offerings all over the walls of the ruin.

Retrace your steps. For the return from Mato Grande to the *vila*, you can either go back the way you came (35 minutes) or go via the *miradouro* as described in the last part of the previous walk. The latter route takes about one hour.

3 VILA NOVA SINTRA–MATO GRANDE–MONTE FONTAINHAS–MATO– NOSSA SENHORA DO MONTE–COVA JOANA–VILA NOVA SINTRA
Distance: 9km; time: 3 hours 10 minutes; difficulty: 2 (CW)
This walk takes you to the heart of Brava, to its highest peak, from where you will get superb all-round views if you are not shrouded in mist. It is a steep ascent to Mato Grande, followed by a further steep ascent (on a cobbled path) from near Mato Grande up to the Fontainhas Plateau, where it is cool and green, and the air is heavy with sharp pine scents. Note: Mato Grande and Mato are different places.

Walk from the *vila* to Mato Grande (35 minutes) using the directions in the first five paragraphs of the Vila Nova Sintra–Mato Grande–*miradouro*–Cova Rodela walk.

For the 50-minute walk to **Fontainhas**, begin from the social centre in Mato Grande and take the road that leads up to the left of the tapstand. You will see Vila Nova Sintra below you on your right. After about 400m, you will pass a green church on your right, and, cresting a rise, you will see the path you are to take leading up from the left of the road about 200m in front of you. This is the beginning of a steep ascent on to the Fontainhas Plateau.

The path ascends the right side of a small valley. After about 200m, a path joins from the right. Your path bends round to the left at the top of the valley, and zig-zags upwards. Some 15 minutes after leaving the main road, the path flattens out and you pass to the right of a small peak with a large antenna on top. Directly after that, a small path joins on the left.

Five minutes after passing the antenna peak, take a right fork, and pass along the right edge of an undulating plateau, where the mist trails through spiky aloe vera and among the red flowers of the cardeal bushes. There are some farming huts, and occasional cattle grazing on the coarse grass. The air is sharp with the smell of pine.

After another ten minutes, you reach a T-junction. The right turning heads down to **Mato**. Turn left, and very shortly you will pass a whitewashed house on your right. Bear right at a fork shortly after this. Follow the path upwards, and after less than ten minutes, you will reach the peak. To get to Mato, which takes about 45 minutes, go back to the T-Junction before the whitewashed house, but instead of turning right to retrace your steps, head straight on. After about seven minutes of descending from the T-junction along a winding path, you will emerge on a low saddle, and will see the upper end of Mato down on your left.

Continue along the saddle for another five minutes, and then take a deeply worn path leading down on your left. After five minutes, this path will lead you past a concrete water tank on your left.

After another few minutes, the path becomes cobbled, and you are descending through the first of the houses in Mato. Five minutes later, you reach a T-junction with a telephone box on the right. From here, your aim is to reach the main road through Mato. Mato is criss-crossed by any number of small paths, and the best way to the main road is simply by asking.

Once on the road, follow it to the right, descending past a school on your left, and joining at last the main road to Nossa Senhora do Monte at a sharp hairpin.

Turn right on to the main road and walk for an hour, passing through **Cova Joana**, **Cova Rodela** and eventually reaching Vila Nova Sintra.

4 VILA NOVA SINTRA–SANTA BARBARA–VINAGRE–MATO GRANDE– JOÃO DE NOLE–VILA NOVA SINTRA

Distance: 5km; time: 2 hours 20 minutes; difficulty: 3 (CW)

In this walk, you descend almost to sea level by a zig-zagging cobbled path, and then climb back up again by a very rough (and in places precipitous) ridge path. It is not a walk to undertake if you have dodgy knees or don't like getting out of breath. Vinagre – a village nestling in the mouth of a *ribeira* – is the highlight of the walk, with its old lime kilns and air of decayed grandeur. The mineral waters that flow from a natural spring taste like a mild mixture of lemon juice and soapsuds, and have given the village its name. It is said that those who drink of the waters will never leave.

For the 40-minute walk to Vinagre, set out on the road east from the main square of the *vila*. After five minutes, you will reach the stone boat looking out towards Fogo.

Take the little cobbled path down to the left of the boat, and after just a short distance, you will join the main road snaking its way down to Furna. Cross the road, and double back a few metres to pick up the cobbled path continuing its descent on the other side. Your path is actually the old road to Furna – watch out for the stray vehicles that still use this road. After five minutes descending, take a cobbled turning on your right towards **Santa Barbara**, which you will reach after another few minutes. About ten minutes from the turning, staying on the same path, you will round an outcrop, and catch a glimpse of Mato Grande above you on the hill.

At this point, you will begin a series of sharp zig-zags down towards **Vinagre**, which you will reach after about 25 minutes.

The one-hour hike from Vinagre to Mato Grande is a scramble, and some may prefer to turn round and retrace their steps up to Santa Barbara. The undaunted should cross over the bridge in Vinagre and follow the main path past a white house on the left with a brick kiln behind it. Immediately bear right up a rough path that looks as if it ends in a small rock quarry a few tens of metres from the main path. Pass through this area of broken rock, and, after a few minutes pass a ruin and follow the path as it doubles back up a ridge.

About five minutes after leaving the main path, you will pass an inhabited house on your left, and directly ascend past a ruin. The path is indistinct at this point, and does not look promising, but turn directly left behind the ruin, and you should be able to follow it.

This is the beginning of a very steep ascent on a rough path, where you will sometimes be looking for handholds. After about 20 minutes of arduous zig-zagging, you will emerge at a T-junction on a more major path, where you turn right along a contour. Following this path around the side of the hill will bring you to a small settlement after about ten minutes. From here, you can see Mato Grande on the hill on your left.

Follow the path as it doubles back on itself through the settlement, and then follow the path up the hill under the phone line. After about seven minutes, you cross over a small ridge, and your path improves. Three minutes later, you pass a water point with taps, where you turn left uphill.

After another two or three minutes, a path joins you from your right in front of a white, two-storeyed house. Go straight on, following the path uphill. Five minutes later, you cross a small valley, and then bear left at a fork. Two or three minutes later there is a white cross standing on a wall on your right beside a white house. Pass in front of the house on your right, and immediately turn right beside the house, following the path uphill. Within a couple of minutes you will reach a telephone box, and a larger cobbled path through Mato Grande. Turn left at the phone box, and after five minutes of ascending, you will reach the Centro Social de Mato Grande (social centre) on your left.

To get back to the *vila*, via **João de Nole**, takes about 40 minutes. From the social centre in Mato Grande, take the road up to the left of the tapstand. After about 1km, turn right at a T-junction.

After a further 400m, turn left down into João de Nole. After 100m, go straight across a small T-junction. After this, the cobbled path gets smaller as it starts to zig-zag sharply down towards the *vila*. About ten minutes after the small crossroads, the path emerges on a cobbled street at the edge of town. Turn left on to the street.

5 VILA NOVA SINTRA–LEVADURA–FAJÃ D'AGUA

Distance: 6km; time: 2 hours; difficulty: 2 (AI)
This is a classic, downhill Cape Verde *ribeira* walk, with your destination sparkling beside the sea during the brief glimpses you snatch as you descend. Before you reach it you have to negotiate a lot of superbly crafted cobbled paths, ghostly villages and

the echoey sides of the harsh valley walls. There is a short patch towards the end where there is no clear path and the going is slippery.

The first 25 minutes of the walk is on the road. From the town square head west on the town hall road. At the end of the street turn right up the Nossa Senhora do Monte road. Follow this for just over 20 minutes, passing through the village of **Cova Rodela**, with its superb dragon tree, on the way. Stop at a fork in the road: the high road continues to Nossa Senhora do Monte; to the right is the road to Fajã d'Água.

Walk for two minutes along the high road, then take a track to the right beside a sizeable tree. Follow this for about five minutes, ignoring another track up to the left, until you reach a crossroads of paths. To the right a track leads to a few houses on a nearby peak. Take the middle path, downhill, which leads you swiftly into a hidden valley of stark cliffs and, beyond them, the sea. Some 25 minutes from the crossroads you reach a water tank around which the path forks. The left path goes to the village of **Tomba Has**: take the right one instead. You are in a deep valley world of steep, stone wall terracing and startling echoes.

Within a couple of minutes of leaving the water tank you will have your first proper view of Fajã d'Água, the archetypal nestling village, snug and green between the hostile brown Bravan mountains. Keep going, past two water tanks, through a settlement and, 15–20 minutes after the first water tank, past the quiet village of **Levadura** (to see it take a small detour on a path to the left). Now you are deep in the valley and the path is steep and winding.

Some 15 minutes from Levadura, when you are about level with a wood and a few houses on the other side of the valley, the path crosses a watercourse (generally dry) and a small dam, often full of water. Don't take the little path down to the left but go straight on, crossing, after a few minutes, a concrete barrier and following a path up through the houses ahead. In this jumbled settlement you will find someone who can lead you through to the other side where there is a well-trodden path the villagers all take down to Fajã d'Água. Beware: it is gravelly and slippery. For half an hour you descend on a path that is a mixture of rock, landslide and gravel, criss-crossing water channels, dams and stream beds and passing a big water tank, until you arrive at the road through Fajã d'Água.

6 VILA NOVA SINTRA–SORNO–SÃO PEDRO–VILA NOVA SINTRA

Distance: 9km; time: 4.5 hours; difficulty: 2–3 (AI)

This spectacular walk encapsulates the essence of Brava: the remote valley hamlet of Sorno making miraculous use of its little stream to farm extensive green terraces up the mountainsides; the vivid, slightly menacing sea; the barren mountains; the ghost villages that are testament to livelier times; and, periodically, big brother Fogo looming from across the sea. The walk is suitable for any walker of average fitness, with just a very small slippery stretch to be negotiated. There is a two-hour walk downhill, mainly along a road, and 2.5 hours on a remote path that is steep but not difficult. There are no facilities in Sorno.

From Vila Nova Sintra walk for 25 minutes to the fork, as described in the first two paragraphs of the walk from Vila Nova Sintra to Fajã d'Água.

Take the right fork (the Fajã d'Água road), passing a big white water tank on the right after 20 minutes and, after a further 15 minutes, reaching a turning to the right. This road on the right is of much poorer quality and takes you past a small quarry and various houses. You may pass the odd person harvesting grass or loading it on to a donkey but soon you will leave even these few behind, and there is just you, the sea and the odd hawk. The dull brown of the mountains makes a huge contrast with the rich blue and harsh white of the sea.

Eventually one of the road's twists will reveal **Sorno** below, improbably tame below the ominous Brava slopes. The Sorno road takes 1.5 hours to cover, dwindling to a path – slippery in places – some 20 minutes from the village and, all the while, the ingenious village reveals itself in the form of irrigation channels, neat water tanks and endless squares of tended terraces. Follow the path round to the front of a square white building and then follow your nose, and a set of stepped irrigation channels and water tanks, to the sea.

After a break on the beach, it is time for the ascent out of Sorno. Finding the path, which winds out of the other side of the valley from the side you entered, takes a little care. Use as your guide Sorno's first (more southerly) bay. With your back to the water and its twin-peak stacks behind you, gaze up the valley and look for the little path that mounts its left side. For the first five minutes it is a small dirty

WHALERS AND THE PACKET TRADE

For a young man with nothing but a peasant's struggle against hunger ahead of him, the prospect of a job on one of the New England whaling ships that pulled into Brava provided excitement and escape.

The first such boats arrived towards the end of the 18th century. Throughout most of the 19th century, a new vessel would arrive perhaps every three days so that the crew could resupply, drink and deposit their genes in the ever-absorptive pool. Crucially, the whalers would also be searching for crew – as replacements for obstreperous crewmen who would be abandoned on Brava. The Cape Verdeans were disciplined and took lower wages than their American counterparts, and developed great skill in the arts of whaling.

Stories of life aboard the whalers are full of excitement, courage and horror. The shot of the harpoon sinking into a 30m-long beast; the cries as the men rowed frantically to escape the thrashing of the whale's tail; the speed with which their little boats were towed through the ocean by the fleeing animal until they won control and sank a killer harpoon home. Men frequently died during these battles.

Some used the whaling ships as brief stepping stones to jobs in the USA – manual labour in the ports, in the cranberry bogs of southern New England and in the textile mills of New Bedford.

As steam replaced sail, the schooners and whalers could be bought or even 'inherited' for nothing. Cape Verdeans in the USA took them over, did them up and began the era of the Brava Packet Trade – a regular link between the USA and the islands. The boats would take Bravans to work in the cranberry bogs and return loaded with goods and with *emigrantes* visiting their families. The Packet Trade became an independent link by which Cape Verdeans could keep in contact with their families without depending on the transport system of another country.

There are plenty of dramatic tales about these ships – of charismatic captains, of tussles with disaster and of tragedy. The *Nellie May* was the first to begin a regular journey between the continents, in 1892. One of the longest recorded journeys of such a schooner was 90 days; the record for the shortest crossing was claimed to be 12 but was probably longer. World War II halted the trade, but afterwards one of the most legendary of the packet trade captains, Henrique Mendes, resurrected a sunken schooner and named her *Ernestina* (see box, *The schooner* Ernestina, page 20).

track, but it then becomes paved and walled, if old and crumbly, soon crossing a concrete water channel and tank.

As you leave Sorno its colours dull and, after a good 20-minute walk, you turn to see its vivid greens already merging with the dull surrounding browns, its charm retreating. Half an hour of climbing out of Sorno brings you round into the next bay, a new set of jagged peaks ahead of you and, after entering a little wood, a turning to the right past a stack of dry stones. Take this and, in less than five minutes, you pass another prehistoric old home on the left – the path goes up and round behind it.

You are now entering the loneliest part of the walk, its stark remoteness made more poignant by the carefully crafted path, with its implication that someone once thought it would be useful. Some 50 minutes from the right turning at the stack of stones below, you reach the ghost village of **Tez Cova** – decaying old piles of stone houses from which folk used to try to farm the now-abandoned terraces. One half expects the ghost of an old Bravan crone to emerge from one of these hovels and share a thought on the fate of the island.

At Tez Cova you should walk through the village, broadly following the contour, rather than heading upwards and inland. The path dips shallowly and then climbs gently, passing on the left No 26, a building with a pale pink door. At the edge of Tez Cova, the final house is inhabited and you pass it on the left and go over a saddle, which reveals the vista of **São Pedro**, the busy overflow from Vila Nova Sintra. From here, it is half an hour to the *vila*, initially through a maze of paths (keep asking for the *praça*).

7 VILA NOVA SINTRA–FURNA

Distance: 3km; time: 50 minutes; difficulty: 1 (Al)
This walk follows the old, little-used cobbled road from Vila Nova Sintra to Furna. It is an easy descent, steep in places, and is a good alternative to being rattled around in the back of an *aluguer* when you are descending to the port for home.

Set out on the road east from the main square. After five minutes, you will reach the stone boat looking out towards Fogo. Take the little cobbled path down to the left of the boat, and after just a short distance, you will join the main road snaking its way down to Furna. Cross the road, and double back a few metres to pick up the cobbled path continuing its descent on the other side.

After five minutes descending, you pass a cobbled turning on your right towards Santa Barbara. Some 25 minutes later, the old road briefly joins the new road, but leaves it again after a short distance.

Just before entering Furna, you rejoin the new road for the last time.

OTHER WALKS There is also an easy path from Fontainhas to Cachaço; and there is said to be a path from Cachaço to Casa Eugénio Tavares: enquire locally.

THE ILHÉUS DO ROMBO

These islands have been nature reserves since 1990 and are protected by law. The smaller ones are Ilhéu Luiz Carneiro, Ilhéu Sapado and Ilhéu do Rei.

The islets are, along with Raso Island near São Nicolau, the only home for the Cape Verdean shearwater (*Calonectris edwardsii*). Bulwer's petrel (*Bulweria bulwerii*), known locally as *João-petro*, breeds here as well as on Raso. And the Madeiran storm petrel (*Oceanodroma castro*), known locally as the *jaba-jaba* or the *pedreirinho*, breeds only here and on Branco, Raso and islets off Boavista. For descriptions, see *Birds*, page 6.

Until 2007, it was possible to visit the islets on a fishing boat from Fajã or Furna, which would do the round trip for about 2,200$. Most people chose to camp overnight, taking their own water and eating fish that they caught and grilled there. However, in 2007 the government tightened up on access to protected islands. Written ministerial permission is now required and is unlikely to be given. Fishermen could get hefty fines if discovered taking a tourist to the island. The restrictions may be relaxed sometime so it is worth checking.

ILHÉU GRANDE Some 2km², Ilhéu Grande's highest point is Monte Grande, at 96m. It has a rounded shape. Seabirds used to breed here – the island is covered in thick layers of guano.

ILHÉU DE CIMA This long and narrow rock of 1.5km² is famous for its seabird colonies. It has a big lump sticking out of its southern end, 77m high, and some smaller rocky outcrops.

10

São Vicente

Four o'clock in the dawning
São Vicente folk are there
To cry their sorrow
For sons who are sent away
To São Tomé

Mindelo lament

For many people Mindelo, the island's capital, *is* São Vicente. It's a fine city, full of life and a certain grace. In some ways it is one of the most pleasant cities in west Africa. Mindelo's buzz contrasts with a dead hinterland – as dry as Sal but more extraordinary, as it has died at a younger age, while still covered in sweeping hills and mountain ranges. The British called São Vicente the 'cinder heap'.

Wander outside the capital and that haunting question evoked by the flatter islands returns once again: 'How did people end up here? How have they survived?'

HIGHLIGHTS

Many Cape Verdean writers and thinkers were educated at the São Vicente *liceu* and Mindelo is proud of its intellectual and artistic tradition. It has a liveliness – visit for the music, for the occasional performance, for hanging around in the bars. Cape Verde's two most exuberant annual festivals are here: the exotic Carnival, a miniature Rio, in mid-February, and the beach music festival in August.

Also go for watersports, in particular windsurfing (if you have your own gear) but surfing and fishing as well. If you love desolate rocky coastlines and deserted beaches you will enjoy wandering here. It's also the ideal jumping-off place if you have a hankering to visit one of the few uninhabited islands, such as the nature reserve of Santa Luzia.

SUGGESTED ITINERARY AND NUMBER OF DAYS Wandering around Mindelo, including going up to the fort, takes about half a day, as does a trip by vehicle to the top of Monte Verde and back. A tour of the island taking in Baia das Gatas, Calhau and São Pedro also takes a day. If the landscape appeals to you there are a few hikes or wanderings that could occupy another day or two. If you just have a day in São Vicente, for example from a cruise ship, and you arrive early enough, visit Santo Antão, across the channel, instead, and enjoy its glorious scenery by taking a trip along the mountain road to Ribeira Grande and back. Otherwise, if it is a clear day, then a walk or drive up to the top of Monte Verde is the most scenic activity; failing that go for a meal at Caza Azul or a drive up Fortim for a grand view of Mindelo. For a day on the beach jump into a taxi and go to São Pedro (for details, see page 272).

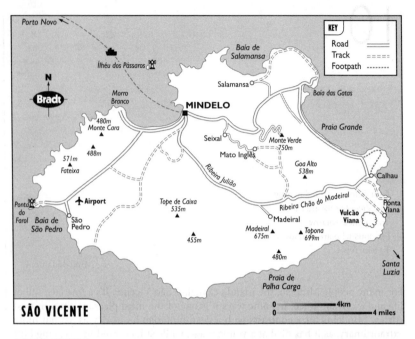

KEY
Road
Track =====
Footpath --------

Porto Novo

Baía de Salamansa

Ilhéu dos Pássaros

Baía das Gatas

N

Brandt

Morro Branco

Salamansa

MINDELO

Seixal

Praia Grande

480m Monte Cara

Monte Verde 750m

Mato Inglês

488m

571m Fateixa

Goa Alto 538m

Calhau

Ribeira Julião

Ponta do Farol Baía de São Pedro

Airport

São Pedro

Tope de Caixa 535m

Ribeira Chão do Madeiral

Vulcão Viana

Ponta Viana

Madeiral

455m

Madeiral 675m

Topona 699m

480m

Santa Luzia

Praia de Palha Carga

SÃO VICENTE

0 ————— 4km
0 ————— 4 miles

LOWLIGHTS

If you love greenery, avoid São Vicente. If you are on a tight schedule and long for the mountains you may regret having allocated time here. Swimming is treacherous on many beaches. There are some sandy beaches but, at present, only one luxury beach hotel.

BACKGROUND INFORMATION

HISTORY This rock in the ocean was of little use to anyone before the end of the 18th century. After its discovery on 22 January 1462, and the traditional release of goats to prey on its delicate vegetation, humans forgot about it, except to land there occasionally with dogs and spend a night goat hunting. An attempt to populate the island was made in 1795, but it failed and just a few people remained, at the top of Monte Verde.

But São Vicente has one superlative natural resource. The island's harbour is a sweeping curve formed by a crater rim over whose northern side the sea has breached. A headland to the northeast of the harbour completes the protection while the ring of hills blocks wind from almost any direction. Thus Mindelo is a fine stopping point for ships crossing the Atlantic. When coal replaced wind as the main propellant, Mindelo became the ideal place for refuelling mid journey.

It was the British, by then the lords of the Atlantic and creators of the steam engine, who began to realise Mindelo's potential. By the early 1800s, they had established a consulate and depot there. One John Lewis, a lieutenant, brought coal and set up a refuelling station for ships crossing from Europe to South America or to southern Africa. His arrival was followed by the Royal Mail in 1850. Soon Mindelo was busy, and in its heyday thousands of ships a year would pause in its harbour to load with coal brought from Cardiff to São Vicente. At any time 5,000 tonnes were waiting in lighters ready to load on to ships – part of the constant reserve of 34,000 tonnes. A 100,000-gallon tank was kept in the harbour, filled with water ferried over from Santo Antão.

John Rendall, one of the British involved in the coal business, reported of São Vicente in the 1850s:

> There is space sufficient to anchor 300 vessels. Two steam packets run to and from England with the Post Office Mails, calling here every month for a replenishment of coals. The place is improving daily, and will no doubt, in a short time, become the wealthiest of all the islands.

São Vicente was also chosen, in 1875, as the site for the submarine cable that allowed telecommunications across the Atlantic, and it filled with British employees of the Western Telegraph.

Yet the trade did not bring much prosperity to ordinary people. Cape Verde earned some money by charging for water and anchorage and exacting coal taxes, but the refuelling was in the hands of foreign companies and many locals scratched a pittance from the sale of rum and from prostitution and dingy guesthouses, though some earned livings heaving coal. For their part the authorities made little attempt to develop São Vicente: there was no investment in a proper pier to ward off competition from Dakar, and little thought was given to the possibility of taking advantage of world events rather than being their victim.

When Alfred Burdon Ellis visited in 1855, he wrote at length about the antics of the characters in his bawdy and squalid lodgings. On leaving, he concluded:

THE ANSWER IS BLOWING...?   *Alex Alper*

Sweeping across the Caribbean and Africa, the alize tradewinds have brought ships to Cape Verde's shores and dust into newly swept homes each summer for centuries. Now they look set to provide a clean, renewable energy.

Today, only 3–5% of Cape Verde's energy comes from wind. But with high average wind speeds and electricity demand increasing by 8–15% per year, wind might be the solution. The national energy company Electra built its first wind park on São Vicente in 1989, and today there are three functioning wind parks on Sal, São Vicente, and Santiago. They contribute 15,000kW to the electricity grid.

One major constraint is financing. With each turbine costing US$5,065 and producing at best 322kWh per month, each one will pay for itself only after 4.5 years. But Infraco, a US company, in collaboration with the Cape Verdean government, will invest €40 million to build new plants on four islands, increasing the power to 17–25% of total energy production. Wind power will then total 20–25MW.

Wind is highly erratic – changing direction and intensity – and thus is an 'intermittent generator'. Its guaranteed output is therefore zero, and diesel capacity must be able to meet 100% of demand. The wind's intermittency is what prevents it from supplying more than 25% of any country's total energy.

But a proposed thermo-wind-solar power plant could provide constant, storable energy by generating thermal energy. Wind would be used only as a cold source, while the soil, oceans or warm-water sources on Santo Antão would provide the warm source.

Taken as a whole it is, perhaps, the most wretched and immoral town that I have ever seen; but what can be expected of a colony which is rated at such a low value that the salary of the governor is only four shillings and sixpence a day?

Thus, at the same time that it was the fourth-greatest coaling station in the world after Egypt's Port Said, Malta and Singapore, the city became a place of beggars, prostitutes, starving invalids and smugglers.

Unfolding world events dealt São Vicente a series of blows. The opening of the Suez Canal between the Mediterranean and the Red Sea in 1869 diminished the port's activity, though it bounced back after a while. Technology advanced and the cable connection became mechanised, so the employees of the Western Telegraph returned home. Ships' bunkers were built larger so they could carry enough coal for their entire journeys. Finally, oil replaced coal, drastically cutting the amount of labour required for refuelling. Drought and famine bit viciously and in 1941, the British consul at Mindelo, Captain J L Sands, reported:

A large number are emaciated, worn out and have lost both heart and hope... the starving seem to accept the situation with an oriental fatalism. They do not press their claims to live, they scarcely beg, may ask you for alms once or twice, and then simply stare at you as if resigned to what is to happen.

It was from Mindelo at that time that the *contratados* were recruited in their thousands to go and labour on the plantations of São Tomé and Príncipe, islands to the south. But the conditions there were akin to slavery and few ever returned.

Mindelo was the intellectual capital of the archipelago, so it was here that despair and education came together to create the idea of revolution (see *History*, pages 24–5).

SÃO VICENTE TODAY Mindelo, the capital, has an air of importance about it these days and is growing wealthier. *Emigrantes* are returning and there is inward migration from other islands. A marina has been built, as well as a new international airport. Currently there is only one flight a week from Portugal but there are hopes that São Vicente will make great strides once more airlines begin operations. There is a scenic new road from Calhau to Baía das Gatas.

Much of Mindelo's terrain feels like a vast natural building site and, accordingly, there are some mesmerisingly huge foreign development plans for the island. The grandest was the brainchild of investors from Dubai who want to build the Cesaria Resort, a €1.5-billion tourism and real-estate development at Praia de Palha Carga and Calheta Grande in the south of the island. It seems unlikely now that this will go ahead.

Resorts planned for Baía das Gatas, São Pedro and Calhau all appear to have ground to a halt. As for Alto Fortim, in town – this is supposed to be transformed into a Nikki Beach Village and Casino Resort. In all, five international golf courses are planned. In total there are plans for four more marinas in São Vicente in addition to the new one in Mindelo.

GEOGRAPHY The island is 227km^2 and lies about 14km east of Santo Antão. It is extremely dry. Its highest peak, Monte Verde, is 750m. There is irrigation in some of the principal valleys – Ribeira de Calhau and Ribeira da Vinha. Earlier this century there were irrigated plantations in Ribeira Julião. The population is 80,000, overwhelmingly in Mindelo. There have been many attempts at reafforestation, particularly along the road to the airport.

NATURAL HISTORY São Vicente has one protected area: Monte Verde, which is a natural park.

Turtles used to nest prolifically on São Vicente's beaches and one of their last remaining beaches, Praia Grande, runs between Baía das Gatas and Calhau. Here, as everywhere, hunting is a serious threat, as well as the illegal removal of sand for construction. The new road running alongside the shore has storm drains running directly on the beach and the rain will most likely sweep away any nests in their paths. The island does not harbour any bird specialities but there are plenty of interesting waders and migrant birds on the wet sand towards São Pedro, 1km from the airport, and on the sewage ponds 2km from the centre of town (reached by going south along the coastal road until just after the Shell oil storage terminals and following a track inland on the left).

HAZARDS In terms of **crime**, begging from street children can be quite persistent, and some have a habit of attempting to help themselves to the contents of your pockets before you are quite sure that is what you want them to do. They are common in Praça Amílcar Cabral and along the coastal road. Watch out in general for pickpockets and don't go up to the fort on your own.

Many **swimming** areas are dangerous: take local advice.

FESTIVALS

22 January	Municipality Day
February	Carnival
3 May	Santa Cruz
24 June	São João (St John)
29 June	São Pedro
8 August	Nossa Senhora da Luz
August full moon	Baía das Gatas music festival
September	Mindelact theatre festival

GETTING THERE AND AWAY

BY AIR There are several flights a day with TACV to and from Sal and Santiago. Halcyonair also operates a link between Sal and São Vicente. Mindelo's international airport receives one international flight a week from Lisbon, the rest being domestic. For guidance on arriving at a Cape Verdean airport from overseas see *Red tape*, page 52.

Taxis to town from the airport (✆ *232 3715*) cost 600–700$ (and 1,000$ at night to town). It is 10km to Mindelo and 1km to São Pedro.

BY FERRY There is, theoretically, a regular ferry connection between São Vicente, Praia and São Nicolau but this needs to be checked just before the trip with one of the ferry agencies: try STM, which operates the *Sal Rei*.

Cargo ships regularly go to Praia from São Vicente and, less regularly, to other islands. To find a place on one of these ships try the agents up towards the port and on Rua Cristiano de Sena Barcelos. To get to Santo Antão take the ferry from Mindelo port to Porto Novo. For further details see *Chapter 11, Santo Antão*, page 279.

BY YACHT There is a new marina at Mindelo, and the harbour and anchorage are excellent, offering protection from the northwest winds through to eastern and southern winds. In Mindelo, Shell will deliver alongside and water is available in this way as well. Ship repair is the best in the archipelago – they should be able to repair new instruments here. There is also a chandlery with a range of equipment suitable for crossing the Atlantic. Whether or not this is your first port of call in Cape Verde, you may have to call not just at the *capitania* in the port radio building but also visit the maritime police and the immigration police. The other possible anchorage is at Baía de São Pedro, where it is best to anchor off the eastern end of the beach. There are no facilities.

Watch the channel between São Vicente and Santo Antão, where winds can gust to up to 40 knots, particularly between December and May.

For yacht services try:

⚠ **BoatCV** (see Sailing, opposite)

⚠ **Cape Verde Travel** (see *Excursions*, opposite)

GETTING AROUND

BY PUBLIC TRANSPORT Transcor buses journey around Mindelo and its outskirts (25–30$), visiting Baía das Gatas during July and August. Buses and taxis gather at the square to the west of the Presidential Palace. *Alugueres* gather in Praça da Independéncia.

BY TAXI There are plenty of marked taxis cruising around town, and a typical journey in the city will cost about 120$. Taxis charge about 2,000$ for a return journey to the top of Monte Verde; 1,600$ return to Baía das Gatas and 2,000$ return to Calhau. It's 800$ to the airport (1,000$ at night). Taxis can be hired for about 1,200$ per hour.

🚗 **Dilson's Taxis** m 995 7976

🚗 **Taxi 2000** 231 4564

BY CAR There are many car-rental agencies in town. Many close for lunch between 12.30 and 14.30.

🚗 **Alucar** In Monte Sossego, southwest of town; 232 1295/5194; e alucarsv@ cvtelecom.cv, alucarstrc@cvtelecom.cv
🚗 **Atlantic Car** [262 F4] 27 Rua Baltazar Lopes da Silva, Mindelo; 231 7032; m 991 6229

🚗 **Auto Crioula** 232 8255
🚗 **Avis** [262 E3] Next to Hotel Porto Grande.
🚗 **Belcar** Largo 6, Chã de Monte Sossego; 232 7330; m 995 7101; e belcarlda@cvtelecom.cv
🚗 **Joel Evora** Madelrazino; 230 0303

WHERE TO STAY

Virtually all hotels are in Mindelo. There's a resort in São Pedro, a hotel in Calhau and a couple of budget places in Baía das Gatas. A booking service in Santiago, Santo Antão and São Vicente is offered by capeverdebooking.com.

ACTIVITIES

EXCURSIONS There are several operators in Mindelo offering a variety of tours.

Barracuda Tours Rua de Coco, 28-A; 232 5592; e geral@barracudatours.com; www.barracudatous.com. Established family-owned agency that can organise inter-island travel & excursions.

Cabo Verde Safari m 991 1544/2721; e caboverdesafari@cvtelecom.cv; www.caboverdesafari.com. Specialise in taking you off the beaten track & have a variety of island tours, eg: half- & full-day excursions by Land

Surfers love some of the São Vicente beaches and, in 1997, Sandy Beach at Calhau was included in the European professional circuit. However, it is among windsurfers, who have reached bullet-like speeds here, that it has become famous.

For one young windsurfer, it was the channel between São Vicente and Santo Antão that posed the greatest challenge. He gazed longingly across the 14km stretch and promised himself that one day, when the winds were right, he would attempt the crossing. He waited a long time for the perfect day and then set out, just as the ferry pulled away from the pier for the same destination.

He raced across and arrived at Porto Novo before the ferry, much to the admiration of the rest of the windsurfing fraternity back in Mindelo. One man left unimpressed, however, was the local policeman, who promptly arrested him.

Rover from €32, & a full-day trip to Santa Luzia for €100.

Cape Verde Travel Rua Carlos Mondlane; m 998 2878; e capeverdetravel@cvtelecom.cv. This long-serving British tour operator has recently opened an office in Mindelo offering island tours, inter-island travel & services to cruise liners & the yachting community.

FLY Viagens e Turismo [262 E3] 232 2844. At the Hotel Porto Grande, this company does a guided tour of the island including Mindelo.

WINDSURFING AND KITESURFING São Vicente could be one of the world's greatest windsurfing and bodyboarding destinations. World windsurfing speed records have been set in São Pedro Bay. The wind there, at the southwest corner of the island, is the result of an unusual quirk in the landscape: the long straight valley behind the bay acts as a funnel concentrating the wind – a phenomenon known as the Venturi effect. The result is an unusually steady and strong breeze. There are some good surfing spots around Calhau, including Praia Grande, around the headland to the north of Calhau, and Praia Branca, just south of Calhau and Sandy Beach. Frustratingly, however, the market for renting equipment has not yet developed, but there may be kit available to hire at São Pedro from the Foya Branca Hotel.

Itoma m 993 4989; e info@itoma.at; www.itoma.at. This 23m motor catamaran is based in Mindelo & is booked mostly by groups from Europe for week-long windsurfing (winter) or diving (summer) trips. This comfortable boat carries a range of sails & boards & offers a very comfortable way to windsurf in places few people ever see. Comfortably takes 12 passengers. Charters from €600 for 3 days' diving to €11,900 for one-week's windsurfing.

Kitesurf NOW www.kitesurfnow.eu. Offers lessons.

SAILING As with much of Cape Verde, but especially between São Vicente and Santo Antão, the seas can be rough and the winds very strong. Trying to anchor in Porto Novo, Santo Antão's harbour, in a strong offshore wind can be very hairy and there is not the same level of support as can be found in the Canaries.

⚠ **BoatCV** (Kai Brossmann & Cesar Murais) Av Marginal; 232 6772; m 991 5878; e info@ boatcv.com; www.boatcv.com; ⊕ 09.00–12.00 & 15.00–18.00 Tue–Sat. German & Cape Verdean operation offering yacht support services & hiring out a variety of yachts, bare boat or captained.

São Vicente ACTIVITIES

10

ENGLAND TO BARBADOS   *James Ensor*

Mindelo is one of the staging points for the OnDeck Atlantic Adventure, a race from Europe to Barbados. Crews can sign on for any of the individual legs, starting at Portsmouth and continuing to Lisbon, Madeira, São Vicente and Barbados. The entire trip can take six weeks and is staged each November. São Vicente to Barbados is invariably the most popular leg. The boats are half-a-dozen Farr 65s, a thrilling ocean racer, with massive amounts of wind available to fill the spinnakers all the way downwind to the Caribbean. Creature comforts are not what these boats are about but it is possible to check them out beforehand on a day trip in the less balmy but calmer Solent (*www.ondeck.co.uk/transatlantic/ ondeck-atlanticadventure.htm*).

FISHING The waters around São Vicente have international renown for their blue marlin. **Cape Verde Big Game** (m *992 3656;* e *biggamecaboverde@gmail.com*), based at the Residencial Alto Fortim, runs fishing-and-accommodation packages, taking visitors out on its Bertram 33 and Pace 40. Try also Residencial Jenny. Fishing trips are also organised at the Foya Branca Hotel.

DIVING At the moment there are no dive centres open on São Vicente but it is possible that the one at the Foya Branca Hotel in São Pedro may reopen.

Itoma is a 32m catamaran that offers dive charters in the summer (for contact information, see *Windsurfing and kitesurfing*, page 259).

SWIMMING The best swimming is probably at the semi-artificial lagoon at Baía das Gatas and also at Baía de Salamansa. Then there's Praia da Laginha, just north of Mindelo. The Hotel Porto Grande and the Mindel Hotel both have swimming pools, the latter a little small but with great views from its rooftop position. The Foya Branca Hotel in São Pedro has a pool that opens to non-guests (for a fee), but the beach there has a vicious shore break, so you should avoid swimming here on rough days. There is a swimming pool at the new marina.

HIKING São Vicente is not one of the hiking islands but there are several rewarding walks. It has a few small mountains and a breathtaking coastline of black rocks blasted by white foam, and white- or black-sand beaches.

You can walk up to the top of Monte Verde (following the cobbled road), or all the way along the coast from Baía das Gatas to Calhau. There are several walks in Calhau (see page 271), ranging from 45 minutes to three hours. You can also walk from the Hotel Foya Branca, in São Pedro, to the lighthouse at the end of the point (two hours' round trip).

CULTURE Music is a reason for lingering in São Vicente. There is live music in many of the restaurants, and events going on at the various cultural centres in town. There are currently no museums, although there are murmurings about developing one at the fort and reopening the museum on Praça Amílcar Cabral. There is also the Centro Cultural do Mindelo which often has exhibitions on. Wandering around looking at the old colonial architecture is also a satisfying occupation.

SIGHTSEEING BY VEHICLE Several operators offer round-island excursions. Cabo Verde Safari offer off-the-beaten-track Land-Rover safaris (for further information, see *Excursions*, page 258). Another option is to hire a taxi with driver. Outside Mindelo there is not much traffic and, with a good map, it should not be problematic to guide yourself around the main sights. Go to Baía das Gatas, Calhau, Monte Verde and São Pedro.

MINDELO

The wide streets, cobbled squares and 19th-century European architecture all contribute to the sense of colonial history in Mindelo.

Most facilities lie not on the coastal road but on the next road back, which at the market end is called Rua de Santo António and, after being bisected by the Rua Libertadores d'Africa (also known as Rua Lisboa), becomes Av 5 de Julho. Most road names in the centre of town have changed, but many of the old signs linger and firms vary as to which street name they use.

WHERE TO STAY There are many hotels in Mindelo at a range of standards and prices: only a small selection is given here. As with the Plateau in Praia, some Mindelo hotels are in old colonial buildings with central atriums, which means that some of their rooms may be internal, with windows opening only onto a shaft.

Casa Azul (10 rooms) Lameirão; 231 0124; www.casa-azul-mindelo.com. Some 4.5km out of Mindelo off the road to Baía das Gatas, this is an artistic & beautiful place to spend a few days, amidst spectacular views. The French owners are often out of the country, so check the hotel is open before you go. **$$$$**

Hotel Porto Grande [262 E3] (50 rooms) Praça Amílcar Cabral; 232 3190; e pgrande@cvtelecom.cv; www.oasisatlantico.com. The large yellow building on one side of the square, this is a pleasant hotel of international standard in a long-established building, with terraces & a swimming pool. Abundant buffet b/fast. Free Wi-Fi. **$$$$**

Casa Café Mindelo [263 D6] (4 rooms) Rua Governador Calheiros; 231 8731; e info@casacafemindelo.com; www.casacafemindelo.com. A peaceful, cool & artistic 1837 colonial house with a large, book-filled living room with internet terminal, & a sun terrace. The rooms are spacious & tasteful but the shower rooms are not en suite (because of architectural constraints). Several management changes have dented their reputation. **$$$**

Mindel Hotel [262 E3] (70 rooms) Av 5 de Julho; 232 8881/2; e mihotel@cvtelecom.cv, mindelhotel@hotmail.com. Just off the main square (Praça Amílcar Cabral) this is a smart, completely neutral, international hotel with all the trimmings, including satellite TV, hairdryers & AC in good-sized comfortably furnished rooms.

Abundant buffet b/fast. Free transport to airport. Visa & MasterCard accepted. **$$$**

Residencial Sodade [263 G5] (23 rooms) 38 Rua Franz Fanon; 230 3200/7556; e residencialsodade@hotmail.com. Up the hill behind the Presidential Palace, the Sodade commands an excellent view over the town & the bay from its rooftop terrace & restaurant. The architecture is pleasant. Rooms are highly variable, from depressing basement hideaways to excellent-quality upstairs rooms & slightly rickety suites. More expensive rooms have fridge, TV & AC. The new Department of Health building being constructed next door may affect the peace & quiet. **$$–$$$**

Aparthotel Avenida [262 D4] (16 rooms) Av 5 de Julho; 232 1178/3435/1176; e aparthtlavenida@cvtelecom.cv. On the road that heads south from the main square (Av Amílcar Cabral) into the centre of town, this is a rather characterless but adequate middling hotel with rooms that have AC & hot water. There are good views of the harbour from one side. **$$**

Casa Colonial [263 F6] (4 rooms) Rua 24 Setembro; m 923 8206; e casacolonial@thinking-iukmedia.com; www.casacolonial.info. A unique chance to stay in a refurbished historic home in the heart of Mindelo. Casa Colonial is one of the oldest houses on the island & has been lovingly restored by a British couple. The house has 3 four-poster beds & can accommodate

10

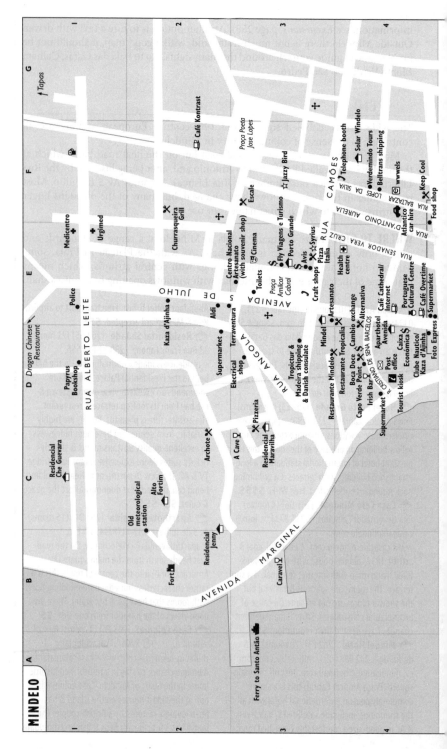

MINDELO

Tapas

Café Kontrast

Praça Poeta José Lopes

CAMÕES

Telephone booth

Solar Windelo

Verdemindo Tours

Beltrans shipping

wwwels

Keep Cool

Food shop

Atlantico car hire

RUA BALTAZAR

RUA D'ANTONIO AURELIA

LOPES DA SILVA

Jazzy Bird

Escale

Churrasqueira Grill

Medicentro

Urgimed

Centro Nacional Artesanato (with souvenir shop)

Cinema

Fly Viagens e Turismo

Porto Grande

Syrius

Avis

Pizza Italia

Health centre

Toilets

Praça Amilcar Cabral

Craft shops

RUA SENADOR VERA CRUZ

Café Cathedral/ Internet

Artesanato

Alternativa

Aparthotel Avenida

Portuguese Cultural Centre

Café Overtime

Supermarket

Police

Kaza d'Ajinha

Aldi

Supermarket

Terraventura

Electrical shop

Tropictur & Madeira shipping & Danish consulate

Mindel

Restaurante Mindelo

Restaurante Tropicalia

Boca Doce

Cambio exchange

Capo Verde Point

Irish Bar

R CRISTIANO DE SENA BARCELOS

Caixa Económica

Post office

Tourist kiosk

Clube Nautico/ Kaza d'Ajinha

Foto Express

Supermarket

RUA ALBERTO LEITE

Dragon Chinese Restaurant

Papyrus Bookshop

RUA ANGOLA

AVENIDA S DE JULHO

Residencial Che Guevara

Alto Fortim

Old meteorological station

Residencial Jenny

Archote

A Cave

Pizzeria

Residencial Maravilha

Fort

Caravel

AVENIDA MARGINAL

Ferry to Santo Antão

262

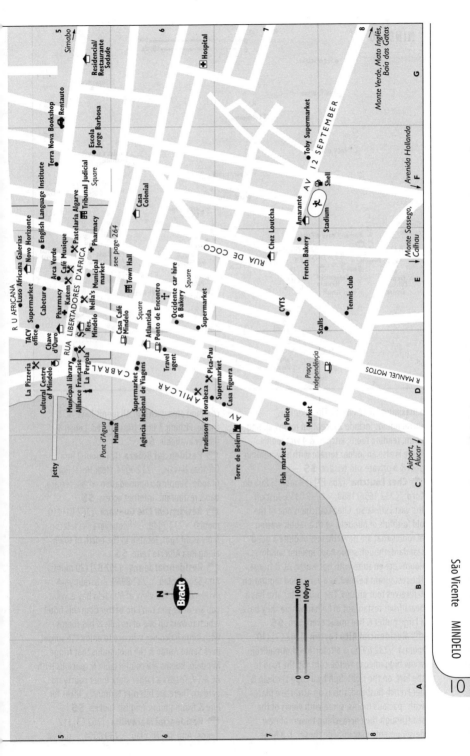

see page 264

São Vicente MINDELO

10

263

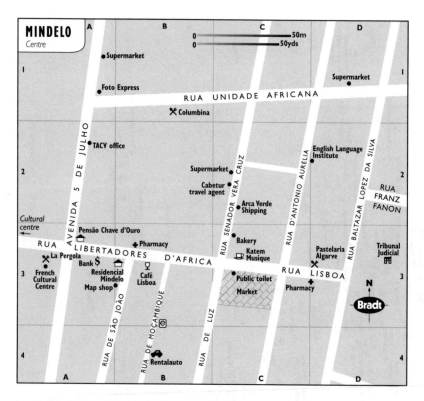

MINDELO
Centre

0 — 50m
0 — 50yds

- Supermarket
- Foto Express

RUA UNIDADE AFRICANA

Supermarket

✕ Columbina

AVENIDA 5 DE JULHO

- TACV office

English Language Institute

Supermarket

Cabetur travel agent

RUA SENADOR VERA CRUZ

Arca Verde Shipping

RUA D'ANTONIO AURELIA

RUA BALTAZAR LOPEZ DA SILVA

RUA FRANZ FANON

Cultural centre →

- Pensão Chave d'Ouro

RUA ✕ LIBERTADORES

- Pharmacy

D'AFRICA

Bakery

Katem Musique

Pastelaria Algarve

Tribunal Judicial

✕ La Pergola

Bank $

Residencial Mindelo

Café Lisboa

Public toilet

RUA LISBOA

✕

French Cultural Centre

Map shop

RUA DE SÃO JOÃO

RUA DE MOÇAMBIQUE

RUA DE LUZ

Market

Pharmacy

N

Bradt

Rentalauto

---

a maximum of 12 guests. The luxurious surroundings include 2 reception rooms, dining room, reading room, kitchen & 4 wet rooms. There is also an indoor terrace with a swimming pool & a private sun terrace. **$$**

Chez Loutcha [263 E7] (24 rooms) Rua do Côco; ☎ 232 1636/1689; m 999 0339. Just off the vast Estrela Sq, Chez Loutcha is one of the old faithfuls of Mindelo, with a rabbit warren of rooms that are nevertheless of quite a good standard, though some have interior windows. Rooms are en suite with hot water, AC & fridge. The restaurant below has a very good reputation, & receives tour groups. The proprietor also has a beachfront restaurant in Calhau where they have a large buffet & live music every Sun. **$$**

Residencial Alto Fortim [262 C2] (10 rooms) ☎ 232 6938; e altofortim@hotmail.com; www.biggamecaboverde.com. Up the road to the fort, on the right. Run by a Cape Verdean & her French husband, this is an attractive place with spacious rooms, some with views of the sea (though the encroaching towers of new developments may impede these), & a huge

common area with bar. All rooms have AC & fridge. Fishing & boat trips offered. Lunch & dinner available. **$$**

Residencial Beleza (21 rooms) Rua Oficinas Navais; ☎ 232 4094. Near Hotel Porto Grande. Simple accommodation with a terrace, bar & restaurant. Internet access. **$$**

Residencial Che Guevara [262 C1] (10 rooms) ☎ 232 2449; e cheguevara@cvtelecom.cv. A pleasant spot, located in the north of town along Rua Alberto Leite. **$$**

Residencial Jenny [262 B2] (20 rooms) Alto São Nicolau; ☎ 232 8969; e hstaubyn@ cvtelecom.cv. If a view of Mindelo Bay is what you are after you can't do better than this hotel which towers up one of its hills & has rooms with large balconies whence to enjoy the sunset over Santo Antão & the mountains that fringe Mindelo. Rooms are comfortable & spacious with AC & TV. There's a rather stark inner courtyard garden. There are internet terminals, bikes for hire & fishing tours. English spoken. **$$**

Residencial Maravilha [262 C3] (12 rooms) Alto São Nicolau; ☎ 230 0094; e gabs@

cvtelecom.cv. Large house with rooms & suites just off the main coast road. **$$**

⌂ **Residencial Mimagui** (5 rooms) Alto São Nicolau; ✆ 232 7953; www.capeverdebooking. com/pub/hotel_lire.php?id=1. Near Residencial Jenny, the Mimagui's studios & apartments offer the same great view of Mindelo Bay & Monte Cara, the iconic mountain of São Vicente. This little *residencial* has large living areas & a terrace. All rooms have kitchens. No meals available. AC & TV. English spoken. **$$**

⌂ **Residencial Mindelo** [264 B3] (11 rooms) Rua de Lisboa; ✆ 230 0863; e djiblam@ cvtelecom.cv. Attractively decorated in white & dark wood, this is a centrally positioned hotel (which can be noisy) with good en-suite rooms with AC, hot water & fridge. Upstairs is a delightful, rooftop b/fast room with views over the harbour & inland over the mountains. Some rooms have only internal windows, however. There's a lounge with TV. **$$**

⌂ **Solar Windelo** [262 G4] (7 rooms) Alto Santo António; ✆ 231 0070; www.windelo.com.

Located in the Praça Nova area, close to the ferries & Laginha Beach, this is the former home of poet & composer Vasco Martins. Offers studio flats & suites. Will arrange excursions & give advice about wind- & kitesurfing. Dinner available on request. Internet. Rooms get cheaper the longer you stay, no charge for children under 5. **$–$$**

⌂ **Amarante** [263 F7] (18 rooms) Av 12 Septembre; e amarante@cvtelecom.cv. Basic budget choice. Rooms are en suite with hot water. **$**

⌂ **Pensão Chave d'Ouro** [264 A3] (15 rooms) Av 5 de Julho; ✆ 232 7050. Centrally positioned on the corner of Rua Libertadores d'Africa & Av 5 de Julho, it claims, at 80 years, to be the oldest hotel in Mindelo & the principal bedrooms still have huge shuttered windows & are equipped with ewers & pitchers. It has great character. Rooms vary dramatically in quality & seem generally on a downward trend; top-floor singles are little more than cupboards with chipboard partitions while it is the first-floor rooms that retain a sliver of old colonial charm. No en-suite bathrooms. There's also a restaurant. **$**

✘ **WHERE TO EAT AND DRINK** Mindelo is packed with restaurants, bars and cafés so only a selection is given here.

✘ **Casa Azul** ✆ 231 0124; ⊕ 12.00–late Wed–Sun. Some 4.5km from the centre of Mindelo: take the road to Baía das Gatas & turn left at Lameirão, following a track up the hill (a taxi should be 300$). Enjoy your meal from this covered terrace, gazing out over the São Vicente landscape towards the mountains & the bay of Mindelo. As with the *residencial*, the restaurant is frequently closed while the owners are in France. **$$$$**

✘ **Restaurante Escale** [262 F3] West of Praça Poeta José Lopes; ⊕ 11.00–14.00 & 18.00– 23.00 Mon–Sat. High-quality cuisine; bookings preferred. **$$$$**

✘ **Archote** [262 C2] At the northern end of town, this is a good choice, with live music almost every night. **$$$**

✘ **Boca Doce** [262 D4] Near the Irish Bar, this is an Italian restaurant & deli. **$$$**

✘ **Chez Loutcha** [263 E7] (see *Where to stay*, opposite) ⊕ 07.00–09.45, 12.00–15.00 & 19.30–23.30. Much-praised restaurant on the ground floor of the hotel of the same name. There is live music Jul–Sep Tue–Thu. **$$$**

✘ **Mindel Hotel Restaurant** [262 E3] Outside on the west side of the hotel. Open-air & a popular place. **$$$**

⊐ **Ponto de Encontro** [263 D6] ✆ 232 8207; ⊕ until 20.00. Smart little cake & coffee shop down the southern half of Av 5 de Julho. **$$$**

✘ **Pizza Italia** [262 E3] Below the Hotel Porto Grande; has a good selection. **$$$**

✘ **Restaurant Saturno** Rua Dr Manuel Duarte; m 991 9185. Thought by some to be the best all-rounder in Mindelo (good cuisine, good ambience) this indoor restaurant is decorated with murals on a planetary theme. **$$$**

✘ **Restaurante Tradissone e Morabeza** [263 D6] On the seafront, Av Amílcar Cabral south end, in an old building; ⊕ Tue–Sun. Has a good selection of meals accompanied by live entertainment after 21.00 Wed–Sat. Also a bar. Arranges dance classes. **$$$**

✘ **Tapas** Fonte Meio; ✆ 232 1656; ⊕ 18.30– 00.00 Mon–Sat. Recently opened, serving a large variety of tasty tapas influenced by Oriental, African & European cuisine. **$$$**

✘ **Pont d'Água** [263 D5] The new marina houses shops selling surf gear, an upmarket hairdresser & a brasserie & stylish restaurant. You can also rent a sunbed & lounge on a terrace by the swimming pool. The restaurant menu includes salads, meat & seafood as well as some rarities such as a vegetarian stir-fry. Live music at w/ends. $$–$$$

✘ **Cantina da Associação dos Marítimos** Av Marginal, Laginha Beach; ☎ 231 9348; m 996 2922; ⏱ 09.00–01.00. When you get tired of eating fish, try this little place with an unprepossessing name; specialities include steak with green peppercorn sauce, & profiteroles. $$

♀ **Caravel** [262 B3] At the northern end of the main beach, just before the road bends away from the coast, this is a slightly windswept esplanade but worth going to for its beachside location. Becomes a disco later on. $$

✘ **Casa Café Mindelo** [263 D6] Under the *pensão* of the same name, this high-ceilinged café, in one of the old colonial buildings of Mindelo, is a vibrant place. Its philosophy, according to the Portuguese owner, is to welcome all; tourists, locals, businesspeople, & create an interesting space where there are sometimes concerts or conferences. Lunches, snacks, drinks. $$

✘ **Chave d'Ouro** [264 A3] ⏱ 12.00–13.00 & 19.00–23.00 daily for meals & all day for cakes. A beautifully designed cake & coffee shop upstairs in the hotel of the same name. $$

✘ **Clube Nautico** [262 D4] ⏱ 08.30–00.30 Mon–Sat, 17.00–00.30 Sun. A vast space in a building beside the old customs house on the coastal road, decorated on a nautical theme & with sails for shade. Has developed a slightly dubious reputation. $$

✘ **Dragon Chinese** Cha d'Alecrim. Serving Chinese food to the migrant workers at the port, this ordinary-looking restaurant has a decent reputation. $$

✘ **La Bodeguita** Rua Camões, near Hotel Porto Grande; m 995 6113; ⏱ 12.00–15.00 & 18.00–late. Little restaurant & bar with Che Guevara/Castro posters on the walls, & Cuban & Caribbean music. Good food with many influences. $$

✘ **La Pergola** [264 A3] (see French Cultural Centre, page 268). $$

✘ **La Pizzeria** [263 D5] ⏱ 12.00–15.00 & 18.00–23.00. Next to Residencial Maravilha. Serves excellent pizza & pasta dishes. $$

✘ **Pica Pau** [263 D6] Rua Santo António 42, 1 road in from the coastal road, to the south of the city; ☎ 232 8207. A bit of a Mindelo institution, this restaurant is as eccentric as it is minuscule, its walls plastered with notes of praise from previous customers. Specialising in seafood, it is most proud of its *arroz de marisco* (seafood risotto). $$

✘ **Sodade** [263 G5] This rooftop restaurant offers an escape from the bustle of town, with a panoramic view that is best before dark. Above the hotel of the same name. $$

⊔ **Columbina** [264 B1] Previously named Luso Africana Galerias, Rua Africana. Tucked away along a passage that opens out into a courtyard, this is a café with other amenities such as a public toilet (with shower), boutiques & internet café. $

✘ **Laginha** ☎ 232 5468; ⏱ 07.00–23.00. At the beach of the same name, this snack bar serves traditional dishes (*cachupa, feijoada*) on a terrace. $

⊔ **Pastelaria Algarve** [264 D3] Rua Libertadores d'Africa. Just down from the Presidential Palace, it has a vine-covered outside terrace from which to watch the world go by. $

There is a bakery near the Residencial Amarante.

ENTERTAINMENT AND NIGHTLIFE Live music abounds in Mindelo and most restaurants have a Cape Verdean night. Try Restaurante Tradisson e Morabeza (above), the French Cultural Centre (afternoons) or Archote, among others. Clubs in Mindelo tend to open at about 22.30–23.00; people start arriving about 00.00–00.30 and they get lively by about 02.30, emptying at about 05.00. On a Sunday people generally stop somewhere for *cachupa* on their way home. Entry to most clubs costs 200–300$. For a discussion of music and dancing, see *Chapter 1, Background Information*, page 40.

♀ **A Cave** [262 D3] ☎ 232 7802. In Alto São Nicolau, close to the Hotel Maravilha, it caters to an older, 30-plus crowd.

♀ **Café Lisboa** [264 B3] Impromptu jamming sessions with DJ at w/ends.

♀ **Caravel** [262 B3] (see *Where to eat and drink*, opposite).
♀ **Jazzy Bird** [262 F3] ⊕ w/ends. Local musicians often meet here for an informal sessions. A good place for chilling out.
♀ **Katem Musique** [264 C3] (previously Café Musique) Opposite the municipal market; ⊕ from about 23.00 Thu–Sun. A very popular venue that mixes reggae & hip hop with traditional music.

♀ **Kav'** ⊕ w/ends. Regarded by many as the best place in town.
♀ **Praça Amílcar Cabral** [262 E3] At 19.00 on Sun, the municipal band plays here.
☆ **Syrius** [262 E3] ☎ 232 3190. Under the Hotel Porto Grande, it is free to hotel guests & 200$ to everyone else. Tends to be under 30s.

A little outside the very centre of the city are some other popular nightspots: **Le Bateau** in Fonte Francês and **Hi Step** in Fonte Ines.

OTHER PRACTICALITIES

Airlines TACV, Av 5 de Julho [264 A2] (☎ 232 1524; ⊕ 08.00–12.00 & 14.30–17.30 Mon–Fri, 09.00–11.30 Sat). Agência Nacional de Viagens, Av da Republica (☎ 231 1115; ⊕ 08.00–12.30 & 14.30–18.00 Mon–Fri). For most internal and international flights.

Banks Caixa Económica, Av 5 de Julho, near Aparthotel Avenida (⊕ 08.00–15.00 Mon–Fri). Banco Cómercial do Atlântico, Praça Amílcar Cabral (⊕ 08.00–14.30 Mon–Fri). Also on Rua Libertadores d'Africa. ATMs at the banks near the Porto Grande Hotel.

Hospital The Baptisto, at the southeast corner of town (☎ 232 7355/231 1879). There are two new private medical centres, both near the police station at the western part of town: Urgimed (☎ 230 0170); and Medicentro (☎ 231 8515).

Internet There are many internet cafés, including one beside the Hotel Porto Grande on Praça Amílcar Cabral, and Global Net on Rua de Moçambique. There is free Wi-Fi in the main *praças*.

Pharmacies Several, including a large one at the top of Rua Libertadores d'Africa [264 B3].

Police (☎ 231 4631). At the market end of the coast road.

Post office Rua Cristiano de Sena Barcelos [262 D4] (⊕ 08.00–12.00 & 14.00–17.30 Mon–Fri).

Shopping A good array of Cape Verdean products can be found at the Centro Culturel do Mindelo (see *What to see and do*, below). Also try walking up Av 5 de Julho, heading north from its junction with Rua Cristiano de Sena Barcelos. There are several places, such as Alternativa (on the first corner) or Terraventura Cabo Verde. Crafts, mainly from mainland Africa, can be bought in many shops around town; music from a shop on Rua d'António Aurelia. For books try Terra Nova on Rua Franz Fanon. Supermarkets are common; try Fragata Overtime, Av 5 de Julho, which is one of the few open over lunch and late at night. There's a big supermarket, Copa, on the same street as the stadium. There are several good-sized mini markets including one near the Shell station on the way to Calhau and an Italian deli near the Irish Bar.

Tourist information Rua Cristiano de Sena Barçelos [262 D4]. Here there is a kiosk (🕐 *09.00–13.00 & 15.00–18.30 Mon–Fri, 09.00–14.00 Sat*), which may have information and definitely sells maps and postcards.

Miscellaneous

French Cultural Centre (Alliance Française de Mindelo) [264 A3] (🕐 *07.00–19.00 Mon–Fri, 08.00–12.30 Sat*). Has a library & courtyard café, La Pergola (**$$**), where there is often live music in the afternoons.

Biblioteca Municipal [263 D5] (🕐 *09.30–12.30 & 15.00–19.00 Mon–Fri, 09.30–13.00 Sat*). On the first floor it has a collection of books on the history of Mindelo, including some on the British presence.

Centro Cultural do Mindelo [263 D5] (🕐 *08.00–12.00 & 15.00–19.00 Mon–Fri, 08.00–12.00 Sat*). Located in the old customs house on the coastal road, it houses the Instituto Caboverdiano do Livro, which sells a wide variety of publications in Portuguese and Creole, a souvenir shop and exhibitions.

Public toilets In the square in front of the Hotel Porto Grande; at Columbina (previously Luso Africana Galerias) (see *Where to eat and drink*, page 266).

WHAT TO SEE AND DO Sturdy English architecture, with sloping roofs and the odd bow window, is pervasive in Mindelo. There is the old **Miller and Cory's building**, now the ferry ticket agency; the old residence of the employees of Shell, now the **Portuguese consulate**; and the **Western Telegraph building**, beside TACV.

A wander through the city should begin with a stroll up to the fort, **Fortim d'El Rei** [262 B2], on the headland to the east of town (Alto São Nicolau). From there you can understand the layout of the city. This hilltop fortress became a prison in the 1930s. In 1934, the militia descended from Fortim on to a food riot incited by a famous carpenter, Ambrósio, who led the looting of the food stores in the Customs House. His story is the subject of plays today. Many of São Vicente's notable rebels, including resistance fighters, were imprisoned in the fort in the 1960s before being deported to Angola. Now the headland affords a more peaceful scene: the busy port and Mindelo beyond it, the hills curling round the magnificent harbour; the strange stump of **'Bird Island'** poking out of the harbour; and Santo Antão. **Monte Cara**, or Face Mountain, on the other side of the harbour, is one of several places in the archipelago where the sharp erosion has sculpted a remarkable human profile out of the mountains. Beside the fort is the radio station, Mira D'Ouro.

On your return along the coast road, just after the port, is a **monument** surmounted by an eagle, commemorating the first air crossing of the southern Atlantic in 1922 by Sacadura Cabral and Gago Coutinho. They stopped here after their leg from the Canaries.

Follow Av Marginal south with its shady trees down the centre of the road. You will pass some fine old storehouses dating from the height of the shipping days: many of them have been transformed for new uses. Opposite the pier is the **Old Customs House**, built in 1858 and extended in the early 1880s. It is now the Cultural Centre of Mindelo.

Keep going and you will pass, on your right, the **Torre de Belém** [263 D7], built in imitation of the monument of the same name in Lisbon and which housed the Portuguese governor from the 1920s. It was restored, thanks to the Portuguese, in 2002.

Ahead and in to the left lies the market and the vast **Estrela Square**. One half of the square has been filled with permanent market stalls, and on the wall at the end of each row an artist has depicted a scene from the history of Mindelo, painted onto ceramic tiles. The pictures are lifted straight from photographs taken in the early 1900s. They allow us to imagine Mindelo at its economic height: great wooden piers, cranes and rail tracks forever hauling coal onshore to the storage bunkers; the grand and busy customs house; the ships' chandlers lining the front street. Old men wandering Mindelo today will reminisce about the golden time in their youth when there was plenty of work, abundant food, ships jostling for space in the harbour, coal piled up high – and it always rained. From there, head north towards the Presidential Palace, passing through the **Pracinha de Igreja**, the oldest part of town where the first houses were built and where there is a pretty church, constructed in 1862.

After the church you will pass the **town hall** (*câmara municipal*) [263 E6]. Built between 1850 and 1873, it initially housed the Aguas de Madeiral water company founded by John and George Rendall.

In front of the town hall and facing onto Rua Lisboa, is the **municipal market** [264 C3], a beautifully light and airy two-storey building begun in 1874, and extended in the 1930s with Portuguese influence. It was restored in the 1980s.

In the middle of town is the spotless, pink **Presidential Palace**, which is not open to the public. The ground floor was built in 1873 as a venue for official receptions. In the 1930s, the second storey was added as well as the frothy white bits – and it became the Presidential Palace. It is now the Supreme Court (Tribunal Judicial).

Behind the palace (ie: to the east) is the **Escola Jorge Barbosa** [263 F5] which has served a variety of purposes since its construction began in 1859. It has been an army barracks (the square was for parades), governor's office, army hospital and then, in the early 1920s, the influential grammar school, Liceu Nacional Infante D Henrique, important in fostering Cape Verde's independence movement.

Just out of town you can walk to **Morro Branco**, 10km there and back along the shore road to the west. This is not scenic – probably only worth it if you have exhausted every other possibility on the island. First you pass the Shell oil terminal, and then rusting shipwrecks close to shore. Do not attempt to take photographs as you approach Morro Branco, as the soldiers in the barracks at the end of the road get jumpy.

BEACHES Beyond the fort, to the north, is the long sandy beach of Laginha, popular with the locals.

OTHER PLACES TO VISIT

Baía das Gatas and Calhau are the settings for weekend parties: vibrant on Saturdays and Sundays, abandoned during the week. Monte Verde is stunning on a clear day but rather unexciting otherwise. A trip round the island is not a conventional aesthetic experience but it is a profound one.

MONTE VERDE A taxi costs 2,000$ return. To walk to the summit take a taxi or *aluguer* along the Baía das Gatas road for 8km as far as the right turn to Monte Verde's summit. A good cobbled road zig-zags up the north and east sides of the mountain to the top. You will see a big tank on the way up, on the left, a relatively young project to gather the Monte Verde mist to irrigate the crops on the terracing below.

THE BRITISH IN CAPE VERDE

Golf, cricket and a smattering of English vocabulary were some of the lighter legacies left by the British in Cape Verde. Their involvement with the archipelago was sporadic but widespread. It included the dominance of Maio in the heyday of its salt-collecting years; the brief 'ownership' of Santo Antão (see page 276); the drastic sacking of Santiago by Francis Drake and the monopolising of the orchil trade in several islands including Brava.

The British have also contributed much to understanding the natural history of the islands. Charles Darwin spent three weeks recording fauna and flora here (see *Chapter 6, Santiago*, page 169) – his first initiation to the tropics on the famous voyage of the *Beagle*. Since Darwin, there have been others. T Vernon Wollaston visited in the 1870s and 1880s, and collected numerous beetles, moths and butterflies which are stored at the Natural History Museum in London. But it is in Mindelo that the British are now best remembered. They left a golf club that claims to be one of the largest non-grass courses in the world. Founded in 1893, it is the oldest sports association in Cape Verde and hosted the first international golf championship, in 1906.

They also left a feisty cricket team, whose members are now in their eighties. English-derived words that have entered the Creole language were gathered by Frank Xavier da Cruz in 1950. They include: *ariope* (hurry up), *blaquéfela* (black fellow), *bossomane* (boss man), *cachupa* (believed to have been derived from ketchup), *chatope* (shut up), *salongue* (so long!), *ovataime* (overtime), *tanquiu* (thank you), *fulope* (full up) and *ovacote* (overcoat).

At the summit the mist may be down, in which case there is little to see but the radio antennae, guarded by three soldiers and a cat.

On a clear day, however, the view is of a forest of black, misshapen crags, and the harbour beyond. Sunset beyond the forbidding peaks of Santo Antão is fabulous.

SALAMANSA Only ten minutes' drive from the capital, in São Vicente terms, this is a thriving place – people actually live here, drawing their livelihood from the sea, and there is a shop. But there is really no reason to visit other than to walk on the beautiful beach and muse on why this fishing village exists at all: it's too exposed for launching boats and the fishing fleet is drawn up some 5km away on the other side of the peninsula. The beach is not always safe for swimming but often has good conditions for kite- and windsurfing. Kitesurf NOW (e *ola@kitesurfnow.eu; www.kitesurfnow.eu*) offers lessons on this beach and others.

BAÍA DAS GATAS This resort is 12km from town. During the week it has the feel of an English seaside resort out of season. In front of rows of boarded-up bungalows, a pack of smooth-haired dogs trots along the wind-whipped sand. There's a children's play area with gaunt metal swings and slides reminiscent of gallows, and at the extreme end of the bay, a low pier. However, it's a brilliant place to fish where you can easily pull in two-pounders from the shore and then light a fire and grill your own supper. It's also great for swimming because of a natural barrier that creates a huge lagoon. At weekends the place is much more colourful.

During the full moon of August people descend on Baía das Gatas for a weekend of music, dancing, eating and general revelry. The festival began as the best of them do – just a few musicians gathering for all-night jamming sessions.

Now bands come from all over the archipelago and from abroad and there is horse racing and watersports.

As you drive back out of the village there is a ruin on the shore on your left. This is the old fish-processing factory – it is here that the Salamansa fishermen draw their boats up. If the wind is in the right quarter you may be lucky enough to see them running home under full sail. They venture as far afield as the uninhabited island of Santa Luzia, staying overnight there and returning with cold boxes full of snake-like moray eels, squid and grouper (like giant, bloated goldfish but more tasty).

Getting there At weekends there are *alugueres* which cost 100$ one-way. A taxi costs 1,600$ return.

Where to stay and eat

✗ **Archote** 232 3916; m 994 2751; ⊕ w/ends for buffets & live music. Look out for the sign on the left as you enter town. Another branch of a Mindelo favourite.

✗ **Foya Grill** ⊕ w/ends only. On the left as you enter town. $$

✗ **Grills Baía** Next to Takeaway Átlanta; 232 6100; e grills@cvtelecom.cv; ⊕ all day. This branch of a restaurant in Mindelo of the same name serves fresh seafood & other dishes. $$

✗ **Restaurante Loyd** 232 6868; m 995 6112; ⊕ 12.30–16.00 & 19.30–23.00. Turn left on to a dirt road before the fishing boats & follow the road for 200m. The restaurant is on the left. International cuisine served outdoors under covered pergolas. $$

✗ **Takeaway Átlanta** 232 7500/6684; m 991 6211. Occupying 2 blue & white buildings, the restaurant has a good view of the beach while the *residencial* is a little further back. Has 9 rooms for rent which are currently being refurbished, but will be en suite with hot water & AC ($$).

CALHAU

Getting there There's a more-or-less hourly bus for the 20-minute journey to the seaside town of Calhau (150$). A taxi will cost 2,000$ for a round trip. You could also walk there from Baía das Gatas, along the coast (two hours).

A drive along the 18km road to Calhau is like a guided tour through all the ecological problems facing both the island and Cape Verde as a whole. The road follows Ribeira Calhau, and takes just 25 minutes.

First the road passes through an area where there is a reafforestation programme. Then, as you continue southeast, you will see Monte Verde on your left. The little village on its western slopes is **Mato Inglês**. Lack of water has driven away all but one or two people.

A few kilometres further on is a right turn for **Madeiral**, a small village in the shadow of Topona Mountain. Old folk claim that the village was once supplied by water running down from the green slopes of the mountain above. Now the mountain has the same scorched, dusty aspect as the rest of São Vicente. Madeiral, like the island's two or three other inhabited villages, is dependent on desalinated water tankered in from Mindelo.

Past Madeiral the *ribeira* opens out and the valley floor is scattered with small squares of green. This is agriculture under siege – strong stone walls keep marauding goats out. The water that the windmills draw from the ground is becoming progressively saltier. In the search for sweet water, wells are pushed deeper, and windmills require stronger winds to keep the water flowing. In such precarious conditions, water-storage tanks are indispensable. Meanwhile the search for water goes on: the piles of earth across the valley floor mark the places where boreholes have been sunk but have struck only dry earth and rock.

It takes a particular kind of personality to like Calhau. The village is a windswept wasteland of gravel and brown sand, protruding from which are the grey carcasses of half-finished breeze-block buildings. Brown peaks tower behind it while, in front, desperate waves obliterate themselves against the black, rocky coast. Nevertheless its proximity to the city makes it a reasonable place to base yourself if you don't like the hustle and bustle of Mindelo, and from here you can explore the rest of the island, occupy yourself with some interesting walks or just relax for a while. The land between the mountains and the sea is just asking to be built on. Down the southern part of the bay optimists have indeed built apartments and there is a beautiful hotel.

A roundabout joining the new road to Baía das Gatas tells you that you have reached the village. People live here still, and fish, but as with every other village, water is the problem. Calhau is alive and bustling at weekends, however, with city folk coming to their seaside retreats.

Where to stay and eat

✗ **Chez Loutcha** ⏲ 13.00–16.00 Sun only. Clearly signposted down a rough track on the right as you enter Calhau (after the turning to the volcanoes), this is run by the proprietor of Chez Loutcha, the *pensão* in Mindelo, who opens up on Sun. There is a buffet spread, with around 20 dishes, you can eat as much as you like for 1,400$, & there is live music. $$$

🏠 **Residencial Goa** (10 rooms) Turn right at the roundabout on the new road; ☎ 232 9355; m 996 2696; e goacalhau@goa-mindelo.com; www.goa-mindelo.com. This French-owned hotel has a stark, minimalist architecture that fits well with the surrounding landscape. The panoramic view encompasses Santo Antão, São Nicolau, Santa Luzia, Raso & Branco. Rooms are huge, striking & of a high quality, with balconies on the first floor overlooking the sea. With its living area

& quiet location the hotel is good for families. B/fast is served on either the seaside terrace or the inside courtyard, & dinner can be arranged. Free Wi-Fi. Charming hosts Stan & Rafael are very knowledgeable & will arrange some excellent walks, excursions & fishing. Prices are on a sliding scale depending on length of stay. $$$

✗ **Restaurant Pepeneró** Close to Residencial Goa, this spot serves homemade pasta but is not always open. $$

✗ **Bar Restaurant Hamburg** m 983 0916; ⏲ lunch & evenings daily. A spot of colour on the landscape. Turn left after the telecom tower & look for a blue building with black-&-white pebbles on the walls. Famous for its simple but good food, this little spot gets busy at the w/end. $

What to see and do There are various good fishing spots within easy access of the village, as well as surfing spots on Praia Grande, Sandy Beach and Topim Beach in the south. In summer turtles nest on the beach directly in front of Residencial Goa (do not go to the beach at night without asking advice as it is illegal to disturb them). There is a natural swimming pool at the foot of the volcano, offering some pleasant snorkelling.

There are also several walking trails. It takes about an hour to walk up to the Calhau volcano, to the north of the village. It takes three hours to do a circuit of the headland to the north (Panilinha). **Vulcão Viana**, to the south, can be ascended from a track that runs down its eastern side: the round trip from the track takes about 45 minutes. The oasis of Santa Luzia Terra can be reached in around two hours (you can arrange to be collected). You can also walk to Baía das Gatas, which also takes about two hours.

From Calhau you can also arrange a trip to the uninhabited island of **Santa Luzia** and have a great view of Raso and Branco islands, and even São Nicolau in the distance. See the São Nicolau chapter (page 307) for more information on Raso.

SÃO PEDRO An *aluguer* from Mindelo will cost 100–200$ to São Pedro, which is just 1km past the airport. It is a little fishing village with a shop and a bar, colourful fishing boats drawn up on the beach and an air of tatty quaintness.

Where to stay and eat

⌂ **Foya Branca Resort** (72 rooms, 6 villas) \230 7400; e foyabranca@cvtelecom.cv; www.foyabranca.com. This is on the other side of the bay & has nothing tatty or quaint about it. The first (& currently the only) beach resort hotel in São Vicente, it is dedicated to seclusion with white walls, well-maintained gardens & 3 pools. The restaurant is very good & caters for vegetarians. Rooms have spacious balconies: ask to be housed in the new complex, where they are bigger & have a better view. The hotel is quiet during the week & more vibrant at w/ends when local families come down for the day. There's a shuttle bus to Mindelo. The hotel offers windsurfing, bicycle hire, diving, horseriding, fishing & boat hire. There is a gym, tennis & excursions. Free regular bus into town. **$$$**

✗ **Bistro Santo André** \231 5100; m 971 1765. Located behind the Foya Branca resort in São Pedro Beach, this tiny restaurant opened by Swedish resident Per Tamm has a terrace where you can enjoy their famous suckling pig or Brazilian *feijoada*. $$$

What to see and do The beach is the main attraction, but there are unexpected currents in the sea so take local advice and don't swim alone.

SANTA LUZIA The smallest island of the archipelago (anything smaller is an islet), Santa Luzia is 35km² and uninhabited. Its highest peak, Topona, is 395m. It is extremely dry and barren. It has a rugged north coast and a south coast of scenic beaches and dunes. No seabirds are known to breed there any more.

Santa Luzia lay uninhabited until the 17th century, when it was granted to Luis de Castro Pireira. It has mainly been used for livestock raising when there has been rain. In the 19th century, about 20 people continued these activities. A family of goatherds lived there until the 1960s. To reach the island, go to Calhau and enquire amongst the fishermen about the possibility of accompanying a journey. To charter a fisherman for the day will probably cost about 12,000$ and the journey takes about two hours.

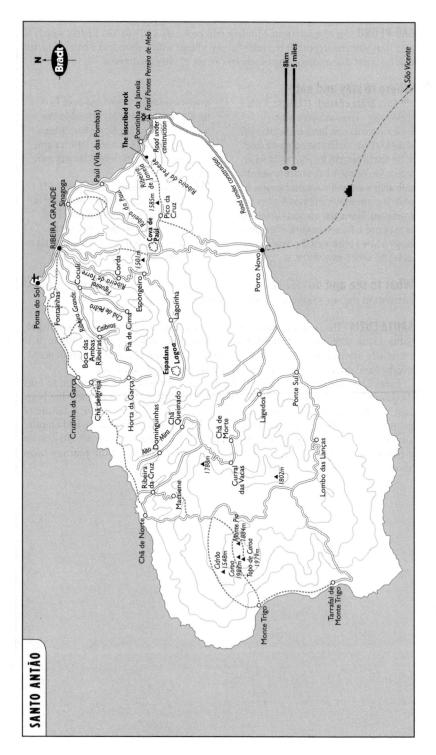

SANTO ANTÃO

São Vicente

8km
5 miles

Ponta do Sol

RIBEIRA GRANDE

Sinagoga

Paul (Vila das Pombas)

The inscribed rock

Pontinha da Janela

Farol Pontes Perreira de Melo

Road under construction

Ribeira de Janela

Ribeira da Prata

Ribeira do Paul

Cova de Paul

1585m

Pico da Cruz

Porto Novo

Fontainhas

Cocull

Figueiral

Ribeira de Torre

Corda

1501m

Espongeiro

Lagoinha

Ribeira Grande

Chã de Pedra

Caibros

Pia de Cima

Espadaná

Lagoá

Boca das Ambas Ribeiras

Chã de Igreja

Horta da Garça

Cruzinha da Garça

Chã Queimado

Alto Mira

DomingUinhas

Chã de Morte

Lagedos

Ponte Sul

Ribeira da Cruz

Chã de Norte

Mattiene

1788m

Curral das Vacas

1802m

Lombo das Lanças

Cidrão 1548m

Coroa 1987m

Monte Pra 1884m

Topo de Coroa 1979m

Monte Trigo

Tarrafal de Monte Trigo

11

Santo Antão

The rugged peaks and canyons of northeast Santo Antão are one of the world's great landscape dramas. Precarious roads trace the tops of its ridges giving sheer views on both sides down 1,000m cliffs. The people live in these deep valleys, their worlds enclosed by colossal volcanic walls. As you ascend the valleys on foot you discover in astonishment that their settlements reach high into the cliffsides, clinging to ledges and surrounded by banana trees and cassava. In the west of the island is an apocalyptic and inaccessible landscape of steep walls, jagged edges and harsh ravines.

There is a legend that Santo Antão's precipices defeated a bishop who, while visiting the more distant of his Cape Verde flock, tried to reach Ribeira Grande from Paúl across the mountains. It is said that halfway through the journey, having scaled a terrifying cliff, he lost his nerve and could move neither forwards nor backwards. And so the bishop remained, supplied regularly by the more sure-footed of the island who would arrive with tents, food and clothing for him. He waited in a crevice until a road was built to conduct him away in safety.

HIGHLIGHTS

There is one overwhelming attraction: **hiking** the *ribeiras*. Non-hikers can also appreciate the landscape from the spectacular **drives** over the ridges and along the *ribeira* floors. The mountain road from Porto Novo to Ribeira Grande is one of the highlights of a visit to Cape Verde and is worth travelling along even if you must return immediately to São Vicente. There are several rare **birds** to watch out for and **fishing** is possible with the locals.

SUGGESTED ITINERARY AND NUMBER OF DAYS If you are interested in hiking, allow at least three clear days in which to tackle some of the classic Santo Antão walks: you could easily spend more than this if you are set on really exploring the island. If you are determined to explore the west, allow plenty of time because roads are bad and transport infrequent. If you are not into hiking, you could still fill a couple of days with sightseeing by vehicle and wandering through the valley of Paúl. A day trip is better than nothing, but ensure it is well organised beforehand to avoid wasting valuable time in negotiations with local drivers.

LOWLIGHTS

Santo Antão plans to have a beach tourism industry but this has not yet taken off. There are sandy beaches but some are hard to access and others disappear during the winter, and swimming is generally only safe in the summer months.

There are virtually no organised watersports, though this may change. The hotels, while perfectly adequate, clean and friendly, are not luxurious (apart from Santo Antão Art Resort in Porto Novo, and others in the pipeline) but this is part of the island's charm.

BACKGROUND INFORMATION

HISTORY Fertile and green but mountainous and inaccessible, Santo Antão remained without much of a population for the first 90 years after its discovery on 17 January 1462. If people knew it in the 15th century it was because of its use in the mapping of an imaginary line down the Atlantic that divided Spanish and Portuguese colonial rights. The Treaty of Tordesillas in 1494 agreed that this north–south line would pass 370 leagues west of Santo Antão. Land to the west of that line was to belong to Spain. Land to the east – including the islands themselves and Brazil, which protrudes quite far into the southern Atlantic – was to belong to Portugal.

A series of people leased Santo Antão from the Portuguese Crown, the first in 1548. In the 1600s, its administration and ownership were granted to the Count of Santa Cruz. It was the son of the fourth Count of Santa Cruz, the Marquess of Gouveia, who was to add brief drama to Santo Antão from as far away as Europe. In Portugal he kidnapped Mariana de Penha de França, the wife of a Portuguese nobleman, and escaped with her from Portugal to England where, having run out of money, he mortgaged Santo Antão to the English in 1732. This went down very badly back in Cape Verde and the Portuguese soon drove the English away.

After that excitement the 18th century granted Santo Antão a little more recognition. Ribeira Grande achieved the status of *vila* in 1732 and, two decades later, Bishop Jacinto Valente chose to settle there, having rejected the crumbling and unhealthy capital of Santiago. It was to be another 120 years before Santo Antão was made capital of the *Barlavento* – she was the richest, most populated and least malarial of the northern islands at this time.

Perhaps it was the effect of living between the high and menacing walls of the *ribeiras*, but the people of Ribeira Paúl and the people of Ribeira Grande had a major argument in 1894 about their representation in Portugal. The people of Ribeira Grande decided to make war on their cousins down the road, armed themselves with guns, clubs and sticks and roared down the coast.

The people of Paúl were ready, though, and destroyed the road so that no-one could cross it. None, that was, but an athletic horse which leapt across the opening, whisking to safety a lucky inhabitant of Ribeira Grande who had been on the wrong side of the road. The people of Paúl fared the worse in the conflict – many of their men were later imprisoned and spent a lot of money regaining their freedom.

The island lost its position as *Barlavento* capital in 1934, when the seat of government was transferred to São Vicente. It also recently lost its important role as supplier of water to its barren cousin across the channel, when a desalinisation plant was constructed on São Vicente. Santo Antão was plagued with an impenetrable interior and also the problem that its only good port – Tarrafal – was a long way from its agricultural area. In recent decades the port of Porto Novo and the road between it and Ribeira Grande have improved the situation slightly.

SANTO ANTÃO TODAY Santo Antão is a poor island with high unemployment and has its eyes fixed on tourism and agriculture as its principal routes to economic success. As a result there are mighty plans for this mighty island. The Minister of Infrastructure, Transport and the Sea has promised a road to Tarrafal and to Cruzinha da Garça, as well as an airport. Developers are talking about turning the east of Porto Novo into a tourist area, centred on Escoralet (also known as Curraletes) beach. Local leaders prophesise tourist developments all along the new road to Tarrafal. Already there is extensive building in Vila das Pombas.

Whether this development can be achieved without blighting Santo Antão's appeal is a moot point. As the co-owner of Pedracin Village (see page 289), businessman José Pedro Oliveira, told *Iniciativa* magazine: 'I believe Santo Antão is one of the jewels of tourism in Cape Verde, if we don't destroy it before. Building a big hotel in a valley or riverbed is the same as destroying it.'

GEOGRAPHY Santo Antão is second only to Santiago in size, at 779km^2, and second only to Fogo in the height of its greatest mountain – the volcano crater Topo da Coroa at 1,979m. It is the most northerly and the most westerly of the islands with a mountain range stretching from the northeast to the southwest.

The population is about 49,000 and the island is divided into three municipalities: Porto Novo, covering the west and centred on the port town in the south; Paúl, and Ribeira Grande, which includes the town of that name (also known as Povoação) and the town of Ponta do Sol. The fertile areas are in the northeast, where there is often moisture on the peaks and intense agriculture, making use of permanent streams in two of the *ribeiras* – Paúl and Janela. The rest of the island is barren apart from around Tarrafal de Monte Trigo to the southwest where there is some water, which is used for irrigation.

Santo Antão's annual rainfall has plunged over the last century by about 45%. Engineers have been considering making better use of the island's one abundant source of water: the annual floods during storms between August and November, which can run off the mountains and into the sea in volumes of millions of cubic metres. Conservation dams in the upper mountains could store the run-off and be used for irrigation lower down the valleys.

NATURAL HISTORY
Protected areas There are natural parks at Moroços, the area encompassing Cova, Ribeira Paúl and Ribeira Torre, and Topo da Coroa; there's a natural reserve at Cruzinha and a protected landscape at Pombas.

An old administrator in Santo Antão and captain of the Portuguese colonial army, Serafim Oliveira, introduced to Paúl a substantial number of plants and trees, most importantly *caneca* (sugarcane – the only ingredient of *grogue*), a type of mango tree and *jaqueira* (breadfruit tree), which grows to be very large and gives fruit all year.

Turtles nest here on the few remaining sandy beaches (almost all the sand has been removed illegally for construction), most notably in Cruzinha da Graça, where the small fishing community has started a conservation programme with the assistance of the fisheries research institute, INDP.

ECONOMY Fishing, agriculture and the extraction of *pozzolana* (a volcanic dust used in cement making) are the economy's mainstays. But the island, which has the largest cultivated area of Cape Verde, has in the past been frustrated in its desires to export agricultural products to the tourist islands of Sal and Boavista because of a 24-year embargo implemented as the result of millipede blight. This embargo has now been lifted for the majority of crops. There are small but growing industries producing *grogue* and its variants, herbs and jams.

HAZARDS The water is calm for swimming at some beaches in the summer months (May–September) but the ocean is wild with a powerful undertow for the rest of the year. Take local advice.

During the rainy season and for some time thereafter, some roads may become impassable and some possibly dangerous.

The west is very remote, waterless and hard to navigate. Hikers should be well prepared and it is essential to take a local guide. Elsewhere, the principal walks, though punishingly steep at times, are mostly on cobbled footpaths which can lull your mind should you decide to explore elsewhere on your own. These are high mountains, remote at the top, with racing mists. Paths can fade into pebbly gullies, demanding a scramble. Between December and February temperatures drop to 10°C above 1,000m.

The hospital in Ribeira Grande is oversubscribed and may not be up to dealing with your hiking injury, in which case you will need to get the ferry to São Vicente to find medical attention.

FESTIVALS The big festival of the year is São João Baptista on 24 June. It begins with a 20km procession of the cross from the mountains down into Porto Novo – done to the accompaniment of drumming. On arrival in Porto Novo, the people begin a party which lasts all week. Paúl's Municipality Day on 13 June is also a great festival, with a month-long build-up, horse races and dancing.

17 January	Municipality Day (Ribeira Grande)
3 May	Santa Cruz (Coculi)
13 June	Santa António das Pombas (Paúl) (see above)
24 June	São João Baptista (see above)
29 June	São Pedro (Chã de Igreja)
15 August	Nossa Sra da Piedade (Janela)
24 September	Nossa Sra do Livramento (Ponta do Sol)
7 October	Nossa Sra do Rosário (Ribeira Grande)
29 November	Santo André (Ribeira de Cruz)

GETTING THERE AND AWAY

BY AIR There are currently no flights to Santo Antão. The runway at Ponta do Sol suffers from dangerous crosswinds.

BY FERRY Almost everyone travelling to Santo Antão takes the ferry from Mindelo to Porto Novo. The hour-long crossing is beautiful: the view of São Vicente, with the forbidding mountains behind Mindelo, and its guardian rock erupting from the harbour, is stunning.

In Mindelo the two ferries, which are run by different companies, have separate offices in the same building down at the port. In Porto Novo they are on the road out of the port. Buy tickets as early as you can as there isn't enough ferry space in high season. There is currently no ferry to Tarrafal.

Mar d'Canal Mindelo–Porto Novo: 08.00 and 15.00 daily, except 08.00 Wednesday only; Porto Novo–Mindelo 10.00 and 17.00 Monday–Saturday, except 10.00 Wednesday only; 17.00 Sunday only; 700$ one-way – car ferry operated by Naviera Armas. Luggage and large hand luggage (more than 5kg and 25cm^3) will be stowed.

Ribeira do Paúl Mindelo–Porto Novo: 07.30 Monday–Saturday; Porto Novo–Mindelo 10.30 Monday–Saturday; 400$ one-way – smaller ferry, liable to suffer in rough weather, with waves crashing unexpectedly over the open deck, so waterproof your camera, wear a jumper, and keep your possessions out of the way of the considerable number of vomiting passengers.

BY YACHT The trip across from São Vicente can be hairy, with winds gusting up to 40 knots from December to May – they are channelled by the two islands, creating a Venturi effect. To anchor at Porto Novo, the only harbour suitable for yachts, requires permission from Mindelo beforehand. It may be preferable to visit Santo Antão by ferry, though leave a watchman back in Mindelo. Tarrafal is a possible anchorage, offering total shelter from the trade winds but constant swell, making it hard to land with a dinghy. Supplies on offer would only be basic (a few food items and water). Ponta do Sol is completely unsuitable for yachts.

GETTING AROUND

BY PUBLIC TRANSPORT *Alugueres* now use the new, fast coastal road, so to travel across the mountains you will have to negotiate this with the driver. Expect to pay a much higher price for this route. *Alugueres* are regular between the two towns but many time their trips according to the ferry timetables. There are also regular connections between Ponta do Sol and Ribeira Grande. Elsewhere they follow the usual principle, leaving villages for the town early in the morning and returning at midday or early afternoon. To access the west of the island it is best to stay in Porto Novo for an early start.

Aluguer drivers in Santo Antão are unlikely to overcharge you but they are likely to insist you have missed all public *alugueres* and should therefore hire them as taxis. Be sceptical and hang around for a bit.

BY TAXI Taxis are in the form of chartered *alugueres*.

BY CAR
🚗 **Motacar** ☎ 222 1021
🚗 **Pegaso** ☎ 222 2460
🚗 **Porto Novo Car** ☎ 222 1490

🏠 WHERE TO STAY

Nowhere on Santo Antão could currently be described as touristy, but the main venue for tourist accommodation is Ponta do Sol, attractive for its coastal aspect and colonial architecture (though ruthless modernisation may erode its charms), and there are also one or two tourist services there. There are several *pensões* in the capital, Ribeira Grande (Povoação). There is also accommodation, including the first four-star hotel, in Porto Novo – not the beautiful side of the island but a good transport hub nonetheless. A few *pensões* dot the valley of Paúl – if simplicity, embeddedness and a cracking view are what you're after, these are for you. There are also some one-off venues elsewhere in the island, which are most useful for those trying to accomplish long hikes between distant outposts. Tarrafal has two *pensões*, as does Chã de Igreja, and you can stay in Cruzinha and Ribeira Grande (the *ribeira* rather than the town). Homestays can be arranged through Alfred (see below) or Casa das Ilhas (see page 287).

ACTIVITIES

EXCURSIONS

Alsatour Paúl; 225 1213; e alfred@
alsatour.de; www.alsatour.de. Alsatour runs
a variety of programmes, mainly hiking (see
Chapter 2, Practical Information, page 52).
Cabo Verde No Limits Ponta do Sol; 225
1031; m 997 9039; e info@caboverdenolimits.
com; www.caboverdenolimits.com. Catalan
Eduardo Gomez was a renowned guide in Europe
before he came to Santo Antão. Now he offers a
range of excursions including canyoning (€35/
half day), hiking, rock climbing (€35/half day),
diving & sport fishing. He is currently building
rooms above the activity centre which will be
available for rent.
CV Natura Ponta do Sol; 225 1526; m 982
5059; e caboverdebikes@cvtelecom.cv;
www.cabo-verde-bikes.com. André offers
excursions by vehicle, hikes, mountain bikes
(hire, technical support & guided tours).
Dany Careca ('The bald') Ponta do Sol (at the
Residencial Ponta do Sol); 225 1238/293 2296;

m 993 2296. Organises individually tailored hikes,
guides, places to stay, vehicle transport all over the
island & fishing trips, for a range of prices.
Hotel Bluebell Ponta do Sol. The hotel has
its own minibus & general guides with whom
excursions can be arranged (see *Ponta do Sol*,
page 292).
Osvaldo Santos Sousa ('White') Porto Novo;
m 993 1809; e sousasantos_99@
hotmail.com; www.santo-antao.net. Offers tours
& arrangements. English spoken.
Protur 222 2895; e aviagenprotur@gmail.
com. Provide tourist information & also rent cars.
Santtur Travel Porto Novo; 222 1660;
m 984 6242; e rufino.evora@yahoo.com.br. With
the port behind you, it's up the hill a little on the
left. Excursions in Santo Antão, hotel reservations,
transfers, ferry information about sailings to Tarrafal
ferry. A vehicle plus a guide for a day is €130.
Viagitur Ribeira Grande; 221 2794. Mainly for
air tickets: TACV, TAP & South African Airways.

HIKING The obvious walks are the grand *ribeiras*. You can either take transport up
the main road and disembark for a steep descent, or you can walk or take transport
along the coastal roads for a steep ascent. After torrential rains these *ribeiras* fill –
take local advice about how to ascend them because there is usually an alternative
path (see *Hazards*, page 278, for safety advice).

The west of the island is unfrequented, a hidden world of ravines and cliffs cut
into bizarre shapes by erosive winds. There are craters filled with lava flows and
looming boulders of white pumice. Interspersed is the odd pool of greenery where
irrigation has allowed cultivation. Now that there is a good map of Santo Antão (see
Maps, page 68), and locals are opening their houses to guests, the west is slightly
easier to explore. However, the area is lonely, the roads are sparse and the traffic is
scarce. The landscape is full of hidden dangers – landslides, sudden cliffs and lack
of water. Plan well and take a guide.

CYCLING With the right kit, mountain biking is a rewarding activity – but don't
underestimate the steepness of the hills or the heat of the day. Biking can be
arranged through CV Natura (for contact details, see above – see also *Chapter 2,
Practical Information*, page 71, for the logistics of getting a bike to Cape Verde).

DIVING There are canyons, lava tubes and tunnels, caves and rock bridges, all for
exploration. For further information, contact Cabo Verde No Limits, above.

CLIMBING AND CANYONING For further information, contact Cabo Verde No
Limits, above.

HORSERIDING This is offered by Pedracin Village (see *Ribeira Grande*, page 289).

BEACHES AND SWIMMING Many beaches on Santo Antão disappear under the rougher water between October and May, and emerge, magically, to be enjoyed during the summer months of June to September. Likewise, the water is calmer for swimming during the summer but once winter starts the ocean is wild and there is a powerful undertow. You may make your own serendipitous discovery of beaches but here are a few:

Praia de Escoralet To the east of Porto Novo.
Praia de Gi Between Vila das Pombas & Janela.
Praia Formosa In the south, inaccessible by road.

Sinagoga Black sand, popular for swimming
Tarrafal The largest beach in Santo Antão (black sand).

Along the coast to the east of Cruzinha da Garça there are several beaches (some black, some white).

FISHING From Vila das Pombas, you can accompany local fishermen as they go out to catch sea eel, grouper, mackerel, octopus and lobster. Cabo Verde No Limits can arrange sport fishing (see *Ponta do Sol*, opposite).

CULTURE Some examples of traditional songs, generally inspired by toil, are: *Cantigas de Guarda Pardal* (songs of the sparrow watchman) and *Cantigas de Currais de Trapiche* (songs to encourage the oxen as they plod around the *trapiche*). Cordas do Sol is a well-known Cape Verdean band specialising in traditional Santo Antão music and hailing from Paúl. Their most famous CD is *Linga de Sentonton*.

SIGHTSEEING BY VEHICLE A lot of Santo Antão's beauty can be seen by vehicle, and an itinerary should include: crossing from Porto Novo to Vila de Ribeira Grande by the mountain road, taking a detour at the top to see the Cova de Paúl and Pico da Cruz; driving up Ribeira do Paúl as far as Cabo de Ribeira (refreshments two-thirds of the way up at O Curral); and driving up Ribeira Grande (the *ribeira*) through Coculi, Boca das Ambas Ribeiras, and round to Chã de Igreja and Cruzinha da Garça (refreshments at Pedracin Village and, with notice, Chã de Igreja) . The road to Tarrafal is very poor.

THE EAST

Destinations are listed in an anticlockwise order, starting with Porto Novo.

PORTO NOVO In September 2005, this busy and windswept town was inaugurated as a city. It is full of smart new buildings paid for by Luxembourg as well as tended gardens and promenades overlooking the channel. But it remains a poor place, without even a steady, affordable water supply.

An enjoyable evening can be spent here watching the sun set on the distant mountains of São Vicente and the glowing harbour of Mindelo. You can even see São Nicolau, no more than a timid relative beyond. There are one or two good restaurants.

Getting there and away To get to Porto Novo from Ribeira Grande find an *aluguer* in the main street. They run all day (contrary to what the drivers will tell you) but the vast majority co-ordinate their trips with the ferry schedules. If you have a ferry to meet in Porto Novo allow plenty of time, as the last *alugueres*

11

to leave Ribeira Grande either sometimes miss the ferry, or arrive to find all the tickets have been sold.

To get from Porto Novo to Ribeira Grande, choose from the many *alugueres* that queue up to meet the ferry from Mindelo – you may even be recruited as a passenger by a zealous tout on the boat. Outside ferry times, hang around outside the ferry offices near the port, or in the *aluguer* park – keep your eyes open as they are generally driving around town trying to find passengers.

Sometimes, during the rainy season, Ribeira Grande can become a lake, roads can be washed out and visitors can become stuck on the other side of the island for several days.

There are several **cars for hire**, unofficially, in town.

Where to stay

Santo Antão Art Resort (73 rooms) Porto Novo; 222 ?675; e santantaoresort@ gmail.com; wwww.santantao-art-resort.com. The first upmarket hotel on the island, wildly different from any other accommodation. It offers very comfortable, spacious rooms with all the services, well up to international standards, & many with balconies overlooking the pool. It is set in a barren landscape just to the west of Porto Novo but if Santo Antão develops as some hope it will, Porto Novo will soon be lapping at its doors, the planting will mature, & it will become more approachable & populated. Offers 2 restaurants, a disco, spa, swimming pool & excursions around the island. FB available. English spoken. **$$$**

Pôr do Sol [283 A2] (16 rooms) Fundo Lomba Branca; 222 2179; e pordosolpn@ cvtelecom.cv. Yellow & grey building in the west of town. **$$**

Residencial Antilhas [283 G3] (17 rooms) 222 1193; m 991 7972; e residencialantilhas@ hotmail.com. Just facing the harbour, to the right, & thus with the potential for great views, this *residencial* is on the up with rooms being upgraded & apartments constructed next door. Rooms are simple, but generously sized & vary in quality, the best having hot water, AC, fridge, balcony & panoramas of São Vicente. Restaurant below also with a sea view. English spoken. **$$**

Residencial Girasol [283 E3] (19 rooms) 222 1383; e girasol@cvtelecom.cv. Good-sized rooms in this inland hotel, fairly basic but not down at heel. Most rooms are en suite & some of them have a view of the sea. All have fans & hot water. English spoken. **$**

Where to eat and drink

Restaurante Antilhas [283 G3] 07.30–23.00 daily (esplanade); 12.00–23.00 daily (indoor restaurant). In the hotel of the same name with a breezy esplanade overlooking the sea. $$$

Restaurante La Lampara de Giorgo [283 E3] 08.00–23.00 Mon, Wed, Fri/Sat, 08.00–15.00 & 19.00–23.00 Tue & Thu. A blue building with no sign, on the first road on the right off the coastal road from the port into town. Italian–Cape Verdean cuisine served on a terrace or inside. $$$

Bar Restaurante Sereia [283 F3] A superb place to while away an hour or two, perhaps while waiting for the ferry, gazing across the water at São Vicente. On the coast road from the port into town. $$

Chave d'Ouro [283 C3] Snack bar serving pizza, cakes & drinks. On the corner of the main square. $$

Felicidade [283 C2] 222 1147. Excellent food including lobster, & great cakes. Dishes take about half an hour to prepare but some take over an hour & may be best ordered in advance. $$

Fresh goat's cheese can be bought on the road to the quay at boat arrival and departure times; vegetables are available from the market at the west end of the main road, beside the bank.

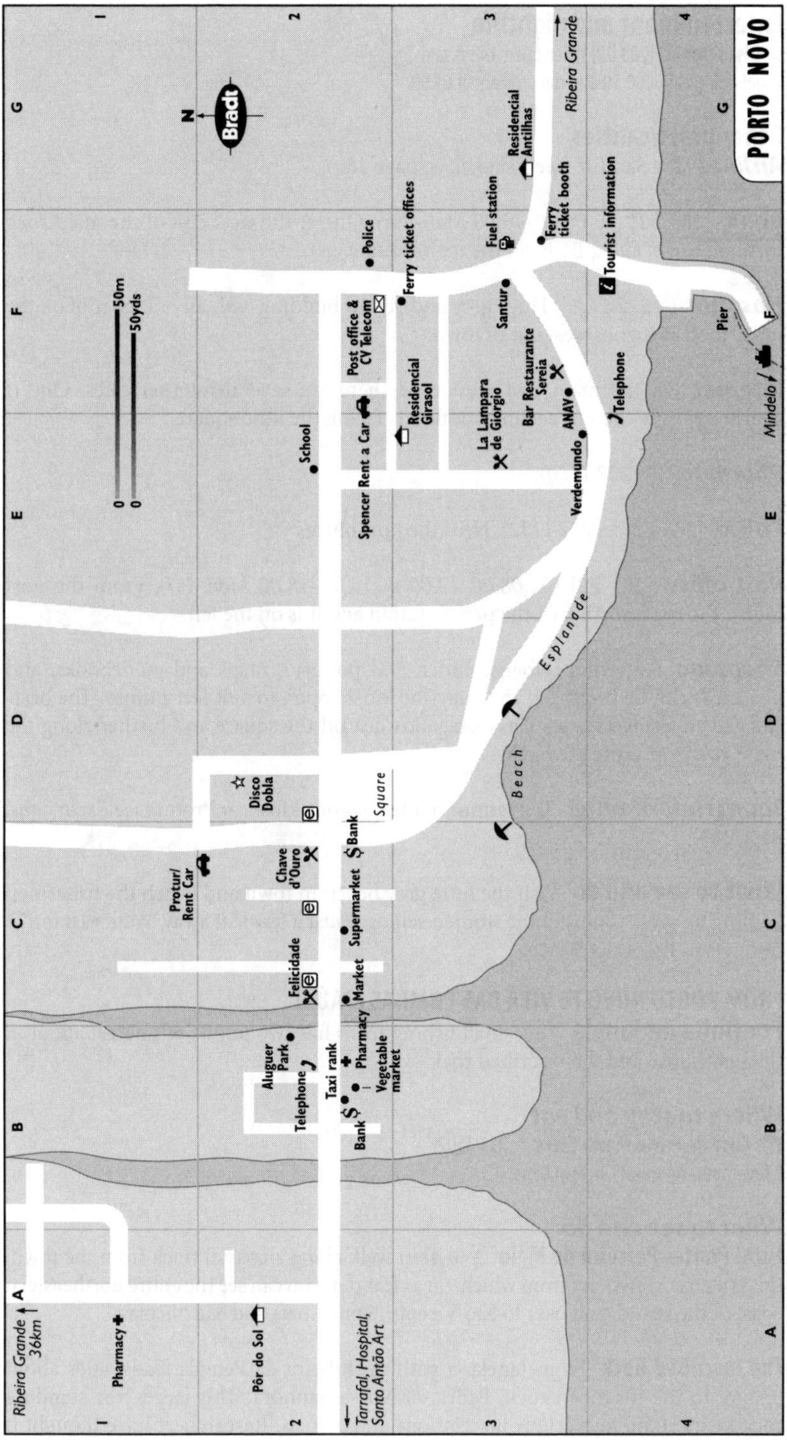
PORTO NOVO
Ribeira Grande 36km
Tarrafal, Hospital, Santo Antão Art
Ribeira Grande
Mindelo
Pharmacy
Pôr do Sol
Aluguer Park
Telephone
Taxi rank
Bank
Pharmacy
Vegetable market
Felicidade
Market
Supermarket
Protur/ Rent Car
Chave d'Ouro
Bank
Disco Dobla
Square
Beach
Esplanade
School
Spencer Rent a Car
Post office & CV Telecom
Police
Residencial Girasol
Ferry ticket offices
La Lampara de Giorgio
Bar Restaurante Sereia
Santur
Fuel station
Residencial Antilhas
Ferry ticket booth
ANAV
Verdemundo
Telephone
Tourist information
Pier
0 50m
0 50yds
N
Bradt
A B C D E F G
1 2 3 4

Entertainment and nightlife
☆ **Disco Dobla** [283 D2] When open, this is said to get going about 00.30 & to run until about 04.00.

Other practicalities
Airlines Try Santtur (see *Excursions*, page 280).

Bank [283 B2] (🕐 *08.00–15.00 Mon–Fri*). One at the west end of the main road through town, and a BCN on the main square.

Hospital (☎ *222 1130*). Huge grey and yellow building with an orange roof on the main road as it goes west out of town.

Internet On the main east–west road there are several internet cafés. One is nearly opposite the market and another is facing the little square.

Pharmacy (☎ *222 1130*).

Police [283 F2] (☎ *222 1132*). Near the post office.

Post office [283 F2] (🕐 *08.00–12.00 & 14.00–18.00 Mon–Fri*). From the port follow the road north past the petrol station and it is on the left.

Shopping Souvenirs (*grogue*, punch and pottery), maps and guidebooks, and postcards can be bought at the quayside kiosk, open to suit ferry times. The best-stocked supermarkets are Casa Delgado's just off the square and further along the main road, opposite the bank.

Tourist information Try Santtur, at the quayside kiosk, or Protur (see *Excursions*, page 280).

What to see and do Visit the little grey beach in town and watch the fishermen hauling up great tuna and the women selling it just a few feet away. Walk east for 25 minutes to Escoralet Beach.

FROM PORTO NOVO TO VILA DAS POMBAS (PAÚL)
Pontinha de Janela This small fishing town has two points of interest about it: the lighthouse and the inscribed rock.

Where to stay and eat
⌂ **Casa de Pasto Maria Clara** ☎ 223 1502.
A few rooms for guests are available.

What to see and do
Farol Pontes Perreira de Melo A 3–4km walk along a coastal track from the town, this is a great viewpoint from which, on a clear day, you can see the entire northeastern coast of the island, and over to São Vicente, Santa Luzia and São Nicolau.

The Inscribed Rock From Janela, a path up Ribeira da Peneda leads, after about 0.5km, to the inscribed rock, Pedra da Nossa Senhora. This large, free-standing rock bears some mysterious inscriptions and a cross. Researchers have thought it to be Aramaic, Phoenician or archaic Portuguese – it bears little resemblance to modern Portuguese or to Arabic, Hebrew, Berber or Tifnaq. Richard Lobban writes in the *Historical Dictionary of the Republic of Cape Verde*:

> The most fruitful investigation rests upon a comparison with the Portuguese inscription of a similar appearance, on a stone at Yellala Falls about 150km above the mouth of the River Congo. This was almost certainly inscribed by Diogo Cão in 1485 [and] appears to have two types of writing systems which range from archaic Portuguese, as well as letters which are in a distinctly different style which is the only form of writing in the case of Janela.

It was also common for the 15th-century Portuguese explorers to mark their landings and passages with stone inscriptions, especially with crosses… In short, the Janela inscription was probably placed there by a 15th-century Portuguese. It is tempting to conclude that it was written by Diogo Gomes or by Diogo Afonso in the 1460s, or by Diogo Cão or his pilots in the 1480s.

VILA DAS POMBAS (PAÚL)
A 15-minute drive south along the coast from Ribeira Grande is Vila das Pombas, which marks the beginning of the majestic valley of Paúl. It's the site of ambitious building projects, including a hotel, apartments, a condominium and restaurants. There is a brand-new bridge built with funds from the Millennium Challenge (and a similar one in Ribeira Grande).

Getting there and away From Porto Novo, the new, coastal road is a spectacular introduction to the stunning scenery of Santo Antão. Following the cliffs and with numerous tunnels hewn out of the rock, you will reach Vila das Pombas (Paúl) in 20 minutes. In Pombas the *alugueres* for Porto Novo currently leave from beside the bridge. Instead of waiting in the bus for it to fill up, you can go to a café and ask the driver to collect you there.

From Ribeira Grande, the journey to Vila das Pombas is about 15 minutes and transport can be found around the mouth of Ribeira de Torre. In Pombas, it can be found by the playground (50$).

To Cabo de Ribeira (up the Paúl Valley) transport can be found along the *avenida* in front of the carpentry workshop (100$).

🏠 Where to stay

🏠 **Aldeia Jerome** (7 rooms) 223 2173; e aldeiajerome@yahoo.it; http://aldeiajerome.it.gg. Bright, clean, inexpensive *pensão*. All rooms are en suite with hot water & fridge. Includes a suite for up to 4 people. English spoken. **$**

🏠 **Residencial Mar e Sol** (5 rooms) Estância; 223 1294; e helderlima@hotmail.com. On the road next to the sea. The owner, Noémia Melo, offers home cooking, & bright new rooms, some with private bathroom (hot water available), others with a balcony & uninterrupted sea views. French & English spoken. **$**

🏠 **Residencial Vale do Paúl** (5 rooms) Vila das Pombas; 221 1319. Also has a restaurant overlooking the sea (reservations necessary). **$**

🍴 Where to eat and drink

🍴 **Morabeza** 223 1790; ⏰ 08.00–23.00 daily. This friendly restaurant offers dazzling views of the ocean & fields. Meals are made to order using locally grown vegetables & freshly caught fish. $$

🍴 **O Veleiro** m 952 0364; ⏰ 08.00–23.00 daily. An offshoot of the well-established place of the same name in Ponta do Sol, this restaurant is right by the sea & offers the usual fish & meat dishes, as well as a few vegetarian options such as soup. $$

✕ Snack Bar Terrace Opposite the Town Hall. $ **✕ Takrida** ☏ 223 1129. Serves the usual
✕ Residencial Vale do Paúl (see above) $ dishes. $

Several *merceárias* (small food shops) around the town act as bars, where you can get a cold beer or shots of *grogue*. Try the one opposite the post office, **Docel** (☏ *223 1428*), for locally made drinks and sweets or **Senhor Ildo's Trapiche**, to the right of the petrol station, for bottled *grogue*, *ponche* and *mel*. There is a new municipal market opposite the *praça* which has a café upstairs.

Entertainment and nightlife
♀ Discoteca Beira Mar ⊕ only occasionally on
Sat. To the left of the police station.

Other practicalities
Bank BCA and Caixa Económica, next to Residencial Vale do Paúl

Dentist (☏ *223 2230/1*). On the main road.

Health centre (☏ *223 1130*). In the central plaza.

Municipality office (☏ *223 1197*). On the main *praça*.

Pharmacy (☏ *223 1972*). On the main road, to the right of the police station.

Police (☏ *223 1292*). On the main road before the playground.

Post office (☏ *223 1397*; ⊕ *08.00–15.30 Mon–Fri*). Beyond the central plaza on the right.

What to see and do The main activity is to travel up Ribeira do Paúl (see below) or to do neighbouring hikes such as that up Ribeirãozinho to Pico da Cruz.
    The statue of Santo António at the northern edge of the foot of Paúl Valley is a 15-minute hike that will give you 180° views of the ocean and surrounding valleys.

Ribeira do Paúl A vast *ribeira* home to thousands of people and their agriculture – sugarcane, breadfruit and bananas – Paúl is renowned for its *grogue*, and one of its *trapiches* (sugarcane-juicing apparatus) is still driven by oxen. Highlights include Passagem, with its charming municipal park nestled among impressive almond trees and bougainvilleas. Beyond the villages of Lombinho and Cabo de Ribeira, up a steep incline, a panoramic view of the valley and ocean opens out. The road ends at Cabo de Ribeira, but a steep cobbled footpath continues to Cova, an ancient crater now filled with verdant cultivation.

Getting there and away *Alugueres* travel from Pombas all the way up to Paúl's Cabo de Ribeira for about 100$. Some *alugueres* do the full journey between Cabo de Ribeira and either Ribeira Grande or Porto Novo – the latter generally to meet the ferry from São Vicente.

⌂ Where to stay Accommodation is listed here in order of ascent up the valley. Most of the establishments below can arrange transfers from Porto Novo in which you are dropped off at the head of Paúl and walk down to your accommodation, your bags continuing by vehicle. They will also give you help planning hikes.

⌂ **Casa Familiar (Sabine Jähnel)** (2 rooms) Eito; ☎ 223 1544. A rare opportunity to stay within one of Santo Antão's great *ribeiras*, this *pensão* can be found by walking up Ribeira do Paúl, beyond Eito, & turning left at the sign for Mercearia Brito. Sabine, who is German, offers 2 rooms that feel like your bedroom at home & open on to a shaded roof terrace (shared bathroom). Excellent Cape Verdean meals *en famille*, & friendly hiking advice. English spoken. **$**

⌂ **Casa das Ilhas** (9 rooms) Lombo Comprido; ☎ 223 1832; m 996 7774; e casadasilhas@yahoo. fr. This Belgian–Cape Verdean-run casa is made up of a series of little houses built on the steep terracing of the mountainside surrounded by fruit & vegetable planting – including sticks of sugarcane, from which their own *grogue* is made. It is worth staying here for the view alone: it is both panoramic & full of the detail of valley life. Rooms are simple & bare, but appropriate, most are en suite & there is hot water. At night great meals are served around a communal table where, during the day, the owners run a small local primary school (see *Travelling positively*, page 79). Casa das Ilhas is reached by a 10min walk up a steep footpath (the owners will send someone down to carry your bags). HB only; vegetarians welcome. English spoken. **$$**

⌂ **Aldeia Manga** (4 bungalows) ☎ 223 1880; e info@aldeia-manga.com; www.aldeia-manga.com. Simply furnished bungalows perched on the side of a hill facing a steep cliff reaching up into the clouds, with spectacular views down the valley. The owner has made a great deal of effort to build in a sympathetic style & power is provided by solar panels (& soon by windmills as well). There is a natural swimming pool. Water is purified by UV light.

A substantial buffet dinner is provided for €8 (order in advance). Jams are made with fruit from the garden. From here at least 6 unguided hikes are possible, including straight down to Vila das Pombas. Collection from the ferry can be arranged in advance for 400$. Wi-Fi available. English spoken. **$$**

⌂ **Covaquinho** (4 rooms) Cabo de Ribeira; ☎ 223 2065; m 998 9919; www.cavoquinho.com. Run by a Spanish couple, José & Belén, this house is wedged, vertiginously, into the mountainside & is easier to spot than to get to: it's orangey yellow & 1 path reaches it from behind the village water pump. Rooms are simple & nicely presented, each with a window affording a view down the valley, & there is also a rooftop bar/restaurant with a spectacular view. Rooms have shared bathrooms with hot water. Wi-Fi available. José also does guided treks. There's a restaurant (🕓 evenings daily); vegetarians catered for. English spoken. **$$**

⌂ **Hostel** (2 dorms) Cabo de Ribeira; ☎ 223 1941; m 981 2478; e sandro_lacerenza@ yahoo.fr. A French–Cape Verdean operation, this accommodation consists of 2 large, 1st-floor rooms, 1 with 3 bunk beds & 1 with 2, that share an en-suite bathroom & are accessed via a long balcony with a superb view. They are simple but bright, clean & attractively done. They are designed with hiking groups in mind, though the beds convert into loft beds with desk underneath. The shop below sells souvenirs: crafts & food produce, *grogue* & liquor. **$**

⌂ **Perla da Paúl** e capvert007@yahoo.fr. Under construction by Frank Roland, who is trying to promote traditional building methods in the area. Sleep through the Paúl night under just an awning. Separate shower. **$**

✗ Where to eat and drink

✗ **Covaquinho** (see *Where to stay*, above). **$$$**

✗ **O Curral** Chã João Vaz; ☎ 223 1213; e grogue@alsatour.de; www.grogue.de; 🕓 10.00–18.00 Mon–Sat, 11.00–17.00 Sun. This café is perfect for taking a break from the long hike of Vale do Paúl. Try various kinds of *grogue* made by the owner, Alfred, buy some of

his cheese & jams & chat to him about his latest ideas (see page 288). **$$**

✗ **Sandr'Arte** Cabo de Ribeira Paúl, in the first village you come to after walking down from the cova. This is a good place to stop for a drink. They also sell local arts, *grogue* & coffee. The owner rents a few simple bedrooms & can do half board on request. **$$**

What to do Walking up or down Paúl Valley is the chief activity and the sights along the way are described in *Hikes*, pages 297–306.

FROM VILA DAS POMBAS TO RIBEIRA GRANDE

Sinagoga This lies on the point between Mão para Traz and Paúl. It is where exiled Portuguese Jews settled in the early 19th century. There are Jewish graves here as well as in Ponta do Sol. Later it was turned into a leper colony. For more on Jewish history in Cape Verde, see *Chapter 1, Background Information*, pages 12–13.

Sinagoga has a black-sand beach where people like to swim. There are plans for a tourist resort in this area.

RIBEIRA GRANDE (POVOAÇÃO) The mountain road from Porto Novo to Ribeira Grande pulls away past the depressing outskirts of town where the inhabitants live amongst permanent, savage and sand-laden winds. It mounts through the cusps of the brown landscape. Already the achievement of the road builders seems extraordinary. As it climbs higher and higher forest plantations begin to fill the higher valleys and a chill tinges the air. But you are still in the foothills – on and on you go until you reach the clouds and the eucalyptus and pine trees which thrive

ALFRED MANDL

Ex-troubleshooter Alfred Mandl arrived in Santo Antão from Germany over 20 years ago and set up in Paúl, building himself a thatched home with walls made entirely from beer bottles. He started offering hiking holidays in Santo Antão – with his partner, Hans Roskamp, he specialises in remote adventures in which visitors reside with local people. But that's only a part of what Alfred is up to. Always interesting and always innovating he can often be found at a table in the café, O Curral (see page 287), which he runs with his wife, Christine, where he loves to philosophise with passers-by.

'When I started here everyone thought I was a little crazy,' he says, smiling. But with his thin form and long beard he retains the aura of eccentricity and the crazy ideas still flow thick and fast. One of his latest is his 'virtuous circle' of *grogue* production: using the leftovers from the milling of sugarcane to feed cows, whose dung is converted to biogas to power the *grogue* production. The remains of the dung, incidentally, are siphoned away for fertilising his vegetables. The cows also produce milk for cheese which he sells in his café.

One of his latest projects involves a new concept in tourism: not five-storey hotels and pizzerias but a site in Lagoa in the centre of the island where he has purchased 64ha of land and plans organic farming irrigated with harvested rainwater. He has planted nearly 20ha of trees there and plans to invite tourists to come not just in body but in mind too: webcams and media conferencing will mean that they can enjoy their holiday before it starts and continue it after it is over.

Alfred is exercised by the need to adapt to Cape Verde's altering demographics and educational levels. 'In 1982, 85% were illiterate; now 67% go to secondary school,' he says. He's trying to develop businesses that can utilise more educated people but he also wants to attract older foreigners to come and live on Santo Antão. '50% of our population is under 29. If you have a car you need a motor but you also need brakes.'

in the cold air. The road skates the ridges of the top of the island and sometimes there are breathless sheer drops on either side as you gaze down into the plunging *ribeiras*. Pinnacles, cliffs, and double bends around spires of rock, mark the descent into the verdant side of the island and you will see the puddle of Ribeira Grande long before you drop past the thatched stone houses to reach it.

The town, known to most as Povoação, is a muddle of cobbled streets crammed into the space between the cliffs and the sea, and overflowing up the mouths of the two *ribeiras*: Ribeira Grande and Ribeira de Torre. For a place of such potential it feels impoverished and run-down. It is strangely lacking in places from which to appreciate the view, and the idea of ending a hard day's hike sipping a quiet beer while gazing at some Atlantic panorama never quite materialises.

A church was first built in the town in 1595. Bishop Valente, who arrived in the mid 18th century, having abandoned Santiago, consecrated the large church of Nossa Senhora do Rosário in 1755. However, the transfer of the See to Santo Antão was never officially approved and it went instead, a while later, to São Nicolau.

Getting there and away To get to Ribeira Grande from Porto Novo take an *aluguer* from the port. You now have a choice between the old, mountain route and the new, coastal road. Take the mountain route at least one-way – it's unmissable.

To travel towards Porto Novo along the coastal road, find an *aluguer* across from town, on the other side of Ribeira de Torre.

There is frequent transport between Ribeira Grande (from where the Ponta do Sol road enters town, near the food market) and Ponta do Sol (from the main square) (50$).

For destinations up the *ribeira* (Ribeira Grande) such as Coculi, Boca das Ambas Ribeiras and Chã de Igreja, wait outside the Caixa Económica Bank (walk up the road that goes parallel to that *ribeira* and you will see it on your left). To the more distant of these destinations the *aluguer* follows the usual pattern (into town early morning, out of town midday). On Sundays it may be impossible to find transport to more remote destinations.

⌂ Where to stay

⌂ **Pedracin Village** (25 rooms) Boca da Coruja; ☎224 2020; e pedracin@cvtelecom.cv. A complex more than 10km out of town along Ribeira Grande (the *ribeira* rather than the town), southwest of town. Take the *aluguer* that is headed to Boca das Ambas Ribeiras – for a little extra the driver will ascend the steep, 1km track from the *ribeira* & drop you right at the hotel. Pedracin is beautifully crafted, with an unusually sensitive sense of place. The accommodation is in chalets in a style evoking the traditional Santo Antão style of drystone walling & thatch, but with most of the mod cons. There's a swimming pool & a restaurant with a view. **$$$**

⌂ **Residencial Cantinho da Varzea** (5 rooms) ☎221 2606. At the southern end of town in a quiet spot, with a shop/café underneath this is an acceptable *residencial* in a fairly modern building, well kept with large rooms. 1 room has a private bathroom, all have TV & some have balconies with a view of a bit of mountain. **$$**

⌂ **Residencial Top d'Coroa** (11 rooms) ☎221 2794; e viagitur@hotmail.com; www.residencial-topcoroa.com. In the southwest of town, beside Viagitur, this accommodation is probably the smartest in town because of its newness, though it doesn't have the restaurant back-up or centrality of the Trópical. Rooms are en suite with AC, hot water & some have balconies overlooking its little square. There is also a 2-bed apartment with a kitchenette but, mystifyingly, no water or sink. **$$**

⌂ **Residencial Trópical** (15 rooms) ☎221 1129; m 993 4116; e residencial_tropical@ hotmail.com. Probably the most comfortable place in town, with a restaurant & internet café below & a small terrace with some thankful

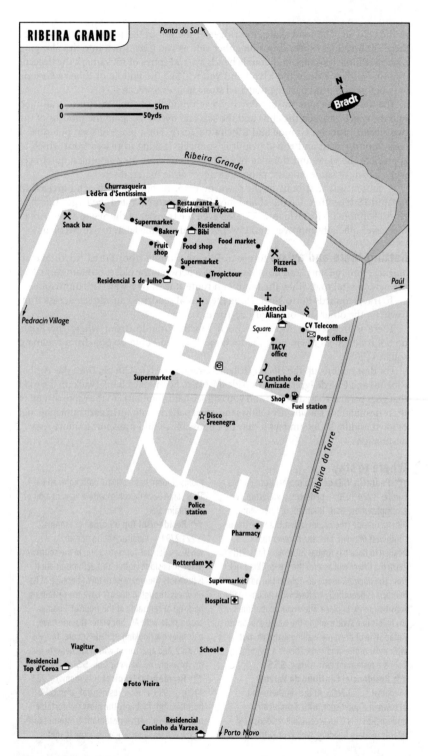

RIBEIRA GRANDE

Ponta do Sol

N
Bradt

0 ——————— 50m
0 ——————— 50yds

Ribeira Grande

Churrasqueira
Lêdêra d'Sentissima
Restaurante &
Residencial Trópical

Snack bar

$

Supermarket
Bakery

Residencial
Bibi

Fruit
shop

Food shop

Food market

Supermarket

Pizzeria
Rosa

Residencial 5 de Julho

Tropictour

Paúl

Pedracin Village

Residencial
Aliança

$

Square

CV Telecom

Post office

TACV
office

Supermarket

Cantinho de
Amizade

Shop

Fuel station

Disco
Sreenegra

Ribeira da Torre

Police
station

Pharmacy

Rotterdam

Supermarket

Hospital

Viagitur

School

Residencial
Top d'Coroa

Foto Vieira

Residencial
Cantinho da Varzea

Porto Novo

shade (but no view). Most rooms are en suite with hot water & all have AC, fridge & TV. Some have a sea view, though no balcony. Accepts Visa. **$$**

🏠 **Residencial 5 de Julho** (14 rooms) ☎ 221 1345. At the end of the main square. It has a maze of down-at-heel rooms, some with private bathroom, & a popular café. Roof terrace. **$**

🏠 **Residencial Aliança** (5 rooms) ☎ 221 2488. Near the post office, this is perhaps the best of the basic options because the rooms are large & 3 of the rooms are uplifted by having great balcony views. 4 rooms are en suite with hot water. **$**

🏠 **Residencial Bibi** (5 rooms) ☎ 221 1149. Down the narrow road opposite the 5 de Julho. Basic, clean rooms, some with balconies. Hot water available. **$**

✗ Where to eat and drink

✗ **Pedracin Village** ⏱ 06.30–23.00 daily. Out of town (follow the directions under *Where to stay*, above), this restaurant has a spectacular view. **$$$$**

✗ **Restaurante Trópical** (see *Where to stay*, above). The most expensive restaurant in town, with both terrace & indoor (AC) seating. It's the best choice for quality. **$$$**

✗ **Rotterdam** Behind the hospital, for widely praised, tasty platefuls. **$$$**

✗ **Café 5 de Julho** ⏱ 07.30–15.00 & 18.30–23.00 daily. Basic, but very good value, filling meals. This is definitely one place to find *cachupa*. **$$**

🍷 **Cantinho de Amizade** Near the petrol station, a pleasant patio bar set in a courtyard. A good place in which to while away an hour waiting for transport. **$$**

✗ **Churrasqueira Lêdêra d'Sentissima** On the road that runs parallel with the *ribeira* (Ribeira Grande). **$$**

✗ **Pizzeria Rosa** Rua do Mercado; ☎ 221 2572; m 986 7877. Opposite the food market, this is a popular place with a good reputation among local expats. **$$**

✗ **Food market** For a taste of real, local, traditional, basic food try this venue above the food market. There are just 2 tables & there's just 1 dish. **$**

Almost everything you need, including bread, can be found at the Shell station. There is a bakery, supermarket and fruit and vegetable shop on the road towards Caixa Económica Bank.

Entertainment and nightlife

☆ **Disco Sreenegra** In a small alleyway in the middle of town.

Other practicalities

Airlines TACV (☎ *221 1184*).

Bank Banco Comercial do Atlântico, opposite the post office at the crossroads on the edge of town (⏱ *08.00–15.00 Mon–Fri*). Caixa Económica, Rua Ponte Lavad: follow the road up the side of the *ribeira* (Ribeira Grande) for a minute or so and it is on your left (⏱ *08.00–15.00 Mon–Fri*).

Hospital (☎ *221 1130*). Off towards the mountain Porto Novo road.

Internet At the Residencial Trópical, Natud's and also the Cyber Café.

Pharmacy Near the hospital.

Police (☎ *221 1132*). Go along the Porto Novo road and turn right before the hospital.

Post office (⏰ *08.00–15.30 Mon–Fri*). At the end of the main street through town.

Tourist information None, but try at Viagitur, next to Residencial Top d'Coroa.

PONTA DO SOL A gracious town, built on a breezy peninsula, this is one of the oldest *Barlavento* settlements. It is becoming increasingly popular with tourists and is undergoing a mini construction boom, with many new apartments springing up on the surrounding hills, most of which appear forlorn and unfinished. An entirely inappropriate six-storey hotel planned for the waterfront is progressing slowly, but all in all development in this little town has thankfully not made too much difference to its charm.

Getting there and away Ponta do Sol is at the end of the road. It is a 20-minute aluguer trip to Ribeira Grande (50$), using transport that waits where the main road passes through the square. Transport leaves at times all through the day, but is most common in the early morning. A taxi from Ribeira Grande costs 500$. A taxi from Ponta do Sol to Fontainhas 500$; to Paúl 1,000$; to Porto Novo 3,500$; to Pico da Cruz 2,500$; to Corda 1,500$. Change at Ribeira Grande for transport anywhere else. Cecilio can be booked in advance (ask your hotel to arrange it).

Where to stay

🏠 **Cabo Verde No Limits** (6 rooms) (for contact information, see *Activities*, page 280). Down the road from the main square, rooms are being built above the activity centre, most of which with private bathroom. Great views over the town from the top-floor terrace. **$$**

🏠 **Chez Louisete** (5 rooms) ☎ 225 1048; m 991 8568; e chezlouisete@cvtelecom.cv. On the road into town from Ribeira Grande, before you descend into the square. Simple but good-sized & pleasant rooms, with a rooftop conservatory where guests can have their b/fast & evening meals. Rooms are en suite with hot water, fan, & 2 have balconies with sea views. **$$**

🏠 **CV Natura** (1 room). On 1 of the 2 roads leading west from the main square to the coast, this room is above the booking office (for further information, see *Activities*, page 280). There's a private bathroom with hot water, & a terrace. **$$**

🏠 **Hotel Bluebell** (23 rooms) ☎ 225 1215; m 994 1153; e bluebell@cvtelecom.cv; www.hotelbluebell.info. Located near the square, this has all the facilities of a modest hotel & some rooms have balconies with a view of the sea. There is a roof terrace with a view of the mountains & the sea. There are 2 suites & some rooms have AC. The hotel offers transfers to & from Porto Novo & can organise excursions, with English-speaking guides. **$$**

🏠 **Residencial Ponta do Sol** (14 rooms) ☎ 225 1238/9; m 993 2296; e residencialpsol@ cvtelecom.cv. On the road towards Ribeira Grande, it's hard to miss the garish green & orange building. Thankfully, the large, bright, fairly modern rooms are not painted in the same colours. All are en suite with hot water & fans. Each room has a balcony from which, for top-floor rooms, there is a sea view. There's also a restaurant which should be booked half a day beforehand. **$$**

🏠 **Casa Vittoria** (5 rooms) ☎ 225 1075. Pleasant clean rooms above Lanchonette Lita. The owner also runs a small shop next door. **$**

🏠 **Leila Leite** (6 rooms) ☎ 225 1056. Opposite the Hotel Bluebell; some rooms have shared bathrooms. **$**

🏠 **Pôr do Sol Arte** (4 rooms) ☎ 225 1121; e porsolarte@yahoo.fr. Slightly basic, hippy place whose rooms have either a balcony or a sea view, 1 with a private bathroom. Also has a café. **$**

🏠 **Residencial A Beira Mar** (10 rooms) ☎ 225 1018; e chefatimaps@hotmail.com. Not far from the harbour, this has one of the best views of all hotels in the town. Each room has a balcony with sea view & there is a rooftop bar that has a panorama of the sea & the mountains. Rooms are ordinary & simple but cared for. Unfortunately, the metalworking shop next door may disturb your rest. Some French spoken. **$**

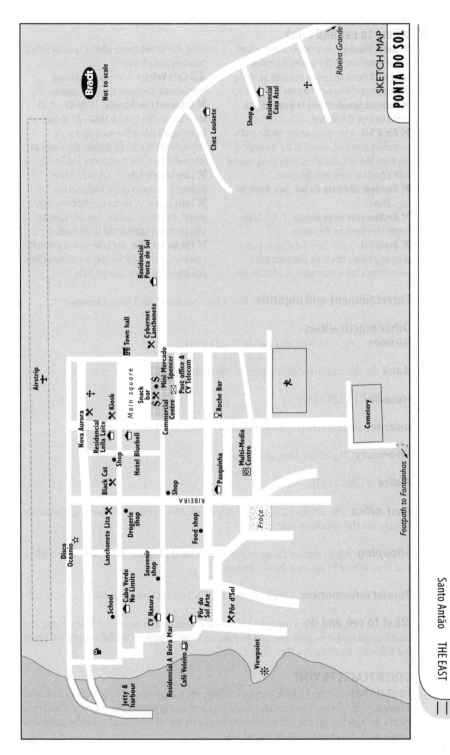

SKETCH MAP

PONTA DO SOL

Bradt

Not to scale

Ribeira Grande

Shop

Residencial Casa Azul

Chez Louisete

Residencial Ponta do Sol

Cybernet Lanchonete

Town hall

Airstrip

Nova Aurora

Residencial Leila Leite

Kiosk

Snack bar

Main square

Mini Mercado Spencer

Commercial Centre

Post office & CV Telecom

Roche Bar

Black Cat

Shop

Hotel Bluebell

Pasquinha

Multi-Media Centre

RIBEIRA

Shop

Food shop

Praça

Disco Oceanio

Lanchonete Lita

Drogerie shop

Souvenir shop

School

Cabo Verde No Limits

CV Natura

Pôr do Sol Arte

Pôr d'Sol

Residencial A Beira Mar

Café Veleiro

Viewpoint

Jetty & harbour

Footpath to Fontainhas

Cemetery

✗ Where to eat and drink

✗ Hotel Bluebell (see *Where to stay,* above). Indoor restaurant on the ground floor of the hotel, with excellent cuisine overseen by Mr Ba, the former chef who now runs the hotel. $$$$

✗ Pizzeria Spaghetteria la Buona Pizza 1 road up from the airstrip. $$$

✗ Pôr d'Sol A tiny place on the north–south road along the coast, owned by the manager of the Hotel Bluebell, this offers really good cooking with a fantastic view over the ocean. $$$

✗ Residencial Ponta do Sol (see *Where to stay,* above). $$$

✗ Restaurante Nova Aurora ☎ 225 1360. Beside the church on the square. $$$

✗ Black Cat ☎ 225 1539. Catering to groups of hungry hikers, this lively place also has a *quintal fresca* (inner courtyard), & often has live music. The French owner offers a range of dishes, including pasta & fish. $$

⏏ Café Veleiro e emanuelrachidsp@ hotmail.com. Overlooks the sea & harbour. $$

✗ Cybernet Lanchonete ⏰ 08.00–22.30 Mon–Sat; 11.00–15.00 & 18.00–22.30 Sun. On the uphill side of the main square, an atmospheric little drinks-&-cakes place with an arboreal theme. Live music every 2nd Fri. $$

✗ Lanchonete Lita ☎ 225 1075. Serves *cachupa* & whatever else is fresh that day. $$

✗ Leila Leite ⏰ all day (see *Where to stay,* above). Rooftop restaurant. Tiny café opening onto the street opposite the Hotel Bluebell. $$

✗ Pôr do Sol Arte Not to be confused with the similarly named Pôr d'Sol, this is a colourful little café where the menu changes daily. $$

Entertainment and nightlife
Not a lot – look out for **Disco Oceanio**.

Other practicalities

Airlines TACV, in Ribeira Grande (☎ *221 1184*).

Bank In the commercial complex in the main square.

Hospital (☎ *225 1130*).

Internet Try Cybernet Lanchonete (see *Where to eat and drink,* above).

Pharmacy Try at the Drogerie shop.

Police (☎ *225 1132*).

Post office (⏰ *08.00–12.00 & 14.00–18.00 Mon–Fri*). Overlooking the main square, on the southern side.

Shopping An extensive range of crafts and food produce is for sale at the Black Cat (see *Where to eat and drink,* above).

Tourist information Very little, but try CV Natura (see page 280).

What to see and do Ponta do Sol is the embarkation point for hikes along the north coast and it is close enough to Ribeira Grande to be a useful setting-off point for hikes up its *ribeiras* (Torre and Grande).

OTHER PLACES TO VISIT

Fontainhas Perched like a fairytale village on a high and precipitous spit of land above a deep *ribeira*, Fontainhas can be reached along a winding cobbled road from Ponta do Sol. Go up the hill to the southeasterly tip of town and take the road that heads west. It's about a 10km round trip.

Cruzinha da Garça This coastal village is more or less the end of the road that runs up Ribeira Grande, and can also be accessed on foot from Fontainhas (see Hikes, page 297).

🏠 Where to stay

🏠 **Pensão Só Na Fish** (5 rooms) ☎ 226 1027. Maria Martins is a returned *emigrante*, this time from Germany. Rooms are simple & 1 is en suite. **$$**

Chã de Igreja This pretty village, with its white church and brightly painted houses, is built on a small promontory of land projecting from the west side of the *ribeira*. A good place to chill for a while. To get there, take an *aluguer* up Ribeira Grande, through Coculi, Boca das Ambas Ribeiras, Horta de Garça and onwards. The best time to try for such transport is about 11.00–14.00. You are unlikely to find public transport back on the same day, as it generally leaves early in the morning.

There are beautiful, large beaches within 45 minutes of Chã de Igreja during the summer months (June to September) but for the rest of the year they are underwater.

🏠 Where to stay

🏠 **Senhor Armindo** (4 rooms) m 996 8942. This returned *emigrante* has created a lush paradise scattered with stone tables & hammocks from which to enjoy it. Rooms have no view. Rent is for minimum periods & there is a kitchen & cook (you supply ingredients). **$$**

🏠 **Senhor Delgado** (5 rooms) ☎ 262 1162. The first tall building on entering the village

from Garça. Spectacular rooftop view, hot water. Evening meals on request. **$$**

🏠 **Senhor Rodrigo** (4 rooms) ☎ 231 6360. Rodrigo runs his beautiful, recently built home with splendid views over the ocean as an informal *pensão*. It has a kitchen & offers HB accommodation. **$$**

✗ **Where to eat** There's no official restaurant but meals can be obtained from the *residenciais* (see above).

THE WEST

The western part of Santo Antão is dominated by one vast volcano which reaches a height of 1,982m. Within its crater stands a younger cone, with a height of 1,979m. To its east, and almost as high, is Monte Pia, at 1,884m.

The west is inaccessible and underpopulated, although, if tourism spreads along a new road west of Porto Novo this inaccessibility might gradually decrease. Currently there is a road from Porto Novo to Lagedos which runs northwest along a convoluted path through Chã de Morte, Curral das Vacas and on to Ribeira da Cruz in the northwest before heading west and then inland again, terminating at Monte Cebola. When the rains are bad, whole sections of road may be washed away.

However, a network of hikes has been put together in the excellent Goldstadt Wanderkarte series (see *Maps*, page 68), and there are local people at strategic points offering basic accommodation. So it is possible to explore, but not without some forward planning: either put yourself in the hands of a knowledgeable local operator such as Alsatour or make your phone calls to some of the people below to organise guides and accommodation (and don't forget to cancel homestays if your plans change as your hosts might otherwise waste a day's journey to purchase food for your dinner).

The views from the hike up and around Coroa are tremendous: down the steep western side of the volcano to Monte Trigo, and across to all the *Barlavento* islands when the weather is fine. The 1,000m ascent is not included in the hiking section because it's not the kind of hike that should be attempted without a guide. The paths are many and easily confused, there is no scattering of locals happy to put you right, and the landscape is hostile, with unexpected cliffs and no water.

TARRAFAL This isolated spot on the west coast is hard to get to but worth the effort. The approach from the sea is beautiful – a small spot of green colour amongst the brown-grey massifs of the mountains gradually resolves itself into the whites and pastels of this sleepy town. Around the shore – the longest stretch of beach in Santo Antão – fishermen relax, fierce games of *oril* click away under the trees, women wash clothes; and hens and dogs go purposefully about their business. Electricity is available only until 23.00 so a torch is a good idea.

Getting there and away Several *aluguer* trucks leave Tarrafal at 06.00 or earlier for Porto Novo (700$), departing on the return journey at about midday. The journey takes about 2.5 hours and is uncomfortable, particularly the half nearer Tarrafal, and the trucks are invariably packed (a cushion is recommended!). You could charter a 4x4 in Porto Novo instead for ten times the price. Generally they do not run on Sundays. There is also a Land Rover which can take eight passengers; ask your hotel for more information on this option. The *residenciais* in Tarrafal will usually give you as much assistance as possible to plan your journey.

Where to stay and eat

Residencial Mar Tranquilidade (7 rooms) 227 6012; e info@martranquilidade.com; www.martranquilidade.com. Run by Frank & Susi, a German–American couple who arrived here on their yacht in 1999 & decided to stay, this is an artistically created little complex of high-ceilinged, stone & thatch cottages, echoing the traditional architecture of the village. Most are en suite. There's a shady terrace in front in which to hang out, & also Praça Tartaruga, a terrace on the beach which they have built as a place for locals, & visitors, to congregate. They are very proud of

their cuisine. Reservations are recommended as they are often full. **$$**

Marina d'Tarrafal (4 rooms) 227 6078; e info@info@marina-tarrafal.com; www.marina-tarrafal.com. Small coastal guesthouse with simple rooms & views of the mountains, sugar cane fields & banana & coconut plantations. **$$**

Marie-Alice and Jaime da Cruz (6 rooms) 227 6002. A newly built, locally owned *pensão* with a terrace overlooking the coast, on the main road uphill, north of the beach. No hot water, shared bathroom. **$**

Other places to stay Try www.bela-vista.net/accommodation-Santo-Antão-e. aspx, for the odd tip on homestays.

What to do Swim, snorkel, fish from a local boat, go by boat to Monte Trigo. Bury yourself in the sand, which is reputed to have medicinal properties. Hike with a guide. Sit. Muse.

OTHER PLACES TO VISIT

Norte This region is remote and inaccessible but the landscape is dramatic.

Where to stay

Casa Isabel and Luciano Neves 222 3118. Simple accommodation with the family

who also offer guided trips up to Topo de Coroa & have transport. Book in advance. **$$**

For the manic, the fourth and fifth hikes can be combined so that the walker goes up one *ribeira* and comes down the next one.

1 VILA DE RIBEIRA GRANDE–COCULI–BOCA DAS AMBAS RIBEIRAS–CHÃ DE IGREJA
Distance: 12.5km; time: 5.5 hours; difficulty: 2 (CW)
This is a spectacular walk, though not as green and cultivated as the other *ribeiras*. You can halve its length by taking transport from Ribeira Grande (outside the Caixa Económica Bank) as far as Boca das Ambas Ribeiras. At the end of the walk you could turn round and walk back, or walk to Ponta do Sol (ie: the reverse of the next walk). Alternatively, you may be able to find an *aluguer* near the church that will take you to Ribeira Grande. If not, you may have to charter one.

Ribeira Grande is at the mouth of two *ribeiras*. The one that gives the town its name is the more northerly one. There's a wide, dusty track that leads up the *ribeira* from where the road to Ponta do Sol leaves town. The riverbed passes through scattered housing and cultivation and on the right, after about 20 minutes, an agronomy station. This was built by the Dutch under an aid scheme but is now run by the Cape Verdeans. A tennis court was included in the package.

Some 45 minutes after setting out there is a large windmill on the left and a small shop which sells drinks. After another ten minutes you reach the little village of **Coculi** with its prominent white church. This village marks the point where Ribeira Figueiral joins Ribeira Grande on the left. Bearing right at the fork just before the village, you will see that Ribeira Grande is joined almost immediately by another *ribeira* on the left, which leads up to **Chã de Pedra**.

The gentle ascent up Ribeira Grande continues and the land empties and becomes less lush, although a lot of sugarcane grows here. Two hours in, there's a slender aqueduct over the increasingly narrow *ribeira*. It was built by the Portuguese in 1956, and is still carrying water today.

Half an hour later is the small village of **Boca das Ambas Ribeiras**, or 'Mouth of Both Valleys' – the small valley of Ribeira dos Caibros leads up to the left. There are a couple of houses here and two prominent breadfruit trees. Breadfruit, which is in season in March, is considered a great delicacy. It has white flesh that is best cut into slices and boiled in salt water.

A cobbled road leads up the left side of Ribeira Grande, but the more interesting (and direct) route to **Chã de Igreja** is along a small path up the right (north) side of the valley.

You start climbing almost immediately, the path ahead repeatedly seeming to vanish as it curves steeply around the wrinkles of the sheer mountain face. Before long, the view of the valley floor far below is vertiginous, with farms and the occasional vehicle spread out like toys on a carpet. In places, there is nothing but a knee-high drystone wall separating you from a sheer drop of 500m. It was the same in the 19th century, when Alfred Burdon Ellis was prompted to write:

> Casualties… are not by any means uncommon, as the numerous wooden crosses that we passed on our way testified.

Watch out for Egyptian vultures (*Neophron percnopterus*) soaring on the thermals towards the head of the valley. They are unmistakable, with a black wing with a white leading edge, and a wingspan of up to 2m.

Santo Antão **HIKES**

11

WARTIME BRITS IN TARRAFAL

When British merchant navy radio operator George Monk's ship, the *Auditor*, was torpedoed by a U-boat in 1941, most of the crew managed to escape into lifeboats. But what then? They had no navigational equipment, limited water and just a few cans of condensed milk to keep them going and they were bobbing up and down in the hostile Atlantic.

Monk, now in his nineties, happened to have a diary in his pocket with navigational charts from which the crew worked out where they thought the Cape Verde Islands might be. Then began traumatic days in which they rowed and rowed, all the time becoming fainter and more dehydrated. They rationed themselves to a few teaspoons of the milk each day.

Finally, one morning, dawn rose on a distant mountain. 'It was vertical black lava rock going straight down into the sea,' says Monk. 'We couldn't land. We rowed for another six hours until we spotted the little village of Tarrafal.

'As we got near they spotted us and two of their fishing boats came out with carafes full of water. We just sat there, drinking water.'

Finally they reached the beach and staggered into Tarrafal where they were cared for so kindly that Monk always yearned to return one day to say thank you.

His dream came true in late 2007 when his story caught the imagination of Ron Hughes of Cape Verde Travel. Ron organised a trip for him, and the Cape Verdean navy offered to take him to the remote village in western Tarrafal.

As the ship approached the green puddle at the foot of the Tarrafal Mountains, Monk reminisced. 'I remember so well walking ashore here on this beach. It's so wonderful to come back,' he told me.

He walked slowly up Tarrafal's main street in the heat of the midday sun and the word quickly spread. Before long a man of similar age, Germano Delgado, was coming along the street to meet him. Delgado had been one of his rescuers.

The two 90-year olds stood smiling at each other, nothing in common but a chance meeting 60 years before – and their age.

'I remember it quite well,' said Delgado. 'They were completely exhausted.'

Then Monk and Delgado put their hands to their chests in Cape Verdean greeting, shook hands like the British and went their separate ways.

Finally, 1.5 hours after leaving Boca, the path finds a nick in the mountain rim at a height of 830m. Over the saddle, look down on the tiny settlement of Selado do Mocho.

It is a hard descent (40 minutes) on a zig-zagging cobbled path to reach the edge of this remote village. Not long after passing around the head of a small valley into the village, the path cuts up to the top of a low ridge, where you find the village standpipe. Straight away, the path begins the descent into Ribeira Garça. Before long, you will catch your first glimpse of Chã de Igreja, on a small promontory of land projecting from the west side of the *ribeira*.

Descend into the deep cleft of the *ribeira*, and find a steep path up the seaward side of the village's promontory.

2 PONTA DO SOL–FONTAINHAS–FORMIGUINHAS–CHÃ DE IGREJA
Distance: 12km; time: 4.5 hours; difficulty: 2 (CW)

This coastal walk makes an interesting change from the *ribeiras*, passing through the village of Fontainhas, perched on a knife edge of rock, and with plenty of exposure to the sound and aroma of crashing waves. A lot of the walk is on the level but there are undulations. At the end of the walk you can either stay the night in Chã de Igreja, or catch the *aluguer* that runs from near the church to Ribeira Grande. If you are forced to charter an *aluguer*, it should be about 2,200$.

At the edge of Ponta do Sol on the road to Ribeira Grande, take the very clear turning to **Fontainhas**. The cobbled road winds in and out amongst the folds of the steep mountains and finally affords you a fantastic view of Fontainhas, perched like a fairytale village on a high and precipitous spit of land above a deep *ribeira*. Some 40 minutes after setting out you will be on its extraordinary main street, built on the spine of the narrow promontory. The houses lining this higgledy-piggledy street have a sheer drop of several hundred metres behind them.

As you leave Fontainhas, and as the path climbs back towards the coast, there is a good view of the *ribeira* with its intricate terracing and ingeniously engineered irrigation channels running across the slopes. On the valley floor the wooden structure is a traditional *trapiche* – a mule-driven contraption used for pressing sugarcane in the all-important manufacture of *grogue*.

In the next *ribeira* the path weaves back inland towards the well-watered but somewhat gloomy village of **Corvo**, 40 minutes from Fontainhas. Another 20 minutes brings you to the prettier village of **Formiguinhas**, where you descend to the shore.

The next stretch of the walk is the most impressive because much of the path has been hacked out of the massive, ancient rock formations. It is a spectacular but desolate walk, with the air full of the sound of the waves and the taste and smell of salt. At one point you emerge in a small, nameless settlement, where there are four houses and fields of rock. Here, there is no evidence of the passage of the centuries.

An hour-and-a-half from Formiguinhas the land opens out again and a broad *ribeira* leads up to the left. A small village (out of sight of the path) shelters in the mouth of this *ribeira*. After 15 minutes, cross a football pitch with metal goalposts and, 20 minutes later, you descend into the small fishing village of **Cruzinha da Garça**.

Pick up the cobbled road here and follow it for ten minutes out of the village, seeing a cemetery high up on a hillside opposite. There's a track leading into the *ribeira* on the left. Although this does not look very promising follow it inland. The *ribeira* is dry, desolate and dramatic. There is nothing but the rustle of parched leaves and the rattle of pebbles falling from the sheer valley sides. Some 40 minutes after leaving Cruzinha, you arrive at a promontory projecting into the *ribeira* with a steep path up its side leading to **Chã de Igreja**.

3 BOCA DAS AMBAS RIBEIRAS–CAIBROS–CHÃ DE LOBINHOS–REAL– LAGOINHA– ESPONGEIRO

Distance: 14km; time: 5 hours; difficulty: 2 (AI)

This walk is a feast of ever more dramatic panoramas and, like the others leading from parallel *ribeiras*, takes you to an eerie, higher world away from the drama of canyons and terraces. No part of the path is tricky, but the unremitting ascent requires a certain degree of fitness. To get to the starting point, take an *aluguer* from Ribeira Grande (outside Caixa Económica) all the way to **Boca das Ambas Ribeiras**, a 20-minute trip. The last part of the hike is a 1.5-hour walk along the road to Espongeiro – you may wish to arrange beforehand for transport to collect you from Lagoinha.

Entering Boca das Ambas Ribeiras from Ribeira Grande, you will find a turning to **Caibros** on the left, just before the cobbled main road ascends and bends to the right. Follow this dirt track and, after about 15 minutes, you will begin to ascend the right-hand side of the valley. Five minutes later you pass a small,

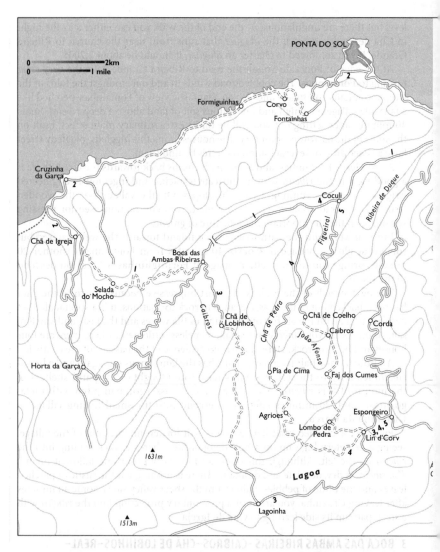

brick aqueduct on the left and the *ribeira* becomes more interesting, filled with palm trees and plantations. The track ends 30 minutes from the main road, after passing between two high buildings and reaching a little turning area. Continue in the same direction, on the footpath ahead, passing up a valley heavily planted with sugarcane, bananas and vegetables. After five minutes, at **Chã de Lobinhos**, there is a path up the hillside to the left which ascends in a hairpin for 20m. Less than ten minutes after beginning this path, you cross an irrigation channel and a public tap. The path ascends steeply and, after passing the last house for some time, you will see your route ahead, darting back and forth, its cobbled walls camouflaged by the rock.

Reaching a ridge, half an hour from Chã de Lobinhos, you can see into the next *ribeira* and you are already eye to eye with the first of the craggy peaks. The path dips slightly and there's a little path to the left: stay on the main path for the

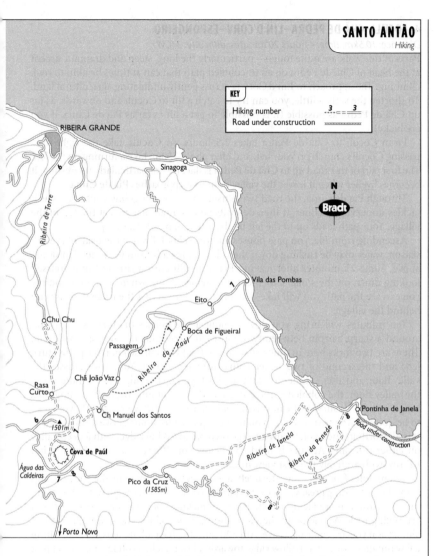

KEY

Hiking number	3 ···· 3
Road under construction	∽∽∽∽∽∽

RIBEIRA GRANDE

Sinagoga

Ribeira de Torre

N

Bradt

Vila das Pombas

Eito

Chu Chu

Boca de Figueiral

Passagem

Ribeira do Paúl

Chã João Vaz

Rasa Curto

Ch Manuel dos Santos

Pontinha de Janela

1501m

Road under construction

Cova de Paúl

Ribeira de Janela

Ribeira do Penede

Água das Caldeiras

Pico da Cruz
(1585m)

Porto Novo

ever more spectacular views of the two *ribeiras* – and of valleys beyond – ample compensation for this breathless climb.

Some 1.5 hours from Chã de Lobinhos, the path reaches a T-junction with a path of red earth. Here is the best panorama so far – you can see both the Chã de Pedra and the Figueiral roads. Turn right and arrive ten minutes later at the upper world, whose beginning is marked by a stone house and extensive terracing. The path is varied, sometimes through open agricultural land, sometimes along narrow ridges with cliffs plunging to either side.

Some 50 minutes from the last T-junction you reach another: turn right and go up the hill towards a green concrete water tank and tap. From here, the path becomes a road which, after 35 minutes meets a fork at which you turn right. Five minutes later you pass a graveyard, and five minutes after that the weather station at **Lagoinha**. Turn left after the weather station and begin the 1.5-hour trudge to **Espongeiro**.

4 COCULI–CHÃ DE PEDRA–LIN D'CORV–ESPONGEIRO

Distance: 10.5km; time: 4 hours 20 minutes; difficulty: 3 (CW)

Parts of this walk are quite tough – particularly the long, steep and dramatic ascent at the head of Chã de Pedra on an uncobbled path that can at times be akin to rock climbing. The approach to Lin d'Corv is across gently undulating agricultural land. To shorten the walk a little, you can try to catch a lift to Coculi and onwards, as far up Chã de Pedra as possible (it is possible to get a lift as far as Pia de Cima, if you are lucky).

From Coculi to Chã de Pedra takes 1.5 hours. At **Coculi**, take the right fork, passing Coculi's church on your left, and after about 700m, take a turning on the left. The first part of this road up to **Chã de Pedra** is flat and not particularly interesting. It becomes livelier when it leaves the valley floor as it approaches **Pia de Cima**.

Through Pia de Cima, the road twists itself into mind-boggling contortions as it tackles unnerving inclines; it then deposits you in a rare flat area at the top of the village. Your path leads up to the left by the low wall beside the shop.

Ascending from Pia, you pass houses and the school. Even at the peak of the dry season, water may be rushing down the sides of the path from the pine-clad slopes above. Some 25 minutes after leaving Pia, you will crest a rise and find yourself looking down on the small settlement of **Agriões**. From where you are standing, you can see the path you will take weaving to and fro across the ridge that rises up behind the village.

Ten minutes will bring you down amongst the houses of Agriões. Carry on around a sharp hairpin between two houses and continue down to a *grogue* still. There are two forks here in quick succession: the first is of two narrow paths (turn left) and the second of two wider paths (turn left again). Your path crosses the valley floor, and after another few minutes leads you up the ridge. Ten minutes from the valley floor, the cobbled surface stops, and you will find yourself battling up a tough incline. To survive the next half hour, up a steep and winding path, you need to be quite fit. The path will take you to the right at a fork, just above a small house. It is all worth it when you finally emerge on a breathtaking ridge, with a deep valley on either side, and Agriões behind and below you. There is a small farmer's hut nearby, with arguably the best view in Cape Verde.

Ten minutes from the ridge, turn left at a T-junction. From here, the path zig-zags up and up, affording great views to the north if you are lucky enough not to be caught in mist. Now you are facing the challenge of making your way up narrow paths of crumbling rock. At one point the path is so narrow and the walls so high that it is almost as if you are entering a cave. After 20 minutes, the path flattens out and, within a few minutes, goes up a shallow ridge towards a low thatched cottage. Bear right past the cottage and, after a few minutes, you will find yourself walking along the right side of a wide, low valley. Some 20 minutes beyond the thatched cottage you will emerge on a further, smaller ridge. Follow the path down towards the valley floor on your left.

After ten minutes bear left at a fork. You are now in a desert-like area barren of greenery, the path at the mercy of shifting winds. The path may be hard to distinguish so confirm the route that follows with passing locals.

Five minutes after the previously mentioned fork bear right at a second fork and start ascending towards the road at **Lin d'Corv**, which you will reach after just over ten minutes. There is not much at Lin d'Corv except a single house and a large area of the hillside concreted over and walled in to collect rainwater.

Turning left on to the road, it will take about 20 minutes to walk the 1.5km to **Espongeiro**. Wait here for a lift back down to Ribeira Grande. *Alugueres* run all day, though sometimes it can be an hour's wait.

5 ESPONGEIRO–LIN D'CORV–JOÃO AFONSO–CHÃ DE COELHO–FIGUEIRAL–COCULI

Distance: 10.5km; time: 3.5 hours; difficulty: 2 (CW)

This hike involves a steep and spectacular descent into the head of João Afonso on a good, cobbled path. It can be shortened by getting transport to Coculi at Chã de Coelho. Get to the starting point by taking an *aluguer* along the Ribeira Grande–Porto Novo road as far as Espongeiro.

Standing on the main road from Ribeira Grande, take the turning at **Espongeiro**, known as the Lagoinha road. Walk for 1.5km until you reach **Lin d'Corv**, where there is a large area of hillside concreted over to collect rainwater. The path down João Afonso begins here. Be careful not to confuse it with the path to Chã de Pedra – the two paths meet at Lin d'Corv. It is important to pick up the right path, otherwise you will end up descending the wrong valley. Stand with your back to the tap at the bottom of the water catchment area, and then follow the path off to your right. The path will lead you down along the side of a low hill through a pine forest, and after about ten minutes, you will see a cottage at the top of a small rise. Take a small turning down to the right about 15m before reaching the cottage.

After less than ten minutes you will reach a few houses at **Lombo de Pedra**. Pass through the settlement and, five minutes later, follow the white arrow painted on a rock to begin a series of zig-zags down the side of the mountain. From here, the path becomes dramatic, sometimes darting backwards and forwards, sometimes tracing down the knife edge of precipitous ridges, and sometimes carving across near-vertical slopes. After a vertiginous 35 minutes, you will pass a tapstand where clear water runs from the mountains above, and will be looking out over the village of **Fajã dos Cumes**.

Continuing the descent, another 30 minutes will bring you to the small village of **Caibros** (not to be confused with the *ribeira* of Caibros) and another 35 minutes beyond that, to **Chã de Coelho**. Passing through here and descending steeply for ten minutes will bring you to the valley floor in João Afonso. From the point where you hit the valley floor, it will take about an hour to reach **Coculi**.

6 ÁGUA DAS CALDEIRAS–RIBEIRA DE TORRE–RIBEIRA GRANDE

Distance: 10km; time: 4 hours; difficulty: 2 (Al)

Torre is the most beautiful *ribeira* of them all: a descent from empty, misty pine forest through the clouds, down a steep rocky path with just the jagged peaks and the more adventurous birds for company, and finally through greenery and cultivation to sea level. Navigation is easy but the path is steep. To get to the start of the walk take an *aluguer* along the Ribeira Grande–Porto Novo road to **Água das Caldeiras**. From Ribeira Grande this takes 40 minutes, and you should disembark at the first sign for the village on the right-hand side of the road. (To do this walk the other way round, leave Ribeira Grande on the Porto Novo road, passing the petrol station, and then the hospital, on the right. Torre is the great *ribeira* on the left.)

Take the cobbled road to the left, fenced off with a chain, and follow it uphill for ten minutes enjoying the sharp coolness. Then take a wide stone track to the left and descend, always through forest. Pine trees were chosen for reafforestation because their needles comb water from the clouds which drips down and moistens the soil.

After another ten minutes there's a clearing. A footpath leads out of the far end. Take it and emerge at a vista of high craggy mountains dropping way below to patches of vivid green, tiny houses and, even this high, the sounds of barking dogs and voices echoing towards you. Two *ribeiras* lie before you – Torre is to the left and after 15 minutes of steep descent you realise you are firmly destined for it as you see the teeth-like crags that now separate you from next-door Paúl. The view is infinitely interesting: crazy terraces inserted into crevices; intriguing local paths disappearing into rock faces.

After 1.5 hours you reach the first cultivation. After this, just continue downwards, through coffee and banana crops and past shallow shelving built to capture water. Sometimes the path follows a terrace – there are lots of people around by now so just ask for the footpath (*caminho*).

Ahead is the strange pinnacle of Torre, a rock that has defied the forces of wind and water to rise out of the middle of the *ribeira*. As you descend you pass the extraordinary hamlet of **Raso Curto**, built on a ridge just wide enough for a row of one-room-thick houses and a footpath. Two-and-a-half hours from the beginning, the path meets **Chu Chu** village, green and damp, with dark cliffs on either side. It's another 1.5 hours, or 6km, to **Ribeira Grande** along the road track down the *ribeira*. If you are lucky the *grogue* distillery 20 minutes down the road on the left will be in operation. Ten minutes before the end of the walk there is a glimpse of the sea through the crack in the mountains.

7 VILA DAS POMBAS–RIBEIRA DO PAÚL–EITO–PASSAGEM–COVA DE PAÚL
Distance: 9km; time: 4.5 hours; difficulty: 2 (AI)

This is many people's favourite, in a huge, abundantly green valley cloistered among vast, cathedral-like cliff walls. It is large that there are many villages on the way up, crammed on to every available ledge. Laughter, barks, clucks, arguments, drunkenness, car horns and radios resound through the valley so that even when you have left them below, and the clouds have intervened, their sounds pursue you into the peaks.

The starting point is **Vila das Pombas** but you can cut over 1.5 hours (and a lot of sweating) from this walk by taking transport up the *ribeira* – the road persists as far as Cabo de Ribeira. Perhaps a good compromise is to take transport beyond Eito as far as the drop-off point for Casa das Ilhas and pick up the hike from there.

From Pombas turn inland at the stadium to enter the valley. Reaching an aqueduct after ten minutes, take the road up to the right, and leave the valley below, filled with cornfields and deep green trees. The road ascends through various villages including **Eito**, the biggest. Some 2.5km after entering the valley, and less than 1km after leaving Eito, the road bends back sharply to the right. Soon after this you will see a little sign, just after a shop, on the wall on the left, to the guesthouse Casa das Ilhas. Take this path, which leads you on a glorious route and cuts out a loop of the road.

You will pass Casa das Ilhas after about 15 minutes of steep ascent. Keep going, the only navigational challenge being a T-junction of paths with a wall in front of you, at which you turn left. The path continues, up and down, and eventually broadens into a road which takes you past flowing water, pools and verdant planting, up through Passagem. Half an hour after leaving Casa das Ilhas, you will reach the main road. Turn left to continue up the valley.

In **Passagem** there is a swimming pool newly filled with water every day during July and August (otherwise, with a day's notice, they'll refill it for you).

Keep going, through the villages of **Chã João Vaz** and **Chã Manuel dos Santos**. There are one or two places to stop for a drink (see *Where to eat and drink*, page 287). A couple of hours later you will finally leave the most vertiginous local house behind and follow the finely crafted cobbled path with its drystone walling, gazing upwards to wonder how it can possibly take you through the mountains above.

Four hours from the start (assuming no stops), your lonely world of cold and cloud will push you over the top of the ridge and you will be gazing down into a fertile volcano crater filled with crops, orange trees, tomatoes and a few houses. Your exit from the crater is on the opposite side; reach it by following a stumbling path down to the right and into the crater, and then a track across it and out on to the road where, if you walk for a few seconds to the left, you find the final spectacle of the walk – the southern slopes of Santo Antão, Porto Novo and São Vicente beyond. Wait here for a lift back to town.

To go down the *ribeira* instead of up, take a lift along the main island road as far as **Cova**, which lies on the eastern side of the road and has two entrances – you want the one nearer to Ribeira Grande. As you enter Cova you will see the path you want leading up and out of the crater on the other side. Once you are on it, it's the same path down to the coast road.

8 PENEDO–RIBEIRA DO PENEDO–ESTÂNCIA DE PEDRA–PICO DA CRUZ–COVA
Distance: 14km; time: 5 hours 40 minutes; difficulty: 3 (CW)
Not for the unfit or faint-hearted, this hike takes you from sea level up to 1,600m within little more than 7km. After that, it is a less demanding one-hour walk to the main road.

LAST CHANCE TO SEE… THE CAPE VERDE RED KITE

When researchers travelled round the archipelago searching for the black kite (*Milvus m. migrans*) and the Cape Verde red kite (*Milvus m. fasciicauda*) in 1996–97, they were startled to find fewer than ten of each across the whole of Cape Verde.

The black kite can be found elsewhere – it is a very successful African and European species, and Cape Verde is its westernmost outpost. But the Cape Verde red kite can be found only on Cape Verde (it may be a subspecies of the red kite or an endemic species in its own right).

Scientists returned in 2000 to search again for kites. As birds go, they are quite easy to spot because they soar away from the ground. After two months roaming the cobbled paths and waiting around potential feeding grounds, they produced their verdict: on Cape Verde there remain just one black kite and two Cape Verde red kites.

The red kites were seen on Santo Antão and the black kite was spotted on Boavista. The researchers, Sabine Hille and Jean-Marc Thiollay, say that this means they are 'technically extinct'.

No-one is sure why the raptors have disappeared. It may partly be persecution – they are known to be chicken thieves and so humans pelt them with stones. They eat rats and mice that, these days, have probably been poisoned as part of pest control. Finally, the days are over when goats roamed freely through the plains, leaving the odd goat carcass for raptors to feed on. Now livestock and vegetation, are so precious that goats are kept penned up.

The researchers want to round up the two remaining Cape Verde red kites, plus any they have missed, and do a captive breeding programme to enhance their numbers. They would then release them and keep them alive through feeding stations and through a campaign to persuade the local people that raptors do a good job clearing fields of pests.

Reach the starting point by taking an *aluguer* along the coast road as far as the little village of **Penedo**, which lies at the mouth of the *ribeira* of the same name.

You strike up the *ribeira* on foot and the climb begins almost immediately, weaving amongst sugarcane plantations and the scattered houses. Follow the path up to the head of the valley and round to where it begins a tortuous zig-zagging ascent up an impossibly steep mountain face. If, as you pause for breath, you look back towards the coast, you will see the smaller Ribeira de Janela running parallel to Ribeira do Penedo, and slightly to the north.

There are small paths that lead off to the right and left but, sticking to the main path, you emerge on a narrow shoulder about two hours after setting out from Penedo. As you continue to ascend, it turns into a narrow ridge with staggering views first down one side, then the other, and a fantastic panorama to the south, east and north. If it is a clear day, **Pico da Cruz** can be seen ahead.

Even at this height (800m), the vegetation has changed – it is much greener here than on the ridges that lead, like dry ribs, to either side. Higher up it becomes cold and alpine with a sharp, resinous smell among the trees.

Along the ridge there are several houses. People have erected frames stretched across with gauze to allow the mist that boils over from the *ribeira* below to condense. After 1.5 hours of walking along the ridge, you pass one of these frames and, at the same point, see the cobbled main road that snakes up from the valley towards the Pico. The road is slightly down to your left. Keep to the path, and, after 15 minutes, you join the road, and emerge, after another 40 minutes of steep hairpins, at a small group of houses in the shadow of the summit. Turn right on the road to Paúl past the old, white painted house. Directly behind the house follow the very rough path which cuts up to the right. It's a 15-minute walk to the summit.

Retracing your steps from the summit to the small settlement, rejoin the road you arrived on and follow it straight on towards **Cova** (crater) and **Água das Caldeiras**. Following this road as it gently descends you will get your first glimpse of the crater about 45 minutes after leaving the summit. Ten minutes later you arrive at a crossroads. This is a good place to wait for a lift, or an *aluguer* back to either Porto Novo or Ribeira Grande.

LESS DEMANDING WALKS The bases of many of the *ribeiras* provide flat walks with mighty views up the canyons. The best such walk is up Ribeira de Torre as far as Chu Chu (see page 303). Ribeira Grande provides a less interesting flat walk. All the *ribeiras* can be ascended quite far by vehicle, at which point you can walk back downhill. Ribeira do Paúl would be a particularly dramatic venue for this option. Finally, it is worth travelling to Cova de Paúl and wandering around the crater (see *Sightseeing by vehicle*, page 281).

12

São Nicolau

Mother dear
I wanted to say my prayer
but I cannot:
my prayer sleeps
in my eyes, which cry for your grief
of wanting to nourish us but being unable to do so.

> Baltasar Lopes, born in São Nicolau, quoted in *Fire: Six Writers from Azores,*
> *Madeira and Cape Verde* edited by Donald Burness (Three Continents Press, 1977)

It was in the shady valley of Ribeira Brava in São Nicolau and along the civilised cobbled streets of its town that the seeds of Cape Verdean awareness were planted towards the end of the 19th century. São Nicolau was for over 50 years the intellectual centre of the archipelago. Yet by 1931, its educational buildings had closed and the scholars had vanished to neighbouring São Vicente. Now Ribeira Brava, the capital, has an air of quiet dignity like a university town in the holidays. For all the island's beauty, it receives just 0.6% of Cape Verde's tourists and its population is declining. It is a victim, as Maio has been, of being the neighbour of a busy centre of commerce. But this makes São Nicolau a joy to visit. The *vila* is pretty and quiet and there are several outstanding walks in the mountains.

HIGHLIGHTS AND LOWLIGHTS

This island has a little bit of everything the other islands have: a pretty main town with colonial architecture; long, deserted beaches; villages frozen in time; dramatic cliffside roads; and verdant mountains. Go for beautiful walks almost undisturbed by other tourists. Go for fishing: the island's waters are famed for their blue marlin. Go for birdwatching, particularly if you are trying to reach Raso Island (though see the restrictions on this, described below). If you are not a hiker, you can still access some of São Nicolau's beauty by road though you will not be able to penetrate the Monte Gordo Natural Park.

It is thought that the diving and surfing potential is high, but it is mostly undiscovered and there are no facilities at the time of writing. There are a few accessible beaches but it is not a luxury beach destination (there are no hotels). The coast offers other joys such as rocky, wave-lashed dramas and the odd *lagoa* suitable for swimming in. Culturally, São Nicolau's interesting history has not yet been gathered together for presentation to the visitor: there are no museums.

SUGGESTED ITINERARY AND NUMBER OF DAYS For hikers, the opening of the Monte Gordo Natural Park, with its facilitation of guiding and advice, raises all

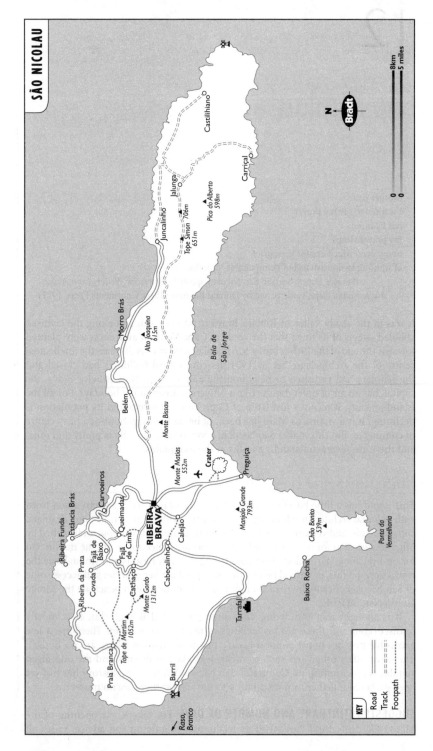

SÃO NICOLAU

KEY
Road
Track
Footpath

Ribeira Funda
Estância Brás
Carvoeiros
Queimadas
Fajã de Baixo
Covada
Ribeira da Prata
Fajã de Cima
Cachaço
Praia Branca
Tope de Martim
1052m
Monte Gordo
1312m
Cabeçalinho
Calejão
RIBEIRA BRAVA
Barril
Tarrafal
Baixo Rocha
Chão Bonito
539m
Maniolo Grande
793m
Monte Matias
552m
Crater
Preguiça
Ponta do Vermelharia
Monte Bissau
Baía de São Jorge
Belém
Morro Brás
Alto Joaquina
615m
Juncalinho
Tope Simón
651m
Jalunga
Pico do Alberto
598m
Carriçal
Castilhiano

Bradt

N

0   8km
0   5 miles

Raso, Branco

sorts of interesting possibilities for hiking across the centre of the island over several days. One could easily fill two or three full days with hiking, with perhaps a day of sightseeing in between. If you are not a hiker you could still fill two full days with perhaps a trip to Juncalinho's *lagoa*, and a drive through the island between Ribeira Brava and Ribeira da Prata, with many stops on the way.

BACKGROUND INFORMATION

HISTORY With a fertile hinterland and several almost permanent streams, São Nicolau was able to produce more agriculturally than the impoverished flat islands. It also has the widest bay of the archipelago, formed by the island's strange long finger that stretches to the east and affording a safe anchorage. Yet São Nicolau has always been overshadowed by others and so, apart from the brief flourishing of its seminary a century ago, it was never an island of importance.

It was discovered, along with the other windward islands, in 1461 – the date was probably St Nicholas's Day, 6 December. Families from Madeira and their Guinean slaves came to settle in the early 1500s. But the island was mountainous and inaccessible – indeed its lush interior is completely hidden from the outside – and so its **productive agriculture and livestock potential** did not attract more settlers until the 1600s. Even then, when the English sailor Dampier visited in 1683, he reported only 100 families on the island. He described the green interior, the vineyards producing good-quality wine, the abundance of wood and the great number of donkeys and goats. By 1731, there were only 260 inhabitants.

One great disadvantage of São Nicolau was the ease with which marauders could attack. Dutch, English and French pirates plagued the people, even after they retreated from their coastal settlement to Ribeira Brava, inland. It was not until a fortress was built in 1818 that security and a soaring population came to the island.

In 1805, the wealthy landowner who governed the island, José António Dias, had a son, Júlio José. He was a brilliant student but returned from his medical studies abroad to spend his life as a philanthropist on São Nicolau. Perhaps his greatest legacy came from his decision to move out of his large house in Ribeira Brava in 1866 and offer it to the three canons, three priests and three students who had arrived from Portugal to found a **seminary** on Cape Verde. This prevented them leaving for Santo Antão, having despaired of finding a building on São Nicolau.

The school attached to the seminary flourished, offering the same subjects as high schools in Portugal. Suddenly the brightest Cape Verdean children were able to learn subjects as varied as the classics, chemistry and political economy. This education groomed them for careers in either the Church or the Portuguese civil service. In this way Cape Verde became the centre for evangelisation of Portuguese west Africa.

The impact created by the generations that passed through this seminary should not be underestimated, for they spread abroad, used by the Portuguese as an interface between themselves and their west African territories. They were articulate and intelligent, wedded to the idea of Cape Verde being part of Portugal, but deeply concerned with the lot of their people. As teachers and administrators they had influence over the next generation, which took their ideas and moulded them into more radical form. The prime example of such a two-generation process was Juvenal Cabral, the seminary-educated teacher who fought for better conditions for Cape Verde and whose son was Amílcar Cabral, the leader of the revolution.

But the life of the seminary was all too brief. It was a victim of the difficult relationship that emerged between the Catholic Church and the government in the democratic republic of Portugal after the Church was separated from the state in 1911. This separation led to the splitting of the seminary – its secondary school function was relocated in Mindelo.

The seminary closed in 1917, reopened in 1923, and shut for ever in 1931. Later, it was used to accommodate 200 political deportees from Portugal. The Bishop of Cape Verde, rumoured to be terrified by 'hordes of deported revolutionaries and anti-clericals', fled to São Vicente. All that remained was a highly educated peasant population. One visitor in the 1930s was astonished when a local boy, prompted by a reference in Creole to a rose, quoted: '*Rosa, vita tua diuturna non est.*'

The 20th century brought desperate **droughts** to São Nicolau, in 1921, 1940 and the 1950s.

SÃO NICOLAU TODAY Agriculture, and the port at Tarrafal, are the economic mainstays. Catching and canning tuna keeps the occupants of Tarrafal and the remote village of Carriçal busy (and is a great spectator sport). The island hopes to develop ecotourism and beach tourism.

GEOGRAPHY The island, at 343km², is mainly barren rock with a large semi-humid valley in its centre, cultivated with maize and beans on the higher slopes, and sugarcane and banana below. In the west is a range of mountains with the highest, Monte Gordo, reaching 1,312m. This peak is the meeting point of two ranges – one runs north–south and the other out to the northwest. The eastern finger of land is a long ridge of barren mountains. Between the central mountains and the western coast are stony plains. Desertification seems to have hit São Nicolau particularly hard – its orange groves and coffee plantations have gone and the old folk reminisce about verdant mountainsides that are now bare – in fact the lines of stone walls that used to divide fields can be traced impossibly high up the mountainsides. There is evidence of much reafforestation. The population is about 13,000.

NATURAL HISTORY

Flora There are 46 endemic species of plant in São Nicolau, of which 32 can be found in the Monte Gordo Natural Park. One of these, Macela do Gordo (Nauplussmithii), is native to Monte Gordo and 17 are on the list of endangered species for the island of São Nicolau.

The fairytale dragon tree (*Dracaena draco*), locally known as *dragoeiro*, is almost abundant on this island – this is about the only place in the archipelago

---

A CHANCE FIND

The endangered Cape Verde warbler (*Acrocephalus brevipennis*) was until recently thought to inhabit only Santiago. Then, in 1970, someone found a specimen of the bird stored at Centro de Zoologia, Lisbon. It was reported as having come from São Nicolau, so ornithologists decided to scour the island in the hope of finding some more. They were rewarded – by 1998, their surveys had identified eight territories in the northwest of the island, though they believe its long-term prospects there are poor. The bird is brown with a creamy throat, a long-pointed black beak and black feet. In São Nicolau it inhabits small, dense stands of cane (*Arundo donax*) along dry riverbeds, often with shrubs and fruit trees.

Although there are 47 protected areas in Cape Verde, enshrined in law, all but Monte Gordo have an Achilles heel: their precise, mapped boundaries have not been legalised. This leaves them vulnerable. In Boavista, for example, there are several areas where land originally allocated for protection has been reallocated for tourism development instead.

In São Nicolau, however, the boundaries of its beautiful heart were officialised in 2007, and work is underway to create a park that is pleasant for tourists and might create some prosperity for the people who live there.

The park occupies some 952ha in the northwest of the island, and includes the peak of Monte Gordo.

It's an important area ecologically because of its rich biodiversity. The unique conditions that have generated this interesting ecology set it apart, not just from the rest of the island but also from the rest of Cape Verde. At the heart of these differences is climate, which affects not just life in the area but also landscape. In the south and southeast there are humid and semi-humid regions. In the north and northwest it is arid.

A key aim of the park is to develop a thriving local economy predicated on conservation of the area. This is why a lot of thought has gone into training guides (who are salaried), and training local people to be useful to visitors, for example by making handicrafts. There is a good visitors' centre where you can get information and purchase handicrafts.

For more information contact e pnmonte.gordo@hotmail.com, or see www.areasprotegidas.cv/montegordo/. You can stay right in the heart of the park at a small pension (see Cachaço for details).

where the endangered species grows naturally. It can reach about 10m high and its flattened top and grey gnarled branches give the landscape the feel of an ancient world – it is said the trees can live for 1,000 years. The 'blood' of the dragon tree has been used in traditional medicines to relieve pain and is also used to colour *grogue*. The tree grows mainly on northeast-facing slopes at altitudes of between 500m and 900m. Conservationists are trying to use it more in reafforestation programmes. The dragon tree is an endemic species of Macaronesia – it grows in the Canary Islands and in Madeira, where it is also endangered.

Birds BirdLife International has defined 12 Important Bird Areas in Cape Verde, of which the central mountain range around Monte Gordo is one. This area, running roughly between Fajã de Baixo and Praia Branca, is an important breeding area for the Cape Verde petrel (*Pterodroma feae*); there were thought in 1998 to be about 30 pairs.

Other birds thought to frequent São Nicolau are the Cape Verde little shearwater (*Puffinus (assimilis) boydi*); the Cape Verde kite (*Milvus (milvus) fasciicauda*) – although there may now be none left; the Cape Verde buzzard (*Buteo ('buteo') bannermani*); the rare endemic Cape Verde peregrine (*Falco (peregrinus) madens*); the spectacled warbler (*Sylvia conspicillata*); the blackcap (*Sylvia atricapilla*); and the endemic Cape Verde swift (*Apus alexandri*).

For birds on Raso (such as the Cape Verde shearwater) see *Raso and Branco*, page 328.

São Nicolau BACKGROUND INFORMATION

12

HAZARDS Some of the walks in this chapter are steep, especially in and out of Ribeira Brava, and the descents can be hard on older knees, no matter how fit their owners are. We have indicated this in the text, but do heed local advice if you are concerned.

Swim in the *lagoas* only when the water is calm. Crime is almost unheard of.

FESTIVALS Festivals reflect the strong Cape Verdean tradition of music and dancing. The February Carnival, held at the same time as the famous São Vicente Carnival, is an exhilarating, exhausting three-day party (see box, *São Nicolau's carnival*, below). New Year is also cause for big celebration, and there is a festival on 6 January. In April there is Pascoela, celebrated in Fajã – mass followed by games, horse races and processions. There are many festivals through the summer, including one lasting two days in Juncalinho. Festival dates are as follows:

February (variable date)	Carnival
April (variable date)	Pascoela (Fajã)
13 April	Santo António (Preguiça)
Early May (variable date)	Nossa Sra do Monte (Cachaço)
24 June	São João (Praia Branca, with horse racing)
29 June	São Pedro (*vila* and Fajã Lompelado, with horse racing)
Sunday following 29 June	São Pedrinho
August	Music festival (Praia da Telha)
September	Sweet Water festival (Ribeira Prata)
First Sunday in October	Nossa Sra do Rosário
First Sunday in December	São Francisco (Tarrafal)
6 December	Municipality Day

SÃO NICOLAU'S CARNIVAL

If you ever catch yourself wondering how people on this quiet island entertain themselves then here is the answer: Carnival. It may last just three days but arguably the other 362 in the year are spent preparing for it.

There is the music, for a start. Songs are written specially for the festival, dispersed, learned and rehearsed. But that's nothing compared with the costumes. The Carnival King and Queen's outfits cost around 100,000$ (€1,000) each to produce – and they look correspondingly spectacular. Anyone who wants to have a costume made, dance in the procession for all three days and get into the sponsored parties must pay 7,000$. The costumes are designed according to the theme of the year. Fittings are conducted blindfold so that the wearer has no idea what he or she is dressed as until the big day.

By the first day of the festival the island has divided into two rival groups who spend four or five hours dancing and singing their way along different routes into the main square. Festivities continue into the next morning – the two rival, post-procession parties don't begin until around 03.00. After sleeping until mid afternoon, the second day of festivities begins: pretty much a repeat of the first. Then there is a day of rest. On the third day of the festival (fat Tuesday), many onlookers emerge in their own costumes.

BY AIR São Nicolau is served by TACV inter-island flights from São Vicente and Sal several times a week. In a land of dramatic scenery, the descent into São Nicolau is one of the best. As it nears land, the plane veers suddenly between a jagged ridge and a volcano cater. The tiny airport (235 1313) is a ten-minute drive from the main town.

From the airport to Ribeira Brava costs 100$ in an *aluguer*. You might be able to charter one as a taxi, which will cost 400–600$.

BY FERRY Currently the *Sal Rei* travels from São Nicolau to Santiago (around 13 hours), and São Nicolau to São Vicente (about six hours) twice a week. It's much cheaper than the plane (3,500$ one-way – but it is not a comfortable boat so it is worth paying the extra 1,000$ for a reclining, padded seat). You can get more information about ferries from the agencies in Praia, or ask around in Tarrafal.

BY YACHT The best anchorage is at the harbour of Tarrafal, and it's where you report to the marine police. There's no marina and there are no buoys. Should there be northeast winds rushing down the ravines towards you, it can be impossible to shuttle to land. There's also Preguiça – for a long time São Nicolau's main harbour – which is more exposed. Carriçal is a tiny, remote village with a pretty bay and shelter from the northeast winds. Anchor outside the cove.

GETTING AROUND

BY PUBLIC TRANSPORT *Alugueres* ply the road between the main square in Ribeira Brava and Tarrafal (50 minutes; 250$). They travel intermittently all day, but are more frequent leaving Tarrafal before 08.30 and leaving Ribeira Brava at 11.00–12.00. Near the check-in time for plane arrivals you'll find *alugueres* destined for the airport waiting in Ribeira Brava's square.

Alugueres also travel along the eastern ridge as far as Juncalinho (200$) and, less commonly, on to Carriçal (700$). They go from Tarrafal north up the coast as far as Ribeira da Prata. These follow the principle: into town in the early morning, out of town around lunchtime. Drivers are very keen for tourists to hire them as taxis. To avoid this, hang around nonchalantly until you are part of a group rather than approaching an empty minibus or truck. A new road made travelling to Tarrafal much easier for a while, but heavy rain caused a lot of damage and landslides in 2009 and they are still feeling the effects.

BY TAXI Taxis are mostly in the form of chartered *hiaces*: Ribeira Brava to Fajã 1,000$; to Tarrafal 2,000$; to Preguiça 600$. A day's hire might be 7,000$.

BY CAR To reach outlying places accessed by dirt tracks, it is best to enquire about a jeep and driver from the *aluguer* drivers or at the town hall.

🚗 **Agência Santos e Santos** Ribeira Brava; 235 1830; m 994 5969; e fsantos@ hotmail.com, fsantos@cvtelecom.cv

🚗 **Monte Gordo Rent a Car** 235 1280

Cars can also be rented from the driving school which is above the TACV office in Ribeira Brava (m 994 5112; e eliolioneves@hotmail.com).

You could also ask in the municipal market about car hire.

São Nicolau   GETTING AROUND

12

BY BOAT A fishing boat can take you from Preguiça to Carriçal and from Carriçal to visit caves down the coast.

WHERE TO STAY

The two centres are Ribeira Brava (*vila*) and Tarrafal. Hikers tend to stay in Ribeira Brava and anglers in Tarrafal. There is a guesthouse in Preguiça and one in Juncalinho.

ACTIVITIES

EXCURSIONS

**Agência e Transporte Santos &
Santos** Ribeira Brava; 235 1830; e fsantos@ hotmail.com. Organises trips & offers car hire with or without driver.
Guides There are a few knowledgeable *aluguer* drivers on the island who speak English, can give advice on major hikes, can drive you here & there & be general fixers. 2 we can personally recommend are **Paulinho** (235 2800; m 996 6191) & **Toi d'Armanda**, who does jeep excursions (236 1804; m 994 5146; e toilopes@hotmail.com).

HIKING Hiking and fishing are the two big attractions of São Nicolau. Some walks are described below (see page 324). The mixture of verdant agricultural land, vertiginous *ribeiras*, craggy peaks and dry, arid landscapes all in such an unfrequented place is what makes São Nicolau so special. By far the most beautiful walks are in the mountainous interior, though we include one or two others as well. The walks can be divided, roughly, into two: those that are based on several steep and beautiful paths in and out of the *vila*; and those that lie west of the main road that runs through Fajã and Cachaço. Since this road runs in a horseshoe shape through the centre of the walking areas, you can alter some walks to suit: you can use local transport to shorten walks or to enable you to walk only downhill or only uphill – or you can sandwich several walks together.

The **Monte Gordo Natural Park** (see box, *Trails in the Monte Gordo Natural Park*, page 327) encompasses many good walks and its office, Casa do Ambiente, can be found in Cachaço (237 1829; e ecotourism.pnmg@gmail.com). It is a white building about 200m uphill along a track from the main road. Here you can obtain information about the park and about hikes, pick up a trained guide (no fee, though tips are welcome), and look at the little endemics garden, where they are trying to grow every plant that is special to São Nicolau. You can also arrange for lunch to be prepared for you at a distant village (500$ per person approximately), discover where the campsites are, and buy some artisanal products. The office also sells water, guidebooks and plant- and bird-identification books, as well as postcards. There are plans to increase facilities for tourists here, including setting up a café and shop.

The principal hikes are signposted. The park regards itself as a resource for the whole of São Nicolau. They may therefore be of assistance with walks that lie outside their boundaries.

DIVING São Nicolau's diving potential is untapped at the moment.

FISHING The quality of the deep-sea fishing is high, particularly for blue marlin and barracuda. Chartering a boat for blue marlin fishing requires a bit of planning because they generally have to come across from another island. It is best to book beforehand. In the UK, for example, Cape Verde Travel advertises deep-sea fishing off São Nicolau for €500 a day. The proprietor of Pensão Tonecas offers blue marlin fishing for €600–800 per day for a minimum of four days and a maximum of four people.

BOAT TRIPS Local fishermen can be hired at Tarrafal and at Preguiça for trips down the coast, for example to caves, beaches or to the village of Carriçal.

BIRDWATCHING Birdwatching rates along with fishing and hiking as one of São Nicolau's prime attractions. For some of the birds that can be found on the island see *Natural history*, page 311.

One of the key attractions, however, was not available when this edition was written. Visits to Ilhéu Raso, to view, amongst others, the Raso lark, were banned in a 2007 clampdown by the government. It is now possible only to hire a fishing boat for around €70 per day and circle the island, and its companion Ilhéu Branco.

As a consolation, it is worth visiting Carberinho (see page 328) where many of the migratory birds found on Raso also visit, and which some ornithologists believe should be given protected status.

TURTLES Loggerhead turtles nest here and are particularly abundant on beaches north and south of Tarrafal, Porto da Lapa and Carriçal. The town halls in both Tarrafal and Ribeira Brava have turtle-conservation programmes in which you may be able to participate. Ask around or email SOS Tartarugas for further information (e *info@turtlesos.org*).

BEACHES If you wander the coast of São Nicolau you may make some discoveries of your own. There are beaches up the west coast from Tarrafal – for example Praia Grande, Praia Branca and Praia Francês. Porto da Lapa has a beautiful beach which is accessible either by fishing boat from Preguiça or by hiking from south of Juncalinho (you will need a guide). There's also a beach at Carriçal and Praia Baixo is a pretty cove and important turtle-nesting beach a one-hour walk south of Tarrafal. Be warned, however: beaches can temporarily disappear in bad weather.

SURFING There can be good surf on the coast north of Tarrafal, for example around Ponta Cascalhão.

HORSERIDING São Nicolau has a proud horse-racing tradition and horses are brought from other islands for the big races of the year at the festivals of São João and São Pedro.

Daniel Cabral Tarrafal, near the port; m 981 6516; e dmcabral7@yahoo.com.br. Offers horseriding & overnight lodging in a typical Cape Verdean home. Speaks English.

SIGHTSEEING BY VEHICLE One of the most spectacular roads in Cape Verde is the road from Ribeira Brava to Tarrafal. This 26km route pulls out of Ribeira Brava and negotiates a series of deep creeks cut into the mountainside of the northern coast before turning inland to the lush Fajã Valley. Mountain ranges spike the right-hand side and you ascend gently through Fajã de Baixo (Lower Fajã) and Fajã de Cima (Upper Fajã), almost completely encircled by a ring of mountains. Then the road turns to the southwest and you enter the stony plains that lead down towards Tarrafal. After Tarrafal the land is flat and brown but it is worth following the odd signposted track down to the coast on the left to witness the beaches or the striking rock formations.

Finally the road bends inland to Praia Branca and out in a semi-circle finishing in Ribeira da Prata. Many sights to see on the way are described below.

RIBEIRA BRAVA

This is a pretty town with houses of ochre, green and blue, and neat gardens blooming with plants and flowers. It is wedged into the steep sides of a *ribeira*, leading to a charming chaos of steep, interlocking streets in some parts of town. Narrow cobbled streets lead away from the large square which contains a bust of the town's philanthropist and an imposing cathedral visited by the old ladies of the town every day. They have first claim to the wooden benches in the square, by the way. Lining the streets are surprisingly well-stocked, old-fashioned shops in dim, shuttered interiors. The *ribeira* – green even in the dry season – towers above and cuts the town deeply in two, its narrow floor functioning as an extra road for much of the year. There is a charming statue of the town's famous poet, Baltasar Lopes da Silva, in the smaller square to the west of the main *praça*.

WHERE TO STAY Accommodation sometimes gets booked up in high season, so book ahead.

Agência Santos & Santos Pousada Mana Guimara [317 A6] (6 rooms) 235 1830; m 994 5969; e fsantos57@hotmail.com. Down near the Shell petrol station above the agency of the same name, this is a comfortable place. **$$**

Pensão Residencial Jardim [317 B7] (10 rooms) 235 1117/1950. A sparkling white *pensão* up the hill at the southern end of town with some charm & a small degree of eccentricity. A terrace offers a shady retreat from which to gaze down on the pastels of the town below & muse on *vila* life. Rooms have fans & hot water. There are 2 mini apartments with kitchenettes & options for families via interconnecting doors. Internet available & there is a rooftop restaurant serving lunch & dinner. It's in a steep part of town, & access is along a 20m, uphill alleyway. **$$**

Pensão Santo António [317 B4] (15 rooms) 235 2200; m 993 4284; e manuelsantos@cvtelecom.cv. Just east of the main square gardens, this has a bright, fresh, new feel with large rooms, some of which overlook the square, & a shared living room. Rooms have hot water, AC & some have a fridge. **$$**

Jumbo Residencial [317 A2] (6 rooms) 235 1315. Jumbo is across the *ribeira* from the old town hall; rouse the owner via the bar on the ground floor. The communal areas are unpromising, & the communal bathroom & some of the rooms are dingy, but a few are almost pleasant – large & clean with balconies. 2 are en suite. B/fast not inc. **$**

WHERE TO EAT AND DRINK Order several hours beforehand if you want something other than the dish of the day. The São Nicolau speciality is *molho* or *modje* – goat meat, potatoes and onions with cornmeal and rice.

Recanto Much-praised seafood restaurant. Just outside the *vila* on the road to Juncalinho, downhill on the right side of the road. Walkable but a taxi might be preferable, particularly if returning in the pitch dark. **$$$**

Alternativa [317 A5] In the south of town nearly opposite the petrol island. A little courtyard bar & restaurant. **$$**

Pensão Jardim [317 B7] ⏲ 07.30–10.00 daily; lunch when ordered, 19.00 onwards for dinner. Rooftop restaurant serving lunch & dinner, with a mostly traditional menu. Above the hotel of the same name. Lunch & dinner should be ordered in advance. **$$**

Pensão Santo António [317 B4] ⏲ 07.30–10.00, 12.30–14.30 & 19.30–22.00

daily, closed Sun evenings. This has a restaurant on its ground floor. $$

✗ **Sila** [317 A3] On the right as the airport road descends into the *vila*, before it crosses the *ribeira* into town. An Italian restaurant. $$

✗ **Bela Sombra Dalila** [317 A5] Down the narrow street that leaves the main square to the right of the cathedral, this serves traditional plates of food such as *modje* & *cachupa*. $

✗ **Market** [317 A3] A café selling cheap *pasteis* & snacks is located just inside the market building. $

✗ **Nameless cheap eats** Rua Seminário. On the road leading northwest from Jumbo Residencial, parallel with the *ribeira*. $

♀ **Ponte Vermelho Churrasqueira** [317 A1] Also a bar & video hall that serves meat dishes. $

⌂ **Sodade Snack Bar** [317 A2] This bar is a good place for recovering from the heat of the day. It is beside the gardens of the *praça* opposite the old town hall. $

⌂ **Van** [317 A2] Popular for evening snacks, the van can be found near the Jumbo Residencial. $

Fresh bread can be bought from the bakery on a little road off the post office square, or from the bakery in Pensão Santo António; vegetables are available from the municipal market in a new building on the street running down from the bank to the *ribeira*.

ENTERTAINMENT AND NIGHTLIFE The population of Ribeira Brava is not generally sufficient to sustain the two Saturday nightclubs, so one is likely to swing while the other fades. Even the owners of the losing venue have been known to give up on a quiet night and go and party at the other one.

♀ **Clube de Ribeira Brava and Atletico** [317 A4] These 2 football clubs regularly hold parties. The first is almost opposite Restaurante Bar Bela Sombra Dalila, the other is further down the same road, opposite the Shell petrol station.

♀ **Good Look** ⊕ Sat. It looks abandoned on the outside but is fully equipped inside. Follow the Tarrafal road off the map & it is about 50m up, on the left.

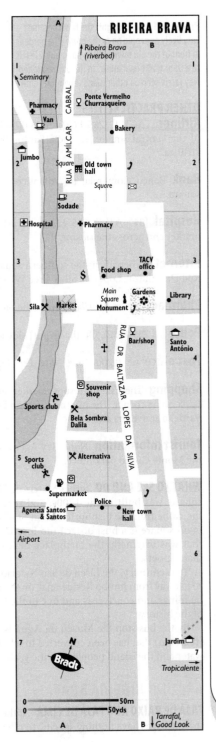

Praça On Sat & Sun nights the town becomes very lively as people go to the *praça* (the gardens in front of the old town hall) to hang out & listen to a DJ or traditional music. In the old-fashioned way rarely seen on other islands any more, entire families arrive to chat, dance, play, & socialise – young & old mixing & everyone keeps an eye out for everyone else's kids – a really lively crowd. ♀**Tropicalente** ⊕ Sat. In Chăzinha, out beyond Residencial Jardim.

OTHER PRACTICALITIES
Airlines TACV (♦ *235 1161;* ⊕ *08.00–12.30 & 14.30–18.00 Mon–Fri*), at the top of the central square. Agência Santos & Santos, for internal and international airlines.

Bank Banco Comercial do Atlântico (⊕ *08.00–15.30 Mon–Fri*). On the main square.

Hospital [317 A3] (♦ *235 1130*). A vast building on the hill past the municipal market and across the *ribeira*.

Internet Cybercafé in the southern square that houses the petrol station; also on Rua Dr Baltazar Lopes da Silva. Free Wi-Fi in the main *praça*.

Pharmacy Cross the *ribeira* from the old town hall, turn right and it's on the left.

Police (♦ *235 1152*). On the airport side of town, beside Agência Santos & Santos.

Post office (⊕ *08.00–16.00 Mon–Fri*). Opposite the back of the old town hall.

Shopping There's a mini supermarket on the road going north that has the BCA Bank on its corner. The internet shop on Rua Dr Baltazar Lopes da Silva sells Cape Verdean souvenirs and music.

Tourist information None. Try Agência Santos & Santos or, for hiking, go up to the Monte Gordo park office.

WHAT TO SEE AND DO Igreja Matriz de Nossa Senhora do Rosário, on the main square, was built in the 1700s, and rebuilt between 1891 and 1898 to become the cathedral: the bishopric was in São Nicolau between 1866 and 1940. In the main square is a bust of Dr Júlio José Dias and also the library, in the building that was originally the birthplace of José Lopes de Silva, one of Cape Verde's major poets.

The **seminary**, the Liceu de São Nicolau, is on Rua Seminário, a little way up the road away from Jumbo Residencial, on the right. You can ask to explore its rambling buildings and courtyards and one of the knowledgeable priests may explain some of the history.

By the bus stop the **Museu da Aguá** is worth a visit. It is a traditional *chafariz* (fountain) that has been converted to tell the story of the relationship between the water and the island people over the years.

AROUND RIBEIRA BRAVA

FAJÃ DE BAIXO AND FAJÃ DE CIMA At the heart of the lush interior of São Nicolau, these villages have nothing specific to offer except some pleasant meandering.

CACHAÇO Here can be found more beauty, the office for the natural park, two viewpoints (*miradouros*) and two small shops, one of which sells a particularly fine goat's cheese: mild, slippery, and with a salty crust.

Cachaço is the confluence of the main road, the track up into the natural park and two hiking paths, one from Fajã de Baixo and one from Ribeira Brava.

There's a small track to a viewpoint at the little church, Senhora do Monte. There's also another designated viewpoint just over 0.5km south down the main road, on the left.

Where to stay

🏠 **Pensão Arlinda** (2 rooms) 237 1176; 998 1533. This small *pensão* makes a good base for exploring the park. B/fast inc, & other meals can be arranged. A Peace Corps project is under way to stimulate business in the area, & the development of this pension & a café are part of this. **$**

TARRAFAL

This impoverished port town lies at the base of stony, barren hills that betray little about São Nicolau's lush interior. The town feels parched and can reach 40°C in the summer. It is strung out along a very long coastal road. At the southern end of this road is the port. A block inland from the port is the long, main square. There are plans to turn Tarrafal into a marina, transforming not just the harbour but also the main street.

WHERE TO STAY

🏠 **Casa Aquário** (6 rooms) Alto Calheta; 236 1099; e info@casa-aquario.nl; www.casa-aquario.nl. Down in the south of town, by the beach, this is a Dutch-owned establishment with simple rooms. Run by an ex-chef, it prides itself on its cuisine & dining is communal. The owner, Henny Kusters, can organise excursions or arrange your entire stay in São Nicolau. HB accommodation only. **$$**

🏠 **Pensão Tonecas** (8 rooms) 236 1220; e tonecas@mail.cvtelecom.cv. Large, en-suite rooms with AC & hot water. **$$**

🏠 **Residencial Alice** (15 rooms) 236 1187. On the coast road, this family-run place is an institution in Tarrafal, having been going

for nearly 20 years. For some it is the only place to stay. Most rooms have a balcony with a view of the sea, & most have AC, private bathroom & hot water. There are a couple of 2-bedroom apartments & a roof terrace. **$$**

🏠 **Residencial Natur** (7 rooms) 236 1178. Going north along the coast road, turn right just before the sports ground & left just after it – the hotel is on your right. Spacious, bright & simple, if a bit clinical, with tiled floors & a roof terrace. Great views both inland & seaward. **$**

🏠 **Hotel Monte Gordo** At the time of writing this half-finished hotel, resembling a cross between a barracks & a fish factory, was closed.

WHERE TO EAT AND DRINK

✗ **Buena Vida** ⊕ 18.00–'the end' daily. At the southern tip of the harbour opposite the old processing factory. Italian food with a Spanish influence, pizza, tiramisu & ice cream. **$$$**

✗ **Blue Dolphin** Opposite Pensão Tonecas. **$$**

✗ **Casa Aquário** (see above) ⊕ 12.00–14.00 & evenings. You will need to give half a day's notice for dinner. **$$**

✗ **Casa de Pasto Alice** (see *Residencial Alice*, above) Thought by many to be the best eatery in Tarrafal, this is like a large living room in which

guests feel like members of the extended family. Serves traditional foods. There is no obligation to order in advance but food other than the dish of the day may be slow to materialise. **$$**

✗ **Pensão Tonecas** 236 1220; ⊕ for lunch & dinner Tue–Sun. **$$**

✗ **Felicidade** ⊕ lunch & dinner daily. In the southeast of town, this is a good place for cheap local eats. Cuttlefish is the speciality. **$**

✗ **Lanchonette Amizade** In the southeast of town. **$**

ENTERTAINMENT AND NIGHTLIFE Tarrafal has a livelier nightlife than Ribeira Brava, with the **Disco Paradise** and **Bar-Restaurante Esplanada** (low blue building facing the water), the main disco in town, popular on Saturday nights.

OTHER PRACTICALITIES
Bank (⏰ 08.00–15.00 Mon–Fri). At the coastal end of the main square.

Ferries Try at STM, near Pensão Tonecas (✆ 236 1170).

Hospital (✆ 236 1130).

Internet Next to Dorado Edileila (follow the road inland from Pensão Tonecas); and Cyberhebr@ico, further inland past Dorado Edileila.

Police (✆ 236 1132).

Post office (⏰ 08.00–16.00 Mon–Fri). At the top of the main square.

WHAT TO SEE AND DO
Medicinal sand Some of the black-sand beaches around Tarrafal and Barril, further north, are reputed to have healing powers, particularly in the alleviation of the symptoms of arthritis. It is thought they are high in iodine and titanium. Sufferers tend to bury themselves in the sand and lie there; some claim they have subsequently achieved relief for many months. The effective period is June to August.

Beaches
Praia de Tedge A pretty, and busy, little beach south of town. There is a plan for a hotel here.

Praia de Baixo Rocha Praia de Baixo Rocha is a 1.5-hour walk south of Tarrafal. A beautiful cove and an important place for nesting turtles – the sticks you will see in the summer are marking nests in the hope that people won't inadvertently destroy the eggs. It's a lonely walk over a landscape like burnt fudge with dramatic views of the mountains beyond. Cross the town's southern cove (Praia de Tedge) and find the track leading south from it. You pass a yellow building on the left and a series of dumps as well as, perhaps, stone-breakers. You are making for a cove that lies between the furthest headland you can see and the second-furthest – a much lower, smaller headland. The trick is to avoid all the bulges of tiny headlands in between you and the cove and stick to the main track. The route is possible in a 4x4 and can be done in a fisherman's boat for around 7,000$.

NORTH OF TARRAFAL

The road northwest of Tarrafal follows fairly close to the shoreline until Barril, after which it cuts inland to Praia Branca, heads north out towards the coast again and then bends east, finishing in Ribeira da Prata. Along the coastal part of this road are several beautiful parts of coastline, including beaches (Ponta Cascalhão, Praia Grande (signposted), and Praia da Francês), and Caberinha.

PRAIA DA FRANCÊS A white-sand beach just south of Barril. It's signposted, and also rumoured to be a great surfing spot.

PRAIA BRANCA An attractive town on the hillside, which has several quaint shops, bars and cafés.

RIBEIRA DA PRATA Driving up from Praia Branca, the road ends in a bottleneck, where you have to leave your car and walk up cobbled streets to this beautiful scenic village – well worth the effort. Ribeira da Prata is an attractive place that will give you the feeling of having stepped back in time. People visit in order to see Rocha Scribida; the 'writing on the rock'. Ask for directions at the top of the village: it is a two-minute scramble up the other side of the *ribeira*.

There you will see a stratum of rock where localised erosion has revealed some intricate darker lines – or, if you must, rock that bears words written by an ancient people who knew the island long before the Portuguese. Historians have plumped for the former explanation.

There is infrequent public transport between Tarrafal and Ribeira da Prata (250$ one-way). There are several shops selling water, biscuits, bread and *grogue*.

CABERINHO/PONTA BROUCO After Barril, turn left off the road and follow the signposted but dusty and desolate track over the rocks, stopping short of the coast. This is a stretch of dramatic rock formations and undulating expanses of smooth black rock on which to sit and gaze at the crashing waves and abundant white foam. There are some steps carved into sandy rock down to the drama below. To the right of them is a deep inlet with stunning rock formations (be careful walking its circumference on the high side as there is a sharp overhang). If, after descending the steps, you head south, you will find after a few minutes a little *lagoa* in which you can swim when the weather is calm.

SOUTH OF RIBEIRA BRAVA

PREGUIÇA From the road Preguiça does not look much – a few half-built houses, a football pitch, a signpost. The bulk of the village is out of sight, clinging to the steep slope above the shoreline. A precipitous cobbled street winds down amongst colourful houses past an old church, to a crumbling pier where sizeable boats berth with cargo from Mindelo. To the right of the pier you can swim in the shingly bay where bright fishing boats are drawn up on the beach. Fishermen dive from boats to catch lobsters by hand at a depth of 10–15m. They wear masks and breathe compressed air piped from the surface, allowing them to stay down for up to an hour at a time.

On the other side of the village is the Portuguese fort, built in the early 1800s, with several cannons. The two memorials (one erected by the Portuguese, the other by the Cape Verdeans) commemorate the voyage of Pedro Álvares Cabral, who in 1500 passed this point on his way to discovering the coast of Brazil.

Getting there The town is a bit run-down and there's not too much to do there but it is a short journey if you have a spare couple of hours. To get there, take an *aluguer* from the main square in the *vila* – they leave intermittently (200$), or you can just walk and hitchhike the 8km. Before dark you will find transport back quite easily.

🏠 Where to stay

🏠 **Dona Maria** (3 rooms) ☎ 235 1582. The large pink house near the top of the village. Large, cared-for rooms, simple but fresh & new; 2 have a good standard of en-suite bathroom though no hot water (yet). Roof terrace with some shade, giving super views of the ocean. The owner speaks Italian but no English. **$**

🏠 **Homestays** A small number of homes take paying guests. For example, the bright-blue house across the way from Dona Maria's has rooms to rent with a kitchen. Enquiries through Dona Maria, above.

✖ Where to eat

✖ **Dona Maria** 🖍 235 1582. Dona Maria's dining room is thought by some to present the best food in São Nicolau, possibly because of the influence of her 8 years in Italy. Because of this, advance booking is essential. $$

What to do Fishing with local fishermen; boat trips up and down the coast to isolated beaches such as Porta da Lapa (a black-sand beach); or to Carriçal; hanging out: some people love this fishing village as a place in which to do very little very pleasantly.

THE EAST

The eastern part of São Nicolau is mostly an arid, boulder-strewn desert. It is hard to believe that just 70 years ago it was well populated and farmed using dryland techniques that yielded crops of corn and manioc. Now, however, just two populated villages remain: Juncalinho and Carriçal. The area has a raw, desolate beauty that will move some and depress others.

JUNCALINHO Juncalinho lies along the eastern ridge which is almost entirely devoid of vegetation. It is a very poor and humble village – some might say desolate – on a plain littered with boulders, some of which seem to have randomly assembled themselves into houses. Only the cemetery and the football pitch have been cleared of stones. It has its charm, though. A dingy sign indicates the *lagoa* – the only sight to see.

Getting there *Alugueres* depart from Ribeira Brava for Juncalinho at around 10.00, taking about 25 minutes to get there. They depart from Juncalinho for Ribeira Brava approximately between 14.00 and 16.00.

🏠 Where to stay

🏠 **Jardim** (4 rooms) 🖍 235 1117 (or through Pensão Jardim in Ribeira Brava). A distinctive, 2-storey house with a tower-like construction at the front, this is run by a branch of the Jardim family who run the *pensão* in Ribeira Brava. Paulinho & Amalia can be found in their restaurant, further into Juncalinho on the main road on the right. $$

🏠 **Homestays** These can be arranged via some of the island's best guides, for example Toi (see *Excursions*, page 314).

✖ Where to eat

✖ **Jardim** ⊕ daily. A local eatery on the right of the main road, this is owned by the Jardim family (see *Where to stay*, above). $

✖ **Lanchonete Caminh d'Lagoa** Off the main road on the route down to the *lagoa*, on the left. $

What to do

Lagoa You can drive the five minutes to the coast, or walk for 15 minutes past circular, stone pig pens, and gaze down at the crater – black rock lashed with white foam. On a calm day the *lagoa* lies just beyond the reach of the swell, full of beautiful blue-green water, and is a pleasant place to bathe. If you are keen to swim, try to choose a calm day by checking with the *aluguer* drivers in the *vila* who can judge the state of the sea as they traverse the main road around the island.

Fajã and its environs are lush and green thanks to technology and a lot of effort. It began in 1980 when, with French help, the people built a 2km tunnel into the mountainside to tap into water there. The pipe did not just transform Fajã's agriculture but also became the source of water for outlying dry areas such as Juncalinho. Initially it gushed 1,000m³ per day but this has now subsided to 400m³. To see the tunnel ask for 'Galeria de Fajã'.

Engineers and educationalists have been working hard to introduce new farming techniques to the area. The key has been to expand the use of traditional irrigation channels (if you are interested, it's worth wandering around the heavily planted terraces of Fajã to see how endless terraces of crops are kept watered by the judicious opening and closing of channels). Some of the water is supplied by boreholes and pumped uphill from where it can descend to do its irrigation.

A second technique, microirrigation, or 'drip drip', is slowly gaining acceptance and can be found in the area too.

Hike to Carriçal There are two extant routes to Carriçal. The first is along the road. It is a magnificent walk. The road turns right after Juncalinho and climbs in a series of precipitous bends high into the mountains inland, over the ridge and down to the sea again. The terrain is dark brown, with heaps of earth and rock, and a frothy coastline.

The second route is along a path that heads directly south out of Juncalinho village, climbing steeply into the mountains, traverses the heights for around an hour and then descends into Ribeira de Palhal and the abandoned village of Urzeleiros (named after the indigo lichen *urzela* which was farmed here – see box, *Orchil dye*, page 16). The latter path takes around five hours and is known as the Caminho de Cinta. It is poor quality and hard to navigate in places. We suggest you either take a guide (whom you could probably pick up in Juncalinho) or use the hike description no 301 on the Goldstadt Wanderkarte 1:50,000 map of São Nicolau (see *Maps*, page 68).

CARRIÇAL Carriçal is a poor but pretty village, probably one of the most isolated in the archipelago. Most families are crammed into two-roomed, concrete houses with hens, pigs, dogs and cats bustling outside. Below the houses lies a tree-filled *ribeira*, a pretty beach and a cluster of boats. You can pay a fisherman to take you out to net a pile of moray eels and bright orange grouper, or to go up the coast to explore the coves and caves.

By the steps down to the shore is a factory. Ask to see inside, where huge pans of tuna are boiled on wood fires and are then canned in tins pressed on the premises.

There is a small shop where you can buy drinks and snacks and it is possible to arrange a room for the night if you ask around.

Getting there In a 4x4, it will take another 35 minutes to get to Carriçal from Juncalinho. Check, however, that the road to Carriçal is open – it is sometimes impassable because of landslides. Just head east where the tarmac road ends. When it is passable, it is spectacular, offering views all the way down the north coast.

Alugueres leave Ribeira Brava for Carriçal at around midday, and depart Carriçal for Ribeira Brava early in the morning.

If the road is impassable (which it often is in the rainy season) a boat operates between Preguiça and Carriçal.

São Nicolau THE EAST

12

HIKES IN AND OUT OF RIBEIRA BRAVA
1 Ribeira Brava–Calejão–Ribeira Brava

Distance: approximately 4km; time: 2.5 hours; difficulty: 1 (CW)

Leave Ribeira Brava on the airport road, ascending past the needles on your left. Bear right at the first junction (the left turn goes to Morro Brás and Juncalinho). After a short distance, bear right again on the road towards the cemetery, which you pass 25 minutes after setting out. The road winds for a short distance in the plantations in the bottom of the *ribeira* before leading you up the other side to rejoin the airport road. Follow it away from the edge of the *ribeira* to the airport, which you will reach 35 minutes after the cemetery.

Some 400m past the airport, there is a signposted turning to the right down to **Calejão**, which lies on the lower slopes of the mountain range.

It is a quiet village, strung out along the old road. After 3km you will pass a path on your left – the descent from Cabeçalinha (described in the next hike, below) which joins your path opposite a graffitied stone on the right. In the building on the corner, just after the path joins you, a craftsman manufactures ornaments from banana leaves. There's a shop selling water, biscuits and soft drinks. The impressive, ochre-coloured building on the left is the old orphanage and bishop's residence.

The road continues, straight at first, and then begins a superb descent into Ribeira Brava along a series of S-bends. There is an excellent view up the valley. The last section of the road is past impoverished suburbia and litter-strewn hillsides followed by some of the biggest houses in town. The track emerges in the São João area of town beside the old seminary and Jumbo Residencial.

2 Ribeira Brava–Cachaço–Cabeçalinha–Calejão

Distance: approximately 10km; time: at least 4 hours allowing for stops en route; difficulty: 2–3 (AI)

This is one of the best walks, at least four hours with a steep ascent and descent. Follow the cobbled road up the *ribeira* out of the *vila* – a fascinating walk through the villages. After an hour and 20 minutes of puffing you pass between some crags on to a small road leading to **Cachaço**. To the right the road winds up to a wonderfully positioned white church. Turn left to reach the busy main road of the island where there are a couple of shops selling biscuits and drinks (and, if you are lucky, goat's cheese – see *Cachaço*, page 319). Here the landscape is green, with plenty of perfectly shaped dragon trees. Turn left on the main road for a fantastic view of Ribeira Brava. Peer down the gullies where vehicles have been known to tumble – and look up at the mountain on your right down which rocks often fall on to the road. There's a great view of the path you took up the *ribeira* and of the spine of mountains out to the east. Eventually the road turns to the right and you begin to see the gentler slopes that lead down to Tarrafal.

Some 35 minutes after leaving Cachaço the road takes a sharp right turn, just before a blue house. The track to the left (see (a) below) is an option for returning to Ribeira Brava, but you can also continue on the main road for another five minutes until you reach a white concrete water tank on the right – this is **Cabeçalinha**. Take the left track opposite this. For a good ten minutes the track ascends until you reach the third panorama of this walk – the southern mountains and sea. Now there's half an hour of steep, zig-zagging descent – not for bad knees – until you begin to sink

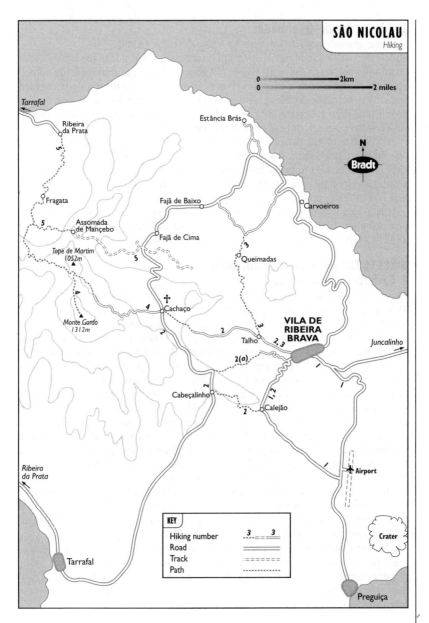

into civilisation again, eventually reaching the dirt road. Turn left at the T-junction, opposite the graffitied stone. From here it is about 40 minutes back to town along the road described in the previous walk.

(a) An alternative is to descend down the first track to Ribeira Brava. On this track it takes about 40 minutes less to reach the *vila*. Leave the main road between Alto António Miguel and Morro Cone Rocha and go uphill for about 100m as far as the pass. Soon you will find yourself in Palso. Follow the path on the ridge to the *vila*.

3 Ribeira Brava–Queimadas

Distance: approximately 5.5km; time: 1.5 hours; difficulty: 2 (CW)

Follow the cobbled road out of town and up the right-hand side of the *ribeira*. After 30 minutes you reach the small village of **Talho**. At the village standpipe (on a small concrete platform with a telephone box next to it), turn right up a small cobbled track. Very soon the cobbles give way to dust and the path begins to look far less promising. Keep following it up the hillside, resisting the temptation to take an easier, wider path which heads left after a few minutes.

As you ascend, the path swings to the left and, 30 minutes from the phone box, you emerge on a saddle. Looking back over the *ribeira*, Monte Gordo is to the right – the massive hump-backed mountain surmounted by radio masts. Turning around and looking over into the next *ribeira* you can see **Queimadas** in the valley. Fajã is through a gap in the range above it.

It is a pleasant, though steep, descent to the village. It is well worth (slightly) provoking any dog you see just to hear the extraordinary echo in this amphitheatre of a valley. At the T-junction by the old school turn left for Fajã to find transport back.

HIKES TO THE WEST OF THE MAIN ROAD
4 Cachaço–Monte Gordo

Distance: approximately 5km (return); time: 1.5 hours; difficulty: 3 (CW)

This steep walk to the highest peak is also one of the most spectacular. You can lengthen it by walking from Ribeira Brava up to Cachaço first.

Take an *aluguer* to Cachaço (30 minutes; 200$). There is an obvious turning on your right, to the southwest, near the village standpipe (clearly marked *Água*). You ascend on a well-made path zig-zagging amongst lush plantations. It is attractive and shady, but this ascent is not for the unfit. After 40 minutes, the path flattens and skirts the right-hand side of a hill with radio antennae on top. After gently ascending amongst scattered houses and fields for 20 minutes, you reach a great view over Fajã on your right. Another 15 minutes takes you to a clearly defined saddle. On your right is the **Tope de Martim** (1,052m) and to the left is **Monte Gordo** (1,312m). It may seem close, but don't be fooled – you are still at least 300m below the summit – which translates into a rough scramble of about 40 minutes. The ascent to Tope de Martim is about 30 minutes.

The view of the archipelago from the summits is the best you will find, including the uninhabited western islands – from left to right, Ilhéu Raso, Ilhéu Branco, and Santa Luzia – as well as São Vicente and Santo Antão beyond. It is said that in exceptionally clear weather every Cape Verde island can be seen.

Floating around the peaks and saddle is the neglected kestrel (*Falco tinnunculus neglectus*), a small, brown bird common in the northerly islands. On the lower slopes you may disturb a flock of helmeted guinea fowl. These birds, rather like grey, oversized hens, were introduced in the 1600s and are found on Santiago, Fogo, Maio and São Nicolau. They are very tasty.

5 Fajã de Baixo–Fragata–Ribeira da Prata

Distance: approximately 6km; time: 3 hours; difficulty: 3 (CW)

This is a magnificent walk with some steep ascents. The only problem is finding transport from Ribeira da Prata back to Tarrafal at the end of the walk: there are only two *aluguer* drivers resident in Ribeira da Prata and you may find yourself in a one-sided negotiation in which you end up chartering a vehicle for an exorbitant sum. Minimise hassle by beginning this walk early in the morning so you can try hitching back from Prata or picking up the mid afternoon school run. Alternatively,

These are three of the first trails delineated in the natural park: With thanks to the Monte Gordo Natural Park office (*www.ecosaonicolau.com*).

SOUTHERN VIEW TRAIL This hike begins and ends at the entrance to the park. You begin by going along the main recreational trail, observing the plentiful endemic flora and fauna, the *caberinos* where local community members tend their fields, alongside the imposing peak of Monte Gordo to Assomada de Ribeira Calhaus. Here you encounter beautiful volcanic rock formations and have a splendid view of the valley below. You make your way down into the green, watery Ribeira Calhaus, and slowly begin to wind your way up the mountainside. You will see *saio* growing out of the rock walls. The hike is a bit steep and rocky, but well worth the effort for the views. After peaking, you come down along the cliffside and make your way to the village of Hortelão after passing more wonderful volcanic rock formations. In Hortelão, you can enjoy traditional foods for lunch, or continue to make your way back into the park.

RECREATIONAL TRAIL This hike takes you from the entrance of the park along the main recreational trail, past magnificent collections of *tortolhos*, through community farms, alongside Monte Gordo peak, winding your way to Assomada de Ribeira Calhaus. You then make your way down through volcanic rocks into a green oasis where you can sometimes see running water. Traverse traditional abandoned homes with views of the cliffs on both sides. You make your way back to Assomada and take the trail off to your left which winds down and along the edge of the farms in Cachaço, giving you great views of this rural village along with the valley below where Fajã lies. You end by making your way back to the park entrance.

WESTERN LOOP From Assomada de Ribeira Calhaus going westward, this loop passes over the top of Mont Desert with breathtaking views of Canto Fajã and the Fajã Valley. The ridge also passes over the mountain village of Fragata (where *grogue* is still produced in the traditional manner) before you descend past Tope de Martim and Tope Moka to the old settlement of Ribeira de Calhaus. Stay awhile to enjoy the freshwater spring and also enjoy shaded relief from the sun under the grand eucalyptus trees. Continuing along the loop you will make a climb back up to Assomada de Ribeira Calhaus along the old trail which was amazingly cut into the hillside. There are also spectacular views of the surrounding islands of Raso, Branco, Santa Luzia and, if you are lucky, you will be able to also see São Vicente and Santo Antão.

take the midday *aluguer* from Tarrafal to Ribeira da Prata and do the walk in reverse. Take an *aluguer* to Cachaço. After Fajã and before Cachaço, there's a large sign on the right for Pico Agudo Canto Fajã. Take this and, after about 50m, bear left. You will see a prominent finger of rock in the saddle ahead. After about 15 minutes, you reach a T-junction with a small grave marked by a white cross on a mound nearby. Turn left and follow the track as it winds towards the saddle and then becomes a path which ascends steeply. You will reach the saddle about 50 minutes after setting out.

São Nicolau   HIKES

12

From the saddle, descend on a beautifully cobbled hairpin track. After about 20 minutes, you reach **Fragata**, with houses built on fantastic ledges and outcrops with sheer drops on either side. The track leads you round the head of the *ribeira* and then begins the descent towards **Ribeira da Prata**. From the saddle to the village is approximately a two-hour walk.

Crops here include sugarcane, cassava, bananas and maize, and coarse tobacco (*erva*). It is smoked in pipes by the old folk, who spurn cigarettes as a lightweight invention.

OTHER WALKS The park staff may be able to advise on other classic São Nicolau hikes. One of these runs north from Tarrafal, past Carberinho and on to Praia Branca, then turns inland towards Fragata, and on across the Monte Gordo Natural Park to Cachaço. Another is to descend from Hortelão to Tarrafal.

RASO AND BRANCO

Just 7km², Raso has sheer cliffs, which rise out of the water to a plateau no more than 164m high. It has the traditional stony plains but also grassy areas. To the south there are colonies of sea petrels and shearwaters, red-billed tropicbirds and brown boobies – but Raso's most celebrated occupant is the Raso lark (*Alauda*

A TASTE FOR BABY SHEARWATERS

Catch a young shearwater while it is still in the nest and eating mostly grass – and you have a creature whose ounce of flesh will fetch a lot of money. This is the reason for the annual hunt of shearwaters (*Calonectris edwardsii*), known locally as *cagarra*, on Ilhéu Raso, during which tens of thousands are harvested and, it is claimed, many are shipped to the Netherlands.

'It ought to be easy to prevent this happening,' says Cornelis Hazevoet, a bird expert and Cape Verde-watcher. After all, he says, the fishermen who hunt the birds come from just one village, in Santo Antão; the cull happens during the same, predictable, short period each year, and it's illegal. Yet it continues year after year, which is a problem even for the fishermen because numbers are starting to plummet. In 2007, they managed to catch only 18,000 chicks compared with the previous year's catch of 27,000.

Shearwaters live for about 40 years, according to Tommy Melo, founder of Cape Verde's first environmental organisation, Biosfera 1. But they lay only one egg annually.

Eating shearwaters is a tradition anchored in famine. During World War II, when imports were difficult, they became a food source. Later, they became a symbolic dish eaten during annual October celebrations to mark the end of famine.

In 2008, Melo was resolute that the hunting should be stopped. He was planning visits to the fishermen to explain about the problem; he had also gathered the resources to police the island during October. Melo has made a video about the cull.

'My despair is knowing that the Cape Verde shearwater, the Raso lark and the Raso lizard are endemic species that exist nowhere else in the world and that in a matter of years they may no longer exist even in Cape Verde if we don't stop hunting them for food or raising them as pets,' says Melo.

razae), one of the rarest birds in the world, which lives only there and is rated 'critically endangered' on the international Red List of threatened species. There are fewer than 100 of these birds, known locally as *calhandra do Ilhéu Raso*; to the uninitiated, they can seem disappointingly small and brown.

The global population of Raso larks was estimated in January 2003 at 93–103 birds and in November 2003 at 76–87 birds. They cannot currently be encouraged to populate neighbouring Santa Luzia Island – though it seems to have suitable habitat – partly because there is a population of feral cats there.

Raso is also known for its endemic Raso lizards.

Branco is even smaller than Raso at just 3km². It is, however, taller, at 327m, and has one small water source. It is one of the most important sites in Cape Verde for breeding seabirds and is white from their guano deposits. Branco was the unlikely host to 30 inhabitants in 1833 – prisoners who were dumped there and left to survive or die.

Branco was, until 1940, the last outpost of the Cape Verde giant skink, a delightful lizard-like creature coloured a mottled white and brown and with a big, heavy tail. It was the second-largest skink in the world, reaching 65cm in length and lived among the rocks eating the seeds of plants and occasionally augmenting this diet with bird eggs. Their numbers began plummeting when the prisoners arrived. After that they were the sporadic victims of local fishermen who trapped them to eat – and their skins were popular as shoe material. The final blow was the series of droughts in the early 20th century. A luckier creature is the giant gecko (*Tarentola gigas*). This lives in cliff holes and burrows on both islands.

The two islands were defined as nature reserves in 1990. Every October, according to Cornelis Hazevoet, one of the leading ornithology experts on the islands, local fishermen from Santo Antão and São Vicente visit the two islets to collect thousands of young Cape Verde shearwaters (see box, *A taste for baby shearwaters*, opposite).

Appendix 1

LANGUAGE

If you are serious about learning a language before going to Cape Verde then the big decision is whether to choose Portuguese or Creole. Creole is virtually impossible to learn outside the islands unless you have access to a Cape Verdean community, one of whose members might give lessons. On the other hand, if you plan to spend some time there and need to win the confidence of people other than professionals and officials it will be essential to learn Creole – learning Portuguese may turn out to have been a confusing waste of time.

In the absence of Creole, having some Portuguese is of huge help – every new word you learn will give you a little more access to people and be invaluable simply in helping you to get around. Most people speak no other European language. Ten minutes a day for a few months will double the satisfaction you get from your holiday. Combined with a smattering of French, to make what we call 'Fraughtuguese', you'll get by.

PORTUGUESE The biggest barrier to the swift acquisition of some Portuguese is pronunciation – it really takes several weeks to master it before learning any words. After that, the rudiments are reasonably simple and English speakers will recognise a large number of words, particularly when they are written down.

Pronunciation The following are basic rules, although there are a lot of exceptions:

- If a word carries an acute (´) or circumflex (^) accent then stress the syllable that carries it. Otherwise stress the second-last syllable.
- Vowels that carry a tilde (~) on the top, and vowels followed by 'm' are nasalised.
- Many vowels disappear, for example an 'e', 'a' or 'o' at the end of a word; and many 'e's at the beginning of words. Tone down unstressed vowels.
- Double vowels are pronounced as two separate vowels.

s   = 'sh' at the end of the word; 'z' in the middle; soft 'c' at the beginning
z   = 'sh' at the end of a word
c   = soft 'c' if there's a cedilla underneath or if it's before an 'i' or an 'e'
g   = soft 'j' if before an 'i' or an 'e'
j   = soft 'j'
rr = rolled
r   = only rolled at the beginning of a word
lh = 'ly'
ch = 'sh'
qu = 'kw', before an a; 'k' before an 'e' or an 'i'
nh = 'ny'
x   = 'sh' or 's' – the rules are complicated – just take a chance

a = as in 'father' when stressed; as in 'air' when unstressed
e = as in 'jet' when stressed; as in the second 'e' of 'general' when unstressed
i = as in 'seen' but shorter
o = as in 'not' or 'note' when stressed; as in 'root' when unstressed
u = usually as in 'root'
h = don't pronounce

Grammar The most basic way of making something plural is by adding -s or -es to the end. The most basic verb endings are as follows:

I buy	*compr-o*	We buy	*compr-amos*
You buy (singular)	*compr-as*	You buy (plural)	*compr-ais*
You/he/she buys	*compr-a*	They buy	*compr-am*

Address all but intimates in the third person (literally: 'could he help me'). You don't need to bother with personal pronouns (I, you, he) unless you want to emphasise them (eg: *I* am talking to *you*).

Common compound verbs

be	*ser* (I am: *sou*/you are, he is: *é*/we are: *somos*/they are: *são*)
give	*dar* (I give: *dou*/you give, he gives: *dá*/they give: *dão*)
go	*ir* (I go: *vou*/you go, he goes: *vai*/let's go: *vamos*)
have	*ter* (I have: *tenho*/you have, he has: *tem*/we have: *temos*/they have: *têm*)
like	*gostar de* (I like = *gosto de*)

Greetings

good morning	*bom dia*
good afternoon (after midday)	*boa tarde*
good evening (after 18.00)	*boa noite*
goodbye	*até logo* ('until later')
how are you?	*como está?*
I am well/everything's fine	*estou bem* ('shtoe beyng')

Questions, answers and useful phrases

What is your name?	*Como se chama?*
Do you speak English?	*Fala inglês?*
Is it possible …?	*É possível …?*
How much does it cost?	*Quanto custa?*
What is this called?	*Como se chama isso?*
Can you help me?	*Pode me ajudar?*
Pardon?	*Como?*
Where?	*Onde?*
When?	*Quando?*
How?	*Como?*
Why?	*Porquê?*
What?	*Quê?*
Do you have a spare room?	*Tem um quarto vago?*
You're welcome	*De nada* ('it's nothing')
I am from London	*Sou de Londres*
My name is …	*Chamo-me …*
Where is …?	*Onde fica …?*

I don't know	*Não sei*	To have coffee	*Tomar café*
I don't understand	*Não compreendo*	To have breakfast	*Tomar o café de manhã*
Straight on	*Em frente*	There is …	*Há …*
On the right	*À direita*	There is no …	*Não há …*
On the left	*À esquerda*	Too much	*Demais*
More slowly	*Mais devagar*	That's enough!	*Basta!*
I have to go	*Tenho de ir*	More or less	*Mais ou menos*

Menus For basic words see the list below. This list is of common dishes:

fish stew	*cozido de peixe*
grilled squid	*lula grelhada*
shellfish cooked with rice	*arroz de marisco*
generally wahoo, a white, hard fish steak	*peixe serra*
dried cod	*bacalhau*
dried cod and chips fried together	*bacalhau à Brás*
maize, beans, chicken, other meat	*cachupa rica*
maize, beans	*cachupa pobre*
a chicken dish	*djagacida* or *jag*
a soup	*conj*
corn bread	*gufong*
a milk pudding, rather like crême caramel	*pudim de leite*
sponge impregnated with coconut, like steamed pudding	*tarte de coco*

Food and drink

bean	*feijão*	cheese	*queijo*
beef	*carne de vaca*	chicken (as food)	*frango*
beer	*cerveja*	chips	*batatas fritas*
bread	*pão*	coffee	*café*
cake	*bolo*	dessert	*sobremesa*
cassava	*mandioca*	eel	*moreia*
eggs	*ovos*	shrimp/prawn	*camarão*
haricot beans	*congo*	spirits	*aguardente*
lobster	*lagosta*	sweet potato	*batata doce*
maize	*milho*	tea	*chá*
meat	*carne*	tuna	*atum*
milk	*leite*	turkey	*peru*
octopus	*polvo*	veal	*vitela*
potato	*batata*	water	*água*
rice	*arroz*	wine	*vinho*
rum (local)	*grogga*		

Days and months

Sunday	*domingo*	Wednesday	*quarta-feira*
Monday	*segunda-feira*	Thursday	*quinta-feira*
	(second day)	Friday	*sexta-feira*
Tuesday	*terça-feira*	Saturday	*sábado*

January	*janeiro*	March	*março*
February	*fevereiro*	April	*abril*

May	*maio*	September	*setembro*
June	*junho*	October	*outubro*
July	*julho*	November	*novembro*
August	*agosto*	December	*dezembro*

Numbers

1	*um/uma*	16	*dezasseis*
2	*dois/duas*	17	*dezassete*
3	*três*	18	*dezoito*
4	*quatro*	19	*dezanove*
5	*cinco*	20	*vinte*
6	*seis* ('saysh')	30	*trinta*
7	*sete*	40	*quarenta*
8	*oito*	50	*cinquenta*
9	*nove*	60	*sessenta*
10	*dez* ('desh')	70	*setenta*
11	*onze*	80	*oitenta*
12	*doze*	90	*noventa*
13	*treze*	100	*cem*
14	*catorze*	1,000	*mil*
15	*quinze*	a million	*um milhão*

Other common words

aeroplane	*avião* ('avi-ow')	change	*troco*
after	*depois de*	cheap	*barato/a*
also	*também*	chicken	*galinho*
and	*e*	church	*igreja*
at	*a*	cinema	*cinéma*
bad	*mau, má*	city	*cidade*
baggage	*bagagem*	closed	*fechado*
bakery	*padaria*	condom	*camisinha*
bank	*banco*	cow	*vaca*
bathroom	*casa de banho*	customs	*alfândega*
battery	*pilha*	day	*dia*
beach	*praia*	diarrhoea	*diarréia*
beautiful	*lindo/a*	difficult	*difícil*
bed	*cama*	dinner	*jantar*
before	*antes de*	doctor	*médico/a*
big	*grande*	dog	*cão*
boarding house	*pensão*	drink (to)	*beber*
book	*livro*	drink	*bebida*
boy	*rapaz*	early	*cedo*
breakfast	*pequeno almoço*	eat	*comer*
	('pekaynalmoss')	English	*inglês*
brother	*irmão*	enough	*bastante*
bus	*autocarro*	exchange (to)	*trocar*
buy	*comprar*	father	*pai*
candle	*vela*	fever	*febre*
car	*carro*	film	*película*
casualty department	*banco de socorros*	flight	*vol*
cat	*gato*	girl	*rapariga*

goat	*cabra*	rain	*chuva*
good	*bom/boa*	rest	*descansar*
he	*ele*	restaurant	*restaurante*
heavy	*pesado/a*	road	*rua*
high	*alto/a*	room	*quarto*
hill	*colina*	room for a couple	*quarto casal*
hospital	*hospital*	room for one	*quarto individual*
hot	*quente*	room for two	*quarto duplo*
hotel	*hotel*	salt	*sal*
house	*casa*	school	*escola*
hurt (to)	*doer*	sea	*mar*
husband	*marido*	sell	*vender*
I	*eu*	send	*enviar*
ill	*doente*	she	*ela*
in	*em*	sheet	*lençol*
key	*chave*	shop	*loja*
lagoon	*piscina*	shower	*chuveiro*
leave	*partir*	sister	*irmã*
letter	*carta*	small	*pequeno/a*
light	*luz* ('loosh')	sorry	*desculpe*
little (ie: 'not much')	*pouco/a*	speak	*falar*
lorry	*camião*	spouse	*esposo/a*
low	*baixo/a* ('baysho')	square (town)	*praça*
lunch	*almoço*	sun	*sol*
magazine	*revista*	supermarket	*supermercado*
man	*homem*	swim	*nadar*
market	*mercado*	telephone	*telefone*
matches	*fósforos*	thanks	*obrigado/a*
money	*dinheiro*	(as in 'much obliged')	
mosquito net	*mosquiteiro*	that	*esse*
mother	*mãe*	they	*eles/elas*
mountain	*montanha*	this	*este*
much	*muito/a*	ticket	*bilhete*
never	*nunca*	to	*para* ('pra')
newspaper	*jornal*	today	*hoje*
night	*noite*	toilet	*sanitário*
nightclub	*boite*	toilet paper	*papel higiênico*
no	*não*	tomorrow	*amanhã*
nothing	*nada*	town	*vila*
now	*agora*	town hall	*câmara*
of	*de*	travel	*viajar*
old	*velho*	travellers' cheques	*cheques de viagem*
open	*aberto/a*	very	*muito/a*
path	*caminho*	village	*aldeia*
pen	*caneta*	visa	*visto*
perhaps	*talvez*	we	*nós*
pharmacy	*farmácia*	wind	*vento*
pillow	*almofada*	with	*com*
please	*faz favor*	woman	*mulher*
police	*policia*	work	*trabalhar*
post office	*correio*	yes	*sim*

yesterday	*ontem*	you (familiar)	*você*
you (polite masc)	*o senhor*	you (polite masc pl)	*os senhoros*
you (polite fem)	*a senhora*	you (polite fem pl)	*as senhoras*

CREOLE *São Vicente Creole translations by 10th-grade pupils at the José Augusto Pinto School in Mindelo, São Vicente, with help from their teacher, Keith West. Santiago translations and introductory material by Steven Maddocks.*

The Creole language varies widely across the archipelago, to the extent that people from São Vicente profess not to be able to understand their compatriots from Santiago. Although every island has its own version, the greatest difference is between the *Barlavento* Creole spoken in the north of Cape Verde, and that spoken in the south (*Sotavento* Creole).

São Vicente Creole is slightly more Portuguese than Santiago, or *Badiu*, Creole – the latter contains more African words. Generally speaking, *Barlavento* Creole is more clipped and staccato, and *Sotavento* Creole is more open, with rounded vowels, and spoken more aggressively. There are differences in vocabulary, with each using its own slang. Among the biggest differences are subject pronouns, 'You' (singular) is *bu* in *Sotavento* Creole and *bo* in *Barlavento* Creole. 'You' (plural) is *nhos* and *bzot*, respectively.

An 'a' in *Sotavento* Creole often comes out as an 'o' in *Barlavento*, as in 'work' (*trabadju/ trabodj*) or 'ill-mannered' (*malkriadu/malkriod*).

In Santiago they tend to pronounce the whole word. Consequently it is much easier for the beginner to understand what is being said. In São Vicente whole syllables – both in the middle and at the ends of words – may be left out. So for example the *-adu* at the end of words in *Sotavento* Creole becomes *-od* in *Barlavento* Creole – so *Kansadu* would be pronounced *Kansod*. In *Santiago* Creole, *v* changes to *b* and *lh* becomes *dj*, so the word for red – *vermelho* in the north – is pronounced *burmedju* in the south.

For more about the rivalries between Creole and Portuguese, see box, page 36.

Below, the Santiago translation is given first, followed by the São Vicente version. The two different versions of Creole have been represented as simply as possible for a novice. All of the sounds correspond roughly to their English equivalents. Peculiarities are as follows:

tx represents the 'ch' in 'cherry'	j is the 'z' of 'pleasure'
dj represents the 'j' in 'Jerry'	k is hard, as in 'kick'
x is the 'sh' of 'sham'	s is soft, as in 'sick'

The only accents used here are to draw attention to stress. For verbs, in *Sotavento* Creole stress is always on the penultimate syllable, in *Barlavento* on the last syllable. This has been represented by an accented final a, e, or i.

Grammar 'You' has familiar and polite, singular and plural forms, as well as gender. It would be rude to address an elderly stranger with the familiar form.

	Sotavento **Creole**	*Barlavento* **Creole**
you (singular, familiar)	*bu* (except *bo e*, you are)	*bo*
you (singular, polite)	*nho* (masc), *nha* (fem)	*bosé* (masc and fem)
you (plural, familiar)	*nhos*	*bzot*
you (plural, polite)	*nhos*	*bosés*

Shopping

Excuse me, where is the shop?	*Undi ki e loja, pur favor?*	*Ondé ke loja, d'favor?*
Do you have bottled water?	*Nhos tem agu di garafa?*	*Bzot tem agua d'garafa?*
How much does this cost?	*Keli e kantu?*	*Keli tonté?*

	Sotavento Creole	**Barlavento** Creole
It's too expensive	*Kel e karu dimas*	*Kel e txeu kor*
I'm not paying that. It's a rip-off!	*N ka kre kumpra'l. Kel e robo!* (strong)	*N ka kre kompra'l. Bo ti ta ingana'm!*

Airport

What time will the flight leave?	*Ki ora ki avion ta sei?*	*Kazora k'aviau ta sei?*
Is there a telephone here?	*Li tem telefon?*	*Li tem t'lefon?*
I'm very upset because my baggage has not arrived	*N sta mutu xatiadu pa modi nha bagagem ka ben*	*N ta txeu xatiod mod nha bagagem ka ben*
I'm in a hurry	*N sta ku presa*	*N ta k'pres*

Taxi

Please take me to Hotel X	*Pur favor, leba'm ti Hotel X*	*D'favor, leva'm té Hotel X*

Hotel

Do you have a vacant room?	*Nhos tem kuartu?*	*Bzot tem um kuart?*
May I see the room first?	*N kre odja kuartu purmeru?*	*N ta gostá d'oia kel kuart primer?*
What time is breakfast?	*Ki ora ki e ora di kafé?*	*Kazora k'e kafé?*

Bank

Where is the bank?	*Undi ki e banku?*	*Ondé k'e bonk?*
Can I cash travellers' cheques here?	*Nhos ta troka'm travelxek?*	*Bzot ta troká travelxek?*
What is the exchange rate?	*Kal ki e kambiu di oji?*	*Tonté k'e kambiu?*
When does the bank close/open?	*Ki ora ki banku ta fitxa/ta abri?*	*Kazora k'bonk t'f'txá/t'abrí?*

Hiking

Where is the path to the peak?	*Undi ki e kaminhu pa piku?*	*Ondé k'e kamin pa piku?*
Is this the path to get there? (hiker points)	*Ekeli ki e kaminhu pa la?*	*Keli k'e kamin pa la?*
Where can I buy water?	*Undi ki N podi kumpra agu?*	*Ondé k'n podé kompra agua?*
How far is it to the valley floor?	*Falta txeu pa nu txiga fundu rubera?*	*Tont temp këgent t'levá pa txigá la na fund?*
How many hours to the road?	*Kantu tenpu falta pa nu txiga strada?*	*Tont temp k'falta'm pa'n txigá strada?*
Go left at the fork	*Na dizviu toma skerda*	*Na skina bo t'v'rá pa skerda*
Go right at the crossroads	*Na kruzamentu vira a direta*	*Na kruzament bo t'v'ra pa dreta*
Can you show me on the map?	*Bu podi mostra'm li na mapa?*	*Bo podé mostra'm li na mapa?*
I need a guide	*N mesti um guia*	*N presiza d'um guia*
I want to go to the *grogue* distillery	*N kre ba ti trapixe*	*N kre bai pa trapixe*
No more grogue or I'll get drunk	*Si n toma mas grogu n ta fika moku*	*Se n tomá mas grog, n ta fuxká*
Is it possible to walk along that path? (point)	*N podi anda na kel kaminhu?*	*N podé anda la na kel kamin?*

| I want to go to the crater | *N kre ba ti kratera* | *N kre bai pa kratera* |
| Is there public transport? | *Tem transport?* | *Tem transport?* |

Restaurant

Could you bring me the menu, please?	*Traze'm ementa, pur favor?*	*Traze'm imenta, d'favor*
We've been here a long time	*Dja dura ki nu txiga li*	*Diaza k'nu ta li*
Could I have the bill, please?	*Traze'm konta, pur favor?*	*Traze'm konta, d'favor*
Do you have any change?	*Bu tene troku?*	*Bo tem trok?*

Personal communication

Hello	*Oi/Ola*	*Oi*
Goodbye	*Txau*	*Txau*
Yes	*Sim*	*Sim*
No	*Nau*	*Nau*
Do you speak English?	*Bu ta papia ingles?*	*Bo t'falá ingles?*
Which island are you from?	*Bo e di ki ilha?*	*Bo e d'kual ilha?*
What is your name?	*Modi ki e bu nomi?*	*Mané k'e bo nom?*
My name is...	*Nha nomi e...*	*Nha nom e...*
Can you help me?	*Bu podi djuda'm?*	*Bo podé isda'm?*
What is this called?	*Modi ki e nomi di kel kuza li?*	*Mané k'e nom d'es kosa?*
I don't understand	*N ka ta entendi*	*N ka ti ta entende'b*
Please speak more slowly	*Papia mas dibagar, pur favor*	*Falá mas d'vagar, d'favor*
I don't have any money	*N ka tene dinheru*	*N ka tem d'nher*
That's enough	*Dja txiga*	*Ta bom*

Miscellaneous

If	*Si*	*Se*
Often	*Txeu bes*	*Txeu vez*
Already	*Dja*	*Ja*
Still	*Inda*	*Inda*
Now	*Gosi*	*Grinhasim*
Other	*Otu*	*Ot*
Sorry	*Diskulpa'm*	*Diskulpa'm*
How are you? (General greeting)	*Modi ki bu sta?* *Tudu bon? Tudu dretu?*	*Manera bo ta?* *Tud dret?*
Excuse me	*Kon lisensa*	*Ko l'sensa*
I'm here on holiday	*N sta li di feria*	*N ta d'feria*
I'm from London/England/America	*Ami e di Londres/Inglatera/ Merka*	*Mi e d'Londres/d'Inglater/ d'Merka*
Collective *aluguer* (often a Toyota Hiace)	*Ias*	*Ias*
Bad/damaged/broken/ill/ mistaken	*Mariadu*	no single word covers the same range
Good/excellent/cool/fine	*Fixe*	*Kul*
Good/tasty/delicious/fun	*Sabi*	*Sab*
That's not on	*Keli ka ta da*	*Keli ka ta dret*
There's a power cut	*Lus dja bai*	*Lus ja bai*
I don't eat meat	*N ka ta kumé karni*	*N ka ta k'mé karn*

Appendix 2

FURTHER INFORMATION

There is little about Cape Verde on the shelves of British bookshops. Two exceptions are Basil Davidson's history, and Mitchell Serel's book on Jewish history, both listed below. If you have a few months it is worth putting a request in to Waterstone's out-of-print-book search facility (✆ *020 7434 1195*) or watching the secondhand books as they appear on Amazon. Alternatively, the British Library has many of the books below (membership is free but a letter, normally from an employer, explaining why no other library is suitable, is necessary). Its catalogue can be searched on the internet (*www.bl.uk*). Also try the Travel Bookshop (*13 Blenheim Crescent, London W11;* ✆ *020 7229 5260*), which has some secondhand gems on its shelves. For the definitive digest of Cape Verdean literature in English consult the *World Bibliographical Series*, Volume 123, Cape Verde, by Caroline Shaw (Clio Press, 1991).

BOOKS
History

Araújo, Américo C *Little Known/The European Side of the Cape Verde Islands*, 2000. Documents European connections with the islands and includes translations of some poems of Jorge Barbosa.

Balla, Marcelo Gomes *António's Island: Missing pages of history for blacks and hispanics* Braiswick, 2002. An idiosyncratic collection of articles about Cape Verde's history.

Berger Coli, Waltraud and Lobban, Richard A *The Cape Verdeans in Rhode Island: A Brief History*. On the same theme as Halter (see below).

Carreira, António *People of the Cape Verde Islands* Hurst, 1982. A detailed analysis of one of the fundamental forces of Cape Verdean society: emigration, both forced and voluntary. It is an academic work by a respected Cape Verde historian.

Davidson, Basil *No Fist is Big Enough to Hide the Sky: the Liberation of Guinea-Bissau and Cape Verde* Zed Press, 1981. A lively account of the armed struggle in Guinea-Bissau.

Davidson, Basil *The Fortunate Isles* Hutchinson, 1989. A one-volume history of the islands from start to finish by Britain's foremost historian of Africa. The book is a very readable, personal account of the emergence of a much-loved nation from the bonds of colonialism. There is a rather detailed analysis of Cape Verde's socialist policies in the last third of the book.

Duncan, Bentley *Atlantic Islands: Madeira, the Azores and the Cape Verdes in 17th Century Commerce and Navigation* University of Chicago Press, 1972. A formidable mass of information about the slave and other trades, spilling over into other centuries and with plenty of interesting titbits.

Halter, Marilyn *Between Race and Ethnicity: Cape Verdean American Immigrants 1860–1965* University of Illinois Press, 1995. Written as part of a larger project to understand American immigrants from a variety of countries, this book is essential for a deeper understanding of Cape Verde, because emigration has played such a large part in moulding the country. As well as fascinating accounts of the lives of Cape Verdeans in the USA, it includes much history of the land left behind.

Lobban, Richard *Cape Verde: Crioulo Colony to Independent Nation* Westview Press, 1995. An excellent book with a broad sweep, by a seasoned Cape Verde-watcher. It is available from Westview Press (*5500 Central Av, Boulder, CO 80301-2877;* +1 303 444 3541; www. *westviewpress.com*) or for individual orders: Perseus Books Group Customer Service (*1094 Flex Drive, Jackson, TN 38301;* +1 800 371 1669; perseus.orders@perseusbooks.com; *www.westviewpress.com*).

Lobban, Richard and Saucier, Paul Khalil *The Historical Dictionary of the Republic of Cape Verde* Scarecrow Press, 2007. Very readable and up to date, this book is ideal for answering a broad spectrum of questions about Cape Verde.

Ludtke, Jean *Atlantic Peeks – an Ethnographic Guide to the Portuguese-Speaking Islands* Christopher Publishing House, 1989. Recommended but hard to obtain in Britain.

Serels, Mitchell *The Jews of Cape Verde* Sepher-Hermon Press, 1997

There are many fascinating accounts written by British sailors, civil servants and entrepreneurs who have passed through the archipelago. They include:

Burdon Ellis, Alfred *West African Islands* Chapman and Hall, 1855. Entertaining and irritating by turns.

Dampier, William *A New Voyage Round the World* Adam and Charles Black, 1937. This is an account of the sailor's visit in 1683, complete with pirates, bandits and a generally unfavourable impression of the Cape Verdean people.

Lyall, Archibald *Black and White Make Brown* Heinemann, 1938. An intelligent and highly entertaining account of the journey this journalist made to Cape Verde and Portuguese Guinea.

Rendall, John *A Guide to the Cape Verde Islands* C Wilson, 1856. Frustratingly lacking in detail given the promise of the title, but fascinating nevertheless.

Roberts, George *Account of a Voyage to the Islands of the Canaries, Cape de Verde and Barbadoes, in 1721* can be found within *A new general collection of voyages and travels, vol I*, collected by Thomas Astley Frank Cass, 1968 – another lively set of adventures.

Valdez, Francisco Travassos *Six Years of a Traveller's Life in Western Africa, vol 1* Hurst and Blackett, 1861. An unusually positive account by a Portuguese sent to report on the islands for the government.

Portuguese titles

Carreira, António *Cabo Verde: Formação e Extinção de uma Sociedade Escravocrata*. This is an important work on the Cape Verdean slave economy, and is available in Praia's Casa de Cultura for 2,000$.

Lopes, Jose Vicente *Cabo Verde: Os Bastidores da Independencia* Spleen, 2002. Also available in Praia's Casa de Cultura.

Germano Lima, António *Ilha de Capitães* Spleen, 1997. A Portuguese-language account of the history of Boavista.

Economy and politics
For factual information on the country's economy there are two reference books:

Africa South of the Sahara Europa Publications. A reference book that is updated every year. *Europa World Year Book*, by the same publisher, where it is covered less extensively.

In addition, look for:

Foy, Colm *Cape Verde: Politics, Economics and Society* Pinter, 1986. A penetrating guide to the working of government in post-independence Cape Verde.

Literature

Burness, Donald *Fire: Six Writers from Angola, Mozambique and Cape Verde* Three Continents Press, 1977. This devotes some time to the exposition of Baltasar Lopes's novel *Chiquinho*.

Clew Parsons, Elsie *Folk Lore from the Cape Verde Islands* American Folklore Society, 1923. In British libraries. A fascinating accumulation of tales she collected from American *emigrantes* in the early 1900s.

Hamilton, Russell *Voices from an Empire: A History of Afro-Portuguese Literature* University of Minnesota Press, 1975. Includes an in-depth look at some of the leading Cape Verdean writers and poets.

Leite, Vicente Rendal *The Booklet (A Caderneta)* Instituto Caboverdiano do Livro. Translation of the story by Baltasar Lopes.

Strathern, Oona *Traveller's Literary Companions* In Print, 1994. Devoted to Cape Verdean poems, it is only worthwhile buying if you are interested more widely in African literature.

Classic Cape Verde literature, which does not seem to be available in English, includes:

Leite, Ana Mafalda, *Cape Verde: Language, Literature & Music* Portuguese Literary and Cultural Studies, 2002

Lopes, Baltasar *Chiquinho* 1947. The seminal Cape Verdean novel and also a leader in the literature of Portuguese Africa. It is available in French translation.

Lopes, Manuel *Chuva Braba* (Wild Rain) and *Flagelados do Vente Leste* (Victims of the East Wind). The latter novel was the basis for the first Cape Verdean-produced feature-length motion picture, which has the same title and was shot on Santo Antão.

Pereira, Celia *Estória, Estória: Do Tambor a blimundo* (*www.tabanka.it*). A children's book and audio book, in Italian, Portuguese and English, including the story of the liberated ox, Blimundo, and an assortment of Cape Verdean sayings.

Language

Gonçalves, Manuel da Luz and Andrade, Lelia Lomba de *Pa Nu Papia Krioulu*, 2003. A lively book that uses poetry, recipes and cultural articles to teach Creole to non-speakers, and teach Creole speakers how to read and write the language.

Natural history For birdwatchers, try these:

Aves de Cabo Verde This useful little orange booklet includes colour drawings of most of the important birds, their local and Latin names and a short explanation in English. Available from CVI (Cape Verde Investments) in Praia.

Bannerman, David and Mary *History of the Birds of the Cape Verde Islands* Oliver and Boyd, 1968. An entertaining book which combines distinguished ornithology with genial accounts of their times in Cape Verde.

Clarke, Tony and Orgill, Chris and Disley, Tony *A Field Guide to the Birds of the Atlantic Islands: Canary Islands, Madeira, Azores, Cape Verde* Helm Field Guides, 2006

Hazevoet, Cornelis *The Birds of the Cape Verde Islands* British Ornithologists' Union, 1995. Order from the Natural History Book Service (*2–3 Wills Rd, Totnes, Devon TQ9 5XN, UK;* 01803 865913; e *customer.services@nhbs.co.uk; www.nhbs.co.uk*).

Hazevoet, Cornelis Sixth report on birds from the Cape Verde Islands, including records of 25 taxa new to the archipelago. Available for download from www.africanbirdclub.org/countries/CapeVerdeIslands/refs.html

Plantas Endémicas A small guide to the country's vegetation, it has been translated into English and is also available from CVI (see above).

Appendix 2 **FURTHER INFORMATION**

A2

Health

Wilson-Howarth, Jane *Healthy Travel: Bites, Bugs and Bowels* Cadogan, 2009

Wilson-Howarth, Dr Jane and Ellis, Dr Matthew *Your Child Abroad: A travel health guide* Bradt Travel Guides, 2005

Activities

Cabo Verde, Santo Antão, Guia dos Circuitos Turísticos. A beautifully produced guide to hikes in Santo Antão, each with a foldout, high-quality map to show the route. Although written in Portuguese, it is of great value even without the text. It might still be available on Santo Antão; otherwise try to get it from the agency Lux Development (*www.lux-development. lu*), which funded the project.

Hammick, Anne and Heath, Nicholas *Atlantic Islands: Azores, Madeira, Canary and Cape Verde Islands* Imray, Laurie, Norie and Wilson, 2004. An essential practical guide for yachties.

For more detail on where to surf, get hold of *The Surf Report*; or try www.surfermag.com.

Cape Verde library collections

The Cape Verdean Special Collection is in the James P Adams Library, Rhode Island College (*600 Mount Pleasant Av, Providence, RI 02908;* ✆ *+1 401 456 9653*). In this collection you find books, newspapers, tapes of Cape Verdean television and radio programmes, photographs and various private Cape Verdean collections. There is about 40 linear feet of material.

The Arquivo Historico Nacional (*CP 321, Chã d'Areia, Praia, Santiago, Cape Verde*) was founded in 1988 and now comprises a large collection of historic and recent books as well as documents of the colonial administration concerning such issues as customs, emigration, and church matters among many other subjects.

MAGAZINES AND JOURNALS

Cimboa A journal of historical, cultural and political articles, published by the Cape Verdean consulate in Boston.

Fragata The in-flight magazine of the airline TACV, is worth picking up. The English translations of its articles are flawed, but the topics are interesting and there are good photographs.

WEBSITES

www.allafrica.com Regular news about Cape Verde is published here.

www.areasprotegidas.cv Information about all of Cape Verde's protected areas.

www.asemana.publ.cv/spip.php?ak=1&lang=en Plenty of news from around the islands from this Cape Verdean newspaper, English version.

www.bela-vista.net A site for tourists written by a German and a Cape Verdean, with an English version. Includes accommodation listings and an update on ferries in the archipelago (not always up to date but worth trying). Also offers a hotel- and *pensão*-booking service.

www.boavistaexperience.com Aimed at holidaymakers and property investors, this site is well endowed with information about where to stay and where to eat, and hosts some forums discussing developments on the island.

www.bravanews.com Information about Brava, in Portuguese.

www.caboverde.com (or caboverdesmart.com) A huge and rambling site, one of the first devoted to tourist information on Cape Verde, with listings for accommodation and restaurants. Put together by Italian Eraldo de Gioannini, it is nevertheless a good first port of call.

www.caboverde24.com A good starting point, with plenty of information about all sorts of aspects of Cape Verde as well as many links.

www.caboverdelove.com. General information including weather and surf conditions.

www.caboverdeonline.com A site for chatting, shopping and catching up on news, in Portuguese.

www.capeverde.com A well-organised website with plenty of information for planning a trip and an online booking facility.

www.capeverdebooking.com/pub/accueil.php. Online booking service for hotels with the facility to pay in advance by credit card.

www.capeverdetips.co.uk Aimed largely at people who are buying or already own property on Sal. It includes plenty of advice about travel and about life in Sal.

www.fogo.cv News, culture and sport, in Portuguese, for Cape Verdeans and the diaspora.

www.governo.cv The official government website, in Portuguese.

www.macauhub.com.mo A news site that aims to link Portuguese-speaking Africa with the Great Pearl River Delta region of China in order to facilitate business, which regularly produces interesting news pieces about Cape Verde.

www.maiocv.com Information about Maio, with an emphasis on land development.

www.mindelo.info Information about Mindelo, in French.

www.sao-filipe.com A more tourist-oriented site about Fogo, in several languages including English.

www.scvz.org Zoological Society of Cape Verde.

www.tripadvisor.com Holidaymakers give post mortems, mainly of package trips to Sal and Boavista.

www.umassd.edu/specialprograms/caboverde This site, though it does not seem to have been updated since 2000, nevertheless holds plenty of interesting information and links. Aims to link Cape Verdeans all over the world and contains information about the islands.

www.virtualcapeverde.net A useful portal for those considering investing in Cape Verde, with links to the relevant bodies, and news from a wide variety of sources.

Bradt Travel Guides

www.bradtguides.com

Africa

Access Africa: Safaris for People	
with Limited Mobility	£16.99
Africa Overland	£16.99
Algeria	£15.99
Angola	£17.99
Botswana	£16.99
Cameroon	£15.99
Cape Verde Islands	£14.99
Congo	£15.99
Eritrea	£15.99
Ethiopia	£16.99
Ghana	£15.99
Kenya Highlights	£15.99
Madagascar	£16.99
Malawi	£15.99
Mali	£14.99
Mauritius, Rodrigues &	
Réunion	£15.99
Mozambique	£15.99
Namibia	£15.99
Niger	£14.99
Nigeria	£17.99
North Africa: Roman Coast	£15.99
Rwanda	£15.99
São Tomé & Príncipe	£14.99
Seychelles	£14.99
Sierra Leone	£16.99
Sudan	£15.99
Tanzania, Northern	£14.99
Tanzania	£17.99
Uganda	£16.99
Zambia	£17.99
Zanzibar	£14.99
Zimbabwe	£15.99

The Americas and the Caribbean

Alaska	£15.99
Amazon, The	£14.99
Argentina	£15.99
Bahia	£14.99
Cayman Islands	£14.99
Colombia	£16.99
Dominica	£14.99
Grenada, Carriacou &	
Petite Martinique	£14.99
Guyana	£14.99
Nova Scotia	£14.99
Panama	£14.99
Paraguay	£14.99
Turks & Caicos Islands	£14.99
Uruguay	£14.99
USA by Rail	£14.99
Venezuela	£16.99
Yukon	£14.99

British Isles

Britain from the Rails	£14.99
Eccentric Britain	£13.99
Eccentric London	£13.99
Slow: Cotswolds	£14.99
Slow: Devon & Exmoor	£14.99
Slow: Norfolk & Suffolk	£14.99
Slow: North Yorkshire	£14.99
Slow: Sussex & South	
Downs National Park	£14.99

Europe

Abruzzo	£14.99
Albania	£15.99
Armenia	£15.99
Azores	£14.99
Baltic Cities	£14.99
Belarus	£15.99
Bosnia & Herzegovina	£14.99
Bratislava	£9.99
Budapest	£9.99
Bulgaria	£13.99
Cork	£6.99
Croatia	£13.99
Cross-Channel France:	
Nord-Pas de Calais	£13.99
Cyprus see North Cyprus	
Dresden	£7.99
Estonia	£14.99
Faroe Islands	£15.99
Georgia	£15.99
Greece: The Peloponnese	£14.99
Helsinki	£7.99
Hungary	£15.99
Iceland	£14.99
Kosovo	£15.99
Lapland	£13.99
Latvia	£13.99
Lille	£9.99
Lithuania	£14.99
Luxembourg	£13.99
Macedonia	£15.99
Malta & Gozo	£12.99
Montenegro	£14.99
North Cyprus	£12.99
Riga	£6.99
Serbia	£15.99
Slovakia	£14.99
Slovenia	£13.99
Spitsbergen	£16.99
Switzerland Without	
a Car	£14.99
Transylvania	£14.99
Ukraine	£15.99
Zagreb	£6.99

Middle East, Asia and Australasia

Bangladesh	£15.99
Borneo	£17.99
Eastern Turkey	£16.99
Iran	£15.99
Iraq: Then & Now	£15.99
Israel	£15.99
Kazakhstan	£15.99
Kyrgyzstan	£15.99
Lake Baikal	£15.99
Maldives	£15.99
Mongolia	£16.99
North Korea	£14.99
Oman	£15.99
Shangri-La:	
A Travel Guide to the	
Himalayan Dream	£14.99
Sri Lanka	£15.99
Syria	£15.99
Taiwan	£16.99
Tibet	£13.99
Yemen	£14.99

Wildlife

Antarctica: Guide to the	
Wildlife	£15.99
Arctic: Guide to Coastal	
Wildlife	£15.99
Australian Wildlife	£14.99
Central & Eastern	
European Wildlife	£15.99
Chinese Wildlife	£16.99
East African Wildlife	£19.99
Galápagos Wildlife	£15.99
Madagascar Wildlife	£16.99
New Zealand Wildlife	£14.99
North Atlantic Wildlife	£16.99
Pantanal Wildlife	£16.99
Peruvian Wildlife	£15.99
Southern African	
Wildlife	£18.95
Sri Lankan Wildlife	£15.99

Pictorials and other guides

100 Animals to See	
Before They Die	£16.99
100 Bizarre Animals	£16.99
Eccentric Australia	£12.99
Northern Lights	£6.99
Wildlife and Conservation	
Volunteering: The	
Complete Guide	£13.99

WIN A FREE BRADT GUIDE
READER QUESTIONNAIRE

Send in your completed questionnaire and enter our monthly draw for the chance to win a Bradt guide of your choice.

To take up our special reader offer of 40% off, please visit our website at www.bradtguides.com/freeguide or answer the questions below and return to us with the order form overleaf.

(Forms may be posted or faxed to us.)

Have you used any other Bradt guides? If so, which titles? . . . .

. . . .

What other publishers' travel guides do you use regularly? . . . .

. . . .

Where did you buy this guidebook? . . . .

What was the main purpose of your trip to Cape Verde (or for what other reason did you read our guide)? eg: holiday/business/charity . . . .

. . . .

How long did you travel for? (circle one)

weekend/long weekend   1–2 weeks   3–4 weeks   4 weeks plus

Which countries did you visit in connection with this trip? . . . .

. . . .

Did you travel with a tour operator?' If so, which one? . . . .

. . . .

What other destinations would you like to see covered by a Bradt guide?

. . . .

If you could make one improvement to this guide, what would it be?

. . . .

Age (circle relevant category) 16–25   26–45   46–60   60+

Male/Female (delete as appropriate)

Home country . . . .

Please send us any comments about this guide (or others on our list).

. . . .

. . . .

. . . .

Bradt Travel Guides
IDC House, The Vale, Chalfont St Peter, Bucks SL9 9RZ, UK
☎ +44 (0)1753 893444 **f** +44 (0)1753 892333
e info@bradtguides.com
www.bradtguides.com

TAKE 40% OFF YOUR NEXT BRADT GUIDE!
Order Form

To take advantage of this special offer visit www.bradtguides.com/freeguide and enter our monthly giveaway, or fill in the order form below, complete the questionnaire overleaf and send it to Bradt Travel Guides by post or fax.

Please send me one copy of the following guide at 40% off the UK retail price

No	Title	Retail price	40% price
1	....	....	....

Please send the following additional guides at full UK retail price

No	Title	Retail price	Total
...	....	....	....
...	....	....	....
...	....	....	....

Sub total	....
Post & packing	....

(Free shipping UK, £1 per book Europe, £3 per book rest of world)

Total	....

Name . . . .

Address. . . . .

Tel . . . .   Email . . . .

☐ I enclose a cheque for £. . . . . made payable to Bradt Travel Guides Ltd

☐ I would like to pay by credit card. Number: . . . .

Expiry date: . . . / . . . . 3-digit security code (on reverse of card) . . . . .

Issue no (debit cards only) . . . . .

☐ Please sign me up to Bradt's monthly enewsletter, Bradtpackers' News.

☐ I would be happy for you to use my name and comments in Bradt marketing material.

Send your order on this form, with the completed questionnaire, to:

Bradt Travel Guides
IDC House, The Vale, Chalfont St Peter, Bucks SL9 9RZ, UK
✆ +44 (0)1753 893444   f +44 (0)1753 892333
e info@bradtguides.com   www.bradtguides.com

Index

Entries in **bold** indicate main entries

354